Digger, Dogface, Brownjob, Grunt

Jill Wallen —

There's much humor in here. Make sure to get to know my boys —

Digger, Dogface, Brownjob, Grunt

A Novel

Gary Prisk

Gary Prisk

Cougar Creek Press
Bainbridge Island, Washington

Cougar Creek Press, LLC
P.O. Box 11159
Bainbridge Island, WA 98110

This book is a work of fiction. The settings are real. Incidents, characters, timelines and names are either the product of the author's imagination or are used fictitiously. Any resemblance to actual persons, living or dead, events or locales is entirely coincidental.

Edited by Laurie Rosin
Cover Design by George Foster
Interior Design by William Groetzinger

ISBN 978-0-615-25343-5
Library of Congress Control Number: 2008911339

Publisher's Cataloging-in-Publication

Prisk, Gary.

Digger, Dogface, Brownjob, Grunt : a novel / Gary Prisk. — Bainbridge Island, WA: Cougar Creek Press, c2009.

p. ; cm.

ISBN: 978-0-615-25343-5

1. Vietnam War, 1961-1975—Fiction. 2. Soldiers—Fiction. 3. War stories, American. 4.War stories. I. Title.

PS3616.R557 D54 2009 2008911339
813.6–dc22 0905

For Linda, the farm girl I married

For Kimberly, the platoon's baby girl

For Karl, my son

For the boys from Philadelphia's
Thomas Edison High

and

For the men I once knew

Prologue

Confusion wasn't the half of it. AK-47s were chopping the jungle into a tossed salad.

While Charlie took aim at his humping tackle, Lieutenant Edward Hardin ran about learning why El Tees didn't live very long. With his vitals in hiding and his life a crapshoot, if ever a man was hunting trouble—in Vietnam, in 1967—he damn sure found it.

His father warned him not to expect much from the world.

Instinctively irreverent when tending war's misfortunes, infantrymen from the Twenty-Fourth Foot in the Transvaal, the Fifth Marines and Seventh Infantry in the Chosin Reservoir, and the 173rd Airborne and Fourth Infantry in Dak To, smiled to mask an altered state of mind.

Lieutenant Edward Hardin was naturally irreverent—a bit of luck he had not foreseen. When Eddie received his deployment orders his father read each word and said, "A dogface needs to know how to eat, dig, shit, and shoot. The rest is just the war."

Scoffing his best scoff while allowing room to avoid the Major's left hook, Eddie replied, "Yeah, right. The trick is not shitting on your boots."

Hardin's men could eat and shoot, dig and shoot, and shit and shoot, all while screaming for a medic. It's not that chaos came with these men—it's just that something did.

They were an odd assortment, boys really—twelve-month men really. Their pictures were familiar—the cocked hats and the melancholy grins. They enjoyed talking about girls and home, rumors and cars, the little things mostly.

They enjoyed a good joke most of all. Caught in a time of chattel sacrifice, the regret that anchored their black humor was the baseline for their survival. Slogging through the mud, in and out of the vines, fighting a war that was mindless, and discomposed, Hardin's men had a duty they could not define: to a smile once remembered.

Sure enough—Vietnam's war sucked.

A noble cause, the old men said, blood and bile curdling in a steel pot, a boot standing alone, mist curling over the fractured body of one paratrooper, then racing to the next. Hollow eyes glistened with tears of fatigue and winced at the roar of small-arms fire.

Infantry combat is a deeply personal, scarring experience.

An infantryman never comes home, regains a sense of empathy, or falls completely in love. He is but a remnant of the boy you once knew—a short-fused remnant.

Coming alive again requires the friendship of time.

* * *

Before I continue, meet my father, Major Edward Hardin. He is the rather lean US Army infantry major standing behind and to the right of Field Marshall Montgomery, the gent seated in the armchair.

These chaps, pictured in Belgium days before the Battle of the Bulge, were the liaison officers charged with tracking the war for Montgomery. Omar Bradley affectionately referred to these combat veterans as Monty's Walkers.

The Major was a golden glove boxer, enjoying a scholarship to Washington State University. He was devoted to my development, lending me his war relics to play with while I trooped through the woods. I was three years old when he came marching home.

That is when I learned where to find "sympathy" in the dictionary.

As if fair warning, the Major died one day in July of 1967. I wish I had known him better, sure enough.

My name is Lieutenant Edward Hardin. El Tee if you like. I fought Vietnam's war as an infantry platoon leader, primarily against the North Vietnamese Army, the NVA.

I am taping this story for my children, Kimberly and Karl. They will transcribe the tapes and edit the words. But this story is for you. Paint a picture of war while your kids listen.

One more thing—if you're looking for sympathy, it's in the dictionary between shit and syphilis. Major Edward Hardin, circa 1946.

* * *

Veterans Hospital. American Lake, Washington. July 2001.

Karl sat down. His dad looked better this morning. The old man woke when he felt his son's weight on the bed.

"Hiya, Pal," he said, smiling through those crusty eyes. "Lemme get my wits about me for a second and I'll show you something." He rolled over and sat up with some effort. He took a long breath before he stood up, then hobbled into the bathroom on bent legs.

"Karl, read those pages on the night table," he said. "I won't be a minute."

Karl read. "As grunts go, Edward Hardin..."

The old man came out of the bathroom just as his son finished the third page.

"Recognize that picture? The one next to my desk at home."

"I never knew that was Montgomery," Karl said, "but I knew he was important."

"Your granddad worked for Monty." He strained to get on the bed. "You bring the tape?" he asked, holding out a paw.

Karl brought out a handheld recorder, loaded with a fresh tape.

"You don't have to stay here for this. It'll take a while, and I'll ramble some too. Your granddad never gave me much about his time in the barrel. A few letters, stories—D-Day and such. And pictures," he added. "I won't get it all in," he said. "Isn't any paper that'll put down the sound and the stench. I'll do what I can, while..." His voice trailed off as he stared out the window, his mouth twisting and working.

"Hell, Karl, you're no dummy. But we never got to talk about this, really."

"You never seemed ready to talk about Vietnam," Karl said, measuring his dad.

"Yeah, I know."

They sat in the silence of that hospital room, both of them wanting to leave, both of them knowing only one of them would make it. Karl showed his dad how to use the tape.

"Piece-a-cake," he said, his great hands fumbling with the tiny controls of the machine.

"I'm glad you want to know about that war," he said. With a sideways glance and the wry grin he liked so well, he gave his son a pat on the back and paused.

"Maybe now I can shoulder my rucksack and drive on in peace."

CHAPTER ONE

Doc Tweed

B-Med Field Hospital, An Khe Base Camp. 0730 Hours. 4 December 1967.

Hallucinating, Hardin's voice thickened. He screamed, then laughed. Suddenly quiet, he bared his teeth. Blessed with the silence of a good dog, he cast about, searching for a sandbag to hide behind. With unrelated details running in the same direction, he was stunned by the news of the North Vietnamese Army body count.

Pleased, as if he had won, he fell in with the beauty of his foxhole.

Hardin was sick with a Fever of Unknown Origin. He was having intense and disturbing dreams about his father. And yet, his men kept dying. A pile of bloody bandages exploded. One man turned black, then another. It's not that these men embraced death; it's just that they had tired, weathered eyes.

As the war raged on, Hardin's body was thrown across the ground. He was swimming in mud, suspended in a floating isolation, drifting in a cloudy substance. Strange, glowing images sparked flashes of recall. One, two... nineteen of his men were dead.

Containing the undulating motion was impossible.

Hardin's heart surged, pushing him through a series of firefights. The fever dragged him in and out of the war. Artillery rounds shattered the trees. He dived between spires of shattered bamboo, scanning a landscape littered with bodies.

Look there, standing alone—a jungle boot.

Hardin's body ached.

Eight men in Hardin's infantry platoon were left standing. Could he keep these men alive? The jungle exploded. The carnage was not as confusing as his inability to return fire. Quiet for a moment, he froze. His weapon—where was his weapon? Men appeared and then vanished. Now he was running from foxhole to foxhole, fighting to secure the platoon's perimeter.

The foxholes were empty.

First Lieutenant Edward Hardin, a stocky, mahogany-faced paratrooper, was a lingering testament to Vietnam's war, a byproduct of an aching, jungle nausea, trapped in a space without reference. The roar of gunfire was deafening as he fought to slow his breathing.

Trying to release his fear, Hardin laughed.

His head cleared in an instant, leaving a jarring pain behind his eyes. The men who littered his dreams now wore blue-green hospital gowns. The jungle screams now came from stubborn hospital carts. The equipment bracketed to his bed had replaced a pile of sandbags.

"Goddamn war," he said, searching the detail of a nearby face.

Watching the wounded who filled the hospital ward scurry from emotion to emotion, pausing to redirect their energies, Hardin knew they were keen to avoid their own reality. Almost all were relieved: they were going home. Leaning forward, a chill rolled over his body.

Grateful, he stared at the man in the adjoining bed. The man stared back.

A sudden scream caused Hardin to recoil. The wounded man, his head and torso bandaged, his left leg pinned in a cast and suspended in traction, was screaming at his missing hand. Stumped for a moment, the man screamed at his missing leg.

Hardin knew his wounded friend was no longer a wrinkle in Vietnam's ribbon of endless shit. This man would hear the sound of the explosion again and feel the shock wave fill his body cavities with gas and debris. *The concussion will hang in the jungle of this soldier's mind as though wet burlap,* Hardin thought.

Grateful for having all of his digits, Hardin took a deep breath, thinking. *Damn, booby traps could vaporize a soldier and leave nary a whisper. It is true that a good grunt is no sudden stew,* Hardin mused, *but how old could a grunt be?*

A tall, thin, rough-looking doctor gave Hardin a nod, offered a gesture of fatigue to the wounded man, and then inserted a needle into his arm. When the wounded man's high-pitched gabbing turned to a muffled sigh, the doctor stepped toward Hardin, nodding his agreement.

With sweat filling the corner of one eye, Hardin leaned on an elbow, took a deep breath to slow his heart rate, and tried to speak. Before he could muster a word, a black soldier stepped forward, pointing at him. The doctor shook his head.

The rafters began to spin, cycling into a blacker void.

Delirious, Hardin found himself screaming at a tree.

When the tree screamed back, a Viet Cong soldier stood to, centered in a ball of light, his face framed in the mouth of a spider hole. Instantly, Hardin flailed through a tangle of bamboo in a blood-soaked rage. He slit the man's throat, then slit it again. Suddenly quiet, he was lying in a wet, dank jungle, in Dak To, his four-inch K-bar, dripping with blood.

His father's voice echoed from the platoon radio, telling him to run.

Frame by frame the paratroopers traced a ridgeline. First Platoon searched the vegetation with a practiced silence, step by step. Breathing was optional.

The canopy stood 140 feet. Bits of sunlight pulsed. Leaves fluttered. Shadows changed from dapple-gray to black, then vanished, leaving the eye suspended.

As if synchronized toys, the paratroopers stalked, boots clamored in silence, dancing, searching uphill in a painful display, trapped in history's gilded funnel. Hardin was afraid. Adrenaline screamed in his ears, drawing him into that familiar sequence of death.

And, as he ran through a vortex of fire, Nuts, the platoon RTO, died.

Hardin watched, shocked for an instant. Nuts' body jerked violently upward and to the right. His right arm tore into pieces and his M-16 flew into the air. His head exploded, spewing his teeth. His body bounced as AK rounds ripped through his chest.

Frame by frame Hardin was running, screaming, fighting. With a guttural rage he returned fire, dropped his rucksack, looked for cover, reloaded his M-16, and searched for his enemy in an instant. The vegetation near his head jumped into a boil. AK rounds snapped at his face. And within the confusion, his radio operator lay in pieces and the NVA were gone.

On his knees, wailing, Hardin gathered Nuts into his arms.

Retching at the smell, he turned away, spewing bile. Brushing at his hair, Hardin found the war clinging to his shirt. His friend lay there in the mud, clutching the radio handset, waiting for his El Tee to ask for the radio, his stature growing.

* * *

Hardin came to in a pool of putrid sweat. His bunkmate lay quiet now, drool hanging from his half-smiling mouth. Hardin pushed himself to a dry spot of the bed, listening to the shuffle of slippers on the wood floor and the rhythmic tattoo of a metal walker.

He motioned to a patient and said, "Is there a chart hangin' on my bed?"

"Right here." The stranger's voice had a hard, northern city twang. His bandaged hands held the metal-framed chart as if handling fine china.

"What's it say?" The stranger glanced at the top sheet trying not to flinch.

With a smirk he looked around the ward and shrugged. After some thought, he said, "Can't tell. Could be anything." Then he stepped to the center aisle, pushed a finger into the chart and yelled, "Oh, shit. Here it is. You're fuckin' gonna die." He laughed a roar and threw the chart onto the bed.

That was a good joke, Hardin thought as he looked around the ward. Ward Two of B-Med Field Hospital was a painted version of the average garage. Wood stud walls topped with screens held a rank of open rafters. A large fan mounted in the end wall pulled air through the ward. The white walls sparred with the red-brown dust that coated the rafters and clogged the screens.

"Why am I here, Doc?" Hardin's boorish tone called attention to his newfound awareness. Noticing a bit of mock disgust as the doctor hung the chart on the end of the bed, Hardin shouted, "Tell me a story, ya big shit."

The chatter on the ward stopped.

The doctor exchanged words with the ceiling lights, angled his head toward Hardin, and stared over his glasses. With an educated tone of voice he said, "You are an FUO, Lieutenant." His long, bony fingers jabbed the air as he announced each letter. Satisfied, the doctor's brow joined his heavy glasses in an expression of suspicious searching.

"FUO. Is that what that chart says, Doc?" The surgeon stood into a silent brace. He looked exhausted. "FUO. Sounds like cock-rot. Wait until the bride hears this one."

Stunned by the texture of a suppressed shout, patients across the ward turned to listen. Some bustled closer, delighted by the sarcasm. As Hardin grew anxious, his head shifted back, and gusts of cold chills ran over his body. When his grin continued, the doctor turned into a tough-guy, grabbing Hardin's chart and waving it about as if it were Hardin's balls.

Hardin laughed. "Tweed's your best shot, Doc—a light brown tweed. Without tweed, no one is gonna buy this shtick you got goin.'"

The surgeon smiled a well-anchored smile and said, "There are strains of malaria and other viruses we cannot identify, Lieutenant." Watching Doc Tweed rise to his toes, Hardin fancied these opening lines of Tweed's VD lecture. "You've contracted one of them."

With a pestering tone, Hardin said, "A light brown tweed with a hint of burgundy."

Ignoring the jab, Tweed said, "You have a fever of unknown origin: FUO. We've been working for days to keep you alive. Ice baths, the whole nine yards."

"The whole nine yards," Hardin said. "You docs wrap a viral sludge into a mystery, then blame me for its origin."

As if being offended was the answer, Doc Tweed massaged his chin with a bony paw, setting his mind to the task. Hardin suspected that FUOs were an integral part of Battle Bullshit, the postulate that the infantry grunt was the origin of unforgiven sin. Every problem a general had was caused by some grunt.

The postulate was fundamentally sound. After all, Hardin had overheated balls, and only a grunt would have such a problem.

With his postulate in hand, Hardin decided to be more aggravating. "Who you tryin' to shit, Doc? Everything in this dump is of unknown origin. Doctors of unknown origin, DUOs. Dinks of unknown origin. And why the hell's that black dude hangin' around here?"

Hardin knew no reasonable man could compete with such all-consuming ignorance.

A raucous crowd of wounded men, Hardin's combat accessories howled, joyously supporting his impertinence with a back-slapping, fist-pounding, hold-your-tools laughter. Doc Tweed shook his head. The hint of a smile crossed his face as he turned and left the ward.

Giving his fans a victory salute to a chorus of "hey, babies" and "dig-its," Hardin smiled at the thought of pussy of unknown origin, and his head sank through his pillow.

Concentric rings of light narrowed to a tunnel and the stranger, the black stranger, was laughing, conspiring with the tweed-covered surgeon. With a fever ravaged body, Hardin's thoughts bounced from the Ranger School at Fort Benning to his home on Highlands Road, then mixed the two into his father's den—only to send him to the slaughter of an NVA ambush.

He was sitting in a Pan American Clipper, behind the right wing: "You are now entering the airspace of the Republic of South Vietnam." Then he was praying in a dark jungle hollow.

Hardin stood-to in his Special Forces beret, a reserve medic accepting his commission as an infantry lieutenant. His father stood-to in his dress greens, ramrod straight, saluting his Pal. The ceremony turned into the airstrip at Guam. Hundreds of sandbagged parapets formed an eerie display. B-52s lined the runway as far as the eye could see.

"Let's go home, Pal," his father said, pulling him away from the plane. "Run, Pal."

* * *

Number #10, Highlands Road. Bremerton, Washington. September 1950.

The guard was changing along Highlands Road with the lengthening shadows of fall. Muted greens and browns and the whispers of war sparred with the warmth of a bright, sunny day. Highlands Road danced with expectant confusion. Maple leaves, pedal cars, baby strollers, and young parents jammed the sidewalks—fearful of a new war, yet thankful to have a job.

Many a danger lurked along Highlands Road. A youngster could find himself buckled to the rush of a good tongue lashing for running through Aunt Dorothy's roses. Eddie ran through her roses because she was blocking the sidewalk, and Jimmy Wiggins, a twelve-year-old monster, was chasing him, threatening to pound him into pulp.

Eddie's dad, the Major, seemed to understand. His mom, the Major's sweetheart, never understood. Because Aunt Dorothy was her younger sister, Eddie's mom enjoyed marching him back to the rose bed for a period of public flogging, landscape repair, and whatever remedial training Aunt Dorothy could muster.

Of course he was sorry. My God, do you think he enjoyed stomping on her roses?

Eddie stomped on them one day just for the brag.

With a border hospitality Aunt Dorothy could shout "Young man!" and make every dog on the block stop and pee. Eddie learned early on not to stop when she yelled young man. Billy Kirkland stopped once and she twisted his ear until he was on his tiptoes and crying. Then she held on to his ear while she marched him home.

Actually, Billy didn't march. He bounced on his toes trying to untwist his ear. Not to be denied, Aunt Dorothy would scold him with hideous words.

And that damn Jimmy Wiggins would pound any kid within earshot. Except of course when Eddie's dad was around. Then Eddie could taunt Wiggins with his best stuff, knowing Wiggins would pound him anyway.

Highlands Road was the best.

Skipping down the sidewalk in front of his house, Eddie tried to miss the maple leaves and the cracks, laughing hilariously at the way his feet seemed to go. Sometimes he would spend the afternoon just to get one clean run to the end of the block. Eddie had to make sure Jimmy Wiggins wasn't around because if he caught Eddie skipping, Wiggins would tackle him, call him a sissy, and then pound him for fruiting up the neighborhood.

Afternoons in the fall on Highlands Road were devoted to tackle football on the grass field at the bottom of the hill. Player selection was rigged; Eddie played center. If all went well, Eddie would catch a pass in the flat and outrun Wiggins to the end zone. He beat Wiggins to the end zone one day and turned to celebrate. Wiggins tackled him and shoved his face in the mud.

Mornings in the fall on Highlands Road were devoted to getting to school in one piece with your schoolbooks free of mud and your lunch not smashed. The bus stop was on Admiral Perry Avenue, one block south of the intersection with Highlands Road.

Getting to the bus stop was a piece of cake. Keeping your manhood intact while you waited for the bus was impossible. You see, Jimmy Wiggins would wait for Eddie to be less than a man, to fruit up his bus stop, and then he would flog Eddie with cuss words and use Eddie's books for roller skates. He would belly-laugh when Eddie tried to put his books back together.

One Saturday morning Eddie was boiling along the sidewalk in full stride, sailing over the cracks, when he skipped past the city bus stop on Admiral Perry Avenue. Mrs. Donnager snorted and hollered, "Young man, you better tend to your knitting."

God, how humiliating. This old bag of gas was one of those neighbors who could accent Eddie's behavior with agonizing clarity. With a twitch and a grin she could embarrass a young man to the point of not remembering a thing she said. She caught Eddie preparing to pee on a rose bush one day, and scared him so bad he didn't pee until the shift horn sounded in the shipyard at four-twenty that afternoon.

On Saturday mornings, Mrs. Donnager and Eddie would ride the 9:20 bus to downtown Bremerton. She was on her way to work at the public library and he was on his way to meet his dad. And because he was a gentleman, Mrs. Donnager got on the bus first.

Billy Kirkland had double-dog-dared him to goose the old bag, but Eddie knew the Major would tan his butt if he did.

That didn't stop Eddie from laughing to himself.

When they got off the bus in front of the public library on Fifth Avenue, the Major would take off his hat, nod at Mrs. Donnager, greet his son with a smile, and say, "How's my Pal?" The Major would watch Mrs. Donnager unlock the large oak door and post the open sign. Then Eddie would vow to never set foot in the library and take his father's hand.

Then Eddie would tell his father he was fine, and they would be off, looking both ways and then back to the left.

The Major and Eddie started their Saturdays with a stroll through the farmers' market, jostling for position to buy the best fruit.

With produce in hand, they turned down Pacific Avenue, heading toward the main gate of the Puget Sound Naval Shipyard. Pacific Avenue was lined with fashionable stores, anchored by the post office on the north end and the main gate of the shipyard on the south end.

Bremerton was a lively town in 1950, day and night. Bremerton was a Navy town—a blue-jacket town, its pulse and mood subject to Defense Department work orders and the security measures required to meet those orders. The intersection of Pacific and First Avenues was not a place to fool around. Whispers of war stirred old fears. Ships were arriving for refit. America was restless, and the shipyard bustled with work.

Coming or going, the Marine guards checked workers and visitors. They searched those leaving for contraband or sensitive materials and those entering for cameras or explosives.

First Avenue was choked with girls, pawn shops, lockers, taverns, and a rambunctious sort of life. Sailors and marines thankful for liberty jammed the street corners.

They were full of talk of war.

The Major seemed to know everybody in town, including the strangers. With a firm handclasp, they passed the Greyhound Bus Station heading for the Black Ball Ferry Terminal, next to the YMCA. The Major went to the YMCA for his boxing workout. He would teach you how to box if you listened, and he would just beat the hell out of those who didn't.

Eddie liked to listen to his dad.

Saturdays ended with a root beer float at the lunch counter in F. W. Woolworth's Five and Ten Cent Store located at the corner of Pacific and Burwell Avenues, across the street from Bremer's Department Store. Eddie's mom sold cosmetics at Bremer's.

The talk of war today was more heated than on previous Saturdays.

"Dad, do you have to go to Korea?" The Major's eyes lost some life.

"No, Pal. These sailors and marines are going," he said, waving down the counter.

The Major died on a Saturday in July of 1967, after a boxing workout on the heavy bag at the YMCA. Major Edward Hardin was worried about his pals.

You see, Eddie's brother, Court, had just returned from a tour of duty in Vietnam, and Eddie had accepted a commission as an infantry lieutenant and was overdue for orders to go to Vietnam.

The Major was an infantryman in World War II, a Dogface. He landed with the first wave on Omaha Beach in Normandy, on June 6, 1944: D-Day. He knew how war could be. He just forgot to tell his pals. And then he died and forgot to say good-bye.

* * *

Ward Two. B-Med Field Hospital, An Khe Base Camp. 1018 Hours.

The lunch counter at F. W. Woolworth's and the look in his father's eye vanished when Hardin's bunkmate let out a scream and was drawn to the stake, gasping for air.

The surgeon stood-to, tethered to a sottish-looking major. The surgeons huddled near Hardin's bed, exchanging inferential comments about his behavior, and then Doc Tweed summarized his condition. Hardin smiled to mask a hunch when Tweed rolled a table aside allowing the major to hold a vial up to the light.

The medicine had a viscosity suitable for muster in Aunt Jemima's kitchen.

"Sir, this is Lieutenant Hardin. FUO. Medevac out of Kontum Province three days ago." Doc Tweed paused allowing his boss to absorb the input, then adjusted his glasses with a wrinkle of his nose. "He's been delirious until this morning." As Doc Tweed's voice settled into a jellied soup, the major let the glow of his title radiate through the ward.

"Could be a new strain of malaria," Doc Tweed suggested, prompting his courage.

Hardin mused: the old boys are in heaven, inflamed by cumulative dominance.

"Is this guy a classmate, Doc, or is this a DUO?" The surgeons exchanged confirming nods, then braced into a well-rehearsed conclusion.

"Shut up, Lieutenant," the major said, showcasing a thick Boston accent. "You're sick, Lieutenant. You've been burning up for days."

"I knew a girl like that once, rolled on for days."

"Shut up, Lieutenant. Take this." He handed Hardin the vial.

Hardin selected a belligerent grin and said, "It's at ease, Dipstick, not shut up." Hardin thrust the vial at Tweed. "You take it, Tweed. It'll cure your constipation."

At this juncture, the major started a "Let's reason with the patient" routine, rambling on about casualties, his lack of sleep and pussy, and a persistent cough he had acquired. The old boy glanced at the chart and then at his companion. With an emphatic breath, he said, "This is probably a strain of malaria. Could be a virus. We aren't sure."

Tweed stood-to with a skewering look, keeping a parade-ground eye on his boss.

Hardin's sit-rep was fluid at best. Flashbacks filled with guilt sacked the hospital ward with searing bars of frustration. And if guilt were not enough, Doc Tweed and Major Dipstick were marketing Texaco's answer to FUOs.

"Look, Major," Hardin said. "I'm kind of dizzy." Hardin laid his head on his pillow and the hospital ward slowly tipped over.

* * *

Vietnamese milled around the air base as if they owned the place, jabbering, smiling at the wrong times. Hardin bumped into one man while staring at another man. They looked shifty. "That's the bus, Lieutenant, the bus to LBJ—Long Binh Junction. The blue bus with mesh on the windows. That's what it's called, LBJ."

"Your overseas trunk will be shipped to An Khe. Your orders were changed, Lieutenant. Well, lemme see. An airborne brigade has invited you to a party they're having in Dak To."

"Chopper leaves for An Khe at 1030 hours. Good luck, Lieutenant."

* * *

The wounded man, his anguish rooted in a blackened self-image, screamed again. Hardin sat straight into a firing position and found Doc Tweed locked in a brace. Tweed's frown forced his unkempt brow to sit on the bridge of his nose the way moss sits on a rotting log, his eyes a pair of glazed raindrops.

Breathing slowly, Tweed cracked a modest smile. Holding the vial to the light, he then offered Hardin the medicine.

Shaking his head, Hardin said, "I'm gonna split, Doc. I gotta get back to my boys."

With a grin and a nod Tweed agreed. "You're my only mystery. The rest are banged, broken, and bruised." With a matador's motion Tweed offered Hardin the floor, then said, "Being the smartass that you are, Lieutenant, makes you a sick asshole."

"Sick asshole," Hardin said with a worn out huff. "No shit. Now I'm a sick asshole. I don't mean to jack ya around, Doc. I'm not takin' that nasty shit." Tweed's face fell tired. He set the vial down on the table, searching the contours of the bandaged soldier.

"I want my clothes, Doc. I'm goin' back to the bush."

Hardin swung his legs off the bed, hoping the change of altitude and the blood settling in his feet would slow his heart rate. Instantly, his vision cycled into a semidarkness, then back to a harsh cone of light as the restless thump of his heart stabilized.

"Look, Doc." Hardin hesitated, working for air. "Stick with the AK holes. The wounds you can mend." Hardin stood, holding on to the edge of the bed.

"I can stop the bleeding, I can't fix the wounds." Tweed's voice carried obvious regret. "The war has consumed any good nature I hoped to have. The amputation rate is high." Hardin fought to keep pace as they turned down a hallway and into a room lined with plywood cubicles.

"That's your gear," Tweed said, apologizing for Hardin's meager assets. The cubicle was assigned to bed number 218. In the end, the scarred jungle boots, socks, weathered fatigues, and his granddad's watch, had stood their post alone.

Doc Tweed adjusted the waistband of his pants, then paused, seeming to ward his anxiety and conclude his business: troubled by Hardin's medical status.

"I'll make it, Doc. There's nothin' to this combat shit."

Tweed took a pull on his nose, then massaged the air with a modest sigh. Saturated with the butchery, more casualties were inbound, and he could not stop the killing. Shackled to a system designed to produce dead bodies, and charged with impeding the process, Hardin knew Tweed struggled with the contradiction.

Being a Doctor of Unknown Origin was one way to hide from the truth.

Tweed shook his head with a quiet laugh, and said, "Doctors of unknown origin. That's a great concept." He shook his head and his eyes registered the humor.

"Understand this, young stud: I want you out of here. Take it easy for a day and you'll be on your way," Tweed said, trying to make the liquid swirl.

Hardin pointed at Dipstick's office. "That med is nasty. Give it to the major."

Tweed nodded. Indifferent, he turned to leave, then stopped. "You're going be hurting for a while. If it's malaria you'll be back." Tweed was looking and talking into an empty hallway.

Hardin dressed and shuffled down the hallway of the administrative area. A sign waving in an air-conditioned stream welcomed him to the army field hospital—B-Med.

Curious faces analyzed his progress. Gravity clung to his boots as if wet tar. His feet slapped the floor, jarring his thighs into his balls. Aiming for the front door, Hardin's vision jumped in and out of focus.

"Where's the Holding Company?" he asked. The nurse backed away, pointing. Were those real tits? "Holy shit, El Tee, look at those trotters." He could see clearly now.

"Top of the hill," she declared with well-seasoned humor.

Hardin's grin annoyed itself into a stare as he perked her nipples, then coached the tightly wrapped cheeks of her ass as they fought for space.

Admiring his clever nature, he took the front stairs with a rush, clinging to the handrail, allowing gravity to bring each step to meet his foot. By the time he stumbled into the dirt roadway his cock had simmered to a gallop. He needed a shave. His fatigue shirt bore no name or insignia, and his boots were scuffed into red suede.

"How far is the Holding Company?" Hardin asked, pestering a passing GI.

"Half a mile." The man shook his head. "No hat, no shave. You're in for some trouble."

Never quite free of supervision, Hardin plodded on. The walk was drudgery, gallons of sweat spiced with a fever narrowing his vision. Spotting the company guidon and bulletin board, and laughing at the circles of white rocks, he comforted his humping tackle and opened the orderly room door.

"Who the hell are you?" the first sergeant shouted, accelerating around the back corner of his desk, closing on Hardin with a hedge for a body that looked to be one continuous muscle.

"Lieutenant Hardin." Hardin raised his right hand. His assailant stepped to a halt, fists clinched, wanting to sacrifice this piece of dirt to a sea of other duties.

"You look like hell, Lieutenant. You better get your shit in one bag. Lots of brass around this area." The old sergeant's head shook with color as he found his chair.

"Fuckin' teenage lieutenants." Top screamed out the back of the tent.

With a short nod, the old sergeant settled into his desk, and after a well-timed pause motioned to his Charge-of-Quarters runner. "Show this officer where he can wash up."

Hardin followed the CQ runner past the mess tent.

Gesturing to his right, the PFC said, "You can crash in either of these hootches, Lieutenant. Here's a razor and shaving cream." Hardin's run-in with the first sergeant had amused the man.

"Somethin' funny to you, stud?"

"No, sir. You look a little ragged, that's all."

The cold water was oily and smelled of Vietnam. Hardin stared into the small mirror, delicately guiding the razor around the wound on his left cheek. Five weeks before, a spire of elephant grass had sliced his lower jaw, leaving a crescent shaped wound nearly one inch long.

Alerted by the sound of the razor, sweat stung his face as he dabbed at the wound. Stray voices filtered around a sandbag wall. The first sergeant was yelling into his telephone.

Refreshed, Hardin mounted the steps. The old sergeant stared at him with a lumbering disgust. Instantly angry, Hardin grabbed a stack of papers from the desk and sat down.

"Is Second Battalion still in Kontum, Top?"

Top reached across the desk and grabbed the papers, permitting an expression of mistrust. Not to be outdone, Hardin bumped the nameplate from the center of his desk.

Pestered by an indifferent shudder, Top said, "The mail chopper flies to Kontum every morning—0700 hours. Chopper pad's down this road. Where's your gear?"

"Kontum, I guess. Blacked out in the bush."

Top smiled with a confirming nod. "Chow hall's that tent, 1730 hours."

Hardin shuffled across a stretch of wooden-slated duckboards to the first barrack and laid down on a corner bunk. With a chilling strain, he listened to his father's voice as concentric rings of light converged, centering his vision on the image of an ornate cross. The eight-pointed iron cross, with its dark purple ribbon, lay in an oak case in his father's den.

* * *

Number #10, Highlands Road. Bremerton, Washington. September 1951.

"This picture is special, shot during one of Monty's briefings for liaison officers. Eight liaison officers worked for Monty on D-Day. During the European Campaign three liaison officers died. Six of us survived from the original group." The Major knocked tobacco from his pipe.

"How come you're wearing a tie, Pops?"

"The Field Marshall insisted on full military dress. The exception was when Winston Churchill paid a visit. I got this cigar wrapper from the Prime Minister when we crossed the Rhine River. His name's engraved on the seal." Eddie ran a finger over the cigar wrapper.

"Churchill made quite a show out of pissing in the Rhine River, laughing through cigar smoke about pissing on Germany." Eddie picked up an oak case from the lamp table near his father's chair and pushed the glass top aside.

"That's a Bronze Star, and some campaign battle ribbons. This one is the Victoria Cross. The VC is struck from a cannon the British captured during the Crimean Campaign."

* * *

Veterans Hospital. American Lake, Washington. 1995.

Karl looked at what he had typed. A British acronym rang in counterpoint from his grandfather's den, exposing one irony of his father's war. VC: Victoria Cross or Viet Cong.

What he heard on the tape was not the voice of the father he knew. The language, the jeering cockiness, the words were foreign. How could these have come from this sober and responsible man? True enough, he wasn't a choirboy. He wasn't a womanizer or a racist either. Did the war put this in him, or did it take it out?

Even his voice changes as he speaks these words.

"Here," he said on the tape, "put in here the piece from your grandfather that I wrote out on the top page. That was his war. I don't think you could talk turds in that war. You can just 'x' out those words if you want, or put funny symbols, like they do in the comics."

"Anyway, after that, go back to the tape. My mind surged..."

* * *

Holding Company Barracks. An Khe Base Camp.

Hardin's mind surged one moment, then marched with the rhythm of his heart, sorting odd bits of memory, randomly selecting an archive to explore. His body shook suddenly, fighting the involuntary tremor of aching muscles. Images confused: first his father, then his family, then the doctors, mixed with snippets of an NVA ambush, mixed again as if searching for a reason.

Any reason.

Hardin screamed as he removed the rucksack from his radio operator's body. The ambush destroyed Nuts in the watered blink of an eye, his death joining an accumulating blur.

Meat and bones had splattered across the jungle, coloring Hardin's face and uniform. The platoon radio lay in pieces. Fish took the radio battery, ammunition, and unit items from Nuts' rucksack. Squeak put the small personal items in the map pocket of Nuts' pants. A medic handed a dog tag to Hardin then tied a dog tag into the boot lace on Nuts' left boot.

The rotor blades of the medevac chopper seemed synchronized with the pulse of the war, as medics scoop body parts into a poncho. Blood flowed from the seams of the poncho: drops suspended in the smoke, then thrown about by the rotor wash. The cabled jungle penetrator drew the litter basket from the clay mud and turned slowly, lifting Nuts through the trees.

Nuts' casket would be closed, stamped with a leprous labeling—non-viewable.

The ambush lasted fewer than thirty seconds. Nobody saw the enemy, the NVA. Hardin's war would last another thirty seconds. The next enemy soldier would suffer a slaughtering meant for hogs. Retribution wasn't killing. Retribution was payback, a responsibility, a moral oath, an obligation, and the purest form of attentive lunacy.

Educated in the woods of the Missouri Breaks, Nuts understood loyalty.

CHAPTER TWO

Dig-it Johnson

Holding Company Barracks. An Khe Base Camp. 0250 Hours.

"El Tee, you been jaw-jackin' all night, cussin' some dude, callin' him all kinds of motherfuckers. Shit's got ya spooked." The black soldier from the hospital ward spoke with a street-corner praise, his large eyes braced for a deal, his expression locked in mock empathy.

The dialog made Hardin uneasy as he pushed at the bunk, mustering enough strength to stand. Struggling with his balance, he took off his fatigue shirt. Covered with dried salt, his waist was rubbed raw. He had lost seven pounds in four days: seven pounds he could not spare.

As the shock of harsh light receded, Hardin asked, "Ya got any water?" Hardin ran his tongue over his dimpled lips. His guts ached.

"Hang on, El Tee." The stranger rummaged in his rucksack and pulled out a two-quart flexible plastic sack; grunts affectionately called a tit-bag. "Here, El Tee, have some tit." Hardin's accomplice stood five-foot-ten, with a wiry build and eyes that seemed quicker than his mind.

"What time ya got?" The brother didn't have a watch, but looked at his wrist, gesturing as if a good officer would have noticed. Hardin had smashed his father's watch diving against a clump of bamboo in Dak To. His granddad's watch had simply run out of steam.

"It's early. You been hollerin' all night, ya know what I'm sayin'?"

Flush with the relief of being exhausted, Hardin stared with a vacant stare. He didn't trust the new men he encountered. How and when they became old men he wasn't sure. He hated the new men he couldn't avoid with hatred that made killing them seem logical.

With a body barely fit for bed rest, he stepped away from the stranger and said, "I was talkin' to my friends." Hardin cupped his head in his hands.

"I can dig-it."

These two men—a white lieutenant and a black grunt—were now bonded. Sacred words, those words of understanding: "I can dig-it" was a phrase spoken as one word. Hardin acknowledged the tribute with a nod and drank, pausing to steady himself with a deep breath.

Finished, he threw the empty tit-bag on the bunk.

"Nice tit. Where're ya headed?" he said, winding his watch. The new comrades had not exchanged names. That would come later, if both men wanted to remember.

"Kontum. Mail chopper's goin' north in the mornin'."

"That's the slick I'm on," Hardin said, waving the man away.

Tired, Hardin lay back on the bunk, letting his eyes search through the rafters. Slick? he thought. The Huey helicopter might be iron-shod, or in full foal: but never slick. Dozens of breeding cycles might produce an offspring that was slick.

Indifferent to speed, the Huey was barely faster than his '53 Ford.

Now his high-school ride was slick: candied gray paint, black-and-white Naugahyde upholstery, white shag rugs, a new Mercury long-block with a Ford truck tranny and drive train, moon hub caps, fluffy dice, and a case of Olympia Beer—Washington State's finest brew.

He got laid in his '53 Ford. In a Huey, he was certain to get fucked.

With skin as thick as a spider web and a windshield made of Plexiglas, the Huey was about as bulletproof as sunscreen—that or a grunt's helmet. Grunts did not care. They fancied the sound of the main rotor blade.

Drumming at the base of a man's balls, the rhythm replicated the pulse of rock'n'roll. The silhouette of a lone slick set against a red-orange ski, two fingers above the canopy, told the story of one last ride. Liberating, the sight brought hope for the grunts the slick drivers affectionately called SOBs—souls on board.

Pilots and crew are mustangs to a man, Hardin thought. In the finest meaning of courage, they would sally forth under fire and green tracers be-damned. "Ask any grunt," Hardin whispered. "About the Ghost Riders, or the Cowboys, or Casper, or Starblazer, and the rest."

* * *

Delirious again, Hardin slept a fitful sleep: covered with blood, he tied ricks of shattered bamboo into litter baskets. Dead men sprang to life, then died again. Four hours passed. When the black soldier woke him, Hardin's body was empty.

"Why are you houndin' me, stud?"

"The big dogs are lookin' for a GI who went missing from Delta Company, Second Battalion: same build, same size, no equipment. Top told me to check you out."

"A deserter. First I'm a sick asshole, now I'm a deserter." Or was he a deserter before he became a sick asshole? Hardin laughed to himself. "This war is nuts."

* * *

Consumed by the smell of sweat and stale garlic, Hardin winced as his stomach rumbled from a low boil into fits of antic barfing. In a resolute act of will, he swallowed and opened his eyes. The mess hall was a mess. Steam from a syrup tray had fogged his glasses.

Fumbling with the realization that a round-eyed woman stood-to in the chow line, he found her tits stretch-testing a helpless uniform. His tongue messaged his lips, lusting to give her the tongue-lashing she so richly deserved.

A frantic gasp creased his senses as he checked his traps, setting his fingers to jump her buttons. His mouth shot into overdrive. "Ma'am, do you know the story about the soldier leaving shortly for the front?" When she turned into his excitement, he was raising a full sausage, his expression reduced to teeth and slobbering and a pimpish grin.

B-Med's combat goddess bypassed the pleasantries and slandered his pride. "Shortly, that's a good one. Your crank's probably a midget." With fire in her eyes, she pulled down the hem of her shirt, accentuating her humor. Her trotters stood the strain as she declared, "One of those porcelain miniatures." She laughed across the tent, throwing her hair in an arc.

"Big Eddie's gonna be disappointed," he said, inviting her to sit down.

Laughing, she was not buying the line. She was flattered, but the words were just a comic interlude. "No short-time this morning, Joe. Big Eddie's on his own. Slap him around." She threw a laugh over her shoulder as she bounced away—a charmingly cordial girl.

Settling for a scramble of chicken eggs, toast, and coffee, his stiffy and the shimmy of her ass gave way to the reality waiting for him in Kontum. Hardin pushed the mess tray aside and folded his arms forward onto the table. With a fever chasing his heart, his eyes closed to his dad trying to skip down Highlands Road.

His father laughed. "I'll give you something to cry about." Then he laughed again. "Listen up. You find a way to be in this house, washed, and at the table when dinner is served."

The mess sergeant shook his shoulder, pulling at the corner of the mess tray wedged under his arm. Hardin sat back with a start, his eyes drawing into a gradual focus. He was trying to stop the man's words long enough to hear them. Then he passed out again.

He woke hours later, back in B-Med.

The black soldier and Doc Tweed talked in the hallway near the entrance to the ward. Fixing the wounded in their place, Hardin turned to find the Black Avenger next to his bed.

After a show of indignation, Hardin said, "Who the hell are you?"

"The name's Dig-it. That's right. Two syllables, just like everything in this fuckin' punk-ass-Vietnam. Ya hear what I'm sayin'? Dig-it, Doctor, B-Med, An Khe, Dak To, Kontum, VC, bullshit, ya dig what I'm sayin', El Tee?"

"You're startin' to piss me off." Dig-it registered the challenge.

"First Shirt told me to put you on the mail chopper in the mornin." Dig-it moved to his left as Doc Tweed barged into the bed.

"How's it hangin', Doc? Dipstick still peddlin' that glue?" Hardin asked.

"Major Dipstick," Tweed said, with a quiet laugh that made his body nod. "Dipstick wants to ship you to Japan. He thinks you might be infected with a dysentery of unknown origin, a DUO."

Tweed was pleased with himself.

"That's a good one, Doc. Really: Japan? Let's see if I got this straight. You're talkin' about a ticket to ride. I can skate because of an Asian rendition of the drizzlin' shits."

Dig-it's thoughts ran full circle, wondering if the lieutenant would skate, walk out on his platoon. "Wha'd'a ya think, Dig-it? Is Japan a two-syllable place to die, or a ticket to ride?"

"Hard tellin'. I got people countin' on me. Don't know how you got it hangin'. Maybe you can sky-up and not look back." Tweed stood in silence as Dig-it left the ward.

"Personally, Hardin, I think you have a fever that will dissipate with time and that exercise and good food is the best remedy. You won't be guilty of desertion. You may die in one of those two-syllable dumps, but you won't have left your post."

"Exercise and good food. What war are you fightin', Doc? Give me my clothes." Hardin stood on the floor, watching a multiple amputee struggling to sit up.

Tweed held out a metal clipboard with a clearance form pinned on top, along with a pen. "I'm not signing anything for you, Lieutenant. If you sign the release form, I'll slip it into the system, and a DUO from B-Med will have cleared you to leave this two-syllable dump."

Grabbing the clipboard, Hardin signed "I. M. Tweed." "Thanks for the memories, Doc. Give Dipstick a kiss for me." Hardin's uniform was one shelf higher and eight cubicles closer to the door.

He still didn't have a name.

* * *

Holding Company Mess Tent. An Khe Base Camp. 0630 Hours.

"You all right, El Tee?" Dig-it's voice reached under the canvas of the mess tent as Hardin fumbled with the complexities of gravity. Combustible enough to maintain trolling speed, he had been cleared for take off by the Holding Company First Sergeant.

"Hard to tell," he said, leaning away from a plume of heavy air.

"We best get steppin'. First Shirt wants us down the road."

Hardin stood into a forward lean, his hands on the table. His hair hurt. His balls ached with a heavy throb as they dropped to the bottom of the bag. Struggling to find a comfortable stride, midway through a spirited march to the chopper pad he walked backwards for a few steps, turned full circle, barfing chicken eggs in a spewing gust.

After a painful series of heaves, his guide's amiability was punctuated with folly.

"Give me some water." Dig-it's face bayed with disgust, watching Hardin wipe a sleeve across his mouth leaving bits of egg smeared on his forearm. Hardin drank in gulps.

"Here, take a white one." Dig-it dropped a malaria pill in Hardin's hand. "Top told me to cover your sorry ass. Pulling slack for a platoon leader is bullshit." He laughed and bounced into a restless grind. "Ya got no gear, El Tee. Top told me if he caught me without my M-16 he'd do a neutral steer on my nuts and send the bag to my mom."

Dig-it began rubbing himself into a slow canter. The men were off, acting commendable.

"Well, Specialist Fourth Class, what I need is some time with my bride and a ride all the way home." Hardin smiled to himself, thinking of Linda.

"Spec-Four Johnson. Friends call me, Dig-it. Can you dig-it?" Extending a fist, Hardin hit it. With the exchange of a modified dap, the two men were bonded on the ebony side of life.

"I lost an RTO named Nuts," Hardin said. "He was nineteen."

"I'm close to twenty."

"Well, Dig-it, the drill goes like this." Hardin assumed a story-time posture. "Went down with a fever in Kontum and landed in B-Med. My gear should be at the airstrip in Kontum."

Dig-it bounced off the outer reaches, laughing and shuffling when Hardin hit the word "fever." Cackling a string of nasty black drivel, he stepped through a well-rehearsed slide and jive routine designed to mesmerize the dummies, while he was careering into a foreign charactery.

"El Tee, you ain't suppose to get malaria. You hear what I'm sayin'? You're in deep shit, my man." With these garlic-gassing words Dig-it lounged into an easy grovel.

"Fuck-a-bunch of malaria. B-Med doesn't know what it is."

Dig-it laughed louder now, his feet tunneling into a boiling fit. Then he slid sideways through a spin. "Not that mystery shit. Your CO's gonna carve two more cracks in your scrawny white ass, and do you a tune. You know what I'm sayin'?" Dig-it, convinced this new lieutenant was history, pumped his fins and rolled into a jumble of flimsy servitude.

"Fuck you, Dig-it," Hardin said, mustering his authority.

"Hey, Baby. Fuck me. This whole mothafuckin' place is one fuck-me after another. You hear what I'm sayin? Fuckin' Charlie's got this block wired, you dig? Mothafucker's gonna bring the damn-damn on our ass. You know what I'm sayin'? You do what ya gotta do. Dig-it. Stick together to get this hip-ass, smooth talkin' brother on down the road." Dig-it dropkicked his rucksack into a heap, laughing to himself. For a brief moment, he was back on the block.

"I got a fuck-me goin' on, and I gotta listen to your nasty black shit. I could turn my ass into B-Med and be out of this shit, but I gotta deal with your jive about doin' it for the boys. Fuck you, Dig-it." Hardin's guts were in hyper-drive. Bile ebbed at his back teeth.

"There ya go. You got it. Fuck me."

"Roger that. Listen up, Dig-it. I don't need to be bagged in one of those grade-A, hex-weave rubber tuxedos with a dog tag fuckin' up my smile. I'm goin' back to the bush because I can't leave. I got jokers like you, and Blood, and Squeak, and Stubbs, and Rap, and fuck knows who waitin' for me to explode." Hardin's voice trailed off. His throat burned with pain.

The grass next to the chopper pad undulated in the flow of the rotor wash as the Huey fired itself to life. The crew chief marked his preflight checklist with a series of quick scribbles, studied the cargo, and gave Dig-it a boarding nod.

"What's the deal with this deserter?" Hardin asked.

"Some blond-colored dude from Delta Company dropped his shit and ran his sorry ass into the bush. Smokin' that wild weed."

"Maybe. That, or his squad decided to kill him."

"Recon teams spotted the dude runnin' with some dinks around Pleiku."

"You should desert, Dig-it. Lay-up on some three-syllable beach."

"I don't need a tan, El Tee. This brother needs his ass back on the block with his balls doggin' mamma's pussy." Dig-it smiled, tongue lashing the side of his rucksack.

"No one cares about your sorry ass." Hardin waved his hand in a lateral arc.

"That's no shit."

* * *

The hot air, the sunlight, the movement of the grass, all encouraging a dream, found Hardin courting a woman's starboard tit. When the slick shuddered into the air, he leaned into the door frame and acknowledged the door gunner. The aircraft drifted sideways, rotated into the wind, and nosed down, accelerating over the perimeter wire.

Rolling into level flight, the chopper found its trace: Route #19, a two-lane asphalt road that ran west from the South China Sea, through the village of An Khe, and north into the confines of the An Khe Pass. Hardin tightened his grip on the airframe.

As if cued by a foul wind, the door gunners leveled the barrels of their M-60 machine guns, adjusted their ammunition belts, and gave the pilot a heads-up.

Dig-it lay sprawled across the cargo deck, his head propped against the back of the pilot's seat, his eyes closed. This ability to sleep when almost all would be alert was a brass-plated reaction to the inevitable, waking up in Vietnam.

Hardin knew that a grunt had two ways to avoid waking up in the Airspace—death, and a continuum of other conditions that would send him home: wounds, malaria, desertion, court martial, insanity. To avoid these alternatives, a grunt would speed-sleep, hoping to wake up somewhere farther east.

When the command to sleep echoed through a grunt's mind, no matter the circumstance, buckled to a bee's ass, or knee deep in beer, the lights went out.

Asleep as he was, Dig-it Johnson was smiling, his dream leaving just enough room for another moment. "He must be gettin' busy," Hardin whispered.

Suddenly, without warning, the slick banked hard to the right. Hardin forced his shoulders into the bird. Rapid flashes of canopy rushed below his feet as the vegetation climbed to meet the landing skids and blurred into a maze.

The slick rocked back to the left, leveled out, and flew through a stream of AK fire. The Plexiglas bubble shattered in an arc. The pilot's visor and helmet exploded, throwing blood and shards of his flight helmet throughout the chopper. The copilot grabbed the collector and jerked the Huey up and to the right. The body of the aircraft shuddered violently, then fell to the right, plummeting toward the canopy.

Hardin grabbed the leg of the copilot's seat.

The door gunners gagged with rage, firing into a void defined by their fear. Within seconds another stream of steel rockets hit the bottom of the chopper, lifting Dig-it off the cargo deck. His convulsive wail pierced the day. He screamed and kicked wildly at the world. Fountains of blood leaped from his neck. Hardin grabbed Dig-it's weapon.

Comprehension gave way to insanity and Hardin became a spectator. He found himself outside of reality in a slow motion display as his friend spewed blood into the air. Dig-it screamed, and his helmet fell out of the chopper.

One door gunner bounced back and forth, squatting, pivoting wildly on the ass end of his machine gun, inventing targets and casting belt links and empty brass casings to founder in an obscure field. The second door gunner was strapped to a rhinoceros, his essentials wired to the gun handles, slinging red streams of tracers into the canopy, his lips moving. He was singing.

Hardin hit the quick release on Dig-it's rucksack and peeled the other strap off his right shoulder. Dig-it stared blankly, his body full of holes. Blood leapt at Hardin's face and pooled at his knees. Rivulets of blood raced across the cargo deck as if frantic tourists, searching after an ever-changing center of mass. Ripping at Dig-it's shirt, Hardin pushed against the wound.

The chopper lost power and fell to the right, in the direction of the turn. The copilot fought for control. The confusion accelerated. The slick was on fire. The screams, the frantic radio transmissions, the smoke, the shell casings, and the blood, all gave way to combat's isolation.

Hardin screamed, "Stop bleedin', goddammit."

Jesus Christ! Blood pumped out of Dig-it's shoulder and leg. War was a joke. If the Tambourine Man were around he'd know how to keep the sky from wearing out.

The door gunners continued to fire, unable to see beyond the barrel of their weapons. The main rotor slammed into the treetops kicking the body of the aircraft in a violent arc, throwing Dig-it and Hardin into the back of the dead pilot's seat.

Spinning, the chopper fell away from the trees and augured into the grass near Route #19, driving Hardin's face and shoulder into Dig-it's chest. The chopper bounced into the air, throwing Hardin into the back wall, then slammed into the ground, collapsing the skids. The grass around the chopper burst into flames as AK rounds stitched the aircraft.

Locked in a ballet, Hardin leapt over Dig-it's body, jumped out of the chopper, grabbed the rucksack and weapon in one hand, and back-hauled Dig-it off the chopper. The air shook with heat and eddies of over-pressured waves of sound.

Dig-it's right boot was on fire.

Frame by frame, Hardin dragged his friend away from the burning chopper. The copilot cleared the slick with his helmet in hand, and fell in a torrent of small-arms fire, AK rounds snapping at the air.

Frame by frame, the sequence was relentless. Hardin ran, dragging his dying friend. "Stop fuckin' screaming, Dig-it. Stop screaming."

Blood gushed from Dig-it's mouth in spurts as his body bounced across the ground.

"We gotta run." Dig-it's incessant screaming was their final betrayal.

Hardin caught himself. "Jesus Christ! I'm the one screaming." This had to be a farce.

Looking away from Dig-it into another dimension, the Huey exploded. The door gunners' doll-rag bodies flopped through the air. Desperate to rescue their pilot, they were blown into the air, christened in JP-4, jet fuel.

Frantic, Hardin started mumbling into the grass. "I must be dreaming. Jesus, this can't be real." He dragged Dig-it farther into the bushes. Dig-it gasped, clutching a letter and struggling to breathe. As he lifted his head to speak, he exhaled through a painful moan, and held out his fist. Hardin hit it. A parting gesture to seal their souls.

Dig-it was dead. His eyes stood wide, propped over his blood-stained teeth. He was staring into the grass, asking for an explanation. Hardin stuffed the wrinkled letter into the map pocket of his pants and dragged his friend deeper into the jungle.

The Huey added a final explosion, a muffled expansion of burning gas. Hardin crouched in silence, his head moved as though a ratchet, one degree, then two. He was searching for the glint of a rifle barrel. The pilot's body was melting in the flames. Hardin shook his head, then rolled Dig-it under a clump of dry brush.

"Shit. Where's your fuckin' weapon? Dig-it, you jive asshole, what are you doin'?" Hardin ripped at the vegetation. Dig-it's letter was gaining weight.

Whispering, his mind choked with fear, the rumors of NVA atrocities came clumping. American POWs didn't make it out of the jungle. The GIs from Alpha Company were executed in Dak To, four klicks south of the Poco River.

Surrendering was not an option.

The AK fire near the roadway was sporadic. A trail of broken grass led to Hardin's feet. Fighting a fear-soaked inertia, he moved in a low crouch back down the trail, watching for movement on Route #19.

Worn free of the echoes, Hardin spotted Dig-it's weapon and rucksack. The smell of burning bodies masked his senses. As if crazy, he laughed at his mounting tranquility.

Dig-it had been shoveled into an early grave. His rucksack wore an expression of fallen intensity, the aluminum frame twisted by the crash.

Hardin searched the far tree line. With fourteen magazines of ammunition and a rented weapon, he ran across the roadway. The smoldering body of the pilot was one with his chopper. The crew chief and door gunner was dead. Hardin ran in spurts, stopping to listen.

Running across the roadway, he found the copilot. The slick driver was banged up, but alive. Blood frothed from the copilot's mouth. He had a busted lung.

Hardin flattened his feet to lower the profile of his heels, then turned his head sideways in the grass. "Easy, baby. Talk to me."

The copilot looked at Hardin then laid his face in the grass. Blood seeped from the copilot's chest, staining the ground. The blood was nearly black. His liver was shot up.

Hardin inched closer, squeezing the copilot's hand to force him to respond. "Stay with me, baby." Enemy fire was light, searching for a target.

"Breathe, damn you." The copilot's fists were cinched in pain. "I hear a chopper, two choppers." Track vehicles raced down the roadway and another crapshoot began.

"Stay down, baby. Stick with me."

Huey gunships hovered off to the west, firing Vulcan machine guns into opposing tree lines. Two armored personnel carriers fired into Dig-it's tree line. A tank rolled to a stopped between the APCs and fired its 90mm cannon, carving a tunnel in the jungle with a Beehive round.

The gunships worked their way from east to west, saturating the opposing tree lines. Three GIs landed next to Hardin, firing short bursts from their M-16s.

Minutes later the firing stopped.

Dig-it was in one piece—his mama could caress his face one last time. As fear percolated through a cycle of shock, pushing at his reason, Hardin's throat had tied itself into a knot. He sucked at the saliva in his mouth and swallowed.

"Come on, Dig-it. Your black ass is goin' home." With his friend on his back, Hardin trudged along the trail of broken grass, again among the vines, in and out, stepping as if Dig-it had become much larger. Blood pooled in the hollow of his collarbone, then ran across his chest.

Hardin stood in silence, alternately checking the tree line and the copilot.

"Everyone's dead," he said to no one. In the end, he found the pilot flying the ashes of his wounded aircraft. The charred hands of the door gunner, burned stiff and brimming with smoke, curled above the grass, reaching for his mother, God maybe, weeping for his pilot.

The day began with the normal maddening, with young men mixing inexperience with too many guns. Now the day would never end. Hopping on the dust-off, Hardin tucked himself into a corner reserved for door gunners, waiting for the airframe to explode.

The medics worked on the copilot's chest, their hands moving from wound to wound, celebrating the completion of each step with a slight pause. Dig-it stared in silence, peering through a jiggle of IV tubing.

A quieting despair consumed Hardin as he focused on the odd sense of understanding in Dig-it's eyes. A mild turbulence in the airframe made him laugh. He was grateful for the shock. Once away from the war he would look for the words: words to foster a smile, private words of well-rehearsed humility. For now he held the image of a dead friend.

The medevac lifted off the roadbed. The battlefield seemed small.

Dig-it's eyes glanced at him, then raced away.

Minutes later the chopper landed in a sandbagged enclosure behind B-Med Field Hospital. Hardin sat without emotion, huddled in the corner of the chopper, recording the scene.

The copilot groaned as the stretcher absorbed his frame.

Doc Tweed looked at Hardin with a leveling stare that led to an assuring nod. Tweed saw war's heroes clearly: he drew pictures of their bodies, and labeled their wounds.

Climbing off the chopper, Hardin's heart rate surged, sending his feet through a series of stumbling strides. He stopped to draw a breath, then leaned against a sandbag wall. The crew chief splashed water across the cargo deck. A stream of tinted water fell from the chopper, splashed onto the PSB, and disappeared through the holes in the metal surface.

Working with a practiced, determined rhythm, the crew prepared their Missouri Mule for its next mission: IVs, bandages, morphine. A pile of used bandages lay against one of the skids.

"Thanks for helpin' us," Hardin said, extending his hand to the crew chief.

"No sweat, GI. You're the only one who's gonna make it out of this deal. We're doin' what we can." He looked away and continued to restock the slick.

"Thanks, anyway."

"Anytime, GI."

Strolling past his former ward, a likeable crew idled about, exchanging wounded gestures, consuming one reaction with yet another, plotting a complete lapse of discipline: men worn thin, hiding from the vibrations of trauma.

Accepting another day's rest, Hardin sat on the front steps of the field hospital, engraving Dig-it's memory into his heart. What energy he had salvaged from the fight was gone. No one knew that Specialist Fourth Class Dig-it Johnson—Eugene Johnson—was his friend.

"That's enough!" His father liked this command. "Pipe down." The Major had a booming voice. "Stand tall." He missed his father, not for the past, for what should have been.

Pals, that is what they were.

Surges of adrenaline forced Hardin to his feet.

With a seeping ache in his nuts, he realized the Methodists didn't have their own flag, and that was the worth. Old Glory's stars represented fifty religions ranked according to social equity. This revelation was bound to be a shock to Buffalo Bob. Hardin was losing his grip.

While he listened to the dusty hush of the empty street, the copilot continued to cry, and the walk back to the Holding Company went unnoticed. Today he earned $2.17 in nontaxable combat pay above his base salary, and the temporary use of an M-16.

No other man could speak about this morning: about getting shot down, or waking up to the sounds of tearing fiber, or riding the unexpected floundering of a wounded bird. With sarcasm on the rise, he said, "I wonder if Uncle Sam pays a full day's pay when a GI gets killed in the morning?"

Collapsing in the first chair inside the orderly room, he drew a labored breath. His throat felt as if he were gargling marbles. The smell of blood forced him to lean away.

Top stopped working with a gust of short desk organizing moves and surveyed Hardin's uniform, his eyes locking on Hardin's bloodstained knees.

"What time ya got, Top?" Hardin rubbed his face into an expression of relief.

"0814 hours." Top acknowledged Hardin's fragile grin. Top knew how to gauge luck and misfortune, and Hardin knew the precise time of day had no meaning. Whatever their fate, these two men were secondhand stock, marginal barter.

Hardin strolled aimlessly along the duckboards. The air was bitter, as if drawn through a straw. A faint echo sounded. Leaving Dig-it's rucksack at B-Med had not stopped the sequence.

Sitting on the edge of a bunk, he tried to relax. Dig-it screamed a melancholy scream, then laughed at Hardin's way. Hardin could have saved Doppler some time. The whistle of a passing train matched the scream of a friend dying in combat, dying alone.

These mental gymnastics were not driven by a fever of unknown origin. Burning with efficiency, Hardin had factored, categorized, and stored thousands of still-frame holographs, a library of the sights and sounds of slaughter: the smell.

And to think he had enjoyed watching *Victory at Sea.*

Bathing in a composite that drew his features into a similitude of voiceless regret, he considered embracing his fever, claiming it for himself as a profound remedy.

He was tired of war.

When Dig-it's replacement—the fucking new guy, the cherry—arrived in the jungle his face would be fresh and full of life. The proximity of death would bring wisps of curious fear. The FNG's hometown would project from an undecorated expression, his eyes filled with anticipation, nervous enthusiasm, and the need to make new friends.

With time, the new man's words would be minced into this and that, his eyes hollowed to expressionless mirrors bounded by recurring events. They were so foolish.

Hardin hated the new men.

The fever forced sweat through his pores as though juice through a cloth sieve. Scenes of Dak To played at random. Rows of empty bunks passed in review. His father was putting on his Victoria Cross when the circles of darkness narrowed his vision to zero.

Highlands Road was the best.

CHAPTER THREE

Top Sergeant

PeeWee Baseball Field. Bremerton, Washington. July 1951.

Our white uniforms glistened in the sun. The smell of bleach made us stand taller. The red pin stripes made us look taller.

Chief gave orders as if he was preparing the team for the county championship. We called him Chief because he told us to. A player could call him Chief or Coach. Today was picture day at the ball field. Two baseball dads wrestled with a navy blue blanket, each coaching the other, one dad cussing his best cuss as they tried to mount their stepladders in unison while raising the backdrop for our picture.

These baseball dads were not like any other dads on the planet. From a bleachered bower, these baseball dads could coat a ballplayer with wordless curses while their foul sighs pooled in the corner of the bum's dugout. Long past the yearn for hustle, they were relegated to shagging for Chief when he practiced the outfield.

Many good men missed the baseball draft back in '42. These dads blamed the war.

Picture day ended with a hamburger feed and a barrel of soda. When young Hardin got home the Major was stalking around his den, tracing the front lines of a mock battle for a lecture he was scheduled to give at the Army Reserve Training Center.

"Hi, Pops."

"Nice looking uniform young man." Eddie picked up a new letter from Murphy and read the salutation out loud: "Dear Major." The Major smiled.

"Murphy was my jeep driver. Called me Major, never sir. I guess that was my first name. When I overheard him talking, I was referred to as 'The Major.' He was a good kid, a young man I guess. None of us seemed old before D-Day."

"Do you miss him, Pops?"

"I miss our talks about the little things: our sweethearts mostly, flowers, a cool sunny day in fall. Murphy would talk for hours about, Katherine O'Brien. Murphy smiled a wistful smile when he talked about his, Katherine, with her red hair, and fiery green eyes."

"It's the little things you miss the most, Pal."

* * *

Walking with his father in downtown Bremerton was like walking with a celebrity.

Everyone greeted them as they passed F. W. Woolworth's. At times the Major belonged to his friends. Today he and his son were going to have a boxing workout and a swim at the YMCA. Then they would walk to the American Legion Hall for a game of pinball and a Coke.

Hand-in-hand they walked, talking about the day, Eddie's baseball game, their swim, his mother's birthday party, and being positive about life.

After a swim at the YMCA, they walked north along Washington Avenue to the headquarters of American Legion Post #201. The all-night diner across the street, with its neon lights and bright red booths, was filled with men waiting for the wail of the shift horn.

The used-clothing store, once a classy tailor shop catering exclusively to officers, catered now to the down-and-out, the windows filled with hundreds of discarded items, each harnessed with a small, round, white tag tethered to a short string. A set of false teeth sat in a dusty white dish. Eye glasses marked five cents and ten cents sat atop faded velvet posts, watching would-be customers pass by. Used clothing stood in rows at parade rest, waiting to be dismissed.

The store looked lonely.

The three-story brick building that housed American Legion Post #201 anchored the east end of Second Avenue, just down from the Rex Theater and the Rialto Theater. For Eddie, the legion hall meant twenty games of pinball. For the veterans, the legion hall was a dimly lit world of memories refined by years of unwanted corrections.

Greeted, they approached a small round table in the foyer, with membership card in hand. An old man grinned and extended his hand.

"Nice to see you, Major," he said as he sat up and smiled.

"Thanks, Andy. My pal will be playing pinball. Don't worry about him being in the bar."

"Never worry about you and yours, Major," he said with a mounting pride.

When Major Hardin entered the bar at American Legion Post #201, the routine was the same: a man in the lounge would holler, "Come on over and sit down, Major," and the men at the bar would look around, stand silent, and turn back to their drinks.

Signaling the men in the lounge a just-a-minute gesture, he would walk to the bar to get change for a dollar, a barstool, and a Coke. Then he would walk to the pinball machine, set the Coke and twenty nickels on the glass top, set the barstool in front of the machine, nudge Eddie on the shoulder and say, "Make the nickels last awhile, Pal, then give me a shout."

That done, he would buy a bourbon and water and join the men in the lounge area. The Major never sat near another veteran. If a single chair were not available, he would stand with his drink in his right hand to keep his left hook available.

When the nickels ran out, he was ready to go home to Highlands Road.

Riding in the car, Eddie said, "Why do those men wear ribbons and pins on their hats?"

"I guess their war isn't over just yet, Pal."

* * *

Holding Company Barracks. An Khe Base Camp. 1420 Hours.

Finding Hardin's face parked in a pool of saliva, Top shook him and said, "You've been out for a while, Lieutenant." Grains in wooden floor carried the rasp of a thousand boots. Hardin crawled onto a bunk and rubbed his eyes. Somehow the hours away from the war seemed to hurt him more deeply. His hands, wrists, and forearms were caked with dried blood: Dig-it's blood.

The keepsake his granddad gave him, the silver watch with the loose-link band, was smashed. Dirt filled the cavity between the jagged crystal fragments and the face of the watch. At 0719 hours the mail chopper had crashed near the roadway, and his body had slammed into the back wall of the burning airframe.

At 0719 hours, Dig-it was sentenced to death fighting for the last day of his youth. At 0719 hours Hardin had smashed his granddad's watch. War time had a clear reference. The watch fell away from his wrist exposing a brighter ring.

"What time ya got, Top?"

"It's nearly 1400 hundred. C'mon, you're going to B-Med." Hardin pulled away from the old sergeant and put the watch in his pocket. Frustrated, he turned less cheerful.

"Doc Tweed said I'd be hurtin." Hardin brushed at the odd bits of coagulate tangling the hair on his forearms. Dried flecks of Dig-it's life fell like confetti, wavering, forming a winged pattern on the floor between Hardin's boots. A raven perhaps.

The flakes lay glistening on the worn wooden floor. Top didn't notice.

"How about a cold Coke."

Hardin stood, avoiding the raven-shaped etching. His balls ached. "A Coke might be just the ticket, Top," he said. Tired and discouraged, he scrubbed at his face. Jelly-legged, he leaned into his stride. His step was heavy, sure enough. Drawing air deep into his lungs, he stopped to allow his heart rate to simmer.

The mess tent was empty except for a hard-boiled cook pestering a meat loaf. Washing his mouth with Coke, Hardin gave his tools a comforting massage, remembering that "don't let your meat loaf" was a high school expression, a parting challenge for the best of friends. He smiled, wishing he were still in high school. Friday nights were one hell of a lot of fun, dancing to rock'n'roll music and chasing a friendly skirt.

With Top perched on a stool as if the pond toad, feigning sleep, Hardin decided to pester the old soldier's need to find the deserter.

"Is that deserter for real, Top?"

"The first shirt from Delta Company thinks so. According to the story, the bastard told his fire team he was going to take a dump. They never saw him again."

With a look to caution his conclusion, Hardin said, "Or maybe the story has a twist: a squad feud, with paybacks."

"Intell reports have a Caucasian operating with a Viet Cong unit near, Plieku."

"I'll believe that when I kill him."

Hardin shifted his weight to relieve a cramp and felt a drag in the map pocket of his pants. Dig-it's blood had glued his dog tags, a gold wedding band, and the tin chain into a crusted tangle that resembled fishing gear left in the sun after cleaning the day's catch. Dangling the mess away from the table, Hardin rubbed it between his hands.

A mist of dried blood fell to the floor.

Shaking his head, Hardin had no memory of ripping the dog tags from Dig-it's neck. A soft pain eased into his chest as he closed his eyes and rubbed his face. Cast in a pale light, a set of World War II dog tags, yellowed with age, hung from the yoke of a brass desk lamp, next to a picture of his father's mate, Major Thomas Poston.

Staring, as if the horizon would become clear, he let the chain run through his fingers and read the inscription on the dog tag: Dig-it; Religious Preference: Baptist; Blood Type: A+. A chuckle caused Top to cock his head. Hardin dropped the dog tags onto the table.

"I guess you thought you might have to leave him behind," Top said.

"Check out the tags, Top." The old sergeant raised a brow as he read the nickname, not caring to create an emotional tie to another dead soldier.

"Damn kids." Top examined the gold band for an inscription. "The ring must have been a girl friend's, or for luck. Bad luck I guess." The age lines at the corners of Top's eyes softened as he placed one of the dog tags in Hardin's outstretched hand.

Hardin smiled, then laughed a short laugh, remembering the look on Dig-it's face when he asked him for a drink of water. "At least it's over for him, Top. No more mysteries."

Measuring the wear on his glasses, Hardin rubbed the lenses with a napkin, and said, "Can ya order glasses for me, Top? This is my last pair."

Top spoke without thinking. "Yes, sir." Top left the mess tent with an encouraged stride: determined to help Hardin.

The condition of Dig-it's letter brought instant shame. Dig-it had crushed the paper in his bloody fist, creating a lasting impression of his will to live. With the envelope pressed flat, Hardin read one word and then another.

The three-by-five-inch white envelope bore a black ink impression of an airborne logo. The lower left-hand corner portrayed four paratroopers with full equipment moments before touching down on their landing zone. A bold VIA AIR MAIL stood above his mother's name: Mrs. Almira Johnson, 1523 West Madison Street, Rutherfordton, North Carolina.

The envelope was unsealed. Hardin pressed the letter to the table:

Dear Mama,

How are you today? I've been in An Khe waiting for a flight. A young looking lieutenant is waiting for the same flight. The medics say he's got a fever of unknown origin. I think he's got malaria. We're heading for Kontum in the morning.

I'll be home in forty-nine days. There isn't anything around here to buy you for Christmas, so......

So numb his heart would not ache, Hardin wanted to finish the letter, to say he missed Almira Johnson's boy. This kind of sorrow, sorrow away from the war, was truly devastating. Combat sowed such seeds—tired soldiers, incomplete expressions, temporary friends, silent bells.

With shoulders too heavy to carry, Hardin stood into a sigh. This bloodstained letter, this remnant of a man's life, contained a due diligence clause—to be delivered safely from hell.

Living to keep such a charge would not be easy.

Hardin raised his Coke, drank a savoring toast, and promised God and Dig-it that he would deliver the letter to Mrs. Johnson. Shivers ran through his soul as his finger touched one bloodstain and then another. A trace of blood had soaked through the envelope onto the face of the letter, touching the salutation, touching Mrs. Johnson.

With words to sanctify his love: Specialist Fourth Class Eugene Johnson never swore in front of his mother. Dressed for church, he would dance around a pillar, waiting for his mother's inspection, waiting for her to adjust his tie.

"See ya on the flip side, Dig-it."

Delighted, without knowing why, a burst of energy brought Top into the mess tent, searching the empty chairs as if he had lost his hat. Waving his cup in the air, he stepped away from the coffeepot, allowing a nurse to fill her mug. Top smiled, registering a "ladies first," then complimented himself with a nod. Confused with impulse, he swirled his coffee with a short circular hand motion, teased out those familiar thoughts of romance, glanced at the nurse again, then ran his tongue around the lip of the cup. He loved this game of chance.

Mindful, as if he was out of time, Top checked his watch as he raised a hand. "I'll get you some clean fatigues, Lieutenant." His image filled the tent as the canvas fell back into the doorway. The old sergeant was winding something besides clean fatigues.

Having thought of Dig-it at every turn, Hardin tried to quiet his hands, forcing his palms flat onto the table. Coveting his despair, the shock of being alive took hold: recall, and the smell of blood consumed him. His chest heaved, then settled through a protracted shutter.

Hardin closed his eyes to a group of frightened men.

A chaplain stood near an altar, straining a soldier's bowels, singing a canticle. Hardin shot the chaplain. Then he was screaming, dragging Dig-it. Then he was holding the copilot's head, trying to cut off his ear.

Seven AK rounds had ripped through Dig-it's body from his crotch to his shoulder. His black matted hair, shaped with a permanent ring by the sweatband of his helmet, was soaked with blood and plastered with dry bamboo leaves.

Hardin's body fell into itself.

The faces of the men in his platoon appeared in the shadows of a stand of elephant grass. Their faces bore chalky white expressions of puzzled defiance, their images warped from paper-thin mirrors twisting in a stiff breeze, bobbing like corks. Instantly the scene miniaturized: soldiers, choppers, and grass. One man stood alone—the platoon sergeant.

Stubbs was taller than the rest.

Sergeant First Class Oscar B. Stubbs was a hawk-faced man with gray, penetrating eyes. He spent each day as the last, forcing GIs to pay attention, mixing caution with suspicion. He smoked Lucky Strikes and used each lighted butt to emphasize his orders or accentuate his point of view. The GIs in First Platoon respected Stubbs for his sense of honor, and his uncanny ability to appear next to a GI without the man knowing he was within earshot.

Cherries unwilling to listen to Stubbs found their lips wired to a bulldog's ass, licking non-stop until they saw every detail the way he saw every detail. A cherry who took his case to a higher authority got his ass whipped. Stubbs was easy to get along with. His battle-hardened formula was simple: the grunts did the gettin,' and Stubbs did the gettin'-along.

It cost money to watch Stubbs chew on his men. He was harder on his enemies.

Stubbs moved through the jungle like a snake, carrying his rucksack as if it were empty, in and out, winding through vines and elephant grass without as much as a brush of sound. And, as if born to the war, he could sense the silence that brought danger. He could hear the birds not singing. He could smell the changing mood of the jungle floor.

Stubbs stopped smoking only when he had to—on ambush.

Eight days before his thirty-fifth birthday he was posted to the platoon from the Airborne School Instructor Group at Fort Benning, Georgia. Stubbs swore he trained Hardin in 1964. He was sufficiently demented to be a jump-school instructor—a black hat.

Hardin knew this kind of dementia well. His brother, Court, thought God invented the airborne. Court was in charge of jump week training at the parachute school at Fort Bragg, North Carolina. A man cannot be more demented than the men assigned as jump-school cadre.

Oscar Stubbs had a natural appetite for new boots.

With a cold hollow stare, with a jaw shaped by a dull chisel, he relished the extremes of combat. Enemy contact was inconvenient, and casualties needed some slack-time.

With Stubbs on his mind, Hardin's guilt dwindled. Squeak and the rest were in good hands. Hardin surveyed his bloody uniform. In the end, he was just another grunt.

* * *

Outside the mess hall two chaplains stood locked in a circle of white rocks. After they spotted what looked to be a bewildered dolt, they welcomed Hardin into their midst.

"Good afternoon, sirs." Hardin offered a salute, expecting an over-world reply.

"Airborne," they chimed, mustering a half salute. "Do you need help, Troop?" They stood to each flank, surrounding Hardin with the Word.

"We need your help in the bush," Hardin said, mindful of his mood.

"We're doing what we can, son." Rage kicked at their choirboy nature.

"Son? Infantry platoon leaders aren't anybody's son." Hardin's sudden anger pushed the chaplains into a posture of stern patience.

"You have got to be more positive, Lieutenant."

"Sweet Jesus. You gotta be kiddin."

Seconds passed before Hardin could find another thought. The silence created by his assault left him with an absent stare. Top stood to Hardin's side.

"I got some fatigues, El Tee. You better get cleaned up." The men from the East agreed.

Focused on the tiny brass cross on the chaplain's collar, Hardin said, "Why haven't you been in the jungle when the poor fuckers are dying in the mud, with their shit blown off? When all we can do is wash their face and tell them it's okay?" Short-tempered, Hardin resented their lofty calling. The whole business was too cleverly managed.

Top sensed a change in Hardin's posture. Without verbal communication the chaplains agreed on a response. "With the hospital, and services, we're doing what we can."

Hardin tossed Dig-it's beads at the nearest chaplain. "Nice catch, Colonel. That's a black man's rosary. That GI knew why you weren't around. We all know. The only life-ever-after you're into is life after you're out of Vietnam. Maybe Jesus isn't real." Hardin turned and started walking.

"Lieutenant." The chaplain wanted to end the meeting with a prayer. Top snatched Dig-it's beads from his hand.

"Give it a rest, Chaplain." Top caught Hardin near the orderly room.

"God damn you, Lieutenant. Those two half-birds are here all the time." Top was pointing at the back of a fading religion, east, toward the Officers' Club.

"Relax, Top, God has already damned me and every other grunt."

Infantry soldiers, regardless of rank, were General Issue—GIs. Over the years, they earned many monikers—Foot, Ranker, Jimmy, Digger, Tommy, Dogface, Brownjob, Grunt, Boot, Eleven Boo, Boony Rat. No matter the handle, infantrymen knew they were special and that fear led to survival if luck would have it.

Curious to know how good luck might flourish, infantrymen prayed as if they would be forgiven, confident that bad luck waited near the next clump of bamboo.

* * *

After three wash cycles, Hardin rinsed Dig-it and the Ivory soap out of his hair—the soap anyway. He threw his shredded fatigues and what was left of Dig-it into a dented, olive drab garbage can. As he slid his butt into the clean pants, a jeep bursting with female-type nurses drove by, laughing at the sky. Or were they laughing at Big Eddie?

It would be tough to get laid in the back seat of a jeep.

Oh those nights spent in the back seat of that '53 Ford, swapping spit with his main squeeze, Johnny Mathis cushioning those wondrous night moves. Hardin had traded young romance for rice soaked carnage.

War Time, 0719 hours, a time of genuine sacrifice for a noble cause.

Reminiscing about stateside pussy, he opened the orderly room door. "Any word from Kontum, Top?" he asked, not caring.

"Uncle, your battalion XO called. He knows you're on the way back." Then, with a start, Top asked, "What happened to the mail bag?" Top searched Hardin's expression for complementary concern, hoping the lieutenant would finally be a soldier.

Not a chance.

"Are you shittin' me, Top? Jesus Christ. The pilot took a round in the face." Hardin grimaced in disbelief. Top had crossed into the tidal zone restricted for christening the elite.

"Fuck-a-bunch-a-mailbags."

"Malaria pill?" This old soldier would never stop pushing GIs back to the jungle.

"Dig-it gave me a white malaria pill this morning. I could use a spare."

Mailbags, chaplains, fevers of unknown origin, none of these would help Hardin get home to his bride—his farm girl, his Linda.

The walk to the mess tent triggered a familiar sequence of thoughts; the time of day in Washington, what Linda was doing, was she at the farm, was it snowing? How was Linda doing with her pregnancy? Their fifteen-month marriage seemed illusory, nestled in a stack of fresh hay on the other side of the world, where the civilized people lived. He longed to be home, to make love to his Linda.

Army chow was no match for Linda's cooking

Army chow was no match for Hardin's favorite long-range patrol ration either. Seasoned with a stick salami, eating a Lerp turned a foxhole into a world-class pizzeria.

Vacuumed wrapped in multicolored packages, salami sticks were stored in a cul-de-sac near the lower reaches of a grunt's rucksack under his spare socks, away from intruders. Hardin enjoyed fingering the oily spires, licking at the beads of spice.

With a packet of steaming spaghetti tucked in the confines of his inner thighs, he would pause, look about to ensure the safety of his treasure, savoring the combined aroma of salami and hot spaghetti. With a jeweler's eye he would hold the salami between his knife and his thumb, and slice eighteen pieces from each stick.

Hardin loaded eighteen rounds into his M-16 magazines. No one else knew he counted the pieces of salami: the two numbers had to match. When the numbers matched, luck would walk with him. Luck was not stepping on the chalk when he took the field in baseball, or bouncing a basketball the same way before taking a foul shot.

With every meal being a grunt's Last Supper, being superstitious made more sense in Vietnam's war than being prayerful.

After a grunt ate his fill and jealousy had faded, he would boast, "Hey baby, I have somebody who cares." A box of cookies, a tube of cheese, salami sticks, a bottle of Tabasco: the treasure brought a measure of civility to the chaos. The illusion brought harmony for a moment.

A gift from home could secure a grunt from disharmony for an hour or a day.

Laughing quietly, he sipped the mess hall coffee. Remembering his dad inhaling through conjuring breath when he sipped coffee, Hardin thought of the Major's favorite command: "Listen here." Since this command was impossible to follow, Hardin would make light of the mood and step in the direction of his father's gesture. Recognizing the insolence of his son's posture, the Major would issue his order again, and follow up with an "And no ifs, ands, or buts."

Hardin enjoyed offering one "but" to prompt his father's ire.

By the time he was driving, the Major's "listen here" had evolved to "listen up," which Eddie assumed was a counter-command for "pipe down." By the time Hardin graduated from high school, he realized his father's den was a sanctuary.

Locked in that den, World War II comrades stood their post, ramrod straight, in full fig. Major Edward Hardin cherished their loyalty. He spoke to one photograph with soft, reflective words: the flag-draped coffin of a British officer, Major Thomas Poston, a fellow liaison officer killed in action. Glory encased Tom Poston's sacrifice. Often, as if a ritual, the Major would sit in the soft light of his den, pensive, smoking a pipe, holding his dog tags, talking to Tommy, falling prey to a lingering guilt.

* * *

An ice cube chilled Hardin's teeth as he left the mess tent, heading for the Officers' Club. At length, his run-in with the chaplains had Jesus on parade. The day could not get worse.

"Freeze, Troop. Where's your cover?" Cover was an army term for hat. "Your boots are a mess. What kind of troop are you?"

Seeking his future in this full colonel's pattern of words, Hardin decided he was an uncovered, misdirected, bootless trinomial with attentive tremors and aching, sagging nuts. And really, considering his low career, his boots were in damn-good shape.

His aggressor was a weathered, full colonel with a polished metal hook for a right hand: nicknamed, the Claw. If the stories were true, the Claw was a legend.

"What unit are you assigned to, Troop?"

Being the odd man about the street, Hardin plunged headlong into the exchange. "Sir, I'm a platoon leader with Second Battalion. Dusted off from Kontum with a fever of unknown origin, FUO." Demonstrating remarkable restraint, the gold stars on the Claw's jump wings served their notice: combat jumps.

Hardin set his feet, staring absently at the old soldier's face.

"What are you grinning about Lieutenant?" he screamed, stifling Hardin's ability to think.

"And stop that goddamned bouncing. Are you trying to piss me off?"

Hardin bounced on the balls of his feet whenever he was trapped. The colonel gusted out a delayed conclusion. "Fever, you probably have malaria. How can you lead troops? Leadership: it's leadership, goddammit. You're too young to be commanding troops."

The Claw intended to increase the delirium until Hardin either pleaded for mercy, begged for reformation, or pissed in his pants—maybe all three. And since the old dog would send him afield anyway, and he didn't have to piss, Hardin started bouncing on his toes again, triggering a dramatic rise in combustion rates. The colonel's timing-lights ran red, and a bell clamored registering total disbelief.

Having concluded that Hardin originated from an unfathomable realm, and that his officer commission was distilled from a bovine mist, the Claw continued.

"Where I come from, Lieutenant, you couldn't burn shit."

Hardin could hear his father exclaim, "Don't get smart with me," as he collapsed in a heap. Any right-minded superior would have been satisfied with causing such an outcome, but the Claw was not finished. With voices in the distance, Hardin was grateful he didn't know where the old soldier called home.

"First Sergeant." The orderly room door opened. "First Sergeant, give me a hand here." Top rolled Hardin's face out of the dirt. "Private, get over here."

The Claw's boots were spotless. The old bastard was pigeon-toed.

"Get some water from the mess hall," Top said.

Scrubbing his face, Hardin twisted into the colonel's starched fatigues, scattering dust onto his boots. "I'm okay," he said. "Everything went black. I can get up, just give me a bit." He rolled over, crawled to his knees, then to one knee and, after a pause, stood into another of the old man's questions.

"What's wrong with you Lieutenant?" Jesus, what a great question. As Hardin's unctuous grin set Top's survival instincts to gassing, the colonel tried to speak.

Top was too quick for him.

"Sir, I checked with the surgeon at B-Med. This officer does not have malaria." Top was playing near the edge again, swirling his coffee with great abandon.

"He's got something."

Well no shit, Hardin thought.

"I'll get him squared away, sir." Top was at attention. The Claw was at attention. And Hardin was bouncing on his toes. Everything is permissible if you keep it to yourself.

"Do that, First Sergeant." The old soldier spun in place. Hardin let Top help him to the orderly room and waited for the screen door to slam shut.

"Cut loose of me." Hardin pulled away and dusted himself off. Top stepped back, his reaction going from shock, to disbelief, and then laughter.

"You piss me off, Lieutenant."

"Was that the Claw?" Scanning the firebase, Hardin found a maze of military trackways. A crucible mixing silent benedictions with the opposing forces of superstition.

"The deputy brigade commander, the Claw," Top said, his brow emphasizing his relief.

Years ago, in 1950, when Top embraced the Army's tradition of ordered compliance, the character of each day was identical. In 1967, in Vietnam, he could not assimilate the attitudes of incomplete soldiers. The misconduct of Vietnam's war—and the war's many elements of farce—had turned well-tended soldiers into scavenging, sarcastic men, willing to challenge any convention.

"I'll be glad when you leave, Lieutenant." Top looked out through the screen door, over the hospital, into the mountains south of the firebase. This wood-framed door would form his view forever, its screen faintly tinged with a red-brown haze.

Hardin smiled. His father searched the horizon when he summarized life's lessons.

* * *

Officers' Club. An Khe Base Camp. 1840 Hours.

Hardin massaged the beer can as he had a new baseball, stroking the surface with both hands, then pausing to read the graphics. The tension in his chest dissipated as the beer worked its magic on his mental junkyard.

With Jesus sparring with the Claw, Hardin set Dig-it aside and thought of Dak To.

Twelve paratroopers from Charlie Company stood-to after the Thanksgiving slaughter. Hardin called these men the Hill People. They were his mentors, his family. The rest... well, the rest were gone—dead or wounded. PFC Billy Kramer had called in air strikes. Before he took over the radio, a short-drop had killed the chaplain and forty-one other GIs. Thirty-six were already wounded, some had died waiting for a dust-off.

One hundred and seven paratroopers from one infantry battalion died on that hill in the central highlands, just south of the Poco River, in November of 1967. The NVA wounded another 282 paratroopers. Ten paratroopers were missing. The brigade held a memorial for the dead.

The Ceremony of the Boot was a macabre gathering of ragged faces. Survivors stood-to in a state of resentful collapse, baring witness. They were lonesome and estranged. Untested men filled the ranks, standing where their friends once stood. Empty boots stood erect, new boots dressed in rows: polished boots, one pair for each of the fallen.

Not enough boots—how could that be?

Beaten into a canyon of despair, their spirits dissembled, the survivors ranked themselves by order of misfortune. Dead to a man, Lord knows what their eyes might have done when they were closed. Consumed by the roar of the small-arms fire, sparring with the stench of death, their view of the world would be forever framed by the splintered spires of a wounded jungle.

Fierce in their own nature, mangled NVA soldiers, each still willing to argue, lay rigid in the steaming heat. Brown-skinned soldiers slouched from their bunkers, awkward, their uniforms casting a yellow-brown hue.

* * *

Veterans Hospital. American Lake, Washington. September 1995.

The tape ran out, and he didn't notice. I didn't tell him, so there may be something missing from his story. I found myself not wanting to delete a single word. As I listened and typed, I began to hear the sounds, began to smell the odors, and began to feel the depth of sadness he carried each day.

I've tried since then to ensure he had a new tape every morning and every afternoon. He's looking tired now and talking while he lies on his side, his feet curled under him. He stares out the window as he talks, seeing only the past.

* * *

Officers' Club. An Khe Base Camp.

With private words, for Stubbs and the rest, Hardin sat waiting for the next blue moon when Doc Tweed barged through the door, bought himself a beer, and sat down at the table with a billowing thud.

Neither man spoke.

When Tweed finished his beer, he said, "I told you not to send me any people and you fuck me over the very next day."

"That's the first time I've heard you swear, Doc."

"I don't do it much," he said, crushing the can.

"You drink much, Doc?"

"I don't need your festering shit, Lieutenant. We lost that pilot."

Doc Tweed and Hardin drifted into separate worlds, each man trying to let go, each man wishing for a solution. Hardin paid a dollar and bought four cans of beer. Tweed gave a grateful nod, holding the cans as if he might lose his grip.

"Beer, whiskey, grass—what's your pleasure, Doc?"

"At this point it's beer. It's anyone's guess where I'm headed."

Hardin moved his can around in a pool of water on the tabletop, then looked at Tweed. "We're scared, Doc." Hardin shrugged as if to apologize. "Drugs are easier than an AK."

The evening ended with a pledge to be safe.

For luck, Hardin chose a different bunk and curled into a poncho liner, caressing the smooth fabric and fondling his borrowed M-16. At first he slept without dreaming. Curiously, as if they were searching, faces began to appear. Nuts screamed at Dig-it, then died in a flurry of slop. At every turn, grunts lay strewn across the jungle floor.

The Army called the men in Hardin's brigade Sky Soldiers, designating the unit as one of the rapid-reaction-force units fighting in the mountains of South Vietnam. "You are good-to-go anywhere in the airspace," Hardin said, mimicking a general's speech.

Awake, he thought about the mess he was in.

As infantrymen from across the centuries, he and his men had volunteered to die in any bore-hole their country fancied. America's most powerful men, from America's greatest generation, had wagered that US Army grunts could pacify the two-syllable hamlets of Southeast Asia and out-fight agrarian peasants the world over. Dak To was such a hamlet.

The Major would be worried, Hardin thought.

Eight of the twelve men left standing were in Hardin's platoon. They were worthy men: sure enough. Good soldiers. They were the men who must not die. Generals from times past, these men were the best soldiers to ever step through the wire.

Hardin plus eight: they found the continuum of expectant death the perfect sanctuary for the friends they had lost and the men they could not find. And yet, they were alone.

An inner torment was the core of their longevity—longevity garnished with echoing screams and shattered lives. Braced by the roar of gunfire, they waited for someone to raise a flag, any flag. Hardin laughed a muted laugh. He had not seen an American flag since his father's funeral.

Dancing with death in the mists of this remote jungle, Hardin and his men had become travelers, drawn down a precarious path, choosing one direction over another, questioning the choice, knowing the probability of making the right decision at every cluster of bamboo for a year was absolute.

The probability was zero.

With minds flash-fed through such a maze, Hardin and the men like him, eventually became one, the spine of their courage laden with doubt, the right choices saved for another day.

* * *

Hardin woke in a frenzy, fighting to focus on the target in front of him fumbling with the selector switch on his weapon. The man stumbled, then fell into the bedsprings of the adjoining bunk. Hardin stood into his enemy with no sense of reason, his weapon empty.

"You fuckin' dumb ass!" Hardin screamed. "Get the fuck away from me." Bits and pieces of chaos converged as Hardin's face contorted in pointless fury. The stranger screamed.

"Jesus, stop tryin' to fire that gun!" The GI extended his hands, then turned and ran. Hollering as he stretched into a frantic stride, his feet barely touched the floor.

With a piss-pressured hard-on clamoring for work, Hardin laughed at the intrusion, stretched to message the alcohol from his neck, then repositioned his crank, dressing his essentials to the right as he entered the orderly room.

"Where's Top?"

"B-Med, makin' sure that dude's shit gets sent to the world." Dig-it was almost obscure.

The walk to the chopper pad, steps filled with the blood that stained Dig-it's teeth—his last smile—found Hardin searching for someone to kill. Anyone would do.

The Huey's crew chief was conducting his pre-flight check. Half-throttled rotor blades pushed the grass with a rhythmic ease. Hardin sat on the cargo deck and said, "You gonna follow the road?" The crew chief laughed over his shoulder and plugged his helmet into the chopper's commo system.

The chopper slid sideways, gained altitude, and nosed out over the wire. A hard right turn brought the canopy under the skids so close you could hear Charlie breathing. Courting a blank mind, Hardin found himself singing, oblivious to his circumstance. Today was a soft rock format: "Are you goin'... to San Francisco. Be sure to wear some flowers in your hair. On the streets... of San Francisco... there's gentle people."

Flowers were forever; the rest was just the war. Dig-it died whispering about his mom, his life a fetch shortened by curiosity.

Hardin would miss him dearly.

CHAPTER FOUR

Uncle

Battalion Headquarters. Kontum Airstrip. 1123 Hours.

Hardin jumped from the chopper and ran into the dry grass bordering the airstrip at Kontum, his senses keen. A clatter of dusty tents sat untended, like abandoned bunkers. The day packed a haunting toughness, forecasting an impending exchange. The heat made the air dance, muting the landscape with a continuous waving motion. Hardin looked back at the crew. They were relaxed by the routine of shutting down the chopper.

Deciding the slick drivers were asleep, he switched his weapon to semiautomatic. He hadn't seen or heard a jot. The tents seemed to crouch. The grass was a blend of short and tall stubble that announced his step with a cracking rush. He stopped abruptly, searching—first left, then right.

"This coffee sucks." The declaration rang with delight. Hardin laughed at his one-oared mind and turned toward the personnel tent to find the local deanery.

"I'm Lieutenant Hardin," he said, plowing through the canvas flaps. "You got my rucksack and weapon?"

"Yes, sir," the clerk said, pointing to the rucksack and M-16 parked in the corner.

Reunited, Hardin stood in silence, consumed by a special kind of loneliness. The shoulder straps of his rucksack were spot-painted with the quiet of a dead man's blood: Nuts' blood. Expanding the drawstring at the top of the pack, he paused, then frowned. His most treasured keepsake, his necktie, was wrapped into a ball and stuffed into his canteen cup.

He shook out the blessed totem, then admired its symbols. Musty odors of lost time sparred with tiny warming explosions as he slipped the drive-on rag over his head and centered the knot on his chest. More erect, he was now a worthy scout.

The drive-on rag was fashioned from a standard army bandage designed to tie off wounds, sling an arm, or secure a tourniquet. This particular bandage was embroidered with Hardin's name, the Sky Soldier patch, a set of jump wings, and a combat infantry badge, embroidered with black thread, now faded to a sunburned brown.

"Everything should be in order, sir." Stepping with a curious urgency, the clerk secured Dig-it's weapon. "I'm glad you made it back," he said, forcing an end to the encounter.

Of course he was glad. A combat rucksack parked next to a rear-echelon desk was tenacious, making alarming insinuations about the clerk's honor, his philosophizing to hide his fear, and his playing slap-dick with Louie.

With his rucksack over his left shoulder, Hardin grabbed his M-16—his Sweet Pea—by the carrying handle, draped the olive-drab towel guarding her lovely midsection over his right shoulder, and walked to the airstrip. He sat in the grass halfway between the mess tent and the chopper, determined to be an unworthy target.

Emptying the rucksack, Hardin sorted the items, ranked side-by-side. Sweet Pea was laid on the towel to field-strip her body, and oil and tune her firing pin. Hardin gave her bolt a kiss for luck, stroked her black butt, then put every piece back in its place. Sweet Pea glistened in the sun, laying freshly oiled on her towel, ready to rock'n'roll.

After four days of fighting in the steep, jungle mountains southwest of Dak To, Hardin had filled two Claymore bags with twenty-round, M-16 magazines. Twenty magazines fit in each bag. One bag hung around his neck and one sat in his rucksack. Eight additional magazines sat in the side pockets of his rucksack.

The magazines were short-loaded with eighteen rounds to keep the following spring inside the magazine as lively as possible. Round by round, he unloaded the magazines, testing the strength of the spring and cleaning each round. Almost all grunts carried forty to sixty magazines of ammunition in the central highlands for good reason: resupply in the triple canopy jungle was difficult, and keeping track of empty magazines during a firefight was impossible.

Wiping at the sweat on his face, he scrubbed the stained borders of his fingernails. Shredded at the edge, stained with salt and blood, the odor of his drive-on-rag was stimulating and precise enough to bring his memory to a boil. With an imprisoned breath, he slipped the rag over his head, accepting the inevitable.

Talking to himself as if a stranger might hear, Hardin said, "I bet Squeak is so short he can't find his cock." Hardin tossed his helmet over in his hand to see if it had lost any weight.

"A three-pound piece of steel shit," he said.

With a huff, he put his helmet on backwards, let it settle, and then jerked it back and forth until a comfortable grove was pressed into the side of his head. He laughed at the Army's logic: camouflage covers, camouflage bands, green fatigues, and green boots, worn by GIs carrying bright white toilet paper.

The camouflage band was a half-inch-wide rubber band covered with an olive drab fabric that stretched over the helmet, designed to keep the camouflage cover in place, anchoring any attitude a GI wanted to express. The

Army expected the GI would camouflage his helmet with branches, grass, and such. Not a chance.

The GI used his helmet as a billboard: the ace of spades, a unit patch, a pack of cigarettes, a postcard, a red plastic flower, a bottle of mosquito repellent.

On the morning of 20 November 1967, in a fit of depression, consumed by the smell of death steaming from the jungle floor, Hardin inked death's final proclamation on the camouflage band of his helmet: "Flowers are Forever."

That night, in the black of the jungle, a fresh grave appeared. The headstone was hollow, devoid of form, floating in a religious half-light. The epitaph was dedicated to him, to Lieutenant Edward Hardin. The date was hidden behind a single red rose.

Linda kneeled near the grave, admiring the tiny blue crystals outlining the headstone. She was crying, her hands gently consoling her unborn child, admiring a bouquet of white roses sitting atop an adjoining grave. A crystal blue vase sparkled with frost.

Hand grenades echoed throughout the night. The sounds of men dying alone were mixed with pleas for water and whispered prayers. The company was out of morphine. They wanted to run; there wasn't anyplace to go. Hope, they had hope.

"One more grenade," he whispered, then accepted his fate. "Maybe the dinks will plant flowers. Red geraniums would work—red geraniums, with yellow stars." He laughed in the dark. His enemy didn't like gardening; they liked killing GIs. They were good at it.

Wearing sunscreen, and a light coat of oil, Charlie seemed to evaporate at will. Charlie would defend Dak To—he would defend his home.

The metallic rage of a machine gun bolt announced an end to Hardin's dream. One of the door gunners was pestering his whore.

Hardin lay in the warm grass, searching the tree line on the far side of the airstrip. The day seemed too quiet. Heat waves boiled from the airstrip like water falling uphill. The sun-baked grass filled the air with pollen-laden currents.

"Come on you rat bastard, shoot me," he said, looking for the enemy scout that watched the airstrip. The air was heavy with silence.

Suddenly, men burst from the tree line on the far side of the airstrip. AK rounds stitched a path across the ground, throwing patches of grass and earth into the air. Hardin's shoulder shattered. Time leapt into another dimension, then ripped Nuts' body apart. Hardin shook his head, then rolled onto his back and covered his face with his drive-on rag.

Silence was abnormal in the jungle: not something a GI could barter with. His memories would stalk about, hiding at times, wired to the revenge of close quarters.

"Hey, Troop, get off your ass. Mess sergeant needs a hand."

A rear-echelon captain was addressing Hardin rudely, ordering that he work in a kitchen. Hardin's first reaction would have sent eighteen rounds next to the captain's boots, but Sweet Pea was sunbathing. Instead, he fumbled with his helmet and stood up. The captain's uniform was clean, trailing a hint of soap at the corners of the shirt. With disrespect on the rise, Hardin decided the captain's name was Clyde.

Without thought, he broke into the Lord's Prayer. "Our Father, who art in the airspace." He stopped and glared at the captain. Do rear echelon captains come from a mass birthing tube somewhere east of Biloxi, for whites only? Yes they do.

Unshaven, insubordination was the answer.

"Ease up, Clyde. I have an FUO." When he grinned and put his helmet on backwards, the captain fired into a four-inch hover, extending his hands for balance.

"What's your name, Troop?" Clyde tallied Hardin's flaws with unvarnished glee. Sending his shoulders through a series of cocksure postures, he ended on the tips of his toes.

"Hardin."

"Get your ass over to the mess tent, Hardin."

"Anything you say, asshole." On that note Hardin grabbed his gear and started walking.

"What was that?" Clyde's eyes were like ductile mush, dull-minded.

"What?" Hardin looked across the airstrip, his expression fishing with concern.

"What did you call me, Troop?"

"Inspiring. I called you inspiring." Hardin followed him to a sagging, general-purpose tent with rolled sides, surrounded by sandbags. He selected a chair with arms and dropped his gear at its feet. Clyde had disappeared.

"Mess Sergeant, you got any cold soda?"

"I think we do." The mess sergeant plunged his hand into a barrel of ice, then raised the can as if he were lifting a precious stone.

"Thanks, Sarge." Hardin toasted the air.

"Anytime, GI." Skating on the rim of a sexual fantasy, Hardin was enjoying the intricate phase of tongue-searching his combat goddess, when Clyde made his reentry.

"Get on your feet." His mouth was reaching for another word when Hardin screamed.

"Get outta my fuckin' sight." Clyde scrambled into a withered foreskin, his eyes registering a flagging authority.

"I want you in my tent, now."

"Why not?"

Rucksack in hand, Hardin found himself toggled to a specimen of blue-green algae, pond scum, marching off to a tent marked, S-3, which was battalion operations. "Capeetan, every time your left foot hits the ground, order and discipline explode into the air."

Clyde was juggling reflexive prattle when the two men entered his domain.

"Hey, El Tee." Willie Spencer, a GI from Charlie Company, flashed a smile of recognition. Willie had survived Hill 875, wounded.

"How's it goin', stud?" Hardin hit Spencer's extended fist with enthusiasm. The joy of meeting another man who understood the war was unexplainable.

"Kinda spooky." His eyes darted from corner to corner, keeping track of the captain.

"Around here, you're pretty much on your own." Hardin motioned to the captain, who had assumed a more determined posture.

"Yeah, I know." They laughed and hit each other's fist.

"At ease, Specialist. Go get me a Coke."

"Yes, sir!" Spencer cleared the door, relieved to be away from the bilge.

"Get your own fuckin' soda, Captain." With extended eyes, Hardin waited.

The man was stupid. Out of habit, he continued categorizing Hardin's violations of the Uniform Code of Military Justice. Hardin laughed, wondering what the captain thought he was going to do, send him to Vietnam? Jesus, Hardin would be fighting for his life within an hour.

"You always this cozy with enlisted men, Lieutenant, or is this a special occasion?" The occasion didn't seem special; he was rogering off to Battle Bullshit.

Revelations 1: Clyde was a cherry. Now that was special. Hardin leaned against the desk opposite the captain. With his Sweet Pea on hold and his rucksack on the floor, he conjured an analytical look, then erupted with a declaration.

"You're a cherry, a fucking cherry!"

"You're an insubordinate son of a bitch." Clyde was swearing at an insubordinate subordinate. *That isn't possible,* Hardin thought. After Clyde chewed on the details, he would find his confusion. Hardin experienced such confusion in high school: soft, hard tits.

"Top thought I was a deserter, Doc Tweed said I was a sick asshole, and now you claim I'm an insubordinate son of a bitch. I may be all three. But believe this: there are degrees of reason you can't measure until you've been in the jungle long enough to lose part of your mind. And understand this: there is no one in this tent that works for you, that cares what you think, or cares what happens to you."

The captain was geared to respond when Spencer returned.

Hardin grabbed the captain's Coke and drank, then toasted his adversary. "Thanks. We don't get many of these." No one spoke, so he set the can down, grabbed his rucksack, and looked the captain in the eye. "Don't come to the bush. If you do, I'll kick your sorry ass."

The words were still floating when Major Bowden—Uncle, the battalion executive officer—entered the tent dragging another captain by the commission.

Willie Spencer left the tent in a rush.

Uncle was a short, husky sort who forced his communication on you with a load of gravel. He stuck life in a man's face, and the man either handled it or he didn't. Uncle and Col Dimmick, the battalion commander, had ferried ammunition in Dak To for twenty-two days. They lost four slicks in the battle, two of which they procured from the Fourth Division.

"Hardin, good to see you. How's the body?" Uncle asked. The two men exchanged handshakes, trying to ignore the rest. The major was a classy, full-speed kind of soldier.

"About as stable as my mind, Uncle," Hardin said.

"That's not good. You were lights-out when we dusted you off."

"It's a mystery to B-Med." Clyde farted with the realization that Uncle and Hardin were more than old friends.

"What's this about hammering my new captain?"

"Some other time, Uncle."

"Get your gear. We'll talk on the way to the chopper," Uncle said, lighting a cigar.

"This place is spooky. No birds, no aircraft, just hot air." Out of habit Hardin scanned the tree line on the far side of the runway.

"Lots of reports of enemy units moving south and east," Uncle said. The two men chattered like old friends must, trying to promote each other's well being while gradually saying good-bye. "Charlie Company picked off three NVA near a blue-line."

"Water and pussy—dangerous stuff."

Uncle agreed with a smile, fondling a memory, then shook his head, as if Majors were more proper. "The NVA have elephants packin' their heavy weapons." Uncle raised his brow. "That's a first for me." Uncle picked up a spent cartridge, involuntarily searching the tree line.

"Elephants, no kiddin'. The studs must be lovin' that."

"We dusted off Watson. The stud in front of him tripped a booby trap. He caught a bamboo stake in the thigh, one hair below his nut-sack. Lots of blood."

Hardin opened the bolt on his M-16 to check the chambered round. "The dust-off wasn't Webster, was it?"

"No. Don't miss your ride."

* * *

Alone, as if drawn into a hush, war's echoes ran wild along an ancient circular path.

Hardin's anger surged as he found himself entering the S-3 tent to show the captain his shadow. "I appreciate the cold soda, and the pleasant conversation." Clyde lightened his clipped expression and sat virtually immobile, countering Hardin's stare. "Say you're welcome, Clyde."

"Fuck you, Lieutenant."

"There ya go. That's the spirit. Fuck me. Fuck you." Hardin stood-to, placed the empty can on the captain's desk, turned the label toward him, and grinned to piss him off.

"Don't come out to the bush. We got time-tested deals for people like you. You and that fuckin' deserter." Hardin hit the tent flaps without looking back and headed for the airstrip. Clyde was the kind of man who got his rocks off in typing class.

Hardin laughed out loud.

* * *

One boxing match he remembered well was a smoker he would have remembered no matter where the match took place. Spring semester, 1958, four days before summer vacation. Hardin sat in his high school typing class, grinding out twelve centered words per minute, desperately trying to concentrate. His shirt was wet with sweat.

This was the final exam.

Suddenly, two senior girls were screaming. A double-dog-dare was thrown and the fight was on. Joyous roars met whirling jugs as typewriter after typewriter crashed to the floor. Desks gave way under an onslaught of screeching expletives. Echoes reached across the quad as these voluptuous two-baggers ripped each other's clothing, tortured each other's tits and kicked each other's box.

Holy horseshit, what a wonderful day.

Naked except for the strings, two sweat-ridden beauties stood braced in the sun, exhausted: neither willing to concede. With their chests heaving, their tits glistened and shook: marvelously unsupervised.

Hardin was consumed by thoughts of this tag-team flogging his manhood.

High school memories were great sport: rock'n'roll dances, parties at the fairgrounds, covering your hard-on at the concession stand at the drive-in movie.

Highlands Road was the best.

* * *

Hardin withdrew as the sidewalk in front of his boyhood home became a vacant airstrip.

Stifling heat dampened the chatter of the chopper crew. With a mounting sense of isolation, Hardin sat in the grass to check his gear: Jungle sweater; three smoke grenades—white, red, and purple; two trip flares; a strobe light; a four-inch K-bar knife; compass and map; two frag grenades; two one-quart canteens; three Lerp rations; air mattress; poncho; grease pencil; matches; lighter; a quarter-pound stick of C-4 plastique explosive; thirty feet of det cord; one Claymore firing device with blasting cap; one homemade bamboo grenade filled with C-4; forty-eight twenty-round magazines; bush hat; drive-on rag; and helmet.

Two items were missing—belted M-60 machine gun ammunition and a radio battery.

Asleep, Hardin heard footsteps in the dry grass. Willie Spencer squatted five feet away.

"What's up stud?" Hardin followed Willie's eyes.

Tentative, incomplete, and fragile, Spencer mustered his best smile. "Ah," he said, forcing the question. "I was just wonderin' how Hippie was doin'?"

"Hippie took the point squad. He's doin' all right."

Watching for relief to register on Spencer's face, the young soldier's throat seemed to fill with a bayful scream, his boastful youth left near an empty sandbag. Spencer looked to the mountains. Grief seemed to be pushing at his heart.

More of Spencer's friends will die in the mountains of the central highlands, Hardin thought.

"Do somethin' for me, Willie." The request was an instant adhesive.

"Yeah, sure," he said with an audible sigh, then brushed at his sweat-matted hairline.

"I'm on my last pair of glasses. And who knows where my mail is?"

"No sweat." Spencer would take Hardin's place if he asked him to. "You're gonna need this, El Tee." Struck with familiar assurance, Spencer touched Hardin's wrist, and then unbuckled a leather-backed watch from his arm.

"You're right." Hardin flashed on the crystal of his granddad's watch, smashed into a jagged testament, marking Dig-it's death: 0719 hours.

"That watch made it off the Hill," Spencer said, nodding good-bye. "Take care of it."

Hardin strapped the two small rusted buckles into place. "How many days ya got left?"

"Sixteen and a wake-up." Spencer shook with fear.

"Get out of Kontum, Willie, before it gets overrun," Hardin said, waving at the mountains. "The boys are good to go, Willie. We'll make it."

"Yeah. Makin' it." Willie's voice faded. The young trooper spun around, still in a crouch, then stood and stepped away, keeping the burden of forsaking his friends. Guilt, his reliable companion, made leaving the war the hardest thing he would ever do.

"Hey, Spencer," Hardin yelled. "Tell Uncle to send you to An Khe to track down my glasses, medical emergency."

He smiled immediately, then held up a thumb. "Get fat if you can, El Tee." Willie Spencer turned into a quicker step.

Hardin's new watch was a Seiko, a Japanese reflection of war, with tiny blue crystals instead of a rising sun. The blue crystals seemed familiar.

With the exception of his cocking cam, Hardin was asleep when the chopper crew fell in for the resupply run. The double diamond on the tail boom of the chopper, a large white diamond with a smaller red diamond in the center, was the symbol of an aviation unit affectionately known as the Cowboys.

"The Cowboys know how to fly," Hardin declared.

Hardin hopped into the chopper and sat tight against the right door frame, his usual spot. After lustful words for his weapon, he surveyed the chopper. Setting his rucksack aside, he cinched the sling along the left side of the magazine housing and laid the weapon across his lap.

Taking stock of the vertical struts attached to the landing skid, the rivets looked solid and the distance to the skid had not changed. To short-hop from the cargo deck to the landing skid while the chopper was in flight required the suspension of good sense. That, or Charlie firing AK rounds through the aircraft. Wanting a parachute, Hardin took a deep breath.

"Well, Hardin, you wanted to be a Brownjob."

Placing his helmet on the cargo deck, he read the inscription on the camouflage band, "Flowers are Forever," then exchanged a conclusive nod with the crew chief.

The young warrant officer driving today was a legend in the central highlands, a real-time hero. Mr. Ballard wore a bright, white flight helmet with Alfred E. Newman painted on the back, a Chinese 9mm strapped to his chest, and a facetious grin. The AK-47 strapped to the back of his seat was brand new. Mr. Ballard and his mates had saved a lot of lives.

Checking the time as if he were late, Hardin laid back against his rucksack and closed his eyes, loosening the strain in his forehead. He was anxious to see his friends.

Beads, earrings, bamboo grenades, and drive-on rags: the grunts in Hardin's platoon were awash with defiance. The Army couldn't threaten these grunts, or give them a gun and send them to war. And if their earrings didn't do the trick, they would parade around with their helmets on backwards while crippled with an expression of puzzled disorder, an expression akin to a demented teenager whose balls had just dropped.

Deviltry had twisted their minds beyond the abstract, so far around the bend you could hear them when they were talking to themselves.

* * *

Shadows started reaching for the airstrip.

Breaks in the bordering vegetation nodded sporadically, alerting Hardin's stare. Day or night, the mountains of the central highlands sat in semi-darkness, emitting an air of conviction, reminding the timid that a year was more than enough time to die.

The chopper blades accelerated, clawing at the over-heated air. The radio traffic brought no relief. Hardin resettled his weight.

A soldier ran to the chopper, threw a mailbag onto the cargo deck, and gave Mr. Ballard a thumbs-up. Hardin's throat went dry. Ghosts of An Khe stomped through his chest. He pushed the mailbag into the center of the chopper, away from his rucksack.

With a haunting sense of recognition, his eyes narrowed, and a dull, heavy feeling gripped his stomach. Dig-it bolted off the cargo deck and arched into a scream. Top's mailbag fell over the edge of the wounded chopper, dragging rivulets of Dig-it's blood into a rush of brutal foliage.

Staring at the mailbag, he wondered how many Dear John letters it contained, and how many letters would go unanswered. "Dear GI: I tried to wait for you, but your friend at the lumberyard kept handing me his stick."

The rivets in the airframe shuddered as the chopper accelerated to full power, rocked from skid to skid, hovered off the ground, nosed down, and fought for altitude. Hardin creased his eyes and looked back over the encampment.

Virtually immobile, he snapped Sweet Pea's selector switch to semi-automatic, pulled her bolt back to check the chambered round, snapped her dust cover closed, clutched her pistol grip, and fingered her trigger. Sweet Pea's butt was beautiful. She would whore for her GI.

She yearned for the sweat of his grip. She would take off everything but her earrings.

Reading his dog tags aloud: Hardin, Edward R., OF 108848, A+, Religious Pref: none, he laughed into the cool breeze. If the tags were stamped with a stranger's name, he could go home. Hardin's face flushed with sweat. He was dizzy.

Worried, he closed his eyes and leaned back into the chopper. The flowered eagle guarding his father's grave stood erect, admiring the white roses and the blue crystal vase glistening in the morning frost. The eagle cocked its head, then spread its wings, challenging a gray haired man in a black robe who stopped to trace the inscription on Hardin's grave stone.

The old man was praying.

As a religious paradigm, war permitted the transition from civility to chaos without requiring a reason. "This war is rude," Hardin said. Thinking about jumping from the chopper, he said, "And, it don't mean nothin." And if this war's outcome flowed from the postulate that the grunt was the origin of unforgiven sin, then why count the bodies?

Hardin had learned to laugh at his mounting insanity. Sometimes he laughed during firefights. Time spent looking for the meaning of this, or that, added weight to his rucksack.

Fighting for Dak To had proved meaningless. Hell, even the dead men seemed relieved.

The shadows of the triple canopy jungle and the proximity of death soon brought a series of faces onto his radar screen.

Specialist Fourth Class Glen "Squeak" Adams was First Platoon's RTO. A short, southern white man, Squeak carried the radio so he could run the platoon. His deeply lined brain shuddered with his step, echoing with a confusion that led to nowhere. The chill in his eyes forced the new men to brace.

Significance for Squeak occurred between the conclusion of one breath and the beginning of the next. Death occurred between someone else's footsteps.

He smoked grass for the abstraction. If you asked him, the balance of his war was too much to absorb. If you asked him, every GI in the airspace wanted more dormant senses, including Hardin. Squeak liked his medicines—some prescribed, some more effective.

At first blush, a new man would think that Squeak would be embarrassed if his horse took a shit during the Fourth of July parade. New men were foolish.

Squeak was the medic, frozen on his knees in the Chosin Reservoir. He was the Jew staring through the wire at Bergen-Belsen. He survived the death march at Bataan with snow-white hair. He was a bugler at the Somme, a Digger in the Transvaal. He stood-to with the 24th Foot, the 94th Rifles, the 5th Marines, and the 503rd Infantry. He jumped into Corregidor, Normandy, Belgium and Laos. He was the Godfather of the Hill People.

Squeak was a Digger, a Dogface, a Brownjob, and a Grunt: a composite of the men whose names were forgotten in the monsoons of years past. Squeak was a traveler. And Squeak had one friend—Paul Albert Webster.

Webster's mind was suspended in a foggy stew, and Squeak knew why. After prying his platoon sergeant's hand from his weapon and scolding the headless corpse with curse words, Webster tried to find the man's head. After hours and days of searching, Webster decided the head was put in another man's body bag.

Now, he couldn't talk without singing "The Shadow of Your Smile" somewhere in shallow memory, in sterile solitude. He couldn't even smile and hide that he was nuts.

Webster entered the battle for Dak To with an echo-virus that turned to constipation when he found a stairway cut into the steep red clay near the base of Hill 875. The steps had been cut with a jeweler's precision. The handrail was neatly tied with strips of bamboo.

"Oh, bullshit," was Webster's favorite thing to say.

He was on point when he found the stairway. He didn't say, "Oh, bullshit." He said, "Fuck me." and that's what happened.

Days later, after a short-drop killed forty-two men, Webster stopped talking; his memories bound to the men who survived the battle, stained as they were.

Half price was the most he expected. Silence marred his good-byes. He eventually fell into a repetitious mood, his footsteps softened by a meaningless chorus of false hope. And then he started singing his song, day and night, on ambush or in his foxhole. That's when his name became, Shadow.

A new man told him to shut up one day. That's when Shadow hit him with the butt of his weapon. He resented the new men, those replacements with their foolish courage. Holding his eyes motionless, drawing stamina from the confines of a dark place, he wanted to kill the new men before they became familiar.

Shadow ate his meals alone, thwarting even casual intrusions. He talked on the radio as if the words were more trustworthy. Some nights he would talk for hours, mostly about his family. His father, a dogface with the 29th Infantry, died near Omaha Beach on D-Day plus one.

Shadow resented his need to communicate, even when he prayed. For him, fighting Vietnam's war wasn't easier after praying. GIs like Squeak and Shadow joked about offering their lives, knowing how nicely their combat pay, that extra $2.17 per day, would secure their family when they stood tall in the ever-after.

Shadow asked Squeak to read his letters from home. He was afraid someone else had died and with a last scrap of madness, his fears would be confirmed.

These two men were not ready to die. They were tired of expecting death and fighting its charm. They prayed they would not be crippled. Squeak liked to dance and cover his nuts when he talked about wanting life or death, and nothing in between.

This made Shadow smile—Hardin too.

Squeak carried his equipment as if he were about to break into a run. Set in a forward lean, he would push his helmet to the back of his head and nod, then smile as if in balance. After taping the radio handset to the left shoulder strap of his rucksack, Squeak held his head to the left so he could monitor radio traffic without breaking stride. This forced him to wear his helmet on the right side of his head.

Within a week Squeak's head lay to the left whether he was carrying the radio or not.

Captain Joe would tip his head to the right when he talked to Squeak so they could see eye-to-eye. Larceny being in favor, Squeak would straighten up with a jerk and surprise the captain, erupting in a high pitched laugh. Joe didn't think he was funny.

Being Welsh-Irish gave Squeak a Celtic rage and a voice that could make the shoulders of a dead iguana wrinkle into its head. Shadow gave Squeak the radio because seven men had died in Dak To carrying it, and he figured Squeak could whisper and still be heard over the roar of small-arms fire. That, and Squeak could hide within the framework of his rucksack.

Squeak carried a small leather pouch of dew in his rucksack. He opened it at night. Not to roll a fat-one, but to use the fang he had cut from a bird spider to pick his teeth. Squeak showed the fang to the new men, boasting that the spider died trying to walk across his face.

Shadow never sang when Squeak told this story to a new man. Squeak liked to puncture the skin of a new man's hand with the spider fang, then tell the Cherry that a bird spider killed a GI in Alpha Company. Then he would say, "No one goes home from No-DEROS Alpha."

* * *

Giving his tools a nudge, as if to say hello, Hardin examined a ridgeline, admiring the rugged terrain. Flying 1500 feet above the canopy with the wind pushing at his face, Hardin knew that spotting an LZ from the air was about as easy as finding a rabbit in a cornfield.

As if on cue, the door gunner pointed to the right front, then pulled back the bolt of his machine gun, ejecting the chambered round and loading a new round. Fear seeped into Hardin's chest. Whiffs of yellow smoke filtered from the canopy.

Approaching the smoke, the chopper hovered to the middle of a thirty-meter vertical shaft. Without hesitation, Mr. Ballard lowered the chopper into the tube. Hardin butt-walked off the cargo deck and eased onto the skid. The tips of the main rotor blades tore at the small limbs of the perimeter trees. If the blades caught a large limb, the chopper would slam into the trees and Hardin and the door gunners would be tossed into the jungle.

Unable to back off, Hardin registered each sound. Slowly, too slowly, the chopper approached the shattered trees at the bottom of the shaft. The irregular tattoo of cracking limbs brought rushes of fear. The landing zone looked like the beginning toss in a game of pickup sticks. Trees shattered by C-4 plastique explosive lay fifteen-foot deep.

The slick hovered to within inches of the top log. The crew chief moved to the center of the cargo deck, signaled Hardin to stand-fast, and began unloading the cargo. After each item, Mr. Ballard re-stabilized the aircraft. The last item was a body bag.

With the crew chief's nod, Hardin stepped onto the nearest log. Standing twelve feet in the air with a seventy-pound rucksack on his back and a Huey hovering two feet from his left shoulder, he moved quickly, scrambling away from the shattered trees.

The chopper looked like a cross between a hummingbird, and hedge clippers. The vegetation at the tips of the rotor blade cracked like AK rounds snapping at the air. Captain Joe had fashioned a typical triple-canopy landing zone: the sounds, the garbage, the confusion, and the uncertainty.

Focused by the tight quarters, Mr. Ballard's face creased into a hardened grin as he fought to keep the aircraft centered in its own turbulence. The cylinder of plant-free air brought rays of sunlight slashing through the canopy, forming an inverted conical glow.

The turbine-driven wind pushed across the jungle floor.

Hardin leaned into a tree watching two medics put a Vietnamese male into the body bag. Sergeant First Class Oscar B. Stubbs stood-to and extended his hand in an expression of relief. He was a darkly tanned, skinny man, with a hook-nose, a long weathered face, and large ears. His ancestors fought for the Confederacy, at Gettysburg and Cold Harbor. The Stars and Bars were tattooed to his right forearm.

"Good to have ya back, El Tee," he said, smiling through a knowing stare. "We've been on point since ya left. Maybe the captain will cut us some slack to get ya back in shape." In silence the two men watched the medics work.

Remembering that Lima Six was his radio call sign, and that El Tee was his given name, Hardin pointed at the body bag, and asked, "We baggin' dinks now?"

Instantly, Stubbs began beating a pack of Lucky Strikes against the palm of his hand. Angry, he lowered his head, concealing a pair of steel-gray eyes under the rim of his helmet.

"NVA: a Chieu Hoi," Stubbs said. "We've got four more dinks just like that one, except they ain't dead yet. They like GIs so much they changed sides."

Stubbs shifted his head with a warning, watching the medics dragged the body bag up the log pile. The Huey hovered up the tube to give the medics room to reach a high point, then settled back down. Easing the body into the chopper, the pallbearers bounded off the log pile and fell into a cluster, watching the slick rise out of the canopy.

"Troops will move easier now." Stubbs lit a cigarette and snapped his lighter shut, pleased with the sound. The burden of making combat decisions landed squarely on Hardin's shoulders.

"What Chieu Hois?" Hardin rolled his rucksack off and dropped it.

Stubbs took a drag on his cigarette, slid into a half grin, and arched his brows in mockery. "While you were layin' up on your malaria-bound ass, Uncle gave us five dinks. Captain Joe's got 'em with the point squad, and Hippie's been jumpin' like a hog pissin' turpentine."

"If mama's boys changed sides once, they'll ride again," Hardin said, pointing at the resupply chopper. Mr. Ballard's face stretched the tube, his door gunners locked in a directed chatter, relaxed by experience.

Stubbs laughed; his memory often set him off. "When we blew the trees for the LZ, one of the butts kicked the wrong way. Hit that dink right in the head." Stubbs dragged on his cigarette and moved into a conspiring posture. "Ya know those little bastards can break down and assemble our weapons with their eyes closed. They even cut hair."

Stubbs punctuated his comment with the butt of his cigarette.

"No dink is cuttin' my hair," Hardin said.

Stubbs looked about, nodding his agreement.

The resupply chopper popped out of the canopy into clean air and flew down the ridge, the rotors' music instantly replaced by the hum of the landing zone. Normally desperate for silence, refining movement, and communication to that of a mime, the noise of a Huey meant that any NVA within three ridgelines knew where the company was digging foxholes.

"Looks like a cheap circus," Stubbs said, flipping his cigarette into the log pile.

"Which one of those dinks are you gonna shoot when the lead starts flyin'?"

Stubbs knew Hardin meant business. "The smallest one. He's got uneasy moves. Just don't feel right." They laughed. Neither man liked being around the people or the language.

"I'll take one of the others," Hardin pointed to the dink who was staring at Stubbs. "We still dancin' on the same sheet of music?" Hardin asked.

"Company's moved maybe six klicks since ya left."

Handing Stubbs his map, Hardin said, "Put the Papa Oscars on the map sheet for me while I talk to Six." Gear in hand, Hardin asked, "Six still got good moves?"

"Not bad for a skinny old man." Stubbs was tired of working point and wanted his lieutenant to buy the platoon some downtime, some slack-time. Hardin let Stubbs' voice trail off as he savored the odor of the moist jungle floor.

Charlie Six was the radio call sign for the company commander, Captain Joe Winningham. GIs shortened Captain Joe's call sign to Six, because they could not call him Charlie for obvious reasons. Outsiders called him, Charlie Six.

A GI's relationship with his company commander was a sacred expression of trust far more profound than any religious commitment. Six—Captain Joe—

would get them through the war, no matter what. Captain Joe was special—he had earned the reverence of his men.

Hardin picked his way through what looked like Third Platoon, acknowledging familiar faces. Sharing mail or dividing rations, these grunts were boiled dry.

Captain Joe looked blank, sitting against a large tree, boiling coffee. With his usual sarcasm and a sense of futility, Hardin dropped his gear, sat on his steel pot, and held his canteen cup next to Joe's coffee. C-Ration coffee was a known cure for any virus. Joe gave him a splash of mud, too busy plotting artillery defcons to do more than nod.

The company commo chief was coordinating radio frequencies for the night operation with the platoon RTOs. Squeak was cleaning the contacts on his radio with a pencil eraser.

Hardin tapped Squeak's helmet, and said, "Squeak, how ya doin'? Does the captain know ya smoke dope?" Hardin held out a fist and Squeak hit it, nodded, and blew eraser bits from the contacts on his radio handset, leaving his lieutenant with a disgusting huff.

"I got forty-five days and a wake-up left in this fucked-up war, and I'm scared shitless," Squeak declared, looking behind Hardin, giving Joe a humorous nod.

"I'm shitless—ask B-Med," Hardin said. Squeak agreed that his El Tee was full of shit, then glanced at Joe again, offering an open palm.

"That malaria's tough duty," Squeak said, spicing his pesky brand of lowercase humor with a sour Virginia twist. When Joe finished with the artillery recon sergeant, Hardin grabbed his gear and started to move to Joe's other side.

Wet-nursing the first step, mindful of his coffee, Hardin fell into the jaws of a ninety-five pound blur of hair and teeth. A black hulk with slashing white teeth nailed his rucksack when he lifted it to protect his face. The impact knocked him over Joe's rucksack. He stumbled, swinging his weapon up to meet the attack. Falling through a rush of vegetation, Hardin focused on a pair of black eyes.

The dog's lunge was suspended in air, cut short when a stranger back-hauled a leather leash, yanking the dog's head skyward, and dropping the animal on its back. Confused and panicked, Hardin reached out. The dog recovered within a heartbeat.

The stranger screamed, "Back!" and the dog's vicious rage turned to a nervous, frenzied pacing, waiting for the next command, alternating his posture, watching Hardin's every move.

"Ya motherfuckin' whore!" Hardin lay on his back, gasping for air, using his weapon as a pointer, waiting for a gesture of regret.

"I'll short leash him." With no apology, the handler tied the dog's leash to the base of a tree. Bent low at the neck, the animal swayed from side to side, moving with a rhythmic, restless motion, his nose wrinkled into his eyes. The hair on the dog's shoulders stood erect, his eyes raw with hate.

"I'm gonna kill you and that pig fucker."

Hardin's chest bounded from one heartbeat to the next. A stress-induced cramping seized his guts. Shaking through a cold sweat, he labored for air. Captain Joe laughed at the dirt in Hardin's coffee as he adjusted his gear for the evening.

"Must be the smell," Squeak said, announcing his rural pedigree. "A good dog can tell who's who. A good dog knows before anyone. Dog jumped Nasty yesterday."

Speaking through the butt of a soggy cigar, Joe said, "Dog seems to like the rest of us. He must know you're a smartass." Joe had a weathered way of putting a man on notice.

"Ya coulda given me fair warning."

Squeak continued to laugh at Hardin's gymnastics, happy for this interlude of combat humor. Knowing he still worked for Hardin, for First Platoon, Squeak took a drink of coffee, and said, "I was gonna tell ya, El Tee. I figured since ya get twice as much jump pay as me, I wanted to see how far ya could jump. Dog's too quick for ya."

Squeak and Captain Joe concluded their affair with familiar, nodding laughs, knowing Hardin would pay them back in kind.

"Fuckin' dog's crazy." Hardin dumped the coffee-dirt from his canteen cup, wiped it out with his drive-on rag, and poked it at Squeak for a refill. Joe laughed at the dog.

"Word is he's got five confirmed kills," Joe said, wiping his drive-on rag across his mouth. The dog had more confirmed kills than any GI in the company, even the Hill People. You had to see Chuck to know you killed him.

"Yeah, all fuckin' GIs," Hardin said. "Dear Mr. and Mrs. Grunt, your son was killed by a fuckin' dog." Hardin's nuts clanged with an aching throb.

"Dog hasn't done much except let our new allies drive him gunnysack," Joe said as he folded his map. He looked around the perimeter, factoring each sector image, each foxhole, to ensure the images matched his estimate of the situation.

When Joe finished he said, "I don't like the dog much either."

"Squeak, when ya get the radio frequencies up, make us some coffee," Hardin said. "I need to chat with Six." Squeak caught Hardin's tone of voice and was on his feet and gone.

"What a fucked up LZ. Those damn trees blew in every direction," Joe said, shaking his head, looking at the shaft of light and the maze of shattered tree trunks on the landing zone.

"Uncle said ya tried to stake some new guy's bag to his thigh."

Joe nodded as he exhaled. "New guy is right. I don't even know his name. He had a pair of lungs. Must have been painful. Blood everywhere." Joe offered his lieutenant a cigar. "He was hurtin' until the morphine took hold." Joe stood and stretched, then took a savoring drag on his cigar. After a pause, he waved a hand through the smoke. "His nuts were restin' on that bamboo stake. That's way too close."

"How far back?" Hardin asked, looking down the ridge. Beams of iridescent light the color of foxglove shown through a gathering haze.

"Four klicks. Off the side of a ridge on a second-rate trail for maybe a hundred meters." Joe pointed with his cigar, then continued, "Doesn't pay to run these trails."

"Were ya chasin' the circus when the stakes started flying?"

"Yeah, we'd just picked them up." Dredging up a can of cheese, Joe continued: "Whatever we're chasin' dropped off this ridge runnin' west, 700 meters back. We clover-leafed, but they were flat movin' out. Dinks need water, or they're late for a rally point."

"I could use a rest," Hardin said, pulling a jungle sweater from his rucksack. Cool, damp air welled up from the jungle floor, mixing with the fear of darkness and the steaming coffee.

"Malaria's a bad ride," Joe said, cracking a sarcastic grin.

"Fever of unknown origin, FUO. The docs at B-Med tried to make me lick some of Auntie J's vaginal cream. Some nasty shit." Joe's eyes grew cold, his mood a mixture of concerns. Low clouds swirled in the upper reaches of the canopy.

Joe said, "Higher-Higher will roast us if you come down with malaria."

Hardin stared at Joe with equally cold eyes. Higher-Higher was a facetious nickname for headquarters and their propensity for flying at ever higher altitudes during a firefight.

Joe gave Hardin another splash of coffee.

"It's good to have ya back, Lima. Things should be quiet tonight. It's uphill for Chuck if he wants to play." Hardin stood up and grabbed his gear. "Password's still Rawhide," Joe said, looking into the mist flowing along the ridge. Hardin followed Joe's eyes, then turned into Battle Bullshit, picking his way through the litter. The dog scoffed, as if Hardin was dead meat.

"Dig deep Lima. They got big stuff."

CHAPTER FIVE

Think About Pussy

Charlie Company Night Laager, The Central Highlands.

Troops stood-to dressed in rags, their jungle fatigues shredded by weeks of tracking through a mountainous burl of belligerent vegetation. Hardin, the odd fish, noticed. As the noise of the landing zone gave way to the instincts that marched with fading light, the company sat in a smother of clouds.

Shadowed faces communicated acknowledging well-defined hand signals.

Twilight's sudden hush brought Stubbs to his feet, listening. Stubbs had wagered the NVA could not set their mortars before nightfall, that the dense canopy would prevent short-range mortar fire. Captain Joe was probably right: the enemy was running for water or a rally point.

Stubbs exhaled, watching the smoke, then looked up the ridge.

A thin slant of dusk light worked its way across the perimeter exposing, in a most telling way, the vacant hunger of each man's face. Fog welled up from the valley to the north, fostering a mizzling rain. Hardin dropped his gear near Squeak's. He grinned, then drank Squeak's coffee.

Tired men focused on their task. Exhausted by the steaming heat, they shivered in place.

Each strike of a shovel forced an approval of sufficiency, each foxhole measured with rigid concern. Squeak adjusted the corner of a sandbag, re-stacking those that opposed the hillside, then pounding the seams into a weave.

Stand-to was a period of expectation. Twilight beckoned a darkening mood, sewing a tapestry of blended colors into a familiar frame. The odors of hot food jostled with the odors of fresh shit and urine and the acrid rot of the jungle floor. Hardin smelled of shampoo.

Rapidly cooling air forced this confluence of strength and fear. Prisms formed in the mist above the ground, transforming once familiar shapes. Outposts vanished in the deeper shadows.

One hundred and three men, each fighting a pernicious nature, spared with a memory. Racing the clock, GIs scrambled to fill sandbags, set machine gun positions, string Claymores and trip flares, organize magazines, bunch hand grenades, test radios, change batteries, smoke a cigarette, drink a gallon of coffee, and eat a hot meal.

As with any ritual, individual vagaries lead to the same outcome—be ready to fight for your life. Stand-to was also a period of seeking. Moments before twilight, when the eye hasn't adjusted to the changing hue, GIs sought a pattern for the night they must endure.

All bad, no two nights were the same.

Vacant, reluctant faces, many one or two weeks new, smiled back as Hardin made the rounds. With a rush of fatigue, the men of First Platoon greeted their freshly washed El Tee with words of fatalism, their eyes beginning to dilate.

Pointing at Squeak's rucksack, Hardin said, "Give me some shit-paper." Squeak assumed an expression of sensitive health that jumped into an agreeable grin.

Catching the small roll, Hardin picked his way out of the perimeter thirty meters down the side of the ridgeline, making sure the studs knew he was outside the box. When his fever boiled into a brace, his bowels gave way to complete relief. His outhouse, his place of being, was laced with intense vigilance and an acute sense of vulnerability derived from having one's ankles shackled by one's pants, and having one's scrotum exposed.

Back inside the box, he rehashed the orders for the night. With the foxhole complete, he set sandbags around the end of his sleeping area to keep his head from taking the first round. Lying on his back, he could execute a roll to the left into a firing position without being exposed to grazing fires.

After one practice move, he placed his rucksack, Claymore bag of magazines, and four grenades on the leading edge of the foxhole just inside the sandbags. His rucksack was positioned to the left so he could reach his extra magazines, the strobe light and grenades.

Squeak stood in the foxhole at the back edge on the right side, leaned forward with his left knee braced against the forward edge, and shouldered his weapon. Settling his left forearm into the sandbags, he selected possible targets and measured how rapidly the hillside fell away.

Radio operators exchanged commo checks, as one man and then another went to ground. The company had expected to get clobbered for several days and the uncertainty was reflected in broken conversations, caustic humor, and rapid eye movement. Sipping coffee or hot chocolate, men searched the jungle, scouring the ground in front of their firing position.

With minutes of light remaining, Hardin wanted to touch base with Buck Sergeant David "Rap" Brown, a large black man with a quiet intensity and an impatient posture. Rap liked to jump his El Tee with the street-talk he used to confuse the average white boy.

Rap was a good soldier. Rap was Hardin's black barometer.

As the story was told, Rap was an officer in the P-Blackstone Rangers, a Chicago street gang based on South 63rd Street capable of any stateside combat.

Rap bragged about the brothers and their arsenal of weapons. Excitable, yet rarely excited, his firefights were spiced with "digs," "muthafuckers," "dig-its," and "you-know-what-I'm-sayin's." A staccato "you dig?" forced all but the odd man to agree.

Rap never received a letter from home. When Tag found out, he asked his folks to write Rap a letter once a week. As Tag explained it, he did not like Rap being ignored during mail-call.

Tag was a white boy from Thomas Edison High, in Philly. He was Rap's friend.

Rap and Fish had the OP for the platoon. Rap and Fish were polar opposites. Not a matter of black and white—they didn't talk to each other because they didn't like each other's kind. That said, they would die trying to save each other's life.

Fish was a good soldier—Hardin's white barometer.

Private John Guffey, nicknamed: Fish, was loose linked. Stubbs said he was unhinged. He was the truest reflection of absurdity that a war could muster—a black eye on the verge of recovery. His nickname was Fish, because that was the way he drank whiskey—or because his last name sounded like guppy.

None of the Hill People knew why they called him Fish. LeCotte claimed that Fish couldn't swim. But what would LeCotte know? He was a Canadian.

Rap said something about Fish one day, then crashed into a rage about Whitey. When the ranting got confused, Hardin stepped back and stared.

Whitey was a blond GI who left for Bangkok on R&R and never returned. He was different than most AWOLs. Rap was his fire-team leader and Rap was going to kill him.

Rap's fire team had been trolling through the jungle in the mountains west of Dak To near the border of Laos conducting a cloverleaf recon patrol. Whitey was pulling drag for the fire team when an NVA squad ambushed the patrol.

Small recon patrols were called clovers because their trace was shaped like a cloverleaf. Run light—with weapons, a radio and limited ammunition—clovers left the average GI wired to a quick-fire response that could not be overcome.

Uneventful clovers left Rap wound tighter than a hickory knot, his imagination so keen the balance of his day was a near miss. For weeks after his clover was ambushed, Rap practiced killing Whitey, performing the combat version of show-and-tell while the brothers danced the combat version of the mash potato.

With two GIs wounded and the stock of Rap's weapon shattered, Whitey hid behind a tree and cried about his mama. Whitey didn't fire a shot. By the time the platoon reached the patrol, Rap's fist had dented Whitey's Kansas head. Listening to Rap's rage left Whitey's mother in poor straits and every swinging-dick in the company convinced that Whitey was toast. Whitey left for R&R on the next available chopper.

Laughing to himself about Whitey's predicament, Hardin found himself searching the flank of the ridge, waiting for the perimeter to lose definition. What he could see of the sky was a jumble of clouds. The night grew dark. A mist had formed soaking the foliage and the ground.

Hardin wiped his face. "It is gonna get spooky out here," Hardin whispered. Squeak didn't respond.

The Army Table of Organization and Equipment outlined the organizational make-up of an infantry platoon, authorizing forty-four men divided into three rifle squads and a weapons squad of ten men each plus two radio operators, a platoon sergeant, and a platoon leader. Each of the four squads was divided into two five-man fire teams.

For the past four months, however, First Platoon's combat strength had not exceeded twenty-six men, owing to casualties, R&Rs, AWOLs, and the one-year rotation. They did look good on paper, though—on the rear-echelon morning report.

Shorthanded, the platoon organized itself into two twelve-man squads. Lima One and Lima Two were their radio call signs. A machinegun team was included in each squad.

"Stubbs, did ya check the outpost?" Hardin asked, savoring his coffee, watching Squeak remount the radio on his rucksack frame. He nudged Stubbs into a full squat. Stirring cream into his coffee, he ducked away from glow of Stubbs' cigarette.

"Yeah, the OP's got a cherry in it." Stubbs was casually pleased. "Dumb shit is piss-tight. He'll be awake all night." Stubbs stood up to return to his sleeping area. "I showed him the crease in my steel pot." Stubbs' grin quickly turned into a rolling, barely audible, laugh.

Stubbs was a sick man. He was also left-handed.

Stubbs knew this fucking-new-guy would spend the night trying to identify any noise his mind could muster. Stupid, as if being stupid was good, the FNG would stop breathing to listen. The sound of a swallow would flog his ears. And after the other GIs on the outpost fell asleep, the new man would whisper into the radio.

Waiting for the call, Squeak would say, "I heard something, too." or, "There it is again." or, "Did you hear that?" By dawn the new guy would be exhausted.

With fear on the rise, light rose off the jungle floor like smoke being sucked out of a bottle. Squeak finished his coffee, setting his cup behind the foxhole. Instantly the GIs in the adjoining foxholes vanished. Hardin could not see his hands. With the moon just passed full, moonlight would not help until the wee hours.

"Lima Oscar Papa, this is Lima Kilo, over," Squeak whispered, calling the outpost. The outpost broke squelch once.

Stubbs insisted that Squeak radio the OP at fifteen-minute intervals. If the OP was clear of enemy activity, they "broke squelch" once, depressing and releasing the push-to-talk button on the radio handset. If the enemy was about, they broke squelch twice and waited for a series of yes-no questions designed to determine the nature of the enemy threat.

One break meant "Yes", and two breaks meant "No".

"Are we set, Squeak?" Stubbs asked.

"Yeah, we're good."

Staring into a void, Stubbs stood-to, needing a smoke. When the odd shapes began stalk-dancing in front of his foxhole, Stubbs laughed, waiting for the bushes to fuck their way through a clatter of vague shapes, then leap into the air. Damn, Stubbs thought, the trees are moving. Night after night the demons could see him clearly, laughing as he struggled for a fleeting glimpse.

Stubbs hated the night.

The GIs that fought with Stubbs registered the obstacles in front of their foxhole before twilight, aligning an aiming sandbag with the most prominent obstacle such that the barrel of their weapon would be pointing to the left of the obstacle.

Stubbs claimed that every communist was right-handed, the logic being that the bastards were too stupid to be left-handed. And being stupid, when confronting an obstacle, Chuck would crawl to the right, into a GI's gun sights.

Fish thought aiming sandbags were for pussies. He claimed that when the dancing bears came to call, firing from an aiming sandbag wasn't sporting.

Ski thought Fish could be right.

Besides, Ski claimed any man firing an M-16 or M-60 at night was a moron, declaring that the muzzle flash reached into the night like a spreading web, setting fire to foxholes, and lighting the company's perimeter. And if that wasn't enough, those fucking tracer rounds ran into the night like traffic arrows and the perimeter drew fire like Rap's black hole.

Rap didn't know if Ski's theory was a compliment.

Tag told him it was certainly a compliment.

Hardin laughed at the logic, knowing the NVA would gauge the firing vectors, neutralize the Claymore antipersonnel mines, and shovel grenades at the nearest muzzle flash. All this in the glare of a burning trip flare.

Night after night, at every foxhole, Stubbs repeated his order: "First fire the Claymores, then grenades, and then M-79s."

Squeak was huddled in his foxhole, eating a cold can of spiced beef. Hardin winced at the sound of his plastic spoon scraping the side of the metal can. Hardin drew a breath. His chest and shoulders ached with a deep throbbing pain. He burned with fever.

This night had a cold, fearful sense to it.

"El Tee, is that deserter still kickin'?" Squeak asked, juggling a mouthful of food.

"Hard tellin'. Maybe, if his squad didn't kill him."

"Wha'd'a ya think the Army told his folks?"

"He's MIA."

* * *

Remembering his father's tale of capture and intrigue, Hardin judged the deserter was probably a good man. In September of 1944, the French Resistance had picked up his father after the Major had been shot down near Rouen, France. Assuming he was a spy or a deserter, resistance fighters tied him to a post in the basement of a warehouse while they verified his papers. On the fourth night they lead him back to friendly lines.

* * *

Four hours into an unusually cold night, with men clinging to varying phases of stupor, Joe's radio operator spoke with a frightened tone. "Lima, Mike, November, this is Charlie Kilo."

"Lima Kilo," Squeak caught his breath and exhaled slowly. Hardin drank from his canteen, allowing the noise in his head to dissipate between each swallow.

"Oscar Papa Two has movement. We're firing red-leg with a one-second delay."

Struck by the motion of the cool damp air, men waited in the mist. Nothing could replicate a night of fear in these rugged jungle mountains. Frightened men listened to radios, hoping the movement would go away.

Hardin listened to his breath passing through his nose. Charlie Kilo's hesitant baritone broke his trance, speaking words about movement. Listening to this radio was like listening to The Shadow. Remembering the bedroom he shared with his older brother, a door opened with a grinding noise, and his brother cautioned him to be quiet.

First the sound of a creaking hinge, then the footsteps of a man running, gunshots and screams. A pause and then a hollow voice: "Only the Shadow knows."

Squeak keyed the handset, alerting Hardin by touching his forearm. "Roger that." Squeak calmly sorted the night as he crouched deeper into the foxhole.

"Lima One, Lima Two, get in a hole. Break-Break. Charlie Kilo, give us a splash on that red-leg." Men searched for cover and asked for help.

"Roger, splash."

"Splash, wait."

No water, no Old Spice, just a warning order. With the artillery spotting round just seconds from impact, the company's world was about to get painted. At this point the caliber of artillery was irrelevant. The jungle shut down. Composure was not required when artillery rounds were on the way.

Ignorance was essential.

Men clambered from their sleeping positions into their foxholes.

The spotting round began its scream, its nose crushing the air: modern hysteria matching wits with undisturbed history. The impact was the full-bodied tearing of mindless energy, not the tiny snap of an AK round, more the impact of a locomotive smashing into a mountainside.

A shock wave rocked the perimeter. Debris crashed through the jungle. A battery-one, six artillery pieces firing at the same time, crushed the ridgeline thirty seconds later.

Seeing the elephants produced this response, Hardin thought. *It is the exponential decay of reason, the sequential confusion, and men fighting blindly to survive. Fear is driving the progression,* he mused. *Each step is raising the probability of death.*

"Not much has changed since the Civil War, " he whispered.

Overwhelmed, the outpost blew their Claymores. With no mind left to ponder, five studs ran crashing through an enveloping tangle, whisper-screaming "Rawhide."

Well up the ridge, a trip flare ignited, back-lighting the retreating grunts. Hardin closed his eyes to preserve his night vision and sank to the bottom of his foxhole. Another six artillery rounds pounded the ridgeline, vaporizing the flare. Fear seized the air within the perimeter. Debris rained through the trees. Squeak stood at the rim of the foxhole.

Lima One, Lima Two, everybody up." Squeak knew if Chuck was ready to attack, he would move immediately.

The scout dog churned madly. The radio barked.

"Lima, this is Six." Not even the moist jungle floor could absorb Joe's icy tone of voice.

Squeak tapped Hardin's arm with the handset and whispered.

"Ya shoulda stayed gone, El Tee," Squeak said.

"Tell Joe-Joe to fuck off."

"I'm too short for this shit, El Tee. Elephants and dead grunts. This don't feel good, El Tee." A chill ran through the jungle casting a wake of dead leaves.

"Fuck me." Hardin grabbed the hook. "This is Lima."

"Move out and reestablish the OP." Captain Joe was checking Hardin's head-space.

Hardin threw the hook into the foxhole, spitting out air.

"Im-fuckin'-possible. Fuck-a-bunch of OPs. Did ya hear that, Squeak?"

Hardin covered his mouth with his drive-on rag, cussing at the sandbags. "That rat bastard son-of-a-bitch. That pig-fucking, cock-sucking, motherfucker."

"I can dig it." Squeak's voice was cautiously empty, directed outside the perimeter. With a hometown of Chance, Kentucky, Squeak had run out of time. "This is Lima Kilo, Roger, out."

Hardin stood-to at the rim of the foxhole, then gave Joe both fingers and a two-handed boost on his nuts. "No way to shake this detail," Hardin whispered.

"Your call, El Tee."

Impulse led to a quieting calm as Hardin evaluated his men. Ski, the well-muscled machine gunner, was too short—had to be The Frenchman. Squeak was too jumpy—had to be the second squad RTO. Other than that, becoming brown bread required selective favor.

Calculating the odds, Hardin keyed the hook. "Lima Two, this is Lima." Half-stifled air bled from the members of second squad. They were prepared for Chuck to come visit; they were not prepared to step out on the town.

"Did you dial the wrong number, honey?"

"No, sweetheart, send the Frenchman, Mex, one stud and an RTO over to my house. No bing cherries, no pie cherries, no fucking cherries."

"Give it a minute." The RTO had heard enough.

Pausing to measure his near-term fate, Hardin began reciting the Lord's Prayer.

Men shouldered equipment weighted with fear-born inertia, the night too dark for intellectual repairs. The luminous dial on Hardin's watch galloped in odd confinement, indifferent to the score. He unbuckled the watch and put it in his pocket for luck.

"Frenchman?" Hardin reached for a sound. Frenchman's shoulder trembled with fear. He was a short man with a quick smile and a quicker temper. Born in Cajun country, east of New Orleans, he had eight months to go. Hardin had asked the Cajun to come die with him.

"Yeah. Me, PeeWee, LeCotte, and Mex."

Filled with the illusions of combat, a Cajun, a Canadian, and two Mexicans volunteered to defend the company's honor. Mex was one of the Hill People; he'd be last in line. LeCotte, the Canadian, was an inner-city white with a full-speed mouth; he'd be next to last. PeeWee was a small man with black eyes as big as saucers; he'd be right behind Hardin.

"Frenchman, whose got the radio?" Hardin forced a thumb into his shoulder.

"PeeWee."

"Tell him to shut it off," Hardin released his grip with a jolt. "Lose your helmets."

Hardin had practiced these night patrols, running in circles through the woods near Number #10, Highlands Road. Bang, you're dead. I shot you first.

No matter: Nancy, the neighborhood nurse, could patch a man's vitals. She might sneak in a kiss as well.

"We're gonna go out through Second Platoon, then crawl fifty meters. Hand on shoulder, then hand on foot. Nice and slow." Hardin found Squeak and then the handset.

"Mike, this is Lima," Hardin stared in the direction he last saw Second Platoon. "You got a watch we can see?" To negotiate the foxholes and equipment, the patrol needed a traffic light.

"I'll move it around."

"Got it." Speaking over the top of PeeWee's shoulder, Hardin said, "We got all night. Stick together. Think about pussy."

Hardin jarred Mex's shoulder with a reassuring nudge. "Think about pussy, Mex."

Lieutenant "Andy" Anderson, Mike Six, straddled his foxhole as the patrol approached the luminous dial of his watch, their feet testing the ground: toe, then heel. The watch dial hung suspended, four tiny lights flirting, then dipping, and then moving away.

Hardin was towing a chain of men, each waiting to be pulled into the next stride.

"Lima, there's no Claymores straight out," Andy whispered.

Hardin found PeeWee's head and whispered, "We're crawlin' out. Keep a hand on my boot. Shake it when we're linked up."

"Think about pussy, El Tee."

One by one the five men went to ground. The jungle was closing in. And the more they tried to concentrate, the less they could sense the jungle's mood.

The patrol crawled uphill, inches at a time, expecting a mindless horde of Japs to overrun their position. Scenes from the Battle of Bataan flashed as wave after wave of Japs fell in front of their water-cooled machine gun. Comrades sang that song about passing the ammunition.

Hardin laughed. The British spent twelve years defeating 8,000 guerrillas on the Malay Peninsula. Hardin had 8,000 dancing on his stage, and the bastards had elephants.

Wet and cold, Hardin shivered.

Hardin clicked into real time when PeeWee's hand tightened on his calf. Silence pulsed in his ears. His heart was beating a hole in the wet clay. Trying to relax when fear was consuming your senses was like trying to piss with a stranger holding your cock. Hardin's inner ear rang with the cracking sound. He set his head into the night, toward the sound.

The vegetation near his face had thickened as if under pressure. Hardin spoke without speaking, his thoughts lost in the thick, foggy mist soaking the jungle floor.

Deliberately, he extended his focus into the night, concentrating on the immediate, on a foreign smell. Muted by the mist, a rushing sound rang from the night. Hardin turned to the right. Sensing an object near his face, Hardin sniffed the air. Garlic, or salt. Burnt paint.

Shaken, he stopped breathing and pushed his left hand into the cold clay for traction, waiting. Relieved by the sounds of the mounting rain, his imagination bounced from NVA scouts to unexploded artillery shells. Either way, his enemy was patient.

Hardin laid his weapon in the mud pointing at the target. He was cold now. When PeeWee grabbed his shoulder, Hardin pressed his right hand into PeeWee's neck, pushing him toward the perimeter. PeeWee understood. Turning back into the night in a slow, crab-walking motion, squinting as if he might see, Hardin knew that PeeWee had crawled away.

Hardin lay in the rain for hours, listening for his stranger, his right index finger tight against the trigger. His neck and shoulder muscles suddenly cramped. Unable to stop shaking, he lowered his head to the ground and closed his eyes. The mud seemed warm now.

Enemy contact had started with movement, not the odd patterns of an animal, but the rhythm of a man, the symmetry of practiced steps. Then came thirteen high-explosive artillery rounds and a night filled with odd sounds. Yet, the sequence was logical.

Whatever the outpost heard must be dead, Hardin thought.

With mud inside his shirt, Hardin laughed, only to be treated to the quick movement of branches, then silence, as if something under tension had been released, vegetation adjusting after an intrusion: after a man had moved. Hardin's focus centered on an imaginary point.

Another switching sound rushed from the night.

"Relax, Hardin. You gotta be cool." He opened his mouth to lower the internal sound effects. Poised on the trigger, his finger began to vibrate against the trigger guard. A knot began to seize the muscles near his neck. He had to move.

The mud was cold.

Straining to control his body, the tension in his neck and shoulders caused his arms and hands to shake. A branch snapped with a sharp crack. He strained to see. His chest seized as if the mussels in his back were tied in a knot. Gasping for air, his heart raced in a pounding, hammering rhythm. The mist had turned to rain.

Soaked, he shivered through a spastic vibration. The sounds swelled in volume. Putting fear aside, he crawled uphill using the sound of the rain to mask the noise.

The suction of the mud and the quiet clanging of his fingers shook at Hardin. Inch after inch he cleared the debris from his face, set his weapon on its left side, then pulled his body along. The soil was slick and oily. A tree limb cracked, this time with less gusto. Annoyed by his alarm, Hardin crawled in spurts: inches at a time.

Five hours, six hours, would the night ever end?

Warmed by the dominance of higher ground, he faced downhill, his body and weapon covered with mud. The night was cold. The jungle floor reeked with a pungent tang.

Wedged in a soggy crater, he shivered. Dawn would be dicey. The rain gradually stopped, leaving those large echoing drops and a flirting gust of wind to accent the last scrap of night. First light came with a gray, filtering cast, and the wing-beats of thousands of mosquitoes. Ready to scream, Hardin searched down the ridge. Looking from point to point, he scanned the canopy for snipers, then searched the hollows on the jungle floor.

A collapsed GI rucksack lay eight meters to his right flank. Beyond this green-twill stranger, in a shell crater, a North Vietnamese soldier lay dead.

Hardin scrambled down to the rucksack, dived behind a log and searched up the ridge, tree by tree. Raising one finger he caught PeeWee's eye. Hardin took the radio.

"Take the ruck and the studs inside the box."

"I'm gone," PeeWee said, taking the rucksack and bounding past LeCotte.

Hardin keyed the handset and whispered, "Wake up, Honey. Time to play war."

"I got a clover movin' out to search the ridge above you," Joe said.

"We got one dead scout, with an AK," Hardin said, scanning the ridge. NVA scouts never worked alone. "Looks like a Claymore."

A squad from Andy's platoon picked their way through the debris, each man evaluating the kill zone. Hardin caught the squad leader's eye, held up a grenade and pointed at the shattered body of the enemy scout. With a confirming nod the squad leader moved away.

Grabbing the dead man's shirt, Hardin rolled the body on its side, checked the pockets, then lowered what was left of the man's chest gently on to the spoon of the grenade, holding the spoon in place until the body pinned the grenade to the ground. The booby trap was set.

Joe sat against the base of a tree, worshipping his coffee and rubbing the graying sides of his morning stubble. With mud caked on his fatigues, Hardin decided he didn't care and held his cup near Joe's nose to bum a splash of coffee.

"You got point, Lima. Saddle up," Joe said, spitting through pieces of a chocolate disk, pointing up the ridge. "You trap the dink?"

"Yeah," Hardin shrugged. "The clover knows." Joe didn't respond. "I think Chuck's got a radio behind us. If we run this ridge down to the blue-line, Chuck's gonna be waitin' for us."

Squeak had packed Hardin's rucksack and started breaking down their foxhole. Their eyes met briefly. Except for those moments when GIs were compelled to speak, their thoughts remained shrouded in a black humor fashioned by death's inevitability.

"Thanks for not takin' me out." Squeak was talking, making no eye contact.

"Squeak, you pencil-dicked, short-time, pile of southern puke. You make me crazy when nothin's goin' on. And, dick weed, ya shoulda warned me about that dog."

"Next time, El Tee."

With this exchange, the ledger was balanced. Both men knew that a GI who begged for slack-time was a useless piece of shit. Squeak was one of the best. He was just wearing out.

With the perimeter in motion, preparing for a fight, the scout dog wrapped himself around his handler. Captain Joe's four chieu-hoi allies were coordinating travel plans. Stubbs sat next to Hardin, with Blood and Mex, the platoon squad leaders.

Caked with mud, looking like a wallowing pig, Hardin said, "Stubbs, your dink friends sure are mouthy. Did ya have the little one on the midnight train to Georgia?"

Stubbs laughed through a drag on his cigarette. "They're exciting when they get scared. Kinda like strappin' on a live chicken." The thought of Stubbs strapping a live chicken to his Georgia hog brought expectant laughter from Blood and Mex.

The chieu hois jerked from one expression to another, accenting their speech with suspicious stares. Hardin pointed at the chieu hois and said, "They'll rodeo again, Stubbs. Count on it. Deserters, that's what they are."

Stubbs nodded a so-what nod and laid out his map, then listened while Hardin briefed Blood and Mex on what to expect during the day. Stubbs broke in with a hack, exhaling smoke.

"I got Chuck's main unit movin' all night. Otherwise, their stay-behind unit would have dropped mortar rounds on us. Dinks are in front of us." Stubbs lighted another smoke.

"We're fuckin' surrounded," Blood said, walking away. Blood pushed at the air as if he were replaying a gunfight. Pleased with the image of the dead scout, he searched both flanks of the ridge.

"Did you trap this dink, El Tee?" Blood asked.

Hardin acknowledged the buck sergeant's lust with a short nod. Strung out on the trauma, death's communion was an integral part of Blood's soul: a soul with an evil, liquid center. Blood was a big, Pennsylvania, white. To shoot at Blood was to unleash a rage of monsoon proportion. Killing his enemy was never enough.

Standing stock-still in the solitude of his fractured mind, Blood stared at the mangled carcass of the enemy scout. Tentacles of mud had drawn the body into the earth, its mass pushing at the vegetation.

Blood's lips moved as he whispered the praises of hell and crouched over the body, his knife held as if begging a question. With a sudden thrust, as if awakened from a trance, he cut off one of the dead man's ears. The jungle stopped breathing.

Mindful of the booby trap, Blood forced the dead man's face into the mud, then finished his ritual by laying a boot firmly on his neck. Satisfied, Blood took one step back, adjusted his rucksack to lessen the tension, then finished his ritual by spitting. Somehow relieved, Blood pushed his helmet to the back of his head.

Blood's hair was blond: white blond. His eyebrows appeared when the sun shown at the proper angle. This fact, combined with the squint of his eye, made his face seem wider than his head. Today, in the morning mist, his smile carried a warning.

Hardin took note.

CHAPTER SIX

God Bless the Hill People

Staging North Out of Night Laager. 0618 Hours.

Note or not, Blood put the ear in his breast pocket and waited for the point squad. Drips stopped next to Blood and made Blood give him the ear. Drips thought Blood was dumber than an empty sandbag and told him so. Blood laughed and told Drips that sandbags could not possibly be dumb because sandbags didn't have any brains.

Speechless, Drips opened his palms, looked at Hippie and laughed.

James Arthur Fawcett might have been stocky if he weren't so tall. Boot camp at Fort Polk, Louisiana, had been a challenge for Fawcett because he outgrew the uniform he was issued. Gigged for buttons and threads and such, morning inspections became a ritual, a push-up ritual.

When supervised, he could stand at attention, but his shadow could not.

He wore a size fourteen boot.

James Arthur Fawcett had a thick, curly red shock of hair and a broad, ruddy face. His skin was black where the freckles had fused together. The hair that carpeted his forearms doubled as mosquito netting. The whiskers on his jaw had the texture of forty-grit sandpaper, suitable for striking a match.

If Fawcett thought something was funny he made note of any GI who wasn't laughing.

Captain Joe called him Drips one day on the airstrip at Dak To, and Squeak could not stop laughing. Captain Joe thought a Fawcett might drip. Squeak knew Fawcett had the clap and that wasn't the end of it.

Fish had stipulated that Mex had contracted the clap before Fawcett, and reckoned that Mex be called Drips, not Fawcett. The platoon vetoed the request, noting that Mex had been called Garbage because he spewed trash Spanish into the radio handset, polluting the platoon airways. Captain Joe reckoned that having a third name was bad luck and that was the end of it.

Garbage got his name changed to Mex when Fish convinced Ski that Mexicans never got jungle rot, because Mexican skin was ten times more resistant to disease than Polish skin, and Mexican skin was self-cleansing. Drips thought this might be true.

Ski didn't care. His family was from Hanover, Germany, and he was absolutely not Polish. The man in Alpha Company they called Ski—he was Polish. He was slower than a wooden watch. That's what Blood said to Ski one day—slower than a wooden watch. Ski laughed. He figured his machine gun was faster than Blood's feet.

"Think about pussy" was the platoon's sign-off on the radio when enemy contact was certain. Mex wanted the platoon's sign-off changed to, "Think about pee hole." Fish vetoed the change, declaring that the skanks Mex liked to ball were pee holes that would scare a good dog.

Mex and Drips ate dinner together after Dak To. Mex stopped eating dinner with Drips when Drips started standing in their foxhole with his pants down while he drank his coffee, the connection escaping Mex's inner-city mind.

Drips said that having cooler balls made the penicillin work faster.

PeeWee advised Fish that Drips might be right, so Fish started drinking his coffee with his pants down. Blood started after Fish's cock one day with the same knife he used to cut off Chuck's ears. That was the last time that Fish had his cock out where Blood might see it.

Maunel Rameriz was called PeeWee because Fish thought he was the smallest Mexican in the Army and told him so the first day Rameriz joined the platoon. PeeWee accepted the name with a gracious smile, laughing at the rotten holes in the Gringo's teeth. That was four months ago, before PeeWee fell prey to malaria and missed the battle for Dak To.

Now PeeWee liked Fish. The two soldiers had survived war's hell in common. The tail of a thousand enemy rounds had peeled away their veneer. They made their bones, were true to their salt, and enjoyed a relationship that required no emotion and less talk.

When death was in the air, Fish spoke in the abstract, and PeeWee replied, "How big?" Then Fish, no matter the situation, would launch into a rave about his big cock, or tits that could fill a wheel borrow, or the pussy he fell into while he was looking for his dog tags.

They sat together, alone almost all of the time, huddled near their foxhole, secure yet fearful, as if Sweet Cheeks might catch them happy. Unfettered happiness found its end with some men. Sweet Cheeks reckoned happiness was a form of betrayal. He cut the side pockets off a new man's rucksack, as he told it, to trim the man's sails.

Sweet Cheeks didn't know a sail from butter.

Billy Kramer—Sweet Cheeks—spent almost all of the day on the balls of his feet, waiting to laugh, convinced that an unexpected laugh was valuable for its gathering; for bringing men to a single moment. He had a ruthless way of sidling when he stood close to a new man, smiling a wholesome smile, then insulting the man for this or that. He would tell the new men he hated them, then he would laugh.

Sweet Cheeks was a name he earned gradually, a blend of the chipmunk pouches that kept his smile from consuming his ears, and the romance in his stories about his '56 Chevy.

Sweet Cheeks had a mean streak. His eyes were cold at times, odd times. In an instant, with an icy grin, he could rivet a horse to a barn door. Those gray-brown pools, his eyes, lay calm in the midst of an unexplained silence.

Sweet Cheeks' smile belied the depth of his feeling. He talked constantly, even on ambush, squirrel scratching his Arkansas logic. Most days he talked to Father Watters, thanking the dead chaplain for saving his mortal bones.

"Father, this is Billy Kramer. Remember me? I was in First Platoon, from Arkansas. Tell Moon Man my name is Sweet Cheeks now. Moon Man got banged on November twentieth, the day after the short drop killed you and the wounded."

Sweet Cheeks prayed in a loud way, as if his words needed grit to make it out through the canopy. The thought of God made his friend Bucks nervous.

Felony prone as a new parolee, Andrew Jackson Biggs, with his pale black skin and his sly nature, was Sweet Cheeks' buddy—one man from Pea Ridge and the other man from Detroit, a mountain beaver and a gray hound. Biggs was a gambler. He preferred dice: African Golf he called it. Games excited him. Acey-duecy was his card game.

Squeak called him Big Bucks one day and Ski shortened the handle to Bucks.

Bucks expected to be drafted by the Tigers. With his rotation date out of Vietnam falling after the start of spring training, he figured to catch on with one of the Tiger's Single-A farm teams. His dream lay just beyond his reach, waiting nearby where he practiced his swing and chided Sweet Cheeks for smoking.

"Weight back and drive the ball. That's what you've got to do." Bucks was left-handed. His swing was flawless. When Bucks told Ski that a good hitter hit off a stiff front leg, Ski laughed, and said, "I got a stiff front leg."

Bucks carried a three-foot piece of bamboo strapped to his rucksack frame. He used the bat to demonstrate his hitting techniques. With one swing he drove the ball. With another he lifted the ball. Or, he dug in and made solid contact, went with the pitch.

His meals were prepared with the same precision. C-Ration cans were placed in ordered rows. The C-4 plastique was praised for its purity, then set ablaze. A good diet was crucial for a professional athlete. Stubbs figured Bucks would open a restaurant near the Tiger's ball yard.

Week by week Bucks chipped at Sweet Cheeks' bankroll, tamping a smooth dice-run on the floor of their foxhole, throwing the bones into a side-wall, then spicing the outcome with a cunning grin. With a casual shrug he would give his friend his money back and the game would go on. Sweet Cheeks didn't care. Neither did Ski.

Ski, sporting the vitality of flat beer, sat in a corral of bamboo, hiding from who knows what. He had survived the battle for Dak To with no particular misfortune and withdrew into a realm no one else could find, clutching to his sanity by a thread.

"Get fat if you can," was an expression Ski had coined as a way of saying, "Roger, out." Somehow his mind had synthesized three phrases: roger out, fuck you, and get fat if you can, using the abstract to create a higher form of hopelessness. Stumped, he would drop the radio handset in the dirt without saying a word.

Ski never said much. He talked to himself when he cleaned his machine gun. A friend's words too often spoken made him anxious, as if he were obligated to memorize them.

Twice a week Ski and Shadow shared an evening meal. Today, Shadow was singing, squatting near the base of a tree, watching Ski finish his good-luck rituals. Measuring instincts had become a ritual for Shadow and the rest of the Hill People. The depth of an eye, the length of a stride, the need for water, the weight of a word, the cock of a weapon, these were the indicators of the next man's worth.

Drips and Mex, Fish and Squeak, Ski and Shadow, Bucks and Sweet Cheeks: in the fight to the end, these eight men were the Hill People, the survivors of the carnage known as the Battle for Dak To—the first battle of the Tet Offensive.

They were the quick-eyed men who Hardin measured—at twilight and at dawn, without fail. They hailed from the hurricane decks of times past, and would put lead in a man so fast the man weighed heavy when he hit the ground. Hardin thought he might one day be full-measure, the soldier they had become.

Searching a jungle recess, Hardin wondered how he might find his end.

The soldier he had become bore no resemblance to the infantry officer described in the Army Officers Guide. Hollow-cheeked and exhausted to the point of numbness, unease had crept into his heart. Constantly striving to dissemble his nature, he was grateful that mutilating the dead had not gained his favor. Thankful that he was not so storied at this craft of killing that his vision had become blurred, he did fear his own rage.

Good guys fighting bad guys—for Hardin, the war had to remain a simple process of accepting or denying the relevance of morality. Within the first hours of combat, he had concluded that killing evil people required an ample measure of deceit. That, and a hollow core.

"We've gotta roll, El Tee," Squeak said.

Squeak emptied the last sandbag, snapping the lose dirt into the air. Searching the jungle at irregular intervals, he froze. Hardin froze. Squeak's cigarette fell from his mouth as he dropped the bag and reached for his weapon. Seconds passed. Mex popped through the vegetation, buttoning his pants, oblivious to his near-death experience.

Squeak shook his head and picked up his cigarette.

Knowing the company had another ridgeline to search, Captain Joe had been coaxing Hippie's point squad for over an hour.

The first steps from this night laager would be reluctant etchings on a predictable path. Captain Joe would not retrace any part of yesterday's route. The terrain would dictate which direction might provide a tactical advantage.

Today would be dicey. The NVA were patient, seemingly unaffected by combat, and far less reliant on chance. If the NVA were waiting, the jungle would quickly be confused.

"El Tee, how ya doin'?"

"I'm all right."

Blood bounced into a full squat, as if he were about to dispense a favor. He enjoyed talking with his lieutenant. Any officer would do. His blond hair was stuffed into a bunch, centered on a pair of hollow, anxious eyes. His incomplete smile seemed at odds with his large thick hands and oversized forearms. His fatigue shirt was missing a right sleeve, leaving his well-proportioned face cocked in protest.

Hardin looked at Blood's knife and then at LeCotte.

LeCotte's angular face bore the trappings of a little-used smile. His uniform looked as if someone had slit every panel of fabric. Slated as a possible replacement for Mex as squad leader, he was a nervous sort, barely able to stand still long enough to take a piss.

LeCotte, in an ordered, corrugated way, was too specific for Vietnam's war. Tied as he was to the chaos, he struggled for facts and logical answers. With his needs less logical than his war, he was never trusted and therefore never given a nickname.

For a Canadian from Pittsburgh, LeCotte was an enigma. As with almost all northern-city whites, he tended to be uptight, sarcastic, over organized and excitable.

"What's the deal, El Tee?" LeCotte said, testing the hinge on a new lighter, his eyes adrift.

"We got point," Hardin said, pausing to put Linda's picture away. "Ridge runnin' is a bad habit. Chuck is gonna bang us where this finger-ridge hits the water." Hardin laid out his map and pointed to the blue-line. Mex stood-to in a patch of sunlight.

"Chuck's figured out our pattern. He's on both sides of us," Mex said.

For Mex, being immersed in Charlie's jungle wasn't as dramatic as realizing that he was surrounded. Mex shoved his fist into the map, then traced a route down a ridge to a blue-line 400 meters farther east.

Waiting for Joe to muster a reason, GIs sat in silence.

Hardin was reading an old letter from Linda when Sweet Cheeks offered him a splash of coffee. Standing five-ten, with dark hair and a crafty demeanor, he was a white boy with even whiter teeth. He was the platoon's Talisman. With forty days left on his combat tour, Sweet Cheeks had an easy motion to his soul that helped balance a mean, derailed train of thought.

He claimed to be from Pea Ridge, Arkansas, when the sun was shining, and from Blowing Rock, North Carolina, whenever it rained. He was equally baffled when his poncho failed to keep him dry, and that wasn't the half of it.

Except for Moon Man, the dead men he knew had gone on R&R.

Sweet Cheeks came to Vietnam with a photograph of a 1956 Chevy, two-door hardtop— his high school ride. He kept the photo in a plastic bag he tucked under the webbing in his helmet liner. If he wanted to be your friend he would show you the picture, and after a moment say, "Ain't she sweet?" then insist you agree by smiling until you did.

"Short-time, eh Sweet Cheeks?"

"Bein' short don't mean nothin'. I shoulda jumped that slick you rode in on. Elephants got me talkin' to the trees." He spoke softly: knowing his luck needed some down time. He looked into the jungle and rubbed his neck. The fear in his eyes pushed against his casual tone.

"You all right, Sweet Cheeks?" Hardin searched his friend's expression for signs of a crack. The bullet crease on his neck had healed like a knotted rope.

"I'm makin' it, El Tee. Good to have ya back."

"Can't do much, I'm packin' a plastic gun."

"Maybe so. But, God's watchin' you, El Tee. You lost some weight." Sweet Cheeks swept Hardin's stomach with an admiring eye.

"You and Squeak are short. Get fat if you can." Sweet Cheeks dumped his coffee and exchanged a worried look with Squeak, knowing the NVA were just one mistake away.

"Commo check?" Squeak and Hardin asked, never assuming, forcing a response.

"We're up." Squeak threw his shoulders forward to resettle the weight of the radio and dropped to one knee. "Charlie Six, Lima Kilo. Want us to cut a chogey?" Hardin watched the company radio operator nudge Captain Joe.

"Take it slow, Lima."

"Roger, out."

Squeak used variable voice patterns when signing off the radio. He was not alone. To survive in the jungle a GI had to master a stepped pattern of radio transactions, each transaction ending with a transfer of speaking rights, until someone ended the call by saying the word "out."

Protocol stipulated that the party starting the call would end the call. Or, the superior officer or noncommissioned officer would end the call. Squeak received incoming calls with a cupped hand, determined to control the call and end it on terms acceptable to the platoon.

Squeak devised word games to correlate rear-echelon fantasies with jungle realities. He used words with multiple meanings to create new perceptions. The two most important words in the game were "Roger" and "Wilco." "Roger" meant Squeak understood the message. "Wilco," short for "Will Comply," meant he understood the message and the platoon would comply with its contents.

The phrase "Roger, out" had become synonymous with the phrase "Wilco, out" to almost all rear-echelon radio operators, commanders and support staffs.

No blooded infantryman intentionally used the word "Wilco."

The game was simple. If Squeak got a call he didn't want, he would give the sender a "Roger, out." This would tell the sender that his message was understood and the call was ended. With this method Hardin could interpret Squeak's translation.

If Hardin took the call, Squeak would sign off with a "You-bet-your-sweet-ass, Roger, out," and Hardin would take the heat if the sender ever found out he didn't comply.

Squeak's "Roger, out" had the rhythm of fuck-you said with a smile. He could end any transmission. Deceiving the handlers was enjoyable and absolutely necessary.

* * *

Reluctant GIs picked their way through the maze of foxholes, setting their intervals and spacing, and staggering their line so one man did not trail another. At the charge, Drips and Fish merged with the point squad, avoiding the dog handler, and signaling an all-clear to Hippie.

The four NVA turncoats fell in behind Hippie. Jabbering hucksters they were, excited, then quiet. Cold eye contact met Hardin's stare. The smallest man looked away.

Stubbs was right.

"Lima Five, this is Lima six, over."

"Five, go." Stubbs was on drag with Sweet Cheeks.

"Keep the drag tight." Stubbs let out a huff of disgust.

A cold, damp fog sat on the jungle floor like wet wool, tying the undergrowth to the gusting wind, masking the definition of the ridgeline. Welling in spurts, the fog made the jungle lunge at the platoon. Trees sprang forward. A thin wash of sunlight set the mist aglow.

Hardin shrugged at the straps of his rucksack, then pulled the collar of his jungle sweater to his neck. By 1000 hours the jungle would be steaming and the company would be out of water.

Shadow stuffed his jungle sweater into his pants, staring into the vegetation, peeling away the layers. "Merry Christmas, Sarge."

"Shut up, Shadow," Stubbs said.

As he eased a foot forward, Stubbs measured the loose dirt piled at the front of the foxholes. He found threats in the perimeter's variegated weave and a grace to its odd pattern of lifeless holes. Seasoned GIs dumped their sandbags to the outside of the perimeter in case the company got hit moving out and had to reoccupy the laager. Stubbs was a stickler.

The dog's pacing brought Hardin back to the canopy, searching for snipers.

The fog and a warming sky had set the canopy in motion, badgering the jungle floor with green iridescent facets of refracted light. The undergrowth sat in patches, first sparse, then dense, with ground visibility under eighteen meters.

Dappled shadows changed form, catching the eye, then blending with the clay. An indignant prayer replaced the fog as Hippie moved the point squad out, fighting the urge to run, stepping without breaking the ground, their movement fluent. One GI alerted, and the others froze, searching their sectors for symmetry, for the shapes that brought death.

With his sector clear, Hardin took stock of the man smiling at him. Fish had survived Dak To, the clap-clap, R&R, and an acute case of the crazies. He lived out of a ramshackle rucksack, bragged about his torn fatigues, and lied when mischief was afoot. That Fish existed was suspect. He hated cherries, and would kill in a hot second. Fish was a loose chipping.

Today Hardin was in good hands. Tomorrow? Tomorrow was a rumor.

* * *

Five hours passed in agonizing silence. With leveling, confirming gestures, men signaled and then grimaced at the worth. The sequence was exhausting. Any movement might trigger a quick-fire response: arms extended, weapons pointed, minds cocked into a frenzy. Hippie's arm shot out, and the point squad sank into a low crouch.

"Bingo, Squeak—we got company." Hippie's voice was urgent. "Looks to be a couple of dinks. Camped here and moved out down the ridge. My guess: they're tryin' to suck us in."

"Roger. Hang a left. Move ninety meters and jump that finger ridge runnin' east."

"Squeak we're sendin' the dog back," Hippie said, gasping through a run.

The dog's head was in a vice—his teeth bare, his neck hair bristled. Saliva poured from his mouth. Squeak pointed at the handler and gave Blood a nod.

"If ya don't keep that fuckin' dog quiet, I'm gonna kill ya both," Blood said. The handler shortened the leash. He would be lucky to keep the dog from starting a firefight.

"There's gooks everywhere," Squeak said.

Searching downhill into a swelling sense of fear forced the question of sequence and timing. The vegetation thickened, cutting visibility to seven meters. With one hour to the nearest water, and two hours to a defensible laager, the paratroopers had to pick up the pace.

One by one the point squad passed the chieu hois, measuring the posture of the turncoats. Without notice, Nasty blasted the small mouthy dink between the eyes with an overhand right and the four quislings clustered into a wad, speaking in tongues.

Fish and Drips checked equipment, searching with their jaws tight, eyes darting, mouths boiled dry with anticipation. Others mimicked them.

"Lima, this is Bucks." Bucks was whispering on the radio, playing *I've Got a Secret.* When he wasn't gambling, he talked constantly: about surviving Dak To, ravaging the whorehouses in Bangkok, and his girl back home—Deon, with her melon-sized tits. Bucks whispered when he was trying to be funny. He moved with moccasin-light feet.

Today was not funny. Today Bucks moved like a timid deer.

"Roger, wait." Squeak grabbed Hardin's arm. "It's Bucks."

"Talk to me, Bucks," Hardin said with a beckoning calm.

"We need water bad, and outta this thick shit." Dry-mouthed and clothheaded, Bucks had jived himself into an on-the-block mess.

"Easy, Bucks. It's thick for Chuck, too." Squeak's eyes locked with Hardin's, registering the mounting pressure. The Hill People knew the company was trapped.

"I can feel dinks breathin'," Bucks said, his voice emphatic.

"Easy, Bucks. Are they ahead of us?" Squeak pointed toward the blue-line.

Bucks' unpolished voice reached out from the handset. "They got their main dudes behind us, and some stall dudes on the blue-line." Squeak shrugged.

Squeak keyed the handset, and said, "Be cool, Bucks. Keep your head down."

Hardin spoke, "Squeak, tell Drips and Shadow to stay tied to the point squad's tail. Have Mex and Ski drop back with Stubbs to keep the drag tight." Squeak cupped his hands around the radio handset to talk privately with the Hill People. Hardin fell into a trance.

Squeak, Sweet Cheeks, and Shadow were scheduled to leave country within forty-five days. Mex was next, followed by Bucks, then Drips, and then Ski, and finally Fish.

"Watching a friend die begging for water and morphine—how bad is that?" Hardin whispered. 13 December 1967—eleven and a wake-up until Christmas. The survivors had nothing to celebrate.

Squeak jarred Hardin's shoulder as NVA mortar tubes sounded, lancing the jungle with their hollow coughs. GIs scattered through the jungle, running at a not-so-quiet pace. The vines and the reedy vegetation reached out, grabbing weapons and rucksacks. The mud ripped at their boots. The point squad burrowed into the water.

The dense undergrowth draped into a wall reducing visibility to a few meters. Columns of men collided, fighting the anxiety of a near-run rage.

With the sting of a viper, Hardin's unknown fever struck, sucking the moisture from his throat and fogging his vision. For an instant the jungle was deserted. He caught his fall, straining to lift a foot, fighting to keep his balance. He was out of water.

Mortar rounds crashed through the canopy, showering the drag platoon with debris and the sequence accelerated. Combat's black hole, with its negative pressure, was sucking the company toward the blue-line, toward their enemy. They would fight for water, fight for a defensible laager, and there would be few surprises.

Hardin was hallucinating as the fever leapt from his bowels to his throat, mixing the slaughter of his radio operator with the touch and smell of the neighborhood nurse. Nancy was standing on the top of her highboy completely naked, framed in the center of her bedroom window, shaking her pussy for troop morale. Shadow and Ski were laughing.

Squeak screamed at the squads: think, react, and stay alive. "Bucks, spread out. Blood, don't lose the point. The party's at the blue-line." Squeak was the platoon leader.

The closer the blue-line, the faster events occurred. GIs, with their eyes full of hate, knew they could not change the rhythm: this act was written by the heralds of time, deep in the bowels of history.

The mortar fire stopped, leaving the echoes. Blood, Drips, and Fish were glued to the point squad's tail. Hardin stumbled. His breathing was erratic. The radio barked.

"Lima, this is Blood." Blood's voice was coiled, anticipating the chaos.

"Squeak, go."

"Squeak, our dinks are fallin' back. Somethin's wrong." Blood's instincts were keen.

"Roger, break. Point, this is Squeak."

"Point, go." Hippie recognized Squeak's tone.

"Half speed, right rudder. When I say bingo, we're gonna take out our friends. Ya got three seconds to get down." Hardin was lucid enough to realize he was falling.

"Blood, ya ready to take 'em?" Squeak said.

"They're right here." Blood's back braced as his quick-fire motion found a target.

"Roger, break. Bingo, Bingo." The point squad flushed like quail scattering through huckleberry. Blood and Drips sprang forward, disarming the first three turncoats. The smallest man bolted to the flank through a burst from the Frenchman's machine gun. The husky stream of tracer rounds lifted the man off the ground, and threw his body flopping across the jungle floor.

Captain Joe found Hardin kneeling, leaning against the base of a tree. With a dancing eye, Joe said, "What in the hell are you smilin' about? You sick son-of-a-bitch." Chewing the butt of a nasty, oversized cigar, Joe was waiting for Hardin to throw up.

Hardin tried to move. "You're down another ally, Captain. Not lookin' good the way you've been killin' your friends."

Joe grabbed the handset from Squeak. "Hippie, move down stream and find a place to cross." Joe looked at Hardin's ragged face and shook his head.

Squeak was lying motionless in a shallow trough, expecting the point to get hit, and forcing the company to run across the creek. Blood was kneeling, talking to the dead man.

Seconds became minutes. The jungle had slipped into a quiet spell. When Joe's two other lieutenants popped through the brush, Squeak grabbed his gear and dashed away.

"We gotta ambush these bastards," Gator said, looking for a reaction. Joe ignored him.

"I say we stick together," Stubbs said, countering the man he claimed was a dumb shit.

Lieutenant Gates wanted to be called Gator: Alley-Gator, the main man at the watering hole. Mex figured Alley-Gator didn't know pee hole from peanut butter. Gator was a fresh experience, a walking warehouse. Essentials dangled from D-rings, straps, leather strips and nylon cords. He was so new his helmet had a lieutenant's bar sewn on the front.

"Bucks thinks the dinks are behind us, tryin' to pin us to this blue-line," Stubbs said, pouring water over his head, watching Lieutenant Anderson's expression.

Andy flipped his map toward his rucksack and looked toward the blue-line, gauging the chance of combat. An intense tranquility ran through his face, his flyweight build chiseled with definition. He moved through the jungle like a fox, quiet, with a bounding ease.

Andy's a good man, Hardin thought.

"Six, this is Cue Ball. We're across. Drop down about eighty meters."

"Roger. Any signs of Chuck?" Squeak asked.

"Nothin." Joe grabbed his gear.

Squeak assigned Bucks left flank security on the blue-line and Mex the right flank. The stream crossing bunched and released GIs like an accordion, increasing the platoon's exposure. The stream was six inches deep and four meters wide. An enclosed canopy hung into a weave of vines, stiff grass, and long-leaf scrub. Visibility varied from eight to ten meters.

The scout dog laid in the creek with a splash, then stood into a rigid pose. The scout dog alerted. Death was near—in the substrate below the obvious, just beyond the last tree. This scout dog could smell the jungle's mood.

"Six, this is Squeak, we're wet. Stay close."

Having gained his feet, Hardin drank the cold water, one swallow at a time, one eye on the scout dog. His head ached, throbbing from temple to temple. His feet were cool.

The dog alerted again. The handler let him run free. The dog bounded, then stepped uphill, away from the water, his step measured by a scent in the wind, dragging his leash. The damp ground absorbed his stride, allowing a steaming silence to mask the dog's search.

With a sudden burst, he exploded into a thrashing guttural lunge, then stopped.

Spotting his prey, the dog flew across the jungle floor and launched himself into a fury. A weapon slammed against a tree. The scout dog killed the man.

A ninety-pound man with no throat and no rucksack lay in a tangle. His bamboo hat was shattered. His life gurgled out a spastic message, bleeding into a messy death, his hands and feet swimming along the soggy floor of a shocked jungle. Blood was not shock.

Stubbs shook his head. Where in hell was the man's throat?

The soulless brutality splattered against Stubbs' most exaggerated images of war. The dog's blood-soaked face glistened, his shoulders straining against the handler's weight, anxious, straining at the end of his tether.

Hardin stood over the dead man, his eyes clearing.

Squeak keyed the handset, whispering as he filled a canteen. "Six, the dog killed a scout. They travel in threes."

"Move uphill. Take it slow." Joe sounded as though he was running.

"You stay tight, goddammit." Squeak didn't blink when he ordered his captain to pick up the pace. With Squeak's focus, Captain Joe's rank made no difference.

Voices were strained as boots fought for traction, hands snatching at the damp ground. Men whipsawed uphill, their tools resisting the climb. With Joe and the drag platoon low on water, the lead elements of the company mounted the steep face of the ridge. GIs were hanging onto the vines and roots, fighting to keep pace, and running away from the trap.

Squeak reached for a clump of grass, lost his footing and the radio slammed into the back of his head, sending his helmet rolling into LeCotte's hands.

Drawn as they were by wounded spirits, the Hill People cursed the misstep of a new man's stride, knowing their enemy might change form: become semi-fluid and seep out of the foliage. Frantic minds constructed one ambush and then another. Friends disappeared, then reappeared, their weapons caked with mud, their eyes reflecting what others had described.

"Slow down, Squeak. Tell Hippie to stop." A gash on LeCotte's face glistened white and red. His glasses were missing an ear-piece, and his drive-on rag was soaked with blood.

"Gator's in the water," Squeak said. "I can hear their feet." Hardin nodded

"Hippie, stop the parade." Captain Joe was breathing hard.

One by one the point squad set into the ridge, each behind a large tree, framing a sector, watching for movement. Hardin set an ear to the top of the ridge, trying to segregate the sounds of the jungle from the anguish of the men climbing the ridge. His head ached with fever as he drank the cool water.

The hollow expansion of mortar tubes rang out again, forcing men to curl into the ground. Mortar rounds, erupting in concert, crashed through the canopy on the far side of the blue-line. Bits and pieces of vegetation slammed against the GIs on drag. The hollow sound was replaced by silence.

The drag platoon and the headquarters element bolted from the ground, plunging headlong through the blue-line. Running with heavy feet, the blue-line may as well have been empty.

"Point, stand fast." Hearing the exhaustion in Joe's voice, Stubbs lighted another cigarette and dug at the mud on the dials of Squeak's radio. GIs reeled at the impact of the mortar rounds, waiting for the inevitable screams. The mortar tubes barked again, then silence.

All hands were scrambling now, sheltered by the panic, their eyes rushing ahead, uphill, caught in a dilemma: stifling heat and limited water. Boots fought the moist soil. Steam sucked the fluids from their bodies. The aching silence had a raw edge.

Mortar rounds fell farther down the blue-line with soft concussions. GIs scurried into a hasty perimeter, laminated to the jungle floor, searching the ridgeline. Listening to the whispers from the nearest radio, GIs laid into the ground.

Whispering as if they might have an answer, it was time for a fight.

Eight minutes later, Joe dispatched the dog, Hippie, and half the point squad to billy-goat the ridge heading west, in the opposite direction of the mortar rounds' trace. The dog picked its steps with a rush. His muzzle tight to the ground, blood matted the hair on his left shoulder.

That dog is a curse, Stubbs thought.

With weapons drawn, searching in overlapping folds, the recon patrol stepped into the jungle. Waiting, without a word being uttered, the roar started with AK fire. The recon patrol was pinned down and fighting for their lives.

"Let's go, Mex," Ski yelled.

With his weapon and ammo, Blood flew past Fish. The rescue team broke into the fire uphill from the fight. The dog and the handler were down and motionless. Cue Ball was writhing in pain, screaming. Hippie and the rest of the patrol were bottled behind a series of bamboo clusters.

Stubbs pushed Mex and his squad toward the fight, mindful to stay uphill. Five GIs, including Ski's machine gun, opened fire. The North Vietnamese broke contact and disappeared.

Mex bounded downhill in a series of lunges and dove next to Ski. "Ski, work the uphill side. I'll get the handler." Ski rotated to his right sending short bursts of five and six rounds into the unknown. Mex crawled around his boots and over to the handler.

The dog sighed through the vibration of his last breath, still straining at the end of the leash. Mex checked the handler. Squeak wouldn't have to shoot the handler or the dog.

Blood, firing from his hip, landed next to Mex.

"Grab a shoulder." Blood set his feet and the two men started dragging the handler out of the line of fire. Doc Collard worked on Cue Ball's shoulder and thigh with those efficient motions combat medics could muster in the middle of downtown traffic.

With a brief flash of guilt, Blood realized he didn't know the handler's name.

Hippie grabbed the handler's weapon and pointed at the dog. Stubbs shook his head, pushing the patrol out of the kill zone with rapid hand signals. As GIs bounded from the kill zone, Stubbs took a last glimpse. Lying motionless on the jungle floor, the scout dog died. This canine soldier deserved a ride, a bit of respect for sure, but the company was packing its dead and wounded. If nothing else, he could finally rest: no more killing.

Mex thrust his weapon into Stubbs' chest, and lifted the handler's body over his shoulder. Cue Ball took more time. His right thigh was torn apart, along with his left shoulder.

"What happened?" Joe asked.

"A gunfight. Dinks banged the dog and these two," Mex said, taking his weapon from Stubbs, closing the dust cover.

"The dinks just fuckin' vanished," Hippie said. "They're gonna stomp our ass."

Scared, Squeak said, "We got another klick to high ground. We better get there first."

Knowing the company was one bad move away from extinction, Joe nodded, and asked, "Where's the dog?"

Hippie ignored the question. "Merry Christmas, Captain."

"Go get that fuckin' dog," Joe screamed, his breath seething.

Blood, Mex, Fish, and Hardin carried the dog back. Captain Joe had it right.

Eleven reluctant men, nearly half of Andy's platoon, packed the handler, the dog, and Cue Ball. Their pace gradually increased as the pallbearers accepted a steady rhythm.

Hardin took his leave with his FUO raging and Jimmy Durante singing "Any Dink'll Do." With feet like lead anchors he was delirious again, staring at an ice cream sundae, then at a pizza. With his heart rate soaring, his eyes blurred, and his world slid into slow motion.

Hardin was down and he could not do anything about it. Squeak and Mex crouched beside him, then left. Other men raced for cover. His eyes would not hold a focus. Captain Joe and the senior medic appeared and propped him against a tree.

"Get him up, we gotta keep movin'." Joe was screaming, as if his words were compressed, pestering Hardin's ability to focus.

"Get up, goddammit!" Joe mouthed the words.

Frustrated, Hardin pushed him away. Joe grabbed Hardin's shirt and stumbled into First Platoon's mental junkyard. Confronted by Hardin's men, Captain Joe backed away.

Rap and Drips picked Hardin off the ground with one possessive scoop, making their intentions clear: no one fucked with their El Tee. Rap pinned Hardin against a tree with his left forearm. Mex grabbed Hardin's weapon and rucksack. Drips and Rap carried Hardin to the top of the ridge.

Filling sandbags brought moments of listening. The jungle billowed with a steaming heat and the scriptural grief of impatient shovels: D-handle shovels sharpened to a razors-edge with a bastard file.

Fuzzy, urgent figures dug in silence, recreating the security of a familiar premise.

Hardin drank slowly. With his lower abdomen on fire, the water settled into a boil. Getting to his feet was an experience close to realizing his girl friend wore falsies. Fluids rushed to parts of a body ransacked by dysentery. With a center of gravity fluctuating between his knees and his shoulders, he leaned against a tree and gently massaged his nuts.

As the rotors of the medevac chopper got louder his body grew stronger. Picking the first steps carefully, he gained his feet. Rap gave him a fist and Squeak mumbled his trash about pussy lieutenants.

"Ya need a ride, Gravy?" Joe asked. Hardin shook his head, trying to activate the balance of his palsied mind. "Next time we don't leave the dog. Not for a fucking second."

Hardin's system surged as he searched the vegetation across the jungle floor. He knew the NVA were waiting just beyond the next clump of trees, and that Joe was wrong about the timing. With or without the dog, next time was now.

"Ya gotta have a short memory, Captain."

Hardin turned away to keep his thoughts moving. Joe seemed to have more grief for the dog than he had for the handler. Shit-fuck, Cue Ball was banged hard as well. Where's the grief for, Cue Ball?

"Fuck this shithole," Hardin whispered to himself.

The rotting smell of compost mixed with sweet tang of human blood found Stubbs staring at the bloody poncho. The handler's body looked awkward propped over the roots of a large tree. Cue Ball sat next to the body, as if he were responsible for the dead man's passage.

Stubbs dropped Hardin's rucksack. "Best not be leavin' this behind, El Tee."

Stubbs had two cigarettes going. Surprised, he flipped the shortest one at PeeWee, then turned a long drag into a nod and set his face to the sky. The sweat and dirt on his expression was streaked with anticipation. He had wiped his drive-on rag through the debris so many times the mess had developed into a natural camouflage.

"Charlie Six, this is Three Yankee. Give me your location, over." Squeak grinned, lifted the hook and keyed the push-to-talk button. He had an opportunity to annoy a Major.

"Well, Mother, we're right here in Viet-fuckin'-Nam."

"Unknown caller, what's your call sign, over?"

"Well, Mother, if you knew my call sign, I wouldn't be an unknown caller."

"Unknown caller..." Squeak keyed the handset for a few seconds, slapped it on his knee three times for luck and threw the hook in the dirt. Unknown caller, unknown origin—FUO, DUO. Jungle Time was nuts. Three Yankee hollered on, whistling into an empty foxhole.

"Squeak, save some water for my chili," Hardin said, covering his weapon with a towel.

Squeak set fire to a chunk of C-4 plastique, looked at Hardin as if Hardin were stupid, then shook his head, twisting his face into a grimace, letting his shoulders shudder with disgust.

"Chilly! El Tee, you'll either throw up or shit your pants."

Hardin set the open ration next to the foxhole and Squeak shoveled dirt into the packet.

"You fuckin' Spec-Four prick."

"Grab a sandbag and stop whinin', El Tee," Squeak said, alerting to the sound of a machine gun bolt slamming home, then to the smoke grenade. A medevac chopper settled overhead, washing the top of the canopy. Anxious hands reached out to guide the litter basket; their faces clouded by swirls of purple smoke. LeCotte, the expatriate from Canada, dodged the incoming basket, arguing with Boyle over Boyle's inability to argue without stuttering.

This argument was in its third week. Somewhere between the harsh sounds of frustration, Boyle declared LeCotte an idiot and started unloading machine gun ammo from the litter basket.

Three medics tucked Cue Ball into the basket and gave the crew chief a thumbs-up. All eyes followed Cue Ball's rise through the foliage, the basket turning slowly at first, accelerating as it cleared the trees. He waved his good-bye to Hippie and disappeared above the trees.

"El Tee, Captain Joe wants to talk." Squeak dumped the chili ration into a sandbag with an offhanded smirk. "I got a spaghetti if ya want it."

Focusing on Shadow sharpening the leading edge of his shovel, Hardin stirred the spaghetti noodles to life. Joe was talking to the S-3—Major Swanson, the battalion operations officer: Mother. Joe's right eye narrowed to a slit when he talked to dun-colored people.

The four rifle companies called Major Swanson "Mother," because the name was more acceptable than calling him motherfucker. Mother's radio call sign was Three Yankee.

"Chuck knows where we are, Captain. Give Mother our loc-stat in the clear," Hardin said, shoveling spaghetti into his mouth. Gagging, he dumped the ration into Joe's foxhole.

"That's papa oscar four." Joe, blind in one eye, listened as Mother clutched at procedural turds. Joe looked at the mess in the bottom of his foxhole, cocked his head with a smirk, and then gave the medevac crew chief a thumbs-up.

"Three Yankee, did you get our loc-stat, over?" Joe asked.

Loc-stat was short for location status, a mystery well rooted in the soils of Battle Bullshit. Because Mother failed to understand that Charlie Company's location, like the time of day, was meaningless, he would continue to ask where the company had been and where they were now.

"We got it, Charlie Six."

Joe laughed, and dropped his cigar butt in Hardin's coffee. "Here, you talk to these jokers." Wiping off the mouthpiece, Hardin took a deep breath. With a chilling deceleration, he stared at the body bag, keyed the handset in silence, and then dropped it in the dirt.

* * *

Stubbs stood-to: opening and closing his right hand. "Rap, run a clover out on the right, in on the left. Check out and in with the OP." Rap's fire team knew the recon was a good idea, but no one wanted to walk up this ridge. Rap hit Squeak's fist, as did the next man.

Pozniak, the patrol's radio operator, was fidgeting with an empty magazine. His nickname was Nasty because he referred to his cock as a "nasty hog." Nasty was short, dark haired, and olive skinned.

Squeak grabbed his arm. “Keep talkin’ to us, Nasty.” Pozniak’s eyes were empty, focused on a spot somewhere in Oklahoma. He acknowledged Squeak with a grunt.

Stubbs dropped into a low squat next to the radio, watching the clover sink into a crouch and glide across the jungle floor. “If we get hit tonight it’s gonna be pure shit.”

“Sarge, you ever notice the way Nasty forces people to step away from him when he starts to say somethin’?” Squeak held out his hand, begging for a cigarette.

“Yeah, I have. Says his dad’s doin’ time for rapin’ his sister.” Stubbs nestled his rucksack into the underbrush and sat down. This night would last a lifetime.

Since Stubbs didn’t know Cue Ball’s Christian name, he decided the man wasn’t a Christian. The morphine and the shock of the firefight had spoiled their good-byes. Years from now, Cue Ball would wonder who else made it out and why the dog handler had died. That, and if the NVA turncoats had somehow betrayed their steps.

Joe’s three remaining allies were tied and gagged. Stubbs checked their location anyway.

“El Tee, you stick with Mex tonight, I got Bucks.” Stubbs took a drag on his cigarette and shook his head, then dropped the butt in the dirt, and exhaled.

“Gooks would’ve eaten that dog.”

The handler’s body flashed in black-and-white, his torso stretched across the bottom of the jungle hollow, his blood staining a bed of gold and brown bamboo leaves, his hand cinched into the black leather leash, twisting his lifeless fingers into a claw. Stubbs rubbed his face with both hands. Cue Ball’s boot had filled with blood.

Lighting another smoke, the old sergeant was frustrated.

“Squeak, how’s it feel?” Stubbs asked. Squeak was in a trance, his coffee perched next to his thoughts. He knew the company was in trouble.

Squeak looked at Stubbs, and then at Hardin. “It stopped makin’ sense when the dinks skyed-up after the handler got hit. It’s like they’re just tryin’ to keep track of us.”

“I’m gonna rack out.” Hardin motioned toward the radio.

Squeak was chest deep in the foxhole, sipping coffee and counting days. Rain started to fall as daylight drew away from the jungle floor, rushing through trees, the canopy blending with the sky.

“You scared, El Tee?” Squeak whispered into his canteen cup, then startled as his voice echoed and became louder. At five-foot-seven, Squeak knew he wasn’t too short to die.

“Fuckin’-A,” Hardin said, searching through the top of the canopy for a cloud, or any diversion. A stiff wind pushed at the treetops. “Is the world watchin’, Squeak?”

"You're shittin' me, right, El Tee? It don't matter if they are."

"Give me an hour. You got the battalion freeks?" If Squeak had to switch to the battalion radio net, it meant Joe and his RTO were dead and Squeak was running the war.

"Yeah. I can jump on the battalion net." Hardin arched his back in pain. His lower abdomen cramped violently; sending chilling sweats through his face.

"You all right, El Tee?"

"Fuck if I know. Doesn't seem like it. We got H&I fires tonight. Delta Company is on a one-hour standby." Squeak gave out a facetious puff of air.

"I don't have enough ammo to last an hour, and Chuck don't care who's standin' by." Squeak was right. Delta Company would not be in time to help.

Deep in the night throughout Vietnam, allied artillery batteries fired shells at suspected enemy targets to harass and interdict their operations. These fires, called H&I fires, pounded the jungle with random precision. Marching along ridgelines and riverbeds, their contrails arced over a pocked and fouled landscape, annoying the NVA to the point of wanting to kick someone's ass.

Tonight it would be Charlie Company's ass.

The jungle grew dark—first the floor, then the canopy. The rain stopped. "We got high-performance pussy for breakfast, El Tee—four calories, and all you can eat. Tac-Air with a stinky smell," Squeak said, admiring his humor.

Squeak was laughing into the dark hollow of an eighty-foot canopy. He laughed then raised his head to gain attention, as if his recall had finally triggered a fond memory. Reminiscing, he said, "I had a high performance redhead once. She was a screamer."

Hardin confirmed Squeak's memory with a smile, "A screamer does boost morale."

"Gettin' laid beats packin' a radio for a cub-scout like you." Squeak was more assertive at night. Hardin gave him the finger and snorted.

"You must like it here," Hardin said.

"Tennessee wants to take the radio. He's been runnin' Mex's horn"

"Tomorrow. Sour Mash can pack the radio and you can run the platoon." Squeak called the squads with a nighttime prayer.

"Claymores, frags, and seventy-nines: no sixteens. Make sure the cherries get it right."

Taking the radio in three-hour shifts, each exchange was more enthusiastic than the last. The pre-dawn cloverleaf closed back in with a negative sit-rep. With a sense of fallen perversion, one GI and then another realized the NVA were gone. Faces showed signs of cautious joy, excited about being alone on this not so special ridgeline.

Living through the night, or enjoying a hot cup of coffee, Hardin craved a simple delight. At this point in time, humor would work.

"The United States Army regrets to inform you that your son, during a high-speed pursuit of North Vietnamese regulars, was dipped in shit and died instantly. No ma'am, it was elephant shit. No, ma'am, we don't have any more details. No, ma'am, he wasn't awarded the Purple Heart, but he was awarded a Silver Star for valor.

"Seems he stepped in the shit several times before he went down. That's right. Elephant shit. Chunks about the size of a top hat. No, ma'am, I don't care for any coffee. I've got other families to see. Yes ma'am. It's some nasty shit."

"You're nuts, El Tee. Talkin' to a fuckin' sandbag," Squeak said.

One hundred five cups of GI coffee steaming in the mist of a cold mountain morning left any hand motion trailing an odd, swirling tail. The air had a damp taste. With weapons at the ready, GIs sat the silence, sipping heavens brew. Birds talked without fear. Men celebrated the new day; relieved they hadn't died in the dark.

Dying in the dark was easier.

Stubbs jabbed the studs—a quick order followed by his Georgia humor, then an order to grab their sacks, "Saddle up girls, it's jungle time. Time to dance."

Joe's radio barked, "Extraction in four days, Charlie Six."

Joe stared blankly at the radio handset, trying to match Mother's words with his own fatalism. He gave the hook to his RTO who keyed the net with his teeth clenched, spitting expletives mixed with a New Jersey brand of protocol.

"We'll call ya back."

Joe looked at Andy, then cocked his head toward the sound of the inbound chopper.

"Anderson, load out the bodies and the chieu hois." Joe sat down next to his rucksack and started talking to the medevac pilot. "Dust-off, this is Charlie Six. We've got two friendly KIAs and three POWs, over."

"Roger, Charlie Six. We've got yellow smoke."

"Roger, lemon. Heads up. We got fast movers comin' through. 800 meters west. Five minutes out, over."

"Roger, fast movers out west." The jungle penetrator pushed its way through the trees.

Having outlined the day for his squad leaders, Stubbs swung his rucksack onto his back, and settled the weight into place. "How come we're on drag?" Squeak asked, strapping the radio to Tennessee's rucksack frame. "It's safer on point, Sarge. Gator wants it too much."

Stubbs' background check on Tennessee made him perfect for the RTO job: young, short, steady, with a country white boy's sense of humor. Tennessee left home and joined the Army after being shot one summer night. As the story goes, he was the town cock peddler. His bride caught him in full stride, butt-stumping a smelly old rhino. She shot him when he tried a rollover dismount move, then pointed the gun at his nuts, making him beg for mercy.

Hardin laughed at the thought of Tennessee holding his power tools, bawling and begging his wife not to shoot him again. Looking at his new radio operator with a disbelieving grin, he said, "So, Tennessee, you wanna be the platoon, DJ. You any good?"

"Cue Ball thought so." A cunning expression consumed Tennessee's face. Or was he working on a deal?

"How come the words in Tennessee have an extra syllable? Like your hick-ass brain needs time to put a thought together," Hardin said.

"You put up with this shit, Squeak?" Tennessee pointed a stubby thumb at Hardin.

"Not for long." Squeak tightened the straps holding the radio in place.

"You married, boy?" Hardin said, pushing at Tennessee's defiance, just for drill.

"I ain't your boy. Besides, a barkin' snap-cracker can ruin a man's life." Tennessee donned his new power with a devious smirk, then took a few steps to gauge the load.

"Lima Five, Lima wants people tight, over," Squeak said, smiling, showing Tennessee how to give orders and jerk on the platoon sergeant's chain.

"Lima Five, Roger, out."

* * *

GIs scoured the jungle looking for the enemy, or Christmas. On the morning of the fourth day, battalion operations established a PZ time: 1400 hours. Charlie Company was being extracted to Firebase Sierra. Stubbs found Hippie in one of his confident explorer poses.

"No trick to this game. Right, Hippie?"

"Dinks like eatin' dogs, Sarge."

"Shut up, asshole."

News of the extraction brought shy men to the dance. With their uniforms rotting, they needed this chopper ride: proof that Mother talked about them in his secret briefings.

* * *

Firebase Sierra was a matted grass clearing, hanging on the tail of a gently sloping ridge, dotted with perimeter foxholes and ringed with three strands of concertina wire. Thirty meters from the wire on the north flank of the firebase the ridge fell into a gorge. The roar of the river below set a steady baritone pitch, sharp near the edge of the gorge. Though muted by layers of jungle, the river noise would mask any night sounds.

Grass filled the concertina wire surrounding the firebase. Hardin looked over the gorge, tracing the tops of the trees rooted near the river below. The opposite ridge rose out of the notch like a wall. A jagged pike of rock overlooked the circular artillery gun mounts.

The jungle in the central highlands in December of 1967 carried the effects of a vigorous monsoon season. Rivers ran full, cold and clear. Trees filled the sky with vibrant greens; their leaves fired with a changing mood, their tree trunks glistening dark-brown spires. Weeds and ground cover choked the trails. Husky grass stood erect, its spines stiffened by wind.

"Squeak, one man per hole awake," Hardin said. "You and the Cock-Peddler take shifts on the box. I'm gonna rack out."

"FUO—Fuckin' Useless Officers."

* * *

Morning brought the expected resupply, plus a hot breakfast, mail, clean fatigues—and a dignitary. General Abrams, the new commander of forces in Vietnam, wanted to meet the troops.

With discipline on the run, the loose-fitting mind of these GIs could easily match wits with Abrams' four-star brace. Hardin laughed to himself, trying to measure what feedback he might suffer. "Shadow is gonna sing while the old boy's trying to talk. Fish is gonna fill his hat with trinkets, and Squeak is gonna offer him a joint. Avoidance is my best shot."

"You better get your licks in, El Tee. Star shine isn't gonna hang around," Squeak said.

"The general's lookin' for a cabin boy like you Squeak."

Grunts hated generals. They would do anything to cock a four-star. And generals were afraid of grunts because grunts were the root of all evil: Battle Bullshit.

"I know a whore in Sin City he can have," Tennessee said.

Hardin pointed at Tennessee's grin. "I heard some snap-cracker tried to blow off your cock." Tennessee spun around and shouted at Squeak.

"You got a big mouth." Squeak had violated the enlisted man's code of silence.

"He's an officer. I wouldn't tell him shit." Hardin tampered with the bonds between enlisted men to create an edge of uncertainty.

"He told me about how you were blown out of the saddle by a hot-tempered snappy. How's the story go when you tell it?" Tennessee wouldn't share anymore secrets with Squeak.

"That's about the way the story goes."

"I don't see any scars. She musta shot ya in the ass."

Tennessee ripped open his shirt, poking at a dirt smudge on his upper chest. "Right there. That foul bitch shot me as I was jumpin' outta the bed. I was in the middle of a move to reason with her and bang, I was on the floor."

"I want to hear her version. Can I write her?"

"Shit, she had me on my knees, bleedin', beggin' for my life. She had this twenty-two rifle pointed at my boys. Oh, mercy. I kept whinin' and beggin' her not to shoot me again."

Telling the story made Tennessee clutch his tools and twist his face as if he'd been hurled overboard. His expression was no match for his harrowing tale.

"Her daddy forced me to join the Army. Said he'd kill me if I didn't."

"You still thinkin' about pussy?" Hardin asked.

"I've got to. Shit-fuck. I'm packin' a radio for some kid that oughta be in high school."

"Squeak, you teach him that disrespect?"

"No way, El Tee. He's a cherry. I don't tell cherries shit."

"Right, especially the one that's your ticket to ride. Here's the deal, Cornpone. Operating the radio is less important than hot coffee and the right C-Rations. Do that and I help dig, fill sandbags, pull point, ambush, OP— and, on occasion, pack the radio. And I cover your sorry ass from any Army shit that comes rollin' downhill." Tennessee looked at Squeak and got a nod.

"Deal."

"Beans and franks, spiced beef, spaghetti, chili, peaches and pound cake, mixed fruit, turkey loaf, every time."

Waltzing through a masturbating move, Squeak was demonstrating the futility of servicing a lieutenant. "Got 'em. Stole the chili from Stubbs. He's readin' his mail."

"One more thing. Anybody caught eatin' ham and motherfuckers gets a boot."

"I hate lima beans," Tennessee said. "Stubbs has your mail."

Stubbs smiled as he read, mincing the pleasures of those summer nights in Columbus, Georgia. He looked up, threw an envelope in Hardin's direction, and reset his paper, pausing to inhale smoke as Hardin moved away.

Sitting alone, Hardin admired Linda's words. The envelope carried the faint scent of her hair. The letter was full of Merry Christmas, and love. Those home-front emotions, now trimmed in a camouflage lace too fanciful to be real, were airmailed with hope, then transformed by death's good fortune into a calculus of fear, then siphoned away by half-naked comrades.

Linda's words brought tears. Hardin was tired. Their baby was due in May. Linda was sewing a fleece sleeper and matching bib, making freezer jam and pumpkin pie. Grandpa Karl was working at the cold-storage plant in Lynden, Washington, and feeding the cattle at night. Grandma Ada May was retiring from teaching fourth grade after twenty-six years to become a full-time grandma.

Snow blanketed the farm. Ice covered the pond where Linda and Grandpa Karl liked to skate. Grandpa had firewood laid in against the northeaster expected next week

Home had become a remote concept, first obscure, then illusive and now contradictory.

At times he pictured Linda skating on the pond, her image fleeting, badgered by a barefoot girl leading a water buffalo, profiled atop a rice-paddy dike, her innocence etched on a rural sunset. The little girl looked like Linda, her shadow cast long among the fresh green chutes of rice, her gentile nature nudging the day along.

Young girls and farms were natural friends.

Smiling at Linda's words, for a moment he was sublime. A patient person could read her writing. With one lifetime to meet his bride, to match her words with his emotions, Hardin's fears were growing. With Linda's image etched on a windowpane, she sat at the dining room table, looking over the concrete bridge and the creek next to the pond. With pen in hand, she willed-it-be-so that her unborn child's father was alive and doing well.

Linda's joy was so easy: her belly-laughs so spontaneous. Her holidays lasted the year round. Christmas shopping started on New Years Day. Eddie wasn't much of a shopper.

Now his holidays would be tempered with the religions of combat, with the sudden silence of a dying friend.

Thanksgiving, that season of hell, echoed with confusion. Two of the platoon's finest had simply vanished. The two men no longer existed, blown into a mist by the insanity of battle. Some did not believe they were gone. They clung to the notion that their friends had hopped on a dust-off and escaped. Only a new man would tell them otherwise.

Hardin set his bride's letter on his rucksack. Hiding in the corner of his memory, on the cover of a glossy catalogue, a bloody boot lay on its side. Near the boot, a rotting hand held a dog tag and a playing card, the ace of spades.

A man's stature diminishes when he holds the hand of a dying friend: rubbing slowly, wiping the mud from a vacant face, wishing the day over. Knowing how to cry would ease the pain of coming alive again. Hardin's tears flowed without notice and at the damnedest times.

Within the roar of battle lay a final madness: an isolation so profound that the soul loses its resolve, stained by insatiable revulsion.

Death had so many faces, each with a special agony.

Sorting incomplete soldiers would be Hardin's recurring burden. That, and dealing with the hatred he held for the paper soldiers, those cynical rear-echelon motherfuckers who expected GIs to enjoy the turkey dinner they prepared for the survivors of the Battle for Dak To. The mermite cans were filled with body parts and vomit.

He wanted to warn Linda—he just didn't know how.

Rummaging through a pile of clean fatigues, the smell of soap, the odd patch, and an occasional name—all these encouraged a renewal. A good sweat would iron out the wrinkles.

"How goes the war, Lieutenant?"

This question was meant to challenge a sane man's misgivings. Few people suspected he was an officer. Holy shit. Here stood a stocky old man sporting a grumpy grin, with four black stars stitched in rows on the collars of his shirt.

The stars glistened in the same sun that was radiating Hardin's bare ass.

Returning the grin, tooth for tooth, Hardin threw his head into a shrug, and said, "The war? That depends, General. If you're dead, it's over. If you're alive, you're just markin' time." Pretending to be modest, Hardin turned, pulling on his fatigue pants, lending a moon to a barrel full of stars. General Abrams had a sock full of Eastern words.

Moments later, huffing as if inflating a balloon, Captain Joe ran flat-tracking toward the podium, coaching a determined smile.

"Six, Squeak and Sweet Cheeks are leavin'," Hardin hollered.

Captain Joe didn't slow down. With a quick clutch and a little scratch, he had a clear shot at the general. As a company commander, he was obligated. As a lifer, this was face-time, not a time to be in name-tag defilade.

"Yes sir—I'm Charlie Company Commander. Yes sir, Captain Midnight."

The Hill People stared at Captain Joe as one, remembering the clatter of generals who had come to Dak To—the old men who stared stupidly at the empty boots, communing with the fallen, examining the survivors.

Those philosophers with their Eastern words, stepping along the ranks, buoyed by the Ceremony of the Boot, energized with spitting puffs of revenge.

CHAPTER SEVEN

Pops

Firebase Sierra, NW of Kontum. 1100 Hours.

Licking a limp envelope and the aroma of wet glue could not replicate a night with his bride, but if it's all you have, then close your eyes and lick it again. Amused, as if pleasantly embarrassed, Hardin knew an infantry platoon held no privacy, and fewer secrets. A pervasive black humor had rooted itself in his mind, assaulting even his most cherished thoughts.

With Captain Joe and General Abrams locked in cordial reflection, Hardin deliberately thought of his father. Even with a World War, the past seemed simpler. His father sat at his desk holding his dog tags, smiling at a picture of Murphy, his driver, perched in their jeep, saluting a dog he affectionately called Tits.

"An audience with Monty bore the trappings of an inquisition," the Major said. "Officers from every quarter paid Murphy enough money to buy his own milk truck."

* * *

Captain Joe massaged Abrams with outsized gestures and a rainbow of animation: big elephants, big guns, and incoming mortars. These illusions of combat led to exaggeration. By the time this war story reached the bar at the American Legion Hall, Silver Stars would be as numerous as cocktail napkins.

Captain Joe was solid, a first-rate company commander, an experienced field soldier. He was also an Army lifer. A good man, but a lifer just the same.

A GI would never fully trust a lifer.

Army lifers fell into one of two categories—field lifer or paper lifer. Joe was a field lifer, a modified grunt. Raised in the swamps of northwest Florida, he could be nothing else. Mother, the battalion operations officer, was a paper lifer.

The two men never saw eye-to-eye because Joe saw the world through turbid gray pools.

Mother ordered GIs around using the simplest of terms, assuming single syllable words were more effective. He talked to GIs as if they were failures, too slow to keep from becoming grunts. In the end, men like Mother were wholly self-centered.

Grunts started the day knowing their life could end between two words, or two cups of coffee—patriots sacrificed on the altar of stern duty, running fearlessly at the sharp end of the enemy's spear.

Men like Mother started the day sharpening a grease pencil.

Charlie Six, Captain Joe Winningham, was an OCS down-home type, driven more by reality than by ambition. Joe did not care what people thought. But, here he stood, rumpled by the suction, laughing at the general's jokes.

Hardin adjusted his drive-on rag, wincing at the retched smell. Longing for clean air, he caught the aroma of good food. Pops, a twenty-six-year-old private, was brewing a steel-pot stew, his kitchen staff, the cast from Our Gang. Bunched like quail, smoking and lying about the joy of unrefined women, six grunts celebrated Christmas dinner.

Hardin laughed. His Infantry Officers Handbook began with a truism: A GI would lie, even if the truth were a better story. When Pops told a story, he would whip the stew into a slurry. When LeCotte told it, Pops made a gumbo. Pops' gumbo was the best, sure enough.

The aromas of Pops' stew were layered, garlic-salts clinging to the jungle floor, beef-salts soaking the shoulder-high scrub, and whiffs of tomato paste filtering through the canopy. Adding stick salami created a meld.

Pops gathered his ingredients during resupply, estimating when the platoon laager might be secure enough for a celebration. With a nod from Stubbs he would strip the camouflage cover from his helmet and begin. Instantly, men would respond. Sandbags, Claymores, trip flares, outposts—all turned on a dime the nights that stew was on the card.

The hours that lay ahead, the night, tomorrow, all became meaningless. The stew's aroma was what mattered, more refreshing than the taste—and infinitely more refreshing than tomorrow. With deep breaths all around, fear was replaced with indifference.

Pops ladled the portions with a flare, careful not to bang the metal spoon on his steel pot or a canteen cup. He would take a breath and looked to his left before nodding that the next man should step forward.

New men weren't given any stew. New men ate dinner one entrée at a time.

At twenty-six years old, rumor held that Pops' cock had fallen off, exhausted by gravity's relentless grind. LeCotte said he saw Pops getting a blow job in Sin City but no one believed him. On Mondays, while shaving, Pops would drop his pants to prove the rumor false.

Pops dropping his pants was the way Fish remembered that Monday was the day to take a large orange malaria pill.

Ingesting this baseball-sized pill was akin to ingesting a blender. Once dissolved, the drug ignited an industrial grade evacuation that forced food through a GI's bowels at speeds only a sick mind could fathom. Fish didn't seem to mind.

If a GI mixed the orange malaria pill with hot chow, within four hours he would be self-propelled.

Pops thought cooking stew on Mondays was a waste of chow.

With LeCotte acting as his business agent, allotting portions of stew, Pops was never alone. He wanted the company. Pops started out wanting to be a hero. When he read the accounts of the Chachin Rangers fighting the Japanese in Burma during World War II, he knew his war would be hard.

Today PeeWee and Amps sat next to Pops cleaning a radio. Boyle and LeCotte stood nearby, arguing over a picture of a nude girl. Bucks and Nasty were rolling dice. All were an over-weaned clatter of ruffians waiting for Pops to sprinkle holy water on their evening meal.

Boyle, a stubby black man with a hellish stutter, countered LeCotte's facetious staccato with a gusting roar, sounding like a sow in heat. Drips enjoyed standing at the ready to finish a jab for Boyle, at LeCotte's expense.

Mex said LeCotte's horn-rimmed glasses pissed him off.

Mex said when LeCotte wrinkled his nose to adjust his glasses; it reminded him of a dry pee hole waiting for Vaseline to make a comeback. LeCotte didn't mind the comparison. He declared his uncle could have Mex deported.

Hardin sat outside the circle, enjoying the humor. With Pops' nod, he threw out his coffee and took a cup of stew: chicken, rice, and spiced beef seasoned with Tabasco and tube-cheese.

"Thanks, Pops."

"No sweat, El Tee." Hardin glanced quickly at the crew as he turned to leave.

"What are you lookin' at, asshole?" Hardin screamed at Amps.

Hardin savored the effect of the parting shot and would direct his assault at the most serious looking GI. Amps was a good target. LeCotte and Boyle tag-teamed him one day, declaring that Amps' southern country mind wasn't quick enough to respond. The profit in calling Amps an asshole was the bond created between the eight men listening.

Amps didn't laugh.

Amps spent half his day hiding in plain sight, and the other half cussing LeCotte's city-boy mouth. Amps was short for amperage, which was something Amps needed more of, according to LeCotte—that and a good piece of ass. Amps despised LeCotte's appraisals of his rural nature and the constant banter LeCotte seemed so fond of.

"The catfish are jumpin' today." The announcement meant Amps was about to tell a story and that it was a good day. LeCotte hated Amps' stories because they were Kentucky bred and had illogical detail. Knowing this, Amps told his stories as if he were talking to LeCotte.

Amps tolerated LeCotte at first, when their stories were new, before the platoon decided that Anthony Michael Phillips had never been with a woman, let alone fucked one. That was a fact. To Amps' way of thinking, women took so much time to unwind a man could never find enough to say.

Eating pussy was out of the question.

According to Pops, Amps' first blow job had him braced so his ass blew wind in great gobs and his knees buckled into jelly. The whore had slapped his ball-sack around like a boxer's speed bag, leaving Amps bowlegged with a sissy grin. LeCotte embellished the story with a mocking, sweet potato smirk, jaw-jacking until Rap finally laughed. This scared Amps. Rap knew that Amps didn't care for his kind. And Amps knew Rap only laughed when one of the brothers wanted him to.

Realizing Amps was praying, LeCotte laughed back at Rap, yelling, "The cunt made him sit down for juice and cookies. All his blood was in his dick."

Ski laughed, and said, "A tee-tee dick don't hold much blood." Ski chuckled crackers from his mouth, combing the hair on his chest, feigning confusion. Rap laughed and hit Lightning's fist.

As if cued by a breeze, the chatter stopped. Twilight was closing in on the perimeter. Stubbs lay on his rucksack, rolling over to slurp coffee and set his ear to the tree line outside of the perimeter.

"Brandy would help," Hardin said, showing off his stew.

"Peppermint Schnapps or a good whiskey would be just right." Stubbs lit a smoke, admiring Hardin's clean fatigues.

"Where's Squeak?" Hardin asked.

Stubbs offered his nonchalance, snap-testing the hinge on his lighter. "He's been hangin' out with those artillery types. I wondered if you were gonna get dressed." Hardin settled against his rucksack and kept eating, wanting to call Stubbs' mama a whore.

"Wanna play some cards, El Tee?"

Stubbs and his young charge played cards until twilight, and then began tucking in the studs. Squeak was asleep when Hardin settled in. He seemed damn relaxed for his last night in the field—21 December 1967.

As with all things a GI might do, at 0200 hours, Squeak broke out with the giggles and a case of the hungries. He had smoked dope with the artillery boys and proceeded to eat all of his C-Rations. With no immediate recourse, Hardin decided to bide his time, hoping Squeak's conscience would take up more room than his brain. Squeak would stay in the bush for one more resupply, a price he would pay for violating Stubbs' rules.

* * *

Firebase Sierra. 22 December 1967. 0548 Hours.

Morning stand-to fell in with a series of insinuations. Squeak, coddling his glassy eyeballs, practiced a wet-diapered impatience, pretending to be helpful, his mind drunk with expectant laughter. He could barely function.

"Stubbs, shake down the rucksacks." Hardin directed his glare at his two radio operators.

"Roger that." Stubbs started his search with the squad leaders.

Any time an infantry company made contact with another unit, searched a village, or stayed in a rear area, pot was for sale. Knowing this, Stubbs had made a pact with the GIs: don't take dope to the bush, and don't steal drugs from the medics.

Squeak had violated Stubbs' rules.

"You slimy pig fucker. I don't give a fuck how long you got left, you're goin' out through the wire." Squeak stood silent, his eyes blistered with hate.

Stubbs whipsawed himself into Tennessee.

"You pull that shit and I'll beat ya to fuckin' death." Stubbs leveled his eyes, first at Squeak and then at Tennessee. Neither responded nor changed expression. "Get fuckin' saddled up." Stubbs threw his hands around in frustration.

Squeak was short. He had earned his due. He celebrated his leaving one day early.

Stubbs ransacked the platoon gear. The butt plate of the M-16, an empty magazine, a Claymore stripped of explosives, repacked cigarettes, any hiding place was fair. If the plant was wet, the best place to dry the leaves was between the helmet liner and the steel pot. The search wasn't a game, but what caused the search was clear.

A GI would do anything to escape the continual expectations of combat, anything to stop the episodic memories, and anything to damn war's tide.

"Get a head count, Stubbs."

Ripe with resentment, the company stepped through a sandbag portal on the eastern flank of Firebase Sierra into the tail of a fog-covered morning, rucksacks filled to capacity with shiny new supplies. General Abrams had wished them Merry Christmas and Godspeed, then flew away to his Three Feathers Whiskey and clean sheets.

Scuffed and battered by nine weeks of continual combat, one man like another, isolated, alarmed by the mere thought of dying on Christmas day, the roar that had seized the whole of their minds was now but an echo. Like well-oiled gears they exchanged hand signals, their eyes hardened like stone.

Without a word 119 GIs had settled on a collective mood: fuck-it, let the war have its way. 22 December 1967: three days before the celebration of the birth of Jesus Christ.

They weren't invited. Instead they were mired in a hopeless bog, mired in the reflections of their blood-sport, racing toward a natural end.

"Six, we need to stand-down." Joe was tired, and Hardin's whining didn't help.

"Mother said a LRRP team spotted a Caucasian northwest of Plieku five days ago." Joe was pleading with the jungle, his eyes questioning.

"Bullshit."

* * *

Filling sandbags on Christmas Eve, Fish erupted from his morbid past, full of rage and stupidity, screaming and kicking. He stopped himself with a jerk, pleased by the attention, then turned shit-house crazy, shooting his rucksack full of holes because the belligerent bag rolled five meters down the side of a ridgeline without his permission.

Christmas mail was inbound and the mailman would not call his name.

"Stubbs, pack up Fish, he's goin' in on the mail chopper," Hardin said.

"Negative. The captain's not cuttin' an LZ."

Mailbags tumbled through the eighty-foot canopy, bouncing from limb to limb. The crew chief waited for a bag to land before he dropped the next one.

Everything is a fucking mystery, Hardin thought.

Moments later he found Stubbs holding a package over his head, catching bourbon drops from the corner of a brown box. A tear ran down Stubbs' cheek. His holiday fifth of Kentucky bourbon was broken during its last flight.

Merry Christmas. Ski handed Fish a bag of homemade cookies.

"Sarge, I gotta get outta here." Squeak's voice was pleading for space.

"Fuck you, fuck you, fuck you. You're not gettin' a bonus for smokin' dope." Stubbs turned away. "Make sure Fish has a canteen without any bullet holes."

Squeak's posture leapt into a slump that he augmented with an abrasive crippled whine. "Oh, man, how ya gonna act?"

Stubbs spun in place, looked at Tennessee to fix his location, and then pointed into Squeak's face with a stubby cigar, his expression nearly exploding. "Hang me out again and you're out here until your last motherfuckin' day." He didn't want to say that, not after Dak To.

"Okay, Sarge." Squeak's tone lanced Hardin's soul, searing in a jagged, beckoning way, with a tone that was almost empty.

The outburst set Stubbs in a brace. "No more bullshit. Tighten up, you might help some cherry survive his tour."

Tennessee laughed at Stubbs: Squeak didn't talk to cherries.

Tennessee turned a cautious eye, listening to the wind in the upper reaches of the canopy. He was coming to understand how quickly moods could change. A chill ran through his chest as he took off his sweater. He had tied his pant legs off just below his knees with boot laces to quiet his movement in dense scrub. This, and tucking the pant legs into his boots, reduced the probability of a leech reaching his cock.

Tennessee had taped the cleaning rod for his M-16 to the left side of the weapon. The carrying sling was drawn tight.

The GIs in First Platoon set their selector switches on semiautomatic outside the wire. When a man pulled flank security, point or drag, every other weapon was set on automatic fire.

Stubbs never put a new man on flank security, point, or drag, because he knew that new men loved two things—the rhythm of automatic fire, and the taste of toothpaste. Stubbs also knew that when new men ran out of ammunition they didn't have enough sense to pray.

Out of ammunition and pinned against a tree, a cherry would turn a blundering eye into one of disagreeable surprise, then fill the jungle with obscene gestures. Staring at a pile of empty magazines, his concentration confused, the cheery would pretend to have a plan, fully expecting good luck to flourish.

Hardin shook his head, wondering if General Abrams believed he could absolve himself by wishing the infantry Godspeed. God didn't know about the infantry—or Vietnam. Hardin shrugged his rucksack into the center of his back; knelt down using his weapon as a cane, then let his search travel across the jungle floor, traversing the ridge in ten-meter increments.

Sweet Pea warmed to his right hand. The black, ribbed ring at the front of her top carrying handle doubled for her starboard tit and fit his hand like a glove. Hardin rechecked the chambered round, closed the dust cover, then pressed the back of his right hand against his leg, leaving a thick yellow pus smeared along his inner thigh.

Jungle rot wounds had minds of their own. Hardin's wounds had decided not to heal.

The company moved out after the mail drop and humped in quiet canopy for eight days. Quiet except for Stubbs' bitching, and Mex translating his dear-john letter into trash Spanish, cussing some worthless pee hole. Fish laughed at Mex and told Stubbs to go fuck himself. That's when Stubbs turned on Mex and burned his letter. All in all, it was a great holiday.

After a PZ time was announced, planning for the good times began. GIs mimed fist-pounding gyrations; astonished by the prospect of safety and cold beer. The folly turned to preparation after a rumor about the next mission made the round.

"Captain, where we going?" Squeak's expression turned raw.

"We are not going to Dak To," Joe said, glancing absently from man to man.

* * *

Landing on a little-used airstrip, the company dug in on the median between the airstrip and a dirt road. Debris from other units littered the verge along the runway. Clumps of spindly twelve-foot trees and shoulder-high grass filled the median to its edge.

Listening to shovels hack at the soft dirt, Hardin analyzed his section of the perimeter. A calm sat over the valley. Too quiet, Hardin watched Joe laugh to himself.

Exposed, yet seemingly content, Joe broke out his shaving gear. With a cigar blazing, and shaving cream covering his mug, he wedged a mirror into the crotch of two limbs and began to dance in place. With no mind for the war, Joe was smoking, shaving, whistling, and dancing.

As if he had applied the finishing touch, Joe stepped away from the mirror, opening his arms with his palms up, then talked to the man in the mirror. Hardin shook has head.

With Captain Joe having his own party, sandbags mounted one on another, some mounds, some molehills, the last bag was beaten into place with a thankful fist.

Across the airstrip, across a hard-beaten stretch of ground, a village glowed with the hue of a brilliant sunset, the thatch a soft golden brown.

Parchment-faced elders stood watch as children popped in and out of doorways. Their voices seemed joyful enough, singing their vowels, children and elders, and no one in-between.

Then, as if by a switch, serenity faded, and the doorways turned into suspicious caves, connected here and there to a wooden walkway. The glow of oil lamps gained strength, giving the village an eerie cast, accenting an occasional void. The spill of a mountain's shadow reached across the airstrip, absorbing one hootch and then another.

The mix of booby traps, punji pits, old people, and kids made these rural cul-de-sacs impossible to predict. Set against a backdrop of an impenetrable jungle, this village was out of place. One note would make it come to life.

Hardin closed his eyes. The Christmas tree at Grandpa Karl's farm was draped with tinsel and strings of popcorn. Colored lights warmed a morning filled with gifts.

Stubbs let a conclusive sigh confirm his notion. With no dirt paths, a boardwalk tied the village into one continuous street. The valley seemed as peaceful as the village seemed odd. The peasants had vanished. A small boy ran from the jungle into one of the hootches. The cry of a night bird rose from a recess near the tree line. Other night birds began to cry.

"That vill is spooky," Stubbs said, looking over the airstrip. His smile slipped into a simmering. Deepening folds flanked his face. He laughed a quiet laugh, struck by the image of Tennessee building a bunker in the middle of Joe's dance hall.

GIs measured war's humor for its savor, waiting for the sound of a casual gun.

* * *

"El Tee—Drips, Mex, Fish, and me are gonna spark into the vill for a set." Squeak's comment caught Hardin in a daze. "Fish was here before, when the airstrip was the temporary battalion headquarters. Fish knows what's happenin', El Tee. Besides, it's New Year's Eve."

"What in hell are you talkin' about, Squeak?"

"Thirty minutes, El Tee. That's all I'm askin."

Without reason, Mex, Drips, Fish, Squeak, and their El Tee checked out of the bubble, raced across the airstrip, ran along a boardwalk, and ducked into the second door on the left. Floating in a dream, surrounded by the jacquard weavings of bamboo and water palms, trembling in the cast of a small oil lamp, images flickered on the walls of the one-room hootch.

Confronted by an exuberant laugh belching from a mouth full of betel-nut teeth, Hardin raised the barrel of his weapon. An old woman raised her hands, extending her palms, her arms were pencils draped with crape paper. Her face was wrinkled in a distant sense of resignation. Her eyes were filled with resolve. Through a bow she ushered the five men to a bamboo table in the far corner of the room.

Permitting a cautious expression, Hardin surveyed the hootch. The oil lamp sat in the center of the table. An old man lay on a bamboo mat in the opposite corner. He stared a cold stare as he surveyed the GIs, his focus settling on, Drips.

Restless, Hardin stepped back outside the hootch and stood into the shadows, allowing his eyes to scan the contours of the village. "What are you doing, Hardin?" he asked himself.

Spotting the North Star, he laughed at his predicament and stepped into the hootch. Standing away from the table he sank into a squat, watching the door, anticipating as he laid his weapon across his knees, timing the firecracker's fuse. The old woman's face framed her eyes to a sparkle as she stood into the recess of the doorway. She would die first.

If he lived, New Year's Eve would always reflect this scene: four GIs soaking in a false bravado, filled with elation mixed with purpose. Surrounding an oil lamp's flame, their faces were lit to the outer edge of their ear. With his breath coming in short bursts, Hardin set his feet to run.

Why was Fish this old woman's friend? How would her ambush be triggered? Her eyes belied a soft-featured grin, her broad brown face accented with barely noticeable spasms.

Fish filled himself with laughter. "Relax, El Tee, no VC, no dinky dau." His childish face hid a mind cracked beyond repair. Building Four at Fort Benning would have no solution to this leadership exercise.

A glint flashed through the door from an adjoining roof and the sky turned dark.

Drips chuckled with misconduct when his host dropped a bag of grass on the table and four sets of eager hands raced to roll the first joint.

"Lots of seeds in this bag." Squeak hesitated momentarily, looked at Hardin, then smiled as he lit the twisted end of paper. The old man sat up and leaned against the far wall, marking the intrusion, as if foreign troops had come to his home before.

Measuring the strain, Hardin waited for a target. Alone, squatting in the corner of a thatch hootch, he laughed through a nod. He realized that Squeak was sharing his friends, blessing the El Tee as trustworthy. Four citizen-soldiers, some of the most courageous men Hardin had known, had invited him to Squeak's going-away party—a compliment sure enough.

With the last seed popped, Hardin suggested they start back. He had consorted with four enlisted men, allowed them to smoke dope in his presence, and laughed at the war.

He didn't know it at the time, but this thirty-minute excursion, this conspiracy of ranks, would be the most critical non-combat event of his war. As an officer, he stood alone, bonded to Drips, Mex, Fish, and Squeak, and in turn, to the men in the platoon and the company.

The rules had changed.

The GIs in Charlie Company knew they could trust Hardin with their secrets.

The five men dashed across the airstrip and bounded into the perimeter. Stubbs jumped Hardin immediately. "The captain thinks you've been takin' a dump. Best chogey on over."

Joe was burning his coffee.

"What's up, Captain?" Hardin smiled a smile as if Joe knew where he had been.

"We're headed for the Special Forces Camp at Ban Me Thuot. A three-syllable flea trap, with no mountains. Intell estimates have thousands of North Vietnamese reinforcing VC units throughout the highlands." Joe was ground thin with the uncertainty.

"Want some coffee?" Hardin declined.

"Nobody's got any fuckin' details," Joe said, dropping his map. Joe lit a cigar and listened for the sound of rotors.

"We've been humpin' these mountains since, September. Get us a stand-down, Captain."

Hardin wanted to go to Nha Trang for a two-syllable, in-country R&R on the white sand beaches of the South China Sea.

"I'll talk to the Old Man."

Joe's face fell to one side. He wasn't going to talk to anyone. He would stand silent and hope the company caught a break. Joe could carry a tune when the notes were optional.

* * *

The company organized in six-man loading-sticks, stacked two-deep along the sides of the airstrip. Almost all of the men slept; some played cards. Hardin sat in silence, hoping he would never go back to the Poco River Valley, or fight in the mountains around Dak To.

"Play some cards, Lima?" Sporting an expression of false humility, Stubbs wanted to entertain a natural habit—laughing at a lieutenant.

"Another time, Stubbs."

"The battalion sergeant major says an enemy offensive is building in the central highlands. Dinks are pourin' down the Ho Chi Minh Trail to kill some GIs—celebratin' some Buddhist holiday."

"Merry Christmas, Stubbs."

As Stubbs found his way, Hardin found himself staring at the hootch he had visited on New Year's Eve. *Too bad the Montagnards aren't Jewish,* he thought. These poor bastards have no particular significance. Given a modest ration of religious equity, Hanoi would be a landfill and Haiphong would be under water.

"Hey, Tennessee, do you know how to spell 'Montagnard'?"

"Are you kiddin', El Tee? He can't even spell RTO." Squeak gave Tennessee the finger and turned with an air of casual tension. Squeak didn't want to die this late in the game.

The distant sound of the lead chopper shook the paralysis from Squeak's mind. Ten slicks roared out of the horizon, nosed up and settled into a hover, then landed—first one skid and then the other. That special sound, that whomp-whomp-whomp, that syncopated thumping rush, that coded urgency announced Squeak's final excursion into the war.

The men of Charlie Company were escaping, ripe with the mockery of false expectations, relieved by the going. An unruly joust ran through one squad, and then another. Men were keen to exploit any lapse of concentration: hitting quick releases on rucksack straps; hitting magazine releases; unscrewing lids on canteens; tying the pin of one man's smoke grenade to the frame of another man's rucksack.

Armed with an endless stream of jive, lies, and combat trash, Hippie's prowess was unchallenged. Hippie could rat-fuck anyone. His best friends could not tell when he was kidding. Hippie would listen to Joe's edicts with rigid concern, then nod and say, "Far out, Jim." If he liked a man, he called him "Jim."

With a laid-back grin, his unshaven mug would swell into a chorus of false rage, then compliment itself for verbal artistry. "Ain't that bitchin'?"

Hippie never spoke the whole truth. Simply put, he was full of shit.

Hippie had an aggravating habit of second-guessing Stubbs, then denying what he had said. Once a week, as if triggered by a reckoning, Hippie would fall in as if he had just run out of time. Recognizing Hippie's penchant for giving up, Stubbs would drop a cigarette butt in his coffee to piss him off. Hippie never crossed Stubbs—or Captain Joe.

* * *

Fish told Hippie to take the point squad the same day he accused him of stealing a can of peaches. Hippie told Fish only fruits ate peaches. When Fish shot a hole in Hippie's tit bag, Hippie said, "Far out, Jim." Then he pinched one hole closed, raised the tit bag, and drank the raspberry Kool Aid squirting from the other hole. Fish told him he was so stupid his shadow had gone home. Hippie said, "Far out, Jim."

At six-one, 170 pounds, Hippie had to lean into his stride. Fish told him he was so skinny an AK round wouldn't even know it hit him.

Hippie tried to show Boyle how to stand on a surf board one day, but Boyle's stutter wouldn't let him decide which foot to lead with. LeCotte told Hippie that blacks could not swim, let alone surf.

That's the day Rap held LeCotte off the ground describing how he was going to stuff LeCotte's head up his ass while LeCotte was wearing his helmet. Rap said that LeCotte's future didn't include going home.

Hippie took the point squad because the point squad never had to dig foxholes. That, and Nasty was the point squad's radio operator. And, he knew that no matter how bad the firefight, Nasty would find a way to laugh about it. Nasty preferred fat women, ugly fat women. Fish described Nasty's lady one day, and the one word Boyle could say clearly was, "nasty."

First Platoon was on the first lift out along with Captain Joe and Hippie's point squad. Hardin sat in the right door of the second slick, day-dreaming. The slicks started down, banked over a blue-line, and landed on the airstrip next to the Special Forces Camp at Ban Me Thuot.

The camp didn't look big enough to make a difference.

Concertina wire wrapped the camp in a taunt complex trace of high and low construction laced into three concentric circles, twenty meters deep. The camp shook with the dust of a rutting frenzy: trucks, concertina wire, bunkers and antennas.

The company dug in, sandwiched between the camp's perimeter wire and the airstrip to the north. The soil was a soft, sandy loam.

The vegetation on the far side of the runway was a sight to blast your buttons. A wall of fifteen-foot elephant grass bordered the runway—ample concealment for the enemy. With no signs of worry, and a bright sunny day, Stubbs and Tennessee settled into a game of pinochle.

"Good to have you boys around." A Special Force's staff sergeant with a heavy Texas drawl was smiling and checking out the foxholes.

"I thought Texans could do it all," Stubbs said, emphasizing his Georgia twang.

"We can. Do you boys dig in every night?"

"We don't have all that sissy wire."

"NVA's runnin' through these woods in big bunches. I got a radio, thought you boys might want to listen to some music, get the latest out of Saigon."

"Thanks, Sarge." Tennessee took the radio to Mex and PeeWee's foxhole. By the time he sat down, The Lovin' Spoonfuls were balling some mousy little girl.

Stubbs lit a smoke and pointed the butt at his new friend. "Are we here to cover your ass, or stump the outback?"

"Hard tellin'. Probably get inserted somewhere." He turned to leave.

"What about the radio?" Squeak asked. The big soldier shrugged and kept walking. Squeak gave the Texan a thumbs-up and said to Stubbs, "I don't like it."

Stubbs stared, waiting for Hardin to speak. Then Stubbs took a drag on his cigarette. "I don't like it either. Why would some Special Forces sergeant give us a music box and not want it back? He must know we're gonna get whacked."

The music box had Sam the Sham doing *Robin Hood* with, as back up, the entire Second Platoon. Stubbs used the music to ignore Hardin and lay back on his rucksack to enjoy a smoke.

The platoon sector was impeccable—weapons cleaned, with rucksacks at the ready. Hardin could not stop worrying about the wall of vegetation on the far side of the airstrip.

"Pops, ya think we need an OP in the weeds over there?" Collin "Pops" Tilman was working on a spaghetti, chili, and spiced beef stew. He glanced across the airstrip.

"Can't solve it all, El Tee. Besides they'd shoot up Dick Clark's dancers first." American Bandstand was swinging into the *Green Grass of Home,* and the studs were working it hard.

"Besides, SF's probably got the grass wired somehow."

Pops was a PFC, two years older and somewhat wiser than his lieutenant, an elder statesman as grunts go. No matter the situation, Pops could muster a smile and a reassuring gesture. A rare individual, Pops had a bits-and-pieces brand of counsel, which he fed to Hardin or Stubbs in the privacy of his office.

"Get a cup, El Tee, this stew is near ready."

When Hardin returned, LeCotte sank into a full squat, begged for his share of the stew and said, "Jesus H. Christ, Pops says the El Tee gets first dibs on stew when he's cookin'."

"It's an investment in your future, ass wipe."

"Gotta get outta this dump to have a future. Your mama might have a future here."

LeCotte would squint when he emphasized war's folly. Using the ridiculous to buoy his spirit, he had a habit of denying the obvious, no matter the nature of the reward. LeCotte used a half grin to segment his more laughable arguments.

Savoring the stew, Hardin caught Boyle's eye. LeCotte's glasses looked as if they had been coated with bile, then covered with dust, then baked over a purple smoke grenade. Boyle didn't know what Hardin was suggesting, but he laughed anyway.

"LeCotte must be talkin' to you, Pops." Pops smiled into a sigh. He had listened to LeCotte for so long he knew more about him than LeCotte's mother.

"LeCotte's a virgin. That's why he talks about his mama. Dreams about climbin' back up the chute." Pops ladled LeCotte's stew, softening LeCotte's response with a look of caution.

Amps laughed. "LeCotte's still suckin' tit." The prospect of tits forced a moment of silence.

"Thanks, Pops." With a raised-cup salute, Hardin turned. He sat against his rucksack, facing the airstrip, eating his dinner, and guarding a can of mixed fruit. Desert was a chocolate disk sporting the texture of Borax, washed down with a cup of coffee.

Lying in the sun, Hardin waited for the far side of the airstrip to erupt. Joe hollered a rebel yell when he cleared the Special Forces headquarters bunker. Joe roared with laughter.

Nearly running, Joe was looking uncomfortably tight: new uniform, fresh shave, shower with soap, new maps, and that grin he used to fondle a used cigar. Hardin check the bolt housing on his weapon.

Joe waved at Hardin with a fist full of maps.

New maps, chopper rides, dry socks and clean sheets are cousins, Hardin thought. Too comfortable for a guerrilla war, any war. Hardin set fire to his map of Kontum, hoping he would never find another. Replacement maps became suspicious, as if their accuracy had gone missing.

The same suspicion one finds reading the box scores a second time.

Hardin examined the map for Ban Me Thuot. Optimistic, he highlighted the blue-lines. The terrain was a piece of cake compared with Dak To—flat ground with an occasional plateau.

Joe interrupted with an insult, insisting Hardin and Stubbs attend a meeting with lieutenants Gates and Anderson. After issuing his summons, Joe cocked around the perimeter, preening his new fatigues, landing with a smile and the smell of lilac mothballs.

"Six, you're lookin' mighty clean. What's happenin'—you buy a ticket to this war?" Joe ignored Andy, spread his map in the grass, and pointed to a black circle, labeled LZ Hammer.

"The battalion commander's due in any minute." *Ah yes, a field lifer would mooch-suck a frog for face-time,* Hardin thought. "Insertion is fifty minutes after first light. A Special Forces Mike Force is workin' a ridge system three klicks north of the LZ. Recon figures there's gonna be a gunfight."

"A hot LZ?" Andy said, having a Pepsodent moment.

Hardin rubbed the fabric on Joe's new shirt, tugging on the sleeve so Joe could not ignore him. Joe jerked his sleeve free, letting the concept of a hot LZ percolate.

With a scathing huff, Stubbs declared, "What's so fucking exciting about a hot LZ?"

Hardin's personnel jacket listed seventeen combat assaults, with four of the LZs hot. Hot meant Charlie was shooting at him when the air speed of his Huey dropped to zero and he tried to exit the aircraft with seventy pounds of junk.

Tapping his map, Hardin closed his eyes. The echoes roared. A slick was flopping wildly out of control, its rotor shattered on short final. The bodies of the door gunners arched through the air. A bloody battle would kill a lot of new men.

Joe looked anxious, as if the story had a twist.

With valor in full fig, Stubbs said, "Andy, which one of you wants to lead the charge? We're talkin' Silver Star, or a Distinguished Service Cross." Stubbs laughed through a cloud of smoke, wincing as if he was watching two monkeys fucking at the city zoo. Gator and Andy looked as if they were posing for a recruiting poster.

Hardin shook at his fear. "Hot LZ? I knew a girl with a hot LZ. She'd fire up your rocks in a hot second."

Joe chuckled. "Shut up, Lima. You're in first with part of the point. It's a six-slick insertion with a heavy gun team flying cover—four gunships and a 105mm artillery prep. The last round, the marking round, is white phosphorous. I'll be on your last slick."

"I knew that." *If I could puke on command, now would be a good time,* Hardin thought.

Gator cut loose of his vitals, his martial self-image now cast in muted tones, his leadership judged lacking for such prizes as known enemy locations. These hideouts were trophies reserved for the warriors with archery skills worthy of a maiden's hand, warriors who would not die.

Joe rolled up his sleeves a notch. "I'll be on your last slick." Joe was repeating himself, rehashing because the Old Man was coming to town.

"You're gonna ride on my last slick?"

Joe's eyes narrowed into a grin at the insinuation. "That's right. This operation could get hairy." Joe was prompting the same old sweat.

"I knew a girl like that once. Got my braces caught in her hairy LZ." A lone Huey popped over the treetops east of the company.

"Any questions?" The Captain Joes of the Army were the curators of this particular stratagem. When a subordinate was challenged with the words, "any questions," he knew that he was not to have any questions. If he did have a question, he certified what his superior had already written on his officer efficiency report: that he was stupid.

"I have a comment. I'll run the platoon. I don't need a proxy yelling orders after we get hit." Challenged, the two men stepped apart.

"Fair enough, I'll work the gunships and platoon insertions." Joe headed for the inbound Huey, and Hardin left the others wondering why their world was flat.

Stubbs had corralled the squad leaders, team leaders, and radio operators. They sensed the catch in Hardin's grin. Hardin paused, then looked at Joe honey-sucking the Old Man.

Mex and PeeWee stood slack-jawed, gawking.

Hardin threw five maps into the center of a grumbling undercurrent, spread his map, oriented it to north, and looked at Mex with eyes Mex had seen before—fair-warning eyes, hang-on-to-your-ass eyes.

Pointing at the map, Hardin spoke without looking up. "Here's where we are now. Here's where we're goin' at first light. There's a Mike Force somewhere in this ridge system. These three map intersections are points of origin one, two, and three. It's a six-slick insertion with a heavy gun team, and 105mm artillery prep. We're in first with part of the point. Six'll be on the last bird. LZ Hammer is gonna be hot."

Squeak braced at the words. He surveyed the palms of his hands. He was looking for his future, knowing he would die at first light. Squeak exchanged glances with Drips and Bucks.

"Oh mercy," Tennessee said, looking across the airstrip at the wall of grass.

"Just seems like our turn," Hardin said. Mex looked at Rap. Stubbs stood up.

Mex broke in to share some of his street-wise logic. He started with a short slide to the right to gain the proper posture. "The only hots I want is some pee hole." Rap hit his fist as the harmony of thought was reinforced with nervous shrugs and a consensus "what-the-fuck."

Hardin looked at the Hill People, at their eyes. "It's our game. Post your maps and get 'em folded. Full stand-to tonight. Make sure the radios are clean." All hands were busy checking and rechecking coordinates, and plotting points of origin.

"One more thing," Hardin said, creating the desired emphasis. "If Six gets hit on the LZ, Stubbs, find Joe's RTO and direct traffic. The rest of the platoon secure the LZ."

No one wanted to make a commitment to the operation. Hardin's warning was greeted with a tribal dialect used to isolate intruders.

Hardin's men had style. Stubbs had a well-groomed summation, "They don't know we're comin', so it can't be too bad." LeCotte had city sarcasm—"We'll probably fly right in their fuckin' front door." Rap had camouflaged heroics—"Ma fuckers best be steppin'." Mex had a nervous jab—"I'm gonna do Chuck, and his mama, too." And Blood had anticipation—"They're dead meat if they hang around." These GIs were dealing with death—making sense today so tomorrow wasn't impossible.

"Blood, send Doc over."

Doc Collard was an enigma, a well educated pool-hall man. He was a stocky five-foot seven-inch gorilla, a white man whose bushy eyebrows parked atop his infectious smile. His humor was short, sweet, and obvious.

"Hey, Doc, what's happenin'?" Hardin asked.

"Same basic shit, a little rot, a leech, Darvon, massive trauma, blood and shit. What's in this deal, El Tee?" Doc Collard wore black t-shirts—he wanted to blend.

"We're hot in the mornin'. Gonna need your bag of tricks."

"My shot-bag's full. Happy New Year, El Tee." Hardin hit Doc's fist, turned to leave, and then hesitated. Doc rolled around his left foot, raised his right shoulder, and settled into a stooped, hanging-arm posture.

"Make sure you're wrapped tight in the morning, Doc." Collard gave out a sarcastic, pointless chuckle and left to guard his aid kit.

With the Special Forces camp at their backs and the open ground of the airstrip, Hardin focused on the road that ran into a tunnel of vegetation leading to the village of Ban Me Thuot, nine kilometers to the west.

Dave Clark's lyrics rolled across the sandbags: "The name of the place, I like it like that." Squeak topped his spiced beef with cheese, watching Shadow singing with the music box.

"Squeak, is Sour Mash any good with that radio box? Can he walk and talk at the same time?" Squeak smiled as Hardin's voice struck an unfamiliar chord.

"Long as he ain't smokin' anything."

"Extra batteries?"

"Got two sparklers, just cleaned the handset." Squeak talked with his mouth full.

"Whose got the battalion push?"

"Inked the freek on Tennessee's pot." Pushing crackers through his lips, Squeak tapped on Tennessee's helmet with his spoon.

"Great. Pack your shit, you're outta this deal." A tidal wave of contradictory emotion swept over Squeak as he fought to fill his lungs with air and slow the reaction.

"You're not shittin' me, are you, El Tee?" Squeak said, throwing the spiced beef into their foxhole, then standing to pull up his pants and straighten his shirt.

"Get fat if you can, Squeak." The spare batteries came at Hardin like inside fast balls.

"Hot damn." Squeak held out a fist, and Hardin hit it.

"You're leavin' on the Old Man's chopper."

With no elation, Hardin let the words drift off and turned away. The joy and the agony were complete. The confluence of anguish and relief brought tears of fatigue as he pushed the spare batteries into his rucksack. Squeak's good-byes with Ski, Drips, Shadow, and the rest of the Hill People would be shaped by instinct—sincere yet fragile. See you in the world, sure I'll call your folks, I'll fuck your wife for you too: I'll be seein' ya.

Squeak had so much to say, so much he needed to do, and the chopper's rotors were calling, beckoning him to travel east, out of the airspace. Squeak kept checking the meeting between the Old Man and Joe, nudging his captain with emotional morphine.

To a man, the other men wished they were leaving, but none of them wanted Squeak's memories. Squeak ran by Hardin on his way to the slick.

"Take care, El Tee." For the first time, moisture welled in Squeak's eyes.

"Rip off some round-eye for me, Squeak."

"Take care of my friends." Squeak wanted a commitment from the El Tee he had worked so hard to train, to make his leaving easier.

"They're my friends, too."

"I know." Squeak let his breath ease through his teeth to temper the shudder in his chest, then said, "I'll see ya next time, El Tee. You and Captain Joe."

Squeak reached into his rucksack with a suspicious grin. He stood-to with a jump and tossed a soft leather pouch over in his hand. Then he hesitated through a shrug and handed the pouch to his El Tee. "That's a bag of dew. Stubbs knew I had it. Keep it next to those beads you count every night, for luck." This time the two men shook hands.

"There's a bird-spider fang in the bag. I bug-fucked the cherries with it."

Squeak would cry, Hardin thought, *he just doesn't know how.* With his fear of giving up tomorrow mounting, Squeak's tour of duty was nearing an end. Hardin would miss his friend, his instinct.

He would miss hearing his voice.

"Keep the world turnin' for us, Squeak."

"Here's a turn for ya, El Tee." Squeak looked into the sky. "That deserter story. I figure it's just to shit-scare the rest of us." Squeak seemed to glide as he ran to the chopper.

As if silhouetted in the open end of a barn, Squeak's stature began to grow. The bond between men who lived savagely, communing with death, created a fidelity that was armored by the acceptance of whatever might come their way. War's wretched nature brought Squeak and Hardin together as one, an officer and a radio operator: friends.

Clutching Dig-it's rosary, Hardin counted the beads: sixty-eight. He would leave Vietnam in 1968. Dead or alive, the numbers had to match.

Squeak hopped onto the slick's cargo deck and started a slapstick routine with the crew, laughing, never looking at the wall of grass on the far side of the airstrip. Hippie and three GIs from the point squad along with Fish, Sweet Cheeks, Drips, Mex, and Bucks ran to the slick to absorb a last scrap of harmony.

Ski stood silently with his machine gun, watching Squeak laugh. Shadow sat alone with his back against the concertina wire. His lips were moving. With his selector switch on semi-automatic, he searched the grass across the runway, covering Squeak's back.

In that instant, Squeak was gone, glued as he was to the chump-end of life.

"Each to their own," Hardin whispered. His friends will file Squeak into memory, one salty bit at a time: the ritual preparation of his evening meal, cleaning the rounds in the magazine he loaded into his weapon at twilight, backing his Claymore with sandbags, making coffee as soon as he stopped to laager, cocking his body and head to the left when he used the radio, putting peanut butter and jam on his spiced ham, laughing uncontrollably through those pot-induced hungries, ordering Stubbs around like a PFC, and the nervous tic in his speech.

The satisfaction of this friend leaving the war in one piece and the proximity of a Special Forces camp created an illusion that allowed Hardin to fall into a deep sleep.

* * *

Number #10, Highlands Road. Bremerton, Washington. September 1954.

The Major's den buzzed with enthusiasm—calls to the dispensary to arrange Court's West Point physical, calls to his friends in Army Reserves, and premature talk of Plebe Christmas.

"Hey, Pops. Things are getting hectic around here." The Major was reading a letter from Murphy, his old driver.

"Nothing changes. Murphy disappeared in France for nearly four days. He met a young girl and stood-to for her until he could not muster another round. He was an old soldier by then, four months and the Normandy invasion old."

"Did you give him hell?"

"I made him stand a short-arm inspection in front of the headquarters nursing staff. The nurses made him drop his pants so they could check his pecker for VD."

"Murphy just took off without telling you?"

"GIs yearn for the company of a good woman, for a long-haired dictionary—a dictionary that opens to the same page. Pussy is powerful stuff, sure enough."

CHAPTER EIGHT

Secrets

Ban Me Thuot Special Forces Camp. 0135 Hours.

Dreams of randy wenches carried Hardin to the apex of glorious passion. Panicked by a sudden burst of foreign expressions, he scrambled to his feet like a tormented pig. Moon-eyed, with his senses fogged, he realized his dick was about to erupt.

Ecstatic, with his fist buckled to an unholy tremor; he ripped open his pants and seized his cock. His balls exploded. The wet dream, complete with the aroma and moisture package, was wonderful. Spasms jarred his knees as he spread his feet into a brace. The pulsing of a steam-driven piston left a seeping ache in his lower back.

Weak, he laughed in the dark, wondering if his mad-minute went unnoticed. Content with his secret, he resolved to dream again. The perimeter seemed empty as he fell asleep.

At first light, when Joe's radio operator alerted the perimeter for stand-to, he also announced that First Platoon had gone missing.

"Stubbs, what in the hell is goin' on?"

"Hard tellin'." Stubbs stared at Tennessee, and his glare caused a response.

Tennessee started talking to his rucksack as he fumbled with the straps. "They hooked up with the point squad and humped to the vill just after midnight."

"What freek did they use?"

"The SF gave 'em one. I monitored the horn until the signal faded out."

"Give me that handset," Hardin said. "Six, this is Lima. We got problems. My boys and your boys are in the vill gettin' laid."

Joe's face carried a disgusted grin. "Lima, Mike, November, come to my location."

Without answering but pointing at Tennessee, Hardin said, "You and the girls think you're shit-hot, don't ya? You're fuckin' with the wrong GI." Stubbs stood silent as Hardin headed for what was bound to be a ridiculous exchange.

Joe straightened his uniform, mustering his authority. His grin had a checkered, ceremonial cast that screamed for relief. "Don't say a word, Hardin—nine fuckin' klicks." Joe turned to Gator, and asked, "How many are you missin'?"

"One."

"How about you?" Andy flashed a fresh, army-green smile.

"None." Another perfect answer. Hardin didn't wait for Joe.

"I'm missin' twenty-two GIs. How about you, Captain?"

"Hippie and the gang—nine. The fools must have humped down that road." Joe was proud of the boys, his spirit buoyed by their initiative. "Last thing Chuck would expect."

With a trace of mock humility, Hardin opened his palms and cocked his head in a relinquishing shrug, passing warrior rights to those who hadn't broken the circle.

"One of these jokers will have to take the first lift." Gator's right hand went to his oysters for pretrial motions. Andy started an iteration of the dating game.

"The lift sequence is the same at 1300 hours."

A five-ton truck pulled out of the Special Forces compound with the same Texan at the wheel. Boiling dust from its tires, the truck jumped through the gears. Joe mounted the truck on the run, anxious to rescue the boys.

* * *

After four hours of sunbathing, sipping coffee, and playing cards, Hardin laughed when the truck broke out of the trees, filled to the gills with GIs hollering and singing. Prompting a rush of curious laughter, almost all of the studs were still drunk or stoned.

"Shake 'em down, Stubbs."

"Right." Stubbs lined the studs out as they cleared the tailgate, tore apart their gear, and confiscated eight bags of grass and six cans of beer. Hardin waited in humored isolation, briefly greeting one GI, then another. The lot had been up all night.

Reluctant speech would inevitably betray the chief conspirators. Clusters of men fell silent as smatterings of laughter, turned to fear, and muddled minds somberly began to evaluate the prospects of a hot landing zone. Stubbs had the task of arranging the truth, balancing reward and punishment to establish discipline, and illuminate any deep-seated resentment.

Stubbs started with Bucks and Rap, his black buck sergeants.

"Did the SF help you with this trip?"

Bucks responded. "Yeah." Both men were sober.

"We lift out at 1230 hours," Stubbs said. "You dickheads got an hour to get the gear straight. Send Doc over here." Proud and relieved, Stubbs wanted some of the whiskey he could smell.

"Doc, we're gonna need more penicillin," Stubbs said.

"Believe it. They were doin' some hard-core broads in that vill. Whores were comin' out of the bamboo." Stubbs cocked his head. Doc Collard seemed to be retracing events. He was worried about something that had happened in town.

"The trip was worth it. Their minds are back, except Fish. With him there's nothin' left to salvage."

Evaluating the job Hardin was running on Mex and Blood, Stubbs didn't believe their answers. They had fucked with his authority, and he would make them pay. He was a hard-stripe E-7. The source of his power originated with King Richard. Stubbs was on point when Perceval found the Holy Grail. Stubbs had sixteen years in the Army. His edicts were absolute.

Stubbs yelled with a smoke filled rage. "Drips? He's a fucking private. Are you telling me Drips was runnin' your squads? You motherfuckers think you can double-clutch your sorry ass down some fuckin' dirt road and leave me hangin', and blame it on a fucking private?"

Stubbs stopped yelling and started a quiet, seething monologue. "I owe you dirt-bags and believe this, I'm gonna get even. You're gonna have to kiss my ass on main street, and then suck my dick with your mama watchin' before anything but shit rolls your way." Stubbs walked away, leaving Bucks, Rap, Blood, and Mex wondering if he was gone for good.

"Are those your squad leaders, Stubbs?" Hardin said.

"Can you believe they left us hangin'?"

"I can't believe I didn't hear 'em. They're good. They slid away without makin' a sound." Hardin waved his hand over the platoon sector.

"Explains why their gear was so squared away last night." Stubbs lit a smoke and blew the exhaust toward Bucks and Mex.

Speaking as he searched the far side of the airstrip, Hardin said, "And they blamed Drips. I'll bet Squeak set the recon. That rat-fucker spent the afternoon in that SF camp." The water was crystal clear, and Squeak was gone. Given that the whorehouse romp was worthy of recognition, Hardin had to identify the key players.

"Tennessee, who set the push?"

"Squeak, just before he split. Told me to listen all night. Told me Drips would be sendin' in sit-reps." As Hardin approached Drips' fire team, talk of boom-boom sobered off into odd bits of annoyed motions.

"Drips, when did Squeak turn the recon over to you?"

The big Norwegian paused to register surprise and determine whether he should tell an officer how things went down. His dotards were farting with lip-licking idiocy, awkwardly registering their postured concern by forming the silent third of a three-sided dialogue.

"Wha'd'a ya mean, El Tee?" A slippage of trust marked Drips' gesture of guilt.

"I know ya don't have enough sense to get yourself killed, Drips, so why didn't ya tell me about the recon?" The entire ward exhaled a disarming conclusion. Hardin's jab caught Drips flat footed. Drips now knew Ban Me Thuot was history, and the next time the unit was planning a trip the El Tee wanted to know.

"Squeak told me to cut ya in, but when he left I didn't know what to say."

"Next time tell me what's happenin'," Hardin said, relaxing with a familiar expression.

"Okay, El Tee." Both men turned when Joe screamed and threw a D-handle shovel at Hippie. Gator was railing at the one man who had joined the raiding party from Third Platoon.

"That platoon leader doesn't have anybody that trusts him," Drips said.

"He's new. Make sure he doesn't hang us out. We're on at twelve-thirty, tighten 'em up."

"No sweat, El Tee." Sweet Cheeks threw the bolt of an AK-47 to Drips with a short nod. "I banged a dink near the edge of the vill. I was catchin' a smoke and the dude walked around the corner of this hootch." Drips tossed the bolt onto his rucksack.

With a twitch in his eye, Sweet Cheeks was lying to his El Tee.

Sensing the lie, Hardin pressed the issue. "Where's the rest of the weapon?"

"I didn't feel like packin' it."

Secrets in an infantry platoon had the half-life of a gnat. Drips would talk, even if he didn't want to. Whatever happened in Ban Me Thuot, whether a GI had gone nuts, or Mex had killed a civilian, Hardin wanted the answer. Not for a tribunal, but to balance the problem with a solution. Months could pass before a secret boiled into a problem.

Someone was dead.

* * *

Avoiding the reality of LZ Hammer, cackling about steam baths and booze, sharing tidbits of morbid humor was an integral part of preparing for death. Groups of GIs sat as one, exchanging nervous barbs: girls and home, rumors and jokes, and what might happen before the end of the day.

Sweet Cheeks kept standing up and sitting down, glancing at Hardin.

The Hill People knew what had happened in Ban Me Thuot.

Anxious minutes rolled into silence and gradually turned to fear as thoughts turned inward. Reluctant men moved to the airstrip and formed themselves in loading-stick order. Four gunships set down at the far end of the field. Six cargo slicks flew over the top of the gunships, billowing rolls of red dust. Staring, as if they had a choice, men mustered their gear.

The filth that came from not washing for weeks on end now had a purpose—absorbing the shock of dying in the mud.

Hardin sat on the deck in the right door of the second slick, with PeeWee, Boyle, LeCotte, Tennessee, and Mex scattered about. The choppers nosed down to the east, fighting for altitude, and turned north over a broken, scrub canopy. The mountains of the central highlands had been replaced with grassland and an occasional knoll. A blue-line ran deep—dark and calm.

Nature's details were changing. The gunships, the artillery, and the door gunners were center stage. Hardin sang, throwing his words into the wind.

The insertion choppers dropped into the long-final approach to Landing Zone Hammer. Treetops slapped at the landing skids. The lead gunship team flew level with Hardin's eye, fifty meters flank to flank, firing streams of tracer rounds into the trees bordering a lush green marsh.

Tree limbs leaped into the air. Patches of earth erupted in duets of pointless insinuation. Exploding randomly in a patterned rush of chaos, fountains of water and marshy soil burst into the air leaving small ponds and potholes.

Hardin leaned into the doorjamb, adjusted his Claymore bag of magazines, gripped the circular hole on the inside skin of the chopper, re-checked his selector switch, slid his finger over the trigger, glanced at the door gunner, and then hopped out onto the skid.

The six-inch pipe seemed smaller.

A softer concussion announced the impact of the artillery marking round. White-hot phosphorous mushroomed from the marsh, then arced into a beautiful flower, showering the ground ahead of the lead chopper. First Platoon sailed into short final with GIs screaming into their helmets, searching for the nearest muzzle flash.

Gunships charged down the tree line. Rockets lanced the canopy, tearing holes in the jungle floor. Vulcan machine guns, firing thousands of rounds per minute, slammed lead into the tree lines, tossing foliage aside like chips off a chain saw. Door gunners stitched the walls of LZ Hammer, their rounds ripping at the ground. The troop choppers plunged below the treetops, descending into the grassy marsh.

With no mind for the noise, his men were alone. "Think about pussy," Hardin screamed.

Hanging at arm's length from the side of the slick, standing on the landing skid, pointing his weapon into the tree line, Hardin was singing, yelling really: "Are you goin' to San Francisco... be sure to wear... some flowers in your hair."

The door gunner fought frantically with a box of ammunition, desperately trying to unjam his machine gun. The pilot gave a nod to himself and the bottom fell out. The chopper's skids sliced through the top of seven-foot marsh grass. Reeds slapped at Hardin's boots.

The gunships appeared again. Solid streams of red tracers hosed the tree line—a giant pissing red streams. The drag of the marsh grass grew heavier, snapping at the skids, stinging his shins. Hardin looked over his left shoulder through the cargo bay. Boyle was standing outside the chopper on the opposite skid with his weapon raised in defiance.

AK rounds pierced the skin of the chopper inches above Hardin's left hand. For that instant, when the air seemed too dense to breathe, the holes seemed an illusion. He jumped from the skid. A second burst of enemy fire caught his rucksack as he fell below the skids, spinning him clockwise, his body flying backwards.

Suspended for a moment, as if on display, his body plunged through the grass into the marsh, out of the line of fire. He screamed in agony as his body tumbled with the drift of the chopper. His seventy-pound rucksack collapsed on impact, stuffing his ass into his boots, his left shoulder and head then stuffed into the marsh. Soaked and covered with mud, small-arms fire pinned him to the floor of the landing zone. His glasses were destroyed.

Pushing at the stiff grass, he fought to find a prism to see through. Blind and pissed off, he stuffed his broken glasses into the mud, scraping at the leeches on his face. Enemy grazing fire increased, searching for a target.

Pinned in the marsh, he waited for the slicks to lift away, then scraped at the leeches again. His door gunner hung at the end of a harness, his face wedged into the bolt-housing of his machine gun, his arms draped in bloody repose, hanging on each side of his gun.

The door gunner was dead, his body dragging at the airframe. Crawling, as if he knew where he was going, Hardin stopped to listen to the gunfire near the river.

Crawling, spitting mud from his mouth, fighting the rotting stench of the marsh, firing through veins in the grass, he aimed at the base of the vegetation bordering the marsh. He ran in spurts, dragging his rucksack, fighting the black mud, each rush ending with a splash.

Hardin had no idea where his men were, or if any of them were dead.

Isolated in a sour bog AK rounds ripped the marsh grass around his head, snapping. A searing pain gripped his shoulder. Mud clogged the cooling chamber of his weapon. Leeches covered his forearms. The cracking sounds of death roared at his mind.

In the wake of the gunships' final pass, he lifted his body out of the mud and sprinted to the tree line. Behind a clump of bamboo, he listened. He heard the rush of a man passing trough the vegetation, then dismissed it. As if he knew what he was hearing, he started dragging his rucksack in a low crouch.

He slipped deeper into the tree line and let his body ease into the ground, searching. Blind and alone, he rummaged in his rucksack for a pair of glasses.

A seeping ache had worked its way from the base of his neck into his left shoulder.

Stubbs was yelling, "Spread out" on the far side of the LZ. Bursts of small-arms fire mingled in counterpoint with urgent bits of silence, then rushed into shouts and more fire.

Hardin froze.

Paralleling the tree line, ten meters from the open marsh, fresh scuff-marks ran in both directions on a hard-beaten trail.

First things first, he muttered, ripping a leech off of his lower neck, crushing it with his fist, watching his life soak into soil. Warm blood spread across his chest as he searched along the edge of the trail, looking for broken grass. His left shoulder burned at the joint. His eyes began vibrating. He wiped at the base of his neck. Blood ran between his fingers.

His faced burned with sweat. His chest heaved involuntarily.

The Viet Cong were close, within a hair. He could smell them. He could feel their breath, their eyes tracing the contour of his helmet. Calculating, he measured the killing zone, marking probable enemy locations. His next move would expose him to grazing fire.

The ground in front of him ran flat for thirty feet, then ran a twelve-foot rise to what looked to be more flat ground. Weeds and grass choked the ground behind him, forcing his search back to the trail.

The trail coursed along the lower ground, paralleling the base of the rise. He relaxed, estimating the distance to a tunnel of broken grass. His enemy had gone to ground.

"Think, El Tee," he said, trying to ignore his isolation. Broken patches of knee-high grass ran in both directions from the verge of the trail. Chunks of lava rock littered the crest of the low rise. Chuck wouldn't take that route—too hard to run.

Barely seconds passed before the jungle was empty, sucked into a vacuum. The small-arms fire near the river was M-16 fire. One by one, Hippie and the point squad filtered into the tree line and went to ground along the trail, forty meters to Hardin's right flank.

With not so much as a hello, bobbing from the bottom of the soup, three enemy rucksacks popped onto the trail, thirty meters to his left flank. He had searched that sector three times without seeing the rucksacks, or the wooden folding chair. Whiffs of smoke filtered off the ground from a campfire. Trail watchers were runners—they did not hang around.

Tag crawled from the marsh looking like a salted slug, dragging mud and stench through a slot in the wedge grass. He smiled at Hardin with a "Where the fuck have you been?" look, then followed Hardin's eye to the enemy equipment. Within seconds he had shed his gear.

Tag, bouncing on his haunches in an odd quiet way, twisted from side to side, first stepping, then squatting low, and then crawling toward the rucksacks. Without so much as a reason, fury gripped Hardin's chest: Tag's body was exploding.

"Freeze, Tag." The tone of Hardin's voice brought a wild search, Tag's eyes widened with understanding. He gave a nod when Hardin pointed toward the top of the rise. "Come straight back and get up on that rise. Cover our backs."

Tag loped through a series of groping, searching movements, wildly scared. Then he bear-crawled to the top of the small rise and lay prone, covering the high ground.

Mex and Boyle crashed into the tree line as though they were flushed from a sewer and dove into the ground. PeeWee crawled from the marsh, covered with mud. The marsh grass had sliced his cheek below his left eye.

Boyle shed his rucksack and started forward in a low duck waddle on the left side of the trail. Mex followed suit, taking the right flank. Hardin motioned PeeWee to join Tag and fell in between Mex and Boyle. Lowering his rucksack onto the trail, Hardin eased his finger past the trigger guard.

The three men moved in lock step toward the enemy camp, each man covering a sixty-degree sector. With weapons extended, they searched for a target. The smoke from the cooking fire curled with a slight breeze, drawing Hardin's eye.

Warm blood oozed from the leech wound on his neck. His left shoulder ached.

The confusion of the landing zone continued near the river. Tennessee, still stuck in the marsh, whispered into the handset, telling Captain Joe he'd have to call back.

Magnets, the enemy rucksacks drew the three GIs closer. Mounted in a quick-fire pose, Boyle, then Mex, then Hardin stopped. The enemy was close, within ten feet. Tuned to the movement of the leaves above his head, Boyle crouched near the first enemy rucksack, instantly turning to his left, his weapon pointing into the mouth of a spider hole.

Mex's search jumped ahead, leaping into another hole. He sank into the grass.

Hardin stopped moving, his mind factoring the details. The silver threads of a spider's web fluttered in the mouth of two spider holes, one web more complete than the other, one web torn by a passing body. The caverns shook with a sinister calm. Bunkers, spider holes, the drums were pounding.

Soon. Someone would die soon.

One-man spider holes flanked the trail, each with a firing lane cut through the vegetation to the trail. Fuck, oh shit, these dinks are good.

Mex pointed at the first hole, the one with the broken spider web, and signaled Boyle for a frag. Boyle pulled the pin and bowled the grenade across the ground with an underhand finger roll. The grenade bounced, rolled to the rim of the hole, hesitated, and dropped into the void.

Hardin's hands ached as he held his aim on the second hole. Boyle's frag exploded sending a slight tremor through the ground. Gray dust coughed from the hole.

Excited, in a vicious sort of way, Boyle kicked his stutter. The second frag hit nothing but net and exploded with a musty growl. A Viet Cong bounded out of a third spider hole on the far side of the cooking fire, barrel first. Some things in life are not well timed. Mex, Boyle, and Hardin spun as one, synchronized by a need to kill.

Still turning, they fired fifty-four rounds at the man. They shot one-for-fifty-four, right in the head. The other fifty-three rounds bit the vegetation. The roar lingered in the jungle just long enough for the dead man to smile. Boyle kicked the carbine from his hand.

Instantly, as if from hell, three women rose from the earth screaming a volley of vowels. Boyle, Mex, and Hardin spun into the noise, fingering their guns with maximum zeal. They hadn't reloaded.

The partisans wore black pajamas. Their black silken sleeves collapsed in folds. Their spindly arms hung in the air, pleading, bawling out broken and incomplete words. Begging for their lives, they screamed at the GIs. Boyle stuttered himself into a speechless ball, frantically trying to reload. His pudgy face twisted spastically, his saucer eyes bouncing from woman to woman.

Fish grabbed the barrel of Boyle's weapon and pushed it to the ground. "Relax, dumb-ass." Fish pushed the ladies into a squat and spoke, bringing their wails to a low chatter.

Hardin stepped toward the campfire, then backtracked down the trail. His rucksack lay near the verge of the trail. An AK round had ripped through the right side pocket, tearing the spoon-handle off of one of his frag grenades, blowing a hole through Squeak's bag of dew.

Hardin took a deep breath. Less than a sixteenth of an inch of the metal spoon remained below the pin. Carefully, he pulled the pin and threw the grenade into the marsh.

With his shirt heavy with blood, and his left arm at half-mast, he sat near the cooking fire. Stubbs had pushed the platoon into a hasty perimeter.

Boyle's first frag had blanched one VC to a frosted-gray, severed his legs below the knees and blew off his right forearm, the hand the man grabbed the frag with when he tried to throw it back. His AK-47 had misfired. The weapon was loaded with a thirty-round banana clip. The butt end of the casing on the chambered round was indented where the firing pin had slammed home.

The weapon was set on full automatic. Chuck had tried to shoot Tag to doll rags.

The second spider hole was empty, filled now with a cold, damp powder. The spider was gone. Stubbs examined the layout of the spider holes and the cooking fire. The firing lanes intersected at the foot of the trail-watcher's chair.

"This gunfight could have been worse, El Tee." Stubbs flipped a cigarette butt at Rap.

"My door gunner got blasted. His body was hangin' at the end of his harness, floppin' in the fuckin' breeze." Stubbs lit a smoke and turned away.

Two VC were dead, two VC escaped, and three VC were captured. The platoon took no casualties. The door gunner's weapon had jammed and he died trying to keep a promise.

Nasty, PeeWee, LeCotte, and Tag huddled around Boyle, trying to coach his stutter into a credible story. His protracted gibberish brought duets of laughter. But someone had been the target of the misfire, so Hardin decided to drive the lesson deeper.

"Tag, you're a lucky man." They opened their cluster into a mingling posture. "That AK misfired. Chuck was aimin' at you."

"Damn, you gotta be jokin'." Tag was a big man, an easy target.

"Don't be wanderin' down these trails. Not without help." Tag listened, his eye surveying Hardin's leech wound, his feet moving a mound of dirt, his head nodding.

Mex held the AK round with the dented casing up for Blood's inspection, waiting for Sweet Cheeks to sprinkle holy water on his luck. Watching Sweet Cheeks finish his ritual, laughing at the men who held stock in his edicts, Hardin issued a facetious amen.

"How was Ban Me Thuot?" Hardin asked, wanting to know more.

"Good booze." Fish grunted his concurrence. Sweet Cheeks gave his balls a nudge.

"Yeah, right. And the blow-jobs sucked." With smiles all around, Hardin asked, "Anything happen in Ban Me Thuot I need to know about, Pops? Gunplay, maybe."

Pops set his weight back onto his right foot and cocked his left shoulder into Hardin's question. As easy as Pops was, his eyes had gone cold, sealed against an officer's intrusion. Happy to share his wisdom and his stew, he would never give up a platoon secret: not even to an officer he respected.

"There's lotsa GIs gettin' shot these days, El Tee."

"Maybe next time, right, Boyle." With his eyes locked on Pops, Hardin held out a fist. Boyle and Pops responded. Pops fell in with Ski, and then Shadow.

The Hill People had a secret. A stranger was shot in Ban Me Thuot.

* * *

As the second lift of choppers set down on LZ Hammer, the Frenchman and Ski began organizing their guns. Stubbs slogged from the marsh with Captain Joe at his heel.

"Hardin, what's goin' on? I've been callin' for ten minutes." Captain Joe's challenge had been primed with fifty meters of bog-walking. Mud covered the lower half of his body.

"I'm not packin' a radio, Captain." Joe's body telescoped with anger.

"What's the deal here?" Joe was pissed into a curdle by Hardin's insolence.

"Two dinks, three chippies, an AK and carbine, four rucksacks, and Johnny's gone marching home."

Joe stopped listening, then shook his anger into a grin watching Fish grab a woman's snatch, pull his hand back as if he had been shocked, then roar with laughter. Fish was indispensable, rather like bacteria in a septic tank—nasty but necessary. Amps gave his power pack a toss, guffawing a rural version of copping a feel.

"Amps, go through those rucks," Stubbs said.

"Drips already did, nothin' but junk."

"What the fuck is this?" Stubbs asked, grabbing the bandage pack Drips was holding. Inked on the side of the pack in bold black script was Delta Company's unit designation.

"Where'd you get this, Drips?" Stubbs asked.

"It was in one of those dink rucksacks." Drips was lying. He adjusted his shirtsleeves when he lied. "It don't mean nothin', Captain." Hardin and Joe looked at each other. The deserter from Delta Company was walking with long strides.

"What do you think?" Joe asked, looking at Stubbs.

"Hard tellin'," Stubbs said, tossing the bandage pack to Amps. "I think the fucker's dead." Bucks and Mex eased away, not wanting to talk to Joe.

Stubbs moved off to check the platoon sector. Hardin's insolence and Joe's frustration had collided on LZ Hammer. The two men stood braced, as if laying in wait might help.

Hardin was tired. The step-by-step exhaustion of Vietnam's war seemed to march on at a steady pace. The accumulating vagueness of being too long in the jungle seemed to blur a man's will to survive, surpassing anything his enemy might do.

Hardin sat next to a stranger at the crest of the small rise. The stranger, the senior medic, seemed remote, tension lacing his face.

"I get withdrawals when I don't have to cover for stupid people," the medic said to nobody, picking at the mud on his boots.

"My door gunner's dead," Hardin said, unbuttoning his blood-soaked shirt.

"That leech picked a good spot to drill," the medic said. He would talk to Hardin today. Tomorrow he might want to kill him.

Demented in an impulsive way, the dead man with the head wound was lying face up across the top of his spider hole, twitching whenever Joe looked his way. As LeCotte might, he cheered the dead man's persistence until stupidity gained the day and he stuck an ace of spades in the dead man's mouth.

Captain Joe, taking fortune by the foreskin, summoned a commanding tone. "Hardin, get control of your people. And send a medic over to look at that man." Hardin's face went blank, staring past his captain, wondering why Joe was suddenly as stupid as LeCotte.

"I got it covered, El Tee."

The senior medic, a Specialist Fifth Class, a second-tour medic with the sympathies of an ex-con, vaulted down the small incline, circled the cooking fire, bounded up to the dead man, and kicked him in the head, hollering into the canopy.

"Stop jerkin' around, asshole. You're makin' the captain crazy." The words sounded across the marshy landing zone and crashed into the next day. GIs turned and stared. No house calls: GIs were not keen on sympathy. Captain Joe turned, staring at the medic.

"What in hell are ya doin', Doc?" Joe's mouth twisted into a defiant expression that was keenly out of place. His conscience had consumed his body and its shadow.

"Fucker's been dead since he got hit. I don't do fuckin' brains."

Straddled over the dead man, the medic's face seemed urgent and strained, the war's message buried in an odd smile. "Damn good thing we didn't bang those broads," Hardin said to himself. Battle Bullshit sucked: shoot a dink and Captain Joe turns back into a Christian.

The medic caught his breath, then screamed into the canopy, his reflections supplanted by rage. "I'll tell ya what, I'll tell ya what." Doc's arms waved spastically at Joe. "I'll stick this sin loi motherfucker in a hole and roll a stone over it. If he's the right dude, he'll be out in three days—no fuckin' surgery, no fuckin' shit. I should cut off his dick and start a fuckin' chain letter."

Doc was reduced to a low-class functionary, punching out the rhythm of a post-firefight sequence he could control, decelerating into a thoughtful center, and then pulling the bubble in around him. He was prepared to work on his friends. When he knew he had no friendly casualties, he shut down his reactive motors and flew away, his brain on autopilot.

Joe had interrupted his flight and Doc could not handle the turbulence.

Hardin laughed when he remembered his father's words: "That's what I told Murphy when the war got rough: in December of '44, during the Battle of the

Bulge. I told him if he was looking for sympathy it was in the dictionary between shit and syphilis."

The company picked up and moved a kilometer through loose chunks of lava rock to hide from their latest kills—Sin Loi Motherfucker and his buddy, Hot Wheels.

* * *

Yesterday, with the whores of Ban Me Thuot servicing the mob, the company drew gas masks from battalion supply. Intelligence reports from Saigon had featured an enemy threat that warned of the possible use of poison gas. Anxious staff weans parsed the intell this way and that.

A report of poison gas required no confirming data.

The Army's obsession with hiding had generated a range of accessories: camouflage sticks spanning the green and brown spectrums; olive-drab helmets; green and brown camouflage covers; green mosquito netting; green fatigues; green rucksacks; green C-Ration cans; green and black boots; multicolored Military Pay Currency; and white toilet paper.

As if a GI's ass wasn't bright enough.

Data analysis and probability calculations, rather than experience, led rear-echelon staff patches to use words that had no basis, pledging their careers to a false premise. What made their conclusions seem accurate was a false constant: that enemy activity percolated within the green shaded areas on their briefing map and was therefore a perpetual threat to the unit's mission.

Poison gas added urgency with no bounds.

And, given that infantry operations were derivatives of the stealth provided by the color green, probabilities dictated that enemy units used the areas colored in green to hide in. Amplifying on this logic, staffers concluded that almost all of Vietnam was shaded green. Following this logic, gas masks were issued to infantry companies whose locations were a continual mystery, the decision based on a long-range-recon report from Laos, that an NVA unit was spotted carrying gas masks.

The probability of an NVA unit deploying gas in the open jungle against an unknown enemy they bumped into was low. The probability that Captain Joe would bump into this particular NVA unit was zero.

Hardin looked at his gas mask and laughed. He saw the briefing clearly.

* * *

"Gentlemen, that concludes the G-3's portion of the situation. I'll be followed by Major Brown, the brigade G-2," (G-2 being military for intelligence).

"General Abrams, Colonel, Colonel, I'm Major Brown, Two Corps Assistant G-2 for outside intelligence." A calculated pause followed so staff officers could scratch an appendage and wonder why the briefer's name wasn't Major Green, and wonder who was responsible for inside intelligence. My God, even envy was green.

"A Spike Team spotted an NVA unit moving southeast at this location." The Major pointed to a green area on the map. "Carrying what looked to be gas masks." Another pause forced the general to look for a trusted aide. "This report has an 'A' classification. I advise we issue masks to all units southeast of the sighting."

Realizing that nearly all of South Vietnam was southeast of the sighting, the general took charge. "G-4, issue gas masks to our forward units." So gas masks were issued to GIs who were already carrying seventy pounds of green shit.

* * *

Watching, as if from a distance, Hardin found Tennessee piling lava rocks around their sleeping area. Front and back, he was covered with dry mud.

"Where's your gas mask?" Hardin asked, his hands offering a gesturing guess.

"I said a prayer when I buried it." Tennessee's high-pitched laugh inflated his half-civilian, cornbread character. "No shit, El Tee. I ain't seen one today, except on you lifers."

Stubbs sat near Tennessee as if he knew a secret, then demanded a share of his coffee. "Mex has the OP," Stubbs said, his eyes fixed in a reflective stare. "Boyle won't sleep anyway. Might as well give him a reason to stutter in the dark." Nudging Tennessee's shoulder he said, "I'm a hard-stripe E-7, young stud. Be careful how ya talk about lifers."

To change the drift of things, Tennessee pointed at Boyle, who was rotating around an image of the dink he had fragged, handing Rap a full-speed line of jive, complete with interruptions that allowed his mouth to translate what his mind had already said. His antics were accentuated with fist-pounding dances from Chicago's streets and a high-pitched cackle Rap found when one of the brothers was on a roll.

"You catch what they're sayin'?" Tennessee asked.

Stubbs ignored the antics created when the brothers played straight man for one another. The energy in Rap's laugh attracted levels of curiosity, with those less tuned-in standing somewhere outside the outer circle, unable to join that inner circle created by Black English.

"Nothin' to catch, just brother-bullshit."

Stubbs broke up Rap's cluster, signaling GIs to go to ground. When Mex told Boyle they had the OP, Boyle's eyelids retracted, and his jaw dropped, then his mouth coughed up a flurry of hyphenated questions about how his number got picked again.

"Shut up, Boyle, get your gear," LeCotte said, shoving Boyle aside. Since walking in the lava field was impossible, and Boyle was wound so tight, LeCotte figured he could sleep.

"Mex—no more ears, ya got that?" Stubbs said. Mex shook his head and smiled, his eyes projecting a futile understanding.

"Yeah, Sarge, I got that. Some of these dink-ass-dudes come without ears."

"Right, like the two we banged today."

Mex glanced at Stubbs with a be-careful eye, then picked up his rucksack. He was a quiet, nut-brown man with a smooth loping gait. His stoic reaction to combat, born on the streets of Los Angeles, had him wired to an attitude he called home. Rap didn't scare Mex, and Rap knew the knife Mex carried had a history.

Mex and Bucks spent their day with larceny in drag. Neither man showed signs of stress. Having reduced Vietnam's war to a giant rat-fuck, they devoted their life to the worship of pee hole. They blamed Drips for their wayward habits—but really, the Hill People were floating in a space well beyond normality.

LeCotte had come back to pick up chow and challenge Hardin's wisdom.

"You're damn lucky you didn't fire up those three broads. If you'd of been reloaded they'd be history," LeCotte said, competing for last rites. "I saw you and Mex dry-firin' their ass." Stubbs picked up a hot C-Ration from Pops.

"Shut up, asshole," Stubbs said.

"Dickheads like you always get a dry ride, LeCotte," Pops said. LeCotte let out a disgusted grunt, adjusted his glasses, and stuck a finger at Hardin's chest.

"I should be runnin' this outfit."

Hardin stared at LeCotte's finger and said, "I agree. Tonight you're runnin' an outpost."

LeCotte, a good card player, always raised the stakes. Hardin had to call his hand or muddle his future with each encounter. LeCotte would have blown away the women, too.

Quick-fire was a reflexive fallacy designed in a classroom to promote and insulate unsupervised behavior. You're dead: I shot you first. Boys in training preferred this argument. While fighting Vietnam's war these boys had to shoot first.

They winced when the women screamed, their tiny arms reaching out of the silken sleeves of their well-worn shirts, their screams accelerating, then warping. Mex, Boyle and Hardin had turned as one, their quick-fire palsy reaching for the sound, trying to kill. They had heard these screams before, those silent screams from the night. Now the screams packed the contorted faces of three young women, faces that would reflect a GI's regrets.

"Stubbs, are the gun-sets staked?" Hardin asked.

"Ski's still workin' on his. Blood's pissed about missin' the gunfight."

"Blood and Joe were givin' guided tours of those spider holes. Blood's eyes were on fire," Hardin said. Stirring hot water into a chicken and rice ration, Hardin added a squirt of Tabasco.

"Shit, Stubbs, where's your gas mask?"

"Must be a combat loss."

Stubbs' cigarette butt bounced off Ski's shoulder, then landed near PeeWee's foot. Satisfied, he tipped his helmet back on his head and lit a Pall Mall, exhaling smoke under the rim of Tennessee's helmet, filling the liner until smoke rolled out the sides.

Sudden cramping in his lower abdomen brought Hardin to a quiet spot outside the perimeter—magma. He cherished these interludes for their siphoning reality. His body shook with fever as he stood, breathing deeply to keep his balance. Hardin closed his eyes. Dig-it was singing with the ladies.

"Have some coffee, El Tee," Tennessee said.

"You handled Joe real well today." The coffee was warm and friendly.

"He chewed my ass somethin' fierce when you were outta ear shot."

"Don't hang us out; not for anybody. Ya hear me?"

"I hear ya. Why do ya get more jump pay than me." Squeak had left the jump pay mystery for Tennessee to solve.

"That's easy. You're not circumcised." Tennessee sat up and looked at Amps.

"How would you know?"

"Just a guess."

With his mind racing, Hardin flashed on the dog lying in that bloody jungle hollow—three holes through his chest. At times, deep in the night, the dog's final sigh rang like a bell. Alerted by a familiar sound, he stared into the jungle at the last spot he saw, LeCotte.

Finding a dark recess in the foliage, he found himself chasing his father's ghost.

Highlands Road was the best.

* * *

Number #10, Highlands Road. Bremerton, Washington. September 1954.

The Major was alive with expectation. Court's nomination to West Point had the phone ringing. Court would earn a Regular Army commission, a status the Major longed for. Eddie read the beginning paragraph of the letter the Major was writing to Scoop Jackson, thanking him for Court's nomination.

"Murphy spent his down-time looking after this Yorkshire terrier. He found the dog in France. Called him Tits. Here, Tits. Here, Tits. He loved yelling that around the Twenty-first Army Headquarters. The damn dog was a male and would have a go at your leg without warning."

"Did Monty like the dog?"

"He did. Once Murphy snapped to attention, saluted, and hollered 'Private Francis GI Joe Murphy, sah.' In the excitement the dog peed on a British General Dempsey's leg. Monty laughed, proclaiming Tits, one of The King's Welshman."

"Did Tits make it through the war?"

"Yes, I was glad for that. The time spent with that dog were separated from the war. When Tom Poston was killed in April of '45, Tits knew. That dog's friendship seemed to transcend the loss. For a time, a dog named Tits drew me away from the brooding, and the self-loathing that comes with losing a friend."

CHAPTER NINE

This One's for Dak To

The Outback Southwest of Ban Me Thuot.

Days folded into a nether dimness with hardly a sniff of Chuck. The dancing girls of LZ Hammer had faded with declining reviews. The lava bed had run on flat ground for three kilometers and power-rolled ankles into tender, inflated spasms.

The ground bordering the lava field had a light brown, wet-sand tinge, and a dusty clay texture. A stringy canopy draped into a low, wattle pattern, blocking the sunlight. The air was stagnant. The heat waves were making more noise than a passing pant leg.

Not one gas mask survived the march.

The leech wound at Hardin's neck had oozed blood for days. Now he was cleaning the wound morning and night, fighting the smell of rot.

To accent their boring trace, Doc Collard had splashed water on his face from a seeping spring and captured a tiny leech with his eyeball. Listening to Doc screaming sweet Jesus over a mini-motherfucker waltzing on his eyeball, Hardin laughed, took off his fourteenth pair of glasses, reset Willie Spencer's watch, and tried to gin up a second wet dream. No luck.

A new guy named Butterfield had arrived during one of the resupplies and Rap had christened him "Butt"—"Brother Butt."

"Sweet Cheeks."

Sweet Cheeks was busy applauding Doc's leech, hollering Sweet Jesus, setting a betting line with Bucks, and Nasty on how long it would take to catch the little bastard. Between outbursts of vagrant chitchat, Hardin absorbed the laughter. *Ernie Pyle had it right,* he thought—"Soldiers are made out of the strangest people."

They are nuts.

"Sweet Cheeks, there's a slick inbound, you're leavin'," Hardin said.

Cherry Brother Butt was his replacement. On McNamara's tally-book they looked the same: same commodity, and both men were alive. People talked to Sweet Cheeks. No one would talk to Butt until he lived through a day and Fish sprinkled holy water on his passage.

"Hot damn." Sweet Cheeks kicked Bucks' rucksack and laid a full-speed dap on Mex as he began to separate from the glue. Emotion welled up in Hardin's chest. Tears began to form.

Sweet Cheeks' joy was nearly too much to bear.

Sweet Cheeks jumped him with his Tar Heel charm. "You're a good dude, El Tee. Not like the rest. Thanks for keepin' me alive." Hardin knew they kept one another alive.

"The war's not over, Sweet Cheeks. It won't ever be over."

"Yeah it will, El Tee, just ride 'em hard. They dig that no-shit style." The two men hit each other's fists. "Here, I want to give you somethin." Sweet Cheeks handed his lieutenant a short piece of parachute shroud line, frayed at one end and taped at the other end. His shoulders settled into a gesture of giving.

"It's for luck, El Tee. Hang it on your rucksack," he said with a quick grin.

"You're not outta here yet, Sweet Cheeks."

"No sweat. That's the leash off my fuck-you lizard. He got hit on the Hill. Screamed fuck-you just before he died." Hardin tied the shroud line to his rucksack frame and shook Sweet Cheeks' hand, then looked away, absorbing the sound of the inbound chopper.

"Take care of yourself, kid. See ya in the world. Arkansas is still part of the States isn't it?" Mean as he was, if Sweet Cheeks left his infectious smile behind someone would pick it up. Raised where the four-leaf clover grows, his luck was priceless.

"Flowers are forever, El Tee. I watched you ink that on your helmet."

Sweet Cheeks waded through a gauntlet, leaving Hardin with a hand he could barely close, holding the ragged end of a shroud line, and swearing never to doubt another man's superstition. Sweet Cheeks smiled when he told the story about a girl from Blowing Rock, North Carolina. And with a sparkle in his eye, he'd brag about her blowing his rocks.

A GI would lie about anything.

Hardin flashed on his father's den. His dad was holding Murphy's picture. "I said good-bye to Murphy near the Bergen-Belsen concentration camp. I didn't realize how close we had grown until he was gone. Murphy was parading around like a general by war's end—Murphy and his dog Tits."

Sweet Cheeks sat on the edge of the cargo deck saluting his friends as the slick hovered into the air. The Hill People stood as one, returning his salute. Hardin's salute brought a smile.

* * *

When a GI joined his platoon, he was issued a fuck-you lizard before he was issued his platoon-essential gear. The lizard might be a soprano or a bass. Good dogs and lizards, they followed a GI no matter where he might go.

The name "Gecko" portrayed an incomplete picture of the little bastard. "Fuck-you" was a fitting moniker—a short, two-syllable, easy-to-pronounce, rapid-fire handle that rolled off a GI's tongue. Derived from a guttural call the lizard made at twilight, the call was a spiritual gesture according to Fish—a blessing for the evening meal.

Stubbs, a self-professed reptile expert, could not determine whether the sound started with an "H," as in "Huck-you," or started with an "F," as in "Fuck-you," as he preferred. His dilemma stemmed from the problem the Vietnamese had pronouncing the word "fuck"—"Numba huckin' one GI." After all, these were Vietnamese lizards.

The keepsake tethered to the end of Sweet Cheeks' shroud line was lost in Dak To, and he had transformed the broken bond into a reason to live. Somehow his rucksack and this piece of shroud line had saved his life, and he passed the charm on to his El Tee.

Two of the veterans of the battle for Dak To from First Platoon were out of the jungle—Squeak and Sweet Cheeks. Ski and Shadow, Bucks and Mex, and Drips and Fish stood in the killing zone.

* * *

The dry streambed concealed the day's impatience, exposing those raw edges torn by dancing too long in one spot. Trails laced a flat draw, intersecting in hidden arenas where hundreds of soldiers could rally, rally points the French had not found.

Heat sapped the moisture from a weave of thinning vines and left the soil a dry crust. The trees looked sickly, as if dwarfed. The trees, white with bark, were spiked with awkwardly small limbs. The sunlight glowed in the upper reaches of the canopy.

The trails in Charlie's jungle are well tended, Hardin thought.

Tired feet clamored over stones, snapping one stone against another. Exhausted by the need for water, Hardin searched the three men in front of him. One boot followed another, dissociated from the other by a moment's madness.

"Six, this is Lima," Hardin said, cupping his voice into the handset.

"Wha'd'a ya want."

Mex mouthed the words "pee hole," then keyed the hook and said, "I want outta these fuckin' woods."

"We've been invited to spend Tet guarding the Special Forces camp at Duc Co."

"These camps aren't that fuckin' special." Amps agreed.

The Special Forces had been running Go Teams and Spike Teams out of Kontum, Ban Me Thuot, Duc Co, and Dak To across the fence into Cambodia and Laos for more than two years. Recent after-action reports from the teams detailed a massive infiltration of NVA troops and equipment down the Ho Chi Minh Trail. Inserted and extracted as if they were riding yo-yos, the teams were running for their lives.

Hardin sat in a clump of vegetation so dense the air he found had already been used. The water in his canteen was a tepid mix of Halazone and gritty clay drawn from a stream near LZ Hammer. The water trickled from his head, washing down both sides of his neck. He washed his face and neck, pushing at the silky film coating his skin. The leech wound on his neck was beginning to rot.

"Jesus, Hardin. What are you fuckin' doin' here?" *The Z-Special Force water assault teams his father had trained with in 1938, in New South Wales, must have had similar problems,* he thought, *one boot following another.*

The company searched south, skirting a well-used trail, then mounted a small ridgeline to find higher ground for a night laager. The Hill People were still talking about their excursion to Ban Me Thuot. Some of their talk was serious.

Boyle stopped espousing the art of fragging spider holes after Fish wrote him a note threatening to kill him if he didn't. LeCotte read the note to Ski, suggesting that Ski intercede on Boyle's behalf. Ski told LeCotte to go suck on a dead dog's ass. LeCotte read the note to Rap, and Rap laughed. Then Rap told LeCotte that if Fish killed Boyle, he—Rap—would stuff LeCotte's head up his ass with his helmet on.

Tired of the hassle, LeCotte took Boyle's pound cake and told him Fish was kidding.

"Lima, this is Six. I want you to drop off and bush this red-ball. Join us in the morning."

"You hear that?" Tennessee jerked the radio handset out of the dirt and wiped it on his leg, his shoulders nodding into a slump.

"This is Lima Kilo, Roger, out." Joe spoke again, but Hardin was out of earshot. "He's takin' a dump." Tennessee listened, then keyed the hook and said, "You made him sick."

"What'd Joe want?" Hardin asked.

"Told us to drive safely."

"I got bad vibes over this drill. This puppy's built for loggin' trucks." Tennessee alerted Mex, Bucks, LeCotte, and Blood and stopped the platoon fifty meters south of the trail.

Hardin took Stubbs, Bucks, and a fire team back to the trail and located an intersection of a dry wash and the trail, providing washed stones for panicking men to stumble over if they got caught in the killing zone.

"This area is spooky," Stubbs said.

"Chuck's been here today." Bucks pointed at a series of scuff marks, then bent down and snapped off a thick blade of dry grass, and said, "We better move up the ridge and circle back. Come into the 'bush site from uphill."

Hardin nodded his decision. "Set up an inverted L, Stubbs. Bucks—take the short side on the wash, plus the junction. Ski's gun's on the junction. Leave the rucks uphill with an OP."

Stubbs added a note of caution. "Bucks, every man takes a piss."

Hardin and Tennessee stayed at the ambush site. The platoon circled forward, ran a counter-clockwise clover up hill, dropped off an outpost, peed in a hole, and picked their way down to the trail. Silently, nineteen men began digging shallow troughs, replanting displaced vegetation. Stubbs inspected the gun sites, rearranging dirt and adjusting vegetation to mask a face or weapon. Then he back-swept the trail to mend any disturbance.

Detail, death was in the detail. Small trenches were dug to lower the profile of the odd boot heel. The smooth, round silhouette of the GI helmet disappeared behind bouquets of well-placed vines. Finally, one by one, GIs took a drink of water, set their canteen within reach, and secured their ammunition.

Overlapping firing lanes merged into a web. The inverted L-shaped ambush had the long leg of the "L" fronting the trail, the short leg running down the wash.

Stubbs set Mex's squad with the Frenchman's gun on the trail. Stubbs took the last position with two Claymores and twelve frags to seal that end of the killing zone.

With Stubbs manicuring the Frenchman's gun site, Hardin set Bucks' squad at the junction and along the wash. Ski's gun was covering the wash. LeCotte had the last position with two Claymores and eight frags.

The temperature was rising. Any disconcerting movement or cracking tattoo brought silence. Men froze, waiting, searching. With weapons calibrated, men watched: right and then left. They sat in a steaming daze, their bodies melting in a pocket of sweat and powdered clay.

Tennessee's face burned bright red. Short of breath, his head fell into the sharp stubble. He was in trouble. Without disturbing the vegetation, Amps unscrewed the lid of his canteen and held it over Tennessee's head. Drops of water fell near Tennessee's ear. As if surprised, he woke with a start. He drank the water and thanked his friend. They were alone.

When a grunt dies on ambush, he dies in absentia, isolated from reality.

Dense and sparse vegetation brought the trail in and out of focus. With a background of sinuous vines and tangled foliage, sunlight filtered through a small leaf canopy. A breeze pushed gently at the treetops. Patches of shadow sparred with shafts of refracted light. Rising waves of heat drew at the last scraps of life on the jungle floor, the temperature over one hundred degrees.

Stubbs signaled Hardin, rubbing his eyes, giving notice that visibility was limited.

GIs lay so close to the trail junction, Ski could see twenty meters of the wash. Hot and dry, the jungle seemed to hang into the wash like thousands of fish lines, waving their lures.

Hardin gave LeCotte the finger when their eyes met. Tennessee had passed out again. His rough and reddened face lay across his left arm. His lips were burned dry. The men of First Platoon had been too long without water.

A mounting intensity brought flashes of recognition. Hands began to move cautiously. Hardin alerted, then stared into the wash. As if to see better, he pressed a narrow seam into the grass in front of his face. The obvious became clear. The rocks in the wash had been removed where the trail passed by. A trail watcher had manicured the intersection.

Hardin searched the length of the ambush site. Ski's gun lay in a natural wedge of scrub at the point of the L, covering the wash and the intersection. The Frenchman's gun lay deep in a man-made blind covering the main trail. Stubbs and LeCotte lay at opposite ends of the L, ready to cut off the outer edges of the ambush, and the two primary escape routes.

Hardin lay prone, midway between The Frenchman and Ski.

Stubbs raised a finger, then waved off his warning, resisting the balance of his thoughts. As if to see better, he raised his head. With his eyes darting across the dense vegetation, then staring into the tunnel formed by the main trail, sonorous echoes sounded in Stubbs' mind.

He knew if the ambush was triggered, all bets were off. The platoon was stranded 300 meters from the company, all up hill.

And, with the enemy buildup for Tet, the ambush could draw anything from a small patrol, to recon units, to supply units, to a regular battalion. If the platoon ambushed an NVA battalion, not one GI would be alive by dawn.

Without water for an hour, exhaustion forced a deeper silence. Hardin wiped the salt from the corner of his eyes. Amps signaled that the platoon radios were turned off.

Jesus it's quiet, Hardin thought, lowering his head to his forearm to relieve the tension in his neck. A sharp kink grabbed his right shoulder blade, then subsided. Fungus stirred in the wounds on the back of his hands. A sticky fluid wept from his neck where his shirt collar had aggravated the leech wound. His bloodstained shirt was heavy with sweat. And, indeed, as bad as his breath was, a stench hung in the stagnant air.

With the shear notes of a clarion, the sudden silence of the jungle consumed the men of First Platoon. The inmates of the jungle had stopped talking. Hardin swallowed to clear his ears. The sound rang like cannon shot, then slammed into a memory—the dog's shattered body. Surges of adrenaline threw his mind into an involuntary spiral.

Sweat fell from his nose and wrists, soaking the soil beneath his neck. His face and eyes burned. The platoon needed water.

Stubbs had strung warning-twines, linking Hardin to Bucks and to Mex. If Hardin pulled a warning-twine, the ambush would be triggered.

Laughing at the thought of Stubbs being without a smoke for over an hour stopped when Blood's hand shot up, covering his face, fingers extended, hand cupped. Blood lay motionless, anticipating, looking as though he had just run out of time. Enemy soldiers were approaching the kill zone in the dry wash and Blood was signaling the news.

Breathing was no longer an option.

Death could be gradual: noises, feet moving across stones, stones cracking together, sonic tattoos, the rustle of branches, vines clinging to passing bodies. Nothing on the outer edge of the Eastern Sea, or in the academics of Christminster, was more frightening or more exhilarating than watching the enemy you are going to kill walk into your trap—nothing.

First a pair of boots, then the point man popped into view, right out of a catalogue, right out of Hanoi. Main-line North Vietnamese regulars, the motherfuckers really existed. Hardin processed the information rapidly, his mind flying, correlating variables, factoring data into probable events.

The point man stopped, his expression running from haste to fatigue. He was staring at a flat mat of vegetation, looking directly at the barrel of Ski's machine gun and he could not see it.

A livid white scar ran the length of his left cheek.

With but seconds to determine the probable threat, the chop in Hardin's chest sounded in the hollow of his throat. Wanting to stop and start, he eased his trigger finger into place.

"Think about pussy, Eddie—it's payback time. This one's for, Dak To, asshole." Hardin mouthed the words to validate his commitment.

A murmur rose from the dry wash.

Strung out like ducks on parade, seven dinks argued casually, their words punctuated by brief fits of silence, their feet just fifteen meters from Blood. Quiet and not alert, the seven enemy soldiers stood in the heart of the kill zone.

Brightened by a conclusive nod, the point man stepped toward Ski, then stopped at the trail junction. The next two men joined him, ten meters from Ski's machine gun. The patrol leader was selecting a route. If the NVA turned left, The Frenchman would take them out on the main trail. If they turned right, Ski would kill them in the wash.

The enemy's sing-song jabber was out of synch with their new reality.

A radio operator was fourth in line carrying a Prick-25 GI radio—just like Tennessee's. Hardin listened; his senses geared to the enemy radio. An intermittent rush shot from the handset. Other units were using the frequency. Hardin focused on the radio operator and the last man. They listened intently, searching the vegetation, waiting for their patrol leader to choose a route, not caring which route was chosen.

The radio operator dropped into a squat, startling Hardin. His AK lay across the top of his knees, the muzzle pointing into the platoon's ambush position. The trail man, the man on drag, was more casual, drinking water, and watering his face and upper body.

The obvious struck Hardin like a bolt. None of the NVA were carrying food, their tube-sock filled with rice, their staple bandoleer. Fire fueled Hardin's mind as more pieces fell into place. The RTO had not used the radio. The drag man had not looked back along the wash for another man or a trailing unit. This was a recon patrol. A company of NVA regulars was within 500 meters.

The third man in line ended the conversation with a quick lateral hand gesture, and the NVA started down the wash. The first two men were within ten meters of PeeWee.

Suddenly, the third man's head whipped into a panic and the barrel of his AK swung into a firing position. Hardin jerked the warning-twine attached to Bucks' hand, Bucks squeezed Ski's calf, and the dam broke.

A roaring eruption of small-arms fire expanded the jungle's dimensions. Hardin shot the patrol leader in the face, one-half second before a volley from Ski's machine gun blew the patrol leader and the two men in front of him to shreds.

The point man's jaw and tongue arced away from his face and his brains blew into a spray, dripping from the vines. Claymores sealed the ambush and grazing fire leveled the vegetation hiding the GIs.

The radio operator and the drag man took head-shots with the first volley. The others met a frenzied blending of shredding bodies and evolving reality. The instant roar of the ambush sucked the air from the wash as dead men and their equipment flopped into cheerless heaps.

Their mind's camera would have set a shutter speed high enough to capture the trace of a M-16 round as fire leaped from the foliage. The NVA soldiers pitched and thrashed as the rounds ripped at bone and meat, slaughtering their vitals. Blood and meat plastered the wash. The seven soldiers died in fewer than four seconds. Not one AK round was fired.

Tennessee was stumbling and First Platoon had to run for their life.

GIs bounded from the ground in a passion of fear, scouring the wash, stripping rucksacks, searching wildly for information.

With his heart raging, assaulting his ability to breathe, Hardin screamed, "Roll it up, goddammit. We're outta here." He rolled the radio operator onto his stomach and opened the radio. The back of the man's head was gone. His brains had flowed over the dials on the radio.

Twenty-plus flashlight batteries hooked in series powered the radio. Leaving the radio on the dead man's back, Hardin fired four rounds into the transceiver housing. Satisfied, he ran from the killing zone. Bucks had sealed off the main trail with the two machine gun teams. Drips, Fish, and Mex had grabbed weapons and whatever else was available.

Hardin, suffering the initial chattering of diminished rage, stopped, then ran back into the wash. Honoring a duty he could not define, he shot the one enemy soldier who still had his face in tact. The round blew the man's eyes out and left his nose hanging by a thread.

"That's for Dak To, you rotten pig-fucker." Blood stood stock-still, stimulated by his lieutenant's unvarnished behavior.

"Blood, trap the RTO," Hardin said, bounding out of the wash.

"Rap, take point. We gotta run."

Stubbs pulled the machine gun teams and the platoon started up hill, knowing the roar of the ambush would bring trouble. Swarming through Hardin's senses, thousands of the bastards were ant-racing over the ground, challenging his blunt mind, streaming over his body.

"Six, Lima Kilo. We got seven dead November Victor Alphas with AKs and a sandbox full of shit." PeeWee fell one step ahead of Amps, wheezing and throwing his guts into air. LeCotte and Pops lifted him off the ground, straining to drag his body up the steep incline.

"Roger. Roll up and run." Captain Joe's voice was coarse.

"No shit, we're rollin'. Where are ya?"

"South on top of the ridge."

Drips and Bucks were hauling Tennessee. Amps had the platoon radio. The GIs fought for altitude in a tight formation. Stubbs and Blood had drag, pushing men with their weapons, trying to outrun the point.

Fifteen minutes out of the wash, the booby trap exploded, and desperation surged into personal expressions of disbelief. Knowing Chuck would stomp their ass into pool of pig slop, fear became the lighter part of their run. Stronger, bigger men, towed and coaxed their friends. No one would be left behind. Tennessee was waking up.

"Pick it up, stay on the ridge, tighten it up." Panicking men crashed through gathering seas, pushing their bubble away from the killing zone. No one needed coaching.

"Six, we got Chuck at the bush. Where are ya, baby?"

"One hundred strokes south once you're on top. Bet you never needed a hundred strokes before." Now Joe thought he was funny. Pussy was powerful stuff.

"Roger, put red-leg on the bush. A ride on a red bush would be nice." Hardin was gasping for air, his endurance strapped to a mysterious fever, his fear hauling Amps by the hook.

"You got twenty minutes of light, best kick it in the ass," Joe said.

The ground flattened out. The platoon was almost home. Rap stopped the platoon to count bodies. Shadow hurriedly set a flare across the top of the ridge, and the GIs pushed their pace to a dash with squads abreast. Tennessee was lucid and out of water.

"Six, we're strokin' her top. Don't light us up," Hardin said.

Artillery rounds pounded the ambush site.

"Roger, no OPs on your end."

Stubbs screamed Rawhide, Charlie Company's secret password, and a herd of running grunts screamed with relief. The platoon was ushered to four foxholes and started filling sandbags. They weren't safe, but they were home.

"Tennessee, when your ex-wife shot ya were ya on top?"

"Fuck you, El Tee. Jesus, get real." Tennessee dropped to his knees and sat back on his heels. He was burning with fever, trying not to throw up.

"Amps, make coffee. I gotta talk to Six."

Joe had that here-come-the-elephants look as he and his artillery recon sergeant set the grid locations for defensive concentrations. Hardin stuck a finger on the map where the ridge topped out.

"We put a flare right here." Joe adjusted a def-con to match the flare location. To a man, the company wanted to run.

"We're gonna find out who was chasin' who," Joe said.

"Shit-fuck! We're the only assholes around."

Hardin's eyes set hard, watching the NVA radio operator's body bounce with the impact of the rounds he fired into the radio. Then the patrol leader's head disintegrated and Ski blew his body parts across the screen. Vietnam needed more dead Viet Cong.

Joe pushed Hardin's shoulder. "Hey, dumb ass. You're not listenin'. I want one of those pith helmets. Was their gear new?"

"Yeah, squeaky clean. GI radio, Prick-25 with flashlight batteries hooked in series. Check out the AKs, AK-Ms, right out of Cosmolene."

"We'll talk in the mornin'." Joe was trying to keep fear from gathering disciples.

Hardin found Amps trying not to puke. "Commo and OP?"

Amps smiled a sickly smile, massaged his neck, then spoke with his mouth full. "Gator's got the OP, commo is locked, and Polly wants my doodle all day."

"That ain't funny, Dip-Shit. Bangin' those dinks was a fuckin' mistake. If they find us, our shit is gonna get stomped." Amps shook his head and whispered for mercy, then jumped into the foxhole to finish his coffee.

A void engulfed the jungle. The sounds of sun-dried vegetation being soothed by cooling air interrupted the night. Hardin crawled out of the foxhole and lay down.

Amps jostled the radio from its sandbagged enclosure. Shadow's flare was casting an eerie glow, filtered by vines, trees, and grass. Chuck was close. He was on the right track.

"Our Father, Who art in heaven."

Hearing the exhaustion in his own voice, Hardin stopped his prayer and scanned the backdrop. The top of the ridge was laced with linear shadows, a graveyard with light reaching past the tombstones through a fog. Hardin set his head near the ground.

"Ya know, Amps, I'm beginnin' to miss my dad," Hardin said. "He whispered when he talked about the Battle of the Bulge—the Ardennes Forest, the Ghost Front."

"My old man died in the Chosin Reservoir: on my second birthday."

Firing artillery on def-con one brought six high-explosive artillery rounds into the ridgeline. The jungle turned black on impact. White-hot shrapnel and debris blew through the perimeter.

Instantly the artillery recon sergeant began screaming cease-fire over the radio.

Being scared was easier at night. Men lay prone, glued to a radio handset. One of the six artillery rounds fired on def-con one had landed between the perimeter foxholes and the outpost. On impact, Hardin and a stranger entered the airspace above the foxhole at the same time. This wouldn't have been a problem if they had entered feet first. Cussing his best cuss, Hardin took a butt stroke in the neck and a knee in the stomach, landing in a tangled heap.

"Amps, you got the radio?" Hardin was yelling at the tongue of a boot.

"Are ya shittin' me? It's right where you left it."

"Southern prick," Hardin mumbled through clenched teeth, groping around the outside of the foxhole until he found Amps' rucksack and the handset.

"Who's the stranger?" Hardin asked.

"Carpa. Second Platoon."

"You're lost, asshole."

Listening to the artillery recon sergeant whispering into to his radio handset, quietly screaming, ordering the artillery battery to shift fire, then to fire a right-by-piece so he could identify the gun tube that was out of alignment, Hardin shook his head.

With artillery rounds falling in front of them and behind them, the outpost blew their Claymores. Instead of infiltrating back to the company perimeter whispering Rawhide, the outpost started a two-phase operation called, "Grab your shit and run."

Hardin started laughing.

The Soldiers Guide clearly stated that shitless did not mean a soldier didn't have to take a shit. Shitless meant that one's asshole was suffering from extreme compression, generating pressures of 400,000 pounds per square inch.

With death shaping his instinct, a grunt with a tight ass could barely lift his leg. But here were the boys, screaming "Rawhide!" Five General Issue, GI studs, were running, jumping, crashing, and falling. With their weapons banging from tree to tree, they were screaming, "Raw-fucking-hide," "She-ii-it," and other split infinitives that grunts used with clarity.

Plunging headlong through the jungle, five grunts traded slang for slang, from rat-fuckin'-shit to Rap's Chicago street English.

"Amps, where's the Greek?" Hardin said.

"He crawled out mumblin' some shit about you bein' crazy."

* * *

Morning brought a recon patrol to secure the gear the OP left behind. The new men inspected the impact crater between the OP and the perimeter.

"Joe, you look like hell this morning." Stubbs was coddling a fresh cigarette.

"Thank you," Joe said, searching the ridgeline to the north.

"The dinks we banged were in a dry wash headin' south, not too alert," Stubbs said. With a thought striking him, he looked past his coffee.

"The dinks you banged were carryin' the new model AKs—AK-Ms," Joe said.

"That makes me feel better," Stubbs said.

Cigarette in hand, cigar in mouth, Stubbs and Captain Joe stood into a singular thought, wondering why the sleeves on Drips' jungle fatigues never reached the midway point of his forearms. Drips was so large his helmet looked like the top of his head, and his shirt would not button past the second button.

Odd as Drips was, Stubbs could laugh, deciding Drips' attitude matched his uniform.

Whether ginning up a bout of mischievous mockery or flogging an officer with exasperating nonsense, Drips intended to solicit a reaction. He was restless to keep from concentrating. Amps was his current target.

"Hey man, how's the El Tee doin', still shakin'?" Drips pointed his weapon like a toy pistol to emphasize his comments. Amps nodded and kept cleaning the handset.

"Why don't you ask him yourself?" Drips didn't like officers.

"What's gonna happen today, Amp-Man?"

"Chuck's gonna rub us into a shit-blister, then carve us up with a limp cob."

"You're a hick-fucker, ya know that? Those were main-line dudes we banged, straight outta Laos. We're better off in the boonies; believe it. Some base camp's gonna get whacked."

Drips whispered, "Ya got some dew?" Not talking to Drips when he expected you to brought a burst of hot air forced through a tight jaw. Drips' body filled Amps' field of vision. He expected Amps to be happy about their chat.

"Shit," Amps said. "The El Tee would waltz on my nuts if he caught me doin' that shit. You too." Drips dropped into a full squat to inspect Amps' work.

"Yeah, maybe he does care. He reminds me of my kid brother. Now, if Fish had some whiskey," Drips said, wetting his lips with his tongue, nodding with a pleasured expression.

"Some sour mash, that'd be good."

Drips scratched at the stubble on his face, his mind trying to locate a reason to talk to Stubbs. Drips scooped a handful of dirt, sifted out the leaves, stepped into his "travelin' man" routine, and said, "What's happenin', Platoon Sergeant?"

"The senior medic is givin' shots." Stubbs waited for a smart-ass reply, his deeply lined face packing a renewed intensity. Stubbs had classified Drips' allergic reaction to the clam-surprise he had sampled in Ban Me Thuot as a self-inflicted wound.

Watching Drips strangle a tree while he tried to piss and keep from screaming gave the brothers more than enough reason not to talk to him. Clap-clap was not recommended for hiking either. Asian clap produced a bowlegged version of the airborne shuffle, complete with short steps and howling.

"We got commo?" Stubbs asked.

Amps snorted. "Of course. I could use a blow job."

"While you're on your knees, Amps, take care of this," Stubbs said, as he gave his balls a toss. Amps jumped away and shouldered his rucksack.

Joe jarred Hardin from his trance. "Hardin, we're bein' extracted. PZ, ASAP. Another Special Forces camp. Ever heard of Duc Co?" Joe asked.

"Duc Co, Dak To, Dip-Shit: who fuckin' cares? Mother best make up his mind."

Joe cracked a grin and said, "Duc Co's got flat ground."

"That don't mean nothin'. Duc Co's just another two-syllable place to die." Hardin turned, sidestepping a tangle of bamboo, knowing his friend Dig-it was right.

Reynolds, a Harley-riding GI from Baker, California, PeeWee, the shortest Mexican in Vietnam, and Nasty, the dark-skinned Mediterranean, were hovering in a confidential wad, talking secret enlisted-man blather when Hardin approached. Continuing to hover, they stopped talking and stared when he got close enough to hear.

"What are you fuckers lookin' at?" Hardin said.

"What are we doin,' El Tee?" Reynolds was the current spokesman.

"Wha'd'a ya gotta know for, Cowboy? We're outta here. Pickup in an hour."

"Where we goin'?" Hardin could not resist stirring their tools.

"You boys should be flattered. We're goin' back to Dak To." Silence fell over the group. Hardin laughed to myself. He knew the word would spread. That'll teach the nosy bastards to roger-off and mind their own business.

* * *

The chopper ride to Duc Co found the six remaining Hill People searching the terrain for familiar landmarks; their faces lined with rigid concern. The Dak To Special Forces camp, the Poco River, Rocket Ridge, the landmarks they would not forget.

Hours later, the company sat in platoon sectors near the end of the airstrip at Duc Co, waiting for orders. Joe was escorted to the Special Forces command bunker. Once the rush of this new AO subsided, the field judges for Hardin's rumor came calling. Shadow and Ski crouched near his rucksack, courting a special brand of poison.

"This ain't Dak To." Ski never embellished his words.

"Who said it was?" Hardin asked.

"PeeWee said ya told him we were goin' back to Dak To." Hardin had them now.

"Duc Co, this is Duc Co. This is where we're goin." Ski looked at Shadow for guidance. "PeeWee heard what I said. He's fuckin' with ya."

Paybacks. Not even Reynolds would back PeeWee on this one. Don't fuck with the Hill People: they'll wash your mouth out with lead.

CHAPTER TEN

Hippie and Fish

Airstrip, Duc Co Special Forces Camp. 1550 Hours.

With an area of operations somewhat larger than Abigail's ass, the company sallied off the end of the airstrip with files abreast, heading for a flat high ground that overlooked the SF camp. Within thirty meters the point squad was forced into a single file, slashing at stiff spires of eighteen-foot elephant grass, each pass of the machete's blade swelling in volume.

Eighty meters and fifty minutes later, with visibility reduced to one meter, Hippie's point squad and First Platoon stood exhausted, dominoes in a raceway, trapped in a tunnel.

LeCotte, boiling with frustration, plowed from side to side, throwing his body into the grass, his mouth hissing like air pulsing from a donkey's ass.

Tag, a large white man from Philly, enjoyed rolling up his sleeves to show off his biceps. He seemed oblivious to pain. With his hands and forearms shredded and bleeding, his machete kept a steady pace. Dusty, yellow pollen stained his uniform to an odd shade of brown.

A blood-sweat mixture ran down Amps' cheek. His forehead had a nasty gash. Tennessee had fallen and slit his ear. Pops' lips were sliced, his tongue wagging like a snake.

Hardin grabbed the hook and spit out, "Six, we're on the compass, visibility zero."

"Roger, out." Joe and his cabin boy were still standing on the airstrip.

Eighty meters into a meandering tube of razor-edged grass, blood splashed as freely as the first whispers of dawn. GIs huddled, then dispersed, confused and frightened by the alarming noise of the machetes. Groans of pain rang like claps of thunder in a canyon clogged with bodies. Men stumbled, then lashed out, hacking wildly at the grass, screaming, straining for another step, their senses clear one moment and fogged the next. The tunnel smelled of ripened blood and something much more profound.

"Fire! The grass is on fire!" Shadow's scream lanced the day.

The roar of expanding air amplified a sudden thrust of exploding grass. The fire's heat swept over the GIs, consuming oxygen and reason. Currents of air forced the upper reaches of the grass to whip one direction then another.

Men panicked. Weapons were useless.

Above the roar, Shadow kept screaming. Shadow never screamed.

They were climbing a small rise. Hippie was crashing toward clean air, Nasty on his hip.

Spirits ruptured like eggs, splattering shell and yoke against an inevitable madness. GIs threw their bodies into the grass, the tunnel mushrooming with rage. Uniforms hung in rags, boots and shirt collars were soaked with blood, and rucksacks clogged the tunnel as GIs collapsed in the heat, gasping for air.

No platoon leader, no platoon sergeant, just men fighting to survive, reaching out for another man's courage. The fire expanded and contracted, pushing gusts of smoke and debris deeper into their starving lungs. Burning alive, with their flesh and fat boiling amongst charred rags, with their teeth wedged out in proclamation, these soldiers knew the drill.

Weapons were untended. Medics scrambled up and down the tunnel, stumbling into the next GI without finishing with the last, bouncing like vultures tending a knacker's yard.

Death gave the orders now. The killing zone was perfect.

With the collapse of reason, fear pinched Hardin's features. His men were strangers. They were fighting the grass like rats trapped in a flooding sewer, clawing at each other's progress. The medics seemed detached, like feverish wards.

Hardin looked ahead for Amps. Hippie recoiled, then fell. Tag and Nasty returned fire over the top of Hippie's body. The ambush brought confusion to its knees.

A man could drive nails with the sound of Hippie's scream.

Up and down the line, GIs fired blindly to their flank, the roar of gunfire concentrated by the density of the grass. Magazine after magazine, M-16 rounds rip into the void. Ski and The Frenchman mowed their sectors flat. The firefight ended in seconds. The grass was burning and Charlie was gone.

Medics stumbled forward following Stubbs and Pops. Their kits were depleted.

Hippie, the California dreamer, was dead, a piece of elephant grass clinched in his teeth.

Pissed, as if any target would do, Fish sank into a squat and grabbed Hippie's hand. These two grunts had fought the war together with an impulsive instinct that shapped their destiny. They had lived with a frail appetite for life and a luck they could not fathom. Hippie had survived the Battle for Dak To and died in a shit hole called Duc Co. Hippie had thirty-six days left on his tour of duty.

Two GIs from the point squad were wounded—Snoopy and Jinx.

Wasted by survival's urgency, the bodies of the men left standing were a latticework of cuts, their uniforms a sweat-soaked collage of blood and debris, their expressions locked in a sterile sneer, their faces coated with a red-brown sheen. These impressions would never fade.

Drips set Hippie's body to his shoulder and plowed forward on point, daring the enemy to fight. Mex and Blood ran hard at his heel, covering Hippie's final hump.

"I didn't think Hippie would die," Amps said to no one.

An hour before twilight, with sandbags in hand, the company dug in. Drips sat in the middle of the perimeter watching the medevac chopper fade from view. Drips, Mex, Ski, Shadow, and Bucks were saying good-bye. Fish sat apart from the group, slowly sharpening his machete with a bastard file, his stroke delivered with a jeweler's eye.

Fish needed to kill somebody.

The radio barked, bringing Amps awake.

"Hey wake up, El Tee. Captain Joe wants to talk to you big-timers." The lieutenants drifted to Joe's foxhole with no sense of purpose.

Fuck the war.

"You got some great digs here, Captain." Gator's outburst took Joe by surprise.

"Shut up, Gator. Brigade is sending out a field-order for the defense of the Duc Co Special Forces Camp during the Tet holiday."

Jesus, Hardin thought. *Now we get fucked in writing.*

The five-paragraph field-order was a rear-echelon illusion filled with well-known secrets, laughable numbers and coded circumstance. Spawned through the bowels of careering expressions, these field orders were an antic attempt to detail a game of chance. Paper lifers used the field order to bring folly into a slightly sharper focus.

After all, what was more preposterous than an operations officer—a major who had never been shot at—standing in front of a spot-lighted map, in a darkened sandbag bunker, his face hidden in the half-shadow of a hooded lamp, holding a rubber-tipped pointer, telling a general what the Viet Cong planned to do and how they planned to do it?

Hardin offered Joe a splash of cold coffee. Andy and Gator sat in a blended intensity, rocking on the purchase of their ass, delivered safely from disaster without a scratch. Hardin stood to show off his shredded uniform, making sure his balls were exposed. Blood soaked the front of his shirt.

Captain Joe surveyed the cuts on Hardin's jaw and forearms. "Andy, you got the outpost on this rise, forty meters out. Any questions?" Gator was raising his hand.

"Why Duc Co?"

Joe turned on Gator like a drunk sniffing hot pussy. "Get the fuck away from me, Gator." Hippie was Joe's friend. They shared cigars: saluting the men they had known.

Sapped by fatigue, Joe sat alone in silence, fighting the residue of losing hope.

* * *

For the next four days, scantily clad GIs stalked through a low canopy jungle and occupied an abandoned firebase, complete with bunkers and one strand of concertina wire.

The encampment echoed with life, the musty bunkers offering evidence of the complications of fear. The doorways, the gun ports, the connecting pathways, and the straggling debris, all witness to the secrets old forts seemed to keep. Tired sandbags formed a meandering mosaic of stoop-shouldered posts, the tombstones of a front-line trace.

Completing a rigorous check for booby traps, Captain Joe sounded the all clear.

The night sky exuded a glow like the unblemished depth of a clear mountain lake. The starlight was so crystalline a man could whirl the stars into pinwheels or send them chasing with a burst of air. The heavens sat like holographs in a magic lantern. The moon arced to the left leaving just a sliver to hang a rucksack on. Starlight pierced the canopy along the edge of the wire. Leafy shadows danced.

Alone, Hardin sat with his chin perched over a steaming cup of coffee, watching the wire. As usual, his thoughts were of home, picking wooden pins from a clothesline. He missed his bride, his Linda. She was a beautiful woman, with deep brown eyes, full of love: a good friend.

His dad, the Major. Well, Stubbs would have to do.

The old sergeant was trooping a hard-beaten path, bunker to bunker, back and forth.

He found Shadow singing "The shadow of your smile, when you are gone." On this night the melody rang a haunting chord. The words could jostle the last tear from a good man's soul. The words, like a stranger's poem, embraced what a friend might miss the most.

Stubbs didn't have a best friend. Once a week, as if triggered by a reckoning, Stubbs would fall in with a new man, to tighten his grip. Then, without warning, as if pissed off, he would seethe through the confines of the new man's mind and rip him a new asshole. Stubbs did not want to be too close.

"Not so loud, Shadow. How ya doin'?"

Paul Albert Webster was Shadow's Christian name. Alone, as he preferred, he would watch the wire throughout the night. Since his time in Dak To, he sang softly of his memory and rarely spoke.

"I'm doin', Sarge." Shadow's voice begged for yesterday.

"Wha'd'a we got out there?" Two men, two dark spots, parked side by side in a full squat, cradling their weapons inside their thighs, staring vacantly into the wire. Shadow rocked sideways to resettle his feet, then looked toward Stubbs.

"Nothin' out there, Sarge. Dead men, draggin' their chains around. Losin' Hippie, that's somethin' to think about." Shadow turned back into the night to wait for what might come next.

"Hang in there, Shadow." Stubbs leaned on Shadow's shoulder as a gesture of dependence, and stood with a sigh.

"Too short to give it up now, Sarge."

* * *

Toggled to Hippie's death, the GIs of Charlie Company waited, coffin-faced, savoring the prospects of revenge. With the battalion commander's war room set in the center of the encampment, the other three rifle companies in the battalion were scattered around the Special Forces camp. Captain Joe had volunteered to be the reaction force for the operation. Two things made nursing the Old Man tolerable: good resupply, and good artillery support.

"Sarge, mail and rations are inbound, five minutes out," Tennessee said.

Radio transmissions burst with cautious joy; an in-country R&R. Fish, Amps, and PeeWee ran toward the chopper pad like kids racing to touch home plate for a game of work-up. Hardin watched the chopper land, wondering if the home front had sent him a Christmas treat. He laughed. "Be hard to get what I want in a cardboard box," he said to himself.

Captain Joe had Gator and Andy locked in a con-fab.

"Hardin, we have new maps: easy terrain." Joe handed him four maps.

"Easy for Chuck. Bet the terrain at the end of the airstrip looks easy, too."

"What's your problem?" With this challenge from Andy, Hardin held up the maps.

"My problem? Let's see: no comics for five days. Some SF pukes walk me into a tunnel of fire. And you dickheads never seem to be where Chuck is when Chuck's scatterin' my shit. I guess you're my problem, asshole."

Joe raised a hand. "Lighten up."

"Lighten up," Hardin said with a huff. "We're lucky Chuck wasn't ready to bring the damn-damn on us. He could have stomped our shit in that grass. He just wasn't fuckin' ready. He's ready now, and he's gonna DX our nuts."

Air gushed off the rotor blades as Amps grab the packets of mail. "El Tee, you got a package," he said, permitting his eyes to register envy.

Hardin looked at Fish, and said, "Fish, find some jizz. We need to clean some guns."

The return address listed Linda's mother, followed by the address at the farm. The parcel was wrapped in a recycled grocery sack, covering a box the size a sweater might be wrapped in for Christmas. Farm-style chocolate chip cookies had been promised for months. Hardin shook the box, then sniffed at the corner. Knowing that Grandma Ada May had a farm-girl's sense of humor, the box was too light for cookie dough.

Stubbs and Tennessee were half-heartily playing pinochle. Stubbs had one eye closed, guarding against the curling smoke of his cigarette. Blood and Pee-Wee stood near Hardin's shoulder, waiting for the sight and taste of real home-made cookies.

"Chocolate chip cookies, no doubt. Merry Christmas. You dickheads can suck on your C-rats, the El Tee is movin' uptown."

Energized by the news, LeCotte brought Boyle, Butt, The Frenchman, and Nasty to mooch. Hardin did his best to taunt them, careful not to damage the contents of the package. Pops sat in a full squat talking to Shadow, watching Hardin out of the corner of his eye.

Hardin raised the box, and said, "I'll save ya a couple, Pops."

Beyond reason, childishly laughing, he surrounded his booty and tore off the brown paper sack. The contents were sealed in clear cellophane, and he was looking at the bottom of a white cardboard box. This was not a box of cookies. Hardin had been browned with an off-the-shelf surprise. He flipped the box over: unbelievable.

GIs leapt into a raucous dance, then began a rhythmic chant of "horseshit." The brothers exchanged full-speed daps, cackling and slapping each other around. The white dudes were laughing and holding their tools. LeCotte led the cheers.

The El Tee had been handed the rat-fuck of the war.

Hardin sat stock-still, like shit set in lemon Jell-O, staring at a dozen horse turds neatly arranged in a four-by-three brace, and sealed in clear cellophane. A gold and black elliptical logo proclaimed the goodness of Rambler's Road Apples. The twelve symmetrical turds had been dried and placed in prissy, dark-brown fluted cups.

Horse shit from his mother-in-law, what a great shot. Now he had a reason to live through the war. He could hear Grandma Ada May and Linda laughing their belly laughs when they mailed their fun. Misty was Grandpa Karl's horse.

Stubbs put out his cigarette so he could laugh. The brothers continued to work the El Tee's dilemma with a thigh-slapping dance. Tennessee now had the material he needed when Hardin talked about his ex-wife's shooting spree. The story swept the firebase.

Gawking bursts of laughter brought a parade of boonie-rats to check out the El Tee's chocolate chip turds. Squads of GIs passed Hardin's bunker en masse.

"Jesus, El Tee, looks like you get the bone today. Horse shit beats an AK." Dark shades of combat humor that made an officer the chump would last a lifetime.

Hardin jumped to his feet. "Stubbs, I'll be right back."

With the gait of a rebel, Hardin was up to the eastward, horse shit in hand, sallying down the way, waving the box around to clear his path, stomping off toward the Old Man's command bunker. With no mind for the judge advocate, he barged through the front door. The battalion commander's inter-sanctum, with its radio whips and secret people, turned instantly dark and suddenly quiet.

Colonel Wild Bill Dimmick sat with his muscatel mug perched behind a small wooden field table, surrounded by the chatter of radio traffic and his concerned staff. The ambush required a cobra's precision and fast feet. Hardin's sudden appearance brought challenging eyes which he countered without thought of circumstance or consequence.

"Here," he yelled, then slammed the road apples on a field table, announcing to the staff, "That's what I think of your battalion." The Old Man grinned instantly.

The impact was immediate. Staff patches sat speechless, their clean-shaven mugs at odds with the day. By the time any sound filtered from the bunker, Hardin was halfway back to his rucksack. Majors one through five would never forgive the challenge. Not a matter of disrespect or of insubordination—more of a test to validate a covenant.

"Wha'd ya do with the horse shit, El Tee?" Stubbs' natural instinct started covering Hardin's tracks. "El Tee, what are we in for here?"

Hardin shrugged, and said with a risible gesture, "Hard tellin'. This puppy could go either way. I slammed the horse shit on the Old Man's desk and told his staff that's what I thought of their battalion." Stubbs pinched his cigarette. With his balls churning, Stubbs tried to imagine his lieutenant in shackles doing bad time in the Long Binh Junction stockade.

"You did that?" Stubbs methodically shaped the excess ashes at the end of his cigarette into a perfect cone, gathering his thoughts. "You did that in front of the Old Man?" Stubbs flipped the cigarette over the crest of the hill.

"Yep, the staff sat there like green gas locked in a plastic sack."

"Green gas locked in a plastic sack," Stubbs said, coaxing a weary grin. He paused and turned toward the wire to talk to the breeze. "Jesus Christ. I've been in this man's Army a long time, and I've never heard of anything like that. El Tee, you better hope the Old Man likes you."

"Wha'd'a ya think, Stubbs?" Stubbs continued to stare at the wire, shaking his head and taking a draw on a new cigarette.

"I think the colonel is gonna talk to the captain and that box of horse shit is gonna roll downhill and bury your smart ass. That's what I think."

Tennessee stuck the forked end of his M-16 barrel under the packing wire around the C-Ration case and twisted. The wire snapped. He paused, then twisted off the second wire band, and said, "My ex-ol' lady's got a gun better than this one."

"She's a better shot than you, too, Ace. That's no lie."

Charlie Company spent the next nine days walking in quiet canopy, sorting through the memories of a man they called Hippie. A new man decided to start saying, "Far out, Jim," as a tribute to Hippie. That's when Reynolds, the Harley driver, pinned the new man to a tree, lifted the new man's balls with the blade of his knife and told the new man a story.

He told the new man, that if he wanted to see the inside of his ball-sack, all he had to do was keep rankin' on Hippie. When the new man whined, he cut the buttons off his pants.

Stubbs told the new man that he could pray. Or, he could shut the fuck up.

McGregor was the new man. He was a married man, but whether he had a family or not, no one knew. It would be better if he didn't. With his balls on parade he knew the men of First Platoon were his friends.

Or maybe he knew he was alone.

Blood gave him a boot lace to stitch his crotch.

With Pops and LeCotte monitoring the repairs, McGregor laced his crotch closed, wondering if Reynolds was finished with his lessons and listening to the radio reports that the Special Forces camp at Kontum was nearly overrun by North Vietnamese regulars.

* * *

Duc Co Plateau. 0640 Hours.

The glimmer of dawn painted the riverbed with streaks of orange, brushing the air with pollen and light wisps of mist. The riverbanks ran flat for twenty meters. Washed rock and clumps of shoulder-high grass stretched to the base of a sixty-foot bluff on the left flank. Dense jungle choked the right flank forming an intermittent tunnel.

Charlie Company moved north, scouring the western flank of the blue-line. Shocked at times, the sound of their boots intensified, amplified by the merging vegetation. Round worn rocks tapped out short, cracking shouts. Frightened men joined the heat of the jungle.

The birds had gone quiet.

Brittle wedge grass, mottled with gold and whites, brushed at their boots scattering broken bits of straw across the rocks. Islands of small trees stood with their roots exposed. The bluff, a composite of layered clay, rose as an abrupt complication.

If not for a protruding, powder-gray stria that ran its face at a thirty-degree incline, the bluff would force Joe to stay in the wash.

The morning was filled with changing prospects straining the frayed cords of discipline. Tempers were short. Unwilling to be led, or driven, grunts searched the wadi with an aimless eye; their instincts fowled by not caring. With limited visibility, grunts ambled along.

Alerted by a sharp crack near the base of the bluff, Mex froze and sank into a deep squat. Searching the wadi his eye anchored itself to a point near the base of the bluff. Mex moved forward and set in behind a rock hollow.

Death's dance erupted into a concert when Tag pushed the point squad into an arc and went to ground. With cold stares grunts waited and the riverbed fell silent. Ten minutes passed, with Tag and Fish exchanging signals and shrugs. Captain Joe pointed at Hardin and then at the top of the bluff.

Hardin mouthed the words "no way," then gave his commander a quick nod. First Platoon crawled to the left flank and mounted the base of the bluff and started climbing. The side of the bluff left GIs exposed, waiting for the impact of the first round.

With temperatures rising, Amps breathed in short gusts, his throat clogged with dust. A breeze rustled through the jungle. The chatter of the water was precise and concealing, marking the platoon's progress with bits of anguish. Fighting a short patch of vines, Shadow swore softly. The top of the bluff rolled away from his eye into a thick blanket of dry grass and a grove of spindly trees.

Drips, Fish, and Mex crawled over the crest of the bluff. A breeze flowing out of the gorge billowed the leaves creating a continuous motion in the canopy. Within fifty meters the platoon had spread into two staggered files, paralleling the river. Pops and PeeWee had point.

Stepping high to silence the grass, PeeWee covered his face with extended fingers, then extended one finger, signaling Drips forward. A hard-ridden old man stood near a large tree at the edge of the bluff, watching the company trace the blue-line.

Sporting a small pouch, a bolt-action carbine, shorts, a ragged khaki shirt, a flop hat, and sandals, the old man didn't know he was in trouble.

Drips moved in three electric steps, grabbed Chuck, spun him around, knocked the carbine aside, and pinned his neck against the tree. Chuck's feet were off the ground and Drips was choking the life out of the now-defenseless scout.

Fish pushed himself into Drips' face, quietly yelling. Tired of the abuse, Drips threw the VC into the base of the tree, knocking Fish on his ass. Slapping the man to shut him up, Drips ripped open the pouch. Holding a fist full of money, Drips gave Stubbs a questioning shrug then stuffed the money into his rucksack. The would-be scout was a tax collector.

"Six, we bagged a scout," Tennessee said, watching Stubbs tie the prisoner's hands.

"Say again..." small-arms fire erupted along the blue-line clipping Joe's words.

First Platoon bounded into a run along the top of the bluff, dragging the tax-man. Searching for a route to the river, Rap found a draw and signaled for a hasty perimeter. Small-arms fire ran in spurts at the base of the bluff.

"Stubbs, gag the dink," Hardin said, whirling his hand through the air, signaling for a hasty ambush. Ski took the draw on the right flank. The Frenchman took the trail on the left flank. Rap set his fire team to cover the Frenchman and his back. Pops and PeeWee were covering Ski and his back. Stubbs filled the gaps with two-man teams.

Blood, in a fit of rage, grabbed a cherry, forcing McGregor's face to the platoon's left flank. Blood would beat this new man until his instincts were honed like a ferret's.

Anticipation chipped at the layers of the jungle. Alone, men peered through lenses of dry stubble, refocusing with the sound of each breath. Magazines of ammunition lay side by side, waiting in the bleached grass next to a helmet. Trees marched in place, marking time. The platoon was hiding in a straw maze, lost in the faded-green flickering of an exhausted jungle.

Shadow's lips were moving, singing his song. An odd man would shun the pain of that old song. An odd man had little to remember. An odd man would die on this bluff, a man new to the violence.

With Butt trying to sneeze, LeCotte pushed his face into the grass.

Pops worked to hook an ammunition belt to Ski's machine gun, his movement barely noticed. The air in the grass was dry to the touch. The ambush set took less than a minute.

Hiding in an open patch of knee-high grass next to a trail was an enigmatic exercise akin to hanging your ass over the flame of a blowtorch and farting. Hardin's patch of grass was on fast forward. The one sound he could hear was Hippie's scream.

Guts were retching, pounding an ancient drum. The sequence surged forward, and then accelerated. A silent scream rocked the canopy when Viet Cong exploded from both flanks. The first three flat-landers caught a burst from The Frenchman's gun, and Ski blew the lead man from the draw back over the bluff.

The VC disappeared, then recovered in seconds.

McGregor, Blood's Seventh-Day cherry, his would-be ferret, stood up. His cheek ripped wildly. A barrage tore chunks of flesh from his head. Dust bounced from his shirt as the AK rounds pierced his chest. His body folded. His knees buckled, the force of a round throwing his chest backward, lifting his hands.

His weapon fired blindly through the canopy.

Spitting his words, Rap fought the dancing end of the Frenchman's ammunition belt. As McGregor's face fell in pieces, outrunning his helmet, the lower part of his jaw landed near Rap's forearm. Recognizing the row of teeth, Rap fired into the jungle as fast as he could load.

In that moment, the Viet Cong vanished, creating a frightening, shocking calm, leaving but faint silhouettes on the edge of the glen. A drum roll of sound followed as empty magazines were replaced, and machine gun bolts were reset. Expanding the perimeter, GIs began to crawl outward, pushing their search into the jungle.

Blood trails from the killing zone ran in vectors, like radiant heat.

Stoic, as if imprisoned, Rap and Doc put the pieces of McGregor's face on the poncho next to his neck. McGregor, the tax collector, and four VC were dead. Mex cut the twine binding the tax collectors hands and rolled his body over the bluff. He didn't want anybody to cut off the old man's ears.

Blood may have been looking for redemption as he crouched next to McGregor's broken body to register his fractured image. McGregor's hair did not look red now—more a crimson brown. Blood stood away from the poncho, reeling as if he had found revulsion. Nearly shaking, he drained the poncho into the grass, measuring the stain. Or maybe he was praying.

Frustrated, Blood held his rucksack under his arm as if he had stolen the contents. *There is something odd about him,* Hardin thought. Blood's abrupt shoulders had collapsed. A grit seized his face as he touched McGregor's body, examining the wounds, first one, and then another. Hissing out a batch of private words, the big buck sergeant put his knife away.

Walking to a private spot in the foliage, he took the time to look at the blood on his boots—Hippie's blood. The blood had not bothered him yesterday, but it bothered him now. He brushed at the dark brown stain, scuffing the ground.

Yesterday had passed without a hint of passion. Today, before he could warn McGregor about his faithful virtues, the new man was dead. Blood crouched into a pointless rage; his anger focused on an intangible. How could McGregor's head be so tortured?

Having lost the hope of this new man's dream, Blood stood into the heat of the jungle, his expression searching, his body rocking in an agreeable motion. McGregor's campfire burned heavy with charred steaks: fresh biscuits, his laugh echoing like a shift horn.

Blood's dream had vanished long ago. Another new man would come along. Ski wiped at the tears welling in his eyes. He too had hoped for McGregor, for the jovial nature he seemed to have, for the instrument he seemed to be.

"You let this cherry get too close to ya, Ski," Stubbs said, watching as the medic covered McGregor's head with a towel.

"For some reason we knew his name," Ski said, standing, adjusting his machine gun across the front of his waist. Slowly he placed the ammunition belt over his shoulder, then draped a towel over the bolt housing. After a breath he tapped McGregor's boot with his own.

"Charlie Six, this is Lima, we got a dead friendly," Tennessee said, his eyes darting, searching for movement, symmetry in the surrounding vegetation.

"Oh, God. On the way." The sadness in Joe's voice carefully maneuvered through a noticeable deceleration and laminated itself to First Platoon's heart. The war was at them again.

"Sarge, Joe's comin' up the draw." Stubbs scrubbed at his beard looking for the tax collector. He concluded his search by shaking his head and lighting a cigarette.

As the medic covered McGregor's body, Hardin's fever set sail, spilling his breath and forcing him to one knee. His tears wouldn't stop. *Holy shit,* he thought. *What's up with this? Snap out of it, El Tee. You gotta to have a short memory.*

Hardin's mind was cluttered with incomplete portraits, with team pictures of boys too reluctant to smile. Obscure, elusive, contradictory boys, each hoping for one at-bat while grandpa was in town: waiting at the dugout door, scratching a rut with their cleats, watching the outs and the innings slip away.

"Next time, El Tee." Stubbs' voice trailed off.

Stubbs was speed-smoking, holding McGregor's near-empty rucksack, nagging death's latest iteration. His face looked like an aged piece of rough-sawn lumber. He cocked his head as if he had another thought, then tucked the rucksack into the blood soaked poncho.

"Hey, Hardin, we got three dinks, easy as pie." Andy stood-to with disgusting glee.

Knowing Andy's braggadocio would eventually turn to self-loathing, Hardin offered a gesture of grief and lay an open palm toward McGregor's body.

"Nothin' to this combat shit is there, Andy?" Hardin said, letting his shoulders slump. Then, as if following form, he began to read the bloody dog tag. "McGregor, Cameron; Blood Type, A-Positive; Religious Preference, Catholic. You want to read it, too, Andy? For practice maybe. Or maybe your friends are bulletproof."

Shouldering his rucksack, Hardin turned on his friend and said, "Do me a favor, Andy. Stop gettin' excited about this motherfuckin' war."

Andy declared he had done his job. Killing people had become his job: how fucking insane. And what about next time? This band of grunts could do a proper job, next time.

The company nearly ran from the bloodstained glen, racing toward a pick-up zone. Mac's feet hung out of his poncho, bouncing lifeless and free. When grunts carried their dead, a collective despair evolved, and this cumulative process made them look so much alike: hollowed of their core. Their shakes and aching sweats sparred gently with their belly cramps. Their blank faces preached in unison.

They would never have their victory.

Charlie Company had been in the jungle, bush ranging, running at the sharp end, for ninety-eight days. Resisting the calm that came with sleep, they were losing their ability to reason, and losing their willingness to be reasonable.

"We're being extracted for a three-day stand-down at Camp Enari: Fourth Division's base camp at Pleiku. Pickup zone's 300 meters south, as soon as we get there."

Captain Joe was captain-talking. Nobody cared.

CHAPTER ELEVEN

Little Farm Girls

Airborne, Enroute to the 4th Infantry Division Base at Camp Enari. 1115 Hours.

Amid the relief and the freedom of flight and the prospects of a safe haven, disquiet deepened for Hardin. The caricature of his radio operator killed in Dak To donned a rust-colored hue. Black as coal, Dig-it laughed at the sky. McGregor's eye arced away from his head.

Resonant pangs of guilt washed Hardin into a deeper depression, unable to shake war's recurring obligations.

The dead men... their screams were perfect now.

The sun warmed his face as the chopper bounced through a gentle head wind. Sidesaddle, Hardin leaned against the door frame of the Huey. A parched jungle passed below the landing skid. Tears formed in the cradle of his eye.

A sudden jar brought Hardin upright to catch his helmet. His wallet slipped out of the map pocket, and fell away from the aircraft. He tracked the dark brown square with its worn leather corners as it sailed toward the canopy. With a defiant turn, the wallet caught the air and unfolded, tumbling and flapping.

Hardin's keepsakes burst into a cluster.

One by one the pictures he spoke to at twilight filtered into the treetops and vanished. Linda's picture would not last a week on the jungle floor. Linda was a farm girl, accustomed to the rigors of hard work, the vagaries of weather, the serenity of cornfields covered with snow, and the gentle nature of Grandma Ada May.

Linda would find violence in the jungle—violence, and a flimsy replica of humankind.

Linda was Hardin's hope, life's reason. Plus, she was a knock-out: drop-dead gorgeous. At five-two, her long brown hair could turn a man's head. Her true beauty was that she did not know she could consume a man's thoughts. He missed his friend.

Now he would miss her smile.

He wiped a tear from his eye knowing he would miss the ritual of saying goodnight. As the airstrip shaped the horizon, he vowed to say her name as he said the Lord's prayer. After all, Linda was five months pregnant, nurturing a facsimile of his dreams.

From the tarmac the company route-marched to a staging area for a combat re-fit: clean fatigues, radio batteries, food, and ammunition. Poncho tents mushroomed in rows, dressed right and covered down.

"El Tee, I need eight magazines," Tennessee said, feeling a bit inadequate.

"Annie Oakley said ya needed five inches." Hardin slid his air mattress under the poncho pup tent, along with his rucksack and weapon.

"She'd'a just blown it off."

"You and Amps don't talk to each other much, Tennessee."

"You're right, El Tee. Cumberland roots run deep. Folks from the hollow don't trust those folks from Kentucky. Me talkin' to Amps would be like Davy Crockett talkin' to Daniel Boone."

* * *

With unpolished brass and a man left to watch the gear, 412 men from the four infantry companies of Second Battalion sallied off to their watering holes to wrap their minds around two minutes on end, and step one more pace around the bend.

The Officers' Club throbbed with perverted purity. The club manager met the battalion officers at the main entrance with a proclamation: non-neutered stock would not set their hooves where the wild bush roamed. Translated, the main portion of the club was off-limits to the visiting bushmen.

Ushered through a luxurious room containing a formal bar, stained-glass lamps, pool tables, a jukebox, a stage for visiting entertainers, and a sea of tables, the herd found itself in a bare cubicle with mess-hall tables and metal folding chairs.

"This is bullshit," Andy exclaimed, assuming a beer-scoffing pose and waving his arms. "Let's drink outside the fuckin' wire."

"Easy, Andy. We can use the rest," Joe said.

"Who needs a rest?" Andy shouted. "I need booze and pussy. One of 'em ain't in this empty room." Andy stomped toward the door. Joe caught him by the arm.

"Lighten up, stud. When the time is right we'll take over this pop-stand and shuffle down their precious fucking bar."

Officers lied as if they were GIs. Facing a mountain of empty beer cans, Hardin found himself on the outer edge of an olive-drab junkyard. One story mounted another, as if derived from parallel occurrences. Andy's brand of distinction bore the trappings of a siege.

With the reflexes of the geezer he had come to be, Joe rang the bell, announcing a call to arms. The heathens were taking over the bar. With a crash and a holler, as if on cue, the battalion commander burst into the room through an outside entrance, his ice-blue eyes laced with scotch.

"We got trouble." The piercing-eyed glare the Old Man liked to use when danger was afoot kept jumping into a grin. "The enlisted bucks tore down the Enlisted Men's club: put the god-damn roof on the ground. The sergeants tore apart the inside of the NCO club."

"Who cares?" The Old Man shrugged and continued.

"The MPs formed a riot wedge and waded into the fight with their batons. Sixty-three MPs are in the hospital."

Drunk to a man, the officers stumbled into the street, right into a corral of MP gun-jeeps, complete with M-60 machine guns locked and loaded.

"Holy horseshit," Joe said, adjusting his shirt.

"They look fuckin' serious," Andy said. A bullhorn broke in.

"Listen up. The division commander has ordered us to get you animals off his base camp. We're gonna escort you back to your assembly area. Now move out."

"Fuckin' leg-pussy motherfuckin' cock suckin' son of a bitch." A stranger screamed at the bullhorn. Another stranger grabbed his arm.

"Back off, Lieutenant." A third stranger pushed the man away from the MP.

"Pig fuckin' cock sucker," he screamed again. The MP started forward. Another MP pulled him back. "Come on pussy. I'll kick your fuckin' face in, you and your fuckin' general."

"You watch your mouth, Lieutenant." A major said, swinging his rank around.

"I don't work for you, asshole, so you can hump on outta my airspace."

Hardin wanted to sky-up but had no place to run. His father's Army was holding him at gunpoint, throwing him out of the first secure area he had seen since the second battle of Shilo—or was it Vicksburg?

This purest form of Battle Bullshit, this perfect wrinkle, demonstrated why the grunt was the root cause of any problem a general could possibly have. Under the headlamp of a dozen gun-jeeps, a battalion of drunken paratroopers wrestled with their gear. Shouts of laughter mixed with shouts of anger as the grunts shook at the cobwebs.

Hardin found Tennessee exchanging words with his air mattress, sucking on a near-empty bottle of bourbon. Bombed into a pile of giggling rubble, knee spasms had him turning in circles, snorting as if a sudden noise might help.

"Don't forget the radio," Stubbs barked, fondling a welt under his left eye.

Spitting whiskey, as if to make a point, Tennessee yelled, "Fuck the radio. You want it, Stubby, you carry it." Then he raised his bottle. "Just kiddin', Sarge. Want some whiskey? This shit ain't as good as that sour mash old Dickle makes down in Cascade Hollow."

"I can't find my weapon. Come on, we gotta move." Stubbs was sobering fast.

"Shit, Sarge, I'm already movin." Tennessee's poncho jumped into a heap and threw him to the ground. Stubbs threw his poncho on top of Tennessee and laughed.

"Those MPs want to fire us up," Hardin said.

"They'd be dead in seconds. Besides there aren't many of 'em left." Stubbs was right.

GIs fell into a sobering, rumpled silence, staggering down a dirt road in the dark: a cluster-fuck of the highest order. No longer young, the battalion marched back to hell, playing flourishes with half-empty bottles of booze.

The formula for their despair was exponential. Dak To had blood soaked red clay and shattered towers of jungle. Wounded men died waiting for a dust-off, and a short drop killed forty-two soldiers. Kontum had elephants, mortars, an ambush, a counter-ambush, the dog, and grunts running for their lives. Ban Me Thuot had a hot LZ, an ambush, and thousands of NVA hiking through the weeds. Duc Co had elephant grass, a fire, a dead Hippie, a tax collector, a hasty-ambush, and McGregor.

Marinating in whiskey, with grapeshot in their ass and pussy on their mind, the GIs knew they had been fuddled and fucked by the frogs running the train. After losing eighty-one grunts killed, and thirty-four grunts wounded from Dak To, to Ban Me Thuot, and then Duc Co, a general with polished boots and a sissy belt decided the best remedy for their infectious despair was a walk in the woods.

What a shit-hot war.

The uprising would inspire the company until the next firefight. And inspiration, no matter how shallow, fostered hope. And with hope, a grunt might survive.

Uncle stuck around the base camp to resolve the damages and pay the bills.

* * *

The moon mounted the upper edge of the canopy casting a glow on the airstrip. A night chill found GIs huddled in a drunken haze, savoring the last sweet scraps of whiskey and the echoes of glee. GIs lay on the tarmac like rusting hulks, waiting for spare parts.

"Amps, wake 'em up," Stubbs said. Amps nodded and turned on his radio.

Splashing water on his face, Hardin said, "My head feels like it's filled with mud."

Joe slapped the tarmac with his comics and said, "Lift off in fifteen minutes. We've got one map. We're close until we get more." No one responded, so he rubbed his neck and stretched. His face looked like a chattered piece of rusted steel.

"Any questions?" Joe creased his brow, then fumbled with the smell of stale whiskey.

"I had a question yesterday," Hardin said, boosting his rucksack into action.

"I can't believe we only lasted eight hours," Gator said.

"I want some real chicken eggs," Stubbs said, looking into a freshening sky.

Before coffee was served, slicks appeared on the horizon from four points on the compass. Hardin sat in the doorway of a Huey, staring at a blank horizon. The beans-and-franks C-Ration can mounted on the left side of the door-gunner's machine gun was worn thin where the ammunition belt slid over the can into a feed tray.

Suspended on a swivel mount, outside of the chopper, the barrel pointed toward the ground. The bipod legs on the front of the gun were folded back along the barrel, as was the top carrying handle. Hardin took note of the ammunition belt hanging across the can: solid red-tipped tracer rounds.

After thirty minutes of cutting circles in a clear sky, the platoon was inserted on a deserted plateau with a squad of men from Alpha Company.

"Amps, who are these fuckin' immigrants?" Hardin asked.

Muck-smeared, like pigs in heat, nine strangers stood in a tight circle. Unable to move without breaking wind, they were suffering from rectal thumb lock, complete with swollen tongues and disconnected eyeballs. Nose-deep in indignation, they stared at Amps with their foggy defiance.

"You dumb shits are fuckin' lost," Amps said, shucking his rucksack.

"We're from Alpha Company, Second Platoon, sir." Holy fuck, Amps thought, the dumb ass called me "sir." Bad-luck Alpha was two-bits south of a dime.

"Well, Fuck-stick, spread out and find a hole."

Aware of the curse this encounter with bad-luck Alpha might portend, Hardin lay in a small depression surrounded by Mex's squad. He was brave until Mex told him he could not avoid the curse. "Look what happened to Hippie," Mex said. "Hippie got drunk and passed out in Alpha Company's orderly room. Now he's dead."

Try as he might, Hardin could not ignore the strangers. First they wanted the platoon's radio frequency, then they wanted water, and then they wanted to set out Claymores. And then this bastard touched Amps' radio, suggesting the two men talk about war.

Hardin scrubbed at the crust on his face, listening to the odds and ends. Alerted by what was an empty laugh, he turned an ear to the source.

With bad-luck Alpha rooted to the ground next to his shoulder, Hardin mustered a caustic tone. "Today is not a good day to talk about combat. If you see Chuck, blow him away. Otherwise, take a break." The stranger's real problem was that his perfect sobriety was not dealing well with Hardin's need for another beer.

The morning leaked away with all hands playing hide-the-landing-zone. After the boys from bad-luck Alpha flew away, Stubbs stood-to, counting bodies. Eleven helmets were listed as a combat loss. Nasty, LeCotte, PeeWee, and Fish were wearing simonized black helmets with bright white letters: MP. Taking an MP's helmet, like taking an ear, inured a grunt to a spectrum of false colors and heightened the intrigue of his war.

Holding tight to their tools and lying through their teeth, folklore put the platoon body count at twenty MPs. LeCotte bagged four. According to Tag, Amps started the riot.

"El Tee, Captain Joe wants a heading of 315 degrees. We're lookin' for a blue-line in a klick." Amps nursed a bruised right hand.

"Ah, the tuneful stench of bullshit in heat," LeCotte said. Grabbing the hook from Amps, he started singing. "Red shit, green shit, round the town... Found my dick, on the ground... Met a girl that sucked so well... Couldn't stand that nasty smell."

Prepared for the second verse, wincing as he fought to keep his balance, LeCotte fell over a tree root and lay face down in a thicket, cussing Boyle's mama.

The sweatband inside Hardin's helmet liner had compressed a one-inch ring into his skull, making his hair follicles itch. Weak-kneed, without a map, left him chasing a bobbing needle around the compass face. Catching his balance with the hand that held the compass, he recovered then fell over the same tree root to a chorus of cheers. His authority was sewer bound.

Tennessee keyed the handset, blew air at it several times, and cleared his throat. "Roger Dodger, puddin' and pie... Fucked the girls and made them cry... It's jungle time and you know why... Bad-luck Alpha just went by."

Amps shook his head. Stubbs lit a cigarette.

The point squad stepped into a timid gait with one accordion move followed by a rush of tender steps. Repeating the pattern, Hardin settled into a nut-jarring wobble behind Fish, the newest MP. Fish had a burlap bag strapped on top of his rucksack, filled with cans of beer.

At odd intervals, Fish would stop, take off his rucksack, check the security of his load, and then make a warning gesture at anyone he could see. Laced with the peculiar coursing the world of Fish's brain was a black and bloody sojourn. A cherry touched his rucksack once. Fish cold-cocked him without so much as a "what-the-fuck."

Fish was put in a body bag in Dak To. Two ammunition drops occurred before a medic found he wasn't dead. Fish was somewhat rational until the medic refused to certify his Purple Heart. Fish drew down on the medic, then told Mex to find a hole for the body. Mex told him he was crazy. That's when Fish decided that being crazy was worth cultivating.

The day turned into a grumpy walk in the woods. What else could it be? One headache led to another. When the point squad found a small blue-line that had taken a direct hit from a bomb drop, Tag decided to take a bath.

"Six, Tennessee here. We're gonna do a test. This one's kinda spooky." Captain Joe's mind was buckled to a scruff of tender whiskers. Tennessee knew if his message was garbled in the unknown, Joe would be too slow to understand.

"This is Six, say again, over." By this time First Platoon had established a thin perimeter and five GIs from Tag's point squad were swimming in the pool.

Tennessee turned off the radio, and Fish issued a can of beer to each man in the platoon and the point squad. Tag was drinking and splashing in the pool when Captain Joe gave out a ridiculous huff, shook his head carefully to keep his eyes from banging together, then told Gator and Andy to establish a perimeter.

Castles of shampoo drifted down stream. No one cared.

"Fish, thanks for the beer." Surprised by the generosity, Hardin struggled to make his gratitude sound gracious. Fish accepted the gesture with a nodding grin.

"Anytime, El Tee." Coming from Fish, this was a compliment. Reckless and outrageous, he was a much better soldier than his lieutenant was. Hardin often wished he were a private, so he could fuck off as he pleased, so he could have a best friend.

Hardin sat in a heap, chugging his beer, watching a curious lot wallow in a state of euphoria. Nasty stood at the edge of the pool talking to his helmet: his MP helmet. Satisfied with the conversation, he filled the helmet with water and threw it into the pool. When it sank, he crossed himself, smiled at the sky and put on his boonie hat: A Chicago Cubs hat.

One boonie hat led to another, each one admired for a moment of satisfaction. The straw hats, cowboy hats, baseball hats, bush hats, bandannas, scarves, and jewelry signaled a level of defiance, of self worth—a reflection of time spent away from the war.

Nuts had donned his father's World War II overseas cap when he cooked his evening meal. When he was killed in Dak To, Hardin kept the overseas cap for luck. He wore it at times—when he picked his teeth with Squeak's bird-spider fang, or talked to Sweet Cheek's shroud line.

The grunts fighting Vietnam's war used their appearance and their superstitions as tools, challenging the Army lifers who wanted to practice their leadership skills. Boonie hats were tailored to a man's antics, clues to the rituals he might use to isolate one man from another.

Humorous disjointed communication added spice to the isolation. And with or without drugs, the humor ran counter to the reality of the jungle and the reality of paybacks. At times, black humor could draw men away from getting even—and once away, draw men together.

To date, those times were rare indeed.

Shedding his Christian name could draw a man from his past and allow him to be lonely. His new name, his nickname, would match his nervous demeanor: Fish, Sax, Dig-it, Squeak, Sweet Cheeks, Tennessee, Amps, Grumpy, Lightning, Blood, Bucks, Whitey, Pops, Rap, PeeWee, Mex, Shadow, Stormy Norm, Ski, Wolf Man, Mr. Monty, Nuts, Linus, Drips, Nasty, Hippie, Tag, Doc, Water Buffalo, Sergeant Snorkel.

Grunts died whispering their nickname, making sure God knew who they were. In the finality of death they prayed, wishing themselves back to places like Highlands Road, wishing away the sheen that coated their memory.

Tennessee kicked Hardin's boot. "Party's over."

"We movin'?"

"Nope." The self-admiration captured by southern-country logic came wrapped in the furls of the Confederacy and oozed from Tennessee's padded, tonal whine.

"Then give yourself a hand-job and quit fuckin' with me." Hardin flashed a grin that was hard to read, and waved him aside.

Joe hollered at Tag, then started ventilating the point squad with nasty, whiskey-stained expletives, arm-waving the instructions for a police-call, fussing over littering the outback by cheerlessly monitoring a cleanup that gained momentum with each empty can. Wanting to help, Hardin threw his beer can into the pool and threw a rock at it.

The rock hit the water with a sucking sound. Hardin stopped for a moment, watching the waves expand and roll into the grass at the crater's edge. The next rock hit home. A knife of clear sunlight flashed off the white and gold label, carving refracted trails of light across the surface of the pool as the can sank into the deep blue hole.

Next time, he thought. *There's gonna be a next time.*

* * *

Moonlight absorbed the colors of the day, mixing the company into a primed silence. GIs crept two-by-two up a long, rolling ridge. The open expanse increased the sense of solitude. Tired boots sketched ribbons in the ankle-high grass and the damp green backdrop faded to a moon-eyed glow.

Shadows stretched across the pale knoll as though long, thin giants.

Clumps of black objects brought fits of urgency. A man's shadow would stall on his right flank then trace an arc around his back, nagging his step. Doc's shadow followed a waveform consistent with the medic's nonchalance.

The company stopped in the lea of the knoll overlooking a cluster of pole-mounted hootches that straddled a meandering draw 200 meters off the left flank. Hardin cupped his ears away from the wind. A creek curling through a draw made enough noise to cover the sound of the running men.

"Six, two men carryin' guns just booked out of the hootches. Want a look-see?"

"Why not." Joe's voice scratched with a dull rasp.

"Tennessee, wait here. Come on, Rap, ditch your pots." Mex, Pops, and Rap followed Hardin deeper into the shadow of the knoll, into a crease, and down into the hollow.

A high pitched voice filtered from the hootches on their left flank.

Skirting a bamboo rail fence, touching each post, Mex stopped, his body folding as if he was built on hinges. With a quick thrust he pointed to his left, the white of his palm flashing in the moonlight. An old woman squatted in a field fewer than thirty meters from the fence. A stream of urine splashed from her ass. She lifted her face toward the knoll. Deep lines weighed on her like troubled times. A hand beckoned her into the recess of a hootch.

Voices and shapes bobbed in and out of the moonlit doorway; their tranquility mixed with urgency. The old woman stepped into the doorway with a carbine in her hand. Again she searched the well-lit surface of the knoll.

Hardin's throat began to knot. The ghosts were gathering.

Rap began to crawl toward the trail, to listen. The rounded shape of his boot heels rolled from side to side. Pops grabbed his right boot. A P-38 can opener was wedged in the tread of the boot, refracting moonlight like a strobe. Pops tapped Rap's leg, signaling an all-clear.

A hard-beaten trail traced the bottom of the hollow near the edge of a creek. A strong flow of water purled through a border of reeds. The trailhead at the top of the draw pushed at the recon team like an oncoming train.

The sing-song voices, the splashing of the creek, and the rustling of cooling vegetation, combined with Hardin's drumming pulse, could easily mask the sound of on-coming feet. The enemy could be at his side before the glow of the moon gave up their stride.

Crawling with empty, deliberate motions, Rap huddled near the vegetation along the trail. Confident he had found a good ambush site, Rap turned his white teeth into the moon's glow. Mex spotted Rap's signal and nudged Pops forward.

As the four men set their ambush, small-arms fire rang in the distance, several hundred meters to the east. The silence that followed was perforated by the old woman's voice.

The metallic rush of the carbine's bolt rang from the hootch. Feet were scurrying across a bamboo floor. Anxious villagers watched the trail, an oil lamp back-lighting their forms. A small girl burst from the hootch and ran past Mex and down into the hollow. Her sandals slapped at the ground until they dropped into the night.

Covering the moonlit half of his face, Hardin wished he were as black as Rap, blacker than a bruised crow, blacker than blue coal. Hardin asked him one day how he got to be so black. "Workin' the streets," Rap said.

Alarmed by the outline of his shadow, Hardin lowered his head, placing his glasses in the grass below his chest. Whispering, he said, "The dinks are comin' back. Don't fire up the little girl unless she's packin' an AK."

"How we gonna know?" Mex was right.

"I'll take the kid," Hardin said, nudging Rap for agreement, hoping the almond-eyed little girl would not come back. "Rap, cover the hootch."

The four-man ambush-set lay on the uphill side of the trail, leaving each man's reflection buried in its own shadow. Inching toward their right flank away from the three hootches, the moon was low enough to blend their shadows into one form.

Waiting was never enough.

Fear drew the recon team to a bead as the weighted shuffling of feet grew louder, echoing from the trailhead. Two VC appeared in the moonlight, struggling with their load. A third VC hung between them, stumbling as he tried to catch his step. Hardin rubbed his eyes to clear his vision, then set his glasses to the bridge of his nose.

The little girl's body took three rounds. Hardin didn't want to kill her.

Moonlight framed the VC like a picture, their movements strained, laden with their wounded friend. Clear one moment and obscure the next, the glint off a weapon keyed Hardin's grip as his finger tightened on the trigger. Hardin took a deep breath. Where was the little girl?

Hardin gasped as the muzzle flash from his weapon seized his chest. The three Viet Cong fell onto the trail. Seconds passed. Rap shot the old woman when the barrel of her carbine came level with the floor of the hootch.

Pops and Mex scrambled up the trail to retrieve the AKs.

Running out of the hollow, the recon team stopped in the shadow of a crease to listen. The dead VC looked like a clump of vegetation. The golden thatch of the hootch cast an odd light, as if a lamp burned inside.

"I was worryin' about shootin' that little girl so much, my fucked-up brain went ahead and shot her anyway," Hardin said. "I'm started to see shit. That ain't good."

"That kid was watchin," Mex said, scanning the hootches.

"If she was older, green tracers would be chasin' our ass up this knoll," Pops said. The little girl's hatred kept the music playing. She had the third AK. In time, she would kill a GI.

Little girls in America wanted to play guns with the boys. They wanted to be the nurse. Little girls in Vietnam wanted to play guns, too. They wanted to be the shooter.

Laurel was one of the girls on Highlands Road who played army. She would mend wounds with softening gestures, then stand naked on her dresser, shaking her thing for the boys. Laurel had a gun.

Tennessee was blathering in tongues when the patrol reached the company perimeter. Overcome by the wonders of diarrhea, LeCotte had lost what few tiles he had left. His bowels working overtime, he dribbled on about fulfilling his destiny—covering Vietnam with shit.

Third Platoon had killed a VC and took credit for wounding another. After morning stand-to, Gator ran a clover and the rest of the company lay back to enjoy hot coffee and a rare morning ration.

LeCotte continued to fart about, accenting his disdain with a bowlegged version of Pops' stride. He asked Boyle for toilet paper and Boyle burst into a hyphenated stutter, laughing as he tried to speak. Forty seconds later, Boyle said, "Use your hand." He said it twice without stuttering, bringing a moment of elation to measure against LeCotte's sarcasm.

Time and time again LeCotte dropped his pants. His friends found his agony refreshing. Doc offered a field-expedient Kotex. Blood offered to set up a target to test his range. Rap added comments about LeCotte's family. Amps blamed the stench on the yellow fog that dogged LeCotte from shit pile to shit pile.

With each barb, Fish would rejoice, then hesitate, waiting to laugh in unison if LeCotte tried to respond. When LeCotte dropped his pants, cheers would erupt, a timer would record the burst, and a radio operator would monitor the seismic disturbance.

Stubbs lit a cigarette, shaking his head. "LeCotte's ass is gonna glow in the dark. You're short, Mex. Maybe you could use LeCotte as a decoy."

Mex exhaled and said, "I got forty-eight and a wake-up, Sarge. I'm gonna fuckin' sky-up. El Tee's gonna wonder where my slick-ass got to. Me and Bucks, ridin' those bones."

Listening to Mex, Hardin found himself in Dak To, out of water, out of food, unable to cry, hoping for a ride out of the war. The emotions spent trying to escape simmered, testing his salt. Mex and Fish and the rest were more important to him than Jesus Christ.

"Ya think Shadow's gonna make it, Mex?" Stubbs asked.

Mex took a step back. "If he don't off himself, he'll ambush his neighbor. Dude's just lookin' at another fuckin' day. Shit don't mean nothin' anymore."

With fewer than thirty days left on his tour, the obligation of carrying a weapon mixed Shadow's emotions into a substrate of unfulfilled obligations. Shadow was beginning to crack.

"You think Shadow's gonna kill himself?" Stubbs asked.

Mex looked away. "Hard tellin'. If we'd'a banged that little girl… maybe."

"Sarge, we still got those bamboo grenades?" Mex asked.

Turning away from Mex, Stubbs took a drag on his cigarette, exhaled, and nodded. "Yeah, we got 'em." Stubbs tapped the aluminum frame on his rucksack and looked at Hardin.

"Shadow's leavin."

* * *

Charlie Company searched the plateau for another four days, bouncing their crucible of democracy from village to village. Shadow was content to walk in the sun and sing, separating from shared emotions. His voice sounded small as he spoke to no one, measuring his mistakes. Alone, he had embraced much of what he disliked, content to drift to his death.

Snatching bits of camaraderie, Shadow hid behind the veil of a timid smile. On this day, his day of reckoning, he hit one fist at a time: Ski, then Fish, then Bucks, then Drips, and finally Mex. When the resupply chopper touched down the men scattered.

"Why did you come to Vietnam, El Tee?" Shadow asked, his head cocked.

"I don't know, Shadow. Circumstance I guess," Hardin said, not believing his answer.

"When's Doobie coming back from R&R, El Tee?" Shadow's expression turned blank, then suspicious as he surveyed the perimeter and the confusion around the chopper.

"Doobie got whacked in Dak To, Shadow. He didn't make it."

"No way Doobie's dead."

The two men shook hands. Shadow stepped through a turn, a song on his lips.

Shadow sat in the door of the chopper alone, looking at his past. The Hill People, his fellow survivors, knew he would be alone for the duration.

Hardin wondered if a new memory might put a sparkle in his eye. He nodded when Shadow's lips began to move. Unable to hear the melody, he tried to sing along. Shadow's shoulders embraced themselves as the slick lifted away.

A lanky, white, agile GI named Willits was Shadow's replacement. Fish decided the new man's nickname was Clyde. Clyde had a tin ear.

Shadow left Hardin doing a solo act, keen for the sound of Dig-it's laughter. Shadow's question would linger: "Why did you come to Vietnam, El Tee?" Beyond the anger over his father's death, the answer was too complex. The reasoning for going to war had been reduced to the victory he could claim as his own.

The Hill People, the eight men from the battle for Hill 875, were still alive.

Amid tears of fatigue, Hardin laughed at his fate. His father won the Victoria Cross, a cross for his son to bear. Hell, he couldn't even die in vain. His country wouldn't let him.

* * *

Number #10, Highlands Road. Bremerton, Washington. July 1967.

While stationed in Germany, in July of 1967, First Lieutenant Edward Hardin received a telephone call from his brother Court announcing the instant death of their father. Court's words rang out from a field phone in the empty tent. The announcement took fewer than four seconds.

The Major had suffered a heart attack after a boxing workout at the YMCA.

Young Hardin wore his dress blue uniform to his father's funeral. With half a month's pay he purchased a wreath shaped like the eagle his dad wore on the shoulder of his army uniform. Saturday after his father's memorial he strolled through downtown Bremerton. The buildings were smaller now; worn by perspective, free of the joy he once cherished.

Some words did linger: "Learn how to take care of yourself, Pal. Life's a lot simpler."

The American Legion Hall was damp. The veterans at the bar sat slouched on their stools. They didn't turn around.

A jukebox had replaced the pinball machine.

Hardin ordered a schooner of beer, punched the buttons for "Heart and Soul," "Moonlight Serenade," and "Misty," and sat in a single overstuffed chair in the lounge area, to be near his Pal. The gathering spot that was once so inviting was empty now.

Singing to himself, he strolled along Washington Street, lingering in front of the used-clothing store. A pair of wire rimmed glasses claimed to be worth fifty cents.

The all-night diner was nearly empty.

The main entry of the YMCA was scarred and unkempt. The pool tables stood erect at parade rest, unused. The lone attendant did not recognize the young soldier. The boxing ring was inviting. The heavy bag hung still. The speed bag danced on the end of his father's fists, announcing each tag. The shower where his father fell showed nary a trace of their footsteps.

Hardin stood near the ferry dock and threw a rock in the water, as if to finish a wish.

Angry, he searched his father's keepsakes: the brass statue of a naked boy, pictures of war, letters from Monty and Murphy, marquis posters of his boxing days, the boxing smokers, the leather chair he read in, his Manhattan glass. Remembering their laughter over root beer floats, and pin ball at the American Legion, he weighed the details of his father's life.

Chalked full of resentment, he left his mother's home to return to Germany. With thirty days of effort, as if time healed wounds, he was not able to see his father and say good-bye. And he was not able to stop his mother's crying. Major Hardin was her sweetheart.

His mother's tears led to a reassuring embrace and a rendition of his father's warning: "Take care of yourself, Eddie."

Returning to his unit in Schweinfurt, Germany, Hardin stopped at OCAR in Washington D.C. and volunteered for duty in Vietnam. Volunteering guaranteed a soldier combat duty with an American unit. And the time had come to stand-to.

His father had died and didn't say good-bye, taking with him his stories of the French Resistance, Montgomery, Eisenhower, Bradley, Churchill, D-Day at Normandy, the British, Murphy, the Nazis. Gone were the stories of growing up poor, the boxing, the football and track.

Gone were the Major's reminders: "Driving is a full-time job" and "Honesty is the best policy." "Listen up," "Pipe down," and "I'll give you something to cry about."

The Major was Eddie's first point man, his best Pal.

* * *

Stubbs approached Hardin with his cigarette going full speed, and a look of regret in his eye. "Shadow gave me a warning." Stubbs cocked his head into a pause, swallowing as he did so. "Said we're gonna pay for leavin' that dog." Stubbs shook his head in frustration and exhaled a smoke filled laugh. "Then he started singin' and walked away."

Stubbs and Shadow had been close.

"Shadow's over the edge. He's the one that put that dog in the litter basket with the handler." Listening to the fading sound of the chopper, Hardin became instantly angry. "Ya know, Stubbs, if the rest of my tour is pure shit, I'm gonna regret losin' that dog."

The company searched another kilometer of jungle and dug in on a low ridge to prepare for extraction. Palace guard, a stand-down at the brigade's administrative base camp in An Khe, was described as a week of one-hour stand-by duty for one rifle company at a time. GIs would have a chance to relax, see a dentist, and have a few beers.

Charlie Company was designated to stand down first, which meant the Old Man wanted the most probable chaos out the way within the first seven days.

"You ready for this, Stubbs?"

"What?" Stubbs gave Bucks a smoke.

"We're goin' to An Khe for palace guard. Charlie Company gets a one-week stand-down starting tomorrow." Stubbs' eye grew distant, then focused, his body involuntarily assuming a disbelieving posture as he told himself jokes about his future in the Army.

"Just our company?" Stubbs asked, moving his finger around in a circle, pointing to no where as his brow arched in astonishment.

"We're on a one-hour stand-by." Stubbs shot his cigarette at Drips.

"Fuckin' impossible. Be a lot safer out here."

"They got a mini-PX." Stubbs lit a smoke, irritated by the proximity of more frustration.

"We'll get trampled if we get between these dickheads and Sin City. You and me, El Tee: we're in for some serious ass chewin' before this week's over—serious ass chewin'."

"If we get the studs refit by noon, we might get 'em back inside the wire before dark." Stubbs blurted out an absurd roar, muddling smoke through his laughter.

"These dickheads don't give a shit about bein' inside the wire. We're gonna meet the ladies in Sin City. Bet on it—every whore on a first-name basis."

"Who's got the OP?" Hardin asked.

"Big Bucks."

The two men drifted into their evening routines. In the oil patterns curling across the surface of his coffee, Hardin found two pajama-clad VC, struggling in the moonlight, their wounded comrade suspended between them.

Hardin shot the wounded man knowing that Mex and Pops would start with one of the other targets. After the first shot, Hardin shot the man on the left with three rounds knowing the recon team would move to the right side of the target after their first shot. Pops probably stayed on the right.

Odds were that only Hardin shot the wounded man.

A young girl with a seven-pound AK had crouched in the night, peering from a patch of trees, afraid to fire. Next time she would collect her paybacks. The recon team had killed her father and her brothers. And then they shot her grandmother.

Yesterday she was a young farm girl. Today she was a soldier.

CHAPTER TWELVE

That's it, and You're First

0640 Hours.

The sun began to shine upon the ridge as the company dropped into the ravine. By the time they reached the valley floor, white birds were swirling in the treetops and the mist that hung around the river at dawn began to die away.

"Have you been in Sin City, Stubbs?" Hardin asked.

Stubbs nodded, gesturing crudely, as he had never done before, striking the pose and motion of a mongrel dog. "It's a dump." Stubbs wanted this fictitious rest, his anticipation registering the static rush of commo checks. The day seemed brighter. The birds were singing.

* * *

Hardin's conscience grew heavy as the chopper pad at An Khe took center stage. He took off his helmet. Satisfied that Dig-it's letter was secure, he let his thoughts turn inward. By the time he had another thought his feet were mounting the stairs to the orderly room.

"Morning, Top. You find that deserter yet?" Top turned from his typewriter, his expression non-committal until he recognized the challenge.

"Damn. I forgot you were with Second Batt. You stayin' long, Lieutenant?" With a conspiring look, Top threw a wad of papers in the garbage.

"Seven days and seven nights. Can you believe it?"

"No, I can't. You'll be glad to know the brigade headquarters moved to Bong Son." Top was anchored to a desk laden with reports.

"You mean the old man with the hook isn't around to get me a hat?"

"The Claw stops by now and then. He'd remember you." Top's demeanor was barely stern, tempered by administrative drivel and a company of the Queen's Rifles standing on his graph paper.

"Does the Cav still have a club on the knoll?" Top nodded indifferently, not caring to create familiarity he might regret.

"You're on your own, Lieutenant. Don't use my name for any reason." Uncomfortable with trying to dismiss Hardin as a problem, Top settled back in his chair with an audible sigh. "Is there anything else the prince requires?" Top asked, raising a toasting finger.

"How about gettin' the studs out of Sin City."

"MPs can do it." Top laughed. "We'll figure something out."

The cold shower left Hardin with the yearnings of a lonesome man. Smelling like sweaty soap, he spread his towel across the frame of his bunk. Suspicious, as if waiting for parole,

GIs paired up in threes, cleaning weapons, packing C-Rations and ammunition. With all hands busy, the barracks burst from joke to joke. Flanked by garbage cans full of iced beer, the platoons stood inspection for their stand-by mission.

Stubbs and Hardin stood near the doorway talking. Forty feet and five bunks away a new man hurriedly cleaned his twelve-gauge. He was ready to party. The gun discharged, shredding Bucks' rucksack and bed mattress.

One double-aught-buck pellet entered Hardin's fatigue shirt above the left breast pocket and tore across his right tit. Reeling, the impact threw his feet over his head and slammed him into the wall. The barracks echoed with a gasp.

Reaching for words, Hardin framed the new man's face with a glare that could fry eggs. He pushed his back against the wall to ease the pain. Instantly his rage was gone. Trying to breathe himself into a calm heart rate, his mind seemed to haggle with itself.

Stubbs had not moved.

Confusion erupted in a duet of anger as GIs poured into the tent. Focused on the pain, Hardin opened the shreds of his shirt. Beads of blood sat on his chest. If this was grazing fire, a full load of double-aught-buck would definitely be a bad ride.

"I've seen worse," Stubbs said.

"Fuck you, Stubbs. What are you fuckin' dickheads lookin' at?" The new man had disappeared behind Drips and Mex.

Top barged into the tent. "What happened?"

"Cherries are fuckin' stupid," Pops said.

Hardin's heart rate slowed as he rotated his shoulder through a series of painful motions. He ignored the mockery in Top's posture, wondering when he stopped wanting to kill the new man. Since killing the bastard was his initial reaction, how and when that emotion ended was important. That all-consuming rage could be regulated by some mechanism of memory, was a phenomenon he had not considered.

The incremental exhaustion created by too long searching for death had left him with a focus no longer than the sound of a rifle shot. Given this limited ability to focus, he realized he never wanted to kill the new man. His quick-fire personality wanted to kill him. His combat buddy, that bivalved son-of-a-bitch hiding just below the moment, wanted to kill him. Quick-Fire, that loony bastard, was bent on exposing Hardin's advanced stage of misfortune.

I hope we don't become one, Hardin thought.

Picking the pellet off the floor, he studied the disfigured piece of lead: his memento of valor. Somewhat less than a Victoria Cross, lead was lead.

Top and Doc Collard escorted Hardin to Doc Tweaton's meat shop. The crusty old surgeon was delighted to have something to mend. With Collard howling into a scrub sink, the surgeon applied an eight-inch by eight-inch gauze bandage to the wound, tying the mess together with a crosshatch of white tape.

"I'll put you in for a Purple Heart," the surgeon declared, scrubbing his hands.

"Not for this, ya won't," Hardin said. "Not for this."

Halfway back to the barracks, Hardin threw the dressing and four ribbons of tape into a trash barrel. Collard smiled with his eyebrows, trying to control his laughter.

"You might want to let that scratch air out a bit."

Standing in the midst of Bucks' rucksack, Stubbs examined two frag grenades that had taken a direct hit. When the war was close, superstitions ran full circle. Bucks' dice were in tact but his wooden crucifix was shattered. He had carved it in Dak To. Gathering the pieces into his drive-on rag, Bucks tied the rag off and stuffed his good-luck into his pocket. He had decided to keep carrying the rucksack no matter what fell out.

"The surgeon was gonna give me a Purple Heart." Stubbs ignored Hardin's words.

"Accidental discharge. Drips put the new man through the drill," Stubbs said.

Wanting to pout over being shot, Hardin smiled instead. The laughter on Captain Joe's face jiggled, and then leapt into a riot as he and Stubbs joined forces.

"What's wrong, Gravy, some new guy try to bang your sorry ass?" Joe shouted, admiring the smoke of a new cigar. "Dogs, dinks, new guys—ain't much difference." Hardin's shirt packed a quiet message. He had decided to wear it until it disintegrated.

"Ya know, Captain, you had that same sorry grin when that dog tried to rip my nuts off."

"That was damn funny," Joe said, his expression assuming a trace of concern. Reticent, as if calculating his next move, he stood into the frame of the doorway. "I want the studs to survey their personal gear, call home, whatever they need to do as soon as possible."

"They're doin' that whatever shit right now. What's the rush?" Squinting one eye, Joe grinned. The rest of the story was under his bush hat.

"Conversion Day is Thursday. Today is Saturday."

GIs were not issued US currency. They could draw 200 dollars of Military Pay Currency each month, which they could exchange for piasters to spend on the local economy. Almost all GIs paid for services with MPC, and local merchants exchanged the MPC for greenbacks or piasters on the black market.

On Conversion Day, new MPC was issued and the old MPC became instantly worthless. Piss-tight so to speak, whores would run about screaming, waving shoe boxes full of bad paper.

* * *

Stubbs woke Hardin for chow, praising the chaos in town, sporting the odds of having the studs inside the wire by evening stand-to. The minimum bet was five dollars.

The incident at Pleiku had been studied during a Pentagon analysis of the effects of prolonged exposure to guerrilla warfare, prolonged uncertainty, and the mental illness caused by living too long in a red-brown membrane, shooting at dinks with a plastic straw. The study had no conclusion and gave no recommendation, just a heads-up: these grunts are nuts.

A host of field grade NCOs, along with the battalion sergeant major, had gathered in the mess tent to dismiss the carnage at Camp Enari. Extrapolating that riot into images of Sin City left images of whores fleeing the incorrigibles of Hannibal's army.

Top had organized a sweep of Sin City complete with trucks, medics and radios. The plan was to drive the herd out of town and through the front gate of the firebase.

Stubbs laughed at the thought of finding Fish or Drips.

"Ya listenin', Stubbs?" Top shook his head as Stubbs and Hardin sat down with their Swiss steak. Stubbs introduced himself and started eating his dinner.

"Does his platoon respond to that grin?" Top asked.

Stubbs assumed a defensive posture, swallowing as he gathered his thoughts. "We just watch his feet. Hear he pissed off your friends."

"He did do that—doctors, preachers, deputy CG."

Delighted by the story of Hardin getting chewed out by The Claw, Stubbs sobered quickly with Top's account of the bad chopper ride. "You didn't mention a chopper, El Tee." Stubbs didn't abide secrets, even personal ones that didn't count.

"Bad luck, that's all. Fuckin' thing fell outta the sky."

"You're not doin' too good around here. An FUO, a bad chopper ride, and a cherry blows you down with his fire stick." Stubbs pushed his mess tray aside.

"At least the girls haven't given him the clap," Top said.

"Yeah, the clap," Hardin said. "I found my college buddy standin' in the shower, holdin' a can of Raid and a bar of soap, hollerin' about crabs doin' chin-ups on his nuts." The three men were enjoying a laugh when Captain Joe sat down with a cup of coffee.

"Tell me about the horse shit, Hardin." Stubbs crushed his cigarette into silence.

"That took a while." Stubbs sat back in his chair, evaluating his tactics, not wanting to bail out on his lieutenant unless he had to.

Hardin covered the road apples with carameled humor. Then, with a slight pause to beg the question, he constructed the scene of a staff unable to respond before he escaped.

"The Old Man said to tell Lima Six that he owed him. He won't forget."

"This could be a pisser." Stubbs left the tent.

* * *

Full of beer and freshly laid, the brothers had organized a smoker near the back of the platoon barrack. The sound of bare fists striking home brought Hardin to the screen door. The white dude at the smoker was a cook, and he was the one getting smoked.

"Knock it off. Rap, Bucks?"

"We got it, El Tee." Rap stopped the fight. Actually Rap's voice stopped the fight. The night was so black the voice fit right in.

"Another time." Cookie let out an audible gasp. Rap spoke in hushed tones, postponing the outcome. The brothers were changing bets.

The longer he knew the man, the more he understood the worth of Rap's stature. Rap could settle a dispute with silence—or with rapid expletives. Hardin turned away with a confirming nod trying to decipher the muted tones of Rap's voice through a grated texture of Black English. The words he heard didn't match the inflection or the situation.

When the screen door slammed behind him, the barracks' center aisle caught his attention, lined on its flanks with weapons and gear. Rucksacks stood upright, balanced on scarred aluminum frames, straps drawn tight secured essential supplies—clues to the bearer's shortcomings.

One rucksack carried eleven quarts of water, another carried three. One carried five smoke grenades; another carried none. Some carried fragmentation grenades, the pins held in place with tape or rubber bands.

Sweet Cheeks' shroud-line lay coiled on the floor.

Hardin laughed at his inspection, and then crossed the street to the officers' bar. Four hours later, restless and full of booze, he and six strangers marched to the First Cav Officers' Club. Their mission: measure the ball-weight of the local slick drivers. Eager to be in a crowded bar, they cleared a table near the entrance and began erecting a pyramid of empty beer cans. The display was topped with a placard declaring the Airborne as the best units in Vietnam.

The proclamation gained volume, spurring the paratrooper's quest of the illusive Round Eye. Outnumbered fifteen-to-one, the troopers ordered their big man from supply to go forth and entice the ladies standing at the bar.

He returned, sniffing with the prospect of bagging two nurses. He gifted a set of 34-Bs to Hardin because, as he explained, Hardin's grin was touching her fancy.

While outlining the affair, tempers became confused and accelerated. A full can of beer brushed the bridge of Hardin's nose and crashed into a quartet of slick drivers at the next table. While Hardin filed a disclaimer, the big man from supply filed a rebuttal.

"Shut up, asshole, or I'll rip that mustache off your fucking face."

As fights go, the fight was not fair. Hardin's exit was a classic however: hit in the face, flying backward through the screen door, boonie hat thrown in the street, followed by a resounding, "Don't fuckin' come back."

His face ached as he dusted off his boonie hat. He didn't land a punch. His father's left hook would have cleared the bar. His father's advice, like his left hook, was right on the button: "If you stand women on their heads, they all look like sisters."

Hardin spotted the Big Dipper and the North Star. They were more reliable companions. The flowered eagle guarding his father's grave was alert, scanning the bone yard. The honor guard fired a salute. The soldiers were remote, detached. Who in the hell were they?

Hardin's thoughts returned home to visit his father.

* * *

Number #10, Highlands Road. Bremerton, Washington. September 1959.

Hardin stood in the Major's den, reading the latest letter from Montgomery. A yellowed ivory pipe lay on its side, patient, waiting for its evening call to duty. The armchair was cold.

The concrete block wall facing the entrance ran sixteen feet into a closet on the left and a series of small windows on the right. The wall was brighter today—fresh paint. The khaki-tan masonry absorbed the lighting used to accent ninety-one World War II photographs.

History's famous people stood-to at parade rest. A photograph of General Omar Bradley with a personal inscription hung next to a picture of the Major with General Eisenhower.

An "I Like Ike" button gathered dust near his reading lamp.

The ornate oak frame in the center of the long wall held a personally inscribed photograph of Monty. The wall over the Major's desk was filled with boxing memorabilia. The boxer on the card looked much younger than before. The tabletops were covered with souvenirs.

Although Monty's letter was discouragingly short, the Major was grateful for his morsel of British nobility and discouraged at being somewhat less than a footnote in Monty's memoirs. The Major was proud of his pictures and his contributions.

Hardin had transformed his father's comrades into a righteous guard. During newsreels of the Beaches of Normandy, the Falaise Gap, the Battle of the Bulge, or the liberation of Bergen-Belsen, he watched for his father. The Major was the one carrying the fight to the Jerries.

When he talked to his father again, he would tell him how discomposed Vietnam's war had become. He would ask if Bradley and the others were brave men.

* * *

Holding Company Mess Tent. An Khe Base Camp. 0530 Hours.

Chewing bacon with a stiff jaw was akin to laughing with a hangover. The welt on his left cheek bulged beyond the rim of his eye. After checking his buckshot bruise for rot, he caught himself tongue lashing the rim of a porcelain cup. Yawning for the first time he could recall, he relaxed, ignoring the activities of the base camp.

Finding his overseas trunk was the order of the day.

At 0932 hours Stubbs announced that Charlie Company was scrambled for a combat assault in support of a scout platoon of the First Cav. The NVA had taken a small hill controlling Route #19 where the road turned from west to north into the An Khe Pass. Hardin had seen tanks on this hilltop moments before his slick was shot out of the sky.

Stubbs and the platoon stood-to on the chopper pad, pissed off and short of machine gun ammunition. A black grunt named Riggs presented himself to Hardin with eyes wider than his shadow. Wounded in Dak To, he had returned to the company from Japan and was assigned to First Platoon.

He was whiter than scared.

"I got twelve and a wake-up," Riggs declared. "I can't be doin' more shit. I can't be doin' more shit. You hear what I'm sayin', El Tee?" *You can always hear Black English,* Hardin thought. Riggs shook himself into a frenzy. His lieutenant was too young to be out of diapers.

"I hear ya, Riggs. You got ten minutes. Get us machine gun ammo and you're outta this deal." Riggs' tried to talk. His eyes grew wide as his body tried to outrun his feet.

"Okay, okay, okay." Riggs raced toward the nearest building, screaming a low howl. He would be back. His friend Fish needed the ammunition. Within two minutes Riggs dropped four ammo boxes at Hardin's feet. Ski and Bucks took the ammo with nothing more than a nod.

"Take care of yourself, Riggs," Hardin said. Riggs searched in disbelief.

"I'm outta here. I can't be doin' more shit." Riggs backed away, his shoulders pleading for space. Riggs was a good man. He had done enough.

Hardin gave him a nod. "Take care of yourself, GI."

Riggs turned and bounded onto the roadway, then turned to watch. As Fish trudged up the loading ramp of the Chinook, Riggs took off his helmet. Fish ignored the gesture. Nobody cared. To a man they had withdrawn into combat's hangar, preparing to die.

Hardin retraced the briefing Joe had given him: small hill, First Cav's three attempts to retake the hill had failed, 155mm artillery battery was in support, and the NVA were dug in.

Hurled into the soup, the turbine scream from the Chinook's engine forced Hardin's mind into a crucible: weapons check, prayer, fear, prayer, fist-pounding, prayer, weapons check.

The chopper started into its decent, banked through a 180-degree turn and settled on the hardball, Route #19, 400 meters west of Dig-it's last stand. GIs were milling about, watching God-bobbing volleys of artillery crush their next stop. Tanks and armored personnel carriers were perched on the roadway.

Captain Joe braced himself in front of Hardin, pointing over his shoulder at the objective. Joe screamed, "That's it, and you're first."

Historic forces kept some men at the sharp end until they died, or their valor had more value than their death. Hardin leveled his eyes. Death and circumstance were colliding.

"The Old Man is upstairs coordinating artillery fires," Joe shouted.

"Are you talkin' to him?" Hardin pointed toward a wad of Hueys suspended in the sky, toward the Old Man's floating press box.

"Commo's locked." Hardin looked at Joe and turned to find Stubbs.

* * *

An infantry officer's formative months were spent studying the confines of the five-paragraph field order—how one paragraph reinforced another, and how critical the order was for successful combat. Building Four at Fort Benning, Georgia, housed the classrooms where infantry combat became a science.

The titles of the paragraphs were branded on the officer's butt. Paragraph 1: Mission: must be well defined. Paragraph 2: Objective: topography and routes, etc. Paragraph 3: Situation: enemy and friendly. Paragraph 4: Logistics: resupply. Paragraph 5: Command and Signal: who talks to whom.

Joe had the no-bullshit version, one word per paragraph: "That's it, and you're first."

Hardin pointed at Bucks. "Let's do it." The Hill People knew where they were going: up a nameless hill to die with a friend.

Tennessee caught Stubbs' eye and motioned toward the rear of the platoon. Two columns of men moved in silence, tracing flat ground through shoulder-high vegetation. Fish and Drips stopped at the base of the hill. Hardin dropped his rucksack, letting Sweet Cheeks' shroud line pass through his fingers.

"Bucks, Mex, drop rucks. Think about pussy." A metallic symphony clattered through the brush as gun bolts slammed home.

Twenty-six frightened men stood-to in a firing line, facing the hill, eight feet apart. Aware of what the day might bring, Stubbs trooped the line, setting every other weapon on full automatic: "Stay spread out, keep eye contact, don't get ahead of the man next to you."

Artillery rounds continued to crush the air above their heads. Tremors shook the ground. Debris fell through the canopy.

"Stubbs, you got center left. I got center right."

"I'll buy the beer, El Tee." Their eyes locked for an instant, perhaps for the last time.

"See ya on top, Stubbs."

The jungle's dapple shadows reduced visibility to a fraction as one man and then another mounted the hill. Alone yet together, men fought to keep their spacing and stay on line. The hill was steep. Mex and Bucks screamed at their friends. Blood screamed at the air.

Gunships pounded the hilltop with rockets and streams of tracer rounds.

Jerked onto center stage, the hill crested away from the firing line and boots began to run, plowing full-scale through the debris. The air was filled with dirt and confusion. GIs fired blindly into the final volley of artillery fire. Shrapnel hummed passed their heads as men crashed into the earth. A white phosphorous artillery round hit the hilltop with a muffled thump spewing white-hot burning stones across the NVA trench line.

AKs stitched the ground and ripped at the trees.

The brutal reports of the AKs, the splintering bamboo, the incessant screaming, all gave Hardin strength. He was a warrior. He could not see his enemy. No matter. Hardin's laugh cut short. His throat locked and he reloaded his Sweet Pea.

Fish pointed skyward, laughing through a scream.

Jet planes crashed toward the hilltop—silver F-100s. Staring, as if he had ordered the attack, Hardin stopped breathing. Tied as they were to a cloud of white phosphorous, three fast-moving, meat-pounding streams of blistering shit burst from of the edge of time. Belly-to-the-treetops, the first pilot's wrinkled face burned into Hardin's memory.

Nose guns fired 20mm cannon rounds into the trench lines. Three F-100s in trail assaulted the hilltop, sixty feet off the deck. The trench lines erupted into a boil, then again and again. With each pass, the surface of the ground rose and then rushed into stillness, creating that precious lapse that allows one man to race ahead and kill another man.

Drips and Rap scrambled forward into the jet-wash, dragging a wireless wave of warriors behind them. The NVA had vanished.

Hardin fell against a dirt mound with an agonizing gust and gave his nuts a hostile inventory to stop the aching. He rolled onto his back, listening to the silence. Voices filtered through the leaves. Amps spoke with his high-pitched brilliance, announcing the victory.

Stubbs popped from the haze, too alert to be afraid.

A scout platoon charged, clanging their tracks, stumping up the backside of the hill to survey the battlefield, chattering like tourists. White-hot shrapnel at fifty meters, white phosphorous at forty meters, F-100s at thirty meters, AKs for garnish, and the scout platoon came clanging to inspect the scene.

In the dismounted mode, Custer wandered in close tack, California rowels jangling, a 44 Russian tied low on each leg. With a Coke in one hand and a camera in the other, Custer circled the hilltop on foot, recording the battlefield.

"Nothin' to this combat shit, is there?" Drips declared, poking the barrel of his weapon into the middle of Custer's crotch. He lowered his camera. Drips stood up and spit.

With a cigarette blazing, Stubbs stood-to. "You okay, Drips?" Stubbs gave Custer a hip check, forcing the man to jump over a trench line.

"Yeah," Drips said, spitting an acid spew. "Give me somethin' to smoke, Sarge, before I smoke that worthless pig-fucker."

Stubbs gave Drips a cigarette, then screamed a tired scream, "Saddle up. We're outta here." First Platoon crashed off the hilltop. The company stumbled along.

Hat in hand, Hardin, Blood and Rap popped out of the tall grass onto Route #19 next to a tank. This particular tanker was making an eight-millimeter movie. Rap's hand tightened around the pistol grip on his weapon.

"Damn, my man. That was just like Fort Benning." Rap's arms extended as if in slow motion, and his weapon re-aimed itself at the tanker's balls. Rap wasn't anybody's man.

"Muthafuckin' crack-ass muthafucker." Blood stepped between the two men, forcing the barrel of Rap's weapon to the left.

"Easy, Rap. These dumb fucks don't know no better." Rap looked at Blood with eyes that screamed with hate.

"Find me a muthafuckin' ride, ya dig what I'm sayin'?"

Hardin lay down on the side of the road, knowing if he laid there long enough someone would notice. Blossoms of white phosphorous flourished at the back of his mind.

Creases in the pilot's face ran five deep as the G-force pulled him across the top of the hill. The folds bounced with the turbulence of the airframe, his teeth bared in a painful smile.

* * *

The company landed in the holding area at An Khe just before noon. After a cold shower, Hardin and a lieutenant from Bravo Company set sail for Sin City. By 1300 hours Hardin had ordered a second beer and was sitting against a plywood wall in a dump called the Los Angeles Bar. He stared vacantly, listening to a three-piece rock'n'roll band.

Unattended weapons lay scattered throughout the bar.

Three white civilians with hair down to their ass banged on two guitars and a set of wasted drums. GIs galloped across the floor. Whores plied their trade with long black hair and skirts that barely covered the fuzz on their snatch. Booze, pussy, and rock'n'roll—the tonal force consumed all speech, the aromas enticed the dullest mind, the booze stripped the senses, and the pussy had too many hands.

Hardin rubbed his eyes with his palms and laughed. In England his father was issued a red membership card printed with the logo of the Mayfair Hotel in Piccadilly, in London, along with a white membership card for the Gardenia, a nightclub in Piccadilly. Night or day, the Major enjoyed Piccadilly without paying a cover charge. London's nightlife was well attended.

The Los Angeles Bar didn't have a cover charge, a membership card—or running water.

As he sat defenseless, his weapon cradled between his legs, a young, black-eyed girl crashed in the adjoining chair, her right hand grabbing Hardin's nuts. With no rank or name-tag on his uniform, the bar-girl assumed he was a private.

"How old you, GI?" A second girl chimed.

"Eighteen." They were delighted.

"Baby San, numba-one Baby San." They giggled and said Baby San several times while the first bar-girl massaged his program. "Numba-one blow job, GI."

Hardin waved for another beer. The paper-thin walls diminished his instincts. Quiet sexual urgings, punctuated by the orgasms of the other tourists, began to cripple his resolve. The sunshine girls smiled a practiced smile as he paid them ten dollars in soon-to-be-old money and sent them off to jump some other stiff.

"I'm gettin' a little crazy with these dinks dancin' around," Hardin said, gesturing toward the door. "Besides, the money's startin' to fade." His friend wasn't married.

Rows of tin shacks marched in place, then merged with the main gate of the An Khe base camp. Hardin laughed at the day, knowing the studs would be nose-deep in shit if they found their feet in Sin City on conversion day.

Hours later, Hardin was asleep, dreaming about his bride. Stubbs woke him.

"How are we doin', Stubbs?" Hardin waved a hand through the cigarette smoke.

"We're inside and tight," Stubbs said, toasting himself. "Drips crawled through the main gate on his hands and knees with Fish carryin' his weapon."

"Probably outta money."

"NCO's got a barbecue with beer out back." Stubbs opened the screen door and shot his cigarette butt at Amps. "Why don't you join us, Eltee?"

Enjoying the friendly banter, Hardin watched Bucks work the crowd. Cards or dice, the platoon sergeants were easy marks. Drips and Fish had fallen into a pile of sand bags, each embracing a fistful of the green-twill beauties—out cold.

With Stubbs on a roll, empty beer cans were tossed on Fish, the logic being that Fish would cherish his new friends.

Hardin and Bucks were playing cards—Acey-Ducey—stealing and lying with gusto, drinking their brains into a stupor. Bucks was celebrating being short and Hardin was tired of being sober.

When Bucks drifted off, Hardin crawled into his hootch, mounted his bunk, and caressed the stale mattress as if it were his own.

Hardin fell into a reflective sleep.

CHAPTER THIRTEEN

Captain Weber

An Khe Base Camp. 1640 Hours.

The jeep drove itself as Hardin scanned the perimeter bunkers. News that his overseas trunk had followed him to An Khe offered a day of reunion. Rummaging through a storage building he found his well-traveled friend wedged under a cascade of duffel bags. His footsteps echoed as he crossed the wooden floor. The Christmas sticker his mother had placed next to his father's name was worn at its edges. Santa Claus smiled his best smile.

The words were plain enough: Merry Christmas Eddie.

Home held a cold, clear autumn day—a day devoted to raking leaves and securing the house for the winter. Eva Hardin gave her son a hug. Standing in the garden near the pond, the tears on her cheek glistened in the sun. Her chest heaved and then shuddered as she exhaled.

With comfort for her son she said, "Your father wanted you to have his overseas trunk, Eddie. So he could be with you, for luck. He was lucky, you know."

Alarmed that his mother's tears might portend an inevitable fate—third time's a charm, three on a match and all that—he remembered she would pat his hand whenever they said good-bye. This time she cupped his cheek. Somehow she knew her son wasn't coming home.

"I'll be seeing you," were the last words she spoke that September day. With that, and a borrowed tear, Lieutenant Edward Hardin and his father were on their way.

The leather carrying handles were covered with mold now, the leather hinges and leather knife case as well. He had intended to stencil his name and service number next to his father's, to claim equal status, but this was 1968 and he was fighting Vietnam's war. He was a grunt, something less than one of the King's Welshmen.

Equal status was not possible and would be forever denied.

His father's generation, commendable at the turn, promised to bring force to bear in Vietnam as soon as they could determine when and where. And so the war continued, rife with dense confusion, a partial compliment of twelve-month men hoping to survive.

Reminiscing, evaluating his essentials, wondering why he might pack wooden matches, a needle and thread, a D-ring, and fish line, re-packing the trunk required organizing the items by type and purpose. The types were obvious. Except for the tennis shoes, the purpose was lost.

Bouncing on the balls of his feet, the tennis shoes massaged his feet. Deciding he was alone, he broke into a run, then caught himself. Laughing, he opened a card from his brother. A dog tag punched with his father's name and service number fell to the floor. Anxious to compare the tag to the stenciled numbers on the trunk, he read the tag again. Delighted, he hung it with his dog tags and his wedding ring.

The message on the card jumped from the past.

Dear Eddie:

> *Vietnam's war is a mess. Mom will have a hard time with the news each night. Keep your head down. The beads are worry beads from Morocco. Dad carried them on D-Day on Omaha Beach, and the Battle of the Bulge.*
>
> *He loaned the beads to me for luck. I can't take his place, but these beads are from the Major.*
>
> *Take care of yourself, Pal.*

Love, Court.

Hardin stared at his brother's signature, rolling the beads over in his hand. He laughed through a wail when he counted the beads—eighteen. The number matched the number of rounds he loaded in his magazines. The same number of pieces he sliced from his salami sticks.

With luck in full fig, Hardin was a mannequin, a walking trinket.

Deciding he was bulletproof, he adjusted his drive-on rag and stood into a lumbering sigh. Folding his brother's card, he looked out of the window. "Take care of yourself, Pal." His father's words had a natural fiber, a hard-beaten tone spiced with the gravel of good tobacco.

Hardin could make a meal out of his father's den, when his mind would let him.

Posting the trunk near a wall away from the duffel bags, he paused to reflect, to read the Christmas sticker one more time. The leather handle smiled as he closed the door.

* * *

Driving the jeep as if his ass was on fire, racing toward the Holding Company orderly room, visions of his bar girl got his crank tangled in the steering wheel. The jeep slid through the turn by the main gate, shot past B-Med and slid to a dust-billowing stop when he stomped on the brakes. The nurse he had met in the mess hall before Christmas stood in the street, stretch-testing a faded fatigue shirt.

"We talked in the mess hall," he said, smiling his best.

She assumed an intriguing pose—hip cocked, trotters on parade. With a trace of recognition in her eyes, she managed a colder response. "Oh, really. Have we met?"

"Yes. I was flying to Kontum, trying to get to know you in the chow hall." Hardin's grin and frantic eyeballs had her wondering.

She nodded slowly, altering her posture into a guarded, arms-folded challenge. "With a short porcelain crank as I recall."

To counter this shriveled salutation, Hardin surveyed the high points of her uniform, waiting for a suggestive notion. "Can I buy ya a beer?" Hardin asked. He should have been embarrassed, but his cock was frog-marching across the seat of the jeep. His persistent grin made the lady smile.

"Are you with Second Battalion?" Her question caught him unbuttoning her pants.

With a gesture of apology, Hardin hesitated, then said, "Yes."

"Were you on the slick that went down on Route #19?" She asked, looking away.

"That was a bad ride."

"I'll stop by your club. That way you won't get your ass whipped." Her body language was forceful, insisting, sporting a strike zone the size of a hatbox.

"The Cav has no class."

"They did whip your ass. 2100 hours: I'll buy." She pulled at the front of her shirt, accenting a pair of guns fit for a dogfight.

"Yes, Ma'am." Hardin gave her a salute, which she returned with some humor.

Thank you, God. The specs on this woman read like *Hot Rod Magazine's* Car of the Year—a round-eyed captain-type female, complete with four on the floor, pos-attraction, and two of the biggest side-draft carburetors a cam could handle.

She'd buy. Holy shit. Sexual fantasies leapt from the corners of Hardin's twisted mind. He raced from one flag to the next, each lap faster than the last. She was conducting the orchestra, her baton insistent, demanding more from the percussion section.

"What are you up to, Lieutenant?" Top caught Hardin looking spic-and-span; smiling as he looked past the food in the chow line.

"A nurse is gonna buy me a beer."

"What's her name?"

"I don't know, but she's got airborne-sized tits. Makes me nervous just thinkin' about those puppies." Hardin's excitement plowed through the scalloped potatoes.

"From B-Med. Must be Captain Weber." Top's look turned serious.

"She's hot for my body. I'm gonna let her modify my linkage."

"She's a friend of mine. Treat her right."

Top swirled his coffee and looked at Hardin over the rim of his cup. He had fired a warning shot—mumblety-peg with a large knife.

Top knew he could not provide guidance to a man prone to confusion. Hardin had expected violence for so long, treating someone right meant not killing them. The social grace he retained had been subverted by the forces of regeneration, needs that had him yearning to be alone with this woman and take the sex he had fancied, the sex he had conjured on the ridgelines of the Central Highlands.

With Top's guardianship role established, Hardin quieted his smile. The thought of playing sausage with this woman had compressed his mind into a blistering toil. Teasing out her tits would rank well above the rush of peaches and pound cake.

Supper was a splendid mystery chased with fresh toothpaste, and eight packets of Chiclets gum. Hardin arrived at the club early to prime himself with beer, capture the best table, and set the mood with music on the jukebox.

Willie Spencer's watch kept a solid pace. One song led to another, evoking memories of a good time past. Hardin stood at the jukebox, his power tools jousting with his conscience.

Two hours past the scheduled rendezvous he had progressed into a sphere of foolish banter with three other platoon leaders. When the war stories flowed in rapid succession, he decided to buy his sixth beer. "I… guess… you'll say… what can make me feel this way… my girl… talkin' 'bout my girl." Hardin was pounding beer to escape.

"I hope you're sober. Can't stand a drunk." Her voice was windy. Her challenge teased his senses. His body danced with excitement.

"I'm okay. I could use a little company." He couldn't hide his anticipation. He wanted to touch her hair and have the smell wrap him into a rhythm.

"What kind of beer?" He showed her the can. "One more?"

"That should do it." Boy, that's no shit, he thought.

"Well, Lieutenant Hardin, my name is Captain Weber." The woman was focused.

Her walk to the bar captured the eye. She sat down with a gentle slide keeping the table between them. Hardin's balls jumped into a spin, cycling in opposing elliptical orbits. A surge of blood slammed his cock against the table leg. His mouth filled with mush.

"What else do ya know about me?" *What a shit-hot start,* he thought.

"I know you went down in that slick with a friend of mine."

"Must have been the pilot." Hardin closed his eyes and the pilot's helmet shattered.

"Did he have a chance?"

"No." Moisture welled in her eyes. Hardin looked toward the jukebox.

"The one morning I didn't say good-bye." Her chin quivered, then wrinkled briefly.

"That can hurt." She wiped her eyes. "There's a lot of that goin' on." Hardin gulped his beer, selected three more songs, and sat quietly admiring her courage.

"Let's go for a walk," she said. "Get some air." Captain Weber wanted some company, too—that and the quiet of a million stars. She continued to cry softly as they passed the barracks heading toward B-Med, exchanging a word now and then: occasionally touching shoulders.

"We were going to get married this month, in Australia. He was a good man."

"A lotta good men are gettin' whacked."

"Bob Fox. His name was Bob Fox." Captain Weber turned her grief toward the entrance of B-Med, then said, "You made it."

"Like I said, good men get whacked. Besides, I'm gonna be a daddy come, May."

Captain Weber lectured herself, evaluating her misgivings, deciding that this GI she fancied was an honorable sort, and that she would hold on to her warrant officer for as long as she could. She opened the door to B-Med, then turned and said, "When we meet again I expect you to be in one piece—and you can buy the beer." She leaned forward and gave Hardin a kiss on the cheek.

For that moment Hardin drew at the smell of her hair, then lowered his head as if to apologize. Civility was the last thing on his mind.

* * *

For all that, and before the sun could rise, pangs of guilt crept through Hardin's conscience. He was ashamed of his intentions. His dog tags said he was the man who was married to Linda. For all his resolve, he had strained his limits. The wain ropes of an ox cart could not have kept him from his thoughts. He closed his eyes to his wedding ring teasing the nipple of Weber's breast.

Breakfast seemed a false reward.

With Stubbs complaining about convoy duty, Hardin stood sipping coffee, aimlessly watching the trucks arrive. Blood and LeCotte stood in separate trucks, yelling obscenities.

"Fuck you, Blood," Stubbs yelled. Nervous laughter laminated itself into a meld. None of these Brownjobs wanted to ride in open trucks.

Stubbs glanced at the truck following his. "Holy shit," he said, whispering.

The bed of the deuce-and-a-half was consumed by a quad-fifty machine gun mounted just forward of the rear axle. The gunner was incidental.

The convoy jumped through low gear into an inevitable focus. Trapped, Hardin stared at the dash, waiting for the explosion. As a rocket-propelled grenade tore the cab apart, Weber's tits took center stage, exploding from her shirt. *Pussy is powerful stuff,* Hardin thought.

On the side of the roadway, waist-high grass ran unbroken for sixty meters into the jungle foothills. As much as he tried to search the vegetation, his thoughts were consumed with sex. Given the choice between a gunfight and sex, Weber's breasts would leap at his face, demanding his touch, her tongue tracing a ridgeline.

Hardin opened the door of the truck, and yelled, "We're gonna get hit."

Fish and Bucks scrambled to the back of the truck and dropped the tailgate, then dropped to a knee, searching opposing tree lines. Hardin sat sidesaddle into the doorway to organize his feet as if he were standing on the skid of a chopper. With his weapon wedged in the door, he lowered his rucksack into the door well.

"You drive this road much?" Hardin pushed his rucksack deeper into the door well. He was zero-for-two on reaching the An Khe Pass, and he could feel a series sweep in the making.

The F-100 flew by. The pilot wasn't smiling this time—he was screaming.

"I got sixty-one and a wake-up. Ain't been shot at yet," the driver said. Not having been shot at set the probability of being ambushed well beyond the ken.

"You better hang on to your ass, my man, cause you're due." The driver searched the roadside as he shoved the transmission into a higher gear. "Where's your weapon?"

"Kontum." With a shrug, the driver threw his cigarette out of the window. Trying to reach Kontum without a weapon was a game Hardin knew well.

Thoughts of danger were disconnected. Captain Weber leaned over Hardin letting her nipples caress his lips, her padded whispers naked with lust, the sounds and smells of her body pushing him to respond. She was a snowy clean elixir sent to enrich the lot of an unfinished warrior. The sudden downshift and the chattering exhaust centered Hardin on the roadway.

"You're due." The hillbilly would be ripened fruit before he reached the An Khe Pass.

The lead truck followed a bend to the right and then turned back to the left. The moment the lead jeep carrying the convoy commander started into the first bend, ambush fire raced from the right flank, hit the convoy commander between the eyes, and blew his helmet out of the jeep, splattering his brains over his radio operator's face, belching gray matter from the windshield to the spare tire.

Relaxed by the intensity, Hardin dove from the truck and rolled to a knee. Screaming, he began firing into the grass at the base of the tree line. Wading through the grass, visually detached, AK rounds snapped at his face.

The quad-fifty roared, the rounds shredding the vegetation and the darkness beyond. Uprooting small trees, tossing bits of jungle about like confetti, the four-tongued dragon was snorting blue smoke and casting shell casings from its lair.

Slogging through a tangle of insanity, with Blood at his hip and a squad on either side, Hardin fired magazine after magazine, firing at undirected sounds. In the light of this perverted logic, his new medic exploded. A shoulder and half of his neck burst into the air, dragging tails of his uniform as streamers.

This replica of Dak To left Hardin in a guttural palsy. Reflex hurtled him under a dead tree. Frantic, he lunged ahead. His glasses shattered. Removing his helmet, he shed his rucksack. With seven magazines left, he fired through a latticework of grass prisms at sounds he couldn't segregate, hollering some medieval dialect.

Time seemed suspended as he bounded through the chest-high scrub, standing at intervals, firing at sounds, looking for Blood on his left and Tennessee on his right. With the lurch of a sudden fall, he was out of ammunition. The one magazine he had left was empty.

Mingle-minded, with his guts in a boil, he slumped into a heap, searching the grass for a bullet to put in his weapon. Exhausted by his defeat, he sat staring at the empty magazine.

The clear crystal face of Willie Spencer's watch was shattered. The second hand was bent and lodged against the tiny blue crystal that was number three. Gently, as if Willie knew, Hardin doctored the second hand and set it free. *Holy shit,* Hardin thought. *Damn, it still runs.*

Mex hollered. The enemy was gone. Hardin stood.

Ah-Shucks, his hillbilly truck driver, was shedding speed, glaring at the jungle from behind bullet-riddled sandbags, squatting in the bed of his truck. No longer an apprentice warrior, he could measure his margins by counting the holes in his windshield. Ah-Shucks was bounding toward mental deficiency. If he stopped to cling to a memory, a grunt would run him down.

Road kill.

Captain Joe had promoted Doc Collard to senior medic the day before the convoy operation, without giving Hardin so much as a countrified grin. Amps recoiled as Doc rolled the dead medic's curling hair into the poncho and tried to hide his missing shoulder.

Hardin followed the procession, retracing his movements, looking for empty magazines. Laughing, he reached into the grass to secure a magazine and found a chunk of the medic's shoulder, waiting for orders. With a slight hesitation, he grabbed the magazine and stepped aside. By the time he reached the roadway, he had recovered twenty-two magazines, and the dead medic was starting to rot.

Why the dead man was Hardin's medic was not clear. No one knew his name. If he was not on the morning report, he was not a member of the platoon. His rumpled imprint on the poncho was inflated, as though he had taken a deep breath.

He died at 0814 hours, moments before Hardin smashed his glasses.

"Amps, log in ammo and magazines. I need eleven. Check the squads," Stubbs said.

"What about the medic?" Amps asked.

Hardin rocked on his haunches between the truck and the roadside, hoping the shade would temper the next few minutes.

"What's his name, Stubbs?" Stubbs didn't answer. Detachment rushed to anger, then futility. With eyes that looked oily, the dead man's mouth curled at one side, toward his missing shoulder, as if he had something wise to add.

"Drips," Hardin said, loading a magazine. "You, Mex, and Big Bucks are goin' home when this caravan reaches, Kontum."

"We ain't gotta prayer of makin' Kontum in this truck." Drips knelt down and hit Hardin's fist with a hint of humor. "Got some cherry as good as me, El Tee?"

Alerted by an uncertainty he could not measure, Hardin detected a hitch in Drips' speech, a hitch that wasn't there before. He was hiding something. Knowing Drips wasn't crafty enough to keep a secret, Hardin answered his question.

"No. I figure if I get you jokers outta here, I'll get the clap whittled down to Fish."

"PeeWee's gonna get somethin' special the way he's been flaggin' his cock around." Drips glanced at the poncho, then smiled through a nod.

"Tell me somethin', Drips. Is it true red-haired pussy is an eight-second bull ride?

"Screamers when ya give 'em a little dew." Drips laughed as he turned into the roar.

The two men bolted from the ground facing the direction of the fire. Bravo Company's radio operator had emptied a magazine into the side of his jeep.

"He's fucked," Drips said, taking off his helmet. "Got blood and shit in his mouth."

Drips inventoried the faces he could see. He admired the courage he found in other men. He admired his own courage most. Drips nudged the dead man's boot as if to say good-bye. When he found Hardin watching, he shrugged and looked away.

"Ya want me to tell Mex and Bucks you're cuttin' us lose, El Tee?" The two comrades conspired instantly to issue Mex and Big Bucks one last ration of shit.

"Send 'em over." Drips turned into the confusion.

Truck drivers scurried along the roadway collecting fifty-caliber shell casings, and throwing the brass into the back of the gun truck. Infantrymen lay scattered in the brush, each man focused on one thing: reloading their magazines as quickly as possible.

"Tennessee, you shoot anybody today?" Stubbs asked. Tennessee sat motionless, staring at the shattered trees the quad-fifty had killed.

"Fuck if I know. I was shootin' 'cause you were." Stubbs tossed a small bag of marijuana at Hardin's feet and pointed at the dead man with a disarming conclusion.

Watching Mex and Bucks pick their way down the flank of the roadway, Hardin knew that Drips had primed his friends for an ass chewing. Their innocence was couched in a simplicity they could not sustain. Mex took the lead, cocking his body to the left.

"Ya want us, El Tee?" Hardin remained quiet, serious. His grin was gone.

"Step away from me. You pull that shit again and I'll bang ya myself."

Bucks started to retreat, then decided on a clever shuffle. Hardin laughed to himself. Mex and Bucks always looked bewildered when he chewed their ass. He tossed the bag of dew at their feet. A roar of muddled shock spiraled into alarming street-trash: Sin City had too many whores and too much whiskey. Bucks was mustering a glimmer of honesty when Mex became indignant: in Spanish.

"Shut the fuck up. That dew was the dead guy's. I know you don't smoke dope."

Drips laughed with a howl. Bucks caught the trap. Mex was still thinking in Spanish.

"You dickheads." Hardin paused to enjoy sound of the words. "You dickheads are outta the bush when we reach, Kontum."

Only in Vietnam could you find an inner-city black working his Black English on an inner-city Mexican talking trash Spanish, the two alternately inventorying their nuts, shuffling through an on-the-block dance routine, the show performed on an open roadway, moments after an ambush, under the glowing barrels of a quad-fifty, next to a dead medic.

Normal they were, they're antics dedicated to preserving what might be left of their day. Unspoken were the times of their best friend's death. Hippie was the last best friend to die.

They were a rough bunch indeed; as almost all grunts were, but they had some virtues. They could be kind when it occurred to them. They might even be honest, though they preferred a good lie.

Putting luck aside, the grunts who kept living did not lie when it counted.

Stubbs dropped nineteen magazines and 600 rounds on Hardin's rucksack. Pops, Boyle, PeeWee and LeCotte grabbed the poncho. Crimson blood splashed onto the roadway. A rivulet reached the grass along the shoulder.

Hardin closed his eyes. Dig-it's blood raced across the deck of the burning chopper.

"God damn war," he said to himself. "Tighten 'em up, Stubbs."

Stubbs had two cigarettes going, the dust-off holding his thoughts. "Knock it off, Bucks," Stubbs hollered. "Get 'em saddled up. Check their ammo."

Amps stepped around a pool of blood.

* * *

The resupply was completed before Captain Joe spoke into the smoke of a new cigar. "Glad we didn't have point," he said, his voice carefully empty as if more grain might tip the scale. "Dinks blasted Bravo Six right between the runnin' lights, perfect shot."

Hardin motioned for Joe to sit. "Bravo Six's RTO jumped on the net, screamin', 'Six is hit, Six is hit'. The silly fuck is nuts," Joe said, waving smoke away from his face.

"That RTO is gonna be our next deserter," Hardin said, savoring a scrap of disgust. He didn't want to talk to Joe. Joe had volunteered the company for convoy duty.

"Could have been me," Joe said.

"You big-timers asked for it, ridin' in jeeps, talkin' on radios, wearin' your rank, lettin' Mother put us in trucks. This is the same road we had to fight for 'cause the Cav couldn't get it done. I don't even know that poor fucker's name." Losing his temper, Hardin grabbed his rucksack and stomped into the grass south of the roadway.

The medic was a new man, a new dead man, perhaps from another time: Korea, the Battle of Little Round Top. He would stand in line, well behind Hippie and Dig-it. Nuts would never meet him. With morbid zeal dead men picked at the strings of Hardin's soul, tempering the weight of his brow. For all he tried, his burden sat in plain view, along a furrowed ridgeline, kicking at this and that, taking more room than the rest of his body.

Hardin took a deep breath, allowing the weight of the stranger to settle. He laughed a false laugh. As if to conclude his business, Doc Collard laughed, then burst into his Groucho Marx imitation, arching his eyebrows, waving a cigar.

"What are ya celebratin', Doc?" Hardin and Collard gave each other their best grin.

"I'm yours 'til the rivers all run dry, or ya get another quack."

"I didn't know you were gone."

Collard lay against a tree, watching Drips, Mex and Bucks dance, glad for the distraction. The old friends set a fanciful line as they talked about being back in the world. A rare occasion indeed, finding these men happy at the same time. Habit had forced the segregation of their joy, as if being something other than ruthless brought retribution.

And so, the men of First Platoon relished the rhythm of their leaving.

Tempted by hope, their wishful banter gathered steam, countering stray thoughts with bits of foolish bravado. The trio had been through hell. Their unspoken words set their eyes to a horizon that scared the new men. At times they scared Hardin. Today they were just foolish.

Bucks' dance throbbed with purity, as silk might float on a soft breeze. He had mastered a pattern of quick steps, followed by a slow gathering into a spin, then exclamations of joy, his hands pushing down on his program while his head shook with laughter.

Surprised by Amps' foot, Bucks landed in a pool of the dead man's blood, freezing as if misfortune had wings. Crossing himself, he began apologizing to the dead man, his hands held to his sides as if to make room. Begging Fish for a word, Bucks reckoned aloud: since the dead man was a stranger he didn't know who to curse. Fish thought this might be true.

Relieved, Bucks resumed his celebration. Drips told him not to touch him until morning, just in case Fish had it wrong. Mex told Bucks it was bad luck, and that wasn't the half of it. Mex told Bucks he was gonna die in Vietnam.

That's when Drips screamed, "Oh bullshit," and started to dance.

Drips, a rhythmic dwarf, used trees, bodies, and other obstacles to stop his motion and change direction. At odd intervals, he would stop and extend his palms toward his feet, declaring he had finished on the assigned spot. After an appropriate pause, he would jump into a squat and utter a noise as if he was suffering through a cheese-log shit, then stand with a roar and make his audience pound his fist.

Mex couldn't dance. Rock'n'roll music mystified him, sure enough; too many drums beats; but he had an answer for his critics; trash Spanish.

* * *

"We're walkin' south from here. Convoy-time is over." Joe paused so the platoon leaders could plot the new points of origin on their map. His boots were covered with blood.

"I don't see any paved roads." Hardin couldn't resist.

"Knock it off. We'll search south toward this blue-line. Gator, followed by Andy. Hardin you got drag. Ten minutes."

"Why aren't we goin' to Kontum?" Andy asked.

"A LRRP team spotted a Caucasian south of here," Joe said.

"That dude didn't walk here from Ban Me Thuot," Gator said.

And so the story goes, good men chasing a ghost. The convoy mission was critical until two men were killed less than a mile from the An Khe base camp.

Captain Joe was a good commander. His instinct had been a guide through a disordered world, sewing seeds of trust with faint threads of assurance and confidence. The mosaic he wove was a fragile blend of cold reality and black humor.

Combat left no quarter for sympathy. Rap would kill Whitey because he tore the fabric of Rap's fire team. Convoy Duty had stretched the company's fabric. If one of the Hill People had been killed, Joe would have been isolated and ignored.

Just following orders was not an excuse in Vietnam's war.

Hardin looked at his captain. Twice he started to speak, only to find the words he might choose unreliable. For the past four months, trapped in war's partially illuminated environment, Joe had made good decisions. His boss, the Old Man, would write a glowing efficiency report.

Joe's men would add a reminder.

They weren't running false colors, converts as they were to a vicious cult—temporary men honed to a psychosis of mutual fidelity, no longer dutiful to a flag, but to a twelve-month commitment, to live or die. Vietnam's war was not complicated.

If a grunt made all the mistakes one time, he would be sent home in a box.

Hardin looked into the jungle. Remembering the words that Montgomery had written in his father's officer efficiency report, he missed his dad.

Times spent on Highlands Road were the best. Too bad he was in such a hurry.

* * *

Number #10, Highlands Road. Bremerton, Washington. September 1954.

The Major's den was littered with colored pencils and map overlays. He was preparing a lecture for the Army Command and General Staff College at Leavenworth, Kansas. Pipe smoke hung atop the highest row of pictures like a fog bank.

"Hi, Pops."

"How are you doing, Pal?" The Major banged his pipe against a heavy glass ashtray. The battle overlay was titled "The Fulda Gap."

"What's this?" Eddie asked, looking at a letter signed by Montgomery.

"It took me four years to get that efficiency report for my service as a liaison officer. Look at the date—20 June 1949." Young Hardin read the one sentence and shrugged.

"That's the report. One paragraph for fighting from Normandy to Bergen-Belsen?"

The Major took umbrage, then read the words with pride. "The efficiency with which Major Hardin carried out his duties of liaison officer for the 21st Army Group was of the highest order. From the War Office, Whitehall, London. S.W.I."

"My coach said I had some decent blocks today."

* * *

The Jungle Southwest of An Khe Base Camp.

Looking west along Route #19 Hardin thought he could see where Dig-it had died.

Dig-it and the Major—that would be a pair. Deciding Dig-it was his friend he looked hard down the roadway, puzzled, as if he were trying to remember something. Charred bodies came to mind.

The sky was fusing with heat.

After a map check and a warning from Joe about dry vegetation, the company started south through a maze of low limb-infested trees. The jungle floor was baked to a crust. The temperature beneath the canopy had reached 110 degrees.

Wallowing in putrid sweat, GIs spread and staggered their files. Weighing heavy, Hardin's boots whispered across the flat ground. Fear set his step from one balance point to the next as he hunched against his load. Hot dry air seared his throat. He could barely swallow.

With the day low on water, Hardin began to search for a blue-line. Rap and Blood set the pace at inches per step. Paralleling a well-used trail, stepping high to soften their stride, Mex and Bucks froze as if their batteries were connected. Hand signals forced a period of silence.

Amps ran his hand through the dry grass, then shook his head, watching Reynolds crawl toward the trail.

With no scuff-marks or broken vegetation to judge, Mex turned an ear into the dense foliage. A blue-line ran west into a tunnel of vines.

"Lima, I'm wet, over." Mex whispered when the jungle was close.

"Roger, water-up and keep steppin," Tennessee said.

"We got a water buffalo in the blue-line, fifteen meters on our right flank. We're gonna break left and hunker down while you slide through," Mex said.

Stubbs crouched in ankle-deep water. The water buffalo, its tail switching casually, fed on sedge grass. Water curled quietly around Stubbs' boots as he set his ear into the jungle, listening. Watching the vegetation for movement, he threw a rock at Old Blue. The buffalo lifted its head and extended its neck, shook its head and continued to graze.

The platoon moved through the blue-line to the edge of a meadow that stretched into a tangle of spindly white-barked trees. Just inside the edge of the far tree line the roof of a hootch stood as fair warning.

Stepping into the blue-line to flush the buffalo, Fish and LeCotte fired at a rushing sound. A dink bolted out of a thicket in front of Rap, running toward the hootch. Twenty-four GIs fired in turn. Lightning said he saw the man fall. Too hot to care, the platoon filled the blue-line with their boots.

Filling his canteen Hardin found Tennessee talking with Joe. *Tennessee is a slut,* Hardin thought. He and Joe had been cozy for months.

"You southern boys fit like a cartridge and a bore. Wearin' a Klan hat must be like wearin' a helmet," Hardin said, pouring water down his pants.

"At least the Captain knows where to find Murfreesboro," Tennessee said.

"Amps has a country face. A brief-bloomer if you catch my drift. Amps said Murfreesboro had one outhouse, a two-holer." Hardin laughed a huff. "You and Captain Joe can hold hands."

"Hell's Half Acre is where I'm from. Captain Joe knows where that is."

"That's where we're headed."

CHAPTER FOURTEEN

Amps

Jungle, Southwest of An Khe Base Camp.

Proud of his lack of guile, Amps stood burbling sharp reports, laughing as if shooting a target he saw yesterday. With his boonie hat cocked he let go a barrage, jumped away from the colored air, extended a palm to excuse the mess, then joined his frolic with a home spun sonnet—Kentucky Windage.

Twilight brought GIs like Amps to the verge.

The jungle was plain enough now. The company's night laager sat on a knoll overlooking the blue-line and sixty meters of the surrounding landscape. This patch of jungle was a seedy, wrinkled maze. Exhausted, as if they could not sweat another drop, one GI and then another stepped out of the perimeter to service his bowels. With no wind, the close canopy gathered a heavy mix of coffee, garlic, and shit.

Even the foliage seemed annoyed.

Admiring the salami he had sliced, Hardin stirred the chunks into a can of beans and franks. Squeezing a ribbon of tube cheese brought a smile as thoughts of pussy sent his crank snaking down his pant leg. Would it be the Cockney ladies of Piccadilly Circus, or the black-haired Baby Sans of Sin City? He squeezed his thighs together.

Faces hung in the still air, their voices filled with a humored pain. The coffee was as bitter as Ski's mood. Complaining about the rash on his ass, he told Doc Collard to kiss it.

The image of a burl of a man stood-to in Ski's mind as members of the night ambush walked by. In silence, with a reluctant grin, they exchanged nods. Amps and Ski were their gatekeepers. Andy was the last man to make eye contact. Amps gave him a thumbs-up. Ski gave him the finger.

You could hear Ski blink as he gave out an uneasy sigh, not lifting his eye. Carrying a look of alerted exhaustion, his expression sparred with his unrelenting rage. His day had been crippled with periods of prolonged silence, interrupted by animated communication with any object that happened to be in front of his face.

Ski could be dangerous. He could rip the heart from a new man whose dreams were persistent. Ski could walk tracer rounds into a knothole.

News had reached the platoon that Stump was dead. According to Ski, Stump was the best assistant machine gunner. Being wider than he was tall, Stump carried an extra 400 rounds of ammunition. The AK round that hit his chest had driven a belt link into his lung. He died in a hospital in Japan. Stump was Ski's best friend. He was Bucks' friend, too.

Bucks held eighty-seven dollars of Stump's markers and considered all time lost when he wasn't rollin' dice. When he told Ski to make good on Stump's markers, Ski held Bucks off the ground suggesting that Bucks lose the markers and swear that Stump was a good dude.

One day Stump told Bucks the dice were golf clubs—African golf clubs. That's when Bucks asked Rap to shoot Stump. Rap told Bucks that Stump liked to skin snakes and that Bucks might be packin' the shortest snake Stump would ever skin.

Fish thought this might be true.

Ski had taken Bucks as his friend after Dak To, as he said, to keep the dude from stealing his money. Bucks tolerated the big machine gunner's moods, as he said, to keep the dude from shredding his bamboo baseball bat.

"Have Mex run a light clover around Bucks' OP. Gotta be quick," Stubbs said. Amps grabbed the hook, setting his dinner aside.

"Lima Two, Fiver wants a quick light one around the outpost, over."

Four studs grabbed their gear and exited the bubble.

Stubbs lay against a tree with his hands resting on his weapon, watching LeCotte dig and listening to PeeWee bitch about running out of Tabasco. Hardin tapped a plastic spoon on the handset. "That radio's power. Drop a name and things happen." Tennessee shook his head.

"No, El Tee. Tits are power—tits and pussy. One thing's fer sure: you bein' a dickhead don't help." He pointed at Hardin with his spoon.

"You callin' me a pussy, boy?" Hardin asked.

"No, El Tee. You're a dickhead." Amps agreed.

"A dickhead maybe, just not a dick. Is that it?" Hardin said, dropping into a full squat next to Amps to quiet his laughter.

"I never thought of that, but yeah, okay." Amps nodded and glanced at Tennessee.

"Squeak had it right. You weren't on top, were ya fuck-stick? She shot ya because you couldn't get it up." Amps changed sides and laughed again.

"Squeak had nothin' right. I got a rod stiff enough to chop cotton."

"Chop cotton. You're a fuckin' hick, ya know that?"

Amps sighed a comfortable sigh. Whenever Hardin talked about Squeak or Tennessee he became smug and self-assured. As if having the goods on one of his friends was part of Amps idea of himself. And from what Stubbs had told him about Squeak, Amps spent much of his day trying to ignore what anyone said: even his lieutenant.

Amps never seemed to shoulder his work on purpose, more as if he was the platoon radio operator by mere chance. Occasionally he would slouch around, whining about having no idea where he was going. Annoyed by this behavior, Stubbs would take the handset and haul Amps around until Amps became more of a soldier than he would have been without the aggravation.

Avoiding Stubbs, Amps brewed his coffee, resolved to another night at jungle central. He finished his C-Ration and listened to Mex's radio transmission.

"Lima Two is back, Jack. Situation is negatory." Mex had made a speed recon.

"I shot that water buffalo in the ass and the damn thing didn't move," Amps said.

"This gun couldn't punch a hole in a fuckin' balloon," Tennessee said, reading the serial number on his rifle.

Warned about the M-16 rifle, Hardin chaffed at his bonds.

Never mind the lack of penetration in thick jungle surrounds, Hardin thought. Grunts dying with a more reliable weapon gave their civilian handlers more believable statistics. These grunts were, after all, twelve-month men—merely green-carders indentured to ensure the fidelity of their nation to a semi-Christian band of strangers.

The nation's fidelity bond required the physical presence of an army to ensure the security of South Vietnam. The bondsman's actuary managed the war's statistics to keep these grunts in the game, awarding Golden Rifles, Brownjob of the Year, Best Body Bag: the Bronze Star the equivalent of a cocktail olive.

In some circles, Purple Hearts were issued for well-tended scars. In some circles, the M-16 rifle produced more Purple Hearts than the AK-47.

Faced with ritual fatigue, the jungle reduced a grunt's world to survival, producing a mistrust of anyone outside of his line of sight. And with life day-to-day, grunts found the tax-free savings account and combat pay laughable. Alive or dead, a grunt was a piece of equipment with a variable cost. High-priced grunts got their names chiseled in granite.

Wicked men just got paid.

Bursting with self-hatred and tired of parsing his war, fatigue reached out to settle the day. Hardin was asleep before stand-to. His dream nurse was working on his program, gently massaging his thighs.

"El Tee, give it a rest." Amps kicked Hardin's shoulder with the heel of his boot. "Roll over. Your cock is wavin' in the breeze."

"I was leadin' the choir." A tenor quartet of lizards sang out "Fuck-you, fuck-you." The lizards were a welcome, lyrical warming, as certain as Sweet Cheek's shroud line.

Tennessee shook out his boots. “Those lizards gotta be workin’ with that buffalo.” Amps lay with his hands behind his head, looking through the trees.

“Ever see ’em?” Amps asked. Tennessee shook his head and turned to reheat his coffee and fluff up his rucksack.

“No, man. They change colors.” When Tennessee lied he used a scholarly tone.

“This place sucks,” Amps said. “Spiders big enough to eat birds, singin’ lizards. Look.” Amps pointed into the jungle. Fish was perched in a squat, his ass parked over his Claymore.

“No one’s gonna touch that Claymore,” Tennessee said. Fish cocked a lustful leg, looked at his work, then with a pleased grin, started wiping his ass with gusto.

“Fish is one sick fuck,” Amps said, wishing he was as short as Fish.

“Ya gotta love this war. Tennessee, you call your o’lady when we were in?” Hardin asked, lighting a ball of C-4 plastique.

Amps laughed. He enjoyed laughing to himself. Being a bit timorous, he avoided one-on-one exchanges, standing on his dignity. He would wait for a conclusion—any conclusion would do—then add his concurrence with a brief nod or a jealous shake of his head.

Pondering the odds, Amps would sit with a fist posted near the side of his mouth, covering his expression while he listened. If he agreed a second time, he would point a finger at the right man, then give his nuts a toss.

“Why in hell would I do that?” Tennessee had raised his voice because Amps had sided with Hardin.

“She’s gonna want ya back. The pride of Dixie.”

“Fat chance. Her daddy’s gonna shoot me. Figures Chuck’s gonna take care’a things.” Amps nodded, then drank from his tit-bag.

* * *

Stand-to passed into darkness. Tired men waited, as if they knew when fate’s targets would appear. The night ambush was locked in a large cave, over there.

A Claymore exploded. The concussion echoed through the canopy. Scenes of death flash in rapid succession, replete with comrades mangled by fragments of bamboo and steel. A scream followed. Screams from the night have no origin. They plunge into a man’s memory and race to the deepest pool of his imagination.

Drops stood-to in Hardin’s mind. Drops died before he could scream. Drops was killed in Dak To. He wasn’t called Drops because he had the clap. Drops was called Drops because his last name was Sprinkle. Drops could be mean, drunk or sober. He was shot in the forehead. As Stubbs reached his side, Drops' face collapsed into an empty cavity.

Hardin took a deep breath, trying to find a night focus. His friend Andy was in trouble.

Quiet now, the night jerked from one radio check to the next, followed by a morning walk in bleached twigs to rescue Andy. Wasted by the sleepless horror of expecting Chuck to stomp their ass, Andy's boys stumbled and cussed themselves into a rocky stride. They had blown a man into a putrid blur—720 steel balls had cut him in half.

Assuming the stride of a lost dog, Stubbs was happy to be on drag, channeled by a river of broken grass. When the old sergeant analyzed the ambush site, he could not resist his own humor. With the tone a wizard might use, he keyed the hook.

"Andy, Lima Five. Are ya there? "

"Mike go." Andy's breathing was audible and his voice was hostile.

"Andy, is this the asshole that kept you dancin' all night?" The challenge.

"Fuck you." The rebuttal.

"You're not suppose to say 'fuck' on the radio." Tennessee was right.

"Who said 'fuck' on the radio?" Amps joined the fray.

"No one said 'fuck'. Andy said 'fuck you,' over," Tag chimed.

Nervous chatter hovered over a body spread through the jungle like spaghetti after a food fight. The dead man's face carried no expression. Rats had eaten the meat from his left hand.

Suffocating heat forced the company to trace the blue-line. GIs ate salt and prayed for a break. By late afternoon the company laager was complete and the lizards were back. Amps was gutting an iguana he'd plucked out of the blue-line. "Just like chicken." He dropped the legs into a canteen cup of boiling water. "Are these the dudes talkin' to us?" Amps asked.

Tennessee keyed the handset, and said, "How would I know?"

"The soprano has a southern accent. Must be a fag," Stubbs said.

"No way, Sarge. She's one of those tight little company jobs," Tennessee said, brushing off the handset and shoving it in his rucksack.

"She's perfect for that tee-tee dick you're packin' around." Amps slapped his thigh, laughing through a mouthful of beef and rice.

"I got me an auger, Sarge. A purebred puss-hog. The ladies get excited just knowin' Boss Hog is in the yard, spring-loaded and grain-fed." Amps shook himself into a daydream.

"You don't know pussy from knotholes. Give me the hook." Stubbs took the handset, threw it in the dirt, leaving Tennessee mumbling about the Sarge not being worth a shit and talking to Amps about paybacks.

"What are we doin'?" Hardin asked, watching Captain Joe drip cheese on his comics, trying to keep a nasty cigar butt on fire.

Joe muttered through a studious huff, "How's the fever?"

"Comes and goes, like most things around here." Joe agreed.

Running across the perimeter, Doc Collard signaled for water. A new man had collapsed with heat stroke. With three men fanning his naked body, Doc poured water on his chest and balls. The cherry was convulsing. Head to toe, his body was rigid.

"Doc, I've got some alcohol," Hardin said, untying his rucksack. Doc worked frantically, struggling with his inability and a jungle that was losing light. Hauling the man to the blue-line to save his life was not an option.

Worried and alone, Linda had mailed her soldier four bottles of antiseptic for jungle rot and dysentery. At the time the gesture was humorous. Now she was saving a stranger's life. Hardin had kept the rubbing alcohol, and dumped the two jars of powdered shit-stiffener.

"Is he gonna make it, Doc?" Hardin spoke to a dark form.

"Yeah, I think so. Ya got any coffee, El Tee?" Long past their coffee break, Doc wanted to let Hardin know he was tired. "We better dust him off, El Tee."

Tennessee keyed the handset. "Charlie, we need a dust-off first thing."

"Charlie, wait." Seconds passed. "Resupply at zero-niner across the water."

"Roger, break, Blood, ya listenin'?"

"Blood, go." Before Tennessee could speak, Blood said, "We're dustin' off the cherry at 0900, strip his gear. Right on. Fucker's a pussy."

"I need eight magazines."

"You need more than that, asshole."

* * *

Bucks and Rap loaded out the heatstroke, and Captain Joe got a medic named Taylor and three cherries in trade. Second Platoon took a pair of five-foot-five ivory bookends, and First Platoon took a black GI named Richards.

Fish decided to call the man Boo because, as Fish explained it, Boo was the first brother he had run across who looked surprised about being a grunt.

With round, dark glasses, and heavy-looking eyes, Doc Taylor had a slow, easy nature. Doc Collard inventoried Taylor's medical bag. Rap gave Boo his black-on-black briefing: Rap was the main brother, and nobody messed with the short, white dude with the glasses.

* * *

The Hill People gathered at Drips' foxhole, gratified that luck, fate, and circumstance had brought them safe from disaster. With the trail of dusk nesting on their shoulders and night nudging their words, the five remaining survivors of the battle for Dak To shared a steel-pot stew, whispering the words that made sense in those places where there is no sun.

With time gnawing at their heels, they wished one another a safe return to life. Ski, Fish, Drips, Mex, and Bucks—three whites, a brown, and a black. They would pray tonight, perhaps for the second time. They would witness the start of one more day, knowing they were brothers, paratroopers. They would mentor their El Tee with bits of caution only vacant eyes could convey.

With his soul pleading for a return to life, Hardin whispered the Lord's prayer. He spoke the words to the prayer a second time, adding Linda's name. And, as if he knew better, he apologized to his bride for leaving out their baby.

Sitting against a clump of bamboo, he wished he were part of Drips' fire team. Expecting the death of these men—his dearest friends—had become so exhausting, so intensely personal, the medic's death was a relief, a reprieve. A brusque end for a stranger—his death welcomed by men hiding from a yellow-gray dusk.

Hardin did not know what manner of man he had become amid the noise and the fear, amid the rumors and the hopes of home. He did know he missed his father and that the fabric that held his life together was giving way. His farm girl, his Linda, she was his hope.

With his fever of unknown origin on the mend and cringing at the prospect of being alive, the saga continued. Who would die next? Was death their rigid due? Hardin sucked at the saliva in his mouth, wished for earlier times, and decided to live no matter who he had to kill.

* * *

At dawn the temperature at boot level was ninety-four degrees.

"Tighten 'em up, Stubbs," Hardin said, realizing the jungle had gone quiet. "Get the girls ready to dance. Time to rock'n'roll."

"The plantation owner wants Tennessee for his code-talker—fried chicken, grits, incest."

"Captain Joe can have the cock peddler," Hardin said, staring at Amps.

"We're slack for Second Platoon," Stubbs said.

* * *

Bodies whispered and occasionally screamed as the loose, dry, knee-high grass fell away from their boots. The intermittent canopy left irregular patches of light on the jungle floor. A thin, reedy sound echoed with a sense of desperation. Death had a quieting effect in a world baked to a tinder crisp.

The jungle was calm when Joe decided to stop and fill canteens, to sit and listen for the reason for his fear. "If you find yourself in trouble," he liked to say, "relax and do whatever is most likely." When Mother hounded him for more detail, he liked to say, "A man running for his life can't see much, Mother."

Packing a ready-made grin, Joe let his dog-eared drawl jimmy the butt of a nasty turd. Captain Joe was happy with the flow of the creek.

Replenished, grunts cut along a flat with one of Andy's new men on flank security, billy-goating a small rise forty meters to the left front. Through a series of strides he froze, sank into a half-crouch, searching. Ignoring the antics of the stupid new guy, other GIs coursed along on autopilot, sorting the smells of burnt sweat.

When a Viet Cong soldier lunged out of the grass, his AK at the ready, the new man emptied his M-16, pulverizing the man's chest. Andy charged toward the flank, his body oscillating with the weight of his rucksack. The company raced after him, and then formed a perimeter around the dead man to wait in silence.

God's newest warrior sat on his helmet, sobbing into his hands, shaking. The other new men wanted to cry, too. Then and there, Fish decided to call the new man Short Round—because, as Fish explained it, the man was short.

Hardin shook his head. Instantly this new man's dreams were broken.

To look your enemy in the eye and shoot him, in a one-on-one quick-fire duel, on your second day in the jungle, would stall any grunt's mind. Andy ducked as he knelt near the new man, whispering. Short Round would spend his tour floating between acts, expecting to die—in the shower, in the mess tent, on R&R.

Eventually Short Round would embrace Hardin's world—a world of increasing disorder.

Soaked with sweat and decorated with waving patterns of dried salt, the GIs left the dead man for the rats, searching south into tighter vegetation. A yellow dust coated their skin. Smelling of stale garlic, the odor of their passing lingered in the air near the jungle floor.

Damn that brittle grass, Hardin thought. Then he laughed. Even hyper-alert, he had lapsed into a daydream. Tennessee jerked his arm.

"El Tee, are we still lookin' for that deserter?"

"I'm not."

Perched as if on rubber bands, grunts wobbled along just to wear themselves out, knowing they would either find themselves dead or sitting down at the end of the day. Short Round's nagging wail drew them into a patch of dense vegetation. Single file, one man followed another, wondering how the crying might end.

On the morning of the fourth day, First Platoon was assigned a cloverleaf. Hardin gave the recon to Rap. Mex was still in charge of the squad and Rap wished he wasn't leaving.

"Relax, Rap. Trace this route and come back down through the water—piece-a-cake." Hardin outlined the route on Rap's map, emphasizing the trail junctions.

"Go light, stay off the trails, keep in touch."

Rap looked at Mex and found the usual uncertainty. In a curious turn, Rap hated the Mexican's wily ways. Admiring the man's ability to stay alive, Rap would have liked Mex if Mex were afraid of him. As of yesterday, Mex even scared Fish.

Rap had called Mex "Cisco" on the airstrip in Duc Co to see if Mex knew the Cisco Kid. That, and to listen to Mex threaten to slit his throat in Spanish. Laughing at the brown man's antics, Rap threatened to kill Mex if he tried to leave.

Mex had listened, slowly closing his left eye. Laughing at the black man, Mex threatened to kill Rap while Whitey watched. Then he slit the nozzle off Rap's tit-bag. When Mex stood into a brace and smiled, Fish erupted into a fit and Hippie jumped into a dance, all on an empty airstrip the day Hippie died.

"Okay, El Tee," Mex said. Hardin smiled, holding his palms up.

"Get a commo check." Amps called PeeWee to ensure they were receiving each other loud-and-clear. Lima-charlie, and lickin'-chicken were Amps' slang for loud-and-clear.

Amps yelled into the hook, "Lima One, ya hear me?"

"I got ya lima-charlie, sweetheart. We're gonna bring the damn-damn on Chuck and pop a cherry." PeeWee's tough talk on the radio was designed to solicit a response.

Joe's radio operator responded. "Charlie's gonna scatter yer shit, baby."

"No way. Lightnin's our slackman."

"Hey baby. With Lightnin' pullin' slack, Charlie better sky up. Di di mau, motherfucka."

Hardin spoke quickly. "We got good commo?"

"So far." Sweat was dripping from Tennessee's chin.

Fifty minutes later Mex checked in using his best quiet whispers. "Lima Six, Lima Two." Trapped in a dark cave, he tried to outrun his fear. When the alarms sounded, he could speak perfect English.

"Wha'd'a ya got, Mex?"

"Piles of bamboo sticks on the side of a trail."

Hardin could feel the texture of his squad leader's voice. Piles of bamboo sticks—symmetry in the jungle. "Put Rap on the horn." Hardin had to get used to talking to Rap when the spiders were on the move. Mex had the handset keyed and Hardin could hear his voice.

"Get Rap. Fuck you, he wants Rap. Get him goddammit."

"Rap, are there any trip wires?" Hardin asked.

"No, ..." Rap said, barging into a slurry of Black English.

"Two piles of bamboo sticks. How far apart?" Hardin asked.

"Twenty, thirty feet." Logic focused Hardin on the space between the piles.

"Lay quiet, Rap. Get on the uphill side of the trail. Set your gun covering the trail. Ya gotta be quiet. Chuck is less than a hundred meters from you. I'm bringin' the boys out, Rap. Look for us east of your location. Don't fire us up."

The trail Mex cut through the carpet of straw was easy to follow. Forty minutes later, Bucks found Rap and his bamboo play-set. Staring at the piles of bamboo, voodoo had Bucks' mind on the run. Bamboo sticks the length of a post card were stacked in piles the shape of pup-tents, with a longer top piece protruding into the trail, pointing toward a small blue-line.

Bingo, Hardin thought. There's a rally point on the blue-line.

Hardin threw the bamboo sticks into the brush, then scanned the trail. The trial-heads disappeared into tunnels of thick vegetation.

"Rap," Hardin said, pushing LeCotte toward the trailhead to the west. "Blood, we got dinks on the blue-line, maybe a small base camp like Ban Me Thuot. The dinks that are late for the party will be lookin' for those sticks, for their road sign. Check it out."

"Gonna be slow," Rap said, staring into the dry brush between the trail and the creek.

Boyle was stuttering because the look on Boo's face made him crazy. He wanted to stick a finger in Boo's eye. He rolled a grenade over in his hand in front of Boo, hoping the new man would run. Stubbs grabbed Boyle's shirt and pushed him toward the trailhead.

"I'll go with ya, Rap," Hardin said, signaling Stubbs to hang tight.

Rap ran his tongue over his lips, pushing his search into the vines, fighting the roar in his head, taking ten- and twelve-inch steps, barely longer than his boot. With six abreast, Drips on the left and Rap on the right, keeping the line was critical.

Boo cracked a twig. The squad froze. Eleven GIs sank into a squat, listening and searching. Visibility was limited. Hardin rose and signaled right and left. Allowing time for Drips to get the signal, he stepped forward.

The first hint of sound was discarded. A metallic tick brought the squad up short. Hardin stepped forward. With thinning vegetation thirty meters to his front, the blue-line was bare. A maddening pattern of voices grew louder. Rap's hand formed a cone to cover his face. Pops went to ground. Four men and two women sat tending a fire.

Rap's vantage was slightly higher than the semi-circle of bare ground.

A tendril of smoke curled from a fire pit. A burned cooking bowl sat near the water's edge. An anchoring tree stood into the blue-line across the clearing from the fire pit.

The Viet Cong sat across a forty-foot front, pinch-scooping rice from wooden bowls and talking with their mouths full. A matted marsh grass accented the blue-line with a yellow-green hue. Shafts of sunlight formed a cage around the clearing.

Drips moved a cupped hand to his face. He had spotted an outrider twenty feet from the clearing on the left flank. Four GIs had clear shots. The odds were not good for hitting seven targets. Hardin laid his helmet on the ground.

The inscription was clear: Flowers are Forever.

Pops eased his weapon into a slot between two trees. PeeWee was trapped in vegetation too dense to move. Boo stared blankly at the sole of Fish's boot. Blood laid his sights on the one VC who had his AK leaning against his chest. Hardin pushed the grass away from his face. The female squatting near the blue-line had the best chance of escaping.

A shout echoed from the right flank: an eighth dink bounded down the creek bed.

Drips dropped the outrider. Rap dropped Paul Revere. The Viet Cong in the base camp were caught in a frenzy, an uncontrolled acceleration of fire. Such carnage did not have a beginning—rather snippets of indescribable horror. The head of Blood's target burst into Hardin's view, dragging at his front sight as he moved his weapon left across the kill zone. Boo's frag caught two VC as they bolted across the blue-line. One fell, then scrambled to his feet.

Drips shot him.

The echoes pulsed as they died away. Fish fired one round into the female lying in the marsh grass on the far side of the blue-line. Fish did not abide women who packed AK-47s.

"Lima Five, any signs?" Hardin whispered into the handset.

"Negative," Stubbs said.

"Stay tight." Hardin signaled Rap and Blood to nail down the far side of the water while the squad covered the campsite.

Twenty minutes of silence was enough for Boo. "What happened to 'em?"

"Shut up, Boo." Fish crawled to Boo's side and smiled his Hill-People smile. Blood and Rap popped into view on the far side of the stream carrying a rucksack.

Pops and PeeWee stepped into the campsite, searching for trinkets, their movements pushed by a mounting intensity. Hardin stood into the stream, staring at eyes blacker than a raven's ass, his rage screaming across the top of a pair of dead, chiseled cheekbones. Water slapped at the dead man's face, his shadow badgering the stones on the bottom of the stream.

"Bad day for a ride, asshole." Hardin slid his finger into place and squeezed. The dead man's face erupted. Scarlet bits of flesh lapped at the rocks.

"That's for Dak To."

Blood's expression creased with concentration as he measured his lieutenant's next move. Hardin leveled his eyes on the campsite. Boo knelt next to a dead woman, examining the AK she tried to shoot him with. Pops grabbed Boo's shirt and back-hauled him to his feet.

"Keep movin', Boo."

CHAPTER FIFTEEN

Drips

Charlie Company Night Laager. 1740 Hours.

Sheltered by the stifling heat and a jungle dense enough to trap their obscure thoughts, the satisfaction of killing the enemy had diminished. Abrupt hand motions countered voices, rigid with concern. Hand signals replaced the banter of preparing for stand-to. The significance of stumbling into a Viet Cong rally point had spiraled into expressions of faith.

With the lieutenants gathered at Joe's coffee cup, Andy jumped in with a plain-sailing look and said, "These dinks don't know we're here." Gator said, "They don't have much ammo."

These are good men, Joe thought, each expecting the other to care what they said, as if their insight was born from a good idea. Hardin turned to leave, looking uneasy, then stopped.

When Gator shit-sticked Joe by declaring the VC were stupid; Joe cocked his head, took a thoughtful draw on his cigar, and became a professor. "There's a plaque on a pedestal near the base of that hill we took back for the Cav on Route #19. One fine morning the Viet Minh ambushed French Field Force #1, killin' 1300-plus French soldiers at the base of that hill."

Not caring about the history of things, Hardin left the classroom.

"Get Drips for me, Cornpone." Tennessee gave Hardin the finger.

Drips coaxed his way between foxholes, walking as if he had acquired a hitch, acting as though he was out of film. He dropped into a tired squat, then settled on his helmet.

"Drips, you're leavin' on the resupply slick."

"I kin dig it." The big redhead held out a fist. "What about Bucks, and Mex?"

"They got the next ride."

"You're a good dude, El Tee."

Drips held his council. Haggard, something ate at him. He stared at the ground between his boots, hesitant for the first time Hardin could remember. Drips started with a sigh, then thought better. With Shadow gone, he could not find the words to keep his promise. Perplexed, something stirred in his heart. Padded chatter put on weight as he wiped his drive-on rag across his face. The hair on his forearms had burned blond. His hands were nearly black.

"You got one more night, Drips." The big Norwegian shook his head.

Giving a short nod, he said, "Roger that."

Reynolds, the Harley driver, was hard like Drips—a nasty nature with a wry grin. A lank man with a steel-tying disposition, the time had come for Reynolds to stand-to. They stood together, Drips and Reynolds, passing the chisel. For a moment they looked at their El Tee, agreeing that the secret Drips was nursing had ragged edges.

Noting their covenant, Hardin found Tennessee sitting cross-legged, boiling an Iguana and kissing Joe's ass with a share of it. Captain Joe had been an instructor at the Florida Ranger School for so long he talked of retiring near Field Seven at Eglin Air Force Base, the Ranger School Headquarters for the Florida training phase. Being fond of the subject, he talked to himself—fishing in the Gulf mostly.

"You like that lizard, Captain?" Stubbs asked, not caring. "Any word on extraction?" Stubbs opened his pants to air out his crotch.

"The Old Man got pissed-off when Bravo Six got blasted." Tennessee scooped a lizard leg into Joe's chili Lerp. Joe nodded, and said, "Stubbs, send Drips over here."

Desperate to demonstrate that his nature was tail-first, Drips assumed a defiant posture. When Joe made a friendly gesture offering the Viking a seat, to a man the GIs in Drips' fire team registered his folly.

Fraternizing with an officer was an actionable offense. The GI handbook forbid such encounters. Written in the mid-forties for the Chindits in Burma, the handbook tracked the evolution of a Foot, from a Digger to a Brownjob. The handbook ended with a warning. The next generation of infantrymen would be difficult to control: they would be Chimeras, imaginary monsters with incongruous parts.

Thirsty or mud-bound, this incongruity defined the parameters for a grunt's behavior.

Missing too many links, like their predecessors, grunts were not altogether bad. Leaning against a comfortable sandbag, a grunt might end his day with a fond memory. Mostly they were glad to keep from thinking.

Pestered by yesterday, Drips lived in the extreme. He could not put two minutes on end, let alone tie a fire team of mixed nuts to a company commander.

"Hardin says you're leavin' in the mornin," Joe said.

"Yes, sir." Fish stood and methodically folded his arms. Drips turned to avoid his stare.

"You're a good man, Drips." Drips wanted to run. "You taught me a lot. Thanks."

Drips was speechless. He had been given praise and gratitude from the one man he'd worked so hard to piss off. Captain Joe was the officer who made him hump the boonies with the clap, the officer who laughed when he clung to a tree to take a piss.

Captain Joe was the man whose cunning was much like his own.

Joe held out his hand and the Viking shook it. "Take care of yourself, Drips."

Drips nodded quickly, looked at Fish, and then straightened his helmet. Drips looked at Stubbs as if to say, "Hey, baby, me and the captain are buds."

Stubbs returned his grin.

"You still work for me, Drips, and you got one more night." Drips was off, helmet backwards, shirt half open and a toy gun in his huge fist.

"Third Platoon isn't makin' much contact," Stubbs said.

"They're lucky—long straw." Joe offered Stubbs a cigar with a boss-eyed nod. "They're ghostin' this deal."

"How's the new medic?" Joe asked, changing the subject.

"Taylor: he's laid way back. Studious, glasses, fits in with LeCotte. Doc, wha'd'a ya think about Taylor?" Stubbs scrubbed his cheek with the back of his hand.

Doc Collard grinned through a casual shrug. "He knows what's in his shot-bag." Collard arched his eyebrows, struck an agreeable pose, and dug into his aid kit. "Far out. Drips doesn't need it, but I'm gonna give it to him anyway." Collard held up a syringe, and said, "Clap-Cleaner," then stomped across the perimeter to mess with his friend.

The sight of Drips' freckled ass forced PeeWee and LeCotte to step away. Drips laughed and spun around hoisting his pants. LeCotte erupted into a tirade about social sensibilities, dragging Boyle stuttering through a chorus of black gibberish, with Fish adding his advice on life-after-Drips.

Doc Taylor smiled a wry smile and adjusted his glasses. He had not decided which cluster of GIs he preferred. Odds were on the more calculating one—Pops' crew.

With warning gestures to circle the wagons, Stubbs, Mex, Blood and Rap started setting guns, sandbags, Claymores, and the outpost.

Bucks cornered Hardin. "When do Mex and me get extracted?" Bucks was struggling, alerting without stimulation, worried about the dead medic's curse and the pieces of his wooden crucifix.

"Roll some dice, Bucks," Hardin said, pointing to a smooth run he had carved in the ground. The dice looked like the friend a drunk might find in an alley: snake eyes. "Now, Bucks, tell me a story about that deserter. Take your time."

"That dude's in Vung Tau, layin' up on his ass. Mothafucker skyed up."

"Those snake eyes belonged to that deserter," Hardin said. Bucks grabbed his dice, took almost all of Hardin's coffee, stood with a toasting gesture and stepped into the night.

Big Bucks was a superstitious man. He was also a liar.

* * *

Hardin woke with a start, dripping with sweat, fighting to focus on a tree or a star. He guzzled water to stem the confusion, then sank back into a vortex of unbaked dreams. One moment the old woman cried smoke-colored tears, the next she fired her carbine at Rap, the next she cradled a lifeless little girl. The fever of unknown origin had blackened the night.

"Let's go, El Tee."

Awake, he had slept through morning stand-to with a heart rate off the charts. Stubbs kicked his boot, winced through a long drag on his cigarette, then assigned Amps as his nurse.

The landing zone wasn't special until the landing-smoke caught the grass on fire. With the rotor-wash pushing the fire deeper into the jungle, the pilot faced the fire while the crew unloaded the supplies and a clean-looking major.

Drips gave the major a handful of hell, knowing his slick would not leave until the Man from Glad was on board. Hardin was leaning against a tree, talking on the radio when Stubbs directed the staff-patch with a backhanded thumb.

"Are you the CO?"

Hardin didn't stand. He could barely focus. He motioned the major to squat.

The man's uniform was ironed, his boots were polished, his shoulder holster was glossy, his hair was freshly cut, and his fingernails were clean. He held a plastic map case with zippers and grease pencils, and a musette bag for his nightgown and toothbrush.

The putrid cologne meant the staff-patch wore clean underwear. Keen to exercise his authority, the fire and the confusion of the resupply had his foreskin in overdrive. With no mind for grace, Hardin let the bastard have a taste of combat.

"Do I look old enough to be a captain? I'm a fuckin' grunt. What do you want?"

Suddenly the fire exploded through a stand of trees, forcing smoke across the LZ. Deciding Hardin was his man he spread an overlay. He was pleased with his obvious courage.

"Six Yankee wants you to follow this route and search this area of operations." He looked over his shoulder, startled by the surging fire. "Extraction's in three days."

"That's eleven fuckin' klicks." Hardin shouted as he stood and braced the tree.

"It's flat ground, should be no problem."

Matching the major's let's-whisper sign, with his father's listen-up finger, Hardin screamed, "Are you a test product, no batteries, just a fuckin' grease pencil?" The major was set to respond when Drips barged into Hardin's shoulder.

"El Tee, where's Captain Joe?"

"Who knows?" Hardin stuck out his fist. Drips hit it. "Take care, Drips, see ya in the world." Drips nodded through a bounce and slapped Tennessee's helmet.

"Thanks, man." Drips looked quick and hard at the major.

"I'm your S-3, Lieutenant. Here's your overlay."

"I'm a Brownjob, Major."

* * *

Carrying unopened cases of food, GIs crashed through the brittle foliage, determined to put distance between themselves and a growing fire. Four hundred meters up-wind, the point squad found a dense hollow. Tag stood-to next to Joe holding a soccer-ball sized booby trap made of bamboo laced with punji sticks.

"Five of these puppies were layin' near a trail, 300 meters north," Tag said.

Joe ran a finger along one of the punji sticks and said, "This is the same kind of trap that hit that kid in Kontum. Spring loaded." Joe started to open one of his letters, then stopped and said, "Make sure the studs get a look."

Tag held the trap by one of the spikes as he made the round. The studs didn't care.

Hardin didn't care either. He missed his friend Drips. Finding no sense of satisfaction for Drips' leaving, his energy sank away. Cussing at himself as if his courage would survive such a victory, he shrugged and let his thoughts run along.

"Burn that overlay," he said. The noise barking from the handset was a surprise.

"Lima, this is Six." Joe's voice was inquisitive. Hardin smiled at Tennessee, knowing what the call was about. "You got Three Yankee's overlay?"

"The damn thing caught fire." After a brief silence, the radio barked again.

"Lima Six, this is Three Yankee." Major Fireball, Mother's assistant, was bellowing, anxious to dress down the one subordinate who was out of step.

"Lima, go."

"You lost the overlay?"

"Roger that."

"Listen up, can you outline from memory?"

"Roger that." Hardin tossed the handset to Amps, then struck up a conversation with a tree he decided to call Martha.

"Really, Martha, the major doesn't understand. I can't think of myself the way the major sees me. You see, Martha, my memory caused the destruction of his overlay. Some day, Martha, that memory of mine will seem natural. Burning overlays will be child's play."

The major could either defer to Hardin's memory, or walk in the woods in his polished boots. The company wasn't riding Burma's Toonerville Trolley. Eleven kilometers was an eight-day hump if good water ran at the right intervals.

Hardin looked at Tennessee, stuck out his fist for a rap, and the conspiracy was sealed.

Surviving Vietnam's war trapped a man in a coiled cycle of situational recall, complete with retraced footsteps and recurring atrocities. The film ran uncensored, battering his senses with textured, graphic, real-time death. Not that his memories were memorable, quite the contrary, his memories were simply his—time capsules for his friends.

Burning an overlay might keep his memory from growing for a spell. But historic forces generated overlays as if their ideas would survive any defeat.

Beyond the light in that gathering place for sleepless nights lay the dilemma of a GI's war. Behind him stood a nation poised with memorial chisels, dripping with deathless envy; a nation anxious to record his Christian name, with numbers to quantify his passing and sanctify his service.

For a GI to satisfy his nation's needs, his memory had to grow.

To leave Vietnam alive, his memory had to grow. To be a reliable comrade, his memory had to grow. GIs had to burn overlays to keep the remnants of their soul up to scratch.

"You see, Martha, shooting first does not require a keen sense of fair play."

Joe wondered who Martha might be as Hardin circled the extraction point on the map, then traced a direct route with his finger, a route just shy of six kilometers.

Hardin pushed at the fatigue in his shoulders. His thoughts drifted now, remembering the wounded from time to time. Bravo Six had died riding in Joe's assigned jeep. Bravo Six had pulled rank to be assigned as the convoy commander. Joe was a lucky man.

Joe lit a cigar and said, "That's a long walk; two klicks a day."

"I told you, Martha. Joe's no fool."

"Martha and her overlay." Joe laughed, re-lighting his cigar. The extent of Hardin's treachery had come into focus. "Was it pretty?" Joe blew smoke at Hardin's face.

"She was pretty, nice leggins." Hardin pulled out a dry cigar and flipped it at Reynolds, a man severely hampered by protocol.

"Don't fuck with me, El Tee."

Twins they were, Reynolds and Ski, quiet with a mean grin: ready to roll on anyone. Reynolds told LeCotte a story about a girl who could suck-start his Harley because the story left LeCotte speechless for a time. He wanted to tell Blood a story, but he gave Drips his word.

* * *

The leather leash bore the scars of months of searching. Hardin looked at the new dog with curiosity, and fear, much the way he looked in the mirror. Frantic as he was, the dog's bullet-crazed eyes could hold a focus longer than Hardin could.

The handler was a ragged, torn man; half-sized by comparison, not much more than a gloomy aberration. He paced in nervous arcs, as if being restrained by his dog, his expression both dull and ruthless, his eye laying somewhere beyond his recall. This scout team has been in serious combat, Hardin thought, giving the dog a wide berth.

During the run from the landing zone, the dog had alerted the point squad into suspicious exhaustion, appearing at Tag's side without making a sound, setting his muzzle to Tag's shin, forcing Tag to stand stock-still. The odd smells of a seldom-used trail, the dampening sounds of an active blue-line and the four-meter visibility had slowed the dog's pace.

Shadowed patches of dry stubble held broken footprints. Stubbs knew he had to medevac this dog. Shadow would find out if he didn't.

"That fire will bring trouble," Hardin said.

"Fish has got that look again." Tennessee burrowed closer to the ground.

Stubbs stared absently. He saw neither Hardin, nor the jungle. Voices hung in the dry heat, pricked like suppressed shouts. A rustling of dry leaves pushed through the canopy.

Instantly, the jungle stopped talking.

AK fire near the blue-line broke the day's back. Rucksacks crashed in unison and helmets rolled about as whispered curses joined piercing stares.

Caught in the hurry of fear, laminated to the dust-gray soil, GIs rummaged for ammunition, weapons waiting. The confines of the vegetation swelled in volume, suddenly exploding with color—greens and browns. The blue-line rang like a shift horn. The trail was a minor one, nearly hidden by the encroaching vegetation.

Time stopped. Mex and Bucks lay side by side, facing the fire. They would live or die together. "I bet Charlie shot that fuckin' dog," Amps said.

The gunfight had stopped before it started. Actually, it was not a gunfight. Not one GI had returned fire.

Tennessee raised his hand, listening to the radio. "Six is movin' Gator forward on the right, wants us to move forward on the left behind the point. Andy's on drag."

"You and Stubbs move 'em up. Stay low. Don't pop the blue-line."

Hardin ran the trail with a low, bounding stride. Joe, Gator, and two RTOs were huddled near the blue-line. With his back to the base of a tree on the blue-line side of Joe's conference, Hardin tucked his knees under his chin and cradled his weapon next to his shoulder.

Joe looked through the trees, across the blue-line.

"Dog didn't alert." With a sudden rush of stupidity, Gates fingered the dog for following a trail to a creek, the most dangerous intersection in Vietnam.

"Now a dog is runnin' your platoon." Joe shot Gates a look that could freeze hot pussy. His voice snapped with hate. Once Joe hated a man, the man became a trash sump.

"You're a goddamn idiot, Gates."

Tinsel foliage hung into the blue-line. Familiar odors signaled caution. GIs were crawling toward the blue-line on both sides of the trail. Water rippled on the rocks where the trail crossed the creek. The terrain on the opposite bank ran uphill through thinning vegetation for as far as the eye could see. In the sweltering heat the jungle held a cold cast.

"So far all we got is a couple dinks," Joe said.

AK rounds tore at the right-front trace.

Firing left handed, as fast as he could load, hot shell casings bounced against Hardin's cheek. An empty magazine he tossed aside slammed into an AK round and then slammed into Raps' rucksack. Strung along the blue-line, GIs returned fire, magazine after magazine.

"God *damn it,*" Joe screamed.

Amid spasms of rage, Joe bolted into a gorilla's run, bounding down the front line trace, exposed between Third Platoon and the blue-line, kicking and screaming. Stainless men hid from themselves. Gates hadn't moved.

Joe's boot found a machine gunner's thigh, uprooting the man like a soggy bag. A GI screamed, clawing at the rocky bottom of the blue-line, the man struggling to breathe.

Joe ran toward the wounded man.

"Cover me," he screamed. Unarmed, with his mind in low range, Joe raced into the water. Grabbing the M-16, Joe back-hauled him into the jungle. Joe was screaming. Laying the man at Doc's feet, Joe's eyes seemed to hemorrhage.

Almost running, Joe slammed his helmet against Gates' chest, propelling his carcass through a series of balance-catching steps that ended with Gates rolling into a fall and catching Joe's fist with his chin. Not one man moved.

Hardin looked at Amps, then at Tennessee. They had heard stories about Joe's temper. Joe screamed into the jungle about killing Gates. Gates seemed to be relieved. Humiliated by circumstance, he was no longer responsible for anything the war might do.

Taylor motioned for Bucks to check out the wounded man. The wounds were through-and-through wounds, seven perfect holes. The AK rounds had spun the man like a top: no bones, no arteries, no organs, and both cheeks of his ass.

Bucks resented the brother's luck. The dude stood with a bewildered grin, sporting a gather of bandages, floating on two shots of morphine, looking like a used Christmas tree.

No one cared.

With the blue-line nailed down and the company fifty meters away, Joe pounded the far side of the water with artillery. White-hot shrapnel tore through the trees. Alone, GIs searched the confines of their helmet, afraid that Joe had gone mad.

Hardin should have blessed his luck, yet he was consumed by recollected fear.

After an hour spent dusting off the wounded brother, Joe changed directions and literally ran the company through a patch of dense jungle. Spasms of heat left Hardin shuddering as he passed out.

As if possessed, he could still hear the crushing expansion of the artillery shells. Trapped in a world laden with lost time, the concussions reverberated. His father grabbed his arm, propelling him toward a shelter. "Run, Pal, run."

Mex held Hardin upright, coaxing his steps. Rigid one minute and limp the next, Mex jerked his lieutenant from boot to boot. No one would have guessed, as he plodded in silence, wincing at the impact of incoming rounds, that the fever was killing him.

The water Hardin drank was linked to his pores. Tennessee was scraping dirt from his helmet with his dog tag when Hardin's eyes clicked back into the current time slot. Stubbs and Amps were talking.

"By God, I tell ya they froze. We're the only ones that returned fire. It was their dude that got banged. Can't figure they'll pull slack for us." Amps sounded like an old woman.

"What's happenin', Joe?" Hardin asked.

"Oh, little gunfight, little walk in the woods, little artillery. I'm takin' Tennessee when we get extracted." Joe didn't break stride with his comments. "He's home: from Hell's Half Acre." Joe sank into a full squat. A grimace judged the remnants of his cigar.

"Gator's boys went to ground and froze." Joe looked at Hardin, waiting for a response.

"They're ghostin'. Best you get in Gator's shit and stay there." Joe stood silent. "Every swingin' dick knows they're sandbaggin' this deal. You best tighten 'em up."

Hardin grinned, hoping Tennessee would stop playing with himself and say something.

Joe pointed at the gang-tangle of Fish's gear. "How in hell does he live out of that bag?" Fish's rucksack was an unsettled arrangement that clearly expressed his attitude.

"Fish, you grab that Claymore you shit on last night?" Stubbs asked.

Fish scooped up his rucksack. With three times as many straps as fasteners, the rucksack had no form and the grenades in the side pockets were bunched like potatoes in a sack. Trip flare wire held one shoulder strap in place.

"Meant to shit in front of it. Malaria pill fucked up my aim." Fish was offended by the attention. His logic was natural enough for any grunt.

"The Claymore's empty. Why don't ya just fill it with shit?" Stubbs said.

Fish turned and dropped his rucksack. "Ain't empty—just need another flare."

* * *

Common valor, men fighting for each other—the pledge was their catechism. Death not withstanding, they chose to risk their lives instead of choosing the safe and shameful.

And yet, cowardice had formed a vortex of perdurable indignity.

Time wore on with Joe at the charge. His screaming would not mend the deceit. Twilight stand-to found the company hiding in a thicket so dense one platoon could not see another. Calmed by the isolation, Stubbs shared a cigarette with Gates' platoon sergeant. The two men agreed to pick up the slack: somehow.

Fragmented by mistrust and broken promises, GIs exchanged thoughts of home. The need for relief vied with discussions of payback. Condemned to hump together, they wanted to be brave. For all that, they wanted to live. Months had gone by since Whitey's betrayal. The fungus he spawned had infected a platoon.

"I'm a radio operator. How come I gotta be shootin' dinks while a whole platoon hides in the weeds?" Southern boys had an aggravating grind to their voice when they whined.

Hardin decided to change the subject. "Did you blow your rocks when she shot ya?"

"I gotta cobble me some shit on you," Tennessee said.

"What's with Gator's boys? They'd talk to a whiner like you."

"Those dudes want in this outfit. They figure you're obsessed—ya know, outta whack, diggin' up shit, nosin' around. Lucky when it comes to Chuck." Tennessee's comments included a nod and an exaggerated motion of his spoon.

"Outta whack, what does that mean?"

Trying to ignore Hardin, Tennessee gave out a huff, then said to Amps, "Mex picked up a small piece of shrapnel from that artillery Joe was playin' with—in his forearm."

"Mex don't care," Amps said. "Besides, he don't weigh much anyway."

The calm created by zero visibility was similar to the calm of a night parachute jump. Reality had become the flat mat at the edge of the jungle. With the darkness came silence. Pops refused to cook. GIs withdrew into their core, searching for a way to make old bones.

Bucks and Mex had three nights remaining in hell. Boo had 332. Some R&Rs were a memory. Some were just beyond the next firefight. Some men shot Chuck and watched him die. Almost all men shot Chuck's image and searched for his body. Two facts remained—death was usual, and death's quickening brought purpose.

Not killing—more a cultural exchange that produced dead bodies.

* * *

Morning marched out of the brier patch like a wounded duck, with Joe drawing Third Platoon at point. Bucks and Mex had won another resupply, and Blood had won a lanky replacement Fish named Biggy. Lightning and Biggy were matching ebony spires.

Biggy was so new, LeCotte spent the better part of the day explaining to him that The New Point Queer, Tee-N, was not a queer, and that The Point Queer, Tee-PQ, was wounded, and he was not a queer either. LeCotte got so frustrated at one point he tried to get Boyle to reason with Biggy, causing Biggy to lapse into a sympathy stutter.

Rap finally intervened, declaring, "Tee-N was a good dude." That said, Biggy agreed, pushing LeCotte aside and walking away.

Two days passed. On the morning of the third day the point squad found a trail of broken grass bending to the north. The grass patterns indicated up to a dozen pair of boots. Tracking the prints into a hollow, Tag found a complex of spider holes. Joe stopped the parade.

"Ya hear that?" Tennessee asked.

"What?" Hardin looked in the direction Tennessee was searching.

"That," Tennessee said, cocking his head, burrowing closer to the ground.

"I don't hear anything." Looking along the side of a gradual slope into a sixty-meter stretch of open ground, Hardin thought he saw a man running.

Sitting in the balcony some thirty meters away, Hardin watched Gator's boys frag nine spider holes. He was nearly asleep when a VC sprang from a spider hole firing his AK on full automatic, spraying rounds in an arc as he ran. No one returned fire—not even Joe.

Before instinct could triumph, Beans was dead, shot in the face when curiosity drew him to the mouth of the last spider hole. Stunned, then ashamed, GIs mingled in an aimless display, unsure of what to do with the body.

Parked in a squat, Gates tried to make Beans more comfortable. A shallow trench glistened with blood on Gates' left arm. Confident he was finally a soldier; he let Taylor bandage his wound. Finally wounded, he watched his men lay Beans near the clearing for extraction.

A lone GI stood-to in front of Gates.

"A Purple Heart's all Beans is gonna get for gettin' wasted in this shit-hole. If I find out you got one for that scratch you got there, I'll hunt ya down and put a round in your face. Just like Beans. You're a sorry fucker, Lieutenant."

He whispered over his shoulder when he turned and began his vigil next to Beans' body. Crying softly, his head was buried in the personal items taken from his friend's rucksack—dog tags, pictures, boonie hat, drive-on rag, Bible. The essence of his friend had been reduced to a handful of echoes.

He would remember his buddy as the best boonie-rat who ever humped a ruck. God help the son-of-a-bitch who said otherwise.

Three men joined him at the corners of the poncho, setting Beans on the medevac as if they were bedding a new child. Those who could watched the procession, waiting for Beans to leave so they could declare he was their friend, too.

As the dust-off hovered to full power, Hardin jerked Tennessee's sleeve. "Check it out." Gates mounted the chopper. A silent cheer rose from the jungle.

Hardin flashed on his father's house. Words from his childhood rang out. "Bang you're dead. I shot you first."

Grunts died without notice no matter where they fought.

CHAPTER SIXTEEN

Old Bones

Freedom Bird. The Jungle Southwest of An Khe Base Camp.

"When you're older you'll recognize the girls that liked to play squat-tag in the asparagus patch. Ask your mom." *The Major did have fun telling his stories,* Hardin mused. He closed his eyes and found Linda, radiant as ever, her sweater accepting a full measure.

"You ready, Stubbs?"

Stubbs nodded through a stream of smoke, then involuntarily searched the jungle. Field-striping his cigarette, he checked the chamber of his weapon and closed the dust cover.

Pushing a tuneless whistle between his teeth, Stubbs said, "This AO is trouble."

Hardin pointed to a trail of broken grass that ran north.

Stubbs waited for the last man in Blood's squad to pass, inspecting their equipment with a practiced eye. Hardin grabbed the handset to sing to the troops.

"One more time around Piccadilly Circus, driver, follow that bus. It's a shame the way the rich folks treat us, everybody's rich but us."

Tennessee laughed. "Officer my ass. Your shit came out of a box of grits." Amps dropped into a squat, talking to Mex on the radio, translating what Tennessee had said.

"If you want to be Joe's boy, you best watch your mouth." Hardin stepped behind Amps, whose rucksack had become a Fish look alike.

"Amps, you're not runnin' my radio unless you get your shit together. Your mama know how fucked up you are?" Amps kept walking, knowing the El Tee had more to say. "You're not from Tennessee are ya, Amps? You know, where the girly-men have their balls in separate bags."

"Kentucky." Amps gave his helmet a confirming twist.

Hardin cocked his head with a "big deal" shrug and smiled in mock surprise.

Tennessee interrupted. "El Tee, Joe's on the horn." He tried to give Hardin the hook, but Hardin wouldn't take it.

"Ask Joe what he wants."

Tennessee shook his head and keyed the handset. "He's out of range." Tennessee had to talk to Joe, because Hardin would lie to anybody. "Extraction in forty minutes."

Bucks and Mex started jumping around, copping a feel off of this target and that. Stopping, Bucks raised his hands to silence the crowd. With a moment of mock ceremony Bucks gave his dice to PeeWee, stipulating that PeeWee find a cherry to fleece.

Joe's message brought an end to the party.

"Lima, you got the PZ—two-slick extraction, twenty-minute turn. You got the last ride." Mex would be on the ground with twelve GIs because Bucks was five days' shorter.

"You got the perimeter, Mex—four Claymores." Mex gave Hardin a thumbs-up. Hardin turned to Tennessee. "I'm goin' out with Mex. You and Stubbs are ridin' with Bucks."

Forty-eight minutes later, knowing they would share a beer, Bucks gave Hardin a modified dap and dove on the cargo deck of the second slick. In his heavy-hiding mode, his round face peered over PeeWee's shoulder.

With his helmet on the back of his head, Bucks talked to Mex on the radio, smiling as though he had larceny on his mind. Friends they were, sure enough. Harder than most, they had a soft underbelly. Mex held up a fist and said, "Adios, Bucks." Bucks waved as the slick cleared the treetops. Mex kept waving as if a premonition had crept into his day.

Walter "Big Bucks" Biggs said Charlie would shoot him after he got home.

The jungle seemed to gain weight, as if time was stalled. Minutes passed: and seconds too. The birds were shouting their calls. Faint cracking sounds drifted over the canopy. A muffled explosion followed. The birds stopped shouting. Amps spoke in private tones to Pops in the lead chopper. Machine gun fire burped in spurts. Gunships played their rockets.

Amps translated the story the best he could.

Boyle stood in the waist-high grass with the crew chief, sixty meters from the downed chopper, speaking clearly on the radio with a hollow calm, not stuttering, explaining to Mex what could not be explained. PeeWee knelt under the weight, his radio now an instrument of grief.

Boyle asked Mex if he was listening.

Bucks was dead.

Mex chewed at his cheek for the first time. Drained of his spirit, he struggled to puzzle out the words, staring with an expression not seen since Dak To. Standing stock-still, he spoke in Spanish, as if Hardin would better understand. Five minutes later Mex mustered a labored breath, his eyes calculating: who should he kill? A crease narrowed his expression. The gray of death had taken his face. With a sigh, Mex braced Hardin's shoulder.

"The Nam's a bitch, El Tee. Bucks never did nothin' but pick it up and drive on."

"I'm sorry, Mex."

"Stand tall, El Tee. Get fat if you can." Mex held out his fist and Hardin hit it, grateful that he had been forgiven. "Bucks stepped in that dude's blood. That's why he got whacked."

Watching Mex cross the clearing brought tears of fatigue. Hardin had recounted his father's exploits with an admiring style: to Fish, and Ski, and the rest. Mex enjoyed the stories, adding Spanish spice so the rest would laugh. Bucks enjoyed the stories too, rolling the dice over in his hand, shaking the bones when a story was finished.

Mex and Bucks told their stories to the new men. They would tag-team a man at twilight of his first night in the jungle. Lost in the trace of combat lore, their stories were cloaked in the secrecy that fashions grief, stories meant to scare a man that was already piss-tight.

Mex had nothing more to say as he gave Hardin a thumbs-up.

Fish lay on his back, gazing into a flat sky, singing as if he might smile, laughing as if he too had died. Ski stood in the open grass, cocked into a near-run rage—defiant, his machine gun slung at his hip, one-in-four belted death draped over his shoulder.

Guilt stood-to, full of brass, its image reflected in the men of First Platoon.

Thankful Bucks' death was the result of circumstance, Hardin prayed that luck would recruit her pride and break with his men as she had since Dak To.

Hardin had promised he would take care of Bucks. What could be next?

With his freedom-bird on short-final, Mex popped smoke. He spoke in Spanish again, this time to himself. Within minutes he flew over Route #19, heading toward the western perimeter of the An Khe base camp.

Searching without emotion, Mex spotted the downed chopper laying on its side in the tall grass. The main rotor blades lay in pieces. Two APCs sat on the roadway. Gunships circled, searching for a target. Men were boarding a slick on the roadway—PeeWee and Boyle.

The cool air bristled the few whiskers Mex had on his face. The relief of being above the confines of the canopy brought better odds. Familiar images brought a useless feeling—the wire and guard towers.

With a quick turn onto the landing pad, Mex found his feet fewer than ten meters from the spot where he and Bucks had mounted the sandbagged truck. Four GIs were dead, three GIs were wounded, and he and Drips were going home.

The road to the barracks was cluttered with rugged men, relieved, wishing they were Mex, or Drips, and looking for a way to deal with losing, Bucks. By and by their wish would focus on living another day. With Conversion Day in their rear view mirror, Sin City would be eager to sell them a most favored fantasy.

Hardin skirted the main complex at B-Med, heading for the helipad at the rear of the hospital. LeCotte and Stubbs stood at the front of the dust-off chopper. As the crew chief washed the deck, Hardin watched bloody water cascade onto the PSB decking.

Bucks and Dig-it would be good to each other.

LeCotte spoke with unusual reserve. "Bucks got hit when the slick stopped bouncin'. Nasty got banged when we were draggin' Bucks from the slick."

"Are the rest makin' it, Stubbs?" Hardin asked.

"So far. Nasty took a round in the thigh." Stubbs said.

"I'm gonna find me a dink and feed him to the rats," Pops said. His shoulders shook as if he was shedding water.

Stubbs stared at Pops, knowing that evil had the man in its trace. Few knew the depth of the secrecy required to bury a GI's anguish, or what a GI might do when fully immersed.

Curious to know how Bucks was killed, Stubbs found a surgeon removing Bucks' shirt. He gave the stranger a confirming nod, then let his expression become calculating, warning the man. Bucks lay facing the lights. His hair looked as though it had been scrubbed with a cheese-grater. He was not much of a mess—an AK round had punctured his heart.

The stainless table forced Bucks to throw out his chest and lay in a brace. He looked concerned, maybe uncomfortable. He hated the Army, its marching and formations. He liked to stand with a slouch, as if his being a soldier was impossible. Bucks, Dig-it, and the rest—they were men a grunt could call his brother.

Bucks did expect to die in Vietnam. He did not expect much attention.

"Don't cut that," Hardin said, taking hold of Bucks' drive-on rag.

The surgeon lifted Bucks' head and drew the drive-on rag over Bucks' face.

"I'll take his dog tags, Doc."

"We're gonna keep the tags for processing."

"Ya don't wanna go there, Doc. Give me the fuckin' tags."

If not for the words, then for Hardin's tone of voice, the surgeon removed Bucks' dog tags, wrote down his particulars, and handed them to Hardin. PeeWee and Boyle stepped into the tent. Drips and Mex stayed near the chopper. They did not want to see their friend dead.

Hardin turned to leave, and then stopped and said, "You know how it goes, Doc. These men are his buddies. Treat them with respect." He tapped Bucks on the boot.

Bucks' fists had cinched into tight knots, a pale tan shone around his knuckles. Hardin looked Stubbs into an understanding, and said, "Make sure PeeWee has Bucks' dice, Stubbs. I want those bones workin' their magic—every night."

Hardin headed for the orderly room, juggling thoughts of dead men. Top was buried in paper. "Any brass around, Top?"

"No, thank god." Top settled back in his chair.

"Any word on what we're doin'?"

"Rumor is you're headed to Bong Son, north up the coast, rice paddies and booby traps." The field phone rang, and Top disappeared into another thought.

As Hardin sorted through his gear, listening to the banter of his friends, the skin on his hands reddened and became tight. His heart rate soared. Within that instant the fever consumed his vision and he collapsed next to his bunk. Fevered dreams roared with the sound of battle.

His father and brother were staring at his grave stone, admiring the flowers. His father yelled for his brother to run. Dig-it opened fire on the funeral party, killing his brother and Linda. His father was running, dragging him from a chopper. Dig-it was screaming, his body burning in the grass. The dreams merged with the quiet of his father's den.

Hardin was home.

* * *

Number #10, Highlands Road. Bremerton, Washington.

"British top sergeants exercised strict discipline—no folderol. The Germans were bombing their homes. If you kill a man's family, he'll never stop trying to pay you back."

First he was shooting plastic soldiers with his BB-gun. Then he was laughing, shooting the buds off of Aunt Dorothy's roses. His men were perched in a rose bush in the back yard of Number #10, Highlands Road. Finally, he was winning the day. A splash of cool water brought Top's face into view. Hardin was soaked with sweat.

"That fever's got you by the balls, Lieutenant."

* * *

Hardin wrapped his hand around the pull chain to release a measure of cold water. Blinded by the shampoo and guided by those antique men, he would never find a remedy for his war. He missed his friend Bucks.

Refreshed, Hardin nursed a cup of coffee in the mess tent. Mex was shit-faced, dancing, his slap-sided moves waxed joyous by canine mating rituals. Hollering at odd times, he would grab PeeWee and they would cuss in trash Spanish. Mex said good-bye again and again to Ski and Fish, to Pops and Boyle, to Amps and Tennessee, and even LeCotte. He would leave in a rush, and no matter the end, he would drink to pass the day.

"Mex, buy me a beer," Pops hollered, laughing when Drips fell over LeCotte, ushering a jeep full of iced beer with his arms raised in a triumph, barging through two circles of white rocks and one perfect sign. Even in the rear area, Drips' suit was too small.

If the cleanliness and the right angles of the rear area made a GI uneasy, the remnants on his mess tray reminded him that hot meals led to stomach cramps and an extended tour of duty perched over a dark pool of diesel oil in a six-hole latrine.

For Hardin, the laundered white tablecloth at the officers' table was embarrassing.

"Excuse me, sir. We need to talk to you." LeCotte and Amps stood-to, weaving, and playing with each other's drunken blather.

"Excuse me, sir." LeCotte nudged Hardin's shoulder with the back of his hand, spilling Hardin's potatoes from his fork, then tried to straighten his glasses and stand at attention. His smirk, combined with the tablecloth, brought Hardin to bear. He jumped out of his chair, knocked it over, and screamed.

"Fuck you, LeCotte. You and that silly fucker you're draggin' around with ya."

The GIs in the mess hall rushed into silence, rotated in place, and focused. Amps held his breath. "Excuse me! Excuse me! You touch me again, and I'll kick your fuckin' ass." Hardin turned on Amps. "And, I'll knock your greasy dick in the dirt." Too drunk to respond, Amps knew whatever he wanted to see the El Tee about wasn't worth the drill.

"Now get outta my fuckin' sight."

Finding the door to fresh air involved several directions, one chair leg, and one echoing "Holy shit!" Hardin knew the excursion was LeCotte's idea, and that Amps would never let him forget the pile of snake shit they had stepped in.

Stubbs helped them find the door and returned with a humored smile.

"Jumped 'em hard," Stubbs said, picking up the chair.

"Is Fish inside the wire?"

"He's hangin' with Drips."

Stubbs left the mess hall when the officers from Bravo Company and Alpha Company arrived and the strains of heritage rang out.

Hardin drank a beer and listened to combat tales until treachery consumed him and he yelled, "A toast." The officers rose with pride. "I hereby declare that Second Batt, wherever we gather, will have a Gross Table. To the Gross Table." He raised his beer and they chimed in.

"The Gross Table." Hardin proclaimed that anyone with sufficient flatulence to penetrate the Airspace was a charter member. Others must earn their crest. Putting your dick in the cottage cheese, mooning a general, laying horse shit on the Old Man's staff—any vulgarity sure to end your career was an automatic qualifier.

To further the tradition of the Gross Table, Hardin pledged to teach those gathered an old ditty that fit their situation well: "We're a Bunch of Bastards."

We're a bunch of bastards, scum of the earth
Born in a whorehouse, pissed on, shit on
Kicked around the universe.
Of all the dirty bastards,
We are the worst
We hail from Second Batt,
The assholes of all the earth.

"One more toast. To the paper Dickheads."

"To the Dickheads."

Bursting into a fourth chorus, hallooning on about being born in a whorehouse, Hardin stopped singing when Captain Weber appeared, looking like a reluctant dream. His traps flooded as he joined her halfway to the chow line.

"Hey, GI." Her eyes were tentative.

"Number one GI?" The sparkle was gone.

"Yeah, number one." Her eyes fell to the side, and her smile fell with them.

"Meeting you helped me through a rough patch," she said. "I'm still looking for my pilot. I wanted to say good-bye. I hope your luck holds."

Hope is fading, Hardin thought. The wishful soldiers strolled as they had before—Hardin yearning for forgiveness, Weber yearning for closure. Vacant now, yet selfish, someone had to tell him the killing would stop, that he was a good man. Weber cried.

She has seen her share of broken men, Hardin thought.

"I'm on duty tonight and leave in the morning. I'll be stateside in three days."

"I will remember you, and the docs at B-Med. I have trouble predicting my emotions, but I'm glad you're makin' it out of Vietnam. Remember us when you can. To anyone really."

"Keep that grin workin', El Tee." She brushed his cheek with the palm of her hand.

"You'll be at B-Med as long as I'm alive," Hardin said.

"You lost a friend today, a Sergeant Biggs," she said, giving an understanding nod.

"Bucks. His name was Big Bucks."

"I'll keep you in my prayers, El Tee." An angel leaned forward and gave Hardin a peck on the cheek. He fought back tears as she paused on the porch of the hospital. Weber waved as she closed the door and he began to cry. Rocked to his core, his body trembled.

Brushing off the dust, he gathered his sympathies and headed for the bar.

Maybe the Penguins would sing "Earth Angel." Hardin drew the beer can across the table, wondering if his father had found an angel during his war.

* * *

Holding Company Barracks. An Khe Base Camp. 0240 Hours.

Chemistry 101: malaria drugs mixed with cold beer, and hot chow. The whole thing was so cleverly managed. The concoction left Hardin with the unpolished version of intestinal folly. Unchallenged forces of chemistry coupled with a pulsating form of rectal rifling woke him with a squirt, sending him bounding out of the hootch. Within a stride he had shit his pants from his crotch to his boots.

Setting his boots on a sandbag wall, Hardin left the pants lying in a heap, and slogged to the shower. Being bowlegged kept the jungle-grade sludge from sloshing in his ass crack. Not one thing satisfied a general more than knowing that his infantry was served a hot meal.

At first light Hardin mounted the stairs to the Holding Company orderly room with his boots and shirt on and his dick jogging under a full sail.

"Mornin,' Top." Top turned from his coffee into a bursting howl.

"First Cav take your pants instead of kickin' your ass?" Top shook his head as he sat down, then stretched into a yawn. "Get the lieutenant a pair of small regular pants."

"Thanks, Top." The runner left with an obscene gesture lining his face.

"They said you had big balls." Top laughed at Hardin's compressed features and settled back, confident he finally had the lieutenant under control.

"Lighten up, Top. These puppies are just shy."

"Damn I'll be glad when you're gone. I heard about your Gross Table, and what you got there is gross." Top was pleased with this comic interlude.

"When I make captain, I'm gonna request the Holding Company so I can be your boss." This offering caused Top's head to whipsaw and his eyes to focus.

"You stay the hell away from here." The CQ dropped the pants in Hardin's lap and tried to hide his laughter. "I got a sweet deal here. And a grateful captain as well."

Stubbs barged through the screen door as Hardin finished tying his boot laces. Hardin could hear Reynolds scoffing about PeeWee shitting his pants.

"We're outta here, El Tee. Top." Stubbs gave the first sergeant an understanding nod.

"Right behind ya, Stubbs. See ya next time, Top. Weber's outta here; on her way to the world." An expression of satisfaction crossed Top's face.

"Don't come back here, Lieutenant Hardin." Hardin stuck out his hand, and Top took it.

"Take care, First Sergeant." They shook hands firmly in a roughly fashioned gesture designed to seal their bargain and key their memory.

Drips and Mex were standing at attention near the orderly room steps, the picture of bedlam in low gear, their humble cleverness about to explode.

Mex held out a fist. "Adios, El Tee. See ya in the world." Hardin hit Mex's fist and offered a fist to Drips, cocking his head to solicit the rest of the story.

"I'm sorry about losin' Bucks," Hardin said, feeling his strength subside.

Looking over the faces of the platoon, his chest shook. He slowly filled his lungs with air. The men left standing, those durable lads, needed a tight rein to take up the slack.

"You jack-offs get away from me, before I kick your ass."

Two of the bravest men he had known gave him a pat on the shoulder. Mex lingered. He turned with a palm extended toward the members of the platoon. "Bucks dyin' was bad luck, El Tee. His turn. We figured one of us was gonna get whacked."

"I got paybacks for him, Mex." Hardin alerted to his father's voice. Shaken by what he heard, he spent a few seconds scanning the assembly area. As he slipped his hand inside the pocket of his rucksack, the voice spoke again.

"Take care of yourself, Mex."

"Me and Drips, we got it dicked, El Tee." Mex hesitated. "Bucks ran out of time, El Tee. Sin Loi. Chuck was gonna catch one of us half-steppin'. Walkin'-and-talkin', or bagged-and-tagged, we died in Dak To. Fuck-o-shit: wait 'til the world figures out we're still alive."

Apart from chance or the rigors of war, Hardin's insanity was driven by a simple passion: Nuts, Dig-it, Hippie, and now Bucks. Their deaths would be avenged, no matter the means, no matter the personal cost.

Mex braced when Hardin took hold of his dog tag chain, unhooked it, and attached one of Bucks' dog tags to it. Allowing the chain to drop back against Mex's chest, he gave a short nod, and said, "Adios, Mex. Take care of Bucks for me."

Mex leaned away and returned Hardin's nod, cocking his head in a grateful stare. Had he been a different man, he might have declined Hardin's request. Because he was who he was, a grunt, he would keep Bucks safe no matter what.

As their backs mingled with their friends, Hardin took a series of short breaths. He thought of Dig-it lying in the grass, his eyes searching for one last image of life. He swore softly, wiping the rot from the back of his hands. If time trod more slowly, grunts like Mex could savor their good-byes. If time were more tolerant, they might find dignity in the death of their enemy. They might even fix bayonets, or at least be subject to their issue.

And, so. Two men were leaving the war. They were not going home, they were just leaving. The other men, those left behind, were once again lost in tomorrow's song.

On and on, Eastern calculations ruled the day. Jungle Central, a headquarters exuding the persistence of timed numbers, had warped the data: Robert McNamara's data. Bodies per day: there had to be an average.

Battle Bullshit would brook no delay.

* * *

"Give me the hook." Amps fumbled his way to the handset, yanked it off his rucksack, and handed it to Hardin upside down with a puke-flavored huff of exasperation.

"Lima Two, this is Lima Six. Put LeCotte on the horn."

LeCotte grabbed the handset looking like a scarecrow in drag.

"LeCotte, over." His voice was stained with beer.

"This is Lima. What did ya want last night?"

"Ah." LeCotte turned to Pops, tried to give him the handset, and threatened to kick his ass when Pops walked away. "It was Amps. He wanted to bring a round-eye to the party."

GIs scuffed their boots as they neared the chopper pad, their minds so mildewed the puzzle did not fit. Hardin found himself at LeCotte's side. "Fuck you, LeCotte."

Ecstatic, Boyle skipped with joy. His lieutenant had finally grown a brain. "Tennessee tells me you're a cherry, LeCotte, no boom-boom. Tells me Boyle's been givin' you tips on where to put your dinky cock."

Disgusted with his witless lieutenant, LeCotte said, "She-it, Boyle pisses with a stutter."

Charlie Company was inserted in an unused rice paddy crisscrossed with trails and dotted with clumps of bushes. PFC Wallace, the new man, had recovered from his bout with heatstroke and had returned to the field packing the same frail demeanor. With his brain wired to a fading expression of self-pity, he practiced his misfortune lying next to Amps.

"You scared, Wallace?" Stubbs asked. Wallace glanced at Amps, then back at Stubbs.

"Yes." He nodded, his finger playing with the grass in front of his face.

"I'd hate to look as bad as you do and not be scared." Wallace stared straight ahead. "We saved your sorry ass once. Next time you're on your own."

Stubbs looked past Wallace, watching Ski and PeeWee mime a debate over a chocolate wafer as the sun dropped behind the An Khe Pass and dusk replaced the evening calm.

CHAPTER SEVENTEEN

First Platoon's Baby Girl

Charlie Company Laager. East of An Khe Base Camp. 0655 Hours.

Outside the village of An Khe, at the east end of the valley at the base of a ridge, near the main road—Route #19—a platoon of NVA regulars waited for the GIs. They had spotted Fish and PeeWee at twilight and had withdrawn to a trail junction to set an ambush.

Wedged between a fringe of jungle and a rock outcrop, twenty-nine AK-47s covered an open field. Eleven more soldiers lay in a gully fifty meters south of the trail junction, waiting to flank Tag's point squad.

First light brought a flurry of activity. Tag and LeCotte led the choir, their caustic banter spicing an eerily quiet morning. At the wire of his trip flare Rap found a trace of broken grass. Looking for Mex as if the wily man had never left, Rap showed his find to Pops and then to Tag.

Pops measured the find with a practiced eye, then told Tag to dogleg the next move.

Stubbs wrestled with the starlight scope, finally standing on the case to seat the locking hasps, determined to rid his world of technology's ways. Brushing at the hair on the back of his neck, Stubbs checked the status of his cigarette supply.

Cussing the new words he had fashioned, Blood flipped his selector switch to automatic fire, leveling his weapon on the new man's chest. With his facial muscles playing double-or-quit, he spit at the air. "Ya sorry cocksucker."

Stubbs leapt between the two men. "Easy, Blood."

Eyes bulging, Blood drummed with pressure. The veins above his temples had replaced his ears as he extended his left hand away from his weapon. Losing control, he had no qualms as he waited for the new man to respond. Stubbs was incidental.

"He's gotta know." Hearing a vaguely familiar voice, the new man stepped behind Stubbs, his posture stripped to a pointless gust.

"What's he gotta know?" Stubbs pushed the barrel of Blood's rifle to the ground, jamming his index finger into his chest when Blood tried to resist.

"Wallace does what I tell him, without that pussy mama shit." The words "game over" flashed in Blood's eyes. Wallace was playing the combat version of pinball.

"You're right, Blood. But nobody, fuckin' nobody, shoots my people but me. You hear me? Not you, not nobody."

Blood shifted away from Stubbs' voice, perplexed, then deflated by his platoon sergeant's scream. When Wallace smirked, Stubbs lunged through a horizontal butt stroke, slamming his weapon on the point of his jaw. Wallace crumpled into a heap.

"Wake him up," Stubbs said, pointing at Amps. Stubbs acknowledged Hardin's witness with a nod, then lit a smoke. With a sense of deceleration, he bounced into a crouch to mooch some coffee.

"Blood was gonna bang the man. The studs were gettin' lax. They'll tighten up now." Stubbs gave out a conclusive sigh, took a drag to dismiss Hardin's silence, then exhaled with an upward motion of his head.

"Ya probably broke his jaw."

Stubbs pinched the embers from his cigarette and stood to end the discussion and collect his thoughts. "You watch, he'll get a Purple Heart," Stubbs said, watching Reynolds whisper in the new man's ear. Wallace was a liability. A collegian, steeped in sensible outlooks, set adrift in Vietnam's madness, so fragile that his comrades had calculated his death.

Tennessee expressed satisfaction as he gestured to the mountains and said, "We got drag, movin' northeast." Weak-kneed, Wallace stood aside, trying to adjust his jaw.

"You figure you landed in the wrong spot, Wallace?" Searching the new man's fearful nod, Hardin's voice had assumed a confidential tone. "I'm gonna tell ya how this bullshit works. We're gonna take a walk and you're gonna stop whinin'. If ya don't, I'm gonna kill ya. This game's real. Be careful how ya play it. Fair warning. No more fuckin' slack."

* * *

With dawn painting the trees, Joe changed the company's route of march. The change was logical and illogical: the route took the company beyond its area of operation. Tag said he saw where a man had crawled through the grass, then suggested a dogleg. Arriving at the end of his coffee, Joe fired a battery-two on the next trail junction and followed Tag's lead.

In the days that followed, searching an empty jungle became the normal state, the anxiety worse than being shot. Obscene gestures and vacant stares replaced half-smiles and amusing interludes. Finally, Rap held LeCotte off the ground and Amps laughed, slapping his knee.

The boredom welled until battalion radioed the news.

"We're leavin' the mountains, El Tee," Amps declared, toasting the air with his coffee.

"When?" Hardin asked, slicing a salami stick.

"In the mornin'. Right after I beat the piss out of Wallace."

"Be damned funny if he kicked your sorry ass," Tennessee said.

* * *

Airborne Enroute to Bong Son. 0850 Hours.

Flying north, dragging the sunrise with him, Hardin stared at the eastern sky.

Almond-white sand lay against the South China Sea as if antique lace, separating rich green palm groves from a cream colored surf. Methodically, Hardin admired the landscape passing below his feet. The rice paddies were well tended.

A two-lane road ran north and south, paralleling the coastline, four kilometers west of the beach. Dense stands of palm trees bordered the asphalt.

Thatch hootches pushed away from the roadway, screened by bamboo fences, tied together by wet and dry rice paddies and clumps of palm trees. Resigned that she did not have to wait for rain to walk in the mud, a little girl guided a water buffalo along a rice paddy dike.

Nestled in the western shadow of an island of mountains—the Tiger Mountains—Hardin spotted the village of Bong Son, a one-half-mile stretch of trinkets and false charm. He looked past Amps through the cargo hold of the chopper. A mountain ridge ran a north-south trace, sixteen kilometers from the coast, bordering the rice paddies on the west. The An Lao River ran south out of the mountains, turned east and northeast passed Bong Son and the Tiger Mountains, then east again to the South China Sea.

The Ia Drang Valley, the Poco Valley, and the An Lao Valley were three of the many rugged, strategic valleys that absorbed the flow of NVA troops from Laos and the Ho Chi Minh Trail. Intelligence reports estimated the Viet Cong controlled eighty-five percent of this area of operations—Binh Dinh Province.

Two US Army base camps, Landing Zone English and Landing Zone English North, sat perched on knolls like trophies on a stage, one kilometer west of Route #1 and one kilometer north of Bong Son. Dug into the only hill masses in the An Lao River delta, elevation sixty feet, the base camps could be shelled by any Viet Cong unit worth its salt.

The glint from a mirror brought Hardin's eye to the center of the village. Jeeps were parked at odd angles and GIs were milling in the street. Bending an ear, one could imagine faint screams emanating from the steam baths. LZ English would be trouble for the company—too much commerce within walking distance.

With Hardin's promotion to captain due in twenty-one days, the men of First Platoon knew their chances would fall to a stranger. Tennessee had volunteered to take the company radio for Captain Joe to avoid the uncertainty of a new lieutenant. He was withdrawing from his war inches at a time, not wanting to spend his life covering for a new officer.

Tennessee and Hardin were the best of friends, their relationship laced with chaos-born humor intended to create a balance for the attitudes of the other GIs in the platoon.

As veterans of the nastiest foreign war their nation had fought, Hardin and his men had become something of a young disappointment, their nation's unpolished brass. After winning the lottery they were at first new men, and then simply tired. Weary and superstitious, they found no humor in the prospects of another day—or a new platoon leader.

These GIs were fighting Vietnam's war by fondling the hollow words of paper soldiers. Fish could not wrap his mind around a can of boot polish. Neither could Hardin.

A new El Tee would never scream "Fuck you, LeCotte," to help a black GI with a stutter get ready for the challenge. Or tie a man's rucksack to a tree to mess with his day. Or hog-tie a GI to a bamboo pole and load him on a chopper for R&R. Or assign race relations to the biggest, blackest man in country.

The studs stepped onto the airstrip with an expectant pause, surveying the hootches bordering the perimeter wire and the rice paddies north of the base camp. Dense rows of vegetation interrupted their line of sight as they traced a stretch of dry paddy. A man could get ambushed in a rice paddy from a hundred locations.

Tennessee stood in front of Hardin to deliver his first message from Captain Joe. "Six wants you at a briefing in the TOC." Gaining stature, his words bit the air. His posture smiled with authority. Tennessee thought he had the hammer.

"That's Tactical Operations Center to you, boy." Tennessee's eyes narrowed. "If you want to talk, call me on the radio." Cutting the cord, Hardin's loyalty lay with Amps. Tennessee stomped to his rucksack, looked at Hardin, and keyed the handset.

"Lima Six, this is Charlie Kilo." Amps answered.

"Lima Kilo, go."

"Put Lima on the horn." With a pissy grin, Tennessee fingered Amps.

"Wait one." Amps extended the handset to Hardin with a look of exasperation.

"Tell him ya can't find me." Amps threw his head back, laughing.

"I can't find him." With a rush of satisfaction, Amps seized control. Tennessee's power surges could be absorbed with a lie.

"Oh, fuck you." Tennessee threw his handset in the dirt. The separation was complete.

Anthony Michael Phillips—Amps—was skinny. Even his smile was skinny. His head was so round, if his hair didn't stick out like spikes in a watermelon, you'd expect to see his face anytime. When Hardin had asked him why he was from Kentucky, Amps did not answer.

Amps had a rural, compassionate mind, and might have embraced a more vigorous demeanor if he knew how to speak English. He could speak English—he was just a hick.

Amps didn't have ears. He had ears—they were just too small for his head. For that reason alone, no woman would be seen with him. Even the whore who had beat his ball-sack blue made him pay her up front. She laughed when he wouldn't stop coddling his balls.

Somewhere in the mire of Amps' mind, at the end of a thought, a reset button waited to be pushed. On occasion, when the world least expected it, a voice would speak to Amps.

Stubbs and Hardin learned to listen.

"Have you ever fucked a pig, Amps?" Stubbs asked.

"What, Sarge?"

"Squeak said you were a pig fucker," Stubbs said, passing the challenge to Hardin.

"Squeak's a city boy." Amps' mind was beginning to bog down.

"I heard the Kentucky State flag has a pig's dick on it," Hardin said.

"A fly speck, maybe."

"Think, Amperage Man. Picture it, Amps. A pig's dick, does it have a left-hand thread or a right-hand thread?"

Amps turned in a tight circle, shaking at a thought he was trying to capture. Finally he said, "By god, it's a damn good thing you're leavin'. Fuck-oh-shit, you're makin' me crazy."

Stubbs threw Amps a pack of smokes and continued the argument as if there had been no interruption. "A pig's dick has the same thread as its tail," Stubbs said. "If you'd ever corn-holed a pig, Amps, you'd know that kind of shit."

Hardin nodded as he passed Amps, watching Stubbs scratch-test a rash to see if it would bleed. "Get 'em refit, Stubbs." Stubbs dismissed Hardin's order by lighting a smoke.

Southern E-7s had an aggravating way of disposing of lieutenants.

Hardin set his rucksack by a sandbag wall, checked his weapon, tightened the sling along the left side of the bolt housing, let Sweet Cheek's shroud line slide through his fingers, and set off to see the wizards.

"Watch my gear, Tennessee. Get us some C-Rations."

"Fuck you, El Tee." Amps held up a thumb.

"I know why your ex-wife shot ya."

"She-it," Tennessee said.

"Shit has one syllable: same-same, fuck." Tennessee hit Hardin's fist. "Drive on, GI."

* * *

The battalion tactical operations center boasted live and dead sandbags, straight and crooked antennas, sagging phone lines, generators, staggered doorways, a white flagpole, centering palm trees, a waiting jeep, and enough signs to guide the blind. Dug into the hillside, the facade looked like an earthen dam, the sandbagged roof cut even with the crest of the hill. The entry hall spilled into a communications room lined with situation maps, wall-mounted tables, and radios.

Two radios coordinated artillery support, and three radios tied the rifle companies to battalion and battalion to the brigade.

Conversations were cautious. Historic forces guarded the secrets of war—secrets so special, they gained momentum, then hung about in droopy, reticular weaves, snaring a passing GI and demanding his allegiance. In written form, secrets required classifications and layers of security.

For the GI, joy sprang from realizing a secret didn't have to be true—and that Radio Man would pass them along to anyone who called.

Radio Man was two men. During the day he hailed from the Bronx and had a caustic answer to any question a GI might asked. At night he hailed from Detroit and called himself the head nigger. With either man you got a breath of fresh air.

Hardin stared into the briefing room.

The codes of this inner world glistened when the paper-majors played the fantasies of their youth. Mother stood-to, energized, bouncing between negative and positive poles, feigning neutrality, inspecting his newly embroidered name-tag, then massing his papers into a stack.

Hardin couldn't help himself.

"Mother, how ya doin'?" Hardin settled close to his shoulder. Mother adjusted his stance. Hardin leaned closer.

"We'll close the battalion net by morning."

"That's the spirit, Mother. We don't want to miss any of this shit-hot war."

Glancing around the room, Hardin noted the stark shafts of light aimed at the briefing map, and a hooded lamp mounted on the face of a wooden lectern. The room grew more confidential as he sauntered away from the map. "No place to hide." He let his voice trail off.

Lifting his grease pencil, Mother dismissed Hardin. "The brief's in ten minutes."

Waiting for the Old Man, Mother practiced his brace, fidgeting like a bride in an undersized girdle, adjusting his waistband, keen to keep the starch in his jungle fatigues from harassing his balls. Officers and noncoms from the four rifle companies and the recon platoon milled near the briefing map. The anxiety of past battles played in their words.

When the Old Man's voice boomed through the bunker, Mother quick-stepped to a chair in the front row. Hardin stepped to the back of the room and tucked his ass between sandbags.

The room fell silent. Eight cloth sandbags accented the front wall like the shaded squares of a crossword puzzle, the wall a mosaic of staggered joints, converging on the symbols that dotted a four-by-six-foot briefing map. Small rectangles identified the operating units. Black letters and numbers announced the dead, wounded, or missing at each firefight.

The numbers were old news. How could they be otherwise?

Numbers—no names. Names were too persistent, rude at times. And familiarity might fog tactical judgment. Besides, Dig-it was Dig-it's real name. With little room for peace, Hardin dreamed of a villa on the South China Sea, then listened as his father shouted for him to run.

Reflection sparred with a mood of anticipation as he glanced through the doorway, adjusted his feet, rubbed his face briskly, and launched into an inspection of Mother's world. Excepting the briefing map, the eight cloth sandbags, the lectern, various skin tones, and the footpaths worn into the wooden floor, the room was an olive-drab cocoon. The corrugated steel roof, the wooden floor, the plastic twill sandbags, and the folding chairs—all olive drab.

In front, between the situation map, and the lectern, a stranger stood with his head down, badgering a knothole in the floorboards with a rubber-tipped pointer.

A grain-ridged footpath, scuffed bare by the reluctance of those men running at the sharp end, ran parallel to the front row, ran a circuit around the wooden lectern, then to the map, and then back to the center of the front row. If a man found himself posted to the center of the front row, his unit would in turn be posted to a jungle recess somewhere in the back of nowhere.

The footpaths grew faint near the rear of the briefing room. Finding an inverse relationship between these worn swales and an understanding of combat, Hardin was standing on solid paint.

Paper lifers pranced around these briefing rooms like the Polish Horse Cavalry. Brandishing their riding whips, their helmet plumes laid flat by the winds of war, cannon shot pulled at their sense of reason, dead soldiers clogged their victory—old watercolors too fanciful for the monsoon.

Mother would be shocked to know that blood could stain the earth.

As Mother brushed at a blemish on his shirt, Hardin laughed through a deep breath. Mother sat alone in the middle of three chairs in the front row. Uncle, the battalion executive officer, appraised his options when he entered the room and sat next to Mother anyway.

The Old Man stood-to behind the lectern to jump-start the briefing. The spotlight mounted on the lectern left his face in darkness, adding emphasis when he dipped forward and intrigue when he withdrew.

The Old Man's eyes had a phosphorous hue, a deep white-blue: intense. He didn't wear glasses but you got the impression he was looking over lenses, cataloguing comments as accepted or rejected. Few had ever crossed the Old Man.

"Gentlemen, this is Binh Dinh Province. Major Peters is an intell-type with the brigade that just pulled out. Listen to the words. Smoke 'em if you've got 'em."

To the rustle of lighters, Major Peters sauntered to the map. He was a hard-breathing man who looked as if he had just been slapped, he eyes starving for a focus. With a voice as hard as a base-plate, he opened fire, categorizing village layouts, and terrain features. Emphasizing the success of his brigade, he took credit for the lack of enemy activity, the Pacification Program being ahead of schedule, and the rice crop being good.

"Search and Destroy operations in the mountains around the An Lao Valley and south into the Crow's Foot have been uneventful."

"Thank you, Major." The Old Man stepped into the harsh cone of light, his head canted toward the major, his brow creased, fixing the major. "That will be all, Major Peters." Wild Bill motioned the good major to the door, his snap-smile suggesting Major Peters was misinformed. With a brief pause he stood into a brace, his hands gripping the sides of the lectern.

His eyes looked like cubes of ice.

"This province is eighty-five percent VC. We're here to find 'em. Don't fire up any women, kids, or old people. Find the rest. Don't turn your back on anyone. Smaller patrols, faster hits, company- and platoon-size operations. Any questions?"

Laughing to himself, Hardin had a question about the other fifteen percent.

"Yes, sir. Will red-leg fire into a village if we're gettin' hit?" The new Bravo Company Commander was a good man, two in a row for Bravo Company.

"Yes. Make sure you're right." A rumble ran through the room. Hardin had to ask.

"Sir, the other fifteen percent, are they carryin' signs?" The Old Man seemed to gnaw at the air as he glared at Hardin, issuing one of his "you little bastard" looks. Wild Bill still had paybacks for the box of horse shit—the Rambler's Road Apples.

The look he gave Joe put the captain on notice. "Binh Dinh Province is one continuous booby trap. This is the faceless war you've heard about—homemade Claymores, punji pits, the whole nine yards. Worse than any area we've seen."

Whether the Old Man's nine yards referred to belted fifty-caliber machine gun ammunition for a B-17, or Vince Lombardi's nine yards on first and goal, the meaning was clear.

"Listen up, company commanders stand fast. The rest of you clear the area." *Finally,* Hardin thought, *the secret shit for the Art Majors.*

Listen up—the one order that turned off the receiving functions in a GI's brain.

* * *

The studs had withdrawn into a relaxed banter, lying as fast as the alcohol allowed them to think. Boo's expression had taken him half way around the block. Booby traps had him learning how to stutter. Boyle needed, Boo. Boyle figured the sooner LeCotte was crazy, the sooner he could be the fire-team leader, and the sooner he could tell PeeWee to piss off.

Lately, PeeWee had taken to stuttering in Spanish. PeeWee had Boyle so mad, Boyle asked Rap to shoot the wetback in the ass. Rap told Boyle that PeeWee was Mex's homeboy, and Mex was crazy enough to come back and blow Boyle's balls off.

And, so one story led to another.

Blood was fraternizing with the battalion personnel officer. Rap and Lightning sat to one side to keep Boyle's stutter at bay. Ski, Amps, and LeCotte were guarding Pops' stew. Boo and Butt were badgering Tag with their two-on-one block trash. PeeWee, Fish and Reynolds were interviewing a new man who was carrying a Bible.

The Preacher looked as if he had just gotten off the boat.

Stubbs gave the Bible a tap. "Are you a gunfighter, or is God your shield?"

"I'm assigned to First Platoon."

"You believe in killin', Preacher?" Stubbs asked

"I can shoot." His eyes leveled on Stubbs' cigarette, intent on the challenge.

"Give him to Rap."

PeeWee and Fish exchanged daps, laughing when the Preacher met the blackest man he'd ever seen. The cheeks of the Reverend's ass tightened, vibrating in sync with Rap's mean-street chatter, his expression locked in awkward combat with an abrupt change of mood.

"Stubbs, we must be gettin' these guys from the instructor group at the Fort Benning Jump School." The old sergeant winced into a snobbish grin.

"We use 'em to test chutes." Virtually immobile, Stubbs exchanged words with himself, a flash of recognition altering his expression. Satisfied with his conclusions, he set fire to another smoke and gave Hardin a nod.

"Can Amps handle the company radio?" Hardin asked.

"Amps is a young kid, until you look into his eyes. He doesn't say enough to figure out what's under that grin. One thing's for sure—bein' that skinny makes his cigarette look like a cigar. His dad's doin' time in Louisiana. Least that's what I heard."

"Louisiana beats this shit-hole."

Exhausted by his own predictability, Stubbs finger-coned the end of his cigarette, focusing on the glow as he took a drag. He laughed through a gush of smoke when Rap grabbed the Preacher's Bible. Rap's animated version of black gospel made light of his capacity for killing. Fear had found a home in the Preacher's eyes. Rap pushed the man aside and covered the distance in two steps. The sweat on his face hung in large drops.

"Somebody's gotta do the prayin."

"I don't want that Kansas mothafucker." Rap fixed Stubbs with a hateful stare then lunged away, anger pulling him from side to side, his fists clinched. Whitey was from Kansas.

Stubbs sighed a futile sigh. "The bunkers on the perimeter are gonna be beaucoup trouble. Word is, they been lettin' whores inside the wire at bunker #1, by the main gate. Let whores walk right through the wire."

"I'm short, Stubbs. I make captain eleven June."

"I hear you're leavin' before that." Pleased with his confidential tone, Stubbs snapped his lighter closed and leaned into a knowing brace. "Battalion Sergeant Major."

"Where'd he say I was goin'?"

"Didn't say."

"Old Wild Bill is playin' his horse-shit card. This could be a pisser. A radio relay in Dak To, clockin' elephants for Chuck. Holy shit. I'm fucked fer sure."

"You see the Old Man's eyes? Jumped-up shit, he is pissed about somethin'."

* * *

Battalion Headquarters. Landing Zone English. 1730 Hours.

Flakes of burned shit drifted on the breeze coating their evening meal. The barrels of a nine-hole latrine had been burning for hours; the fallout seemed appropriate given Hardin's latest prospects. Chicken and hot shit—Tennessee's last supper.

"This how the barbecue works down in Dixie?" Hardin asked. Tennessee set his butt on his steel pot with a thud, adjusting his weight so his cheeks would fit on the round top, smiling, knowing he was out of Hardin's range.

"Chicken and grits."

"Grits are a hyper-elastic version of Cream of Wheat. Grits get anywhere near your plate, they jump your eggs, then butt-fuck your bacon. Worse than lima beans."

"You don't like grits?" Tennessee gave himself a massage, and said, "They can't be makin' you a captain. I best get steppin' and keep steppin'." Amps agreed.

"You ever burn shit, Tennessee?" Hardin asked.

"Not on purpose."

"What about your outhouse at home, you scoop it out or what?" Amps changed sides and shook his head, using his fork to accent his joy.

Tennessee gave Amps a warning with his fork. "I'm takin' over this pop stand." The company commo chief, an officious young sergeant with a short stride, motioned Tennessee.

Amps left with Tennessee and Hardin settled into another beer.

His unknown fever had stopped its episodic dance. If he slept at all, his dream replayed scenarios of Bucks' death, time and again.

Except for occasional half-second flashes, no frame-by-frame replays of Dig-it or the others cast their spell. They would return, the dead men, staring through a pallid veneer.

Dropping his plate, Hardin was crying in the dark, alone. The dead men grew in stature at night with each passing day. He was a small man when standing near their memory.

Pushing aside the tears, Hardin had shattered so many pair of glasses he had no idea which pair he was looking through. His purpose for living was less clear. Shouldering the fatigue had left his eyes nearly dry. His chest shook. Desperate, he was too exhausted to resist the Old Man's order that he forsake his platoon, the men he pledged to keep alive.

He wanted to stay and search for the things that mattered, truth and empty magazines. One reality was clear. No one above company level knew whether the GIs of First Platoon found either one. Hardin's truth would remain within the platoon's perimeter. His empty magazines would be scattered with the pieces of their collective soul, each magazine a sanctuary for a mournful echo.

"Third Platoon got a new El Tee," Andy said.

"Andy, what's up?" Hardin considered himself lucky. Lieutenant Anderson was a good soldier. "Is the new guy a cherry or what?"

"Cherry as they come." Andy sat down for a friendly cup of coffee and a gesture of peace for a parting warrior.

"Is he white?" Sergeant Cookson, the platoon sergeant for Third Platoon, a Georgian with shoulders broad enough to wrap a bad day around, carried a crew-cut around like a tattoo, daring a man to miss a beat. Cookson leaned on his men with heavy hands.

"He's scared white."

"Bein' scared is good."

"I suppose. I got crazy when we banged those dinks along that river bed."

"Forget about killin' dinks, Andy. They been fightin' for a long damn time."

"They ain't seen anything like us."

"They know we're here, Andy. They just don't know how we're gonna act." Hardin's stomach cramped into a tight ball as he stood into a clumsy stride.

"You can't miss the new El Tee—six one, skinny, white as a sheet."

"I'll look for him." Andy faded into the shadows. Hardin entered the mess tent to throw away his meal and found the company platoon sergeants surrounding a helpless table.

"This must be a cluster-fuck."

"Nothin' like a wise-ass lieutenant." Cookson returned fire with a southern twang and a whiskey-stained look of mischief.

"They're promotin' him to captain on eleven June," Stubbs said, astounding the group.

"I'm gonna come back and be your company commander, Cookson."

"Good god, a teenage captain." Cookson had the NCOs laughing.

"Anybody know if there's a radio link to the world? I should be a dad by now."

"There's a MARS shack, fifty meters from the TOC. LeCotte just made a call."

* * *

The Mobile Army Radio Station was a soundproof box, a padded cube. After ten minutes of weather bites and restarts, Hardin was patched through to his mother at Number #10, Highlands Road, in Bremerton, Washington.

He was shocked. He was hollering into a funnel, a tube that absorbed his gentler emotions, exposing the raw edges of his speech. He was hollering at his mom.

"Mom, is that you, over?" Silence met his words as they bounced across the sea, trusted to the aim of a stranger.

"Yes, how are you doing honey, over?" Eva Hardin was the real trooper, the Major's sweet heart. Her words were crisp. She was doing a fine job of keeping happy, keeping a steady hand, and keeping the home fires burning.

This was Eva Hardin's third combat assignment, her third time in the barrel.

"I'm fine, Mom. How's Linda? over."

"Linda gave birth to a baby girl, Kimberly Dawn. I stood in for you at the Naval Hospital. Linda and baby are doing fine, over." Hot damn: a baby girl.

"How are you doing, Mom, over?" Hardin closed his eyes. His mom was playing the piano in their living room, singing the words to "I'll Be Seeing You," throwing her enthusiasm over her shoulder, coaxing him to join in. He knew she was crying.

"Oh, Eddie, I miss your dad, but I'm fine, over." And there you go. GIs never told the truth because their moms were always "fine."

"I have to go, Mom, give Linda and the baby a kiss for me, over." He didn't have to leave. Other soldiers were waiting to make calls, but he didn't care. With nothing to say to his mother about the war, he was crying.

"I'll call Linda. She and baby Kimberly are at the farm, over."

"Thanks, Mom. I love you, Mom. Good-bye, over." He waved to his mom as he drove out the driveway. She could throw a kiss farther than anyone.

"I love you, too, honey, good-bye." Eva Hardin's parting 'over' was lost on a southerly fetch somewhere in the Philippines, leaving her son wondering how to raise a baby girl.

He could not control the giddiness in his pace as he skipped past the welcoming signs for the battalion and turned into the canyon of sandbags leading to the mess hall. The stars sparkled from horizon to horizon. The war stood aside. The space in his soul reserved for those he loved rang with joy, sending a chime at each star and a holler at each GI.

Beating the measure of "Hang on Sloopy" with his foot, he knew he could not hang on to good news. He knew the war would claim this glimmer of hope as its own. Each holler brought him closer to the fear of never seeing his little girl. Fatherhood's joy vanished when the artillery battery cut loose.

Twenty seconds later the guns let go again.

Little people died in Vietnam, almost every night. Hardin sat motionless, thankful for his chance at immortality, wishing he were home.

Kimberly Dawn, the darling of the Naval Hospital at the Puget Sound Naval Shipyard in Bremerton, Washington, would skip down Highlands Road, mindful of Aunt Dorothy's roses, knowing the old bag would twist her ear.

Hardin closed his eyes to embrace a summer day, skipping over the cracks, dressed in his red pinstripes and steel cleats, ready for Saturday's baseball game. The Major put Neatsfoot Oil on his glove the night before a game, and gave him a pat on the back on game day.

Happiness for his Linda sparred gently with his pride, then raced into a sullen appraisal of time and circumstance. With Kimberly Dawn's birth, with this glowing sense of occasion, he had one more reason to survive and something to balance losing Bucks.

Lost, as if displaced, he worried. He had to be vigilant, tuned to the platoon's level of despair, hopeful that the birth of his baby girl might keep twenty-two men alive for one more operation.

News from the home front found its way into a GI's rucksack on its own, as if guided by inference, the envelopes awkwardly small, the words but dissonant fragments. Fear soaked the face of these envelopes leaving a suspicious stain. Letters from parents brought momentary comfort. Letters from wives and girlfriends were rarely shared. War's continuum of distrust left warts on a GI's self-esteem, outflanking his ability to keep even heartfelt words.

Stubbs had set the betting line on how many days it would take for the Red Cross to notify the platoon they had a baby girl. The GIs of First Platoon, Charlie Company, would fight for Kimberly's freedom and drink a toast to her good health.

They would fight for anyone's baby girl.

CHAPTER EIGHTEEN

The Crow's Foot

Battalion Tactical Operations Center. Landing Zone English.

A stumpy, mute man in faded tiger fatigues sat on his rucksack near the entrance of the TOC. His nametag said he was Walker. His face said he was a hard man. His knife kissed the wet stone with a smooth caressing motion as death was piled upon death.

"Are you a true man, or a liar?" That was Walker's question. Walker was the Recon Platoon Sergeant, well nigh a legend.

Captain Joe gave Walker a nod as he entered the TOC. New maps were issued for an area of operations called the Crow's Foot; a large valley system southwest of Bong Son stretching fifteen kilometers southwest, toward An Khe. Three finger-valleys branched from the main valley forming the shape of a crow's foot.

Walker stood next to Joe in the briefing room.

"Within hours of their insertion, Sergeant Walker's recon team spotted dozens of well equipped NVA transiting the main valley of the Crow's Foot," Joe said, introducing Walker.

"Their equipment looked new." Walker wasn't talking to anyone in particular. "Charlie has well-trained ground support in the rice paddies and the mountains."

Andy stepped to the map and said, "I bet they got the east-west trails in and out of the mountains wired: spider holes, ambush sites, booby traps." Walker nodded his agreement.

No one interrupted, so Andy continued. "They're using Bong Son for R&R." With Hardin's transfer, Andy's platoon would be the lead element inserted on combat assaults. Andy would take over the company if Joe got killed.

Joe nodded, and said, "Hard to tell how the NVA use these towns.

Gator's replacement swallowed as if an aspirin were stuck in his throat, his yellow-brown eyes trying to fence a world more personal than he had imagined. His reasoning that Vietnam's war was a field application of Officer Candidate School, at first logical, had been replaced by a dry mouth, and no reason whatsoever.

The snag in the sandbag near his shoulder required inspection: for a bullet.

"Lieutenant Bowe is taking Third Platoon," Joe announced.

Wanting to run, Bowe had been introduced as a leader, an example of courage. Suffering his first case of rectal compression, his mouth puckered, causing his eyes to protrude beyond the bridge of his nose. The lanky Virginian didn't want any part of it, "it" being his scrawny body in a set of jungle fatigues. His expression screamed *I was just kidding.*

"Dink patrols are movin' in and out of this delta every night." Andy moved to the map and started in with the rubber-tipped pointer. "If we're near these villages at night we can figure the local VC know exactly what we're doin'."

Andy looked conclusively around the room, stepped into the doorway for emphasis, then shook his head. "That'll make night moves and moves at first light one dicey son of a bitch."

Andy was not finished. "Believe it, kids and women are gonna get banged in this mess." He ran the pointer around the map as if he were stirring soup. "Mix this shit with booby traps, and the studs will shoot anything that jumps in front of them."

Mentally rummaging through the briefing room, Bowe was becoming a carbonated form of delirium. Joe motioned to a chair and Andy sat down, giving Bowe a reassuring nod of confidence. Andy kept the pointer.

Joe did a body-bob and said, "Yeah, I hear the words." He didn't really, but Andy sat a little straighter. Bowe had crossed his legs and cinched them into a knot, choking the sides of his chair with his dishpan hands. If he relaxed for one second, he would shit his pants.

Today was orange malaria pill day—Monday. If Bowe had already taken one, Hardin would do his level best to convince the rookie to take one more. Fighting Vietnam's war with a crotch full of shit was as common as jungle rot and empty magazines. Hardin would be doing Bowe a favor. Two orange malaria pills would blow his boots off.

Joe spoke over his shoulder as he approached the map.

"Any ideas how to handle these villages? Can't afford to hesitate if Chuck is in our face. Eighty-five percent chance of that being how it goes down." Bowe had crossed his arms and looked as if he were holding his breath. With no takers, Joe kept talking.

"I don't feel like dyin' in this mud after some old woman fires me up. The way the vegetation surrounds these hootches is complicated—open-paddy, hootches, open-paddy. A GI could get hit from anywhere." Hardin laughed and decided to seal Bowe's fate.

"Since these paddies are new to us, maybe Bowe learned some tricks at Fort Benning."

Epilepsy wasn't common in Vietnam, but Bowe's reaction was close—a nervous disorder marked by convulsive attacks with loss of consciousness. His legs and arms uncoiled and his body snaked over his chair, he rolled his eyes around the room, organizing a withdrawal. Joe laughed. He had seen these reactions at the Florida Ranger School.

With a straight face, Joe said, "How about it, Bowe—got any ideas?" Andy offered Bowe the pointer. Bowe declined, gasping, trying to keep the numbness from spitting him into a slur.

"No, no, sir."

Joe flashed a smile when Mother settled into the doorway. Knowing supervision was a rating category on Mother's efficiency report, Hardin decided to introduce him to one of his plastic soldiers.

"Quick-fire inside a village and someone's gonna die," Hardin said.

Joe was looking for a point. Hardin stood to the side of the room holding a two-inch diameter, eight-inch-long piece of bamboo he had cut in Dak To and stuffed with C-4 plastique explosive. A homemade grenade—nobody hesitates, nobody goes to the stockade. At first the room was curious. When Hardin unscrewed the top off one of Stubbs' frag grenades and pushed the blasting cap into the C-4 at the top of the bamboo tube, the room fell silent.

Mother disappeared; his bus ticket was shredding. Joe stared in disbelief. Walker's throat started into a low rumble. With five bamboo grenades to account for, Hardin decided to defend his decision.

"How long have you been packin' that around?"

"Since, Duc Co," he lied.

"Where's your brains?" Joe asked, pointing a bony finger.

"Is that what it takes to keep steppin'—brains?" Hardin spoke quietly until he lost control and screamed. "No matter who jumps in front of me, I'm gonna blow their shit away. The dinks who die in front of me are VC by definition: they're dead."

Yelling at the company commander. Andy had seen it before. Bowe was shocked into disbelief, leaning forward to release the gas that had seized his bowels.

"Shut up, Hardin. We've got a 0630 PZ time on the airstrip."

Since Joe had chewed his ass for Bowe's benefit, Hardin decided to mess with Bowe's mind. He extended his hand and Bowe grabbed it without hesitation.

"You are a tall one, Bowe. I don't think those rubber bags come that big. Shit—you'd even hang out both ends of a poncho." Andy couldn't believe what he heard.

"Jesus, Hardin, lighten up." Bowe agreed.

Stubbs cut off Hardin's path to the mess tent and said, "What do ya want me to do with these?" Stubbs held a bamboo grenade near his face.

"Hang on to 'em."

"The captain was pissed." Stubbs took a calculating drag on his cigarette.

"He'll get over it. In a week those bamboo fire sticks are gonna make sense." Hardin turned into the night to think about his baby girl.

"Six was pissed." The night made Stubbs more reflective.

"You said that, Stubbs."

Amps tripped over Pops' foot, then fell, clamoring over LeCotte's rucksack, drunk.

"You're a dumb ass, Amps. Give me a pen and some paper," Hardin said.

"Dumb-ass? Pee-ef-cee Amps is my military title."

"There's nothin' military about you, Dumb-ass, now cough up some paper." Amps coughed a fake cough, then swigged at his beer.

"I got some shit paper. Maybe I'll use it first." Amps handed Hardin a plastic bag filled with paper and waited for a response, swigging his beer.

"Pee-ef-cee: Perfect Fuckin' Cherry. Dumb-ass is a pee-ef-cee."

"I ain't no cherry."

* * *

Praising Linda for a job well done, Hardin scratched at his needles of doubt. After four introductions, the words flowed into a reminiscent chop, barely touching one emotion before trouncing on another. With so many good words to choose from, hugs for his baby girl gave way to springtime on the farm, only to find him concerned about his mom.

Finally the promise stage of the letter: a Hawaiian R&R in September, a transfer out of the jungle, the assurance of false hope, and an antiquated farewell. Communicating with a world suspended beyond the eastern sea left him wishing he could start life over.

* * *

Number #10, Highlands Road. Bremerton, Washington. September 1958.

Young Hardin sat in his father's den conjuring the sounds to match the pictures. The Battle of the Bulge echoed as tank fire crashed through a frozen forest. Bagpipes sounded at the funeral of John Poston. D-Day roared without definition. The Major's conversations with Ike were profound and to the point.

Driving north from Bastogne, he found the second page of a letter his father was writing to his brother. Court was beginning his last year at West Point.

"Monty was a gracious host. Lots of toasts and reminiscing about the good times. A faint mention of the bad times: losing John Poston. After a while, one sets the bad times aside."

* * *

Landing Zone English. 2200 Hours.

Under the peasant norms of farming life, laminated beneath a veneer of culture and time, the most vicious guerrilla war in history was being fought. Little-known religions and seasonal ambiguities masked the metallic anguish of this war.

The complexities of the rice paddy sparred with the simplicities of the jungle.

Sun-parched elders transformed their village from an agrarian wonderland to a political classroom, to a bunkered perimeter with a nod. To America, the village was a country town and the farmer was a peaceful sort who was hard working and seasonally abused.

To a grunt, the village was a trap and the farmer was a Viet Cong soldier.

"She gonna go airborne?" Stubbs sat down next to Hardin.

"What are you talkin' about?" Stubbs leaned back and offered Hardin a beer.

"Kimberly, is she gonna go airborne?"

"I'll bet she's a chubby one. I weighed thirty-one pounds when I was one year old."

Stubbs laughed and stood. "No wonder your mama talks about you the way she does. I can't find Fish, or PeeWee."

Hardin threw out a guess. "Bunker #1, no doubt. Have Drips go find 'em."

Hours passed before Hardin found himself staring into the night, arguing with his fragile resolve. The rice paddies had spread into a black matrix, framing the night. A filtered light shown from a sand bag hovel on the perimeter, highlighting a ribbon of cigarette smoke. As safe haven, the yellow-white hue cast a sense of loneliness.

Distant explosions lingered like the words of a rumor. Dig-it fell clumping from a tree line. Whispers and quiet laughter brought a moment of silence, replaced by the glow of a cigarette on a tired face: Stubbs' face. The war seemed smaller at night: smaller and over there.

Nearby, bunched into a huddle, puzzled by his own nonchalance, Lieutenant Bowe briefed his squad leaders. Hardin sipped his beer. His new comrade would find little in Vietnam to match his obligation. Reflecting on his first night in Dak To, Hardin laughed.

Praising high ground was a derivative of centuries of warfare, of building castles and kneeling to worship God. Bowe would be obsessed with high ground until death or Sergeant Cookson convinced him that his enemy was hiding in a hole. Bowe's platoon would function in spite of him. If a GI died because Bowe was stupid, Bowe would become a pariah.

"Sergeant Major said one of Walker's recon teams spotted a Caucasian packin' an AK, in the Crow's Foot." Stubbs handed Hardin a beer.

"The Crow's Foot: I got a bad feelin' about that valley." Hardin dropped his beer between his boots. "Could be that deserter."

Drips stood-to with Fish and PeeWee. Stubbs lit a cigarette and waved his lighter in front of PeeWee's face. "You two owe me."

Hardin drifted away, only to find Doc Taylor standing stock still, a droop at the corner of each eye, a pot pipe in his shirt pocket, determined to smoke grass before racking out.

"El Tee, me and Mr. Monty and some dudes are havin' a set. The flyboys got an empty tent." The doctor wanted Hardin's approval.

"I'm not into that shit, Doc. Get the studs back early. You, Doc—you make sure. Tomorrow could be as bad as it gets."

"No sweat, El Tee."

"You're my medic, Doc. If your shot-bag isn't straight and someone in this platoon pays a price, I'll deal your ass in a hot second. You hear what I'm sayin', Doc?"

"My shit's good, El Tee."

* * *

At 0635 hours six choppers flew south and west across twelve kilometers of rice paddy and the An Lao River, heading into the mouth of the Crow's Foot. Currents of cool and hot air washed the airframes with a cologne scented with fear. Roaring out of the sunrise, the choppers barged over a ridgeline and fell into an eclectic void.

Set amongst the forces of time, their shadows stained the valley floor.

The main valley was beautiful. Remote and unblemished, the Crow's Foot could have been in Yosemite National Park. Suspended above the Crow's Foot, as if floating on a quiet pond, an ache worked its way into Hardin's chest. A weight hung on his boots.

His lips were moving.

"Are you goin'... to San Francisco." Suddenly wary, his eyes widened into a knowing search and the choppers sailed into short final. A white-phosphorous artillery round landed with a softer thump. Hardin stood out onto the skid, his right hand glued to the pistol grip, his left hand wired to the chopper's door frame, watching the gunships rip at the unbelieving calm.

"Be sure to wear... some flowers in your hair." His door gunner joined the fray as a second gunship flew along the tree line. Combat assault number thirty-one landed deep in the Crow's Foot, on the open floor of the main valley.

"This one's for my baby girl."

The grass on the valley floor lay in one direction—signaling, warning the GIs. The jungle seemed to crouch, measuring the intrusion. The romance of the valley was as brittle as its charm. The slicks dropped into the grass, lifting away as GIs ran for cover.

The sixty meters seemed a mile. Something hot bit Stubbs' throat as he bolted into the tree line. GIs ran from the clearing with Pops on point. The heavy air consumed the sound of their boots. Or, was it the echo of a distant bugle? LeCotte picked his way into a small clump of scrub, pointing Ski to watch a hard-beaten trail.

Stubbs' face was blistered with sweat. A stiffening set gripped his eyes.

Rap and Blood signaled men to spread out.

Stubbs crawled next to LeCotte, a faint burn traced the side of his neck. Pops placed a second magazine in the grass, next to his face. The heat, the silence, and the pendulous canopy became a meld, an incomplete portrait of potions and lucky charms. Death was waiting with its oils and its brush. The scuff-marks on the trail were fresh.

Rooted to the ground, they forced their search deeper into the jungle. Insistent sign language followed each miscue. Fish fingered the surface of his lips, measuring his frightened comrades. Tag rose from the ground creating a wave of movement.

To creep along in toe-then-heel agony required absolute concentration. The mulch on the jungle floor was moist, softening their step. The ground cover was as brittle as dead cedar. The point squad labored from side to side, skirting the trail. Half-cocked in a quick-fire dance, Tag's fist shot skyward.

GIs bent to the ground, unhinged, sweat flowing into the well of their eyes. Searching across a jungle floor that reeked with a soggy tang, they lowered their heads to relieve the pressure and calculate their response. Breathing for a second time, Pops raised his chin and stopped breathing. An enemy soldier was running down the trail, running at Tag.

The stranger was either a poorly dressed NVA or a well-dressed VC. Without breaking stride he took a full load of double-aught buckshot in the face. His head disintegrated along with his hat. Within that instant, his legs flew over his shoulders and his torso crumpled into his feet.

The dead soldier was packing a B-71 transceiver and a SKS rifle.

The point squad dragged the soldier downhill, rolled his body under a bush, and buried what was left of his head. To mock the man as a dumbass, Tag laid a ten-piaster note on his chest and weighed it down with a can of ham and motherfuckers—enough chow for a trip to see Buddha, and enough money to take a bus.

With cold precision the point squad cleaned the trail, freshening damaged vegetation, brushing the ground to hide the blood and gray matter. The smell would linger for days.

The jungle has a hollow tone when there is no breeze.

"Lima, backtrack the trail 200 meters. We'll wait." Joe sounded perplexed.

With Ski pulling slack for Fish, the clover stopped to listen. Not happy with the jungle's mood, Hardin took Pops and Boyle forward to recon a small finger ridge. The ground was covered with a ground-hugging vegetation—a brittle salal. The red-brick soil was damp and cool.

Tracing a patch of open ground, Pops froze. Two AK rounds lay on the dank jungle matting near his left boot. The jungle seemed to sense his fear. Chuck didn't waste ammunition, yet AK rounds lay at the edge of the trail. Without looking down, Pops sank into a squat, searching from tree to tree. The AK rounds were as warm as Pops' skin.

The instant his hand tightened on the shells, death told Pops to run. He threw himself from his squat, lunging to his left. AK fire belched from the undergrowth.

The canopy echoed the roar of gunfire.

Pops' scream echoed through the Crow's Foot as steel rockets chipped at his mud-clogged mind. His upward downhill motion accelerated when an AK round slammed into his weapon above the magazine and below the bolt. The handle of Pops' weapon slammed into his chest, throwing him to the ground.

Tiny rockets broke the soundings around his eyes. The heat from their passing seared his ears. Roots lacing the jungle floor absorbed Pops' fall. Hardin and Boyle returned fire.

"Pops, let's go," Boyle yelled, dropping an empty magazine.

Boyle yanked Pops to his feet as Hardin fired blindly into the brush to cover their escape. The ground sank away from their boots. Stumbling, Pops' chest heaved with pain.

Running backwards, Hardin caught sight of a muzzle flash. A baseball sized chunk of tree trunk slammed into his chest. He fell, then twisted downhill, firing without thought. Something moved. He reloaded and fired low, into the void, then reloaded again. Scrambling to his feet he ran without looking back, using the tree trunks for cover.

The eyes of his men looked like those of a tortured horse, fixed in that certain stare.

Men burrowed into the ground, anticipating, hoping Pops wasn't dragging the war with him. Hardin bounded uphill through the perimeter, motioned Stubbs to take the rear, and continued his withdrawal into the company perimeter.

The weapon Pops had been whoring was history. The dust cover was gone, the bolt and magazine were twisted together. Pops' chest was scarred with the imprint of the weapon's carrying-handle, punctured by the back sight. Bowe stared in disbelief; mesmerized by the bolt housing of Pops' weapon.

"What'd ya see?" Joe asked, his back tucked against the base of a tree.

"Nothin': Pops' gun stopped a round. I got the shakes. Fuck-oh-shit that was close. The bastards must be trackin' us," Hardin said.

"Dinks are tryin' to fix our location. Your heatstroke came crawlin' back when the shootin' started. Thought Cookson was gonna kill him. Used a lot of water." Joe held Pops' weapon as if it were made of glass, then handed it to Stubbs.

Stubbs confronted PFC Wallace. "What am I gonna do? You wanna play heatstroke, and I wanna play butt stroke." Stubbs jerked the weapon from Wallace's hand. "Is it clean?"

"Yes, Platoon Sergeant."

"Fuckin' thing's never been fired." Stubbs let the man's self-pity take hold, then surveyed his options. "I'm gonna kill ya with your own gun, that's what I'm gonna do." Wallace stood silent, frightened by the smolder in Stubbs' eye; the steady hate. He would hide in the tubes until the Women's Volunteer Service turned him out.

Wallace was one of Aldershot's finer lads.

"You're a sorry fucker, Wallace. Without a weapon you got a reason to hide."

Charlie Company hauled ass for the better part of an hour and dug in with three light OPs. With Pops' weapon fused into an alloy of hot lead and pot-metal, Hardin found himself lost in the clouds of cream swirling through his coffee. Sweet Cheek's shroud line seemed shorter, as if a portion of its charm had been spent.

With a heart rate twice the speed of sound, Hardin's fevered dreams were back.

"I'll run the horn," Hardin said, wanting to stay awake.

Amps agreed with a huff and found Hardin's hand with a slapping, it's-about-time-motion, then barked out a sarcastic order. "Eggs and grits, and white toast. First thing." He smiled and settled into a cold can of beans and franks. No one would cook tonight.

Hardin closed his eyes to the sounds of a lone AK-47 barking at point blank range and the dark features of his enemy spread under the irregular shape of a cloth hat. His margin of error could be easily measured. Chuck had given Hardin fair warning; a strawberry-colored wake-up call with a centripetal force vectored somewhere between his eyes.

A cold, blistering sweat consumed his body. He leaned into the sandbags at the front of his foxhole to keep from collapsing.

Stubbs lowered himself into the foxhole, examining Pops' weapon. "We're in Indian Country, El Tee. You all right?"

"Who knows?"

"Livin' through a year of this shit might not be possible." Stubbs ran a finger over the jagged remains of Pops' weapon.

"In the end, Stubbs, if I'm livin,' it's what's left-over that worries me."

"You got the shakes, El Tee." Stubbs' hand shot out in anger, seized Amps' shirt, and with one forceful jerk Amps was standing wide-eyed in the foxhole with the radio handset in tow.

"You got the fuckin' radio, asshole. All fuckin' night."

The fever consumed Hardin in a matter of seconds as he crawled to his rucksack and collapsed. Delirious, he crashed from dream to dream.

* * *

Number #10, Highlands Road. Bremerton, Washington.

Automatic weapons fire tore at the den wall. Shards of glass lanced the smoke filled room. The Major was returning fire. Pictures danced in their frames as the greatest of the great were ripped to shreds.

By the bottom of the fifth inning young Hardin had had three at bats—a line drive to right, reached first base on an error, and a sacrifice bunt. The team was ahead, nine-six. The Major was watching from behind home plate, helping the umpire keep his head steady so he follow the curve ball. Then he stood near the entrance to the dugout.

"Hi, Pops. How'd ya like my hit?"

"Hit the ball hard," he said, stepping away. "I have to go show a house, Pal."

"I'll see you in Piccadilly, Pops."

Dreaming as if normalcy was in flower, Hardin bounced from foxhole to foxhole, tying years and events into a jumble. His father appeared wearing his Victoria Cross—his VC. Then he vanished, first the brave soldier, then full of fear.

His father was charging up Omaha Beach on D-Day, screaming his vengeance, only to turn and run screaming into the surf. What was his father's truth? What was he screaming?

"Run, Pal."

"I am, Pops."

* * *

Somewhere in the morning, when the night turns gray, when the jungle is still enough to feel the air move, Hardin's body began to gush sweat like a geyser. By the time stand-to gave way to Joe's order to saddle up, Hardin was out of water and could barely stand.

Stubbs took charge of the platoon and Hardin fell in behind Amps. Artillery rumbled behind the ridgeline to the north, shouting like hooves on a wooden bridge. By the time he could control his feet, the company had established a night laager and Amps was serving coffee.

* * *

Time was a blur, a tedious waltz on the dark, damp slopes of the Crow's Foot. The air remained heavy with rotting vegetation. Dark gold leaves covered the ground. Barely able to lift his feet, Hardin was content, not knowing what his true measure might be.

Gradually the company picked its way back to the floor of the main valley for extraction. They were flying into the rice paddies for their first exposure to Vietnam's hedgerows. Sitting just inside the tree line, waiting for the first lift, Joe motioned to Hardin.

"The Old Man is transferring you to Delta Company until you make captain." Joe fingered the ashes off the end of a three-day-old cigar, then took almost all of Tennessee's coffee. Their expressions joined in a countrified stupor.

"Bullshit! You know if your dicks were a wee bit longer, you might get a woman to fuck ya. And Cabin Boy here wouldn't have so much trouble walkin'."

"Cabin Boy, is it?" Joe spit bits of cigar at Hardin's boots and ginned up a sidling smile. "Delta Company Commander doesn't have a dick."

"You've gotta be jokin'. That man needs more than a dick."

Joe laughed an agreeable laugh and nodded as he held his lighter under the beaten end of the cigar. A smile emerged from the smoke as his dirty, black whiskered face wrinkled itself into an expression of reluctant authority.

"As soon as we get in, say good-bye." Joe was serious now.

"Just like that. Go baby-sit an outfit that'll get me killed." Hardin shrugged. His anger was bunched in confused patches.

"You don't have any problem tellin' me what to do," Joe said, soliciting agreement.

Joe's eyes cast a prophetic image as his tone spread into hopelessness. Hardin could feel the fabric of their bond tearing. Fear was gnawing at the layers of his mind. With hope shutting down, he could not keep his face from casting a disbelieving grin. His respect for Joe was sagging under the weight of reality.

Hardin had been betrayed.

"Who gets the platoon?"

"I don't know."

"This transfer is payback for that box of horse shit."

Joe stood, handed Tennessee his map, and dismissed Hardin with some impatience.

Hardin barged through the nearest thicket and stood next to Stubbs and Amps. Their faces registered apprehension. Uncertainty kept their eyes moving. They were saying good-bye.

The toe of Hardin's right boot pushed at the damp soil as he visualized the instant that odd-round entered the soft-shell of Pops' weapon. Sweet Cheek's shroud line laid across his palm as his fingers kept pace with the Lord: through the shadow of the valley of death, I will fear no evil.

His tit that was lanced by buckshot in An Khe had absorbed the AK-propelled chunk of wood, reminding him to keep faith with his instincts, no matter how anxious his steps became. Being separated from the men who buoyed his sense of reason frightened him.

Death without them would have no meaning whatsoever.

A little farm girl watched stoically, waiting for Joe, holding her father's AK-47. She waited for all the Joes. Killing this little girl would bring a grunt limitless grief. And confusing fear with this grief was the complication in the enigma that was Vietnam.

* * *

An operations sergeant waited to escort Hardin from the airstrip to the TOC. The Old Man wanted to talk to him in person. Charlie Company was held at the airstrip for resupply and an insertion into the rice paddies north of the Tiger Mountains. Hardin gave Joe a thumbs-up.

"Take care of our boys, Stubbs," Hardin said.

"I'll do that, El Tee." Ski and Fish had huddled with Amps to listen.

Hardin turned to Ski and extended his hand. "You're short, Ski, make sure these dick heads keep ya covered." Ski stood into his massive frame, his shirt open. Then he stepped to the side, smiled, and hit Hardin's fist. Reynolds nodded and adjusted his helmet.

"I'll be around, close enough to make a difference." Rap stood into a brace, dropping his rucksack at his feet. He was paying his respect in silence. Blood was pissed off. He didn't like changes that he didn't get consulted on.

"Thanks, Pops."

Pops' smile sat in the middle of his rough-sawn, cedar-colored face just long enough to turn into resentment. Bleached strips of hair ran the length of the sides of his head, leaving a bright patch in the middle. At age twenty-six, Pops was a wise man.

Hardin looked into his sun-baked face and found Pops' eyes measuring his own. Pops' calipers mirrored his short, testy stature, and gave notice to all: he was a man of positive force. Guru or God, Pops was the reason that many of the men in First Platoon were still alive. Pops had shouldered Vietnam's war. Receiving confessions, he counseled his friends with the comfort of a steel-pot stew. A gold cross hung with his dog tags, lost in a forest of bleached hair.

Unshaven and less forgiving, Pops cocked his body to the right, ready to strike without notice. He was a bit like Popeye, with well-developed forearms and a heightened sense of honor and fair play. He held his coffee in his left hand, leaving his right hand free to stir emotions.

"Take care, El Tee." The tired soldiers shook hands, trying to out-squeeze the other's grip. "Do us a favor, El Tee." Pops whispered and then continued. "Get Wallace outta here."

Hardin found Wallace talking to Bowe. "Get in the jeep, Wallace."

Bowe started to speak, then caught the glare in Stubbs' eye.

Grabbing Hardin's shoulder, Drips said, "Had to come back, El Tee. I missed, Fish." As the story was told, Drips was coming back to the field because Fish was lonely. Truth was, Mother had ordered Drips to burn shit, and Drips told Mother to go fuck himself.

"I know. Besides, it's easier to keep a secret outside the wire."

Drips looked at Reynolds for that moment that defined their pledge. With an imperceptible tick, Reynolds conveyed his answer. Drips' secret was safe. Hardin wanted to know what had happened in Ban Me Thuot, but he knew as an officer, he was not privy to this information. A GI would never betray one of his own.

The two men let their parting simmer.

CHAPTER NINETEEN

Damn, How Ya Gonna Act?

Landing Zone English. 1600 Hours.

Watching wounded men march into the eternity of their survival, staring skyward, their minds bent by the roar of the battle, pushing at the noise and the fear, then accepting the calm of death, left men like Edward Hardin standing in a thinning rank, too exhausted to do other than mark another nameless day.

Before he could muster the courage of a band of strangers, he had to confront a nagging account. He looked briefly at Wallace, wanting to reason the man to be brave. Hardin would sacrifice this man to save any one of his friends. Wallace was expendable.

Scared beyond his ability to function, this new man possessed the capacity to corrupt. Good men died when men like Wallace wallowed in their own piss. The jump masters at the parachute training center had thrown him from the plane on his qualifying jumps.

The jeep lurched forward. Hardin leaned into the dashboard and looked back over the airstrip. His platoon had split into groups, anticipating the worst from a new officer. Who among them would scream, "Fuck you, LeCotte?" Boyle was defenseless.

Hardin escorted Wallace to the TOC and pointed to a corner by the radio operators.

"Sit down." Hardin handed his rucksack to Radio Man—Bronx.

"Am I going to the stockade?" Detecting a stale, cultured contempt in the man's tone, Hardin stared at the man's swollen face.

"They shoot men like you, Wallace." Hardin pointed at the floor. Wallace placed a hand on the sandbag wall and sat on his rucksack, peering about like a helpless child.

The briefing room reeked of cigarettes and Old Spice. The briefing map had been gift-wrapped. Ribbons of pushpins littered the rice paddies. GIs were dying in the mud. Unit symbols and hyphenated numbers accented the war's sacred acronyms: KIA, MIA, WIA.

Hardin extended his hand and said, "Sergeant Major." The top sergeant's face bristled with sweat. His forearms were fenced with tendons and muscle.

"Lieutenant, this is Staff Sergeant Walker, Echo Recon. You know Major Swanson." Hardin shook Walker's hand, reacting to his down-home grip with a nod. He knew Walker well enough to communicate without speaking. "The Colonel will be here in three-zero minutes."

"Sergeant Major, can we talk alone?" Hardin asked. Mother showed Walker the door. The dark-haired old soldier showed few signs of wear as he sat erect, his face cultivating an expression of tempered intensity, his right eye angled outward. Hardin lowered his voice.

"I've got a man out front. He's scared. Gone down twice with heatstroke in firefights." Hardin cocked his head and waited for a response.

"Bad for business. You want me to handle it, Lieutenant?" The old soldier nodded, coaching Hardin's answer, smiling through a seasoned stare. "I'll get him out of the field, make sure he pays a price. Might be bad time, probably something else." Top turned to read the briefing map—eight KIA. The ultimate sacrifice was about to collide with Wallace the coward.

"What was that about?" Mother asked.

"Sergeant's business, Mother."

Hardin nestled into the radio room and asked Radio Man for a soda. Bronx was a lanky, wiry, blue-faced GI with black hair and a New York style. He plunged a hand into the icy water in the mermite can, hesitated as he evaluated the exchange, then tossed Hardin a soda. The situation map fronting the radio desk indicated that Delta Company was laagered east of the village of Bong Son in a U-shaped valley on the eastern slope of the Tiger Mountains, fewer than one hundred meters from the South China Sea.

"Delta move much today?" Bronx looked over his shoulder.

"Couple hundred meters. Had to rest a twisted ankle." Hardin laughed. Only a Bronx accent could brand a man a loser with such clarity.

Radio Man screamed, "Atten-hut." Uncle and the Old Man stormed into the bunker.

"Let's talk, Lieutenant." Hardin found himself back in the briefing room with the Old Man's ice-blue eyes rushing at him like headlights from a dense fog.

"Lieutenant, you're joining Delta Company in the field. Work with the company for a week, get a bead on the troops. I'm relieving that captain. You'll run Delta Company until a new captain arrives from Bien Hoa." In Army lingo this was a major-league compliment, a coveted assignment. "Any questions?" He didn't expect any, so Hardin jumped right in.

"When's the new guy arrive?"

"Four days, five days max."

Hardin nodded his understanding and looked at Walker. He had one more comment. "Those road apples came a long way."

The Old Man laughed a short laugh. "Yes they did. I gave that horse shit to the commander of the First Battalion and told him that's what I thought of his unit." The Old Man smiled to compliment his young charge—then, as if evaluating his decision, he held up a finger and said, "Do it right, and keep doin' it."

"Yes, sir." The Old Man turned and left the briefing room. Mother rushed into the wake of his words, to capture a thing or two. Uncle lit a smoke and stood to the lectern.

"Study the map, Lieutenant." Hardin's grin was barely discernible as he moved closer to the lectern. "Delta's AO is pretty much all of the Tigers." Hardin decided to isolate Mother.

"Walker, have you been in these mountains?" Hardin asked.

"Took a recon team through last week. Steep, some rocks, open sky except on the south half and in the gullies, dry, not much water. This blue-line is active. Hard to figure Charlie campin' in the hills with a town so close. Lotsa tracks. Might be some tunnels."

Mother listened intently, not wanting to defer completely. "Squad-sized operations, mostly," Mother said. "Wasted effort, mostly. Contrary to my estimates, and contrary to the brigade's estimates, I might add." Mother snorted blame around the bunker.

Uncle crushed his cigarette into a sandbag.

Walker stepped without moving. He wanted to hate Mother, maybe shoot him for being less than vulnerable. Smiling for the first time in weeks, he gave Mother credit—not for his value, for his persistence. Absorbing Mother's blame with an imperceptible nod, Walker said, "Uncle planned that operation into the Tigers. Maybe you field-grades should get together."

"Tell Hardin what's goin' on in the AO, Sergeant Walker," Uncle said, motioning Mother away from the briefing map.

"These vills are VC, big time. On the northeast by the coast, at the mouth of the An Lao, there's a break for three-four hundred meters. From here, the hootches run solid for ten-plus klicks, behind Bong Son, then west along the river. On the south bank."

Walker traced the river with his finger. His hand was pocked with dozens of festering sores: an allergic reaction to fire ant bites that had developed into jungle rot.

"Good avenues of escape, good concealment near the river, good infiltration routes," Hardin said, tracing the river's course into the An Lao Valley and the mountains to the west.

Walker agreed, then said, "Where Delta is laagered in this U-shaped valley, that village is abandoned, doesn't look like anyone's been there for a long time. This village at the south end of the Tigers is active, mostly fishing, next to Route #1.

The VC can transit into the mountains south of the river without covering much open ground. We didn't find any sign of Charlie campin' in the Tigers."

Mother tapped the map with a grease pencil. Hardin jumped on Walker's last word with another question. "Bunkers, tunnels, booby traps?"

"Didn't find any. A sniper could cover the vills and the paddies from any of these hilltops." Hardin grinned. Walker meant the villagers could see the hill-tops.

"You won't find Charlie if you run large operations, Major. They'll fade into the jungle." Tired of Walker's conclusions, Mother stood to a brace.

"You're right, Sergeant. Do you understand your mission, Lieutenant?"

The question was so good, Hardin knew Mother didn't think of it. He understood he had to live, but what did Mother want him to understand?

"We'll work it out, Mother." Once Mother left the briefing room Walker's face assumed an expression of trust, accepting Hardin's credentials. "What's goin' on, Walker?"

"Delta Company's been driftin' since that captain got assigned. The troops don't trust him. He's not too sharp."

"Is that deserter for real?"

"There's a man missin'. Third Platoon—Lieutenant Dorell's unit. I'd guess damn near every unit in Vietnam has a man missing that's listed on their morning report." Walker exhaled with a weariness that seemed to grow. "The troops do their best to ignore the captain. They figure on doing whatever it takes to stay alive." Walker offered Hardin a smoke, then lit one himself and leaned against the lectern. "You know yourself, Lieutenant, most officers hump the woods for a few months, then split, leavin' the squad leaders holdin' what's left."

Walker was breathing rapidly.

Hardin remained skeptical. "That missin' man might have changed sides. Or, he might have found his way to Malaya. His squad might have killed him. Or, he might have killed himself. At this point, I don't much care."

"You do have to be careful, Lieutenant," Walker said, checking the doorway to see if anyone was listening. "A deserter is a problem. Delta stands an IG inspection right soon."

Vietnam's war was full of deceit.

The IG, that deceitful bastard—the Inspector General, the Army's Inquisitor—that man had the questions. He was a spy, trained in an Anglican-sterile house near Oxford, England, where the questions with just one answer were formulated. The grunt and the IG were polar opposites.

If a grunt talked to the IG, all bets were off. Within the first exchange, the grunt would start a three-sided dialogue with a dead friend, then start picking bits of flesh from his hair and screaming for a medic. The grunt's company commander might as well kiss his career good-bye.

Finding himself wedged between mysteries, Hardin left the TOC heading for Delta Company's orderly room. The company commander was being relieved, the deserter was listed as missing-in-action, and the Old Man had Hardin rounding up strays, just for drill.

* * *

A water buffalo in harness lumbered across the dry clay surface of the rice paddy. A barefoot old man struggled with his step, nudging the animal forward, the traces of a harness draped over his shoulder. Hardin looked again as Grandpa Karl's image flashed against the red-brown backdrop of his prize bull, his white overalls stained with river-bottom mud.

The family farm near Canada was ripening with spring. The buds of a new crop of peas were beginning to show. Linda was in her bathrobe. A chubby baby girl nuzzled at her breast. The reflection of a snow-capped mountain shone on the pond, clashing with the billows of dull gray dust at the buffalo's heel.

The old farmer knew where to find the missing man.

* * *

Five company orderly rooms sat like row houses just below the crest of the hill. The faded canvas tenting had long-since begun to leak. Hardin was walking by Charlie Company when Lieutenant Wilson yelled from behind a typewriter.

"Hardin, get your ass in here and help me with this write-up for a Bronze Star for Valor." Wilson pointed at the paper in the typewriter.

"Who's it for?" Hardin asked.

"You, my man. For LZ Hammer, in Ban Me Thuot. Bunkers, frags, hot LZ."

"Hot LZ. Who started this parade?"

"The Exec. Uncle wants to clean up your act."

"What's Uncle doin' for Boyle and Mex?"

"Honorable mentions. Seems those boys think you won the day."

"Give it to Boyle. I'm lucky to be alive."

Wilson ripped the paper from the typewriter and threw a hook shot into the trash. Jungle Central was too congested with sunshine to allow consideration of a GI's daily sacrifice. Even though Boyle was deserving of many decorations for valor, for his days and months of courage, he would be passed over for more high-energy events, more self-serving careers, for individuals who would flower with more fertilizer.

My God, man, Winston was a member of The Eleventh Hussars. Hardin's father was a liaison officer for Field Marshal Montgomery. Surely, Hardin would aspire to be something more than Welsh-stuck in the muds of Southeast Asia, the friend of a black GI with a speech impediment.

Although Eddie missed his father's words of encouragement, the memory of his father's war no longer inspired him.

* * *

The slick ride to Delta Company passed without thought. Awed by the azure expanse of the South China Sea, Hardin tracked the whitecaps rushing before the wind. Almond-white sand churned in a seashell-colored surf. Shades of green embraced the beach, each shade checked by another, each as vivid as the next.

The chopper landed in a billow of dust.

"You here to help?" The captain asked.

Holy shit, Hardin thought. A pernicious grin betrayed him as he surveyed the captain's swollen ankle. An attentive numbness blessed the captain's eye. A handshake sealed the lie.

As if introducing his field first sergeant and the artillery forward observer was not required, the captain suffered through a sigh, and then adjusted the rucksack supporting his leg. A nicely timed grimace caused Hardin to turn away, waiting for the enjoyment to stiffen.

"I'm having trouble getting around, Lieutenant." The captain smiled to concede his fate, then introduced Dooley, the company's senior radio operator.

"First Sergeant," Hardin said.

Unsure of Hardin's status, the first sergeant stood-to.

"Get the platoon sergeants." Hardin wanted to measure attitudes. He stood silent until the four men stopped moving. "This perimeter is a jug-fuck. You got ten minutes to tighten it up. When you get back I better not be hearin' a sound."

Top stood to a steady brace, angered by the reluctance of his platoon sergeants. "Get it done, goddammit." His tone bore the trappings of pleasure, his vigil finally reinforced.

"Pick your best platoon, Top. If their outpost isn't perfect, you're goin' out on a clover to search the base of that southern ridge." Hardin wanted to know which platoon the first sergeant considered his best platoon. A clover along the base of the southern ridgeline would cover more ground than the company had covered in three days.

Mood and movement changed. The casual chatter wore to a whisper. With rucksacks refit, the platoon sergeants stood-to, searching Hardin's expression.

"What platoon, First Sergeant?"

Top pointed at the Second Platoon sergeant and said, "Show the lieutenant your OP."

Hardin looked at the other platoon sergeants and said, "You two stand fast."

The outpost was parked in vegetation so thick they couldn't see. Their weapons were lying on the ground unattended, and four men were smoking cigarettes.

When a platoon sergeant screws his first sergeant in front of an officer the paybacks never end. The anger in Top's voice caused the platoon sergeant to step away. Hardin returned to the landing zone with Top at his heels.

"Top, this is NCO business. There's no place to hide. Get the platoon leaders." One platoon sergeant stood fast as the others filtered away.

"You got First Platoon?"

"Yes, sir."

"Any problems with dope?"

"No, sir." The young sergeant's eyes shifted away.

"Bullshit. Shakedown the platoon."

Lieutenants Moore and Dorell were white, five-nine, slender, and too casual for Hardin's liking. Dorell had the deserter.

"I'm runnin' the company for this operation."

Moore alerted and measured Dorell's expression. Looking for guidance from their old CO, the good captain had sense enough to turn and hobble away.

"Which one of you has Second Platoon?" Hardin asked. Moore raised his head. "You better fuckin' learn how to put out an OP. You shit-stick this outfit again and you're doin' squad-sized night patrols in these vills. I've been here less than an hour. In another hour your people are gonna be doin' it right. If it doesn't happen that way, your platoon sergeants will be runnin' your platoons, and you'll be high-paid grunts."

The shakedown was a new experience for Delta Company.

Top crouched near Hardin's shoulder and dropped a plastic bag filled with dope and an M-16 magazine on the ground. Hardin slid the plate off the bottom of the magazine. The following-spring belched out, sending marijuana flying into the air.

Detecting signs of humor and recognition, Hardin asked, "Either of you smoke dope?"

"No, sir." Taken in unison, Hardin couldn't discern whether they were lying.

"First Platoon sergeant told me he didn't have a dope problem. Either of your platoons have a dope problem?" Hardin had trapped them. The answer was either yes, or I don't know. Moore stepped to the plate.

"I'm sure we got some somewhere."

"Not in the jungle, not ever." Hardin motioned the lieutenants to stand fast and left with the first sergeant.

"I'll handle the problem, sir."

"Burn the dope, Top." Hardin handed the old sergeant the magazine. "The magazine needs a new spring. Pull out every helmet liner. Make sure nobody's dryin' new weed."

"Yes, sir."

"Run this outfit the way ya know how, Top." Hardin threw his words at the lieutenants. The shit they were standing in had an unfamiliar odor.

"You know what an outpost looks like, Dorell?"

"Yes, sir."

Hardin dismissed Dorell and zeroed in on Moore. "Word I got was you were squared away. Get your map." Hardin waited for Moore's reluctance to gain speed before he spoke again. "Run a platoon clover into the middle of the valley, then cut south across the blue-line. Check for trails from the blue-line to the southern ridge."

"No problem," Moore said.

"I don't expect any problems. Come back inside the vegetation near the beach, go light, sit-reps every hundred meters. Top is goin' with you. I'm Delta 5."

"Anything else?"

"Yeah, don't lie to me." Hardin's eyes danced.

"Top, have Third Platoon take the perimeter, three, four-man OPs, and get the First Platoon sergeant for me." Top moved out.

"Moore, bring your rucksacks into the center and leave a man with them." Hardin had a glimmer of trust stirring with the NCOs.

"Sir." The First Platoon sergeant stood-to.

"Get your platoon ready for a light clover. Check the base of this northern ridge from the head of the valley to the beach." Hardin lined out a route on the map.

"How long you gonna be around, sir?" Hardin grinned, then paused to absorb the implication. In this war, in this land of mystic rituals, where every action seemed counterbalanced by a leveling reaction, the platoon sergeant's question rang a sentinel's bell.

"Long enough. There's a new captain inbound in four days."

"The troops are bitchin'. Keep your eyes open."

"Who's the old man?"

"Pop, First Platoon. He's thirty-two. Got a voice that could crack steel." Hardin flashed on Pops' steel-pot stew. The weathered stranger caught sight of Hardin's gaze, then nodded, accepting the responsibility he knew was his.

An ache pressed into Hardin's chest. Instantly, grief for Bucks mixed with a haunting loneliness. He missed the men of his platoon, the men he could trust—Stubbs, Amps, LeCotte and the others. He measured the new faces, the darting glances. Each man had a best friend. Tonight, when the star shine accented those tiny crystals of sweat, combat buddies would decide whether to trust the new officer. Their decision would be guarded.

The captain shouldered his rucksack and said, "What do you think, Lieutenant?"

"Grunts are an odd bunch, unpredictable. Like that deserter." Hardin studied the captain's face. The old boy knew more than the rumor would allow.

"The colonel said you'd force the issue."

"Is there a deserter, Captain?"

"I'm leaving in fifteen minutes, Lieutenant." Hardin's throat went dry.

"Did the Old Man know you were leavin'?" The captain nodded and threw out the dregs of his coffee. He introduced his commo chief and the change of command was complete.

The chopper lifted off twelve minutes later.

* * *

Morning stand-to was ragged, but the day hump was solid, spread out and quiet. The operation covered two kilometers, a search of the blue-line, a bath in a large bomb crater, and a difficult climb to the highest elevation on the center ridge of the Tiger Mountains.

Radio transmissions from Charlie Company's search-and-destroy operation in the villages and rice paddies north of the Tigers were rife with booby traps, captured weapons, and Viet Cong firing from spider holes near the An Lao River.

Hardin sat alone, perched on his helmet, his back tight against a tree, his weapon cradled against his chest, enjoying a can of peaches with Stubbs on his mind. A GI fired a full magazine from his M-16 into the brush, finishing his tirade by hacking the brush with his weapon, screaming five kinds of motherfucker.

Shot from his boots, Hardin landed ten feet from his helmet, facing the fire, holding his weapon and the can of peaches, complete with plastic spoon. With heartbeats to spare, he seized on the betrayal, and found himself charging at the GI's wide-eyed face.

"You sorry fucker. You're tryin' to get Chuck to bang us!" Hardin didn't wait for a reply. "If you think you're gonna fuckin' play crazy with me, you are fuckin' crazy." Hardin studied the face of another GI, measuring his intent.

For a moment Hardin thought of Rap, then lowered his voice.

"You don't know me, Buckwheat. You better ask around. I'll fuckin' deal your sorry ass in a hot second." Buckwheat didn't speak. His block-bullshit was gone.

Hardin whispered, his grin pushing air through clenched teeth. "You bought your squad a night ambush." With Buckwheat's weapon empty, Hardin turned and walked to his rucksack.

Within seconds the man ran scrambling at Hardin, his legs scissoring, weapon in hand. Exploding with rage, Hardin squeezed the pistol grip of his M-16. The black grunt and the white lieutenant, suspended in a void, sealed in an awkwardly small clearing on the brink of death.

And where was Lieutenant Dorell?

Intent on the chaos, a shudder rolled through Hardin's chest. His fever of unknown origin was dancing a jig, etching a carotene web on the lens of his glasses.

Buckwheat stopped and set his feet. He wanted to ebonize Hardin's cracker ass, but the barrel of Hardin's weapon had found his crotch. Hardin set his selector switch to automatic fire.

Buckwheat's platoon sergeant spoke rapidly. "Me and Top, we can deal with it." The first sergeant was white, so ebonizing the new lieutenant was on hold.

"Top, maybe. You, no-way. You've been kissin' this brother's sorry ass. You're not the first poor excuse I've run across." Looking away with a wry smile, Hardin whispered. "If one more of your brother-mother-fuckers steps in the wrong spot, you'll be the first one I shoot."

Hardin laughed at the islands of dirt floating in his can of peaches. Buckwheat's taunting image brought Hardin to a spot in the platoon sergeant's face.

"You better ask around, sergeant. Find out who you're dealin' with."

Coaxing the man's defiance, Hardin dumped the peaches between his boots, one peach at a time. He smiled the badgered smile he had borrowed from Fish, then whispered, "If I have to, I'll shoot that sorry fucker too."

Nobody crossed Fish because Fish was obviously crazy. That resonant notion allowed him physical and spiritual latitude only the jungle would challenge. Marching toward an uncertain end, Hardin had embraced many dysfunctional characteristics, communing with uncertainty with a consciousness pervading reality.

"Get your map, sergeant. And Buckwheat's squad leader, and Dorell."

Balanced for a time, Hardin knew if screaming Buckwheat at one of the brothers didn't set off an explosion, the deal was over. The platoon sergeant's dream of racial supremacy faded when Top grabbed his shoulder. If he had a move to make, Hardin wanted the man's best shot while the betting line was hot.

The three men sat on their helmets, each with a map. The squad leader was a young, white buck sergeant trying to get a handle on his war.

"Lieutenant Dorell." Hardin took the map out of Dorell's hand, flipping the corners into the dirt. "First you have a deserter, and now Buckwheat bought ya a night ambush. Charlie Company's been busy, killed two, beaucoup booby traps." Hardin waited for questions, then looked back at Dorell.

"Your platoon sergeant thinks bein' black makes him special. He's goin' on the ambush to make sure no one else in your outfit runs off." The words caught

Dorell off his guard. "You get your shit together, Lieutenant, or you're on ambush every night."

Dorell had been screwed by one of the brothers, and Hardin had called the man out so quickly Dorell was exposed as part of a bigger problem. Dorell remained silent, so Hardin crossed the perimeter to talk with the first sergeant.

"I stepped on some boundaries, Top. Couldn't help myself." With an open palm, Hardin pointed at Buckwheat. "That sorry bitch got dirt in my peaches."

"These studs have been ghostin' since that man took off," the first sergeant said.

Instantly circumspect, Rap's allegiance to the notion of killing Whitey brought Hardin full circle. He cocked his head and asked, "Are you sure his squad didn't bang him, Top?"

"At first. Now I'm not so sure."

Staring at Buckwheat, Hardin said, "Maybe that sorry bitch shot him. He just got done fuckin' the company over."

Raising a brow into a nod, Top said, "Right now, I'm not sure I want to know."

"Dorell's got the next ambush. I want him takin' sit-reps with the company commo chief, tonight." Top smiled and started checking the perimeter.

"Six Yankee wants to talk to you, El Tee." Hardin took the handset from Dooley.

"He can wait. How'd ya get a nickname like Dooley?" The relaxed-looking soldier shrugged, gesturing that Hardin should answer the phone.

"That's what the platoons started callin' the captain, Dooley Six. The name sort of stuck." Dooley responded with satisfaction when Hardin keyed the handset.

"Six Yankee, this is Delta Six."

"Bravo and Charlie are bangin' 'em hard—six KIA, two weapons, four tons of rice."

"We got a dry hole, kinda like bein' last in line." The Old Man keyed the handset, then hesitated through a short laugh. Hardin could hear Radio Man in the background.

"Drive on, Delta Six."

"Roger that. We're gonna drop over the north ridge, work the vills along the bottom."

"Stay close to the high ground."

"Roger that. This outfit needs sandbags."

Breathing, as if he were pulling the slack from his trigger, the Old Man said, "Sandbags are on the way along with Delta's supply sergeant. Keep him for a few days."

As the night ambush grudgingly picked its way out of the perimeter, Dooley sat quizzically inspecting Hardin's bamboo grenade. "I got Charlie Six on the horn," he said.

Eager to engage a familiar voice, Hardin had expected Joe's call.

"Hello, Joe. Ya miss me, don't ya?"

"Roger that. What's happenin' on your side of the ridge, Lima?"

"Nothin' much. There's a man missing. And Delta's got lotsa ghosts."

"That's what I figured. Keep your head down, Lima." Joe's voice was like old times.

"Take care, Joe." Joe's wish for the past left a hollow in the air around the handset.

* * *

Morning stand-to brought an energetic consensus fueled by Dooley and the company RTO, a small man with dusty red-blond hair and glasses. Pushing a positive tone of voice, Dorell coaxed the night ambush back into the perimeter. He gave Hardin a thumbs-up when their eyes made contact. Delta humped east along the northern ridge of the Tiger Mountains, then dropped off the ridge heading north in three parallel routes, searching the hillside above the hootches along the base of the ridge.

The brush was stiff, shoulder high. The air was thick and hot.

The three platoons reached the base of the ridge simultaneously, 400 meters apart. Hardin had Dorell's platoon on the western flank move back uphill fifty meters to cover the trails and hootches. Once Dorell was in place the center platoon moved west. An hour later, with two platoons forming the anvil, Moore's platoon started west.

At five-foot-six, 130 pounds, Bam Bam could step through a mail slot undetected. Easing through fourteen-foot scrub, with a village on his right flank, he sank into a squat, hesitated, listened, then began to step again.

With a closed fist he stopped Sam, then pointed at Sam's face, directing him forward on his left flank. Once in place the two men laid an ear to the sound. Feet were moving on their ten-o'clock. Sam cocked his head. A branch of scrub rushed across the surface of a uniform. Bam Bam set his cheek against the stock of his weapon. Sam followed suit.

The Viet Cong patrol popped into view. With the VC scrambling for cover, the contact turned into a running firefight, drawing the GIs to the edge of the village. Blasting holes across the platoon's sector, hootches, trees and the empty rice paddy took the brunt of the fight.

The gunfight was over in minutes.

Dooley held the handset, waiting for Moore's call. He had learned from the veterans of Dak To that when enough people were firing, someone was going to get whacked.

"Delta Six, Delta Two, we need a dust-off, one penny wounded, two kids are down."

"Roger, wait." Dooley called for a dust-off as Hardin wrote down the map coordinate for the pick-up. The penny was a grunt.

"Delta Two, move seventy meters west to a clearing."

"Roger, Delta Six. Four VC KIA, one AK." Moore's breathing was exaggerated.

"Relax, Delta Two. Spread out, get up on the higher freek, dust-off's inbound."

"Roger, out." Hardin chastised his meaningless words. Moore's penny had become a plastic soldier. Hardin was reloading his BB gun.

Hours later, with Moore's platoon back in the box, GIs dug in on a knoll overlooking a large expanse of rice paddy. Sitting below the crest of the knoll, they searched in silence. The sound of the medevac chopper still hung in the air. The glow of twilight shone on the paddy dikes, carving the field into darker squares.

Fixing the likely targets along the northern edge of the paddy, Hardin's eye stopped. A small white spire stood amongst the palm trees, across 600 meters of open ground. Moore waited for Hardin to speak.

"Dig deep. Chuck's got mortars. How's the wounded?"

"Both legs got hit, hard to tell. The kids got banged hard, stomach and chest." With mounting anguish Moore closed his eyes.

Hardin followed his gaze, then asked, "Who banged the kids?"

"The dinks ran behind them to cover their tracks."

Moore searched again, his soul wounded by the complication. He would see kids flopping about like wounded rabbits whenever the night was quiet. Hardin would see them too, when those pernicious oils lapped at the night. The two men sat facing the rice paddy, their hatred for their enemy gauged by the depth of the hollow behind their eyes.

When they could, they would shoot their enemy to doll rags, not with elation, but with purposeful retribution.

Hardin mustered a breath, and said, "Stay close tonight, good sit-reps. No loose change, especially the penny who banged the kids." Delta Company faded into the night.

Rolling scenes of wounded children unfolded in Hardin's mind. What kind of mongrel would throw children into this hell? And why the combat pay for this endless witness? Dig-it's form emerged, looming through a bank of fog.

Top's mailbag fell over the edge of the wounded chopper.

Nothing made sense: especially the cynicism of a moneyed incentive. A cold, economic review of these tax-free dollars put the sacrifice in perspective. In

1941, German POWs nestled in the prison camps of England were paid $6.19 per month for their labor. Adjusted for inflation and opportunity, these wages in 1967 equated to $81.15 a month, or 1.25 times a GI's combat pay.

World War II was a magnificent affair. The World Combat Championship, sponsored by the makers of grapeshot, was won by a championship caliber team; a team with good chemistry and a well-financed game plan. The team had *Joe Palooka* under contract.

Team members could spar a few rounds, then retire to the Windmill Theater or the Globe, for *Moscow Nights, No Time for Comedy, Night Train to Munich,* or *Gone With the Wind,* knowing the world would celebrate their victories, and fondle their rich memory.

By comparison, Vietnam's war was a mesh of incongruous threads; twelve shrinking months in hell, filled with imagined heroics that led in circles.

* * *

Dooley sat mesmerized, talking to a can of crackers, which was odd only if you had never done it yourself. Hardin laughed at the imperative. Jungle meals did require analysis. With childish animation Dooley smiled at his wonderfully crisp crackers.

"Why do you repeat yourself, Dooley?" Hardin stuck a hand in a side pocket on Dooley's rucksack, searching for Lifesavers.

"What's that?" Dooley jerked the rucksack away from Hardin and laid it behind his back, punching it into shape. "Goddamn officers."

Hardin cocked an eye to register the challenge. "You keep sayin', 'Damn, how ya gonna act?' You say it to the trees, the hootches, people, crackers, anything in front of your face."

Dooley smiled defensively. When challenged, Dooley's free hand would start playing with his P-38 can opener, his right foot would set itself a little deeper, and his eyes would search to the left and then level on the challenger.

"Nothin' else to do. Besides, it don't mean nothin'. Kinda like dyin' in Vietnam."

Dooley embroidered the sizzling spiced beef with a ribbon of squeeze-cheese, concentrating, then squinting, then searching Hardin's face. He smiled as if he had finally found the answer. "Now gettin' laid, that means somethin'. Been so long I don't remember why. I still got an idea what it feels like, though."

Dooley had his P-38 in play.

A metallic toy, the can opener hung around a GI's neck, lost in a forest of hair, swaying with each stride. Much like having a second dick, hanging a forearm away from his elbow, both required a comforting nudge. An assemblage of two short pieces of aluminum, hinged in the middle for storage, the P-38 was the GI's crucifix.

One side was a flat rectangular piece, a half-inch wide and an inch long, with a small hole bored near one end to accept a dog-tag chain. The other piece was the same width, but half as long with a sharpened hook on the bottom. Hooked on the side of a can and ratcheted back and forth around the top of the can, a GI could organize his evening meal in seconds.

The ratchet rate increased as the lid lifted and the can turned full cycle.

Dooley had opened a can of spiced beef leaving a tag of the lid intact, bending the lid until the lid was parallel with the top of the can, then using the lid as a frying pan. He placed a portion of beef on the lid, adding a grin when it began to sizzle. After melting cheese into the beef, he used one cracker as a spatula and shoveled the mixture onto a second cracker.

Talking to the cracker, he said, "Damn, how ya gonna act?" Drawing the aroma through a long breath, he popped the delicacy in his mouth, and started the sequence again.

Dooley was from Kentucky, a derivative of a rural bituminous economy, trapped by family debentures and inducted into the Army as alternative service. His dilemma wasn't quite as complex as being shot by a jealous wife, but close.

Dooley was a lean man, cursed with the pangs of honesty, blessed with a salty, whisky-drinking wit that lent credence to a knotty, muscled frame. He carried an old clipping from the Elkhorn City News, Sports Page. Dooley was in full stride, wrapped in the arms of his opponent, falling across the goal line after running back an intercepted pass. He talked to the faded picture the same way he talked to his food: "Damn, how ya gonna act?"

As light began to fade, a lone fuck-you lizard uttered one sharp call, followed by silence and two less energetic calls. This lizard was giving fair warning. The pattern was unusual.

CHAPTER TWENTY

Get Fat if You Can

Delta Company Night Laager. The Tiger Mountains. 2340 Hours.

From converging streams of green tracers to napalm on a cloud-filled morning, nothing generated fear like a search-and-destroy mission under a Ranger moon. Illuminated by a sense of isolation, memories worked in concert, jarring a man's being from one halting sound to the next.

Within the confines of the next second, death hung on the GI's boot.

Stubbs was desperate for a foxhole. The smells were a matter of habit: dry and moist clay, damp thatch, dung, rotting vegetation, garlic sweat, urine, palm pollen, rice, the South China Sea. Stubbs set his face to the breeze. He could smell it. He could taste the rain coming.

The starshine chased their silhouettes in odd circles. Shadows pranced on the clay surface of the paddy. Muffled footsteps sounded. Ski stumbled on the till, then fell with a dull rasp. Long-bodied images of lost men skirted the flanks of the cream-colored paddy dike. The dike cast a luminous hue as if beckoning Joe's chosen route. The rustling noise in the palm trees rushed their pace; the air was heavy with the coming monsoon. Stubbs and Ski were friends.

"Get fat if you can." That's what Stubbs liked to say goading death's wish.

Two columns of men marched in a synchronous wobble as one misstep, and then another, sounded on the furrowed clods sending a man scrambling for an offended posture. A weapon slammed the ground with a shout. Shadows crouched.

The calm in Tennessee's voice belied his fear as the point squad approached the trail below Hardin's promontory, eighty meters away.

Hardin strained to recognize his friends, breathing through his mouth. He found Rap, then Ski and Stubbs. They were in the middle of the left file. Icy currents of fear flowed over the knoll. The paddy field was plain enough now—empty, except for a band of men, trudging with their muzzle to the ground. "I could shoot them all," Hardin whispered.

Feet began to churn as if they scorned their cowardly pace.

In the penumbra of the night a tenor bell rang out, a clear, sharp note assaulting the gray-black horizon with a gathering knell. The white spire of the temple bobbed in a sea of black palms, shining like a diamond in a goat's ass. Feet began to clamor.

The bell's echo seized Hardin's chest. A thrust forced his fear when the bell rang a second time, sharpening its edge. Hardin set an ear to Dooley's radio handset.

Stubbs was certain. "Get fat if you can."

Hardin drew his weapon to his shoulder, listening, searching. The whispers of panic joined his fear. The weapon seemed to search on its own. He found Stubbs, and then Amps.

Tennessee spit expletives into the handset. Gasping as if he was drowning, his words packed the texture of a worn out prayer. The bell rang a third time. Within the bell's call, a thunderous explosion laminated itself into a sudden hush.

The men of Charlie Company disappeared in a cloud and agony set sail.

Frantic voices poured into the moon-filled night. Four grunts died instantly. Three grunts sprawled in agony, twisting in pain, screaming at God.

Enraged, Hardin lowered his weapon. He was guilty of desertion. Staring vacantly into the pall of smoke, at the shadows of the survivors, he waited for the second Claymore to be fired.

Dust and debris hung in the night air like a tethered fog, billowing from side to side. The vapor of young bodies and the odor of their blood, mixed with the dung in the paddy field. An ocherous glow attached itself to the men left whole.

Frantic men screamed that other men should stop screaming. Stunned, Hardin listened for the voices he might recognize.

Disbelief rang and rang again.

One scream rang louder than the rest: "My legs. My legs."

PeeWee would die in Spanish.

Rap would die silently, seething with hate.

Men blackened by the night stumbled in the luminescent cloud, the cloud first yellow, then orange where the star shine sent light chasing the tail of a running man. In an instant the wounded were silent. Desperate pods of men searched for missing limbs.

Tennessee badgered the radio for a medevac, for gunships, and for mercy. Joe's orders echoed, then hung like an ornament in the confusion. The night air pulsed with shock—soaked by the pleas for morphine and the grief of men still whole.

Broken men clattered in the dark, wishing for strength.

The screams enveloped Delta Company. The war had had its way. Night screams did not travel on oscillating waves. They seared a man's throat like an arrow's shaft, burning, pulsing with pain, each scream the caliber of shattering glass.

For Hardin the screams brought resentment and this resentment became whole as he fought to lay claim to the casualties. The questions would not stop. What really happened, what it meant—and why was Joe moving at night?

Hardin prayed—prayed that his precious friends were still whole. He was dependent on their survival. Pops' sly grin was etched on the pilot's face. Hardin couldn't see it, but he knew that sly grin would last.

The medevac hovered above the cloud, chasing it across the rice paddy. Grunts huddled in black mounds. The radio announced the tally: three grunts were wounded, four grunts were dead, torn to doll rags.

Stunned, Hardin rocked on his heels, locked in a trance. Alone, he was holding Sweet Cheek's shroud line, singing: "The shadow of your smile… when you are gone." Dooley tapped his arm with the hook. He couldn't see that Hardin was crying.

"It's some dude. Said his name was Stubbs." Hardin hesitated, took a deep breath to get a rope around his emotions, then keyed the hook.

"Tell me a story, Stubbs." Quick speech and false courage would help.

"Andy and six of his pennies got banged. Andy's hit bad." Relief surged through Hardin's body. His anger turned on Mother, the soldier who had planned the night operation.

"How about our boys? Ski, Fish, LeCotte, Boyle?" Hardin wanted to mention all of their names and hear their voices ring through.

"We're spooked. Damn good thing you're gone. We'd'a been pullin' point."

"Yeah, well somebody's dead. Take care of 'em, Stubbs."

"Get fat if you can, Lima." Stubbs fought to stabilize his Georgia baritone. Hardin threw the hook in his foxhole and waited for sunrise to expose the battle he could barely imagine.

Charlie Company had been ambushed at a choke point where the large rocks at the base of the knoll and the paddy dike pinched their movement into the throat of a hand-detonated Claymore. Exaggerated boots had stomped the clay till of the killing zone into a circus of blood-soaked folds.

Captain Joe had moved the remnants of his company north and was in the process of burning two miles of village along the An Lao River. The temple with the white spire and the bell was left standing.

Captain Joe refused to bring Charlie Company out of the paddies. Revenge stalked the palm groves, awaiting his order, ready to strike even remote facsimiles. Bastard files and wet stones ground emotions to a razor's edge.

Dooley nudged clay over a pool of congealed blood. A small patch of jungle fatigue rolled under the force of his boot. "Damn, how ya gonna act?"

* * *

Delta Company mounted choppers at 1000 hours and flew back to LZ English to stand-down. The new captain for Delta Company was expected on the morning mail run. Relieved of his temporary duty, Hardin hopped a Caribou heading for Qui Nhon to find his friend Andy.

Andy sat propped in bed, erect and angry, bitching about the accommodations and the Vietnamese being treated at the end of the ward. Hardin recalled his bout with that unknown fever and his bunkmate threatening to kill the VC at the end of the ward at B-Med.

Guilt brought Hardin to a long, chilling moment. Andy's right thumb and right leg were gone. The other wounds glistened, weeping with medicine and Andy's life. Timid and somewhat translucent, Andy's eyes conveyed despair. Andy was embarrassed by his situation.

"Holy shit, Andy, looks like Chuck put the damn-damn on your ass." Hardin's lame attempt at humor didn't temper the frustration of the moment. Andy had branded him a deserter, squinting into an expression of distaste.

"You lucky motherfucker. A two-day turn around, and you'd be layin' here."

This fact forced the question. "Why the hell were ya movin' at night?"

When Andy volunteered to pull point he expected to die. GIs swore never to be crippled and live. Andy was shattered beyond belief.

"Things were goin' all right until we popped that trail. I can feel myself flyin' through the air. Funny thing, I don't remember the landin', just the flyin'." Hardin's incomplete friend would fly again. Andy would need the recurring trauma to keep from being bored.

"Captain Joe's hurtin' fer sure. Lost the best platoon leader in the battalion. I feel like I left you guys hangin'."

Hardin's hand brushed the bed where Andy's leg should have been. Seeing the stump projecting from his hip and the sheet falling flat, he withdrew his hand awkwardly. Andy mustered an expression of wry disgust.

"I keep gettin' surprised to find it gone, too." Hardin wanted Andy to forgive him for leaving the company, but Andy was an honest man. He wanted to trade places, to leave someone else holding the empty magazine.

"I had to say good-bye, Andy." Hardin wanted to curb his agony, and save his grief for a day when he would do his best. Andy's expression fell into a remote hollow, dismissing Hardin's gesture with a dull stare.

"I got your address, Hardin. You'll get a Christmas card if ya live through this shit."

Ashamed now, Hardin turned into the center aisle, he knew Andy would never write.

"We'll see how things work out." Hardin circled the bed. "I almost forgot. Captain Joe torched the village. He left the pagoda and the bell alone." Lieutenant Anderson, call sign, Mike Six, shook his head with a satisfying grin.

"That fuckin' bell won't stop ringin' either."

"I can hear it, too. Sounded like a B-flat. We were dug in on the ridge above the ambush. The ground shook when that booby trap went off." Hardin's shoulders moved through a hopeless shrug, and the two comrades joined in agreement. "Your screamin' woke the boys, Andy." Hardin smiled and looked down the ward. "You got a set of lungs, Andy."

"Yeah. Got a set a nuts, too." Andy massaged his balls and shook his head. "Don't know if any girl will want to play with 'em, but they're good-to-go."

"No doubt, Mike Six has balls. See ya in the world, Andy." Hardin stuck out his left hand. Andy hesitated through an awkward moment, then shook hands with earnest. When Hardin turned away Andy did his best to forgive him.

"I liked the way you stuck up for your troops, Hardin." Hardin nodded. "Say good-bye to Joe and the others for me." Tears welled in Andy's eyes.

"I can do that. Take care of yourself, Andy." Andy turned his frustration to an orderly. Andy's agility had given way to staggered steps. He would sit on the old metal chair in front of the American Legion Hall, Post #201 on Washington Street, in downtown Bremerton.

Or, he would find a way to kill himself.

* * *

Hardin's guilt mixed with anger, and then assumed the chill of the empty hall, reminding him that Andy's wounds were ordinary, that bad cards could be dealt to any GI.

The chopper ride to LZ English was a reflective drum of fallen friends. Dig-it was at the charge. His vitality and joy for life made his death a turning point of sorts. Dig-it's quizzical expression at death was indelibly etched in Hardin's memory: a standard of measure.

Hardin flipped the tail of his father's beads in and out of his hand. Suspicious, he counted the lot: eighteen beads.

The flight droned on as the palm groves along Route #1 mingled with the trinkets along Bong Son's main-street. The Tiger Mountains stood green against the South China Sea. A convoy of trucks filled the road, heading north.

Whiffs of smoke curled low over Joe's bloody field. Two hundred meters to the south the Viet Cong had used children to cover their retreat. Both children had died.

Hardin stepped out as the skids of the chopper settled onto the airstrip.

The walk to the Tactical Operations Center seemed endless, each step drawing him further from Andy's plight. The radio operators at the TOC looked at their watch. Money changed hands. Hardin was late.

The new captain was a large man with heavy dark stubble—Doc Collard without the smile. Hardin outlined the status of the company, including the incident with Buckwheat and the mystery of the deserter. When asked to command First Platoon for an operation into the Crow's Foot, Hardin had but one request. He wanted Dooley to be his platoon radio operator.

With agreements all around, Delta Company would be inserted in separate platoon landing zones, with no artillery preparations. Each landing zone would have a light gunship team for support.

The axis of the platoon landing zones ran east-to-west with a two-kilometer separation. The landing zones were staggered across the open floor of the main valley. First Platoon would have the deepest insertion to work the valley floor, and the northern finger valley. The other platoons would work the northern ridge, running an east-west trace over stiff topography.

While Moore and Dorell toasted Hardin's demotion with barbs of payback, Hardin calculated how spread out the company would be five hours after insertion. He stood to the briefing map, and said, "Is there a rifle company on stand-by to bail us out?"

Mother startled at the interruption.

"We can get Charlie Company to a LZ within an hour."

Mother was so new he thought GIs wanted to die in Vietnam. Mother's expression pushed Hardin aside, massaging the new captain with ferret-preening gestures.

Hardin let out a belligerent scoff. "Jesus. Within five hours I'll be four klicks from the nearest help, 1500 meters from a LZ, with twenty-three studs. We're not a goddamn SOG team, Mother. Chuck is gonna stomp our ass if he finds us."

Mother was determined to show the new captain where the big dog pissed. "You initiate contact, Lieutenant. We'll fly in reinforcements."

* * *

At two-bits a beer, boozing with Mother annoyed even the dullest mind. Hardin christened the new captain "Deputy Dog"—Dee-dog for short, highlighting the man's plodding behavior. Welcoming him to the war, Hardin lied about the pleasure, and pledged the warriors present to be true to their salt.

Laughing, hovering outside the conversation, Hardin realized he no longer belonged.

It was 29 May 1968, his brother's birthday, thirteen days until his promotion to captain and his ticket out of the jungle. Hardin was short: twelve days and a wake-up, the trick being doing whatever was necessary to survive. The others had to get along. Hardin had to move along.

After cleaning forty-eight magazines, 864 rounds of ammunition and his weapon, he began a letter to Linda. He had been transferred from the jungle to a safe place and was papering the walls of a dusty Army tent with forms he didn't understand. He made light of the time remaining on his tour of duty. Except for his love for Linda and their new baby girl, and hopes for seeing them on R&R, the letter was a lie.

Dad, he thought. *I'm a dad. I'll buy the young lady a purple pedal car.*

The artillery battery sounded. His heart sank. This mysterious valley scared him, its special markings, its silent blue-lines, and its deep jungles.

The Crow's Foot might as well be in Laos.

Mother was too handy with that grease pencil. He would send good men to their death and be the dumber for it. Hardin drank his beer looking over the rice paddies at the lights of LZ English North. The prospect of being isolated deep in the confines of the Crow's Foot brought confidential gestures and a restless sleep. Pops was telling him not to go back.

* * *

Somewhere in the gray of morning a thin mist appeared, filling the talons of the Crow's Foot, leaving the ridges draped in black-green shrouds. The helicopter insertion was ghostly.

The rotors and Hardin's song were screened by a slow motion display of unearthly powers. Silence scoffed as his throat filled with fear. He could hear the wandering souls chanting.

Perhaps I'm dead, he thought. *I'm running. Run, Pal.*

He had escaped this valley once before and knew its meadow grass would pulse and sweep with the rotor's wash. That haunting sound would come again: that thin reedy whisper across his boots, that warning from the men who watched the valley, those accustomed to an intruder's greed.

They watched, perched at the edge of the weave, to kill him if they could.

GIs burst from the sides of the four slicks and ran south to a dry gully bed to hide, strung out for forty meters in the seven-foot ditch that drained the northern talon of the Crow's Foot during the monsoons. Quiet faces peered across the valley floor. Covered with dust and bits of seed, they searched the tree line, waiting for the trench to explode, waiting for the trees to run off and leave them naked.

Straining to hear the whisper of a pant leg caressing the grass, no man spoke.

Parched foliage cracked and swayed in the breeze. Leaves fluttered, rippling like waves. The trees along the northern verge of the valley seemed alive. The Crow's Foot was not part of the civilized world. Hardin would die in the Crow's Foot, just days from his freedom.

He was hiding in his grave.

With his face perched at ground level, he could feel the historic forces that governed a soldier's step. Little Big Horn, Little Round Top: same-same, Little Fucking Ditch. Hardin was dismissing another wind-driven illusion when Pop, the platoon's godfather, came gasping.

"El Tee, we got fresh graves, ten or twelve of 'em," Pop said. Hardin could feel the sequence. Chuck was going to decimate the platoon.

The announcement set Hardin's mind racing. "How fresh?" he asked. These would be Chuck's graves—no memorials, just hasty holes.

"Soils powdery, brand new." Dooley tightened the strap of his M-16. Dinks had been digging in the gully when the platoon landed.

A third man was stumbling down the wash. Rapada's eyes were animated with fear.

"El Tee, we dug up a huge dude wearin' some kinda dark sweater." Rapada's nickname was Sam because, as Pop explained, his first name had too many letters.

Sitting like pins in a bowling alley, Pop waited for Hardin to make the call.

"We're outta here. You got drag, Pop. Keep it tight. First Squad, then Second."

"Every man takes a piss." Pop spoke with a calm, graveled voice.

Ten minutes later Sam led the charge across the valley floor, noting the broken grass on the landing zone, then knifed his way into the jungle at the base of the ridge. He could hear the medics counting body bags. Second Squad seemed suspended in the middle of the open valley as he coaxed their run. Pop was carrying the last man's rucksack.

With Pop inside the tree line, the platoon began a cautious recon. Enemy scouts had watched the insertion and would alert the nearest tactical unit. The platoon had to locate the trace of the blue-line in the finger valley to draw water if they hoped to find a laager before twilight.

The soil was dry. The rotting odor was less pungent. And the jungle was too quiet.

Dooley stepped with a jerking stride, calibrating his movement with the breaks in the vegetation. When his helmet sounded along the sweatband he would stop and listen, then push forward with his left hand and step again. Stealth wasn't Dooley's problem. He smelled as though he had bathed in garlic.

The Crow's Foot, with its soft pliable impressions, was roaring with death. Sepulchral engravings of Dak To and Kontum shown through the veins of the dense undergrowth. The NVA knew these twenty-three GIs were a good target. They would wound one man, slow the rest down, then wipe out the unit and mutilate the bodies.

The platoon was in trouble. They would have to run a series of disconnected movements, securing a well-camouflaged perimeter for thirty minutes with each move, and pray they were downwind of the enemy trackers.

Jesus, I'm so close, Hardin thought. Ten days and a wake-up.

Moving along the flank of the ridge, uphill from the blue-line, Pop had taken the point, keeping the platoon close enough to hear the water. A trail that led to the water took an hour to clear. "Life is a bitch," Pop whispered. "I get killed if I make as much noise as that fuckin' creek." Pop stopped to watch the trail, sending Sam with a fire team on a dogleg uphill and then downhill to cross the trail. Then he ran the trail and hid again. The trail was worn bear, signaling the blue-line as a main source of water.

At 1612 hours, Moore's platoon ran into an enemy bunker complex on the eastern end of the ridge and was pinned down.

Charlie Company was scrambled to reinforce them.

At 1643 hours, the command group of Delta Company, including Dee-dog, was pinned down by an NVA patrol 400 meters west of the bunker complex.

At 1705 hours, with both of these units still in contact, Dorell's platoon was hit by an NVA platoon, 1800 meters west of Dee-dog. All three units were calling for artillery support from the two batteries of 105mm cannons in the area. Twelve artillery cannons were firing in support of three simultaneous contacts.

When Dorell's platoon got hit, First Platoon crawled into a thicket and ate without cooking. The firefights were the diversion the unit needed to lose the NVA scouts and regain some measure of surprise. Plotting the grid coordinates of the three firefights, the contacts ran an east-west axis leading directly to First Platoon's location.

A major enemy base camp lay to the south, in the center talon of the Crow's Foot.

The noise of the water in the blue-line seemed to spar with the distant roar of the firefights. Men running would be hard to hear. Artillery rounds pounded the top of the ridgeline.

Dooley checked his watch for remaining daylight: 1836 hours. "We're fucked, El Tee."

"I know."

Rewind the situation, Hardin. Think. We're sitting on the closest water to the firefights. The trail is a class "A" hardball cutting across the blue-line and heading over the next ridge to the south. We're five klicks from Dorell's contact and eight klicks from the bunker complex.

There's no way to reach Dorell before morning and jets are bombing the ridge less than a klick from our hideout.

We're between main force NVA base camps, at a primary source of water, with less than one hour of light. This is bigger than elephants. There are two solutions—find help or run.

We're two kilometers from the nearest landing zone, which doesn't matter because Charlie Company is committed to the fight in the bunker complex.

Dee-dog is isolated and out of the loop. Plus, he's a new guy.

From the tactical decisions transmitted over the radio, Dorell's platoon had the lowest priority for support. That meant First Platoon had no priority. Hardin decided to run.

"Pop, check ammo, spread out, and get us off this trail." Hardin pointed over his shoulder into the deeper shadows and moved Dooley into the brush thirty meters.

The scream of jet fighters filled the valley.

Sam took one man and ran back to the trail to erase the tracks leading into the perimeter. With forty minutes of light remaining no man would blink. Dooley was monitoring the company net, wincing at the sounds coming from the handset.

"Let's turn off the squad radios," Dooley said. An odd squelch might be fatal.

Suddenly, men were running. Hardin grabbed Dooley's wrist and forced it to the ground. Boot after boot splashed through the blue-line, running uphill past the platoon's perimeter, heading toward the top of the ridge. Their foot-beats fell as close as raindrops. These were the strangers whom he knew so well.

Hardin's throat tightened into a knot. He could not swallow. He didn't want this fight and he didn't care who knew it. He moved his hand across the ground, grabbed the handset and plugged his right ear to hear himself talk.

Hardin was breathing through his mouth, trying to swallow as he whispered, "Delta Six, this is Delta One, over."

Hiding in the dense heart of the Crow's Foot, Hardin sat in shock. Dinks were running with weapons a high port. The hollow resonance of their boots jarred the jungle floor.

"Delta Six, this is Delta One, over." When Dooley lifted his rucksack the radio's whip antenna flipped to attention, yelling like the Coca-Cola sign in Times Square. Staring at the parade, Dooley slid his hand to the back of the radio and lowered the whip.

"Delta Six, Delta One, talk to me, goddamnit." Hardin's whisper had an edge.

No response: not even a broken squelch. Hardin could hear Dee-dog, Delta Two, and Delta Three, talking to battalion, each in turn. He had stopped sweating. His balls had disappeared. He stuck his dog tag in his mouth to generate enough saliva to swallow. He lowered his head to his forearm to wipe his eyes, then keyed the handset.

"Three Yankee—anybody—this is Delta One, over." The sun had fallen behind the ridge. Dooley laid the radio down, turned the frequency to the battalion net, then pointed at the sky. He was either praying for divine intervention or a Huey.

"Three Yankee, anybody, this is Delta One, over." More silence, then some distant broken radio traffic with Charlie Six. The day was wearing out.

"Three Yankee, anybody, this is Delta One, over."

"We got ya, Delta One. What's happenin'?" Dooley recognized the voice.

"We're at grid: eight, eight, one, four, five, two." Hardin double-checked the grid, then said, "We got eight-seven November Victor Alphas runnin' north on a hardball, five minutes ago."

"Roger, Delta One. I got your grid greased on my bubble. Will advise Three Yankee. We're kinda busy. You need any help?" Dooley shook himself into a twisted grin.

"Yeah. Who are ya?" The pilot's laugh burst into a song to the melody of "Gold Finger." "Starblazer... we're the ones... the ones with the mini-guns."

"We're in deep shit, Starblazer. Slam some ordinance into the top of this northern ridge about 500 meters east from our location and keep slammin' the ridge movin' east. And tell Three Yankee to shift red-leg fires to cover Delta Two's west flank."

"Will do, Delta One. We shot at some bad guys on the valley floor about a klick east of your location. We'll catch ya on the flip side."

"Thanks for callin'."

Without making a sound, the NVA were back, running in the opposite direction. Hardin traced the point man's face, his determination reflecting a fulfilled promise. Four two-man litter teams shuffled in unison, carrying wounded south across the blue-line. The enemy base camp had a hospital. Hardin decided not to spend the night up this creek, watching Chuck's parade.

Starblazer's mini-guns groaned. Rocket pods ignited. Hardin's NVA were getting a taste of close fire support.

Dooley activated the squad radios and the platoon started shedding baggage. Quietly they tied down gear, organized ammunition, retied boot laces, and prepared for a dash down the finger valley to the open sky covering the main valley floor.

The bed of the blue-line was the best route. With twenty minutes of light remaining and 1400 meters to cover to reach the valley floor, the platoon had to run.

Silent expectations broke in jagged patterns as shock joined the men at the streambed: bodies plunging headlong, eyes rushing forward. Sam pulled slack behind the point. Pop had drag. Tree after tree, rock after rock, the mob ran crashing down the draw.

Chuck might hear their footbeats, but he would never guess the thunder was a pack of grunts running for daylight. Hardin discounted other strategies. Visibility was such that Chuck would have to be standing in the blue-line to identify the noise.

The sound of splashing water deafened the senses as one man and then another fell, desperate to keep pace. Once down, their buddies scooped them up.

Evaluating the chaos, Hardin realized some things were just too quick to remember.

With but sparks of light illuminating the valley floor, with Sam on point, the platoon stepped rapidly through the jungle, skirting the north side of the valley. At twilight's last gasp, Sam emerged from the jungle and stood for a moment at the edge of the open valley looking at the sky. When he had judged the light, he signaled the platoon.

Men ran at heel, tainted by their neighbor, afraid Dooley might lose sight of Sam.

Sam didn't hesitate at the rim of the gully, forming a perimeter as fast as men climbed into the ditch. Real or imagined, the smell of death hung in the valley.

"Those dead dinks are about fifty meters up-stream," Pop said, trying to muffle the rasp in his voice. "We better figure a scout saw us make the run."

Hardin gave Pop a tap on the shoulder, acknowledging the message and nudging Pop toward the other end of the platoon position. Pop was blessed with the short sleep of age, but not its patience. He jerked and kicked at his friends until he had two-man teams stationed at the rim of the trench, placing the machine guns on the north rim, covering the open valley.

Hardin dug footholds with his knife, then mounted his post, clinging to the rim, searching north. His skin began to crawl. He could hear the sounds. Twilight masked their collective mood. Twenty-three grunts, half-standing, half-sitting, watched in silence, motionless. No one would sleep tonight.

The NVA broke contact from the firefights on the ridge, which meant they had run west and then south past the platoon's old perimeter.

"What do ya think, Dooley?" The words hung in the fading light.

"We're fucked, no doubt about it. If one of us panics, Chuck is gonna bang us hard. Nine GIs died in those bunkers." Hardin took a deep breath. His face was lined with recall.

"Nine. No shit. Delta or Charlie Company?"

"Delta. A bad day for Dee-dog, that's no shit."

Wanting to shoot General Abrams between the running lights, Hardin's chest fell through a series of spasms. "You know, Dooley, if it hadn't of been for Grayson, you wouldn't be here."

"Who's Grayson?"

"He's the man that's keepin' you here, Dooley."

"You're fuckin' nuts, ya know that, El Tee?"

"Yeah, I know," Hardin said, and the valley floor lost definition.

Death seemed to march along without meaning. A medevac chopper had crashed near the mouth of the valley, killing the crew. Alone in the night, drawn to the sound of a familiar voice, men listened as the radio announced the names: nine dead and four wounded.

Buckwheat was dead.

Hardin decided that Buckwheat's death was payback for his can of peaches.

Charlie Company didn't lose a man. If Stubbs kept Lady Luck humpin,' and Rap didn't kill him, LeCotte might make it home alive.

CHAPTER TWENTY-ONE

Rear Echelon Folderol

First Platoon Night Laager. The Crow's Foot. 2400 Hours.

The glow from the burning medevac chopper cast a stria like a straight rainbow, gradually giving way to the grip of the Crow's Foot. Beauty and fear seemed pleased with each other. The valley was a tomb, the air dense enough to stir. Star shine cast an iridescent hue, sad and foreboding. The pale grass seemed to glow, its gold-brown color magnified near the tree lines, framing the valley floor. A man could not cross the valley undetected, not on this night.

A Life Saver scraped across the roof of Hardin's mouth, sending echoes through an essentially empty space. Combat imperatives were being replaced as truth and half-truth struck a dissonant chord. Did patriots run from their enemy? Today they did.

At 0400 hours Hardin decided to run again.

Two files of men shuffled in silence, straddling the trail that traced the center of the valley floor, their weapons held at port arms. A rush of grass swept across their boots casting pollen into a wider glow, the cadence of their step hypnotic. The clear night sky pushed Sam to the point. A funnel of vegetation drew his pace to a crawl.

"Now I know you're nuts, El Tee," Dooley said.

"Maybe so. But we're the only target left in the Crow's Foot."

* * *

With a barrage of predictable adjectives, First Platoon joined the remnants of Delta Company on the crest of a ridgeline, one kilometer east of the Crow's Foot. Hardin's theory about an enemy hospital would stay under the rose until he was transferred out of the jungle.

Mother wouldn't believe him anyway.

He had no remorse about leaving this platoon. With the exception of Dooley, Pop, Sam, and the radio operators, good-byes were pointless. The rest were alive and on their own.

"Damn, how ya gonna act?" Dooley was staring at a new black lieutenant.

"You talkin' to me, Dooley, or that tree?" Hardin knew what Dooley's problem was. He didn't want to be the new lieutenant's boy.

"By God, it's damn-awful hard to get a catfish to suck on a dog's dick. The Man just shit in my rucksack. Fuck me. And I got eight months left in this shit-hole." Dooley lit a cigarette, dropped his rucksack, and sat down on his helmet.

"A catfish suckin' on a dog's dick. You're a hick, Dooley."

"Fuck you, El Tee."

"Here's a fuck-me for ya, Dooley. That black lieutenant is the man and you're the boy. You either jump through your ass or you're not gonna make it outta this deal alive."

Dooley was so pissed-off he was puff-smoking and shaking his head, betrayed by Hardin's words. "I knew this fuckin' war would get worse. Hadn't figured this."

"If you're too pussy, give it up." The radio was Dooley's security. Locked in a stare-down, Hardin grinned. "I got nine and a wake-up, Dooley. Don't mess with my program."

"Damn. Damn, damn, damn."

The new lieutenant was a quiet, muscular man with an unassuming posture. After 200 meters Hardin decided to call him Whiplash, because his seventy-pound rucksack was kicking his ass. With Dee-dog spitting about, Hardin laughed. Covering less ground increased his odds.

Pop fell in behind Whiplash to take away his skates. With the effort of a stallion, Whiplash forced his body to respond. The heat was suffocating. The air was still, pressed into the canopy. In his current state, the new man was a liability.

Halfway through the day, with the platoon snaking down a dry wash, baking under a low canopy, Whiplash collapsed. He was conscious, he had ample water, and he was moaning.

"Six, this is Delta Five. Our new oscar is down. How far we goin'?" Hardin asked.

"Four hundred meters. Got a resupply slick comin' in."

"Keep goin'—we'll catch up."

"Sam, take Dooley and a squad and stay with the company. The rest will pick up here."

Dooley wanted to say something, but Hardin's grin cut him short.

Whiplash looked quite content, comfortable with his special status. Checking his watch, Pop kneeled next to his head, leaned into his ear and whispered.

"You're a pussy." Whiplash narrowed his eyes.

Hardin cautioned Pop, then signaled him away. Reaching his limit, Hardin said, "I'm gonna sit here and watch five minutes go by on this magic Seiko watch. If your sorry ass isn't up and truckin', we're gonna leave ya here."

Whiplash didn't believe Hardin would do such a thing until Hardin stepped on his hand, crushed it into the rocks, and signaled Pop.

They crouched in unison beside the patient.

"Pop." Hardin formed the word for the perimeter to hear. "If this piece of shit isn't steppin' in five minutes, leave him here."

Hardin threw the new man's rucksack on top of his own and started off to catch a break. Pop and the squad would not let a new man hang them out. They would foot-drag the laggard through a royal thumping.

Delta Company sat perched on a shelf overlooking a crescent valley, organizing for the resupply. The two rucksacks kicked Hardin from side to side as he stumbled into Dee-dog's coffee shop. Exhausted men stood in their foxholes.

"Where is he?" Dee-dog said, looking in the direction of the wash, one hand caressing a coffee burn and the other gauging the density of bearded stubble so coarse it was tinged blue. He had no mind to nourish a frail officer.

"Last I saw he was fetal-stuck, babblin' about desertion." Deciding Dee-dog was too serious for a disjointed war, Hardin pointed at the rucksack, and said, "That's what's left. He farted and disappeared." Dee-dog didn't laugh. "Good thing I was carryin' his gear."

"You leave a squad with him?"

"I did. Told 'em if he wasn't truckin' in five minutes to leave him." Dee-dog acknowledged the situation. "They'll be along."

The resupply slick hovered into a cloud of purple smoke.

The noise brought the men to their feet. "Is he gonna make it out here?"

"Eventually. The heat got him," Hardin said, not caring what the new captain decided. "Put the man on that chopper. We can't pull slack for anybody."

"Just like that?" Dee-dog waved a paw toward the slick. Hardin shrugged.

Whiplash broke through the vegetation, dragging his tongue, looking as though he had been pin-balled down the wash. Hardin pointed at his gear with an open palm.

Filling sandbags, Dooley was digging in. Dooley tossed the D-handle shovel to Hardin, and set out to corral C-Rations and whatever else he could steal.

"Get me a B-2, a chili, and a spaghetti," Hardin shouted.

Dooley thumbed the air, gave his balls a toss, and kept moving. He accented his return by bouncing on both pads of his feet like an ostrich in heat. The resupply slick was lifting off and Dooley was screaming as it lifted above the trees—screaming into the turbine noise, flagging both middle fingers, and playing six kinds of crazy.

"You do that?" Dooley was ecstatic.

"What, scream at the wind?" Hardin held out a fist. Dooley's problem was leaving.

"No man, that new dude is history. How ya gonna act?" Dooley gave his program a boost and crashed into the ground.

"Yeah, I figured that. His shit was kinda scattered. He'll be back when he's in shape."

Searching, as if he were trying to focus, Dooley threw Hardin's C-Rations into a pile and said, "Got to have your shit in one bag. My man was bad news. I shit ya not."

"Bad luck's got a memory, Dooley. You best be careful."

First Platoon, Delta Company was much like First Platoon, Charlie Company, with one exception—they were someone else's responsibility. Hardin had played so many roles in the past three weeks, his anxiety for Lima Six had faded.

* * *

"What did you see when the rest of us were in contact on that ridge?" Dee-dog's tone of voice implied that Hardin was suspected of quiet aggression.

"We were brave for a while. Until we realized we were outnumbered four to one." *I don't need this bullshit,* Hardin thought. Dee-dog walked three of his four units into contact at the same time and was damn lucky the company wasn't wiped out.

"We learned once you're in contact it's impossible to reach you on the radio. We learned that no one checked our status with a fly-over, or a call. We learned that the available artillery support was dedicated to your firefights, and we learned that Bushmaster doesn't work."

With a slow, pugnacious set to his jaw, the captain said, "We killed nineteen NVA."

Hardin wanted to scream, to tell the new man that quantifying death would not change the turbidity of the war. Alas, four-syllable words were over the top, and what Dee-dog really wanted to know was how many bad guys First Platoon had killed. Steeped in the acid of dead GIs, lifers used these lives to etch legends on stainless microfiche.

"Doesn't mean a thing." Hardin paused to allow the new man to mount his assault, then looked across the valley. "We watched eighty-seven dinks run north out of the Crow's Foot. We gave the sighting to Starblazer and requested fire support. Starblazer hosed them down and passed the fire request on to Three Yankee."

With a vicious grin, Dee-dog let out a facetious huff, sending bolts of anger through Hardin's body. "Should have engaged 'em," he said.

Leveling his eyes on the captain, Hardin refused to back away from the challenge. "Engage 'em—what does that fuckin' mean? You got a lot to learn, Captain. We bang those dinks, and we're dead men. Every fuckin' one of us."

"You'll engage this enemy when I tell you to."

"Answer this, Captain. The dead GIs from yesterday—do ya know their names? Do ya fuckin' know their names?"

Without waiting for a response, Hardin spit his words at the new man. "We spotted four litter teams headin' south."

"Did you engage 'em?"

Hardin poured his coffee into a pool where he thought the captain might want to sit and laughed at the insanity. "Nope, but I'm gonna shoot the next Red Cross volunteer I see." Hardin tried to smile away his resentment, but he liked the taste of this exchange.

Dee-dog was tethered to the respect a combat infantry company command garnered in more glorious times. Hardin was aggravating his potential.

"Next time I want ya to engage this enemy when ya see 'em. You understand?" He used his canteen cup to punctuate his words, poking at the air in front of Hardin's face.

"Well, Captain, every man wants somethin', that's fer sure. With any luck, there won't be a next time." Hardin stood and spit into his foxhole. He waited for a reaction to his grin, and then wiped his mouth. Then he smiled. He had gone from trusted advisor to cowardly accused—worse than being a deserter.

Bang, you're dead.

"The very next time, Lieutenant." What a dick. *This guy is a whistle-blown jackass,* Hardin thought. *This perverted goat fucker is gonna kill beaucoup GIs.*

Hardin executed a fake salute. "Ahh, Roger, out." Fuck-out, fuck-over, fuck-off, and kiss my ass. Dee-dog thought "roger, out" meant, "yes, sir." With nine days and a wake-up left before he made captain, Hardin decided to never see Chuck again.

Dooley had been eavesdropping on the confrontation, pretending to get much-needed information from the communications chief. "Holy catfish. Damn, how's he gonna act?"

"What's that mean, Dooley? 'How ya gonna act?' Does it mean somethin'?" Hardin sat in the sun, grinning over a soothing cup of C-Ration mud, looking east toward the South China Sea, thinking about having a real woman with real tits, not some flat, withered rice-shoot chewing betel nut wrapped in burnt black silk.

"Who knows, El Tee? It's kinda like sayin', 'Are you shittin me?' or, 'Ya know?'." Dooley used the phrase for situational summations, to gather his thoughts.

"That man ain't shittin' ya, Dooley." The two men shared a chocolate bar in silence. Dee-dog called on the radio from seventy feet away.

"This is Delta Six." Hardin grabbed the hook out of reflex. "Tell Delta Five there's a slick inbound to take him out. Six Yankee has some work for him." Relieved, Hardin whispered with delight. He was fired, he was out of the jungle, and he was off the Big Dog's patch.

"Roger, out." Hardin held out a fist. "I'll look up Grayson for ya, Dooley."

Dee-dog rose with satisfaction, pulled at the waist on his pants, rolled his shirt sleeves, stretched to allow the victory to warm his bones, then triumphantly surveyed his domain. He had rid his playpen of the most experienced platoon leader in the brigade.

"There ain't no, Grayson," Dooley said.

Dooley was wrong. Every GI had a Grayson.

* * *

Hardin sat in the right door of the C&C slick, watching the grass fight the rotor wash, then gave Dooley a thumbs-up. The noise in the trees consumed his misgivings. A dream appeared and then dissolved. Strangers held their mail, waiting for the chopper to lift away. Dust-bitten faces stared into a deep nothing. Gone were the rowdy, whiskey-drinking, ignorant men of their youth. They sat now without self-pity, fondling the clippings of their past.

Dead, stiffened eyes could lie so still a watching man might blink.

Pop had grown old the way an oak tree grows old. He acknowledged Hardin with a quick salute. Moore and Dorell huddled with their coffee, anxious to start again.

The wind played with Hardin's resolve, promising his freedom. His colonel, the old war-horse, would have his reward, one of Uncle's ceremonies, with citations declaring that he was a good soldier. It would be Lieutenant Edward Hardin Day, with glad hands and toasts all around.

He would become talkative, salty, and quick-tempered like the other war dogs.

A good dog can tell a good story.

The vibration of the chopper's frame, the steady beat of the rotor blades, and a sun parked in a still blue sky, brought on an orgy of sex—naked women, their tits jogging under a full sail.

His cock began to swell, snaking its way down his pant leg. R&R—six nights of rock'n'roll. Linda was a farm girl. She would be ready for a high-intensity workout. Hardin laughed as he remembered his father's words… "I told the doctors after you were born to put a few stitches in to tighten things up. Nine pounds, eleven ounces—that tends to stretch things out."

"It's dinner time, Pal."

* * *

Battalion Tactical Operations Center. Landing Zone English. 1400 Hours.

Mother bounced with certain mirth. After months of branding Hardin a classless reprobate, he was energized by Hardin's fallen status. He would initiate the young buck's conversion to Army lifer by monitoring his first paper assignment.

They didn't shake hands.

"The Old Man wants you to survey three starlight scopes that Bravo Company lost in An Khe." Mother was pestering his grease pencil for more grease, so Hardin sat down. "The forms are in that folder."

"I've never done a report-of-survey, Major."

Finally the expert, Mother's chin rose, inviting comment. Before he could speak again, Hardin started to laugh, realizing he could not say the word "major" with any tonal reverence.

"It's easy, Lieutenant. You're the report-of-survey officer. You go to An Khe and investigate the disappearance of the starlight scopes. If you determine that Bravo Six is responsible for the loss, the cost comes out of his hide. Otherwise, the equipment is listed as a combat loss."

"What's one of those puppies cost?"

Mother paused, then said, "About two thousand dollars."

"You mean if I drop a dime on Bravo Six, he's gotta fork out six grand? He'll have to extend his tour to pay it off." Mother's expression went blank.

"That's not what the Old Man wants. The IG inspection is on thirty June. Those scopes are a problem." Paper lifers saved the risky cosmetics for the expendable sods like Hardin.

"You're a clever bunch, that's for sure. When's the ride to An Khe?"

"At 0600 hours, from the chopper pad by supply."

"Buy ya a beer, Mother." *Piss in the wind maybe.*

"We'll see how things go." Hardin was rear echelon meat, and Mother intended to play hard to get. *I don't think so,* Hardin thought. Then it occurred to him—Bravo Six was dead.

"Bravo Six got banged in that convoy ambush."

"0600 hours, Hardin."

* * *

Hardin flew to An Khe filled with fantasies featuring the nurses from B-Med. He searched the supply rooms that bordered the helipad, checking serial numbers, and found one of the scopes. A lieutenant at the jungle school signed a statement that the other scopes were lost when a bridge his platoon was guarding was overrun.

When he landed back in Bong Son five hours later he found the Old Man in his tent writing a letter. The old war-horse went into a spin cycle when the starlight scope hit his desk.

"Where did you find that?"

"An Khe, in a supply room by the helipad. Bravo left it layin' in the grass."

The Old Man grabbed the report and raised his head coldly. Undoubtedly angry about something other than starlight scopes, his jaw was cinched.

His hawkish eyes ran to an expression of disgust as he said, "The Exec needs to talk to you in the mess tent." His speech bit at the air in front of Hardin's face—short, crisp, and titled. *Not, wants to talk with you,* Hardin thought, the word "needs" being the operative signal.

Hardin started toward the mess tent, triggering his memory for clues. Uncle was working on a beer, talking with the battalion surgeon.

"You sure about that list?" Uncle asked the surgeon.

The two staff officers stopped short when Hardin sat down. Their reception was cool. A typed list of names lay partially hidden under the surgeon's forearm.

Hardin drew back a chair and grew a lighthearted grin. "Sir, what's up?" Uncle's look of betrayal barked at Hardin's frivolous gesture.

"Nine GIs from your old platoon came down with malaria."

Standing in the dock, Hardin knew he had to be patient with these negotiations. He had to simulate being a chippy lifer. He assumed a tedious, zoo-keeper look, then said, "My, my. That's damn near fifty percent. You got a list?" He pointed and the surgeon slid the list across the table. "Well, lemme see." He flashed a pen that was now part of his uniform, and put a check by eight of the names.

"What kind of an outfit were you runnin'?" Uncle had softened his accusatory tone, permitting his expression a sense of expectation, hoping his boyish charge could massage these allegations.

Pausing to measure the crease in the surgeon's eyes and the cock to Uncle's head, Hardin realized they were prepared to dissect his response. "These wardays just keep comin', don't they Doc? Tomorrow there'll be a new message, a new list. You ever get close enough to know a man's boot size, Doc? In case you need his boots. You ever put on a dead man's boots, Doc? They don't fit: even when they're the right size."

Hardin pushed the paper across the table. He pointed at the surgeon and spoke forcefully. "First Platoon, Charlie Company was the best platoon you ever served with. I put a check mark by the names of the men who came down with Vivax Malaria. One GI has Falciparum."

Hardin paused again, this time for effect. The surgeon looked astonished.

"I'm right, aren't I, Doc? Right on every man." Uncle sat back and shook his head, accepting a sense of recognition as he exchanged a concluding nod with the surgeon.

"You best be thankful they didn't catch a Caribou headin' south and keep on goin'. Nine more deserters wouldn't look good on the Old Man's score sheet."

Suspicious, the surgeon read the list, slowly raising his head. With a smile to lessen the tension, he said, "You must know these men well."

"Doc, Doc. The point is, you don't know them at all."

Uncle disengaged his suspicions to buy a round and lighten his conscience. Uncle bolted three beers to the table with enough emphasis to force ice water to pool at the base of the cans. Hardin grabbed a can, and Uncle's emotion slipped into a grateful laughter.

"Sorry about that, Hardin," Uncle said. "What do you think is going on?" Uncle knew what kind of problem he had to sort out. As the two staff-patches leaned into the center of the table, their expressions became confidential.

Gesturing casually with his palms extended, Hardin said, "Be my guess they stopped taking their malaria pills because they don't trust the new platoon leader. Word is the man can't read a map. Those studs are survivors and they have options. Malaria's a whole lot easier than an AK. What's worse, Captain Joe has three new platoon leaders. Bowe was shittin' bricks before Anderson got blasted. Find yourself some platoon leaders, Uncle. And while you're at it, find a new surgeon. No offense Doc, but you're a jackass."

"Oh, I don't know about that." Alpha Six, the Captain Midnight of Combat Trinkets, sat down. Even without his field gear the man looked busy.

Hardin traced the top of his beer can with his finger, then said, "Alpha Six, how are ya? Ya got any toilet paper?" Hardin tapped the captain's wrist, implying that he needed to excuse himself. Sure as hell, the man reached for the pocket holding the spoon.

"Here you go, young man." Alpha Six sat back with a breath of satisfaction. He was out of sync. Hardin wanted to stall the man's mind and kick his restart button.

Instead, he held up a hand, and said, "Thanks anyway." The man didn't get it.

Uncle smiled, and then turned serious, using the back of his hand to change the subject. With a hollowing surge he said, "Well Alpha Six, those thirteen troopers you caught smoking marijuana are being processed for a special court martial. Is that what you want?" Uncle's voice softened to velvet but a storm was brewing in his craw.

"Yes, sir, that's what I want."

Military law was clear, especially in combat. The use of drugs was an actionable offense, and the sentence was bad time in the Long Binh Junction Stockade near Saigon. Six months of bad time added six months to a trooper's combat tour of duty.

Uncle drank the rest of his beer, staring over the rim of the can.

"When did this happen?" Hardin asked, wondering how an infantry officer, a soldier who knew first-hand what these GIs were going through, could prosecute a GI for trying to escape. Why would anyone intentionally extend a GI's tour?

"I caught them in a tent by the berm last night. Some of my best people." Alpha Six adjusted his chair, attempting to muster his logic.

"I don't get it," Hardin said. "You're goin' out to chase Chuck with thirteen fewer guns, you've lost some key people, and the rest of the studs have a new target."

"Well, Lieutenant, I have heard that you tolerate the use of drugs. I also heard that you smoke dope." Holy shit, Hardin thought. This fucker is sick.

Uncle and his doctor were sniffing at rotten fish. Their heads bobbed in unison as their brows arched, acknowledging the captain's foolish effort to redirect the obvious.

"I know which GIs smoke dope," Hardin said. "I know where that tent is. In the boonies we trust each other, and we fight for each other. You're in trouble, my man."

"My troops are going to conduct themselves in a manner that brings honor to the uniform." Flush-faced into an over-pressured huff, Alpha Six set his jaw. He had a point. The troops should be more circumspect about their rear-area activities.

Hardin had more to say, surprising no one. "There's a military statute about consorting with whores. Have you been snakin' around the steam baths?"

Exasperated, Alpha Six waved with the back of his hand, then said to Uncle, "Now you see what kind of problem I'm up against—young lieutenants letting their troops run wild." Alpha Six was begging for field-grade support, as if Vietnam was a field-grade kind of war.

"Well." Uncle was cautious and a little angry. "I've heard two points of view from two field commanders on a serious topic." He cupped his hands into the center of the table. "And, Captain, you accused the lieutenant of smoking dope. Are you making that a formal charge?"

"No, sir."

"Good." Uncle's hands had closed into fists, and his knuckles were white. "I won't be surprised if someone kicks your ass, Captain." A finger extended from Uncle's right fist.

Exiting on cue, Hardin stood, knowing he'd been given the green light to collect paybacks. As a courtesy he asked, "Sir, do you need any more information about that list?" Hardin pointed at the paper in the surgeon's hand, pretending the list was a secret.

"Not at this time," Uncle said. "You're to work in Delta's orderly room on this IG inspection."

"Yes, sir." Hardin turned and whispered in the captain's ear, "Good luck, asshole."

* * *

Delta Company Orderly Room. Landing Zone English. 0800 Hours.

Tired of ploshing through mind-nagging papers, and trying to make morning reports match the rating parameters for an IG inspection, Hardin decided to create a pretend person, placing odds on how long it would take the brigade personnel staff to discover the ghost.

Brigade would at first grow confidential, wanting to cover any internal errors. Then they would credit the loss of this stranger to "War Time" and its attendant confusions. And after several iterations of "one minute, and then the next" and "first the war, and now this" they would settle on the absolute: It's just "one of those things."

Survival in the rear area required a flat learning curve.

Hardin's insurrection spiraled from a gust of notions, derivatives of his inability to determine where each of the inspection-forms was to be signed. That, and where they were to be stored, which out-box was more productive, who received which copy of which form, and finally how to keep the astonished from putting new forms in his in-box.

He soon realized that if he signed the forms anywhere, anywhere at all, they would disappear, then reappear with red-lettered instructions and an "X" signature designator. Some of the designators had exclamation points, some had underlines. Some had both. When he followed the instructions the forms would reappear with a second set of instructions for filing. If a form appeared a second time without instructions, he threw it away.

Hardin threw away the queries concerning his pretend soldier. The discrepancy concerned Lieutenant Simonson, the battalion personnel officer. His memos contained one of two summations: "nevertheless," or "that notwithstanding." Hardin figured Simonson wanted to be a shyster when he got back to the World.

The ghost's absence punctuated the orderly room with the ultimate summons—Jesus Christ. His absence, without ever existing, defied the urgency of the IG inspection and caused his name to become vaguely familiar. And once an orderly had declared allegiance to his name, his whereabouts became something of a mystery. The ghost was a valorous man, running at the sharp end of accurate accounting, prancing from steam bath to steam bath.

This delightful madness took Hardin into R&R requests, requests for back pay, recommendations for promotions, recommendations for valor awards and service ribbons. He had created his own plastic soldier.

By the time Hardin's promotion to captain came around, one J. T. Ragman, Joe-Shit the Ragman, was promoted from PFC to specialist fourth class, awarded an Army Commendation Medal for Valor, and given orders for a six-day R&R in Sydney, Australia for the Fourth of July.

Today Hardin would start the rumor that Amps had been crying every night since Hardin had left. A good rumor was better than a good question. A good rumor was a lie designed to germinate a rear-echelon fantasy. "Can you imagine a man that dependent on his platoon leader? The stress must be incredible? Some days he cried all day. Hand me another beer."

Paper soldiers were foolish people. They were word-pussys in drag.

Hardin caught himself daydreaming on the front porch of the orderly room, admiring the horizontal gray-blue beveled wood siding on the lower half of the barracks. The upper half of the barracks was wrapped with screens clogged with red-brown clay. The contrast gave the building good curb appeal.

The IG inspection had inflamed the rock painters, sign makers, and guidon washers. This flurry of decency, coupled with extra cans of boot polish, had forced transient GIs to drink before lunch. The sandbags throughout the battalion area had been unstacked, fluffed, and restacked under the watchful eye and survey string of the battalion sergeant major.

A short white wooden foot-rail was installed as a border along the outside edge of the upper walkway to discourage jumping three feet to the lower walkway. A set of freshly painted steps led from the upper walkway to the sleeping tent for each orderly room.

Filled with urgency, the men cleaning the area stood tall: orderly rooms, orderly walkways, orderly rocks, sandbags and signs, dining room orderlies, orderly soldiers with orderly uniforms, haircuts and shaves—and, of course, those transient grunts.

Each orderly room had a four-by-eight-foot plywood ready-board mounted on posts to the left of the front door, advertising company-grade proclamations. Crisp black horizontal and vertical lines sectioned the board into two parts—permanent orders and current orders.

The lettering was perfect.

Grunts never read the orders on the ready-board because nothing could possibly be permanent since almost all grunts were currently crazy. And since none of the current orders addressed their inability to grasp the concept of permanence, anything posted on the current side of the board was assumed to be false because it referred to or led to something else marked permanent.

Next to the ready-board was a wooden stand holding the base for the company guidon. The guidon stayed put because nobody wanted to carry it into battle.

Hardin unfurled the guidon to read the insignia.

The retaining wall supporting the upper walkway was a crosshatched network of sandbags stacked nine bags high, with stair openings for each orderly room and the S-1 shop. A GI could get to the TOC on the upper walkway, walking past the orderly rooms and the S-1 shop, or on the lower walkway, walking past the sleeping quarters and the battalion aid station.

Sandbags flanked the lower walkway, creating a slot that closed just beyond the TOC. The battalion area was a continuum of sandbag frames—one frame for each building—walkway, palm tree, and sign, each frame accented with a white border.

How perfectly ridiculous.

How a disorderly mind functioned in such a structured web was a mystery, unless the individual was himself a mystery? Grunts needed environs that were random and chaotic, uncontrollable. And there they were—mannerless tracings through a square and level world, screaming "needle, ball, and air speed" as they wobbled and wove their turbulence over, under, and around the bumpy texture of refreshed lunacy.

The first tracing seemed to gather weight. The muted-green side-flaps of the GP medium tents that covered the wood-framed buildings were out of place. The side-flaps and dozens of anchor ropes found humor in assuming any swooping pose, whose undoing generated an equally treasonous appearance. No one knew who was in charge of these tent flaps since the man in charge of tent pegs got a clap of unknown origin and was sent to Japan.

The second tracing was more absurd. Power lines and field telephone lines looked as if they had been routed by a public utility from western Pakistan. The wires had no conscience. They ran across stairways, walkways, doorways: three feet, eight feet, on the ground, fifteen feet, straight lines, and sagging lines with never enough slack to pacify their daily aggressors.

Suspicious men knew that these legions of electrons would fry their nuts if they dared to mess with the sorcerer's fire. Tying the wire in a knot was a common solution.

And then, a general's favorite—the likes of Fish, the odd angry grunt. An amalgam of hatreds and fears, postures and attitudes, with reflections that didn't resonate except with other like-minded creatures.

Fish was a reflection of futility and death boiled in a crucible of demented wisdom.

When confronted with synchronized watches, starched hats, clean shaves, polished boots, and parade-ground rows for review, grunts would panic, lust and hate would join, and their minds would shift one counselor to the left.

Attention was not a posture a grunt could organize in a hurry.

* * *

Hardin was fingering the hole in a sandbag when Sergeant Parsons, a friend from Dak To, stood-to. "What happened to you, Parsons?" Parsons' forehead had nearly swollen out of his skin. Hardin searched his hairline and winced when Parsons wrinkled his brow.

"Wait here." Parsons' step was soft as he presented his helmet for inspection. The quarter-sized hole in the front of his helmet looked like the mouth of a road culvert. The groove carved along the steel inner surface arced downward at the back of the helmet.

"One AK round at twenty-five yards. Knocked me colder than a wedge." Parsons ran a finger along the groove and nervously shook his head. "The round must have gone right past my rucksack." Parsons was the short result of Vietnam's war. His searching the confines of a confused memory would leave his heart seizing any bit of solace.

"Remember Willie Spencer? He gave me his watch before he went home."

"So Willie made it. That's good. He was a good dude."

Demming, Delta Company's clerk, stepped around the screen door to adjust the company guidon, then hollered. "Lieutenant Hardin, Uncle wants ya at the aid station by the airstrip. Second Platoon got ambushed. We got thirteen dead and wounded bein' tagged and bagged. Moore is dead."

The two men listened in disbelief. Suddenly shaken, Parsons ditched his steel pot and said, "Come on, El Tee. I'll give ya a lift to the aid station."

Artillery fire rumbled from the ridges near the mouth of the An Lao Valley as they watched the medevac chopper touch down with four bodies. Medics struggled with their grip, fighting with their step, keen to make the final ride for these men as smooth as possible. Another dust-off chopper hovered into view, turned into the wind, and settled on the PSB.

Bloody ponchos could not hide a lifeless form. Twice Hardin started to lend a hand, then sank away, flanked each time by Parsons' silence. Blood surged in cadence from the ponchos, splashed, then flowed through holes in the PSB.

Four grunts were dead. Nine grunts were wounded.

Hardin stood without speaking, listening to a chorus of huddled voices. Squeak, Shadow, and Sweet Cheeks stood-to. Shadow was singing. The melody was diminished: haunting.

His anger surged, then ebbed into a hurtful anguish. Voices from another time were chanting the protocols of death. The remnants of shimmering souls carry a special honor. Hardin took off his helmet and removed Dig-it's letter from the plastic case. He would keep Dig-it's letter, like the cannon shot he found at the State Park. When he read it, he could smell the fire, and the war sprang from a hundred faces.

Putting Dig-it's letter back into his helmet, Hardin's knees gave way as he sat down. He found solace in not knowing the measures of war: what was next.

Counting each man, seven in all, the wounded were being ferried to the airstrip to board a Caribou bound for the hospital at Qui Nhon.

With his bowel tied in a knot and his chest heavy with sorrow, he could feel the wrath of the ambush. His baseball team was wiped out. His team stood-to in their dugout, swapping bubble-gum wrappers, waving their rally caps, memorizing the bunt sign, hoping the opposing pitcher couldn't throw a curve ball.

Highlands Road was the best.

Parsons nudged his shoulder. Uncle was motioning him inside, extending his hand in a cupped insistence. A camera's flash threw its light, pinching his features, his despair recorded before he could respond. The cameraman was smiling. Another was laughing.

Uncle drew the tent flap aside and opened the screen door, nudging his arm. Stark cones of light sharpened the smell of blood and rotting bowels. A metal table supported the body of a well-rehearsed grunt, flawed only by death.

Hardin searched for Dooley, knowing he should not be there. He wasn't.

"I got one trooper I can't identify," Uncle said, his voice churning. "He was on point."

Hardin pictured a man so badly mutilated that his reality was gone. Uncle pointed to the young Filipino with a small hole in his face just below his eye.

"It's Rapada, Porfirio Rapada: Sam. What a waste." Hardin alerted to his undirected voice, the sound crudely fashioned, his words scribed on an impersonal rebuke.

Sam was a cocked-rifle kind of man. Cursed with an honorable nature, he talked of his parents during his evening meal. What made this soldier return to the things that hurt him so? What personal madness required such a sacrifice? He had eight days left. The prospect that the IG might blemish Sam's service with boot polish drove him back to the jungle to be with his friends.

Hardin nudged Sam's boot to say good-bye.

Deeply isolated, he stepped away, avoiding the light, shunning the exposure. His heart ached. Locked in an outer ring of light, as if God had him filling sandbags, Hardin needed air. He looked down the row of cold metal altars, each with its offering. He looked toward the doorway. A body lay marinating on the floor—Lieutenant Moore.

Hardin's voice blurted with rage. "Sam couldn't bide the bullshit." Accepting the declaration, Uncle pushed the grief from his brow. "Uncle, you people gotta quit fuckin' with us. Figure out how to cut us some slack."

Uncle looked away. Ashamed, he drew Hardin's eye to the cold metal slabs. Broken men could lie so still. If not for the smell, their wounds might have been decorations.

The surgeons worked with a controlled acceleration, fingering the bits and pieces of one man and then another, touching each soldier with gestures of shame. Efficiency could not mask their grief as they processed the dead for their final classification: viewable or non-viewable. Not wanting to create a fuss, the dead soldiers proudly displayed their tattered uniforms.

Sam looked relieved. His casket would be marked viewable.

Hardin's throat filled with a fractured scream. "This place ain't worth dyin' for." Absorbing the blame, a bolt ran through him and slammed into his heart.

* * *

He sat near the roadside, trying to muster his day. The unknown fever rushed over him as he fought for air. His body seemed to empty itself. His eyes fell flat. As the jeep approached he looked first at Parsons and then away, trying to be a soldier, history prodding him with the words of muted decorations. His father's Victoria Cross. His father's VC.

He waved Parsons away and stood. "I'll walk."

Dee-dog had lost more grunts in twelve days than Captain Joe had lost in five months. Bad luck didn't have that many iterations. Moore's platoon had mounted a ridge on a well-used trail, ignoring the one absolute of Vietnam's war: if you got lazy, Chuck would punch your ticket.

When the squabbling in his bowel gave birth to cubes of off-colored gas, Hardin laughed a hopeless laugh, then mounted to the crown of the roadway and looked again at the aid station: olive drab canvas surrounded by dusty red clay. The medevac crew scrubbed the cargo deck and the dust-off chopper shut down. Filled with death's image, quiet gripped the landing pad.

The quiet and the smell that was Vietnam were gradually consumed by the laughter of a raucous group of men. Some were dressed in fatigues. Some were dressed in civilian togs. A man in denim grabbed his bag, opened it, peered in, closed it, put it under his arm, opened it, and secured it again. The bag was filled with treasures. Their cameras seemed to smile.

Their laughter packed the grinding tone of intuitive charm—the open-minded had clustered to share linear illusions.

Hardin raced after their deceit. Why, he didn't know. With a collection of alternatives, his face creased with disgust and he lunged across the tarmac. The sorrow for his comrades had descended into hatred for these men. They were laughing about Asian pleasures. One man seemed to lead. He was concluding a story, shaking a cigarette from its pack.

Timed properly, Hardin's fist would meet the man's nose when the man's lips captured a new fag. Aiming for a spot near the back of the man's head, he skipped his step to ensure he would be firing off his right foot. "Bring your punches all the way from the floor, Pal."

With a surge of exhilaration and pain, the knuckles on his right hand compressed into his wrist and his right leg drove his body weight through the stranger's jaw. The man's arms flew outward as his head and shoulders arced upward, taking his camera and feet in concentric orbits around the center of his falling mass, his face twisting with the directional force.

Instantly Hardin looked for another target. Why, he didn't know.

"What the fuck's wrong with you?" yelled a man. He knelt by the side of his friend.

Hardin stood over the fallen man as if he would blow the man's face apart. His mind was cooked. "They were fuckin' ambushed," he screamed. Hesitating through a dizzy spell, he tried to breathe. He waited for a response, then turned into a plowing sense of satisfaction. Spears of pain shot through his forearm. He stretched his hand open and shut, then flashed on his father working the kinks from his hands as they drove home to Highlands Road.

"What the fuck is wrong with you?" a man screamed at his back.

Hardin didn't look back. The question was a good one—it didn't have an answer. The surface of the roadway passed below his feet, scuffing tiny billows of dust to match his rumpled disposition. He sat again on the roadside to search the paddies and the villages.

The placid setting was absurd.

The mild clanging of his thoughts brought him back to the stake—how he died in Vietnam was none of his business. *Holy shit,* he thought. *That's true.* He had offered his life and that was that. He would fight to stay alive. And then he would pray for a non-viewable classification to save Linda further grief. An honorable man could do no less, especially a man setting his cap with British nobility, nagging the glory of the Normandy invasion.

In the end, his war began on D-Day, 6 June 1944. Far behind him, on the beaches of Normandy, Omaha Beach, long since suppressed by the complexities of the Cold War, his father and his father's generals had crafted the standards for combating tyranny.

Tarnished, as if a world without war offered no solution at all, they would prosecute these standards no matter the cost.

To polish their honor they offered their sons.

CHAPTER TWENTY-TWO

Road Apples

Landing Zone English. 11 June 1968.

Promoted to captain, Hardin was gainfully unemployed. He drank himself into oblivion, his future pledged to any game that might seem relevant.

He was a rear-echelon soldier now—a deserter if you like—encased in wire and sandbags, then wrapped in carbon paper, as if a copy of his thoughts might help. Insulated from harm, he barged into his work with no intention whatsoever. He would help with the IG inspection, not caring about the outcome or the man they listed as missing in action.

Being listed as both MIA and a deserter, Hardin found the man commendable and started calling him Frank. For all he knew, Frank was on R&R. The Delta Company clerk didn't care.

Sergeant Demming had been a radio operator until he was wounded in Dak To and shipped to Japan for fender repairs. He was a good soldier. Twice wounded, he had fashioned his clerical skill to match the comic twist to his circumstance. He was short for the war, painfully, obnoxiously short—six days and a wake-up left on his tour of duty. His smirk, his stride, even the coffee he brewed screamed "I'm-outta-here."

"If you keep tellin' me you're short, I'm gonna get you extended." Hardin laughed into the garbage can. The forms he had re-routed didn't seem to mind.

"No way. Can't be done." Demming laughed a felony-prone laugh.

"I'll charge you with insubordination and have you held over," Hardin said, opening the screen door to throw out his coffee. "Besides, bein' shot in the ass requires a thirty-day hold."

"Bull shit. I'm damn near gone." He pointed to a signature block.

"All these forms you've been havin' me sign and you're not gonna stand the inspection. You better not be settin' me up."

"I'll be home with a foxy round-eye by the time you figure it out," Demming said.

"No round-eye is gonna roll with a man who has two holes in his ass."

First Sergeant Parks backed through the screen door with an armload of field manuals.

Demming stood and said, "You must be kidding, Top. Reference books so the boys can learn how to shoot." Parks smiled, stacked the books on a field table, and then ranked the books in numerical order.

"Just part of the show. Captain, you're the only company executive officer I've ever met that was a captain." Top was implying that Hardin was a ne'er-do-well, a fuck-up held back for review. *This is a good strategy for me to build a future on,* Hardin thought.

"They're holdin' me back, Top. Make me read those books. I'll be the first man in Delta Company that ever read a book."

Parks shook his head with a pestered sigh. He straightened the manuals and stepped back to conclude his work. "Delta Six radioed the TOC, wants you out in the field today."

"What did you tell him, Top?" Parks could not make a commitment for Hardin. He wanted to, but he knew better.

"You got the message. It's up to you what you do with it." Top was talking to himself, challenging Hardin's integrity as he cocked his head into a questioning shrug.

"Use that old black magic on him, Top." Hardin smiled and extended an open palm.

"How's that, sir?"

Hardin hated simplistic rebuttal, so he jumped into race relations. "You know. You start jive talkin' so no one understands, and you're so enthusiastic that they agree and walk away."

Top assumed an educated ebony tone of voice, and said, "Senior NCOs have got to be more civilized so we can deal with educated young captains. Call Six and see what he needs."

Hardin spoke with a slight staccato, "I got the message, Top. I'll handle it." That was the end of Hardin's grin. He wanted no part of Dee-dog's version of the infantry.

When Parks and Demming left for chow; Hardin strolled down to the brigade TOC to see how a brigade headquarters could confuse four infantry battalions from one bunker.

The joint was impressive. A long chattering hallway, flanked by office cubes led to an open briefing arena with situation maps, directed lights, opposing lecterns, a row of rubber tipped pointers, theater seating behind an overstuffed armchair, and majors enough for three wars.

Hardin was content to wander around like a pinball until he realized The Claw or some wizened bird might stand him at attention and demand an answer. He left immediately. When he reached the MARS station he wanted to call Linda but the radio link was down. While he was kicking his luck, Uncle yelled.

"Six wants to talk to you. Get some lunch. He's inside eating." Uncle was on his way, happy with Hardin's destiny. Maybe Dee-dog complained about not returning his calls.

"Yes, Sir." The Old Man was reading *Stars and Stripes,* halfway through a handsome-looking mixture of chipped beef and gravy.

"Sit down, young Captain." The old fox had a clever look about him, as if he was waiting for the perfect moment to crush Hardin's oysters.

"They got the box scores in there?" Hardin said, wanting to start with something light. Small tits would work. Box scores were good. They reminded him of high school cheerleaders.

"Not many. What do you think of Binh Dinh Province?"

Hardin's answer was being measured. He was tempted to use some snappy drivel about two-syllable places to die. He selected the short summary instead.

"Bravo lost seven KIA, Charlie lost four KIA, Delta lost thirteen KIA, and Alpha lost one and threw thirteen GIs in jail. We've been here three weeks. NVA killed half and the VC killed the other half. Except for the bunkers, the rest were killed walkin' on trails. Binh Dinh Province is owned by the Communists." Preferring silence, Hardin waited as the Old Man set down his paper.

The Old Man nodded his agreement; shoved his plate aside, and leaned forward with his coffee. His expression took on a devilish-look as a smile traced his face. "You're taking Charlie Company on twenty-four June, a week from today. They're coming in to LZ English on the twenty-third. Get familiar with their status."

Holy jumped-up shit, Hardin thought, gasping inside. The Road Apples turned full circle and hit the table with a sound that thundered through his chest. He was being ordered to retool his quick-fire arsenal.

"Fuck me runnin'. Stubbs told me that horse shit was gonna roll down hill and bury my ass." Hardin was trying to be wolverine tough and whine at the same time. His balls had disappeared so fast they were lodged in his throat.

"You can handle it."

"There must be thirty senior captains in this brigade who would jet-suck a frog to get a combat company command. I've been a captain for a week."

The Old Man smiled, and said, "Charlie Six recommended you. Besides, anyone who needs the job is dangerous. Delta Six said you ran from contact in the Crow's Foot." The old friends sat in silence, gauging the other's reaction.

"Fuckin'-A right we ran. And if the shit looks the same, I'll run again. The man didn't know where we were, and didn't try to make contact. The only commo link we had was with Starblazer, and sky-pilot was singin' to us."

"He's a good pilot."

"There's a hospital in the Crow's Foot. Watched litter teams runnin' south outta that northern finger valley, on a trail wide enough to haul logs." Hardin grabbed the corner of the *Stars and Stripes* and slid the paper to his side of the table. His tour of duty was starting again.

The Old Man dismissed Hardin's comment with a concluding sigh. Then he held up a finger and said, "General Armstrong told me to pass along his regards."

"Armstrong Custer, I'll bet."

"The new Post Commander at Fort Bragg, three star. You punched out his son. Broke the kid's nose and loosened his front teeth. General's been wanting to do that for some time."

As he approached his bunker Hardin could hear Dig-it laughing about the CO carving a crack in his white ass. Dig-it was a prophet.

Hardin read Dig-it's letter again. The bloodstains were as vivid as cracks in a mirror. Why did this man hang on so? He had to look at the envelope to remember Dig-it's last name. And what about the other dead men?

Dying would be a whole lot easier than talking to Mrs. Johnson.

* * *

Sitting in the tactical operations center with his feet resting on the radio table, an ice-cold Coke nestled next to his nuts, Hardin was dreaming about a sweet, hot, screaming piece of ass when an irrational loss of authority engulfed the room. The radios fell silent and Mother was sucked into the briefing room.

Dee-dog, that mammoth rush of intolerance, had arrived with a hankering for subordinate humility, coupled with a dash of frightened obedience.

Hardin had barely tuned in when the captain's lips flew open, his fist pounding the air. "God *damn* it, you still work for me. When I want you in the field, that's what you fuckin' do. I don't give a good God damn what your rank is." Dee-dog's balls were wrapped in a tight sack.

Hardin set his Coke on the table.

"Talk to Six." Hardin toasted the air with an empty hand.

Catching his breath as if his mind was trapped in a pipe, Dee-dog threw his rucksack at the floor and declared, "I'm talkin' to you, goddammit."

Uncle barged through the door flying low cover, shot past Dee-dog as if the situation map might change form, and challenged Hardin with a directed finger. "You and Sergeant Walker are taking an element to recon in support of Charlie Company, First Battalion. A three-day operation into this island ridge in the Crow's Foot."

"How small an element?" Hardin's war was accelerating. Bushmaster didn't work, so he was going back into the Crow's Foot with fewer men.

"Twelve, counting you, one machine gun." The slurry of words hit the map sheet then slid into the pit of Hardin's stomach.

"Fuck me runnin." Hardin wanted to puke. "Do me a favor, Uncle."

"What's that?" Hardin pointed at Dee-dog.

"Tell Fuck-stick to get off my back."

Uncle's head turned over his shoulder and he stood into the room, thrusting himself into Dee-dog's face. Uncle moved closer to the captain, cocking his head, a cinch to his smile.

"You fired him. The man ran away from contact. You're on your own, Captain. You can leave now." With Uncle directing traffic, Hardin gave Dee-dog the finger.

"No problem, sir." Dee-dog was lying.

Sergeant Walker, the staff sergeant in charge of Echo Recon, stood-to, tricked out in tiger fatigues and a bush hat. The three men settled into the briefing room.

Bravo Company, First Battalion would be inserted west of the island ridge in the Crow's Foot. From the valley floor they would search to the top of the island ridge, then north along the ridgeline to rendezvous with the recon team. The recon team would be inserted at twilight, move south uphill out of the main valley, along the crest of a small finger ridge to lay-up for the night, and establish radio contact with Blackjack Three, First Battalion Operations.

Brigade had established the frequencies and call signs. Radio contact with First Battalion was scheduled for 2300 hours, after the team had secured a night laager.

Hardin sat in the briefing room alone, stunned into a husky silence, staring at the map sheet, burning the topography of the Crow's Foot into his memory.

Time accelerated: cleaning weapons, fitting tiger fatigues, applying camouflage, and drawing new ammunition. The standard issue: two canteens of water, two long-range patrol rations, a map, a compass, one hundred rounds of machine gun ammo, two frags, one smoke grenade, and the preferred load of M-16 ammunition.

At 1914 hours two Hueys entered the mouth of the Crow's Foot at full throttle, ten feet above the grass, using isolated trees as slalom gates. Sitting in the right door of the lead slick, Walker caught a glimpse of a bush hat in the northern tree line. Three minutes later the team jumped into the gully bed, 600 meters east of the tombs.

"There's a dozen hasty graves in this gully, half 'a klick west," Hardin said.

Walker looked down the gully. "We've been spotted. I got a bad feelin."

"We landed on their front lawn."

The team sat motionless, eyes level with the valley floor. The noise from the insertion hung in the air. A leaf swirled through an eddy and danced along the rim of the gully. Shadows enveloped a tree that stood alone on the north side of the valley. A trailhead opened into the valley near the base of the tree.

The NVA scout took one last compass reading, set his bush hat, and then began his run. He had made this run twice in the last two weeks. The run took less than an hour.

Night fell in with a thin cloud cover. Far-off sounds started in the west and gained volume, tracing the valley floor. Knowing they had been spotted, frightened men burrowed into the sides of the gully, sitting sidesaddle.

Hardin found the valley too black to see anything other than the white dots on the back of his eyelids. The dots looked like fireflies bouncing and hovering, moving on a stage that had no definition. He blinked repeatedly, but the tiny dots continued to swarm. He rubbed his eyes, then set his glasses and weapon in the grass at the edge of the gully and rubbed his eyes again.

Unable to see, the dots had merged into a string, moving now with a deliberate pace.

When Hardin put on his glasses the dots exploded into a chorus of lights. *What the hell is going on,* he thought. Walker had tied a piece of twine to Hardin's wrist and was walking down the twine. Walker found his ear and cupped his words into the hollow.

"Captain, they're lookin' for us. Gotta be fifty, sixty lights—NVA. We gotta run." The words rang like Joe's bell, surging from both ends of the gully.

Hardin licked at the sweat bleeding through the camouflage pigment around his mouth: three colors, one taste. The muted glow of the open valley stood in sharp contrast to the black tube that was the gully.

Walker whispered hurriedly, startling him. "We'll stay in the wash, run west deeper into the valley. You got drag, Captain."

Twelve men kept faith with the pace, fleeing the oscillating cadence of the lanterns, sensing the rhythmic beat of insistent vowels, the orders of the NVA commander. Hardin stumbled, then caught himself on the side of the gully. The team was running faster than he could see, trying to outrun the stench of death.

The tangy-sweet odor from the graves pushed at their courage, wiring men to the immediate as they fought to define the gully—the sound of men breathing, stumbling, the undergrowth infesting their step. Walker stopped the team. He and Dingo ran up and down the southern verge of the gully, back and forth. Then they ran sixty meters out of the gully, heading south, then backtracked, measuring the broken grass. Then the team ran west into the tree line.

The lanterns swung back and forth, suspended above the valley floor on the flanks of the gully. Half-lit faces scurried in and out of the gully.

After three hours, with their water nearly gone, Walker pushed the team through a blue-line, and then stopped to find the lights. Refreshed by mounting fear, the team ran north across the floor of the main valley, then circled east to double back on the NVA's route.

Running out of the Crow's Foot was getting to be a habit.

Stepping high to silence the grass, Dingo stopped to listen and count bodies. The night marched on without a sound. The lantern lights were fading to the south. Walker let the cover on his compass fall back into place, and then spoke crisply.

"Here we go, half speed."

The recon team ran as one, running at a shuffle, south through the gully. Six hours behind schedule, Walker guided the team into the jungle at the base of the island ridge mass, where they were headed in the first place.

The dense undergrowth forced the team to form a hand-to-belt chain. Single file, with Walker on point and Dingo on drag, the team picked its way uphill. The jungle floor was devoid of light. Visibility was zero. Walker stopped in a hollow to establish radio contact.

"Blackjack, this is Echo Romeo, over."

Hardin listened for sixty seconds, one sweep around the face of his crystal-blue Seiko. The watch seemed so clean, so out of place. Walker flashed a red light on the radio frequency indicator to confirm the dial setting and tapped the RTO's forearm.

"Come on, Blackjack. Wake up and give us some help here."

"Unknown caller, this is Blackjack, over." Blackjack had forgotten the recon team.

"Blackjack, this is recon. We got eighty November Victor Alphas at grid two-three-three-two-four-niner. Our loc-stat from Papa Oscar four: left four-point-two, up six-point-one, over."

"Roger, Echo. We got ya, Lima-Charlie." The handset went dead.

Walker turned off the radio and embraced the ground, expecting the NVA to search the valley throughout the night. Organizing his ammunition, he lowered his head onto his forearm and closed his eyes. The glow of the lanterns took center stage.

By dawn the NVA unit chasing the team would focus on the island ridge, a hill mass that was devoid of water. To complete their mission, the team had to run and conserve water at the same time. Walker sipped his water, rolling the cool liquid around his mouth.

CHAPTER TWENTY-THREE

Dingo Doesn't Know How to Die

Echo Recon. The Crow's Foot. 0450 Hours.

Linear shafts of light knifed through the dense foliage, spearing one team member and not another. Visibility was less than six meters. The ground was cool to the touch. Walker had one canteen of water, the team had nineteen. A stifling heat was gathering strength.

The circular backtrack across the main valley left Echo Recon 700 meters short of their first rally point.

Walker's briefing tied the rags of his beliefs to a packet of tethered words. "Spare your water. Dingo's got drag. Keep eye contact. R&R time—recon and run. Chuck isn't stupid."

A putrid heat oozed from the jungle floor. Sweat-soaked men searched the vegetation. Quiet men listened. Silence painted their faces. Camouflaged features glistened with tiny beads. Walker designated primary and secondary rally points on the eastern flank of the ridge, then briefed the procedures if men got separated.

"The password is Blackjack. The dead will be left behind if the team has to run." Walker drew a nod from each man.

Climbing southeast toward the top of the island ridge, two six-man files held form. A machine gun pulled slack for the right-side point man. The insertion choppers for Blackjack's combat assault flew into the valley and consumed the Crow's Foot. The gunfire from the four gunships echoed down the valley, groaning in spurts like a dull horn.

The NVA would converge on the island ridge with every asset they could muster.

At 1343 hours Walker kneeled in the waist-high grass, examining a bicycle tire-print on a well-used trail. Moving with a keen sense of cadence, no one had spoken for seven hours. Walker rotated his body in place, signaling a formation and sending a warning. The recon team flushed with a quick burst, forming an ellipse facing south down the trail.

Within a minute, three VC popped into view, rifles secured at sling-arms, walking at Dingo. The left front quadrant of the perimeter collapsed on the VC and the right front quadrant sprinted thirty meters down the trail and went to ground in a triangle formation.

The back half of the perimeter stood fast as cold steel viciously slashed hearts and throats. The assault was run with ghostly precision. The Viet Cong were dead in seconds. The bodies were packed into the brush, and the trail cleared. Four minutes had elapsed.

The VC had been heading north, away from the insertion, relaxed and free of the fight.

Hardin looked for a trace of the bodies when he passed through the kill zone. Not one vine was out of place. He stroked the handle of his K-bar and wondered if he could slit a man's throat. With a brief rebuke, he took off his bush hat and wiped the sweat from his eyes. His glasses had developed their own sense of camouflage.

Hardin noticed the winter in Walker's eyes. Walker had driven his knife through one man's stomach with such force he had stabbed himself in the thigh. Yet he carried on—no limp, no fear. Walker had rationed the water from the enemy canteens, forcing his team to respond.

Amid halting steps, Hardin caught himself thinking about Linda.

Wondering when low tide might occur, the whispers and hand signals startled him. Dingo had stopped at the crest of a knoll. The ridge dropped into a dark saddle. The jungle was heavy with heat. Inch by inch. The light on the floor of the saddle grew faint. The point man froze near the bottom of the saddle. Breathing through his mouth, the air tasted like a piece of cold liver.

Walker and Dingo crawled forward abreast, ten meters apart. The balance of the team formed a perimeter. The trail intersection was encased like the junction of two large tubes. The vegetation was trimmed into perfect arches. A fresh-cut bamboo vine was tied to a branch at eye level along the south side of the east-west trail.

Walker lay flat, searching for cleared fields of fire at ground level. Satisfied the trail was not covered by a bunker, he looked for signs of a trail watcher. With a hand signal, the team burst across the trail and cleared it by fifty meters before going to ground.

Hardin flashed on Rap's piles of bamboo. Vietnam's war was simple and complex.

"There's a base camp down this ridge," Dingo said.

Walker registered a nod. With two rapid hand signals, the team bounded out of the saddle. Within minutes, as if scripted, four NVA carrying lanterns ran out of the saddle, turned south past the team's machine gun, heading toward Blackjack's insertion.

Dingo and Walker tracked the NVA until they dropped into another saddle and rendezvoused with a trail watcher. Dingo grabbed Walker's wrist. One of the enemy soldiers had long brown hair and a thick beard. Dingo took a deep breath and let the sight on his weapon settle on the man's back.

"Easy, Dingo," Walker whispered.

"That's gotta be our boy," Dingo said.

"Maybe. But we got a mission to tend to." Dingo and Walker crawled away from the saddle and rejoined the team.

"That base camp's within two klicks," Walker said, marking a grid location on his map. "The VC we killed had new ammo. We got mainline NVA on this ridge."

"There's a Caucasian runnin' with the dinks we just spotted," Dingo said.

Walker ignored the comment and keyed the handset. "Blackjack, this is Echo Romeo, over." A deep tone slammed crackling back into the dry grass.

"Blackjack Six."

"We got three VC, KIA with AKs at grid 982923. And four NVA scouts with AKs running south at grid 971901. There's gotta be a base camp south of our loc-stat, over."

"Roger that."

* * *

The air cooled rapidly. Walker decided not to cook. The smell would hang in the vegetation. He broke the perimeter down and every other man slept. Sometime in the middle of the night Dingo covered Hardin's mouth.

The lanterns were back. Enemy soldiers marched into the saddle from the east, from outside the valley, and searched down the top of the ridge—120 plus figures, their half-lit faces glowing in the jungle night. They were a sour looking bunch.

Suddenly Hardin's bowels cramped. The fever forced sweat through the pigment on his face. "I gotta get out of the Crow's Foot." He spoke softly. Watching the glow from the lanterns fade, his throat tied itself into a dehydrated knot, sending him after his last scrap of water. He lay in the brush on his side hoping for a lower heart rate. The warm liquid didn't help.

Minutes became an hour with Hardin watching the luminous dial of his watch. His guts liked to cramp on schedule and he could barely breathe.

"Blackjack Bravo, Echo Romeo, over." Sixty seconds passed. "Blackjack, Echo Romeo, over." Nothing. "Anybody, this is Echo Romeo. Come on, Baby, answer the phone."

"Blackjack Three, over."

"Your boys are asleep, Blackjack. We're not gonna die in the Crow's Foot coverin' your sorry ass. A hundred-twenty-plus bad guys just jogged past our hide-out headin' south."

"That's not good. We'll fire some red-leg on that base camp." Seconds later, six 155mm artillery rounds crushed the night air. Suddenly Blackjack Bravo was on the horn.

"Blackjack Three, Blackjack Bravo, what's goin' on?" Hardin laughed, gave his face a comforting scrub, and took a labored breath. The diversion had helped quiet his system.

"Stay awake or I'll walk those rounds right over your sorry ass," Blackjack Six bellowed into the radio. "Recon's got 120 enemy soldiers moving south on top of the ridge. If your shit's not straight, I'll rip your heart out."

Hardin laughed at the rasp in the old man's voice. Straight or not, Blackjack Bravo's butt was going to get stomped.

Echo Recon had a bigger problem. The enemy soldiers they had seen the night before had come from the east tonight. The team had to withdraw to the east for extraction.

Hardin's neck and shoulder muscles ached. Sweat poured from his body. The heat had thickened the camouflage pigment on his face. He was trapped. He closed his eyes and found Hippie and Bucks arguing over a game of dice.

* * *

A swarm of mosquitoes boiled from the cool depths of the saddle punching their form in one direction and then another, searching for the blood they knew was on the ridge. The day was too hot for a run. Walker distributed the team's remaining water.

A sallow haze rose from the ridge as dawn turned brighter. Expecting commuters on the main trail, Walker acknowledged the enemy litter-teams and let them pass. A firefight would bring enemy troops from the base camp to hunt the team down.

Walker signaled and the team ran across the trail and went to ground. When the time was right, the team moved, east at first, then south toward the enemy base camp. Two files of six men, spread ten meters apart, held formation like the wheels of an invisible cart. The ridge flattened to level ground. The step-by-step agony wore on the men; their water was nearly gone.

Walker signaled. NVA sat near the main trail. Concentration was absolute as Dingo eased his way through the grass. Once Dingo was in place, Walker eased forward with soft fluid motions, pushing his body with his knees. He returned by the same route.

"I stopped countin' at forty. There's gotta be seventy dinks packed and ready to roll. It's not the base camp." Walker surveyed the trail, waiting for Dingo's assessment.

With a rush of recognition, Dingo said, "Sarge, we moved better than a klick. That base camp's gotta be closer to Blackjack than we figured." Walker agreed.

At 1430 hours Walker called a sighting of eighty-plus NVA, warning Blackjack Six that the suspected enemy base camp was on his front porch.

"Roger, out," was all the old man said.

At 1431 hours Walker requested a battery-four fire mission on the NVA.

At 1547 hours Blackjack Bravo bumped into a hardened base camp with laminated log and earthen bunkers occupied by North Vietnamese regulars. The roar of small-arms fire filled the Crow's Foot. The remaining NVA on the trail bolted toward the fight.

The team dropped off the ridge and went to ground.

Dingo listened. Cocking his head, his eyes locked as he said, "Twenty-eight GIs hit so far. Medevacs are workin': 51s shot the first slick out of the sky."

Walker studied Hardin's face, and said, "Blackjack's got his dead, grunts. We'll get wasted if we try to help, and they won't find our bodies."

Blackjack Six flew in a second infantry company to break contact and backed off the ridge. Thirty-four grunts died in the fight—ductile portraits drawn into a framework of pernicious data, feeding the ever-ready desire for war.

Consumed by frustration, Walker rubbed his neck. "It's time to leave. We can't help." He signaled and the team burst across the trail, ran down hill through clawing vegetation, and went to ground in a tight depression for the night.

Artillery fire pounded the enemy positions with delayed-fuse high-explosive rounds. NVA litter teams and wounded men spent the night running from the island ridge into the main valley and the safety of the Crow's Foot.

In the flat light of twilight, Dingo's voice rang clear in the TOC. Echo Recon had not been marked with a pushpin on Mother's situation map. Echo Recon was "Somewhere in this area." Echo Recon was a secret. And when secrets call, it's like hearing from the dead.

"Three Yankee, Echo Romeo, over."

"Roger, Echo, good to hear your voice. What's your loc-stat, over?"

"I have no idea. Team Leader says we are 500 meters north and 400 meters east of that base camp you've been shellin."

"What's your sit-rep." They wanted to feel the fantasy and create their own.

"Bagged three. We're low on water. No casualties."

"Good news." Radio Man held the mike open so the crew in the TOC could give the team a standing ovation. "0900 extraction, location Alpha, over."

"Roger, out."

With or without water, the team would be at the extraction point. The trick was making sure Chuck wasn't there too. Dingo turned off the radio. His map showed a blue-line 300 meters beyond the extraction point. Men slept in one-hour shifts.

A gray dawn brought the nest to life as Walker chewed on his team, preparing them for a morning run. Dingo rationed water, giving each man a swallow, judging his relief with a short nod. Two men were suspect if the team had to run—the machine gunner and the radio operator.

Dehydrated, the point stepped out of the nest at 0415 hours, drawing the team in a single file on a thirty-foot rope. As the vegetation turned thick and wiry, they abandoned the rope and worked a pace count. At 0835 hours Dingo brought the machine gun forward to cover the extraction point. The clearing was fully stocked, complete with knee-high grass, a hard-beaten trail, and fresh scuff-marks leading uphill toward the enemy base camp.

At 0845 hours Walker called the TOC.

"Three Yankee, Echo Romeo, over." Whispers didn't seem so heavy in the daylight.

"Three Yankee, go."

"Extraction's in place. Approach from the north. Bring a light fire team to cover the high ground to the west."

"Roger that. Casper is ten minutes out. He's got Starblazer in tow."

Walker's RTO hurriedly turned off the radio, grabbing the front of Dingo's shirt, pulling him to the ground. Eight NVA had cleared the tree line on the east side of the pick-up zone, walking toward the island ridge. They would cross the forty meters in less than a minute and be sixty meters away when the team popped smoke. They would stop once they heard the slick's rotors and back-track toward the sound. The radio operator switched the radio on.

"Casper, we got dinks on the PZ. There's gonna be a gunfight. Step on the gas."

"We're damn near there."

Recon opened fire on the NVA. Five men fell. The lead three bolted out of the clearing. The next minutes seemed an eternity. With their weapons silent, the grass seemed to stiffen. Twelve men waited, barely breathing.

"Pop smoke, Echo." Casper's lead chopper crested the horizon in the north.

The instant Walker popped smoke, AK rounds screamed from the ridge. Dingo jumped and fell, writhing in pain. The medic pinned him to the ground and began bandaging his side. The team returned fire. The machine gunner leaned into his weapon, firing from the hip.

"We got AKs waist high on the west high ground, south half, even with the smoke."

"We got green smoke."

"Roger, lime. We got a friendly down." With the announcement of a friendly casualty, the gunships closed on the ridge with a fury, spitting tracers and rockets as fast as they could fire.

Starblazer broke into the net, singing his theme from *Gold Finger.*

The two extraction slicks flew in low and hot, clipping the trees, and dropped their tail into the smoke just as the recon team blew their Claymores. Running as if he would make it, Hardin focused on the man in the door, fixing the door gunner's eyes, searching for a hint of what might happen, what was in the tree line behind him. Diving onto the cargo deck, recon's grunts reached for a chair leg, clutching any handle they could find. The slicks were airborne in seconds.

The door gunner found a wry grin, talking into his mike as he fired tracers into the retreating tree line. With a nod he welcomed Hardin on board.

Hardin looked at the PZ, the billowing grass. Five bodies lay sprawled along the trail.

* * *

Hardin stood on the airstrip for a time, looking back toward the Crow's Foot. The door gunner, the man in the door of the slick, looked like one of the doormen from Dak To. Or, was he the door gunner who was killed in Ban Me Thuot?

Door gunners they were, sure enough. Medics as well. Grateful for sure, a grunt could not measure their courage. Under fire, they stood in that door waiting with an extended hand, sometimes on the ground. *Damn,* Hardin thought, *that takes balls.*

Hardin was exhausted, unable to hold a thought. Fighting to stay alive had become chaotic. The camouflage on his forearms had worn off.

The team medic finished with Dingo's scratch and asked Hardin if he needed help.

"I probably do, Doc." The medic's face creased into a gesture of pointless concern.

The two men stood in silence watching a raft of white birds flow along the trace of the An Lao River, topping the palm trees. Hardin shouldered his rucksack and said, "Most of us don't like gunfights, Doc. Most of us just let the shit happen. Our honor is clean, but we're broken men, Doc—inside and out." The medic looked toward the Crow's Foot and didn't respond.

Hardin found Walker ambling toward the TOC for a debriefing. Walker paused near the door of the bunker to collect his anger. He had a nervous eye. He wasn't glad to be there, but if someone had to talk to Mother, he was on the prod.

Walker found Mother being energetic, claiming this and that, claiming the recon operation as his own—the guzzling-capital he so richly deserved.

Walker resented the man.

Something in the Major's eye made a farce of his words.

In concert or alone, Major Dip-Stick, Major Overlay, Major This-and-That, and Mother were but iterations of war's fantasy, replicas of a dull saw.

Unable to back off, Mother acknowledged Walker's presence. Walker didn't hear him. Mother returned to his briefing map, banging about like dags toggled to a sheep's ass, becoming the essence of Walker's story, determined to win the day with wartime graphics.

* * *

Standing outside that bunker, his uniform torn and splattered with blood, his leg punctured by his knife, Walker was but an imprint, a symbol of the American soldier. Tears welled in his eyes, as if he had lost his family just the other day. A stout man, muscled, and tough as fired oak, his blood-stained uniform and cracked lips told the story of the mission.

Wanting to console his new friend, Hardin began telling him about Dig-it. At the point in the story where Dig-it declared that Hardin's CO was going to carve a crack in his white ass, Walker's expression creased into a wry grin. Hardin looked away and then looked back.

Walker had fallen into a morose mood.

"We're in trouble, El Tee," Walker said.

"I can barely walk," Hardin said, expecting Walker to agree. He didn't.

They shook hands with knowing gestures of regret and relief—glad for each other, more so for the team. Walker slid into disconnected anger as he reset the selector on his weapon, his eyes distant and chilled: with the killing, without reason or reinforcing emotion. Suddenly flush with insistence, as if his purpose was clear, he dusted his uniform.

He paused. Remembering a phrase, he said, "My blade is losin' its edge, and those far off noises are gettin' louder. Camouflage used to help—now it just tastes bad."

"I was excited at first," Hardin said, setting his weapon aside. "At some point I realized I was never gonna leave." Hardin pushed his drive-on rag across his mouth.

Walker scrubbed at the blood-matted hair on the back of his right hand. He squared his jaw to the task and reset his weight. "Stuck a hole in my leg when I laid out that first dink." He ripped open his pant leg to examine the wound. "Knife went clean through him."

Walker took a long, slow drag on his cigarette, watched the smoke curl away, and raised his face into the sun. No one wanted to believe his recon reports, especially the reports that countered their conclusions. His words were shuffled by inferential minds.

Fractured by the weight of these enriched testaments, Walker and his team were fillers, time-slots in Mother's evening briefing—an additional asset to promote intrigue.

The camouflage patterns on his face were well defined; individual hairs were tinged with one color or another. Blood caked the large cavity of his right ear and the top of his knife case. No debriefing would allow that three enemy dead were killed with cold steel by men expected to forget the feeling. No valor awards would be processed.

Men like Walker killed in secret.

"How's your team chief?"

"Dingo doesn't know how to die," Walker said, shaking Hardin's senses with the tone of his voice. "Keep your head down, El Tee."

"That Caucasian you spotted—what did he look like?"

"His uniform was in bad shape—jungle fatigues, ours. Beard, same build as the deserter." Reacting to Hardin's expression, Walker held up a hand. "I know what I saw, El Tee."

Walker's eyes ran to a distant focus, his body desperate for quiet. Breathing as if movement meant detection, he was alone in a place only those who kept living could find, a continuum where he was one with his surroundings, a wave in an endless sea. Hardin knew this place well. He too could quiet his body and his mind—not simultaneously, body first. He could become one with the jungle and step outside his surroundings.

Without dimension or constraint, Hardin often found himself floating, wrapped in absolute silence somewhere beyond the senses of normality. Captain Edward Hardin could feel the presence of his enemy. He could watch his war from the balcony, as if his mind's camera were detached. He could do this in real time.

Walker would kill himself, somehow. Hardin knew this to be true.

Uncle stood in the radio room of the Tactical Operations Center, clutching a Coke, espousing the qualities of a good steak for those who would listen.

Hardin kicked in a rural horse-shit routine, and threw his rucksack in a heap.

"Recon sucks." Uncle stopped talking. Alpha Six assumed a squinting, masterful look, so Hardin gave him the finger. "Today's the twenty-third. Am I takin' Charlie Company, or did you find another old cripple like Dip Shit here?" Uncle's deeply tanned face wrapped into a facetious pause, noting Alpha Six's defiant posture and Hardin's disordered enthusiasm.

"You bastard," Alpha Six said, swinging around as if he had balls.

"Caught ya jackin' off, eh asshole? Fuck-oh-shit, that's glue in your hand."

Uncle let out a consuming huff, cautioning Radio Man's laughter. "That's pretty funny," he said. "Glue; that's good. Tomorrow Charlie Company's getting extracted in the morning. Captain Joe's up in some valley trying to hide."

Tomorrow was a better day in Vietnam's war—any war.

CHAPTER TWENTY-FOUR

Captain Joe's Rag

Landing Zone English. High Noon.

With his gear claiming a corner of Charlie Company's orderly room, working with Echo Recon had reinforced Hardin's decision to run out of the northern talon of the Crow's Foot. And whether Walker had seen the deserter was important only if one cared about finding the man.

Buckwheat killed the man. That, or the man found his way out of Vietnam. These were the stories Hardin preferred. That aside, for an infantry captain to survive he had to ensure he didn't fall pray to being enthused.

* * *

With the Old Man, Uncle, and Mother coaching the day, the change of command ceremony was held near the flagpole under the eye of Old Glory. It would have been a formal affair except for Hardin's inability to stand still and Captain Joe's laughter.

"Stop bouncin', Dick Head," Joe said, looking past Hardin at his band of grunts.

"What makes you smell so bad, Joe?"

Joe laughed a "gotcha" laugh, took off his drive-on rag, and put the dirty, foul smelling triangle bandage around Hardin's neck. With a concluding nod, he stepped back and said, "Lima, if you ever take that drive-on rag off, you'll die in Vietnam." Joe registered his paybacks by sticking the stub of a three-day old cigar in his mouth.

"That's the same cigar you were smokin' when we first met… in Dak To."

"Good luck, Lima. Take care of my boys."

"No sweat, Charger." They saluted each other and Hardin's fate set sail. Complaining about the rank smell and not being able to breathe, negotiations over beer allowed that Hardin could take off Joe's rag in the rear area without the curse being activated.

* * *

Anointed as the company's Field First Sergeant, Stubbs assumed the role of observer, measuring the worth of a new lieutenant and a new platoon sergeant. The task of finding a good soldier had become something of an adventure. Stubbs had decided these new men were hard of hearing. Within twelve hours of his assignment to the company, Lieutenant Dillon, the new man in charge of First Platoon, had become exemplary, hoisting his family's flag as if history had come full circle, challenging common sense for its obvious flaws.

The mood had changed.

Rap and Lightning were arguing. The brothers in First Platoon never argued. Rap's fist landed in the middle of Boo's chest, sending Boo staggering into a clump of bamboo. Rap turned on Lightning again. After talking with Rap, Stubbs dug in with Third Platoon.

In an effort to resurrect old times, Tennessee began ordering lieutenants around like they were stupid, and Amps started rifling through his rucksack looking for the C-Ration he lost in Ban Me Thuot. With Tennessee running the battalion net, and Amps running the company net, straight answers would be rare indeed. Hardin was glad they were alive.

Smelling like used shitpaper sealed in a heated can, with the company searching a new area of operations, Hardin ploshed about as if he were a reporter judging the necessity of this and that, wondering who might be in charge, if anybody.

With twilight closing in, he sat upright, memorizing the contours of the valley, constructing a three-dimensional cube and rotating the cube—east to west, and north to south. The company commo chief and Tennessee stood near his hip, coordinating sit-rep schedules.

Nauseated by Joe's drive-on rag, Hardin said, "God, I can't stand the smell of this fuckin' thing." Pulling the rag over his head, he flipped it into the brush and fell back, gasping with relief. The tail of its smell clung to his face.

Self contained, as if insulated from harm, with his head tucked in a seam of dirt, a lip-licking burst of AK fire, a thirty-round packet of gargled shit, slammed cracking across his belt buckle, blowing four holes through his map, sending him rolling away from the fire. The commo chief took a round through his lower calf, landing in a heap, shocked into silence.

The firing stopped.

With every tile loose, Hardin found himself lying next to the commo chief, facing the direction of fire, estimating the span between the commo chief's boot heel and the hole in his leg—fourteen inches.

With a dust-off chopper in-bound, Amps and Tennessee dragged the wounded man behind a rock outcrop. The incoming fire had come from the First Platoon sector.

Hardin caressed Joe's drive-on rag, praised Joe for his salvation, and tied the rag next to Sweet Cheek's shroud line on the aluminum frame of his rucksack. Then he ran across the perimeter to line out the men he had trusted the most.

"You didn't set an outpost." Hardin crouched low, leaning against the base of a tree. He looked from man to man: Rap, Blood, LeCotte. Turning to the artillery FO, he said, "Take down that fuckin' hammock." A hint of defiance caused Hardin to stand.

"It's comin' down."

"Rap, what the fuck's up? You know how this shit goes. I got holes in my map." Hardin looked at Dillon. "You're a cocky one. You get your shit together." The platoon had relaxed and the company lost a good man. All in all, it was a cheap lesson.

Looking at LeCotte, Hardin said, "You fuckers are truckin' on borrowed time. Chuck was gunnin' for the main man, otherwise one of you is in a bag." Hardin chased his anger from Rap, passed Blood and PeeWee, then pointed at Dillon with a quick motion, and said, "New men have a hard time gettin' from here to there. You best pay attention."

Hardin stood with a sigh. Pops and Ski were huddled behind a wall of sandbags. Without exception the answer was clear. Dillon's coming was a problem.

"Do it right, goddammit." Hardin looked at Rap and Blood for confirmation. "You buck sergeants pick it up or I'll put Fish in charge of this platoon."

Moving his rucksack, Hardin looked back over the perimeter. His map represented yet another symbol of luck. Sweet Cheek's shroud line, more frayed than yesterday, hung beside Joe's drive-on rag like two pilgrims tethered to an aluminum stock.

Hardin looked back toward the tree line and stared for a moment, flipping the tail of his father's beads in and out of his hand.

Decorated with charms, his living room had taken on the trappings of the display window in the used clothing store on Washington Avenue, in downtown Bremerton. He and his father liked to stop and check the prices on the small white tags: five cents for a pair of wire rim glasses. At the time five cents was one game of pinball—an Indian head nickel.

Seeing anything clearly was worth a great deal of money.

His father's beads had been whoring with Squeak's leather pouch and Nuts' overseas cap. Hardin admired the bullet hole in the pouch and counted the beads. He missed his father, his Pal. He missed his father's stories and his smoke filled den—the aura of his Victoria Cross, his VC.

The location of the bullet hole in the commo chief's leg put the offending missile one-sixteenth of an inch above the head of Hardin's cock as he laid cock up. For once, having a porcelain miniature was a good thing.

Remembering Buddha was a crafty bastard; he stared at the holes in his map. One round hit the valley floor of the Crow's Foot just north of the gully bed, and three rounds marched along the An Lao Valley—a damn tight shot group. Twenty-five rounds had blown by the commo chief's left flank.

Feeling the need to be more calculating, with three times the number of GIs, three times the number of team leaders, and much higher attendant probabilities, this near miss grazing would be dramatized by Fish and Ski, using the words they had found in Dak To.

So blessed, the incident would foster cohesion until someone got killed. Then, to a man, they would pause and re-evaluate Hardin's worth.

In combat, perception took the path less traveled. Captain Joe and Hardin had fashioned their perception at every turn, on every ridgeline. Steady and cool or irrational and charmed, the men of Charlie Company followed their lead for one reason: they were still alive.

LeCotte stood silent, examining the holes in Hardin's map. Then he said, "I got some Tabasco sauce if you want some, Lima."

"I'm not Lima, dumb ass."

Hardin confronted LeCotte with his steaming spaghetti Lerp, knowing his friend was guilty of fucking up the outpost. "Put some of that in here." Hardin pointed at the bottle of Tabasco tucked behind LeCotte's thigh. "Come on, right here." He held the spaghetti in front of LeCotte's glasses, hoping to fog the lenses.

With a backhanded wave, LeCotte said, "She-it. I was jokin'. Captain figures he can just go around takin' stuff." He jerked the lid off the bottle and pumped three squirts into the pouch, added a dash of inner-city indignation, then settled into a blank look.

Hardin poked the pouch at him again, insisting on a response, and said, "Is that what I get after you fucked up that OP?" LeCotte pumped a fourth squirt into the bag and tucked the bottle into his rucksack.

Fish tossed Hardin a bottle of Tabasco.

"You nearly get me killed, and this is what I get for not carvin' ya a new asshole." Hardin paused to acknowledge Boyle's joy. "I'm gonna hump your ass in tight circles, LeCotte." Boyle slapped his thigh. "You're goin' with him, Boyle, you stutterin' black bag-a-shit."

Rap laughed and exchanged a dap with Lightning. Hardin acknowledged Rap with a nod, and exchanged a dap with Boyle. Something about Dillon had the brothers on a roll.

After stand-to, unable to sleep, Hardin took the first shift on the radio. "Three Yankee, this is your brand new, freshly circumcised Charlie Six, over." Hardin's chest shook, shocked by the near miss. He needed to mend his isolation. He needed to talk to Joe.

"Yankee Kilo is here for ya, Honey." Radio Man was busy growing grass, timing the flow rate from a tired sandbag. Hardin liked the man because the man made Mother nervous. You see, the night-shift version of Radio Man was so black he could have been The Shadow. Plus, he flashed a devious copy of Dig-it's smile.

"I caught ya fuckin' a crack in that sandbag wall, didn't I, Honey? You grease that crack with butter, or what?" Keeping the push-to-talk switch depressed, Hardin continued. "Lemme talk to Joe, the old Charlie Six."

"Maybe I'll just grease your cracker ass."

"You come out here and I'll give ya all you can handle. Get Joe for me."

After a pause, Radio Man said, "He's drinkin' beer. Give it a minute."

"I got all night." The valley felt empty.

The moon set the valley aglow, contrasting black rivers of vegetation with pale seas of grass. Bushes became stalking men. Tree shadows stretched into undefined shapes, whipped by a breeze that didn't exist. A black curtain dropped behind the tree line.

When night's temperature spars with day's, and humidity remains fast, hush grips the jungle floor, then grows in volume with each passing hour. Phosphorous grass-shoots refract the starshine. A man crawling through the grass leaves a black trail, a snake's trail.

Joe's voice snapped with a joyful slur, jarring Hardin. "Charlie Six, this is Short Time, over." Joe had chewed on so many beers he sounded like he had a mouthful of live shrimp.

"I've been lookin' for a short time, Joe. You gotta take the curse off this rag." Hardin hated whiners, but Joe's curse was serious.

"Not gonna happen. It's rubber-bag city if ya take it off. Take it off and your ass'll get scattered like goose shit in a tight wind." Joe loved his graceless power. Luck had blessed him with unrefined reverence. Only a rural Baptist born in Waterproof, Louisiana, would think that goose shit in a tight wind described the mess an AK-47 could make.

"You backwoods bag of shit. I no sooner took that rag off and some dink pumped four rounds through my map and shot my commo chief." Hardin was using his best down-home tone.

"Bet your ass got tighter than a hard-dick-dog shittin' cinnamon seeds. I told you not to take that rag off. Fuck-oh-shit you're stupid." Joe was a deity, the Father of Eventual Sacrifice. Only Joe could absolve Hardin and exorcise the curse. Hardin had to beg.

"Did you piss on it to make it smell so bad?" Joe laughed as he keyed the handset. Hardin heard him open a can.

"Every mornin'. Doo-dah, doo-dah." Joe was a sick man.

"I tied it to my rucksack frame."

"That'll work, Lima. Keep your head down, kid."

"Thanks, Joe."

"I'll fuck your wife for ya, Lima. You know, give her some Louisiana Lightnin', make sure she doesn't yearn for anything." Radio Man added his two cents for good measure.

"You'd do that for me?" Hardin keyed the handset so Joe couldn't talk, then continued. "My bride has a sweetbread knife she uses on fresh banana bread and the like. You go near her daddy's farm, you better keep a hand on Old Johnson."

In the black of a jungle night, in Vietnam's war, saying good-bye meant more than life itself. Good friends were doing their best to say the words they could not find when they were together. Joe had taught his young charge well and hoped for his survival, but he did not expect the young captain to live.

"See ya next time, Lima."

Hardin would always be Lima Six, Joe's First Platoon leader. Captain Joe would always be an extension of Hardin's father's den—his memorabilia, his Field Marshall. Captain Joe would look for him through weary eyes, his helmet parked atop a rough-sawn stubble, his jaw rummaging the butt of a soggy cigar. He was Charlie Six: Charger to some. Captain Joe was the best infantry officer to ever step through the wire.

"I'm gonna miss you, Joe," Hardin said to himself.

* * *

Number #10, Highlands Road. Bremerton, Washington. September 1954.

The last week of summer vacation marched into young Hardin's bedroom, full of excitement and an expectant sense of occasion. With the beginning of sixth grade, he would finally be a man. He would give a girl a kiss behind the schoolhouse, and if he was lucky get to feel one of her tits. Tits were the most.

His big brother, Court, was already a man and becoming something of a celebrity with his singing and acting. The news from Senator Henry M. "Scoop" Jackson, agreeing to sponsor Court as a candidate to the Military Academy at West Point, meant the Major would supervise his son's senior year of high school like a drill sergeant.

The excitement at home left young Hardin on his own, tempered by a mood of argument among the elementary school gang on Highlands Road. Jimmy Wiggins had grown to be bigger than a horse. Lloyd Grant had landed in reform school for demonstrating the action of his pearl-handle switchblade knife at the counter at Woolworth's Five and Dime.

The energy in the air was that of anticipation and a willingness to fight at the loss of a marble. Jimmy had most of the gang's marbles in a drawer at his house. Jimmy would steal puries because nobody had any money.

On the Saturday before school started, Jimmy organized a football game at the Highlands Road Field, inviting a gang of rival kids from East Bremerton Grade School. One of the kids from East Bremerton looked like he drove the team bus to Highlands Road.

Before the game, young Hardin took stock of his bones and measured his opponents. They lived in the Navy Housing Project. He knew better than to play football with these kids. Most of their dads were Korean War Veterans. And any kid who would ride a bike more than two miles to play a pickup game of tackle football was a kid who would pound him into pulp and drag him through the mud.

Sure enough, each time he hiked the ball, one of three thugs would knock him on his ass, then use his face to change direction and run after the ball. And if this weren't over the top, Jimmy Wiggins would assault what was left of him after they formed a huddle.

Jimmy was having fun, but this was not a friendly game.

Hardin left the Highlands Road Field after the game was declared a waste. His nose was bleeding some, and his mouth was, too. His team didn't score one touchdown. Turning, he looked back over the field. The gang was limping away in pairs.

Jimmy was huddled with his new friends.

"What happened to you, Pal?" The Major asked, lifting Eddie's jaw for inspection. "Looks like you got tagged right on the button."

"We were playing football with some of Jimmy's friends from the Projects."

The Major gave him a jab to the shoulder. "How is the new bike?"

"It's neat. Can I ride it to school?"

"Sure, if you want." The Major held a jump rope he had purchased for Court.

"Wiggins told me that his dad moved away, that he wasn't coming back." The Major looked out of the window and shook his head.

"Jimmy's dad is missing in Korea, Pal. I don't know if Jimmy knows, or if he's ashamed to say, afraid to say." The Major set the jump rope on the hall table and gave his son a pat on the back. "Jimmy's dad is a Marine, Pal. A damned good one, I'd guess."

"Holly cow." Having a friend whose dad was missing didn't seem possible.

Jimmy Wiggins wasn't in school that first Monday. The teacher said he had transferred to East Bremerton Elementary for sixth grade. Saddened by the loss of a good friend, the Highlands Road Gang knew they would see Jimmy in junior high. They knew how to look out for each other.

Dreaming, Hardin sailed on the wind past the school bus stop on Admiral Perry Avenue, glancing at the younger kids, thankful for the status of being a sixth grader. His friends, especially the girls, were excited to give his new equipment the once-over.

After joyous hellos and backslapping stories, he discovered the purpose of sixth grade, and of qualifying for junior high. The girl of his dreams, the girl he took home with him, the girl he wanted to kiss, bounded off the school bus wearing a tight sweater and consumed his reason for living. Carol's new equipment tickled his traps.

Carol stood next to his bike smiling a smile she had found during the summer. He didn't know what her smile meant any more than his dog knew about baseball. Yet there he stood, his eyes riveted on her trotters, cursed with a taste for mischief.

Losing his marbles was a matter of semantics.

* * *

Search and Destroy Mission. 0510 Hours.

An ocean breeze pushed through the palm trees as the company approached the beach and a fishing village filled with silent people. Hootch by hootch they searched north into a small valley and dug in on a terraced rice paddy encased in spindly grass and vine foliage.

At twilight Hardin was negotiating with Reynolds over a can of pound cake when a bell in the village rang once, and then again. The echoes lingered in the valley.

"Sleigh bells ring, are ya lis'nin'?" Ski's words sounded like they were being forced through a sausage skin.

Music was made smaller by Ski's voice, but he sang anyway. He had started singing after Bucks was killed: Christmas songs and James Brown mostly, and then only snippets. He had a square-wheel sense of rhythm. His voice would boom whenever the square side of the wheel hit the ground. Fish said Ski was a natural entertainer, as if Fish would know.

"Shut up, Ski." The perimeter went silent. The bell rang a third time and a stranger fired an AK in four short bursts, tearing at the tree above Rap's head.

Tennessee keyed the hook, and said, "Just 79's, no sixteens." Five M-79 rounds crashed into the jungle. The stranger was gone.

Ski continued to sing as if there had been no interruption. Fish grabbed his shirt and Ski shut up. Then, as if struck by a thought, he jumped into Hardin's foxhole, nudged his shoulder, and held out his hand.

"Every night, Captain. From here on, with Bucks dead, I gotta hold his dog tag so him and me can talk. We kept each other alive in the mountains. I figure he's still lis'nin'."

Hardin slipped the chain over his head, handed it to Ski, and said, "The old tag is my dad's. He landed in Normandy on D-Day."

Ski looked at his captain as if he had met him for the first time, toasted him with Bucks' dog tag, and turned away to read in private. There were seven tags: Nuts, Dig-it, Hippie, Bucks, Sam, Hardin, and his father.

Ski gave Bucks' tag a kiss, handed the necklace to Hardin, gave his captain a pat on the back, and sprang from the foxhole. Acting like a revelation had surprised him, as if one of his annoying murmurs had produced an idea, Ski turned and straightened his shirt.

"Big Bucks was a good man, Captain."

CHAPTER TWENTY-FIVE

The General's Baby Boy

Battalion Mess. Landing Zone English.

Preening the Gross Table for the evening fare, Hardin prompted his lieutenants with a flurry of manners, warning that God-bobbing was required before every meal. Seated one echelon from what looked like a Court Marshal board, he surveyed the men at the head table.

Uncle and Mother had been arguing for weeks.

Mother wanted Uncle to initiate an Article #15 against Hardin because Hardin said Mother had the mental agility of a Louisiana Whitefish. Captain Joe had laughed until he spit beer from his nose, guffawing that a Louisiana Whitefish was a used condom.

Uncle told Mother that Hardin might be right.

A crispy new chaplain sat between the Old Man and Mother, leaving Uncle to coddle-coach a stranger perched at the end of the head table, clutching the tablecloth as if he expected to fall off his chair. The stranger had a tilt to his head as if he were balancing an egg on his ear. His ratchet mug was slamming in jerks from one expression to another, flashing a mild fugitive smirk, his shield garnished with a red rose.

The stranger smiled at the chaplain and made the chaplain so nervous he started fondling the cross on collar, his lips moving with a holy urgency.

The Old Man tapped his water glass and announced that Mother had been posted to the brigade headquarters. Uncle nodded his relief. The stranger pursed his lips, his chest swelling as the words flowed on. After the Old Man explained that Major Magson was a lateral transfer from the brigade headquarters, Uncle fell back into a funk, knowing the stranger had been booze-blessed by the general as the battalion's new planner.

Uncle addressed the chaplain. "Chaplain, would pray for us?" The chaplain stood and the head table bowed their heads.

"Of course. Bless this food we are about to receive and these officers as they make decisions that affect our troops, Amen."

The Gross Table erupted with the field version: "Hiya, Maggie. Rub-a-dub dub, thanks for the grub, yeah, God!" Fists pounded the table in unison. The chaplain waited in silence. The Old Man opened up on his carrots. Major

Magson ruffled his stuffing into a heap with a flurry of nest-building moves, first offended, then content that he was the general's choice.

After toggled introductions, the junior officers followed the members of the head table to the TOC briefing room. Mother and Maggie maneuvered for a vantage in the middle of the front row, each bristling with servitude. Mother's briefing featured the battalion's many glorious deeds, coupled with the notion that planning was the key to killing the enemy.

The proposition that Mother knew enough about Vietnam's war to plan Chuck's death was worth several exaggerated nut rolls, a high-pressure nut massage, and a vigorous tug on the nearest sandbag. To highlight his planning, Charlie Company would be inserted on a ridge along the north rim of the Tam Quan Valley, twelve kilometers north of LZ English.

A class-three intelligence report had pinpointed an NVA headquarters in a tunnel system, the main entrance being tucked behind a rock outcrop near the east end of the valley. Mother recited an eight-digit grid coordinate, a location within ten meters of actual.

A GI couldn't dig a foxhole within one hundred meters of an eight-digit coordinate.

"Any questions?"

"How did you get the location of a tunnel complex within ten meters?" Hardin asked.

"We're going to check this out. And another thing, Captain, a reporter is going out with you." Mother was taking his last shot.

"Baby sittin' civilians is not another thing. What's he goin' out for?" Imagine homemade bamboo grenades on the cover of *Time* Magazine.

"Probably to take pictures." Mother was delighted, the Old Man was amused, Maggie was polishing his chair, and Stubbs was laughing his ass off. "That's all for now." Stubbs waited for Hardin by the radio tables.

"Stubbs, you got a laugh out of Mother, didn't ya?" Stubbs nodded and lit a smoke.

"Mother's gettin' a Silver Star." Hardin escorted him out of the TOC. Stubbs looked puzzled, then set fire to his cigarette again. "Brigade's givin' him a Silver Star for ridin' in a C&C chopper during that contact in the Crow's Foot, while you were playing hide'n'seek with Walker's recon team."

Hardin started back toward the bunker. Stubbs grabbed his arm.

"Wait." Hardin stepped into the glow from Stubbs' cigarette as his brow folded into a questioning squint, and his teeth ground with resentment. "The word's out—Mother drinks every night at the same time. The troops know what's up."

"Does Mother know about the Silver Star?"

"I don't think so."

Hardin was sick of the hypocrisy, sick of wallowing in a bore-hole while the roaches scurried about. Some were more interested in self-promotion than the welfare of the troops, more concerned with data correlation, than the lives of the troops being quantified.

"You want a Silver Star, Stubbs? I can get ya one of those. I can send a war story to the word-pussys. I got a PFC in Delta Company an Army Commendation Medal for valor, and he doesn't even exist. Got him orders for R&R, and promoted to specialist fourth class."

Hardin pounded the sandbag wall as they walked.

"Did anybody find out?"

"Who cares?" Hardin said, slanting his stride toward the Officers' Bar. "The Army didn't care if 'Who' died, so why would the Army care if 'Who' never existed. Besides, enough paperwork will end this war."

* * *

First Platoon had a new man—a short, red haired GI nicknamed Grumpy. Grumpy would stand in for Drips. He would wonder at the words, this wiry man with the clever grin. The doubt that was his companion would be replaced with guilt.

Grumpy would carry his year in a sack, fresh at first, shedding one illusion at a time. In the end, if he survived, the rickety cart that was his year would lumber aimlessly down a vacant trackway lined with vagrant thoughts.

* * *

Airstrip. Landing Zone English. 0620 Hours.

Drips and Fish were jaw jacking—nut grabbing and laughing about bunker #1's brothel, sloshing saliva into the air. Hardin addressed his friend, suppressing his anger. "Drips, you came back to the bush to train that cherry red head, didn't ya?"

"Yes, sir. Grumpy's gonna hump my ruck so I can carry on." Drips stepped into a muscular brace, demonstrating his Atlas pose, stepping to catch his balance.

"I don't think there's a shutter speed slow enough to capture your moves." Drips was easily confused, and shutter speeds were focal lengths beyond his reason.

"What's that supposed to mean?" Fish laughed. Fish didn't know what focal lengths meant anymore than a jackass knew about molasses.

"Say good-bye, Drips. I don't want to be wearin' one of your dog tags."

Fish slapped Drips' shoulder and snorted. Two GIs who fought the battle for Dak To would remain in the jungle—Ski and Fish. No matter what else the war offered, the remnants of Hardin's soul might find solace if they got home alive.

"And keep on leavin' this time. Keep on truckin' back to the world."

Hardin flashed on the aid station. Sam's face imploded and his body shrank away. "Drips. I'm not jokin'. Don't come back."

Confused, Hardin stared in disbelief. The reporter stood alone, dressed in tiger fatigues, propped on the tarmac, manicured like a sullen statue, his camera recording what must have been anomalous events. The general's son carried a camera so new the black case sparkled in the sun. Hardin walked toward him. Instinctively, Drips followed, then Fish.

"Ah, the general's baby boy."

"That's right." Tall, brash, and arrogant, his shoulders were unbowed by the weight of his rucksack. His answering grin brought Drips to the reporter's side.

"The war still funny to you, Hair Ball?" Hardin asked.

"At times."

"Shake down his rucksack, Drips. Make sure he's only smokin' Luckys."

* * *

The chopper ride was a bore until the slicks fell out of the sky and inserted the company in a tangle of snake shit, 1800 meters from their designated landing zone. The remedy required a compass resection, and a location status back to Three Yankee.

"Six, this is Mike Five. We lost the reporter."

"We just fuckin' got here," Tennessee barked, handing Hardin the hook.

"I heard. Circle us up. Have Mike run a clover." Second Platoon searched the ridgeline with no sign of Charlie or the reporter.

"Lima, lead out, we're goin' south into the vill. Try not to shoot up our lost friendly." Lost people traveled downhill. A reporter would be drawn to a village.

The clearing held five unkempt hootches and a gaggle of old women: bags of wrinkled treachery gossiping like farmers after the harvest, transshipping rice into the mountains for their sons and grandsons.

"Tennessee, we found Mister Disney sittin' on the side of a well, wonderin' what took us so long." Tennessee cussed, trying to catch up with Hardin.

"Wait one." Tennessee stumbled as he spoke. "Dillon's got the reporter."

"We need a dust-off, Tennessee. PeeWee's burned down, looks like malaria," Amps said. This was PeeWee's second bout with malaria.

Hardin took the hand set. "Put the filmmaker on PeeWee's dust-off." Hardin's voice signaled an abrupt change of mood. His eyes were vibrating.

"Mister Disney says he's not leavin'."

"Mister Disney says. God damn you, Dillon. I don't give a fuck whether that bastard needs that dust-off or not. Break his fuckin' nose. You hear what I'm sayin'? Either way, you put that sorry bitch on the slick."

"We can do that."

The dust-off came charging, running full-throttle into the Tam Quan Valley at treetop level. The pilot increased the delirium at boot level when he stood the chopper on its tail, rocked the airframe through two lateral swings, then slammed the landing skids into the clay dust, sending GIs and debris burrowing into the surrounding brush.

PeeWee lay huddled in a poncho, clutching Bucks' dice, shivering on the hot clay surface of the trail, his face desperate with fever. Rap and Blood threw the reporter onto the cargo deck of the Huey. The dust-off was airborne in eight seconds.

With the well dry, the village wasn't a village at all. Mama Sans watched the company's seditious two-step with prosaic expressions of authority. They had the answers.

The hootches flanked the main trail that ran the length of the valley. Tucked into a narrow draw, the railhead could easily service a battalion. The trail was worn smooth and densely lined with a leafy scrub. A man could not walk parallel to the trail and see the trail at the same time. Third Platoon ran clovers to intersect the trail at hundred-meter intervals, while the other platoons worked the northern flank of the valley.

Searching again, the day became heavy with heat and ripe with temper. A new guy, a white GI, advised the company it should stop for water, stop for a rest, stop for food, stop for a while, and stop for Christ's sake. LeCotte nudged him but the new man wouldn't stop talking.

Tallying the grieving, as if such might be linear, Hardin's left hand hit the quick-release on his rucksack strap and his body surge forward, weapon in hand. His cussing scream turned the new man's body, and his charge caught him on the left side.

Hardin's foot landed just above his left ankle, and his momentum ran over his knee on the way to his head. His body folded into the ground. His leg fractured on impact. Hardin's weapon swung wildly, crushing the man's face. If not for Blood's quick reactions, Hardin might have killed the man.

"Damn good thing we ditched *Time* Magazine," Stubbs said, pulling Blood aside.

Hardin was more than satisfied. Actually, he was thrilled. The more the man groaned the more excited Hardin became. Fish took off his helmet and gave Hardin a short nod. Stubbs dumped the gear from the man's rucksack next to LeCotte.

Grumpy, the new redhead, had not moved since the attack. He was next in line. He stared in disbelief, slack-jawed.

Hardin spit through clinched teeth. The red-haired cherry boy stood stock-still, wide-eyed, mouth open and speechless: talking to his imaginary friend. "Jesus, my company commander attacked this dude right in front of me on my second day in the boonies... Broke his leg and his jaw... Maybe three seconds... Dude was fuckin' crazy."

"What are you lookin' at, Fuck-stick?"

"Nothin', sir."

"You got the same problem as Drips. That red hair is wound too tight, cuts off the blood to your limp-dick brain." Hardin smiled.

"Yes, sir." Grumpy didn't want to talk to the captain.

"Red hair has a left-hand thread. Same as a pig's dick."

"Yes, sir."

"Does everything you say end with sir?"

"When I'm talkin' to you it does, sir." Grumpy turned and looked for help. Pops and Reynolds didn't talk to cherries. By this time the new man with the fractured fibula and broken mouth was standing on one foot, waiting for a dust-off.

"Is that whiner a friend of yours?"

"Not anymore."

Silence marked the balance of the day and twilight's shovel took heed.

Ski stopped by Hardin's digs to read Bucks' tag. His smiled bloomed toward his right ear when he was content. He had assumed the ease of old leather. "Me and Fish were fixin' to stomp the dude. Guess you just got crazy." Ski gave Bucks' tag a kiss and handed the chain to Hardin. Pleased, as if his loyalty was his pride, Ski gave Hardin a pat on the back.

* * *

Time wore on. Boredom too.

The sun-baked air in the Tam Quan packed a stale taste, thick with pollen and a fine clay dust. Dry grass snapped at the touch, counter to their cadence. One massive GI, a replacement Fish named Sergeant Snorkel, accompanied the resupply. He was a pastry concoction from the Army's cooking school at Fort Jackson, South Carolina: a shake-and-bake, a whip-and-chill, one of Mac's illusions.

The new buck sergeant had been surveyed for mental and physical aptitude, put on a fast track, educated in the rigors of Army tradition, and after ninety days of total service was promoted to the grade of Sergeant—E-5. After ninety days of total service, he was an infantry fire-team leader, able to lead a five-man team in combat.

This low-temperature cooking program was a byproduct of a statistical analysis McNamara designed to fill persistent voids in Army infantry companies. Logic, after all, would prevail. If too many captains were killed, promote lieutenants to captain in two years instead of five years. If too many fire-team leaders and squad leaders were killed, create an instant fire-team leader's school.

The Army had pay grades with declining reviews, making data summaries embarrassing for Mac. His answer—create illusions like Hardin, a two-year captain.

Stubbs made Hardin talk to a new GI before the end of his first week in the jungle to assure them he was actually the company commander. Hardin looked into the big man's eyes, and asked, "How long have you been in the Army?"

"Been five months."

"In five months you're an E-5, a fire-team leader? Most of these studs have been in the bush longer than you've been in the Army." Hardin stopped the man's answer, bypassing an opportunity to laugh. "Not gonna happen that way stud, not out here." He motioned to Stubbs.

"What do we have here, Captain?" Stubbs looked at the whip-n-chill's stripes.

"We gotta talk." Stubbs sank into a tail of cigarette smoke. "This stud has been in the Army five months and he's an E-5." While the new sergeant outlined the Army's accelerated promotion program, Sergeant First Class Stubbs sat stunned, silently reflecting on the twelve years he had struggled to become an E-6—staff sergeant.

Stubbs flipped his cigarette past the cherry's head and reached into his rucksack for another smoke, wincing at the pain of this final betrayal. Being an airborne staff sergeant in the United States Army had become meaningless.

With a dusky hue, Stubbs' face plunged into a rush as he pointed the butt of his cigarette at the new man. "I don't know where ya think you're headin' stud, but you're not gonna lead one of my fire teams—not while I'm alive."

Stubbs took another drag; his sweet-potato drawl had turned to iron.

"This is my jungle," Stubbs said. "I don't care what you get paid. You're a grunt 'til your platoon sergeant gives you a fire team."

With a raised jaw, Stubbs exhaled pensively, then looked at Lightning. He slowly nodded his resignation by playing with the lid on his Zippo. Hardin waited for the fire in Stubbs' eye to fade, waiting for a grace period.

"You got him, Stubbs. Put the word out." Hardin turned, then stopped and pointed at the new man. "Take off those fuckin' stripes."

The rotor wash pushed cool air over Hardin's face. The rotor seemed to pause, as if a capacitor released each blade, leaving an uncertain hollow, leaving a moment to be afraid.

Ninety-day fire-team leaders and two-year company commanders: Vietnam's war was rife with rage and stupidity. If not for Fish and men like him there would be no balance whatsoever.

* * *

Charlie Company was extracted back to LZ English to stand guard mount as berm security on bunkers #1 through #18. For most rifle companies this was a routine assignment. For Charlie Company, berm security would become a ball-busting challenge.

"Remember Mother, Old Silver Star?" Stubbs didn't smile often, but telling this story had him on a roll. "Got in a fight with a sandbag wall and broke his leg."

"Shipped him to Qui Nhon," Amps said.

"They'll pin the medal on him takin' pictures by his hospital bed, and pin a Purple Heart to his pillow. Mother did well. Got his bus ticket punched, a basic load of medals, and a good efficiency report." Mother, the paper lifer, would prosper in Mac's Army.

"He wasn't so bad," Stubbs said, finger-coning the ashes of his cigarette. In a relative sense, Stubbs was right about Mother.

Hardin bought Stubbs a twenty-five cent shot of bourbon and left him staring at a tabletop commiserating over ninety-day sergeants.

Stubbs supervised the berm to ensure no boom-boom girls slid through the wire, and the troops took their jollies to town in turn. With his men refit for an insertion near the western foot of the Tiger Mountains, Stubbs shook down their rucksacks.

Airborne, hoping the faithful wouldn't mind him singing their theme song, Hardin sang as loud as he could. "There's gentle people with flowers in their hair." With his slick on short-final, thirty feet off the ground, a dink with an AK bolted from a hootch. Hardin fired, then the door gunner fired. Chuck dove into a hootch and disappeared.

"Spread out and relax," Amps said, running from the open field

GIs filtered into the village on a patchwork of trails. Small children scampered about. They seemed happy. Women spoke casually, frowning through uncommitted eyes, evaluating the cavalcade of triangle bandages. Four hundred rounds of ammunition had just been fired into their village and the villagers looked like they had just left the movies.

The village was as picturesque as any travel brochure of the South Pacific. Hootches perched on hard clay platforms spread lazily through an endless palm grove. As families gathered to witness the liberation, Stubbs declared the morning a success. More than one GI saw a Viet Cong soldier. News of the sighting brought Major Magson out to visit.

"Wha'd'a ya need, Maggie?"

"It's Major to you, Captain."

"Really? Everybody gets a handle, Major. I'd stick with Maggie if I were you."

"I want to see these villages so I understand where I'm sending you, Captain. It's my first tour. Need to do what I can to learn the ropes." *The first thing you need to learn,* Hardin mused, *is there are no ropes, unless we're talking about the devil's rope.*

"You'll be the first," Amps declared, presenting himself as a tramp, a hack hired to carry a green box that transformed varying degrees of radiant energy into sounds any GI could ignore. Smiling he squeezed his right hand into a fist, admired the fungus swimming in the jungle rot, and then wiped the pus on his leg.

Shaking his head, Maggie said, "I'll spend an hour or so, get familiar with your unit."

"Holy shit!" Amps chimed. "An hour with us will ruin your career. And gettin' familiar with LeCotte will make you crazy."

Hardin laughed to himself, rubbed his eyes, and said, "Chuck knows we're here, Major. About the only thing we'll find is stuff he forgot to take with him."

"Vietnam is a complicated place," Maggie said.

"By God, ain't that the truth," Amps said. Maggie looked at Amps and turned away.

"Major, did you know that radiotelephone was one word?" Tennessee asked.

"I guess it is."

After watching Maggie introduce himself to every worn-out woman in a kilometer of village, Hardin could stand no more. "Get a chopper out here before I shoot the bastard."

* * *

Four hours later, with Second Platoon at the charge, a VC in blue shorts took flight from the village heading across an open rice paddy running toward the Tigers. A GI stood to an off-hand firing position and fired one round, hitting Chuck behind the right ear, blowing his brains into the air as his body reached for one more step then crumpled into the furrows of the rice paddy.

One round, one VC. Mac drafted the right man.

Stubbs liked this man—the look of his modest smile, the shucks of his past. "Lemme guess, Arkansas, maybe Louisiana?" Stubbs asked.

"Alabama." Tennessee was collecting credit for Confederate marksmanship.

"Phenix City?"

"Magazine Point, Alabama."

While Alabama took credit for the dead shot, a team packed the body into the perimeter like a trophy. The man's head was missing the top of the skull, as if he'd lost a hairpiece. The rim of the hole was trimmed with jagged bone and his brain was gone. Being empty headed explained why he was running flank-wise through an open field wearing sunscreen, sandals and blue shorts.

Tag, in a rare display of humor, told Blood that the dead man couldn't have been very smart. Blood didn't get the joke, so LeCotte told the joke again adding a shrug that suggested that Blood should laugh. Fish told LeCotte if he thought Blood was stupid he needed to look in a mirror. That's when Reynolds and Rap decided to beat the piss out of LeCotte if he said another word.

Tag didn't care if they did or not.

The next three days were filled with punji pits, musty spider holes, booby traps, rice, a bundle of WD-1 telephone wire, and hootches where Chuck would be tomorrow. They searched the floors, the rice bins, the bamboo hootch supports, ground vegetation, fencing, freshly turned soils, furniture, thatch overlaps, water jugs, tools, bunkers, and the people: all without a warrant.

Sitting on the verandah of the last hootch, Hardin spotted the pagoda's white spire. Andy's bell seemed to sparkle. The village was nearly reconstructed. Once complete, the village would melt back into the palm grove and they could search it again.

* * *

Generational support for Vietnam's war, although strong in the beginning, had riven like fresh madrona under the mauls of deceit. By July of 1968, America was at war at home and the news found the men of Charlie Company with each resupply, with each letter, with each replacement. Still, for some the effort remained commendable, the cause noble.

By degree, with each firefight, the veterans grew more confidential. With each letter from home they grew more reactive, more contentious. The catechism of their trade grew more demanding; don't talk, don't trust, and don't feel. The questions no longer mattered. Using their foxholes as confessionals, the veterans were mindful of what they had done. With their hearts locked in a shell of diapered sanity, the purchase of their soul was losing hold.

* * *

The point squad broke south along the east side of the village they had been searching, nearly running toward an extraction point. At 1046 hours, with the company strung out through the village, a CH-47 Chinook flew across the horizon. A cable hooked to the belly of the chopper snapped, and a water trailer fell into the jungle just south of the pickup zone.

"Lima, move out and secure what's left. Do it right," Tennessee said, watching Hardin for signs of disagreement.

"Mike, November, tighten up and run. Give us a gun on drag." Moments after the point squad broke into the brush near the water trailer, small-arms fire erupted.

"Tennessee, ya gotta see this. Two dead dinks, one AK and a sandal factory," Pops said, gasping. "Ya gotta see this. Dinks got the tires cut off this trailer and were hackin' 'em up for sandals." Fear and amazement touched Pops' voice.

"Burn the tires, give Chuck a kiss, and get your ass back here."

"Can do." Black smoke worked its way out of the brush, masking the silhouette of the ridgeline. The pilot of the lead extraction slick broke into the conversation.

"Roger, Charlie Six. This is Casper Lead, we got your black smoke."

"Casper, this is Tennessee, and I'll be your controller for this move. I need ya 300 meters north. Should be quiet, over."

"Roger, Tennessee, I got yellow smoke." The VC had thrown a yellow smoke grenade behind a small knoll, 400 meters north of the company, trying to ambush the slicks.

"Jesus, we've got no smoke," Tennessee said.

"Roger, Gray-coat, this is Jesus. I'll be your Savior for this trip, and I've got purple between the lemon and the charcoal." Stubbs had thrown a smoke grenade out into the paddy.

"Grape is good."

* * *

"How many jumps do you have, sir?" SFC Dubitski said. The company's new platoon sergeant, stood next to Hardin's rucksack, his fatigues decorated with stateside multicolored patches: Ranger, Master Parachutist, Pathfinder, white nametag, and bright yellow SFC stripes. The muscular, steel-eyed old sergeant issued a quick smirk as if to mock himself, then stiffened his posture. Dubitski's boots packed the residue of a high shine.

"You recruiting, Dubitski?" Hardin said, waving at the badges.

"You look kind of young, Lieutenant, that's all." The stateside warrior tried to soften his challenge, but his body language betrayed his tone.

"I'm a captain, Sergeant, and you look kind of old. Think you can keep up?" *God,* Hardin thought, *this is fun. A two-year captain could piss off anyone in the Army.*

"Anytime, Captain. I got 4,856 jumps. Hold the record for the most jumps in a twenty-four hour period. I was captain of the Army Golden Knights Sky Diving Team. No sweat keepin' up." Proud of his uniform, Dubitski held his weapon across his chest, convinced that this officer needed his guidance.

Hardin exhaled through a sigh, then set his teeth. "Chuck doesn't care how many jumps you've got, Sergeant. And neither do I. If you're gonna walk around lookin' like Times Square, stay the hell away from me."

"I got your Third Platoon. It's gonna be damn hard to stay out of your way."

"You got me pissed off and I just met ya. You're a primary target, Dubitski. Lose that tight jaw and find a way to camouflage your past."

"Is that an order, Captain?"

"Get one of my people killed because you're dressed like a billboard, and you'll find out what my orders are like. If you're still confused ask around."

Stubbs stood-to in front of Dubitski and the new man walked away. Built like Doc Collard, Dubitski leaned into his stride as if he was headed for a spot beyond his target. Hardin knew their future exchanges would begin with a challenge.

Stubbs joined Hardin for a beer, nursing a stiff knee.

"What was the Sergeant Major jawin' about, Stubbs?" Stubbs took a long drag on his cigarette and looked toward the TOC.

"You're not gonna like it. We're gettin' four NVA Chieu Hois to work with us."

"Give 'em to First Platoon, and the point. Damn, I hate bein' around those bastards."

"You're supposed to be at the TOC. We lift off at 1600 hours."

CHAPTER TWENTY-SIX

Leech Dick

Charlie Company Night Laager. The Fish Hook.

On a plateau overlooking the An Lao River where GIs had searched for years, Stubbs stood in relief against the peach-purple sky. He was thinking of his men, how to guide their steps with purpose and away from a nagging guilt.

No longer curious, he was convinced one of his men had killed the deserter.

Tired yet observant, his ability to be casually cruel had given way not to fatigue but to the weight of futility. Whatever he might find at the end of his year, whatever he might become, he would never be ashamed of his men. Their honor was clean.

The parallax had become obvious as Eastern men proclaimed and GIs prayed. The Grunts fighting Vietnam's war had turned south. Not intentionally, mind you. The variance started at the wire's edge and became more divergent with each empty magazine, with each weary step.

And those Eastern men, those champions of liberty, word-pussys all, were in full retreat, brandishing their papers, suffering withdrawal, praying for salvation—Christians all.

Rap would kill Whitey. That's the way the game was played.

Stalked by this plague of intrusions, Stubbs sparred with himself. His professionalism had ensnared him, his duty larger than his war. Keeping information from his commanding officer set his loyalty after his word, his instinct a burden that sharpened each day. He would protect his men, no matter the cost. If he could protect Hardin, all the better.

A rolling sheet of knee-high grass stretched to the horizon. While GIs dug in on the landing zone, three fire teams ran a clover covering the clock and found no trails or bent grass.

With this news GIs transformed from one spiritual purpose into representative sects.

Most opted for a lighter head, some needed more definition. As Stubbs mapped their faces he traced the steep ridges of Dak To and the hollow expanse of the Crow's Foot.

Accepting the correlation between a GI's religious precepts and his density of stored trauma, Ski and Fish stood at one end of the distribution, and Grumpy and Linus stood at the other. Pops held center court. The rest, well that's what they were, an excellent sampling of the GIs fighting Vietnam's war.

Mindful, as if yesterday might replay itself, they prepared for twilight as they had for centuries clad in the stench of used sandbags.

Watching Ski wipe down his machine gun, Hardin said, "It's not like before." Tennessee set the radio frequency and looked at his El Tee.

"Hard to tell which stud needs a good chewin', you know," Hardin said.

"You invited yourself before, buttin' in, cussin' people's mamas. You're the one that moved to Nashville." At that Hardin presented himself at Pops' steel-pot stew.

"Fuck me, look who's beggin' for handouts," LeCotte said.

"Good to see ya," Pops said, glancing at Dillon.

"How's baby girl Kimberly doin', Captain?" Ski asked.

"I'd guess she's doin' well, Ski."

* * *

At daybreak the company descended into the damp shadows of a finger valley stretching southeast into the An Lao Valley. The canopy spread into a series of overlapping small-leaf umbrellas forming a low altitude roof and a phosphorous glow on the jungle floor.

Sounds echoed quickly.

Stubbs put out his cigarette.

The ground was dark, firm with gravel, and neatly devoid of large plants. Bunches of broad-stem grass and feather-leaf ferns grew in patterns as if they had been planted. The air was compressed and heavy with a cloying moisture.

Mouths were held open. Steps sounded as if in a nunnery. Eye movements were synchronized as quick-fire postures swayed from side to side.

Stubbs shook an unlighted cigarette to his mouth.

Suddenly, symmetry forced the jungle aside and the moving black shadows stood still. Boots gripped the jungle floor in disbelief. A roadbed roared with laughter, its linear figure in contrast to an irregular world. Standing five feet off the jungle floor a clean slate of gravel ran down into the valley, paralleling a small blue-line. The roadbed was plain enough, silent in the speckled light.

The shoulders of this odd ribbon were a mix of grainy clays supporting yellow-green leaf clusters. The plant was absent from the surrounding jungle. Stones on the surface of the roadbed were beaten smooth, covered with a dusting of pollen.

As the valley closed in on their flanks, men moved without breathing, moving into what must be a trap. Boots fell on the sodden ground with a muffled sound.

Abruptly the roadway ended.

"I don't get it," Amps said, staring at the sloped end of the road, his eyes level with the top, searching the road where it turned into a narrowing void.

"I don't get why there's no sign of life, and why there's no vegetation on the road," Stubbs said, scratching his head. "Let's find some daylight. The troops are spooked." Stubbs flipped his smoke onto the roadbed.

"Maybe it was built by the French," Amps said.

"It can't be good luck," Stubbs said, lighting a smoke. "It ain't finished. Let's get outta here. I need some air." First things first. Stubbs was spooked. One by one men filled canteens, then quick-stepped away from the roadway.

Exhausted by the strain of being hyper-alert for too long, Tag held up his fist, stopping the company within sight of the river. Stiff shafts of grass stood erect, seven feet tall, yellow-green spines reached for the open sky, bunched like sedge around a pond.

Relieved to be free of the jungle canopy, seasoned stares and searching eyes measured the sounds of the valley. Birds called from across the river.

Spurred by the silence, the point squad rose in unison. A flock of birds bolted from the trees at the river's edge and the point squad sank back into the grass. An hour passed before the point squad rose again, with Tag guiding the company in a dogleg out of the open field.

Deep green foliage merged into a tangled canopy, the branches so entwined the sun's rays were completely blocked. The floor of the jungle gave off a sheen, as if sweating, its black-brown skin teaming with rot.

The river ran shallow through a ninety-degree turn, six feet below Hardin's boot heels. He sat near a clump of bamboo facing the opposing tree line. The riverbed ran flat across fifty meters of reed grass and washed rock. Tree roots cut bare by the monsoon arched into the rock, as if securing the riverbank from further harm.

The day passed without a word. A pale blue sky lay deep at the head of the Fishhook. Gunships were firing near the barb of the Fishhook, at what it did not matter. Rocket trails hung above the river, their image traced across the black face of a steep ridge.

The valley was beautifully remote.

Recessed inside the tree line, Rap and Pops stepped into their outpost position, searching through the suspended foliage, searching for targets along the river. The water was a distraction, roaring with excitement, splashing and spilling the news of the day, oblivious to the frightened men laying in wait.

Hardin adjusted his butt on his helmet, looking through the mist curling off his coffee, transfixed by the chop and the glint on the water. The head of the valley stood five kilometers to the west. The sun fell behind its shoulders leaving a black void.

Tag's point squad closed back into the perimeter with a nod and a thumbs-up. The company's first night in the An Lao Valley would begin without a fight.

Growing more relaxed, Tennessee pushed his charm at a new man's face, smile-cussing the apprentice he had requisitioned with clinched teeth and threats of death. PFC Baldinger was doing well, fending off the usual pranks. Left alone to prepare his meal, he got sidetracked and started to whine, and then his breath shortened to a pathetic chop.

"Oh, God. Oh, my God. Oh, Jesus. Somebody help me." Hardin looked over his shoulder to find out why the new man was praying with his pants down.

"What's your problem, stud?" Stubbs asked.

Suppressing a laugh, Tennessee covered his mouth with his drive-on rag. Baldinger stood braced with his shirt off and his pants wrapped around his knees, staring at his dick like it was festering with pus.

LeCotte slapped Boyle's fist. Fish told Tag the man's name had to be changed.

"Oh, Jesus. Somebody help me." With GIs thankful for a comic interlude, the cheeks of Baldinger's ass started vibrating and his balls began to swell.

Stubbs spoke softly. "Shut up Dinger and turn around."

Dinger turned one degree with each step, as if to keep his nuts from exploding. With shock in his eyes, he stood like a helpless child, his legs spread wide to keep his pants in place.

"Holy shit. We got us a Kilo with two dicks," Amps declared.

Dinger was sporting a semi-stiff erection, and a black leech about half the size of his cock hung at the right side sucking the blood from his brain.

"You're stupid. No one's gonna hold your cock," Amps said, lighting a cigar.

Dinger was too busy talking to God to take the cigar. As if introducing himself to himself, Amps became the hard-ass he thought he was, holding the cigar in front of Dinger's face suggesting that Dinger become a hard-ass, too.

With a blank expression, this moment would be Dinger's legacy.

"You pussy. Burn 'em off."

Holding the cigar like it was an expensive pen, Dinger measured the distance between his cock and the hot ash. Convinced he would lose at least one ball, he pulled the cigar back and puffed the turd to a glow. Talking to Jesus, he lowered the ember toward his cock torching all of the hairs along the way. He missed the leech.

When Dinger jumped, Amps said, "Ya gotta keep breathin', Dinger." Laughing, Amps was enjoying his new role. "Prayin' ain't gonna help."

Cradling his cock in his left hand, Dinger begged the medics to stop laughing. Gushing smoke, Dinger singed the leech with a quick jab. A squirt of blood leapt into the air forcing Dinger to stagger backward.

Shocked, as if his cock belonged to someone else, Dinger continued his dialog with Jesus.

Meanwhile, Fish had crossed the perimeter to witness the carnage. Accepting a gleeful sigh, the first he had had in months, he pointed at the ground.

The leech had remounted Dinger's boot.

"Mercy, I've heard of blow-jobs," Fish said, opening his pants to inspect his tools. Satisfied, he said, "Leech Dick. That's your new handle. I like it." Ski gave a nod and the christening was complete.

With four medics coaching the day with howling gestures, Doc Taylor said, "Dinger, you're gonna bleed to death. Maybe I should cauterize your dick. Put mosquito repellent on it and light it."

* * *

With river noise in the background, Stubbs checked Rap's outpost facing the river. Back in the nest, he cleared the leeches from his foxhole, checked his cock for drill, and lit a bedtime smoke.

Three men in First Platoon had sworn an oath.

Their secret was a brutal one.

A mist lay on the valley, giving it a look of calm. A metallic sound ran down the river: rocks banging together. Maybe Chuck was on the move. No cigarettes. No hot coffee.

Twilight brought that muted hue when the human eye is blind but for an occasional illusion. A tunnel had formed over the river, filled with a glowing mist. Twilight stood-to with GIs sharing their hope for another day, searching the tree line on the far side of the river.

The moon was just past full and there would be no moonlight until the early hours.

Mental pictures of the open floor of the Crow's Foot sparred with the abandoned roadway that led into the Fishhook. Lanterns hung in rows from an even border of manicured trees. Half-lit faces were searching the finger valley. The company was being followed. A sound came crashing. Blood said it came from down-river. Rap's sound came from up-river. Amps cussed their stupidity, claiming Fish would shoot them at first light.

"Oh, Jesus. I'm still bleedin."

Listening to a murmur bounce from foxhole to foxhole, Hardin cussed himself for not keeping his mind in real time. The dense jungle masked the lanterns and the valley core was hollow. Incoming sounds had no bearing. Camping near the Fishhook was not a good idea.

The river cast intermittent shafts of starlight at Hardin's face. The jungle's muslin facade was laced with suspicious seams. Shadows danced in circles. At first he dismissed the movement, but the figures kept their form, walking.

Enemy troops were on the move, stalking the river bottom, pressed against the far tree line for cover—black on gray.

Footsteps, forty meters long, marched with a determined pace, heading south, away from the company, heading out of the valley. "Where's your lanterns, Chuck?" Hardin said softly. Pops called for a fire mission and the artillery recon sergeant fired a battery-one when the last figure passed dead center, sixty meters downstream. There were no screams.

* * *

A predawn recon revealed no trace of the enemy. At daybreak the company ran across the river in a single burst. After laying up for a time, they worked their way west toward the barb of the Fishhook, destroying small, isolated cornfields.

With a laager on the south side of the river, Hardin gave Bowe a night ambush. Bowe gave the ambush to Dubitski and continued to cook his dinner.

"You got everything, Dubitski?" Stubbs asked.

"We're good to go, Top."

"You takin' a gun?"

Dubitski shook his head and adjusted his sleeves to hide the neon stripes. "We're better off light with Claymores and frags." He's a cocky one, Stubbs thought. He'll take a gun next time. "Piece-a-cake." Dubitski would run the night ambush with precision: nine men, nine M-16s. With a sense of purpose, he resumed his preparations.

"What route are you takin' to the bush site?" Hardin asked, extending his hand. Dubitski laid out a small section of map sheet.

"We're gonna backtrack 300 meters to make sure the company hasn't been followed. We'll cross the water just east of this small island, head north to a rally point in this grassy area." Dubitski spoke with a determined voice, totally immersed in the ambush mission.

Hardin pointed at the map. "That trail runs the length of the river, near the bank on the north side. Chuck will be movin' durin' stand-to. Best be to ground before twilight."

"We gotta go." Hardin grabbed Dubitski's forearm.

"The password's rawhide. If you rawhide, how are you comin' in?"

"We'll rally up on the east end of that small island and hide until sun up. If that doesn't work, we'll keep comin' to this side and lay up. If they're still chasin' us, we'll be comin' back the way we went out." He pointed east, down river.

"Make sure the OP knows." Hardin nodded and started to rise.

"We're good to go."

"I know that. Plot the nearest artillery def-con—def-con four." Hardin shook his hand. "Good luck." His grip matched his expression.

"Roger that." Dubitski said. The former captain of the most elite sky diving team in the world, the Army Golden Knights, nodded his understanding. Camouflage might hide a man's expression, but his fear was in his step. One by one the members of the ambush slipped into the jungle. They didn't expect to return.

"Old man!" Hardin's tone stopped Dubitski's turn. "This war does require some luck, and for you there may not be enough."

Hardin stood mute, watching the perimeter prepare for stand-to, with Sweet Cheeks' shroud line and Joe's drive-on rag telling him to pay attention. Tennessee handed him a fresh cup of coffee.

"Where'd ya get that pussy necklace, you faggot? No radio operator of mine is gonna wear beads." Tennessee found a choker and a naked smile while on R&R in Thailand.

"My playmate gave 'em to me for luck."

"Well, your dick didn't dissolve so they must be workin." Hardin gave the beads a close inspection. "They're fake. She's a whore."

"You don't know shit," Tennessee said, stirring his chili Lerp, stabbing at the beans, trying to gin up an exclamation. "Say somethin', Amps."

"She didn't shoot ya like the last one," Amps exclaimed, sharing a nod with Stubbs.

"Damn, Squeak shouldn't of told y'all that story, of all fuckin' people." Tennessee opened a can of spiced beef and dumped it into his chili. "If I'd 'a invented this can opener, I wouldn't be sittin' here listenin' to y'all go on about shit that crossed your mind."

Tennessee was right. There weren't any Jewish names on the company roster.

"You ever think about that?" Hardin said.

"What?"

"How things cross your mind."

Tennessee looked at the radio, wishing someone would call so he could tell Hardin to piss off. Then he looked at Amps as if he were going to kick him into the middle of next week.

"What are you talkin' about?"

"Do things run across, or walk across your mind?" The radio barked.

"Charlie Kilo, this is Lima OP. The bush is wet, over." The call gave Tennessee a respite while he added more Tabasco and cheese to his dinner.

"Roger, out," Tennessee said, gathering his argument. "In your case, Captain, thoughts just stumble and stumble, haulin' bags of shit. Buncha shit is all there is."

"Where's Collard?" Hardin asked, pointing at Leech Dick's bloodstained crotch.

Tennessee stood, swallowing as he did. "Collard got transferred to Echo Recon. Taylor's the senior medic. Fish is callin' him 'Far-Out-Jim,' in honor of Hippie."

Running with a sense of shame, Hardin's service had become a function of accelerating isolation. He scrutinized the new men with suspicion, regretting his mistrust. Kind words drew illusions of threat, as he factored outcomes, conspiracy upon conspiracy. He was losing his grip without the vaguest idea how to hang on. For him, Vietnam's war had been a hopeless exercise.

Doc Collard said good-bye and his mind hadn't let the man go.

Hardin expected to find his medic sitting on his rucksack with his shirt off and his butt tucked against a clump of bamboo, grinning over a canteen cup, with heavy eyebrows and stubble beard, and a black headband at his forehead, its ragged tails hanging across his chest, and a loose piece of rawhide around his neck. Doc Collard's grin was his challenge; a reminder that authority in combat was a gift from grunts like him.

As his heart rate eased, laughter embraced Hardin's eye, and he grabbed a handful of dirt. "I forgot we said good-bye. Did Joe know their names?" Hardin's hand swept the perimeter.

"Captain Joe knew every man's name," Tennessee said.

Hardin stared for a time into his coffee cup. Alone, he desperately wanted to be demoted, to be Lima again. "As soon as we get a slick, I want Ski sent out."

"Look at Wallers," Tennessee said, talking with a mouthful of beans.

Hardin grinned with a sigh. "Wallers is a saxophone player. Says the Army turbo-fucked him. Says he's suppose to be playin' a saxophone in Saigon." Hardin sipped his coffee and continued. "Made him a deal. If he gave it six months, I'd cut him loose."

Hardin looked at Tennessee, and said, "What do ya think?"

"Is he any good?"

"Who cares: long as he's makin' it?"

Amps raised a finger, and said, "Makin' it easy, that's what my mom used to say. Makin' it easy, that's what counts." Hardin stared at Amps as if Amps had invaded his father's den. "Making it easy." His father raised his finger when he said those words.

Sunset's orange, flat sky brought an odd sense of warmth that lasted until the jungle turned black and swallowed the river.

* * *

American Legion Hall. Bremerton, Washington. September 1953.

A freestanding no-vacancy sign was posted on the sidewalk by the steps leading to the front door of The American Legion Hall. The boarding rooms were full of sailors and marines. Some of the rooms were home to as many as four veterans at a time. A veteran was squatting to one side, begging for food. The Major acknowledged the 29th Infantry Division patch on his right shoulder and gave him a dollar.

"That was a hard way to go," the Major said. "I hope he makes it."

Eddie and his father no longer strolled casually along the sidewalk from the YMCA to the American Legion Hall. The streets of Bremerton had changed. The Major's grip was firm. He held his son's hand nearly to the wrist. Eddie sensed the change. The veterans were rude and angry—no longer the happy-go-lucky men anticipating the fight.

Their time at the Legion Hall started as it had for two years. More men sat at the bar these days, arguing over one thing and another. A last game of pinball was lost when a marine pushed a sailor off a barstool to make room for his girl.

The Major set his drink down and covered the distance to the bar in three strides.

"Are you hunting trouble, young man?" he asked. With a hint of a grin, his eyes centered on the marine's head. "If you are, it's your lucky day."

"Beat it, Pops," the marine said, reaching for the man on the floor.

"You don't want to make things hard for yourself. You don't want to touch that sailor," the Major said, moving within range of the marine.

The marine looked at the Major, and said, with a nodding motion, "All right, Pops, you can take the beating I was going to give him."

The Major circled left and the marine started to jab. The Major kept moving to his left.

"Show 'em how hard things can be, Major," someone hollered.

When the marine threw a combination left-right, The Major pivoted on his right foot, leaning back with his left arm straight and about forty-five degrees to the floor. The Major was leaning back at forty-five degrees with only his eyes showing above his shoulder.

The marine threw an overhand right at his head. He pivoted down, under the punch, and then to the left. Using the power of his turn and his right leg, he drove a right hand deep into the man's spleen. Then, in one fluid motion, he reversed the pivot and drove a left hook into the man's jaw. With the crack of an axe, blood-red teeth rattled against the front of the bar and the marine collapsed in a heap, gasping, blood streaming from his mouth.

The Major stepped into a full squat near the man's head and with no emotion said, "You jarheads sure like to do things the hard way. You learn some manners. If you come around here again I'll take out the rest of your teeth."

The Major stood, working the kinks out of his left hand. "Let's go home, Pal."

When they reached the door of the bar, someone said, "Thanks, Major."

The Major didn't look back. Driving toward Ernie's Service Station, he said, "Learn how to take care of yourself, Pal. It makes life easy. Making it easy is what counts."

"I will, Pops." The Major's knuckles were out of place. When the car turned off Admiral Perry Avenue onto Highlands Road, Eddie said, "How come the veterans are so mad these days, Pops?"

"I'm not sure, Pal. We lost the war, and there's thousands of men still missing."

* * *

Charlie Company Night Laager. The Fish Hook. 2015 Hours.

Hardin searched the depressions in the vegetation bordering the river, the wooded recesses, and the like. Night's deeper shadows had turned these dens into black holes. The valley twisted and turned, opening at each finger valley, then forcing travelers back to the river with narrow draws and dense jungle.

His map was accurate. The valley was shaped like a fishhook, with the shank running north and south and the hook turning west. The barb sat in a tight draw at the head of the valley, in the shadow of a steep ridge. His foxhole sat at the top of the hook, facing north. The Fishhook was a longer version of the Crow's Foot, and just as remote.

The landing zones for extraction were in the open river. The routes of withdrawal from the finger valleys led back to the river. The deeper the penetration, the fewer alternatives the company would find. "Living with fear is a terrible thing," he whispered, scanning the riverbank, waiting for the worst. When the trees along the far bank moved, he rubbed his eyes and looked off angle, using his peripheral vision. Nothing.

Ninety minutes past twilight, Hardin moon-eyed with millions of stars, fire erupted from one and then a dozen weapons. Muzzle flashes lanced the scrub grass near the river's edge, illuminating the jungle for a moment so brief that, except for the noise, no one would have noticed.

"Charlie, November Five, we shot somebody. We're pursuing." Dubitski was running in close tack. Concentration filled his voice. The handset magnified his breathing and the crashing sound of foliage. Amps waited without responding.

"Charlie, we got blood trails running up the valley. Request permission to pursue." Hardin's mind raced. No Claymores had been fired. Dubitski's ambush wasn't set, or he got surprised. Maybe both.

"Negative—roll up and move west along the blue-line and reestablish."

"Roger that."

Morning brought Dubitski and his men back through the ambush site to confirm his suspicions before joining the company for extraction.

The choppers lifted off the riverbed into a glorious sunrise, complete with heavy mists billowing along the seacoast. Watching a Caribou climb away from the airstrip at LZ English, heading southeast, Hardin judged it to be the daily medical run to the hospital in Qui Nhon.

Andy would be back in the world by now.

The troops were held on the airstrip to get refit, and Hardin caught a ride to battalion for a briefing. After introductions, Maggie declared that his new radio call sign was Sector Nine and that the companies should stop calling him Three Yankee. Reinforcing the change, he posted a Sector Nine logo above the briefing map and began outlining the next operation.

Charlie Company would be placed under the operational control of an armored battalion to provide ground security for the armor, while an engineer battalion cleared a road through a valley, southeast of the Crow's Foot.

"Really," Hardin said. "And on my birthday."

"We got a party for ya, Captain." The armor battalion commander took charge of the briefing room with a clang, like he was accustomed to shouting.

Hardin's eyes conveyed his scorn. "Unfortunately, sir, my battalion commander isn't available. If he were, he might temper your sarcasm." The stranger stood instantly into a non-breathing brace, noticeably angry. Hardin's mind whirled with distrust.

"How old are you, Captain?"

"I'm twenty years old." Hardin didn't tell the man the truth, that he would soon be twenty-four. The stranger didn't ask a complete question, so he had it coming. Besides, the colonel had a Sandhurst canter, and Maggie was acting like his staff wean, sniffing after his boots.

The colonel's radio call sign was Iron Horse because, as he explained it, he rode an iron horse. While Hardin wondered if he was serious, Iron Horse outlined the operation using only the finest lingo, clattering on, gripping single-syllable words with jellied speech mechanics, pausing to allow the infantry's four-mile-an-hour, grunt-type brain to catch up with his fast-track tactics. His salvation would be the general misconduct of battle—that and a good driver.

"Is the operation clear so far, Captain?" Hardin set his eyes to a squint as Iron Horse ran his mouth into a grating tone. This colonel enjoyed being unfettered.

Hardin lumbered into the briefing lights and crossed his arms. "So far we've been inserted on a landing zone secured by tanks." Hardin shrugged. "Flat ground, twelve tanks, and Chuck's in the balcony eatin' popcorn." The colonel wasn't impressed with Hardin's impression as he careered away, excited over the prospect of writing Hardin's efficiency report.

"Once you're on the ground, Captain, my S-3 will bring out an op-ord and a route overlay for your mission." Growing more presumptuous, the stranger pushed a chair aside, put a well-polished boot on the chair next to Hardin, and folded his arms across his knee.

Hardin grinned and said, "Make sure you remember to route us through a blue-line now and then, and be mindful of our ground speed."

"We got it covered."

"We got it covered" was a phrase that colonels used when they wanted to say "No shit." Field-grade officers had refined their business and sanitized their art for home viewing. Where would America be if CBS caught a colonel saying "fuck" on the radio?

And where would Vietnam be without Walter's supervision?

"Please, Lieutenant," Walter would say. "You didn't blow Charlie's shit away, you shot him." *"Yeah, Walter, we shot him all right—into fucking doll rags."* Vowing to never salute the Iron Horse because the dumb bastard had stirred the echoes with his roaring, Hardin feigned a bit of servitude and headed for the airstrip.

"Dooley, what are you doin' back here?" Dooley was lolly-walking, aimlessly turning circles in the dirt in front of Delta Company's orderly room, trying to rewire his dick.

"R&R. I'm goin' to Australia for some white, blue-eyed pussy." Dooley gave his nuts a toss and waited for that heavenly surge.

"Takes both hands to ignite your power pack? I'm impressed."

"If goin' down under is as good as I hear, I might just use my whole basic load and extend for another tour." Dooley wouldn't go AWOL because the Aussies wouldn't let him.

"You find Grayson yet, Dooley?"

"You're a crazy dude, you know that, El Tee?"

"How's Pop and the rest?"

"They're still pissed about losin' Sam." Hardin flashed on Rapada's face, pushed himself off the sandbag wall, and stuck out his hand.

"Take care of yourself, Dooley." Dooley hesitated.

"Pop figures Buckwheat banged that deserter. Says Buckwheat found the dude's rifle."

"How come no one knows the man's name?" Dooley stared at Hardin for a moment, laughed as if Hardin should know, and walked away.

* * *

The company landed in a grassy clearing on the valley floor and set sail for the top of a small outcrop in the southeast corner of the valley. A massive rock wall ran north along the west flank of the valley into the heel of the Crow's Foot. A dense carpet of trees filled the east flank of the valley. The mountains were rough, rocky stubs, covered with single canopy jungle. A blue-line ran the length of the valley.

Hardin decided to search the blue-line first, then move across the valley and work a long finger valley running northwest toward the Crow's Foot.

Pops was serving chicken stew when the armor battalion operations officer flew into the valley to talk. Hardin decided to terrorize the man for interrupting his dinner.

"Blood, Tag, bring your teams." Fourteen GIs picked their way in silence through a hundred meters of scrub to the base of the promontory and popped smoke.

"Roger, Iron Romeo. We got green smoke."

"Lime is right."

The major moved with pronounced apprehension. His lightly starched fatigues, shoulder holster, leather message pouch, and polished boots evoked memories of the major in An Khe with the colored overlay. Hardin shook his hand and sat down in the open grass.

"We should move into the trees," the major said, scanning the landing zone.

"Chuck knows we're here, Major. Besides, your tanks were suppose to have this end of the valley secured." Hardin held out his hand and offered the man a patch of grass. "What's on your mind, Major Powers? My dinner's gettin' cold."

Major Powers searched at his back, sat through a half-turn to arrange access to his pistol, and opened his message pouch, handing Hardin an operations order, pausing to look over his shoulder again before he released his grip.

"You're not holding your breath, are you, Major?" Powers flushed red with anger.

"Read that op-ord, Captain. Study the overlay. Memorize the road construction route and daily objectives. The Old Man will be out in two days."

Hardin pointed at the operations order and said, "We don't use these things, so tell me what it says." Powers' eyes narrowed. He shook his head slowly and set his jaw.

"We're grunts, Major. We can't read."

"You're op-con to the armor. You work flank security missions in support of the road building operation. The overlay outlines the construction route. Clear that area first."

Hardin dropped the operations order in the grass, set the overlay on his map, marked six centering grids to trace the proposed roadwork, and handed the overlay to Blood. When Blood lit the overlay on fire, Powers grabbed the operations order and stuffed it into his pouch.

Hardin pressed on. "My call sign is Charlie Six. It's bad luck to change call signs."

The Army should have provided errors and omissions insurance to protect the paper majors from clients who ignored their papers. Powers wanted Hardin to keep the five-paragraph operations order because it was a numbered secret document marked number eight, and Hardin's name was on a list of people Iron Horse wanted to bless.

Powers' problem was keeping Hardin's defiance a bigger secret than the contents of document number eight. Powers checked the brass grommet on his message pouch, twisted the grommet into place, and said, "Your call sign is Iron Horse Romeo, Romeo for Recon."

Blood popped smoke less than a meter behind the major, forcing the man to his feet.

"Like I said. Changing call signs out here is bad luck, Major. If you want to talk, call Charlie Six. If you call someone else, I won't answer."

"Your call sign is Iron Horse Romeo, Captain."

"Fair enough, Major. I'm gonna call your boss 'Hot Wheels'."

Powers clamped the pouch under his armpit, adjusted his holster, and turned into the approaching rotors. He didn't believe the part about the call sign. No one, especially a young two-year disposable, would dare mess with the Iron Horse.

Tag nearly ran to the base of the outcrop, stepping high over ground that was choked with weeds and tangled grass. Pops had reheated the stew, anticipating their mood.

"Thanks, Pops," Hardin said. Pops nodded. "That steel pot is wearin' out your hair, Pops." Pops rubbed his head with an open palm. Boyle, Reynolds, and Lightning hovered in a tight circle, hoping for a spark that might trigger a response.

"You dickheads have been gang-bangin' LeCotte again, haven't ya?" By chance, LeCotte joined the group. "The New Point Queer's gonna be pissed. Right, LeCotte?"

LeCotte glared through the steam of his coffee, sipped to garner time, allowing his expression to roll into a conniving smile, and said, "The last time you were right, Captain, Jesus was makin' wine. Besides, queers don't care about a damn thing." Lightning nodded at Rap.

Lightning had declared that LeCotte was a queer after LeCotte refused to pull guard duty on bunker #1 with Reynolds and Fish. LeCotte's ranting over whores and such caused Lightning to step back, and the further back he stood, the queerer LeCotte became.

Lightning suggested to Rap that the brothers call him Lick Cock, to force his hand so to speak. Fish nixed the idea, assuring Rap that he knew the whore LeCotte was balling, and that Lightning wasn't old enough for the bush to be making suggestions.

Rap told Lightning to mind his own mother-fucking business and assigned LeCotte as his assistant gunner. Lightning didn't smile for nearly a week. Rap finally got pissed off and made Lightning and LeCotte stand in the same foxhole until they pledged to be friends and call the whole thing a joke. Lightning told Boyle he figured that LeCotte didn't like black men anyway.

Lightning held Ski's machine gun in the cradle of his lap, his coffee cup resting on the cooling chamber. Ski had watched him clean the gun, ensuring the parts were arrayed in proper order on a towel, reckoning that he might have to reassemble the gun under fire.

Ski didn't care for blacks much, but Lightning had a way of not being black. Ski had done what he could to challenge Lightning, deciding he could trust the tall, thin, silent man with the lives of his friends. When Ski handed him the gun, Lightning smiled a grateful smile.

Fish stood alone, the last of the Hill People humping the boonies. Before twilight, no matter the circumstance, Fish inspected Lightning's gun, just to let the tall, thin, silent man know that Ski was watching.

First Doc Collard, and then Ski. They had said good-bye and Hardin could not remember when or where. Ski, with his quiet smile and big, blond frame, had vanished. War time, dinnertime, sometime, next time. Hardin was worn out.

Ski crossed his mind and smiled. He never did say much.

Construction security was a series of boxes run at odd angles, mixed with an occasional stationary positioning. The noise from the bulldozers consumed the valley and masked the keenest sensor. Searching the dense underbrush of the valley without being able to hear took a toll. At twilight of the third day, the company crossed the valley and laagered near the blue-line.

Hot Wheels flew in thirty minutes later to bless their supper meal.

"Captain, sit down." Hot Wheels didn't realize his visit was forcing the company to move to an alternate laager before dark. "How come you're packin'?"

"Your slick made a lot of noise, Colonel. We worked hard to find good cover and concealment. We're gonna do it again, only quicker."

Hot Wheels didn't care.

"I want you to work the high grounds on this eastern ridge, make sure nothin's goin' on, no NVA base camps." Hardin studied the overlay. The route-recon covered the ridge above the blue-line, running a near-perfect north-south trace.

"We've already worked this blue-line from north and south. Chuck ain't here. There's not one sign from the water into that high ground. NVA are northwest, in the Crow's Foot."

"Work the high ground, Captain." Big Dog was giving Iron Horse Romeo an order.

"Roger that." Hardin handed the overlay to Tennessee who promptly lit it on fire. Pleased, Hot Wheels nodded, complimenting Tennessee's sense of security.

"We need water, Colonel, just like Chuck. This is the only water in this valley. The next good water's in the Crow's Foot." Hardin shook his hand, as if agreement led to allegiance, and the company crossed the water, moved uphill to a flat, and dug in.

"Six Yankee, this is Charlie Six, over."

"Sing to us, Charlie Six." Radio Man fancied himself as a lead singer.

"Get the Old Man on the horn." Hardin could hear splashes of "Dream Lover" in the background at the Tactical Operations Center.

"Roger, wait." Colonel "Wild Bill" Dimmick was short, another month at most.

Fifteen minutes later the radio barked. "Charlie Six, this is Six."

"These tankers are treatin' us like we're a bunch of niggers, and we're gonna shoot their Ops major if ya don't get us outta here." Hardin used the right word. Black Radio Man had the night shift at the TOC. The word would rivet his mind to the speaker.

"We'll bail you out tomorrow."

In the wake of the Old Man's blessing, Amps keyed the handset, singing, "Dream Lover, where are you? B-Do-B-Do. With a love, oh so true. B-Do-B-Do. I got your tit, in my hand. B-Do-B-Do. I'm gonna fuck ya, where you stand. Because I want, a girl, to call, my own. I want a Dream Lover, so I don't have to cream alone."

"Roger, Charlie Kilo. You got the Head Nigger here. The Old Man left the bunker shakin' his head, lookin' for a shot of whiskey."

"We're all lookin' for somethin', Radio Man."

The morning brought a sensation Hardin hadn't experienced since breaking up the brothers' boxing smoker in An Khe. Rap, Boo, Lightning, Butt, Boyle, Sax, Biggy, and raft of black cherries passed by his rucksack in a line, offering him a fist.

"Tol' the muthafucker. Ain't no niggers out here," Rap said.

Hardin held out both fists and Rap responded in kind. "We got an extraction in one hour, Rap. A three-day rest. Tighten us up."

Boyle stuttered out a happy birthday and stepped away. If Dig-it were alive he'd grab his canteen cup and slide into a rock'n'roll routine, singing his best

Tune Weavers' rendition of: "Happy, Happy, Birthday, Baby." Then he would slang Hardin's Fever of Unknown Origin, and laugh about the new crack in Hardin's cracker ass.

For Hardin, Black English, Street Spanish, and Southern Cornpone had become the same language—the language of his dearest friends.

CHAPTER TWENTY-SEVEN

Dyin's Easy

Landing Zone English. 0920 Hours.

Maggie, that vial of tactical glue, had a surprise for Charlie Company—an operational stand-down, a three-day blip inside the wire. The troops could enjoy a movie, go to town, have a shower, or call home: a no-hassle rest. Suspicious, Hardin headed for the TOC.

"The next operation must be a pisser, Maggie, you bein' nice to us grunts and all." Maggie moved his feet with certainty, scribbling arcs on his situation map with a grease pencil, trapping the ridgeline west of the An Lao River with a chain of green pushpins.

"Maggie, why the hell is your call sign posted above the map?"

"You grunts can't remember it."

"We can't see it, either." Maggie nodded and continued to work.

With surgical precision, a white pushpin found its mark. Maggie stood back to study the scenario. With a concluding sigh, he said, "The Old Man told the brigade commander nobody treats his people like shit. Threatened to run Starblazer out over some colonel's tank."

Maggie liked his new call sign. Sector implied a technical approach to Vietnam's war. Hardin decided to continue calling him "Three Yankee."

"Sounds like you've got other ideas, Major." Maggie turned on his stool. Hardin smiled. "You should let me buy ya a beer, Maggie. You know, swap some lies, comrades in arms."

Maggie smiled a fuck-you smile. "You find Chuck yet?" Hardin asked.

"No, I found you." Abigail was hard stitched to be a smartass.

"Your mind is like a typewriter carriage, Maggie. The part with any storage capacity keeps gettin' kicked back to the same spot, to start over. Sector Nine. Jesus, a spatial wizard!" Hardin left an accelerating trail of semi-dense gas deposited near the situation map.

* * *

Stubbs, Tennessee and Hardin drove a jeep to Bong Son the next morning to get a steam and watch the people. Shade trees reached across the sidewalks along Main Street, a strip of storefronts with trinkets, food, and a hallway to the steam bath out back. Brightly lettered signs in yellows, reds, and blues hung from the facades. Sandwich boards stood their ground, announcing the specials of the day, directing traffic.

Barefoot children worked the street, stealing and hawking their wares—virgins mostly.

The war didn't come to Main Street. The war came to the village across the river, across the rice paddy, the village one hundred meters hence.

GIs bartered for treasures. Laughter erupted in short bursts. An empty jeep stood guard, waiting for a key. Weapons hung on slings as if they were accessories.

A woman took Stubbs down a tight, boarded walk, through a patch of open ground, into a concrete enclosure with half walls and trellises on three sides. The concrete floor was spotless, worn to a smooth shine from decades of use. Three of the four shower heads were missing.

Naked, with his weapon lying on the bench next to his boots, he fought his paranoia. He focused on a palm tree, determined to escape. He thought the beer might be poisoned.

The woman washing him was built like a pile buck, her hands vigorous, gentle yet firm enough to throttle an iron pipe. He was forced to respond. He tried to watch as a mound of shampoo coursed across the floor, but he couldn't hold the thought.

Sitting in the shade on the verandah in a bamboo chair, looking east across Main Street, with a cold Coke in his left hand and his weapon cradled between his legs, Hardin let himself relax. Stubbs sat with a fresh, clean expression of relief.

"Stubbs, check out the dink." A Viet Cong look-alike, trailing a curl of dust as if tomorrow might be coming, caught Hardin's eye. He was holding the muzzle of a carbine he had balanced on his shoulder.

Blowing air across the top of his soda can, listening for the hollow sound, Tennessee said, "A dink is walkin' down the street in broad fuckin' daylight." Stubbs set his Coke down, brought his weapon to a horizontal firing plane, flipped the selector to semiautomatic, laid his metallic whore into the street across his left knee, and fingered the trigger.

"He'd be dead if we were in the weeds," Stubbs said, settling further into his chair.

"I can see weeds from where I'm sittin," Tennessee said, wandering what was next.

The town fell away as Chuck's sandals played double or quit in a hostile silence. Stubbs flipped his cigarette into the street in front of the man's stride. "He looks real to this GI." Stubbs set fire to another smoke, his eye fixed on the man's right hand.

Chuck caught sight of Stubbs' weapon and looked away. Tennessee tipped his boonie hat. Hardin ejected a round from the chamber of his weapon and slammed the bolt forward. Without a hitch in his stride, stoic, the man's shadow raced around his left flank.

"Whatever he's doin', he's done it before," Stubbs said, sipping his soda.

"Probably owns this steam creamer."

With steam all around, they drove back to the firebase. Three GIs, three steam baths—not quite the caliber of three on a match, but then, Normandy had religious equity.

* * *

Wondering why a light bulb would be much help, Hardin puttered about arranging a sleeping area in the corner of a sixty-foot bunker, singing to himself as if he were cleaning the garage at Number #10, Highlands Road. Dug into the hill across from the supply tent, the bunker looked like the press box of an old ball yard.

Complete with bunk and mattress, his place extended to a ring of mosquito netting that hung from the ceiling to the floor. His father's overseas trunk sat against the wall like an exposed crab. The day was devoted to cleaning and sorting the items in the trunk, building a small desk and a bookshelf, driving stakes into the sandbag wall to hang his weapon and rucksack, and posting a *Playboy* centerfold next to a new picture of his bride.

With a ripple of applause, Hardin stepped into a loving hush. This was home.

Linda's smile reached across the waves and made him cry. A warm sun graced her face as she stood in the driveway of her father's farm: Grandpa Karl's farm. The holly tree that provided garlands for the family fireplace, held her shadow, and framed her beauty. Smiling and waving to her GI, she was oblivious to the airbrushed tits mounted one sandbag to her left.

Linda's smile and softening beauty, now remote, were his treasures, more durable for their soothing nature. The other woman, his paper whore, had sexual obligations. She had volunteered to be in Vietnam, lusting for the privacy of a man's foxhole.

Linda would always be too precious to expose to the filth and realities of his thoughts, of his war, of his paranoia. Yet there she stood, watching, ready to forgive him with a warm smile and a dose of farm-bred patience. In the shadow of her smile he talked to his bride, thankful she could hear, not to witness his calamity but to caution his rage when the scars in a friend's eye met his own.

He saved loving wishes for his bride. He gave the centerfold a tongue lashing, promising to rumble-hump her foreparts with the biggest trick bullfrog she'd ever seen. A GI would lie in a heartbeat, even to a paper whore.

One certainty endured: Hardin needed this whore's friendship, her teasing illusions.

The sandbags leaked. With time, they would be reduced to layered dunes, trapping the centerfold. There would be no memorial for this woman.

The corner would be called Hardin's Place. He would read there, or write, enjoy a good wet dream, wonder the contours of *Playboy* tits, plan his R&R, try to sleep, to escape, to sing, wish for younger days, or close his eyes to find his friends—hopefully as they were.

Becoming a company commander had left Captain Edward Hardin subject to his own council. Isolated, he yearned for earlier times—with Squeak and Shadow and the rest. He needed a friend to help him with the war's most annoying wrinkle: hiding from his own orders.

Through fevered dreams he pledged to do his best to shape the outcome of the company's missions, and prevent five-sided immortals from orchestrating combat operations that would get his friends killed. He would use his field-polished guile to ensure tactics minimized casualties. Having completed combat's bar exam with a perfect score, Captain Edward Hardin had dedicated himself to unconventional tactics and lying to the Prince of Wales.

* * *

"What's up, Stubbs?" Stubbs stood-to, braced on the orderly room porch, talking to the Headquarters Company First Sergeant. Fish scurried by, carrying a case of beer.

"Top, how are ya?" Hardin asked the stranger. Shaking his hand, paying his respect to the tiny gold star on the stranger's jump wings, he detected an uneasy response in the man's grip, a tentative sensation. Stubbs looked away with sudden resentment, then spit bits of tobacco from the end of his tongue. Stubbs spoke, fostering a new smoke.

"The first sergeant here caught some of his troops smoking pot last night and wants to have one of them sent to the woods to teach them a lesson." Hardin's eyes leveled on Stubbs, then centered on the first sergeant.

"I didn't get caught smokin' dope and I've been in the jungle for nine months." Hardin paused to weigh the first sergeant's stones and caution the words he might like to offer.

Squinting to match a consequential tone, Hardin continued. "Why don't you come to the bush with this stud, Top, monitor our mobile stockade?"

"Is that what you jokers do back here, follow people around?" Stubbs asked.

When the stranger stood silent, Hardin drew on a practiced resentment and said, "How many studs were caught smokin' dope?"

"I didn't catch 'em. The berm commander, a major from brigade caught five of my men smoking in a bunker on the berm."

"We'll take all five, teach everybody a lesson—you included, First Sergeant." He started to object. "Don't tell me, Top. You can't spare 'em, right? You've got too many details to run. Burn a little shit, mail runs, radio watch, berm security, sandbag repair, supply runs, Batt Man's driver, KP. What else?"

"We can't spare 'em. Yes, sir."

"So you're gonna bone one man to shit-scare the other four into parade rest. Ya think they're gonna stop drinkin' and smokin' because one man gets sent to the boonies?"

"It's the only hammer we've got short of court martial."

"Sort of threaten them with a higher probability of death. A modern-day suicide mission. If they get caught again, these other four, do they get sent to the woods?"

"I don't know."

"What's the stud's name? Doesn't matter." Hardin wondered if Top had picked a man.

"Pluketis, PFC."

Hardin looked at Stubbs and smiled. Stubbs nodded.

"We'll take Pluketis and any other soldier you have that can carry a weapon." Stubbs bounced a cigarette off the sandbag wall next to the orderly room. "Give him to Lima, Stubbs. We get him right away, or what?"

"No, sir, it'll be a few days. We're doing what we can back here. Maybe you could cut us a little slack." Top, the stranger with the gold star on his jump wings, a good soldier, stood-to. Like most of the infantry soldiers in Vietnam in 1968, he knew circumstance would prevail.

"We'll take him, Top." Stubbs wrapped a towel around his neck and began anxiously finger-coning his smoke. "Why Charlie Company?" Stubbs asked, cocking his head.

"Delta's got the deserter, Bravo's lost their captain, and Alpha's bad luck."

To emphasize his anger, Hardin pointed a finger at the first sergeant. "We've found more than a hundred punji pits. Plugetis will find his share. These paddy dikes and ridgelines are laced with intricate booby traps. Dinks hiding in spider holes. Do it right back here, Top."

"It's a mess back here, Captain. Take my word for it."

* * *

Enjoying the smell of diesel required a distraction. Hardin read the *Stars and Stripes* in the latrine to avoid the reality, never for the box scores. Halfway through a story about the Boston Red Sox, a wad of Sergeant Walker's recon troops clamored from their tent and raced off toward the TOC, pulling on their uniforms, dragging weapons and ammunition pouches.

A GI's voice leaped from the speaker of the TOC radio, pleading for his life. The pleas intensified, laced with shell-fire and the roar of small-arms fire. The screams stopped. The men in the TOC listened, stunned. As if from across a grassy plain another distant plea echoed through the bunker. AK rounds snapped from the speaker. Echo Recon's radio operator lay in the river, his fist squeezing the handset. The frequency open.

Gunship fire burst into a series of agonizing groans, only to give way to the sounds of another GI screaming from the speaker, begging for God to spare his life. Pinned down in the upper reaches of the An Lao Valley, where the steep jungle walls turned black, bleeding and out of ammunition, he began to make his peace.

"Tell my mom I love her..."

Running up-river at full throttle, the first set of extraction choppers were shot full of holes trying to land near the barb of the Fishhook.

"Echo Recon's pinned down in the Fishhook. Walker's hit." Uncle's voice swept the bunker to attention.

"Dyin's easy," a recon soldier said, throwing his gear against the wall.

"Somebody's gotta take a six-pack in. Starblazer's got a light team on station. There's another two gunships haulin' out of English North in zero five minutes," Uncle said.

Hardin ran through the bunker, kissed his fingers and extended them toward Linda's picture, gave his paper whore a nudge, grabbed his Claymore bag of magazines, his bush hat and M-16, and then ran to the chopper pad. The slick labored into the air and slid sideways out over the wire. Twilight was closing in.

Fuck, you're stupid, Hardin said to himself, realizing he had left Joe's drive-on rag on his bunk. Perched in the right door behind the copilot, he looked at one face and then another, soliciting a commitment. These men of Echo Recon were strangers.

The door gunner looked familiar.

The slick mounted the plateau east of the Fishhook at treetop level and barged into the upper An Lao Valley, flying west toward the head of the valley at full throttle, into the teeth of the Fishhook at twilight. A mist billowed from the surface of the river, sparkling with shades of orange and red.

The air was dense.

The lush green canopy along the western ridge parsed the sun's rays. Long, narrow, black shadows lanced the valley floor, trellising the river's mist. Choppers bobbed in and out of the mist, scurrying away from the battle, only to arch over and dive again, belching red tracers. A plastic GI canteen ran below his boots, running from the fight, floating downstream.

Hardin sang louder and stepped out onto the right landing skid. White, fragmenting rocket trails hung over the battle. Muzzle flashes sparked in the shadows along the tree line. His door gunner opened fire. The mist billowed, exposing the dead radio operator.

The slick swung north around the gunship suppression fires, let the bottom fall out, and dropped into a tennis court sized grassy area at the river's edge. The grass was kinked, tinged into a neon flutter. Small-arms fire roared as their boots hit the ground. Fear ran to rage as the team scrambled to rescue their friends.

The lower part of Walker's jaw was gone. He was dead. Sprinting, changing direction when the rocks would allow, Hardin reached the dead radio operator. Blood and mucous filled his mouth. AK rounds snapped at the air, then ripped through the dead man's rucksack. Hardin threw himself over the body and pried the hand set free.

"Three Yankee, we got 'em. Fire red-leg fifty meters west of the insertion point and work it in, right-by-piece if you have to. We got dead and wounded GIs. We're gonna run, haul 'em downstream if we can." Another GI fell and started crawling across the river.

"Splash, Baby. Red-leg's on the way."

"Starblazer. Get these fuckers off me."

"Easy, Baby. We got the tree lines."

Walker and his RTO were dead. So was Dingo. Dingo's bowels were being pulled from his body by the flow of the river. Two of the remaining five men in Alpha Team were wounded and screaming with fearful rage. One by one they had been hit. Walker was killed first; the radio operator was killed trying to pop smoke; Dingo was killed trying to drag Walker to cover.

Suddenly, as if sucked from reality, Hardin's mind was quiet. The river was peaceful. The impact of an AK round splattered pieces of the dead radio operator into the air. Hardin screamed a silent scream. Leaving the pieces, he grabbed the dead man's collar. Running, he was dragging the body, to where he did not know.

A slick entered the fight from the riverside of the clearing and bounced on the rocks in front of Hardin. The Plexiglas bubble was shattered, hanging in shards. The copilot struggled with his shoulder wound. The door gunners fired. Rocket and machine gun fire drummed from Starblazer's four gunships. An artillery barrage crushed the jungle on the far bank of the river.

Hardin's radio operator was blown off his feet. He was dead.

The noise, the confusion, the chaos, accelerated into slow motion. Pairs of GIs dragged their friends through the open river, forsaking life. Walker, Dingo, Walker's radio operator, and four wounded were loaded on the dust-off, leaving seven studs running down the river dragging the second dead radio operator.

AK fire roared in front of the patrol. Another enemy squad had joined the fight.

The recon team scrambled down the tree line near the river's edge, dragging the dead man face down, the radio still strapped to his back. His feet hooked the large rocks and vines. His life energy expended, he happily bounced over the rest.

"We're runnin' down river. Come on, baby."

"We got ya, Recon." Goldfinger fired 40mm rockets. He wasn't singing this time.

Enemy small-arms fire exploded when the team scrambled through an open stretch of river, tucked against the jungle on the southern bank, running, dragging their dead. Screaming, falling, firing in desperate fury, one man and then another fell. RPG fire came from a third location across the river.

With two men wounded and one man dead, Hardin took the team into the jungle to find cover. They went to ground and waited.

"Don't let the bastards get across the river." Tree limbs and vines shattered like glass above Hardin's head. Splinters of bamboo pierced his right forearm. The pain seemed to warm his body. Time stopped as he pulled a pencil-sized shaft from his arm.

"I hope the fuckers try," Starblazer screamed.

"Uncle, we need some help. Get us outta here."

"Extraction's inbound with a third gun team. Be cool, Recon," Uncle said, his voice steady.

"We're comin,' Recon. Be cool. Cover our tail, Starblazer."

"I'm shootin' dinks in the tree line on the north bank," Starblazer chimed.

The extraction slick flew in over the top of Starblazer's suppression fire and started a full-speed tactical hover down with the bubble pointed at the patrol, the outboard door gunner firing across the river. Two men hoisted the dead radio operator out of the river onto the cargo deck, then scrambled into the chopper, firing over his body.

Hardin crouched low on the right skid. Overloaded and taking fire, the slick hovered into the open river, accelerated through a left turn, and nosed down, gaining speed, flying east even with the tree tops, door gunners hosing the vegetation along the riverbanks.

Heading east, forever east, water fell away from Hardin's boots. His forearm ached. The bamboo splinter had reached to the bone. Blood pooled on the cargo deck. Two more GIs died in the Fishhook. The gunships covering the extraction trailed by 400 meters, firing tracer rounds into the jungle along the north bank of the river.

Like a cork, the extraction chopper popped out of the valley and leveled out over the plateau. Hardin eased his butt onto the bloody deck of the slick and surveyed the faces of Echo Recon. Older, with their guise cloaked in a torrent of uncut gratitude and colored by the pigments of their trade, the hands not tied to a weapon searched for a reason to be still.

They would never escape the Fishhook.

A tear followed the seam between the light-brown and dark-green camouflage paints on the team leader's face. His lips quivered as he caressed the radio operator's hand. His friend would forgive him one day.

The crew chief and the copilot glanced at their cargo, counting, as if someone was missing. Hardin counted again—all accounted for.

Hardin stood-to, glad for living. His jaw was stiffening with hate. Pushing air from his exhausted lungs, he let his body collapse. After the moments required to release his fear, having run at the battle and lived, he knew the sounds of the firefight would merge with his unknown fever. He also knew that running from the Crow's Foot had been the right call.

The chopper's skids slid across the PSB in front of the aid station at LZ English. Hardin gave the door gunner a nod, then saluted the pilots when the slick lifted away. He stood near the door of the aid station, watching the remnants of Walker's team. Four silent men remained, smoking, guarding the dignity of their friends.

The screen door closed without a sound, their dead comrades out of harm's way. Shouldering their rucksacks, they concluded a whisper, gave Hardin a nod, and walked away, three men staring at the ground, one man looking toward the Fishhook.

"There's not much to say, Dad," Hardin whispered. "I'm damn tired."

Looking toward the mountains, Hardin thought of Nuts and Hippie and the men who fought the battle for Dak To. Examining the jagged crystal on his watch, Willie Spencer's watch, the second hand was bent, lodged against the tiny blue crystal that was the number three.

Gently Hardin straightened his friend. Smiling, with the second hand running free, on its way so to speak, like Sweet Cheek's shroud line and Joe's drive-on rag, Willie Spencer's watch brought Hardin peace... a totem for sure.

"Godspeed Willie," Hardin whispered.

The reporters weren't laughing when Hardin approached. With a nod he ducked into the aid station. Walker was a mess—satisfied, but a mess just the same. His body lay on Sam's steel table. His radio operator lay posted one step to his left. Dingo was on the floor, crawling with death. The medics cut away their rags, talking in a language no GI would cotton. Charts became scripture—eulogies that would stiffen in the stark light.

Hardin nudged Walker's boot, stepped around a pile of bloody bandages, and said, "See ya tomorrow, buddy." With his chest shaking, he took one of Walker's dog tags. For a moment he stood in the open doorway examining the latch on the screen door and the scars on the door casing. Looking back into the room, Dingo hadn't moved.

Hardin set the door as if he were closing the lid of a coffin.

A reporter offered his attention, assigning meaning to the engagement. "What happened out there, Captain?" His voice was sincere. *Perhaps he's a patriot too,* Hardin thought.

"How'd you know I was a captain?"

"Can you tell me about the firefight?"

Looking toward the mountains, he thought of the Major, his best Pal. Hardin took a deep breath, and said, "No I can't... ask the pilots. Maybe they know."

CHAPTER TWENTY-EIGHT

Prejudicial Allegations

Battalion Mess. Landing Zone English. 0610 Hours.

Fevered dreams racked the night, mixing memories and friends into battles that never occurred. Walker's fractured face lay in the mud. Bits and pieces of bodies arced into Hardin's foxhole. Soaked with blood, his father and brother held their ground, covering his retreat, yelling for him to fall back, the Major firing an M-2 carbine, his brother firing an AK-47. The Major's Victoria Cross, his VC, hung from a tattered purple velvet harness, posted near his heart.

Weary, he found the morning reluctant. The air was heavy with the coming monsoon. His feeble malice was fitting. He was spent. Chilled, he shivered, then bunched his eggs and shoveled them onto his toast. Walker was a man who couldn't die—highly trained, a seasoned warrior, tuned to the jungle's mood. Walker shed fear like a goose shed the rain.

Walker did not see the bullet's trace. His jaw was open, beseeching his God for providence. His knife lay buried in its scabbard. His radio operator's name lay on his lips. His voice, like so many others, rang from the Fishhook, yelling their warning: fair warning.

Praying that the monsoon would consume the balance of his war, Hardin thought of Linda and their baby girl. The thought died when Uncle dropped a document on the table stamped confidential, titled "Prejudicial Allegation."

"That reporter you punched out, the general's baby boy, filed an action. You're creating a paper trail." Uncle's face raced into a watchful expression.

"I'm a dead man, Uncle. That's all you gotta know." Without reading a word, Hardin pushed the papers aside and stood away from the table. "Make it easy for us, Uncle. Make it go away." Hardin left the mess tent, his eyes sullen, indifferent, embracing his time.

* * *

The morning roundup at the TOC featured numbers and praise. No names were spoken in honor of the Grunts killed and wounded in the upper reaches of the Fishhook. Kudos were issued for the agility of the air crews and the artillery, but not a whisper for Walker.

Maggie marked the Fishhook with his grease pencils, red then black, drawing arcs depicting the gun-target path of the 105mm artillery rounds fired from Firebase Corregidor. He characterized the fight, his voice fired with soldierly resolve. He lived the battle, reading the transcript of the radio transmissions, accenting the air and artillery support as the difference.

Hardin listened for the words he remembered. There were none.

Maybe Walker was alive.

Hardin caught himself staring at a stranger. My God, his teeth were white as snow. Nobody had white teeth. Maggie claimed the man was a naval intell officer from a ship scouring the coast of the South China Sea. Hardin didn't believe the man was intelligent. He was fat.

Recon required stealth. The slob he was staring at needed oxygen to drink a cup of coffee. When the wave jockey laid claim to the location of a weapons cache in the Tiger Mountains, Hardin laughed. He knew he was going for a walk.

With Maggie keenly puzzled, Charlie Company was inserted along with the overweight, port-side, white-toothed, gray-haze type in tiger fatigues, and spent the day fortune hunting 400 meters of a dingle with flanks that ran eastward into the sea.

"Maggie, Charlie Kilo here, we have no street signs, no weapons, and no shit, over."

"Roger, Charlie Kilo. You got a 0900 extraction, pick a spot, over."

"Where are we goin'?" Stubbs asked, checking his map.

"Firebase Corregidor."

Stubbs dropped the hook in Tennessee's lap. "Hornblower's gonna spend the night." Hornblower's face turned gray, his posture apologetic. A night with LeCotte would be payback for the bad intelligence. LeCotte's sarcasm was relentless.

Blood offered to graze Old Blue with one round so the man would have a war story. Pops told Old Blue that LeCotte was a queer, and warned him that LeCotte liked fat guys the best.

Old Blue sat through the night, watching LeCotte sleep. Kissing the airstrip at LZ English, his chest was heavy with windy enthusiasm.

* * *

Charlie Company touched down at Firebase Corregidor to find an artillery battery naked in a bald crucible, encased in jungle, atop a flat rocky ridge. Hardin and Stubbs stared in silence, evaluating the outer defenses of the base. The clearing was so small; pallets of artillery ammunition were stacked outside the wire on the chopper pad. Foxholes consisted of sandbag hovels strewn about like cow pies.

On the west and north, a coarse, dry, waist-high grass bordered the wire that arced in a random trace, governed only by the encroaching clumps of bamboo. The interior of the firebase was bald, cleared to the ground. The fields of fire were perfect if you worked for Chuck.

Walking in a self-contained way, as if nothing could claim his attention, Stubbs' eye caught an odd pattern in the grass outside the wire. Whispering, he looked in the direction of a breeze as if he had a notion of following it. He laughed and looked away. He had been talking to himself for so many months, talking to himself out loud was natural.

The air touching his face carried a certain motion, a vibration alerting a heightened sense of being. "Dillon—get us some firing lanes," Stubbs said, inferring an order. He lit a cigarette and continued. "Run a clover up this northern flat, 400 meters."

Boo fell into the wire, cussing and throwing his equipment.

Dillon laughed. "What else?"

"Burn the grass. Get us good fields of fire."

Unable to sleep, Hardin became an astronomer. The North Star worked its way around the heavens. Being isolated in the hinterlands provided a measure of autonomy. Morning stand-to brought wisps of fog and a colony of monkeys hollering from a neighboring ridge.

The firebase stirred with scripted confusion, a duel between impetus and inertia, an infantry company and an artillery battery dangling on the end of a radio wave, stemming the red tide, ridding the world of dead plankton, a "Roger-out" away from desertion.

"Charlie Six, this is Sector Nine, over." Maggie's voice was intrusive.

"Charlie Kilo, go." Amps gave Hardin the hook with an expression of mock allegiance. "He's excited about somethin."

"Charlie Six, we have good intell either Corregidor or LZ English is getting hit tonight. It's reliable, over." "Reliable" was a word specific enough to have been a whole number in another life. GIs never used this kind of word.

Hardin drummed a measure of concern and said, "Send out ten cases of Bangalores and 300 feet of det-cord, over."

"Wait one. It'll be there by 1100 hours."

A Bangalore torpedo was a six-foot long, steel-encased cylinder of C-4 plastique explosive, designed to breech barbed wire barricades. When assembled into a dense web and tied together with detonation cord, the Bangalore would clear cut most ground covers.

Blood and Rap assembled the Bangalores into six steel fingers radiating from the northern wire like a fan. The fingers lay ten feet apart near the wire and thirty feet apart at the outer end. Every other finger was booby-trapped with a fragmentation grenade. Stubbs checked the grenades, scattering brush along the fingers for camouflage.

Blood tied the fingers together with det-cord, wiring the assembly into a ring-main. Stubbs wired a blasting cap to the det-cord, then tied the blasting cap to a Claymore firing device. If Chuck gathered for an assault in the midst of this radial plume, he would die in a two-and-a-half-amp surge.

* * *

At 0218 hours, LZ English North was hit with mortar and small-arms fire. The attack lasted less than an hour. The intell report was accurate. With the first rays of light, the company stood-to in their firing positions, waiting, watching for movement, looking for symmetry, and listening for the haunting, progressive rhythm of boots.

Stubbs crouched near Hardin's shoulder with a steaming cup of coffee and a smoke. "Sure be a waste. I say we wake the artillery boys for a spot of tea." Stubbs laughed while his humor clumped around, waiting for Hardin's response.

"Why not."

Stubbs grabbed the clacker and ignited the northern approach. The explosion consumed the vegetation in the kill zone and filled the air with dust and debris. Stubbs held his tools, howling as artillery types hollered, plowing from their bunkers, itching to fight, picking at their focus, rummaging their gun emplacements, bracing for the assault.

"They're gonna remember this," Stubbs said, lighting another cigarette.

The company had been alerted for extraction to fly back into the An Lao Valley for a six-day cruise. Hardin flashed on Walker and the battered faces of the recon team.

"Amps is gonna pack the company radio. I'm gonna do the battalion net with Leech Dick." Tennessee's proclamation packed the typical twang.

"Three southern white boys—Leech Dick, Tennessee, and Amps."

"You'd still be a platoon leader if it wasn't for us."

"Tennessee, I thought your R&R would take the pressure off, but it only changed the texture. You're no longer that obedient scout with that appaloosa stride. Caesar must mind the Ides of each day's feeding. Soon it will be high noon."

Amps looked at Leech Dick, blew bubbles into his coffee, then whispered to his rucksack. Finally he said, "What in hell is he talkin' about?"

Tennessee stood and laughed through a huff. "Who the hell cares what he's talkin' about. Get a commo check. Dubitski's got the last lift."

Tennessee was forcing Hardin to challenge his limits or acknowledge his power. Hardin left without speaking, traced the perimeter of the firebase inspecting the wire, wondering why anyone thought wire would help, wondering why he was guarding a hole in the jungle.

Mud-bound on a remote hilltop, guarding the twisted trace of freedom, each GI, in their own way, was gratified. The faces of friends long gone were in the final stages of recovery; less anguished than they were last week.

History wasn't an issue in Vietnam's war. None of the reports could be verified.

Firebase Corregidor looked small and vulnerable as they lifted away, like a divot in his back yard. He could shoot his plastic soldiers from behind the barbecue. Then he could leave them in the mud and go eat dinner.

* * *

The insertion choppers flew over a grass plateau and landed in the riverbed. Four nearly naked enemy soldiers lay in the open grass, their swollen bodies baking in the sun.

"Hey, Amps," LeCotte said, "That's the honey who gave Tennessee those sissy beads. She's waitin' for ya to get a three-day pass." Amps spit a disgusting gesture into the handset.

Girlfriend's reason was swelling, begging for his attention.

Running as one along the shank of the Fishhook, GIs ducked into the tree line on the west flank of the valley. Dillon took the night ambush.

Stubbs studied the river from a small rise. His vantage was framed by matching clumps of thin bamboo strung with broad-leaved ivy windsocks. The continuous flutter and close proximity of the ivy made it difficult to keep his eyes focused on the far riverbank. Enemy soldiers could move undetected in the star shine with even a breath of air.

A pair of tall, thin trees stood near the river like naked logging spars. Chest-high grass swirled at the base of the trees. Flashes of yellow and green pierced the perimeter as shadows fell across Tag, then Pops, then Blood and Fish.

Fish gave Pops a nod and slipped into the water. The valley pulsed with a change of mood. The wing beats of a flock of birds seemed to draw the air with them, inviting those willing to come along. Reynolds stopped in mid stream. He had seen the faint outline of a bush hat off to the left flank, in the tree line.

Fish pushed the ambush patrol out of the open water.

The Major's war had certainty, Hardin thought. White, blue eyed Austrians were from a more civilized underworld, where the closet doors had pneumatic closures with audible latches.

Hardin was startled into focus by the crack of the handset. "Six, this is Lima." The ambush was across the river. "We've got beaucoup signs headed east, over." Amps nodded, searching for instructions. From the Crow's Foot, dead men chased Hardin with their lanterns and their shadowed eyes. He was firing blanks.

"Fish, your radio push needs cleanin."

"Roger that."

"Think about pussy." Amps turned off his radio and took the handset apart to clean the contacts. Five minutes later he was back on the net. He raised his canteen cup and a fraternal grin creased Tennessee's face. Grits could bond many a personality. Ham and lima beans worked the same way. GIs who ate grits stuck together; they had to.

"You notice how we sound alike, Stubbs?" Hardin asked. "The brothers, Mex, the boys from Dixie—a bunch of cornpone, grits-eatin' horseshitters?"

"Nothin' wrong with bein' from Alabama."

A moment before dark, a lone Huey crested the ridge at the head of the Fishhook, its silhouette stark against the sunset, framed between the ridgeline's trace and a band of thinning clouds. Stubbs listened to the rotor blades pushing the airframe, the nose of the chopper was cocked to the left, the air crew's simplicity, simpler than the men he could see.

Warmed by the chopper's sound, Stubbs exchanged words with his coffee and organized his ammunition. In a fit of regret, the new battalion sergeant major had given Stubbs reason to fear. Maggie was obsessed with finding the deserter, and was determined to push for a resolution. Translated, Stubbs knew GIs were going to die hunting for a dead man.

Screams from the radio broke into the night with the essence of entropic passion. The quiet of the ambush erupted into a roar of small-arms fire and frags. Fish barked orders in rapid succession. The firefight ended as it started, with a surprise: Chuck had vanished. Dubitski landed at Hardin's side, ready to make a run to relieve the ambush. No Claymores had been fired.

Amps keyed the net. "Fish, tell me a story." Hardin grabbed the hook.

"Hard tellin," Dillon said, gasping for air. "Looks like Chuck spotted us settin' in. Turned our Claymores, then jumped out of the weeds, hollerin'. Fish saved our ass. We got nine rucksacks. I don't think Chuck had any weapons." Tennessee was translating for the TOC.

"Rollup and run."

"Roger, we're steppin." No one slept in this pungent valley.

The ambush returned looking like they had not been forgiven. Stubbs started his debriefing with Blood and Fish. Rumors of a deserter sighting ran through the company. Fish told the story as if he and the deserter were friends.

Dillon sat down and took Amps' coffee, accepting a slow, chest-heaving breath and a head-shaking expression of near death. He was exhausted. "We set the ambush. Did it right, quiet, coverin' each other. Chuck must'a spotted us on the trail."

"Any chieu hois on the ambush?" Hardin asked. Dillon rubbed his face to liven his thoughts, then spit in Hardin's foxhole. He didn't like the inference. Hardin laughed to himself, remembering how he had dumped spaghetti in Captain Joe's digs.

"No. Fish went out to shit in front of his Claymore. The damn thing was turned around." Dillon drank the coffee in gulps, then glanced at the point squad working its way into the jungle on a clover to the south.

"Fish screams, 'don't fire the Claymores,' at the same time he's runnin' and hoistin' his pants, firin' his sixteen across the trail at who knows what." Dillon was fully animated as he ran spread-legged in place, mocking Fish's antics. "While Fish is divin' bare dick behind this tree, Chuck jumps up, hopin' we'd blow our rocks. Most of us opened up our sixteens, a couple of frags, couple of new guys just froze."

"What happened to Chuck?" Amps asked.

"Did you see the deserter?" Tennessee asked.

Dillon ignored the questions. His mind was back on the trail. "With no guns, Chuck must'a been packin' rice." Dillon held out his cup for more coffee.

"Boyle will be stutterin' this one for a week," Tennessee said, watching Boyle hand jiving Boo, Rap, and Lightning through a rendition of the contact.

"What were they wearin'?" Stubbs asked. The perimeter was alive with GIs organizing for the firefight they could feel coming downstream.

"Little of everything: VC fer sure."

"Anyone besides Fish see the deserter?" Stubbs asked.

"I don't think so."

"Fish is nuts," Stubbs said, forcing the hot ash from one cigarette onto a new fag. Fish was pushing the sighting and Stubbs didn't like it. The report would not be forwarded.

Trapped between two thoughts, Hardin's eye got caught in the flow of the river. He knew the jungle would consume the deserter. His body would rot in five to ten days, leaving a twisted cage of bleached bones clad in a black, open-work webbing that once was his skin.

Stubbs and Dillon were talking without making a sound. Then, as if plugged in, they became whole. Trying to shake himself free, Hardin stood.

"Fish is nuts," Dillon said, standing when Reynolds waved at him.

"Fish isn't crazy," Hardin said. "He checks his Claymore to refresh his mind. That stand-to ritual is a sanity check. He prays at night, too."

* * *

The company lifted out of the Fishhook and flew back to LZ English for a tour of berm security. They would occupy bunkers #1 through #18 for three days, then ship out. Bunker #1, the whorehouse, was on the south side of the dirt road that ran from downtown Bong Son, through the main gate of the firebase. Bunkers #1 through #8 faced south at rice paddy level, guarding 600 meters of rice paddy and a friendly village.

Bunkers #9 through #18 ran uphill in a northwesterly arc around the brigade headquarters and chopper pad. Bunkers #14 through #18 faced west and had hootches bordering the outer strands of wire. The South Vietnamese Army manned the bunkers around the airstrip on the east flank, and the rest were manned by GIs working on the firebase.

"We got problems," Stubbs said, seriously pissed. His cigarette bounced off Leech Dick's helmet. "Same-same, Ban Me Thuot."

"What are you talkin' about, Stubbs?" Hardin grabbed a case of C-Rations.

"Town's on limits, the whores are off limits." Stubbs lit a smoke and waited for a response. When he didn't get one, he started again. "Did you hear what I said, Captain? The general has put the town on limits and the steam baths off limits."

"I don't much care," Hardin said, wondering why his emotions were no longer touched by reason. Then he laughed. The whorehouses in London and Paris were always busy. Knowing the postulate founding Battle Bullshit would be in full fig when the company reached Main Street, he scrubbed at his face with both hands.

"Me and Tennessee are goin' to town ahead of the stampede," Stubbs said.

"I'm tired of this silly dance, Stubbs."

"Uncle left some papers for you to read in the orderly room."

* * *

General officers generated the longest paper trail in the Airspace because their toilet paper came in unwaxed, two-ply fibrous rolls of soft rectal sponge, which they used without regard to availability because they had aides to wipe their ass.

Grunts, on the other hand, had no paper trail. Their toilet paper was a stack of thin, single-ply, short-fiber, highly waxed, three-by-three-inch, bright white squares which they had to overlap ten deep to increase the surface area and prevent the jungle rot on their hands from penetrating their dysentery. And since these little squares were not attached and were in short supply, a grunt-type paper trail was discomposed, just like his war.

Can you imagine a general with a leech on his dick? General officers had no idea what Vietnam's war was about. And any officer who thought he was going to keep a GI from getting laid was nesting in another time zone. And he wasn't going to get Hardin's help.

Stubbs, Tennessee and Hardin took their steam bath on the lower east side of town. Freshly cleaned and sipping a Coke, they sat watching as the MPs rolled down Main Street. Spit shined, armed, and loaded with vengeance, these MPs would protect the troops from the critters that infested off-handed pussy.

A well-groomed MP sergeant barged past Stubbs and ran Reynolds from the back of the steam bath. The MP paused as he recrossed the veranda. With black cloth captain's bars on his bush hat, a grin, and an annoyed mind set, Hardin waited for the soldier to speak.

"You're their company commander," the MP said, his voice gusting to a pointless rise.

"I am their company commander. I did have a steam bath. And this Coke does taste good. Is there anything else you want to talk about, Buck Sergeant?"

"We're haulin' in your troops, Captain." Stubbs was up the pole, down the street minding four GIs who were trying to liberate another MP helmet.

"Well GI, the stockade has hot chow, and is a whole lot easier than an AK-47." The MP shook his head and continued his search.

"What do ya think?" Hardin asked. Tennessee grinned with spiteful satisfaction, gave his humping tackle a commemorative nudge, and stood into a pose.

"They'll never find Fish." Tennessee was bragging on his boys.

Hardin stood, finishing his Coke. "Come on, we're goin' back."

"What about Top?"

"He's busy. Let's go. I need some, R&R." Hardin was on the second chorus of "Silhouettes" when the jeep turned into the battalion area.

"PeeWee's back." PeeWee stepped out of the battalion aid station, bleached into a cherry by his hospital stay.

CHAPTER TWENTY-NINE

White Mice

Landing Zone English. 1800 Hours.

Berm security duty brought a phone call home to pick a date to meet Linda in early September in Hawaii, and Stubbs juggling the data in seventeen delinquency reports.

Some new men had joined Grumpy in Pops' kitchen: Packrat, Stormy Norm, Pebbles, Wolfman, Linus; some new Docs; Dulles and Cosmo, and a buck sergeant named Knapp. First Platoon was looking good. They didn't know it, but Hardin kept closer tabs on them than the rest.

Stubbs handed Hardin a beer.

"What's with the new battalion CO?" Hardin asked.

"Strac-lookin' big guy." Stubbs could talk, smoke and drink at the same time and still look like a soldier. "I think we're gonna miss old Wild Bill."

"Guess I better shave."

"He's been shod with brass shoes. Boot polish with a shiny smile."

"Won't matter." Hardin held up a finger. "The Gross Table could be in trouble, though. This could be serious. Maybe that's why Charlie Company wasn't invited to the battalion change of command ceremony."

* * *

Hardin wore a clean uniform to meet his new boss. The colonel was talking with Uncle and Maggie in the TOC briefing room. Hardin barged into the room without hesitation, extending his hand and his best grin. A look from Uncle was fair warning.

"Sir." The colonel snapped a curious smile, then blinked with surprise. Captain Hardin looked so young the colonel's West Point bus ticket started gusting in the wind.

"Captain, we finally meet. I've heard about Charlie Company." He was either checking for mumps or to find out whether Hardin had to shave yet.

"So have the Viet Cong," Hardin said, waiting for Uncle to muster a show of force.

Maggie hopped to the map, plugged in like a vacuum, ready to hum those hallowed bars of "Over There." Sporting scuffed boots and a tired grin, Uncle found himself a sanctuary for reflection. Of the three men running the battalion, he alone had witnessed Vietnam's moods. The new Old Man was a desk transfer from a five-sided go-down full of bad data, roistered by rings that weighed more than a GI's steel pot.

"Charlie Company is going to work the Tam Quan Valley with a detachment of White Mice. We think the White Mice can interpret what you find, better and quicker," Maggie said.

Hardin didn't like the sound or the inference of the words: better and quicker.

"What are White Mice?" he asked.

"District police." Rumor had it that the White Mice were assassins—the Viet version of the Gestapo, irresponsible and unaccountable. They killed civilians.

"Do your new toys speak, English?" Hardin asked.

"I don't think so." Maggie glanced at his new boss.

"What time, Maggie?"

The new Old Man took the floor. "From now on it's first light," he declared.

Holy shit, Hardin mused, *is that a hickey on the old boy's ring? Maggie's been busy.* Civilization had never survived first light, and by decree there was to be a new beginning, free of history, free of memorial thought. The new Old Man was delusional.

* * *

The landing zone in the Tam Quan was fenced on the north side with bamboo. Within minutes of insertion, Tag's chieu hois barber spotted a knot tied with a strip of bamboo on a fence rail, pointing into the next field. Working in grids, the barber collapsed the top of fourteen punji pits in a fifty-meter radius. Hardin noted that the Mice didn't find the knot or the punji pits.

The White Mice examined the punji pits and then went gunnysack, storming the village with high-pitched vowels and cigarette lighters. The hootches were on fire in seconds. Women were fleeing the village with anything they could carry—children mostly.

To a man the GIs fell silent, unsure of what to do. Assuming the worst, the shock of the carnage ran its course. When The Frenchman and Reynolds stopped a man with rucksack scars, the District Police beat him until he was unconscious. Then they started beating him again.

Hardin grabbed Leech Dick's arm.

"Call battalion. Get a dust-off, ASAP."

Blood and Rap pulled the Mice away from the prisoner. Defiant, a district policeman screamed in Blood's face. Blood buried the butt of his weapon in the man's skull.

Primed with hate, the Mice wandered in self-directed circles, countering the company's search with intentional noise.

Tag waited for Hardin at the far edge of the village. He was shocked. An old woman lay against the side of a well. Her throat was slit. Reaching for words, Tag could only muster his grief. She was so tiny. Tears stained her gentle face. A dead pig lay tucked under her arm.

Hardin had seen enough.

"Stubbs, set a laager right here. Good holes. Good OPs." With Stubbs staring at the dead woman, Hardin said, "Find a village elder and help with her burial." He grabbed the hook. "Three Yankee, this is Charlie Six. Get out here and pick up these rodent cops."

"First thing in the morning." Hardin expected more feedback.

With Stubbs and Reynolds on one flank and Blood and Fish on the other, the White Mice slept in an aggravated heap. Hardin's orders were clear—if they tried to leave, shoot them.

* * *

The Old Man landed during morning coffee with Maggie hard at heel, dragging an interpreter and a fist full of paper. Amps extended an invitation for coffee and crackers, waiting for a reason to ask them to leave. Maggie's urgency left him exposed: his goal was to iron out the tactical procedures for working with the White Mice.

Hardin's goal was to determine who was responsible for the operation.

Hardin relaxed his posture to ease the tension, then said, "We don't get many visitors: especially in the morning. What can I do for you folks?" He looked at Maggie to accuse him of treason. The Old Man weighed in with an expandable challenge.

"What's the problem with the White Mice?" The Old Man's tone camouflaged the operation's author, attempting to fix Hardin with the solution. Hardin decided a field demonstration of irrational behavior was superior to being subordinate.

"The District Police killed an old woman yesterday. They would have beat a man to death if we'd let 'em." The White Mice stood clustered near a well, talking to the interpreter, evaluating the conference.

Maggie jumped Hardin and said, "Maybe they don't understand what you expect them to do." Maggie was the culprit. The Old Man was going to let him run until he either stepped on his dick or accomplished the mission.

"You don't get the picture, Maggie. You either get those fuckers out of here or I'm going to shoot them. Either way, they're your fuckin' problem." The Old Man stepped to the side. Shocked by the intensity of Hardin's words, he knew now that combat was not a linear function, and staff-patches might be stupid.

"You're going to finish this operation, Captain," Maggie exclaimed.

"There was a murder in this village yesterday—an old woman. She didn't weigh more than ninety pounds. She was murdered when she tried to stop those bastards from killing her pig." Hardin stood into Maggie's face with an insistent rage. "I want a prejudicial allegation filed against you, Maggie. Murder sounds like a good rap."

"They've operated with other companies."

"Well, Maggie, maybe you're complicit in more than one atrocity. If you want to play guns, Maggie, then you and that pussy interpreter stay out here and hold their fuckin' hand. Otherwise, get 'em the hell away from me."

Anxious about what he'd heard, the Old Man had heard enough. Trapped, he didn't know if Hardin was serious. A prejudicial allegation initiated against his operations officer for any atrocity would find its way into his personnel file.

"You're right, Captain," the Old Man said. "An interpreter should be part of the team. We'll take the whole bunch back with us." Maggie would make Hardin pay for this public flogging. Escorting Hardin to a private spot, the Old Man asked, "What's the deal?" His voice was quiet, conspiring.

"You want to see the body? They slit her throat and let her bleed out. You need to get your boots closer to the ground, Colonel."

The Old Man sighed through a reluctant nod. He was not accustomed to being lectured. When he looked off into the rice paddy, Hardin said, "I'm not stayin' in the army, Colonel. If I have to, I'll ruin Maggie's career. Hard tellin' where that might lead. The men in this outfit are grunts, not murderers. Their honor is clean."

"Keep me posted."

The Old Man gave Hardin a pat on the shoulder, a rear echelon give-'em-hell, a gesture meant to curry temporary allegiance. He turned to leave and then stopped, remembering a question he forgot to ask. "The Headquarters Company commander said he sent a man to the field he caught smoking marijuana. How's that troop doing?"

Hardin spoke vigorously. "I sure hope he wasn't braggin'." Alarmed, the Old Man's expression became defensive. When he didn't respond, Hardin continued. "That man's name is Pluketis—Packrat, First Platoon, works point a lot, good instincts. He's as good as any GI, maybe better." Hardin paused, then said, "A grunt knows the smoke never lies."

The Old Man stiffened a bit, involuntarily looking at the White Mice, surprised by Hardin's comment. Then he cocked his head, and asked, "What about the dope?"

This question exposed the sterile rumblings of a centripetal mind, of Eastern men who could not overcome the gravitational force of the nightly tactical briefing.

Packrat smoked dope and would float in its scented curl for eternity—the axis of his life spent fighting a rear echelon fantasy. The headquarters company commander, that bag of bewildered dung, would be up to the eastward until Piccadilly ran out of whores.

The Old Man's face took on a puzzled look, startled by the sound of his voice saying the word "dope." Colonels liked to experiment with the English language when they were beyond the purview of their competitors. Speaking a four-letter word like "dope" loud enough for the troops to hear gave him a sense of belonging, a cosmetic meant to endure and melt the differences.

Tennessee, Amps, and Leech Dick met his utterances with vacant scorn. Grunts knew fancy men never shit their pants.

"Dope is a problem behind the wire," Tennessee said. "We've got too many booby traps to worry about. If you got more studs you don't want to share your grits with, send 'em out."

The Old Man shook his head as he reasoned with Tennessee's declaration: a spec-four's declaration. Challenging a superior who spent his day conjuring excursions intended to create death was no challenge for the sweet notions of southern logic.

Stubbs returned from escorting the Old Man to the chopper and handed Hardin a stack of papers. "Uncle wants you to read this and give him a call."

Hardin read the title: "Prejudicial Allegation Against Captain Edward R. Hardin." With a jerk he turned to Amps and said, "Burn this horse shit." Stubbs laughed and turned away.

The next days were spent running clovers, stay-behinds, ambushes, backtracks, cutting signs, and playing target—dealing with punji pits, a frag booby trap, and a rusty carbine.

Alarmed by his own cleverness, Lieutenant Bowe parked his bare ass over his boot heels and began reenacting the charge of the light brigade. With his sword held high, he was racing toward the enemy's flag when eleven unarmed Viet Cong entered his latrine packing rice.

In the confusion, Bowe bellowed a scream, jumped into a squat to shoot his enemy, dropping globs of shit down his pant leg. Slack-jawed and frantic, he waved his rifle about, pointing at one man and then another, looking like an abused mule, staring at the near naked men as if they were about to flinch.

When Dubitski charged in with reinforcements, the engagement was declared a victory.

* * *

With the tiny old woman's image permanently stained on the grain of life, the choppers carrying the lead element of Charlie Company, crested the center ridge of the Tiger Mountains heading for the South China Sea. When Hardin found his feet, he was standing in the same valley where he had assumed command of Delta Company.

The air reeked of unused pollen—damp, disturbed by the rotor blades. A sea breeze pushed across the beach. The ground was covered with burnt-orange leaves. Something had changed in the valley. Hardin could feel a recurring disturbance in the foliage.

The birds were silent. The landing zone was encased in a tangle of matted vines, and scrub trees parched into a brittle maze, each passage clogged with an odd ground cover. The leaves not blown free by the choppers cast clouds of tiny fibers into the air at the slightest touch. Sweat caked with this cellular mix lay on Hardin's face like veins of gold.

Grumpy and Linus picked their way, parting the vegetation, then stepping over the roots and stalks, landing a foothold, then pushing their bodies through the hole only to regain their balance, check their sectors and take another step.

The heat on the jungle floor was stifling. The air was stale. Hardin could not quiet his breathing. Stiff, brittle limbs grabbed at equipment, forcing one man to follow another, tying the squads to a predictable path. With each miscue a branch would snap and GIs would freeze.

Exhausted, as if the day had run full circle, the point squad broke into a patch of eight-foot grass and found a blue-line and a bombed out swimming hole. The cold, clear water in the bomb crater allowed for one-minute baths. Watching the turbid water flow through a hole in the grass and run toward the sea, Hardin wanted to swim along.

Revived and alert, the point squad changed direction and searched east along the blue-line to the northern edge of a coastal village. Stubbs stopped the company in a steamy palm grove, claiming the lush grass reminded him of Georgia.

Maggie's chopper swung out over the beach and hovered into the clearing, landing amongst a stand of large water palms. Maggie sauntered with an aggravating canter, his expression spiced with the joy of never having been pinned down.

"He's still pissed about the White Mice," Stubbs said. Lighting a fag, he snapped his lighter shut and blew smoke toward the oncoming major.

"Chuck is waitin' for us down this beach, Sarge," Tennessee said.

"Yeah, I know. Things don't feel right."

"Maggie is prancin' like he's been ballin' the neighbor's dog," Amps said.

With a pressed, imprisoned expression, Old Sterling Stuff presented a box of coffee cake to Stubbs, then ordered the company to move south along the coast in the morning and search the village at the southeast corner of the Tiger Mountains. He left without speaking to Hardin.

"This ain't good, Sarge." Tennessee stood looking at the coffeecake. "The last time we got a present was in Ban Me Thuot when that big Texan gave us a music box. This here cake is bad luck. We're gonna get whacked."

"Things don't feel right," LeCotte said.

A coastal breeze stirred mists of steam. Jungle fatigues trapped body salts in their tattered weave. Waves of white caps stiffened the back of Hardin's shirt. Grains of dried salt studded his waistband, burning and tearing his skin.

Abrasions flamed at their hips as GIs poured water down their pants.

Swarms of mosquitoes flowed on the cool breeze as the sun dropped behind the Tiger Mountains. To foil the bastards Amps lay on the broil between a poncho liner and his rubber whore, sweat pouring from his body.

Lusting for blood, the mosquitoes flayed into him like he was the whole of Asia. The first wave tried to lift the poncho liner off his face, but Amps wasn't stupid. He clenched his teeth around a fold. Damn if the little bastards didn't drill holes through the liner and suck blood from his lips.

After hours fighting these draculous pigmies, Amps massaged his swollen lips. Amps counted fourteen bumps on his forehead as he savored his morning coffee. A hankering for cake took him back to Stubbs' pantry. An Army of black ants were gnawing and shitting on his cake.

Amp's mind locked momentarily, then stepped through the phases of his morning stupor, deciding that the cardboard canyon was a visual trick.

Thousands of ants scurried over the cake, their well-rehearsed gnawing designed to mesmerize a GI like an evening fire. Cake squares dwindled into a stream of retreating booty. Fresh troops marched into the canyon with a gamma-globulin confidence and the assurance of glorious rewards, energized by unnamed veterans wearing stylish Eisenhower jackets and well-cocked overseas caps on their noggins. Maggie knew the ants would come.

"By God, would ya look at that." Amps said, as the reality hit home. LeCotte was standing one tree to his left. "Did that cake have nuts in it?" The ants stopped to grab their goolies, howling in the canyon.

"No." LeCotte looked in the box.

"It had nuts last night," Amps said. Microdinks were sucking his blood, infecting his bowels and eating his food.

"You ate that last night?" LeCotte snorted at Boyle, slapping Pops on the shoulder.

Amps strained coffee through his clinched teeth. For all its worth, his mind may as well have been empty. Amps turned on the laughter and issued his orders. "Blood, the captain says you got point. Go slow. We're in a tight area against this beach. Dubitski's got a one-hour stay-behind to bush our back trail. Twenty minutes."

* * *

Accented by the sunrise, the lush green grass yellowed like soft hay near the beach, only to darken in the shadow of the water palms.

Hardin stared into the confines of the foliage, knowing for all its beauty the South China Sea was but a distraction, its soothing calm drawing his eye away from the intricacies of the village. Bright threads of light drew his eye from one color to another. Golden patches of thatch held the image of the tiny old woman. The district police had nearly cut her head off.

The village stirred as if it were deserted. Not far from the first hootch, Pops spotted an old man huddled in the recess of a bunker, hiding. He listened for the vacant sounds, the sounds reserved for the black of night—the sound of a grenade spoon springing from its harness, the sound of a selector switch, the sound of a magazine finding its home, the rhythm of a man stalking his prey, a pant leg brushing a leaf.

A man breathing.

Pops knelt next to Wolfman, blowing air through his pursed lips, listening to the rushing sound, moving his search from the beach to the base of the ridge and back to the beach.

Words don't drift away when the air is still.

A sealed darkness pressed at Pops' chest. Patches of hard-beaten dirt seemed painted, as if the palm fronds were etched on tinted glass, casting well-mannered light onto the village floor. A sudden breeze set the jungle in motion. The hootches were shadowed like boulders on a rocky beach. The elders honed Pops' fear as they appraised one target and then another.

"El Tee, we better spread our files and start leap froggin," Pops said.

"Got ya—spread out," Dillon said.

One file banked right, the other banked left. Within minutes an eel of fear took hold of the village. Something bit Tennessee's throat. First Wolfman, then Linus, then Packrat, then Grumpy—without exception their expression was the same. They were in for a fight.

Dubitski's stay-behind ambush erupted with fire.

"Lima, pick up your feet. We'll wait for the drag," Tennessee said.

The jungle absorbed the churning surf of the South China Sea. First Platoon rose from the ground in a rippling motion mounting the base of a small rise, slanting away from the village.

Ninety-six GIs searched without a sound.

"Tennessee, we got a dead VC and an AK. We're on a rawhide." Dubitski's voice made the grass stiffen.

Hardin leaned into the shadow of a palm tree, his search cutting through the layers of scrub, watching for movement near a trail junction. Death's sequence was accelerating. With his mind riffling through the dangers, a booby trap exploded.

Gasping for air, Pops' voice rang from the radio, carrying the sounds of his body crashing through the brush. "We got two dead VC. Looks like their trap blew while they were wirin' a one-o-five round." Tag had the point squad scrambling toward the ambush site.

"Pops, spread out and wait," Tennessee said.

Curiously, a day in Vietnam's war could start with a firm step or a fall. A grunt could feel the difference coming. This day was one hour old. A friendly stay-behind ambush was successful and a hasty Viet Cong ambush was not. Amps lay behind his radio, his round blond face cinched into a knot, the day more quiet than it would have been without the explosion.

With a sudden pang, Hardin found himself staring at the dead enemy soldiers. Gray with gunpowder and slack with death, they looked surprised—shocked. But for a two-amp surge of electricity, Pops and LeCotte would be dead.

A scarred photograph revealed the image of a mother and two young men.

With the bodies propped against a tree near the center of the village, Stubbs said, "Blood, find the woman in this picture." The villagers had gathered to inspect the bodies.

PeeWee presented the woman in the photograph with a shrug. She was older now, her heart deep in sorrow for her sons. Suddenly stoic, this bamboo feline stood motionless, then nodded solemnly, her face seamed with weathered ridges. Standing in the remnants of what could have been a uniform, her appetite for life stood-to in the strength of her silence.

Reacting to the acrid odor of a burning heat tab, her face fell into a false smile. Her eyes fixed on Hardin. Stepping to the side, as if calculating, a sense of recognition set her gaze, like a tired host welcoming an overdue guest.

Somewhat unnerved, Hardin asked, "Where are the VC?" He waved an open palm toward the Tiger Mountains in a sweeping gesture. She looked over her shoulder at the other villagers, and then at Hardin as if ordering his execution.

"No bic, no bic." Her words carried the weight of the tiny old woman who fell to the knives of the District Police.

Hardin pointed first at the photograph, then at the bodies, and then at the old woman. She hardened her expression. She was Viet Cong to her core. With a patience the world would come to understand, she would avenge her sons and the others in turn.

Leech Dick held up his handset with a waving motion, then pointed at the bodies.

"Maggie's on his way out. Says he wants to inspect our work." Hardin walked back through the village to touch base with Dubitski and Bowe.

"Rap, lay those bodies next to that paddy dike, face up." Stubbs pointed with the butt of his cigarette, watching Lightning and PeeWee set their gun to cover the landing zone.

"Charlie Five, this is Casper Two, pop smoke."

"Smoke it is. Do you have our Three and is he on the radio?" Stubbs had a plan.

"We got him and he's off the net."

"Good. I want ya to land so he has to step over some bodies to come see us." Reynolds had put a hoe near one of the bodies to hide the surgery on his ear.

"We've got lemon smoke."

Casper flew out over the beach, faced the Tigers, and hovered near the bodies. Maggie looked at the pilot and then the bodies. Back and forth, wondering how fate was forming his day. The scene was priceless. The pilot, the copilot, and the crew chief exchanged comments as Maggie hesitated in the doorway of the slick. Realizing he was committed to getting off the aircraft, he decided to step on an arm to clear the obstacle.

Looking back over his shoulder to make sure the dead men hadn't moved he stepped quickly into the village. By the time he reached Stubbs he had regained his stride.

Without regard for protocol, Stubbs said, "What do you need, Major?"

Maggie pointed at the bodies. "Where's their weapons?"

"Most of it's up their ass. They set a hasty ambush that blew their life all over the jungle. Turned them gray. No blood, instant death."

"You called in three VC and an AK."

"We banged one up the beach. He was packin' an old AK."

With enthusiasm, Maggie exclaimed, "I'll take the AK." Even Grumpy knew why Maggie had exposed the company's location. He wanted a trophy.

"Only thing goin' back with you is a female VC." Stubbs was talking to Maggie like the Major was a new boot on the first day of Jump School. He handed the Major the picture and said, "Make sure the District Police don't slit her throat." Angry beyond reason about having the company's location exposed, Stubbs waited for the Major to respond.

Then he turned and said, "Blood, put her on the slick."

"Charlie, Casper here. Thanks for the show, over."

"Get fat if you can, Casper," Amps said.

* * *

Hours later, in the quiet of the village, Stubbs coaxed Hardin away from Amps and Tennessee. Twilight sat on the South China Sea like an ember being consumed; its glow fading as the shadow of the Tiger Mountains reached across the white sand beach turning the sea first purple, then black. Cooler air had come with the change of season.

Muted sounds turned into a vigil as Hardin questioned Stubbs' need for secrecy.

"Captain, you gotta see this." Stubbs handed Hardin a picture that was water stained and worn at its edge. The black-and-white picture featured Hardin sitting on his rucksack on the airstrip at LZ English with his M-16 cradled against his chest. He was sitting with Pops, Grumpy and Wolfman.

"One of the old woman's sons had that picture in his wallet."

"You're shittin' me."

"So far I'm the only one that knows. Grumpy and Wolfman are new guys," Stubbs said pointing to the picture. "Only man takin' pictures on that airstrip was that reporter."

"The general's baby boy." Hardin set his back against the base of a palm tree. "This is a wanted poster. There's money in play, Stubbs."

* * *

Bremerton, Washington. September 1955.

"How are you doing, Pal?" the Major said, watching Mrs. Donnager post the open sign for the public library on the landing by the large oak doors. He looked back to the left a second time as they stepped off the curb heading for the Farmer's Market.

"There's a PeeWee football game at Sheridan Park this afternoon at three."

"I have to work today, Pal. Lots of people are moving out of town." The Farmer's Market was full of optimism and odd splashes of remorse. One of the farmers had a son still missing in Korea. His friends were doing their best to keep his despair above water level.

The Major set a brisk pace for their round of the food stalls, stopping his banter only to donate his sadness to the disabled veterans posted here and there.

"How's junior high school, Pal?" he asked, handing his son an apple.

"I don't know. Our girlfriends are going out with ninth graders and one of us gets pounded just for the heck of it nearly every day."

"I bet some of those ninth graders are big boys." He was talking into the noise on Fourth Avenue as they started to walk toward Pacific Avenue.

"Yeah, they're heavyweights with bad attitudes."

"You're not going to like everyone you run across, Pal." The Major alerted to the shouts, moving suddenly, forcing his son into the recessed entry at Woolworth's Five and Dime. Men were fighting across the street in front of Bremer's Department Store.

"Is your mother working today, Pal?"

"Yeah, she caught the bus before mine."

"Go inside." He shoved his son toward the doors of Woolworth's and raced toward the fight, toward his bride. Eddie tried to watch, but the crowd, the Bremerton Police, the Navy Shore Patrol, and the Marine Guards all converged on the fight.

When the Major found Eddie still standing at the curb, he lifted his feet off the ground, shoved the doors of Woolworth's open with the back of his head, and stuffed him onto a stool at the lunch counter. His fingers drummed furiously at the countertop.

"When I tell you to do something, you do it—is that clear? And no ifs, ands or buts."

"Okay, Dad." The Major stretched his left hand, rubbing the tendons in his left arm just below the elbow.

"Mom's fine," the Major said, motioning to the waitress. "She didn't even know there was trouble." With a jolt, the Major was wired to another place, to another time.

"Those ladies in the cosmetic department talk a blue streak, Pops. It's ridiculous. I can barely stand it. They don't talk about anything either."

The Major stirred his black coffee, banging the spoon on the side, then laughed a relieving laugh. "Get used to that, Pal. Women are born with something on their mind. Most of it's just chatter." The Major looked back toward the street. "One thing's certain. The older a woman gets the more calculating she becomes. You steer clear."

"Who was fighting, Pops?"

"Two marines were trying to cut up a sailor—a Chinese sailor." The Major stared into his coffee, searching as if an answer might appear. When he moved his newspaper aside he pointed to a headline: War Veterans Protest Shabby Treatment.

"Are we going to the YMCA?"

"Let's call it a day, Pal."

CHAPTER THIRTY

Ghosts

Airborne. Enroute to Landing Zone English. 0650 Hours.

Hardin was daydreaming.

Holding a picture of her two dead sons, the old woman was crying through a scream, her face faded like paint running before the rain. Instantly she appeared in profile firing an AK-47 at Linus. LeCotte and PeeWee fell in the fire. Her eyes flashed like transparent crystals, mirrors reflecting a canine nature. Then, as if hollow, her eyes changed shade—pale green corneas suspended in a linen fluid. Her image glared from the bottom of chrysolite pools.

The old woman laughed. As if empty, her faded brown shirt and ragged black pants pulled at her bones. Weathered skin fell in folds, her regret layered by decades of war, her hands callused and firm, her features reflecting the image of a rural past.

The sons of a village elder were dead. Unsure what that might portend, Hardin knew his enemy would wait for him to return to the Tiger Mountains. The son of a general had taken his picture and someone had given it to Hardin's enemy. Which enemy he could not say.

A staff patch, the White Mice, and the Viet Cong… they were a likely concert.

Prejudicial allegations, booby traps, friendly-fire—incoming. If Hardin were a target, a specific target, he would never see Linda or meet his baby girl. With eight dog tags to read, he read his own, thankful the words had not changed. Seven men were dead. He was simply lost.

Mostly he searched for himself only to find a grunt clad in the rags of war, running with the sun, desperate to outpace twilight's certainties, clutching his weapon, death's wax hardened in the hollow of his eye.

His days of war seemed rewarding. His days without war seemed a failure.

How could they be otherwise?

Like the sea grass pushed by the tide he let the jungle have its way. By reputation he could kill without emotion, his features stained with the blood of his friends. In the end, his family would say he had changed. God would find he simply had no soul.

* * *

With the rush of anger, Hardin bounded from the chopper at LZ English, ignored the blather Stubbs was spewing, and nearly ran to the mess tent. After a meal that defied description, he found Stubbs and the GIs of Charlie Company lying in the dusty street in front of the orderly room like a bunch of puzzled losers.

"Stubbs, what are we doin'? Get the studs refit."

"Dillon's at supply," Stubbs said, judging Hardin's mood. "There's no place to sleep. Bravo Company's not leavin' until the day after tomorrow." Hardin stood silent.

"Your call, Captain."

"Strike the flag, Stubbs, we're walkin' out to the south. We're better off outside the wire." Stubbs flipped his cigarette butt at PeeWee.

Hours later, with Maggie in the dark, the company stepped through the wire at bunker #10, crossed 400 meters of rice paddy, and disappeared into the shade of a palm-covered garden. The village smelled of dung and wet thatch.

Clouds choked the mountains to the west. With his back tied to a palm tree, pleased that Maggie would get his ass chewed for not knowing where the company had gone, Hardin smiled, content to spend the time watching his friends relax.

With his cock's recovery supervised by four medics, Leech Dick gave his essentials a thorough inspection, the whole affair being the essence of stealth. The welt on the side of his Johnson had developed a pronounced pucker, topped with an off-colored purple cap.

Having decided on a war story to compliment his wound, Leech Dick had taken to pissing left handed, leaving his brand exposed. He liked to piss where a new man might see it. He didn't have a hole in his helmet yet, but that might come later.

His radio stood atop his rucksack like a klaxon, barking like central dispatch, requesting this and that as if he really cared. The captain, the radio, Amps—they were one and the same, all pushing him to respond.

Baldinger was his given name and he started referring to himself as Dinger when he talked to a new man. Fish caught him calling himself Dinger one day and told him it was bad luck, and that if he didn't change his ways, he—Fish—was going to split his quiver with a machete.

Dinger thought Fish might do such a thing.

Dinger liked Fish at first, the day Fish kept the offending leech from remounting his boot, before Fish told the medics that Leech Dick was his real name and that Leech Dick would have trouble using his left hand.

According to Amps, Leech Dick's first steam bath was worth any money. With his welt on parade, the whore grabbed hold of his bean-bag and hauled him about until he rescued his humping tackle and hollered into the shower.

Banned from the steam baths, Leech Dick was reduced to visiting bunker #1 and begging for boom-boom.

Amps liked to tell that story, and add, "Only a leech would suck that dick."

Boo had his stories, but only Rap would listen.

And so time wore on with one comic interlude and then another. With the company seal stamped on the village, Hardin ordered the troops to saddle up. The time had come to invade Landing Zone English.

Linus, Grumpy, Packrat and Wolfman took point and were approaching the hootches bordering the rice paddy, when "All Hell" broke loose—"All Hell" being a water buffalo with nostrils the size of trombones.

"All Hell" lived in a bamboo corral anchored by palm trees adjacent to the path that ran through the center of the village. As one GI and then another sauntered by his patch, the beast became more agitated. When Boo's shoulder nearly brushed the buffalo's nose, the beast leapt from its daze. "All Hell's" eyes went wide. His front shoulders bolted off the ground, crashing through the bamboo rails. He stumbled briefly. His hooves tore at the ground.

He let out a shrill scream when he found Boo running.

No GI had considered climbing the gabled end of a hootch, let alone climbing the gable to mount the ridge beam.

Boo's feet were on a boil. He climbed straight up the side of the hootch carrying his weapon, rucksack, and helmet. "All Hell" banged at the corner of the hootch with one horn and then the other, shaking the structure back and forth, stirring Boo's oysters into a fry. Boo was speaking a pure form of Black English: as if "All Hell" had a mother. When the ridge beam snapped and started to sag, Boo froze, wondering if the beast had noticed.

Steaming snot and snorting his rage, "All Hell" searched for another GI. The elders in the village were bent with laughter. With ninety-eight of Virginia's finest militia one-eye watching, huddled in the weeds, a tiny girl approached the beast, hooked a tether to his nose ring, rubbed the side of his head, and guided him calmly out of sight.

Rap stood on the trail staring at Boo. Embarrassed that a brother was propped on the top of a sagging hootch, whining, Rap let the shine from his teeth measure his disgust. "I oughta bust a cap in your mama's ass, Boo. Motha fuckin' dickless motha fucker."

* * *

Distracted, as if in a state of prolonged suspense, Uncle could listen or half-listen, his mood drawing flak from his conscience. No smug expression caught his fancy. He enjoyed deprecating humor. For Uncle the predicaments a grunt could fashion were agreeable discoveries.

With small-arms fire roaring in the north, Uncle and Hardin drank coffee and argued the significance of the prejudicial allegation. With the battalion suffering the effects of Delta Company failing the IG inspection, Hardin's refusal to respond to the reporter's charge, with its unapologetic ugliness, was ruffling someone's sensibilities.

"The mess in Delta is bad enough without you ignoring this complaint," Uncle said.

"Who decided to hide the facts from the IG, Uncle? I think you need to find out. If you don't go public with this deserter bullshit, he's gonna turn up on the cover of *Time* Magazine," Hardin said, wondering if he should tell Uncle about finding his picture.

"You're right." Frustrated by his lack of authority, Uncle set the paperwork aside.

"We go back a ways, Uncle, you and I. Whether the Old Man is supporting the cover-up or not, I don't know. I have to assume he knows about the deserter. If so, what's drivin' these allegations? And whose butt is exposed? You need to step back a bit, Uncle, and find out what's goin' on."

Parcing the words, Uncle stirred his coffee and said, "Two men are listed as missing from Delta Company—the deserter whose name is never spoken for fear he might surface, and a decorated soldier named Ragman, who went on R&R and never returned."

Laughing as if he might need a medic, Hardin's expression scrambled around the mess tent and landed with a thud. "J. T. Ragman," he said. "He's a friend of mine. His real name is Joe-Shit the Rag Man. He's a figment of my imagination, a ghost."

"Oh my God. That's not funny. Hardin, you asshole. If you knew the shit I've been through. This has gone to the top. MACV Headquarters has the Australian police looking for the man. There have been reports of sightings. They claim to have nearly caught the bastard."

"There ya go, Uncle."

"The Army Commendation for Valor, the promotion to Spec-Four, and the R&R request—your doing as well?" Resisting Hardin's antic nature, Uncle knew the answer.

"The deserter is dead, Uncle. I don't know why I know that. But I think I'm right. I'd keep Ragman alive if I were you. People that never existed are easier to explain."

"A young captain at brigade has had his ass in a sling over this Ragman affair because he hasn't been able to track Ragman's assignment from the states to the brigade, or from brigade to the company. What's worse, the jungle school in An Khe came up with a certificate of completion for the man. And B-Med has records of a physical they gave him."

"Have they contacted his parents yet?" Uncle began to laugh at his basket of insanity.

Hardin accepted Uncle's urgency for what it might be worth. By the time Uncle was insisting that the prejudicial allegation might be serious, Maggie was swirling through the mess tent, and the war in the north was gaining speed.

"Get your troops on the airstrip, Captain Hardin. We got an engineer platoon pinned down on Route #1. They're reporting khaki uniforms."

Hardin looked toward the fight, and said, "I don't think I can make it, Maggie. I got a lot of paperwork to deal with." Uncle stood and grabbed the prejudicial allegation.

"You lift off in seven minutes. The choppers will be facing north. Route #1 and the ambush will on your three-o'clock across an open paddy. Grazing fires could be heavy."

"Maggie, Maggie, Maggie: it's so dark out that even Walter's band of word-pussys have called it a day. I can't find Chuck when the sun's out, and you want me to fly into the night and capture the bastard when he knows I'm comin'. What are the supporting fires?"

"There will be no suppressive fires outside of the rice paddy."

"Chuck ain't waitin' for us in that rice paddy, Maggie."

"Any more questions, Captain?"

"No, Major, I've got a comment. When a green tracer misses you by thirty meters it looks like it's gonna drill ya right between the runnin' lights. If my people start takin' hits and you don't give us fire support, you better hope I don't make it back."

"Are you threatening me, Captain?"

"I am. Write it down. Uncle is your witness. He can read at your memorial."

* * *

Sounds in the damp night rang with a muted thud as the Huey's rotor blades slapped at the moist air. Standing on the right skid of the second of eight slicks, singing in the dark, his emotions plunged through cracks of fear. Hardin's words would stop to find the rhythm of the rotors, then boom with courage, hoping the confusion lead to nowhere.

Hardin could not hide in this night's secrets.

The short final approach to the landing zone was a race into a hole. Hardin stared at his left boot, shocked awake when rockets and red tracers cut lines in the fabric, defining the assault's lateral boundaries and direction of flight. He tightened his grip on the airframe anticipating the impact with the ground.

Sixteen door gunners joined the fight, stitching the tree lines, searching fires tracing the night, the red streams ninety degrees out of phase, playing tag with

Starblazer's rockets. Braced by a cold sweat, he crouched on the chopper's skid, alerted by the glare.

Mortar-fired parachute flares had turned the landing zone into a carnivale, the muffled explosions marking the edge of the night, the penumbra of each flare ringed with an odd glow. Long, arcing rocket trails hung in the gray-black night as the flares descended. Barely used mortar tubes sounded their cry, echoing, announcing the arrival of replacement flares.

Hardin's mind accelerated, storing data—palm trees, hootch locations.

As each parachute collapsed, the flare's harsh residue sparked, grew confidential, and disappeared with a sputtering laugh. Maggie was playing guns.

Exposed and over exposed, Charlie Company was trapped. Pilot and copilot, locked like robots in trail, were waiting for what everyone expected—the impact of B-40 rockets.

Like cutouts tied to a string, the choppers bounced as one on the dry clay. GIs ran for their lives and threw themselves onto the ground.

As if programmed for delayed viewing, green tracers flowed from the tree line near the base of the mountains, tagging Casper's last slick as it lifted off. The airframe floundered as it slid to the right, trailing smoke over the palm trees near Route #1.

The enemy had withdrawn across the rice paddy. They were running for the mountains.

The ghostly cast on the bordering palm trees shadowed the face of a hootch across the lighted paddy. The jungle turned black within five feet of the hootch. Lying in the open paddy, with nowhere to run, the company waited and prayed, straining to preserve their night vision.

"Maggie, shut off the flares," Tennessee said.

"Roger. What can you see?"

"We're in trouble. Turn off the lights."

"Roger." The mortar tubes fell silent. Listening as the last flare deployed, Hardin's mind ran to the beaches of Normandy, to the GIs lying on the beach, tangled in the wire, some floating dead, drifting in the surf.

The chopper crew had cleared their airframe. They were running across the airstrip at LZ English when their chopper caught fire. The crew chief was slightly wounded. The orange-white glow from the burning airframe highlighted the bunkers on the northern rim of the firebase.

The black outlines of palm trees lay flat on a slightly lighter background. Hardin kept his eyes moving, looking off angle to enhance definition, aware that the outer rods of his eye would burn out if they were locked on one object for more than a few seconds.

Satisfied that the immediate ground was clear, Tag started toward the village, toward Route #1. Meter by meter, GIs fought the till of the dry paddy.

Grazing fire from the village, if coordinated with sufficient volume, would hit thirty men in the first volley. And with casualties coloring the night, those not hit would be hiding behind a dead friend.

"Six, this is Tag. We're at the edge of the vill." Tag was whispering into a cupped handset, his eye etching the faint outlines of a thatch hootch.

"How close?" Amps asked.

"I'm touchin' a hootch. This don't feel good."

"Yeah, I can feel it, too. Move in a ways so we're out of the paddy."

"Thirty meters?"

"Yeah. Stay close."

GIs moved in a crouch, feeling the ground, clearing the space near the ground for trip wires. Convinced he had mastered the rhythm, Hardin had relaxed into a soft cadence when a man fell into a punji pit.

The sound of Wolfman's body falling and his equipment impacting the sides of the pit was sickening. Stubbs groped for wires and vines, crawling toward the noise. He could hear quiet gasping when he reached the pit, his thoughts drumming at the sound. Wolfman's machine gun lay across the top of the pit. His rucksack and weapon kept Wolfman suspended above the bamboo spikes, his chest balanced on top of the machine gun.

"You hurt?" Stubbs spoke at a black spot, relieved the man wasn't screaming at his face.

"Don't know, don't think so." Stubbs lay next to the pit and ran his hand down the side, searching inches at a time for punji stakes.

"Any stakes by your feet?"

"Don't know, I'm afraid to move."

"Hold on, we're gonna pull you out, over the gun." Stubbs felt around and found Linus. "Give me your hand." Stubbs took Linus' hand and placed it on Wolfman's shoulder.

"What are we doin'?"

"We're gonna pull Wolfman outta a pit."

"What pit?"

"We got Wolfman hangin' in a punji pit. You and I are gonna pull him out."

"Wolfman likes hangin' around. Just a sec." Stubbs could hear Linus set his feet and find a handle. "Okay, anytime."

"Fuck you, Linus," Wolfman said.

"Shut up. When I get to three. Slowly, one, two." They lifted Wolfman enough to lean him forward while he pushed against the back of the pit and rolled to one side. Stubbs crawled back to where he thought Tennessee might be.

"I bet you need a smoke, Stubbs." Hardin said.

"That's no shit."

Hardin and Stubbs stared at the ten-inch bamboo spikes imbedded in the bottom of the punji pit. If not for his weapon, Wolfman would have been impaled—feet, legs, and crotch. Stubbs flipped his cigarette in the pit and said, "We don't have any chow."

Searching north toward the Tam Quan through a village spiced with a dual, 105mm, pressure booby trap and hidden rice, Tag and the point squad captured a cow with a square, sullen face. The damn thing looked a lot like Reynolds.

"Tennessee, call higher-higher and tell 'em we need food," Tag said.

"Those dickheads can't get us chow until the mornin." Tennessee gave a signal and Amps stopped the parade.

With Hardin wondering who was in charge, the company dropped rucks. "Lemme have the hook," he said, forcing Amps to shrug. "Three Yankee, this is Charlie Six."

"This is Sector Nine, over." Yearning to be a measure of well-defined space, Maggie was finally a concentric expression of roaring lunacy—a circle jerk.

"We need chow."

"Roger, Sector Nine here. We got chow first thing in the morning." Sector Nine here.

"I know where the fuck you are." Hardin kept the handset keyed, allowing Tag, Amps and Leech Dick to vent their rage. Satisfied with their chorus, he said, "Maggie, we're gonna shoot this dink cow and barbecue his sorry ass." Hardin spoke with an enriched phobic spew, holding the hook vertically in front of his face, yelling scoff, salted with testicle sweat.

"Negative, that's a pacified village."

"Roger, out."

"Do you know how to butcher a cow, Pops?" Hardin asked.

With a rural gesture of determined neglect, Pops held his knife next to his ear. "Do it on the farm all the time." He stood with his head cocked in an expectant expression. Hardin thumbed an open palm toward an unsuspecting cow.

Pops dropped the cow with one shot to the head, and the feast began.

Pleased with larceny, the herd slouched out of their kitchen as if they had no idea of where they were going. Content and exhausted they dug their holes. Leery-eyed outposts, hard pressed for sleep, tucked themselves in, their commo checks replete with aimless drivel.

Knowing that falling asleep on guard duty was an actionable offense prompting a turning point in a soldier's tour of duty, GIs fell asleep, one and then another. Their offense was generally classified because it led to a general court martial as opposed to a special court martial, since falling asleep in Vietnam was not very special. Isolated and uncertain, GIs had to fall asleep on guard duty in Vietnam because they were always on guard.

Hardin laughed into the hollow of his coffee cup. Imagine yelling, "Halt, who goes there?" at Chuck in the middle of Battle Bullshit. Generally, Chuck's answer would be very special indeed. Hardin was mind-winding a second iteration of this general function, agonizing over probable margins of error and tolerance limits, when the handset barked out.

"Charlie Six, this is Sector Nine. I can see where ya are on the map, can you tell me where you are on the ground?" Hardin looked at Amps and then at Stubbs. They were smoking and shaking their heads in unison.

Tennessee ginned up a pesky twang, and said, "What did Maggie say?" Tennessee was boiling water and rubbing dust between his toes. He ate with the same hands.

Hardin turned from the smell. "Sector Nine, that polished vector of hope, is suffering from directional folly. Maggie is cutting circles in a flat blue sky, studying his map, wondering where we got to." Hardin keyed the handset.

"We'll pop smoke, Maggie." This solution seemed reasonable to Amps and Leech Dick: why not help Chuck zero in his mortars? A late-afternoon chopper was a good target.

"Negative, Charlie Six, we don't use smoke in this unit anymore."

"What did he say?" Tennessee said, laughing, powdering his feet with gusto, pulling his drive-on rag between his toes like he was playing a violin.

"He say your mama sucks big time," Amps said.

Hardin keyed the handset to profess his allegiance. "Roger, out." Then he grabbed the hand set on the company radio. "Lima, Mike, November, this is your leader, over."

The three platoons came on the net in the order they were called.

"This is Six. When I tell ya to pop smoke, I want ya to pop every smoke you have, except red and white. Hustle." Hardin could hear the slick's rotor in the south, flying north along Route #1. When the three platoons called back a ready, he said, "Okay, folks, pop smoke." Fifty-four, yellow, green, and purple smoke grenades circled the perimeter, with the smoke drifting gradually to the south.

Casper laughed through a slur when he came on the net.

"We got lemon, lime, and grape."

"Roger, Casper. We got tea and crumpets on the card today."

"Maybe next time."

Hardin laughed at the signaling smoke. "I gotta get outta here. Rap wants to kill Whitey. Grayson wants to hang Dooley. And Chuck is doin' it all."

"Only folk that want us here belong to Tennessee's ol' lady, and everybody's got a gun. They even gave a gun to that major. This place sucks." Amps admired himself for stringing three sentences together. Stubbs put out a barely smoked fag and lit a new one.

Landing through a mixed-smoke hover-down, the chopper disappeared. Out of the rainbow marched Major No-Smoke, holding his helmet, packing a pistol and a map.

"Coffee, Maggie?" Hardin lay against his rucksack, suspicious and damned to be hospitable. Undeterred, Maggie decided to be forceful.

Nomads like Hardin were difficult to govern because they were never home.

"The Old Man wants you to search this village at the mouth of the Tam Quan Valley and establish eleven ambush sites."

Hardin didn't look at the map, his eyes narrowed to comical slits. Busily pointing to the ambush locations, Maggie's announcement forced Stubbs to crouch next to his shoulder. The mission was fantasy in the abstract—payback for the debacle with the White Mice.

If the maps were printed in black and white, men like Maggie would have to learn how to read the terrain and measure the miles. Instead, they fluttered from carpal to carpal, spreading field-grade spores, fertilizing the seeds of combat, intent only on the neatness of their display.

"When?" This question was damn near perfect because the answer was meaningless.

Maggie's head whipped past dead center, skewing his helmet to the left. By the time he leveled his anger on Hardin's comment, his face was purple. "God damn you, Captain. One hundred-plus NVA were spotted in that village." His expression lingered on the word "captain" and then jumped at the word "spotted."

"When?" Hardin rolled onto his left side. Maggie didn't respond so he continued. "NVA troops aren't gonna hang around a village that close to Route #1."

Maggie set his teeth and wrapped a fist around his map.

When he hesitated, Hardin said, "Besides, we'd never stay awake through a night ambush. Fly in a company that hasn't been bustin' brush for forty hours and kick their ass."

"It's only 400 meters, and the Old Man wants you in that village." Maggie was afloat in hopscotch ignorance, casting his stone in the square marked combat. Only 400 meters, what a dick!

Hardin stood-to, threw his coffee toward the chopper, and said, "You got your ambushes, Major." Then he turned on Amps like Amps was stealing his chow. "Tell the studs to saddle up, we're leavin'."

"This operation is bullshit," Hardin said. "If one of my men dies tonight, you're gonna meet every man in the outfit. Count on it." Maggie turned with a huff, heading for the chopper, slapping his thigh with his map.

Tennessee's voice came from the background. "Eleven ambushes—you gotta be jokin'."

The studs weren't laughing anymore. They knew the night would blend their obligations. They were growing more nameless by the hour, wasted by a weariness that forced their scarred shoulders into an irretrievable slouch. The household faces of their father's generation were raging away, certain as ever, calculating victory with no durable memory of defeat.

The Dogface was pushing the Digger and the Grunt.

Hardin adjusted the band of his Seiko, remembered Pearl Harbor, and whispered, "There aren't gonna be any ambushes."

With their route beaten hard by grazing animals, Tag drew the point squad near the edge of the village a wink before twilight. Clouds hung over the South China Sea pushing cold air into the Tam Quan. Hardin had planned to laager in the village, but daylight was dwindling.

Content to hide in the open, the sequence accelerated when the thatch walls of the first hootch exploded. A web of AK fire ripped through night. Nothing mattered now except the tracers. Hardin and Leech Dick lay wedged between a paddy dike and the root ball of a palm tree, listening to the bullet cracks from an enemy squad.

Stubbs tracked a lone tracer into the night.

"Charlie Six, NVA are running northwest into the Tam Quan. Break contact and move west to a PZ. Six birds are inbound."

The company snaked through the low scrub to a small clearing just as the extraction slicks touched down. Amps and Hardin mounted the second slick. Amps reach out but missed Tag's hand. Tag fell from the slick. Screaming, Tennessee fell through a stream of green tracers.

As if watching a movie, Hardin knew that Stubbs was on his own.

Small pods of black figures maneuvered through the brush. A green web converged on the lead bird as the slicks lifted away, hitting the copilot in the chest. Waving back and forth, green and red arcs flowed through the vegetation. Rolling like water from a nozzle, green streams would lift into the night, then fall away.

The slicks banked right, flying blind, deeper into the Tam Quan.

The night was consuming. The void that was the Tam Quan was just that. The instruments in the cockpit cast a glow on the pilot's face. Hardin looked down between his boots, straining to define the shapes on the valley floor. He pushed himself off the cargo deck onto the landing skid, clinging to the inside shell of the slick.

With his best friend down, no one would blame him for getting killed tonight.

The skid held steady: the vibration of the aircraft confirming his fate. Balanced on the six-inch pipe, he leaned into the body of the slick, bent his knees, and waited for the impact. The skids hit without warning. Hardin collapsed into a crushing squat, the weight of his rucksack forced his shoulders into his knees. The slick bounced into the air.

His knees giving way; he floundered and pitched forward onto his face. Instinctively he scrambled away from the slick, clawing at the ground. Gaining his feet, he leaned into his stride, crouched low to avoid the rotor blades. Blind and in pain, he ran as he might. Just as his mind found shelter, his face found a woven bamboo fence.

His eyes burst into a blur. His glasses fell from his nose. Semiconscious, with his face lacerated by bamboo, the warm blood was comforting. Think... he had to think.

The rotor wash pushed at his back. The slick was lifting away. He had to find cover.

With fear beating its drum, he braced himself onto his hands and knees, rolled the rucksack off his shoulders, fell with the weight of the rucksack, and lay still. He needed glasses and then his bearings. Blood seeped from his forehead.

The fever was back.

A shudder rippled over his body as he tried to focus on the withdrawing silhouette of the metal bird. His mind fell through a chasm, focused on a sound, a deep persistent wail. The fever exploded, sending a kaleidoscope of colors through his eyes. Wounded men were asking for water and morphine. They seemed so polite. Squeak was out of ammunition. Squeak was out of water. No one could stop the crying. The stench of death soaked into his skin.

Hardin lay on his back, shivering. His memories were marching full-circle, framed by clumps of shattered bamboo: Squeak, Shadow, Sweet Cheeks, Fish, Ski, Mex, Bucks, Drips. The Hill People stood watching Dig-it being shot to pieces. There's Pops—he's praying.

Pops never prayed. Was he dead?

Hardin found himself crawling, pushing his rucksack in front of him, wiping at the blood near his eye. His rucksack fell over a ledge. He stopped to listen. Night's agony was amplified in an unexpected way. Instantly, he was back in the Tam Quan.

He backed over the ledge, crawling toward a wounded man. Choppers filled the sky with useless confusion. Black figures scurried about like disabled insects, whispering, introducing themselves to themselves, waiting for night's protocol to find a seat.

Tag's radio operator lay face down, moaning. Hardin put his ear to the sound, near a mouth full of blood—near the smell. The night exaggerated the smell.

"Hang on, Baby," he said, turning the man on his side. The man had run off a terraced wall and his load had driven his head and shoulders into the hard-beaten clay.

Hardin removed the rucksack and cleared the man's mouth with a finger. Unable to see, he crawled toward the landing zone to find a medic. He found

Leech Dick, and Amps huddled against the confusion. Cast as an extra, he decided to call a dust-off.

"Anybody, we need a dust-off on the LZ, over."

"Dust-off One-Seven, at your service." Dozens of navigation lights darted like footless stars, each falling through the foolish chatter of traffic control. The sky was full of crazy people. Hardin took off his glasses to keep the odd light from refracting off a broken lens. His forehead was bleeding.

"Charlie Six wants to know how you can fly in that mess."

"Where are ya, Charlie Six?"

"Tell me a story, Doc. I don't have a clue."

"Find a strobe, Charlie Six?"

Hardin sidestepped the impact of the pilot's order. His first reaction was to say, "Have you lost your mind?" He knew the pilot hadn't lost his mind, because dust-off pilots were too brave to be real people. His father liked to ask that question. Eddie's answer was always: "No, why?" If he could talk to his father he would say, "Yes, I have lost my mind. The Coasters will find it."

If Hardin told to his father that he had lost his mind, his father would reply, "If you think you're going to get off that easy, you've got another think coming." He could not lose his mind because he had another think coming. Life was a lark knowing he had mental equity.

The night combat assault ended in boredom. Counting and recounting bodies, squad leaders talked to darker images. If the NVA had been waiting the thirty-four GIs in the first lift would be dead, along with six chopper crews.

Tag was missing. If Tag were alive and running, he would not approach the perimeter at night. Fish would kill him. He would head for Route #1 and wait for daylight to flag down a truck. Tag's radio operator was on the medevac.

Tennessee had fallen on the pickup zone and caught a ride on the next set of slicks.

Waiting for solitude, silent men watched the sky rid itself of one chopper at a time. Hardin unloaded the magazine in his weapon and counted the rounds: eighteen. Then he counted the dog tags at his neck: nine. He counted the tags again: nine. Who else had died?

GIs lay in scattered mounds in a terraced rice paddy, without foxholes, and with little or no concealment. Exposed on the open ground, they fought to stay awake. Total exhaustion gripped the lot as scenes of death folded into an endless medley.

Hardin wrapped one hand around Joe's drive-on rag and one hand around the pistol grip on his weapon. His totems were the currency of a religion only the jungle could ordain.

Exhausted by his capacity for killing, he whispered to himself. "Our Father, who art in the Airspace..." Father Watters could hear him.

Telemachus had retrieved them from the Eastern Sea. Such luck needed no explanation.

* * *

The Tam Quan Valley. 0430 Hours.

Sleep rushed away and dawn exposed their ragged image. Charlie Company lay in odd bunches, propped on an elevated paddy, exposed to higher ground on three flanks and a village on the fourth: asking for misery.

"Oh, Jesus, sorry fuckin' shit." LeCotte was scrubbing the ground, scratching at a multi-colored turd with the toe of his boot and adjusting his glasses to summarize the moment.

"Sorry 'bout that," Leech Dick exclaimed, high-laughing a Cajun cackle at LeCotte.

And, as if on cue, GIs started slang-talking Charlie's family. The company had slept in the village shit-yard, the ground the villagers were fertilizing. Turds lurked behind the weeds, all shapes, sizes, and colors. This was Charlie's shit-works.

"Amps, you asshole, you picked this spot. You're gonna burn shit the next time we're in." Stubbs kicked a dry set of turds, scattering the mess into a fan.

"Wasn't me, Sarge. Besides, the Tam Quan's dipped in shit."

"Battalion called. Food's on the way," Tennessee said, pointing at Tag.

"Tag, where the hell have you been?" Stubbs asked.

"Hit my head when I fell off the skid and by the time I figured out where I was, you fuckers were gone. So I laid up 'til I had some light and cut a chogey up this valley. I coulda popped a half a dozen of ya."

"You need a radio operator. John-John fell on his head."

"Oh, hell, he'll be all right."

* * *

Chow came with strings: the Old Man, and Maggie. Amps followed Maggie, mimicking his stride from a safe distance. With a cultured seal to his brow, Maggie swept toward Hardin, dusting off his credentials. He was zero-for-two on night combat assaults.

"Those were the first night helicopter assaults in Two Corps." The Old Man made the pronouncement with searching pride.

"We missed the NVA. We were close, though." Maggie added.

Maggie must have given the Old Boy's equipment quite a battering last night, Hardin thought. The sunshine soldiers were clutching their old school ties.

Charlie Company had missed the NVA, and Hardin was thankful. But, the controlling "we"—Maggie and his boss—were suffering from ritual failure and its collateral urgencies. Hardin traced the Colonel's face, trying to read his eyes. The Old Man's brow seemed packed with quizzical regret. He seemed to be measuring the worth of the GIs he could see.

Tired of being a poorly fed target, Hardin took a deep breath. "Why didn't you hit the NVA with gunships and artillery, Maggie?" Hardin stood away from his own question, realizing he was exhausted, repulsively dirty, and reeked after marinating in a shit yard.

Joe's drive-on rag no longer packed an unusual smell.

"Gunships don't do well after dark."

Holy shit, Hardin thought. The theme song from Victory at Sea must sound exotic in that cloistered briefing room. The words "night combat assault" must ring as if spoken in a dark cave, then echo for a lifetime.

To tell this new Old Man how out-of-control battalion operations had become, how chaos had become a normal parameter, and that his job was to minimize the confusion, was to challenge a warring ritual that was beyond the scope of a hearing mind. Other unseen Old Men, who believed the warring ritual was a system of stepped sacrifice designed to produce collective valor, fed and coached this lifer's zeal.

Extending a palm toward Pops, Hardin said, "These GIs don't do well after dark, either. I expected to die last night, Maggie, and the night before." Stubbs agreed by mechanically flipping his cigarette butt near Maggie's boots.

"Well, I'm glad you didn't. Where do you suppose the NVA got to?"

Resolute, Hardin stood away from the two men to gather his rage. Expressions of defeat flashed over the Old Man's face, confirming Maggie's inference that somehow the infantry had failed. In time, even this starched soldier would know the difference. Hardin waved toward the upper reaches of the Tam Quan Valley.

"The NVA ran to high ground. Scouts are watchin' us. They'll wait for good targets." The Old Man scanned the ridgelines.

Alone, watching the confusion of the resupply, the Old Man seemed reluctant when he said, "The Exec is responding to that Prejudicial Allegation filed against you concerning that reporter you assaulted in front of the aid station. The allegation has seven supporting affidavits detailing the assault. Do you want to respond?"

In a most telling test of the power of silence, Hardin stared into the jungle, knowing that time was something you got rid of when you were in a hurry, knowing he had no reason to build a friendship with this colonel, knowing his words were meaningless.

"Captain?"

"One firefight is much like another, Colonel. After a while, after enough nameless men march into a body bag chasing their own regrets, nothin' much matters. I can't tell you why I love these grunts. I can tell you this: if you fuck one of them over I'll kick your ass, too."

Hardin stood into the sun and took a deep breath. "You can see death in my eyes, Colonel. You can see the numbing indifference to anything you can muster. Your reporter: the general's baby boy. You tell that rear-echelon-cocksucker if I see him again I'll rip his fuckin' heart out."

"You're on your own, Captain Hardin."

"I knew that the first time we met, Colonel."

The colonel's authority was no match for the searing hate he could see in Hardin's eyes. "Why am I still commanding one of your rifle companies, Colonel?"

"That's easy to answer. The brigade commanding general made it clear that you are one of his best line commanders."

"Really. Well I'm on R&R in twelve days, Colonel. My Second Platoon leader's gonna take the company. My orderly room is cutting assumption of command orders. If he gets hit, the First Platoon leader is good, more experience."

"Can they run the company?" Hardin leveled his eyes on the Old Man's face. If the heat from the Prejudicial Allegation got too intense, Hardin would be relieved of his command and exposed to a myriad of rear echelon retribution.

"My radio operators can run this company. My squad leaders can run this company. We're deep in good NCOs." Both men stopped talking: distracted by the motion at boot-level and the noise of the resupply.

"Where's your R&R?"

"Hawaii. I'm gonna meet my bride and my new baby girl. Actually, First Platoon's baby girl. They adopted her for luck." The colonel turned and left.

* * *

Standing in the Tam Quan Valley on the day of his departure for R&R, the GIs in First Platoon had become mystic, exchanging cryptic messages. At 1500 hours, thirty minutes before he was scheduled to leave, Hardin was standing with Boyle discussing LeCotte's worthless brain.

Blood, Tag, Fish and LeCotte jumped him, wrestled him to the ground, tore his uniform to shreds and tied his hands and feet. Humorous familiarity had erupted into treachery. He sat with his wrists and ankles tied, looking at Pops and Grumpy, registering his right to paybacks.

Clusters of men, each with its level of support and fear, watched in silence, knowing that he would take his luck and his bouquet of imprisoned flowers with him.

Hardin's departure would loosen an avalanche of fears, and familiar companions would suspect the commonplace. Nervous, repetitive comments would dangle unmet. Bits and pieces of memory would trigger gestures of mock allegiance. They wanted him to enjoy his R&R, but Captain Edward Hardin had no fucking right to leave.

"We want you to have a good time, so we're gonna have some folks meet you at the helipad." Pops and First Platoon were wishing him well. Worried as he was, sure enough—Stubbs stood silently, measuring what the next day might bring.

"Sector, this is Charlie. We captured a GI that changed sides, over."

"This is Sector Nine. Say again, over." Unbelievable. Maggie wanted to hear the deserter music one more time. One of his units would headline the general's evening briefing. Maggie would be the general's guest briefer.

"We got a GI that changed sides. Need a slick."

"We'll send one right out." The TOC radio was a-buzz. Cokes were finished in gulps. First sergeants rechecked their morning reports. Maggie woke the Old Man. Cooks added spice to the supper meal. Diesel oil was added to the latrine fire. Orderlies fluffed sandbags and unfurled guidons. Telephone lines burned so hot the sand turned to glass. Starched MPs oiled shackle hinges, sharing joyous outbursts with the sound of each locking ring.

When the prison chopper landed, Hardin was unceremoniously dumped onto the cargo deck under the watchful eye of the crew chief.

"What a great rat-fuck," he whispered, harnessing his smartass grin. The chopper pad at Landing Zone English was crawling with pods of anxious MPs. Hardin was forced to the ground, seated upright, and told to shut-the-fuck up.

At first he told them he was Spec Four Ragman, then he refused to answer their questions, and then he told them the truth. The MPs decided he was either Ragman, or that other deserter whose name they couldn't remember.

"He's too young to be a captain—no ID, no fuckin' way." They wanted to shackle-drag his traitorous ass through the middle of a cheering crowd, but his whining eventually prevailed and a representative from battalion was summoned.

"I can't believe it. Untie him. He's a captain, you dumb ass."

Paybacks. With his helmet on backward and his uniform hanging in strips, Hardin entered the TOC and went straight for the radios. He threatened Amps with bag time, sang a chorus of Doo Dah, and laughed with Bronx and the rest of the boys.

Hardin's rucksack, weapon and helmet were banked in solitude, watching the fragments of Battle Bullshit tug at his conscience. He was emerging from the odors of combat, fighting the drag of his comrades, and ready to experience a capsule of friendship and love.

He laughed while opening his rucksack. "How did ya log this capture on your scorecard? I bet you already turned it in to brigade."

"Yeah, we did. The major drove down there to give them the report in person."

"Hot damn! They'll never believe him again." Hardin held out a hand toward the cooler and a buck sergeant from the Bronx gave him a Coke.

"Where's your R&R, Captain?"

"I'm gonna meet my bride in Hawaii. It definitely beats lookin' at you pukes. I thought you said you were gonna be better lookin' the next time I saw ya."

"And lookin' like you is a good thing?" Bronx smiled.

"Look out for my boys."

"We can do that."

CHAPTER THIRTY-ONE

Linda and Pops

Rest and Recuperation.

Sporting washed and pressed khakis, spit shined boots, rank and branch insignia, a name-tag, and a plastic-encased unit patch at the left breast pocket, Hardin flew from Landing Zone English headed for the naval base at Cam Rahn Bay, one of the largest deep-water ports on the Asian rim, built by Uncle Sam to ensure military supplies could enter the war up-country.

The base at Cam Rahn Bay doubled as an in-country R&R center.

A stewardess with round eyes wearing a Pan American Airline uniform seated Hardin next to an Air Force lieutenant colonel. Hardin was doing well until he discovered the colonel was stationed at Cam Rahn Bay and was going on his third R&R in five months. The pilot ordered him off the plane. The stewardess found him another seat.

Looking down the aisle of the aircraft across ranks of fresh haircuts, Hardin laughed at the symmetry. Battle boys sat dutifully in their egg carton, cavorting in a metal tube filled with lustful anticipation. They sang their songs, these boys. Refreshed, you could barely hear their voices.

Like the whore he had become, Hardin admired his plastic foxhole and found himself alone. The defective sociability of the other grunts seemed obvious. Unable to unfold the napkin, he ripped the soft white paper and scrubbed the pus from the jungle rot sores on the back of his hands—one between each knuckle—and a large sore on the index finger on his right hand, his trigger finger.

Measuring the stranger seated next to him, he stretched his hands, forcing the wounds to weep a milky yellow fluid, nodding with satisfaction. He would force the man to look at his badges of courage. Maybe he would bump the man and leave a pus print on his pants. It was the hatred he enjoyed. His target was barely a man.

Rest and recuperation, R&R, the surreal passage from war to peace, would be paid for with a currency defined by Hardin's inability. How could he transmit the needs of his heart, that piece of meat boiled in the red-brown slop of the most vicious guerrilla war in America's history? Would he be trapped in a rampage of unfeeling regeneration, clawing at the red clay? Or would he set his war aside for a moment and love his bride as if they were new?

Would R&R be six separate days filled with joy? Or just an extension of the hurting numbness of being too long surrounded by the noise and the fear of a remote jungle?

Hardin tried to hold near his heart that moment when he realized he was in love with a farm girl, with Linda. Lately, the warmth of that memory had dissipated, replaced by a basket of recollected fears. Deep in the night, when the jungle was quiet, he could remember their words and where they kissed. Linda's lips parted with a gasp, her beauty shrouded in odd noises.

Vietnam was a war of muslin black, a curtain soiled with the mud of time. The pictures looked familiar, the boys and their hats. That one was Hardin's dad. He was wearing his Victoria Cross. Normandy was easier to find than a distant memory.

Some things were just too quick to remember. Hardin remembered death: that footprint one finds on the jungle floor. Too many men relied on Hardin: too many dead men.

Tired of surviving, he could barely imagine the fondness of a memory, cringing at the prospect of being alive once again. Sitting on the plane he would try to imagine being happy.

Flying toward six days of loving obligation, unable to straighten his wrinkled nature, how could he hide the scars in his eyes and how would he keep Linda's heart from being injured by the truth? Coaxing himself from his fear might be a cruel hoax.

The bus ride to the hotel was an odyssey. His yearning left him afraid to see Linda: afraid she would notice, ashamed of what he had become. His thoughts ran the gamut: Would her smile last the week? Would Kimberly accept her father's touch? Was the odor still with him? Was his FUO contagious? Could they keep from planning the future? He stared at the back of his hands.

The bus slowed and turned into the curb.

As though a diamond perched on black velvet, Linda sparkled with anticipation, glowing with pride. Instantly she smiled. Standing in a spate of confusion, the flowers on Linda's dress beamed with color. Kimberly sat erect in a stroller. Her black-brown eyes shining, she was laughing in the sun. Linda and her baby had come to say they loved their soldier.

Apprehensive, perhaps a bit ashamed, Eddie knew his war would be persistent. And that Linda's expressions of love could never be reconciled with the din of war's paddy-field music.

Eddie kissed Linda gently at first, absorbing the smell of her hair and then kissed her on the neck, consumed by the beauty of her soft skin. Linda's pride in her baby girl, and her happiness, consumed him so much he could barely speak. Crying a bit, he picked Kimberly out of the stroller and held her in his arms. Fear touched his heart when she started to cry.

Eddie smiled his best smile, and she cried louder.

Linda rescued her baby from his grip and coaxed her to a gentle frown. Kimberly kept the stranger in view, then turned into Linda's breast for a reassuring hug.

"She has a little heat rash," Linda said, sensing Eddie's concern.

"She'll need better eyes than the ones she has now to see me."

"I love you, Eddie."

"You look great, Linda." He caressed her shoulder and kissed her gently.

"Your baby girl is a restless sort. Just like you, Eddie. She has a distant, blue moon expression when she's sad. She likes her mischief, and puts whatever she finds in her mouth. When she's not busy, she's asleep on Grandpa Karl's lap."

"She looks like she's gettin' plenty of chow." Hardin counted the ringlets of fat on Kimberly's arm, then tickled her ribs. She frowned at him and set her jaw.

Odd sensual emotions pushed him away from the war into a dimension filled with the odors of times past. He stared at his bride, her chin and her neck, her golden brown hair bleached from a summer spent on the farm.

He tried to corral his astonishment, but the jungle's semidarkness reverberated and the sounds of war rang out. Linda's lips were moving and he was dragging Walker's body. Realizing he had grown more confidential, he turned away. His throat filled with sorrow.

"I love you, Linda." The words seemed distant: pessimistic and joyous.

"I love you, too, Eddie."

He took charge of the stroller, guiding his baby girl along the sidewalk, adding an unneeded touch of excitement with each change of direction. Kimberly was not impressed.

Consumed with Linda's beauty, he showered, basking in the forceful stream of hot water, washing his hair a second time.

Moments flowed from scent to scent, first her hair, and then her breasts. He was lost in a need to be with someone good, with someone clean, with someone gracious and wholesome, with Linda. Making love was so wonderful.

"I'm starving for a thick steak, a baked potato, and a tossed salad with olives, mushrooms, cucumbers, croutons, sweet onions, and fresh blue cheese dressing."

"I arranged for a nanny with the front desk."

"Can we trust them?" Linda smiled and gave him a kiss.

When they were not making love, they were lying on the beach, charbroiling steaks at Mike's Grog and Sirloin, or buying keepsakes for Linda to cherish.

Kimberly is a happy chub, he thought, admiring her overstuffed diapers and her prickly heat rash. The challenging looks she gave him were priceless, her frown tempered by a pair of flashing eyes. This marvelous baby was not impressed with his domestic abilities, crying whenever he tried to set a pin.

Changing diapers required more skill and patience than he could muster.

Linda had made good use of her limited money. The details of Kimberly's being were well tended, from her washcloths and talcum powder to her footies and jump suits.

Radiant at every turn, he found himself touching Linda, searching for a delicate blush. Her petal-soft skin grew flush with heat, drawing him into her love. Like a dog, muzzle down, he ran a course in overlapping circles. He was intoxicated by the fresh smells.

Petal-soft memories seemed to gravitate to the blue end of the visible spectrum where the wavelengths were shorter. He stared at the circle of tiny blue crystals on the face of his watch wondering why they were so enchanting. The time was 7:19 A.M. He had made love to the most beautiful woman on earth and his thoughts were with Dig-it.

The colors of the sunset seemed layered, each shade of blue more dense than the next, fading to a peaceful celebration.

"The stars are brighter in Vietnam."

"What's the country like?"

"From the air the colors are hard to describe. Emerald-green rice paddies lined with neon green palm trees. Mountains covered with 160-foot trees, so steep you have to use the vines to pull yourself along. Wet sticky clay that tears the sole off your boots. And bugs. Damn, there are spiders as big as dinner plates."

"Are the people all right?" Linda said, forcing him to look directly at her.

"I don't know. We only see the old people and the kids. They seem tired. I know I am." Needles of doubt pierced his heart.

"Did the doctors determine what caused your fever?"

"Doc Tweed and Major Dip Stick work at B-Med in An Khe, at the field hospital. Nope, they don't have a clue. They're pretty sure it's not malaria." Linda ran a gentle hand through his short hair and caressed his neck with a breathy kiss. She could sense her friend's grief.

* * *

Hardin searched the blue crystals on the face of his Seiko, his thoughts oscillating between polar opposites—the beauty of his best friend and Vietnam's war. The nights and days had blurred into the rush of limited time. Sitting at a table in the Officers' Club with a combat dentist and his wife, he listened to Linda's banter as she shared stories and likened his tour to the rigors of combat dentistry, happy to compare notes with another woman.

The white-sand beach in front of the hotel was a patchwork of reunions, each burst of laughter tempered with a reluctant gesture. Eventually he became silent, afraid his words would somehow stain Linda and leave her sad forever.

They didn't talk about the war. They did regret his tour wasn't over and pledged to meet in early November to share eggnog and Thanksgiving—God willing, and if luck would have it.

A woman's love, understanding, and patience were all an average man needed to mature. Linda would need an endless supply of each to recapture her grunt.

Linda dressed early and took Kimberly down to the lobby. Hardin finished putting on his uniform, balancing the love he had for Linda and a duty that weighed heavy.

"We'll say good-bye here, Eddie. The baby is cooler, and we have time for breakfast before our bus leaves." Linda looked at the GIs crowding toward the airport shuttle.

"I love you, Linda."

"I love you, too, Eddie." He kneeled and gave his baby girl a kiss, then combed her blond curls with the palm of his hand.

"Take good care of our princess."

"We'll be fine, Eddie." They kissed a final kiss, mixing their tears. Linda's chest shook with grief as she tried to be brave. Hardin held her until she was calm, then kissed her.

"Take care of yourself, Linda."

* * *

Hardin returned to his post wearing good luck beads, clinging to Linda's touch, wondering how the next fifty days would end. With Hawaii locked in a protected cell, Route #1 led the Caribou to Landing Zone English and rice paddies filling with water.

"You said you were gonna be better lookin', Captain." Bronx cast a reliable shadow.

"Forty-nine days and a wake-up left."

"You lost a platoon sergeant—Dubitski." Bronx gave Hardin a modified salute. Dubitski's death number was posted on the situation map, marked with a black pushpin. The former captain of the Golden Knights Skydiving Team was dead.

"Where'd he get hit?"

"Sniper got him at Corregidor, head shot."

Hardin nodded slowly and said with regret, "He was one of the best."

Uncle handed him an after-action report. "Your Second Platoon got hit yesterday. One GI wounded, killed a couple VC."

Bronx toasted the air, and said, "You're walkin' like a cock rooster."

"Got roosters in the Bronx?" Hardin's system warmed as he paused, listening to the far-off rumble of artillery rounds—a soft sound. That wet thatch, wet dung-wet clay smell that was Vietnam filled the hollow in his throat. The radio traffic with the rifle companies drew him to a rhythm. Handset in tow, he reentered the war.

"Charlie Kilo, this is Charlie Six, over."

"Kilo here. Good to hear your voice, over." Tennessee's upbeat tone brought a smile to Hardin. Most of his friends were still alive.

"I'll be inbound in the morning. Anything I need to know?"

"Negative, just bring back the magic."

"I can do that."

The equation had changed. Hardin's promotion had separated him from his friends, his R&R had demonstrated he was capable of leaving.

* * *

"Stubbs, how are ya?" Stubbs squared his jaw to the sun, his rugged features drawn tight as he exhaled a stream of smoke. A shrug fell in with a sense of resignation as he flipped his cigarette into the wire and laid his weapon across his forearm.

"We're all right, Captain. Good to have ya back." Hardin waited as Stubbs scanned the remote hilltop.

"We met like this in Kontum, after a tree fell on one of Captain Joe's cabin boys."

"After that fever flogged your sorry ass. Fever of Unknown Origin. You big dogs sure got the tricks." Stubbs stood away, leaning as if apologizing, then pointed toward the south end of the perimeter that over-looked a long grass plateau.

"Dubitski got hit on that bunker, eatin' chow. Head shot."

Angered by the lank posture of the men, Hardin said, "Get the platoon leaders, Stubbs, and clean this fuckin' place up."

Stubbs hesitated, laughed a sarcastic huff, and then lit a smoke. "Will do," Stubbs said, walking away, pointing a finger at Tennessee.

"I leave for a week and the Confederacy turns the perimeter into a junkyard, kills one of my best people, fucks up a simple operation, and turns security into a surprise." Hardin yelled at Tennessee and Amps loud enough to raise every head on the firebase.

"Good to see ya, Captain. Your wife must have been on the rag when she showed up." Hardin met Amps' challenge with a smile and turned back to Tennessee.

"Give you more authority, let you train a new officer, and you turn on your Captain like the traitorous scum you really are. It's worse than cheatin' on your wife." Hardin sat on the ground, leaned his back against a bunker, and waited as the three lieutenants assembled. After exchanging greetings Hardin motioned to Stubbs, inviting comment.

"Yes, sir?"

"Pull in the OPs and do searching fires with the guns, M-79s, four magazines through the sixteens." The orders amused Stubbs' dormant senses.

"You got it."

Hardin intended to separate the three lieutenants from their attendants, force a rotation of their watch fires, and vanquish their paper maidens. He resented their false claims and their nonchalance.

"Things seem quiet. Chuck on R&R or what?" Hardin said, pushing a tone for the lighthearted. He paused, shaking his head, then looked toward the sound of a passing Huey. "Wasn't the hole in Dubitski's head big enough for you, Bowe? You malignant fuck."

"We haven't found many signs."

Hardin looked at Stubbs, directing the old sergeant to be on his way. GIs from the outposts were filtering in through the wire.

"You three are stupid. When you reset the OPs I want four men and a squad leader. The Army can't replace a man like Dubitski." Hardin's tone matched the hatred in his gray-green eyes. Tennessee and Amps knew the drill.

"You make one mistake and somebody dies. It's just that simple."

"After you set new OPs, I want three squad clovers, 300 meters out, and you dickheads are gonna run 'em. Clockwise rotation through your OPs at twenty-minute intervals. Dillon first." Hardin lit a ball of C-4 under his canteen cup, then scrubbed his face with an open palm. "I'm back, and I owe you douche-bags for tyin' me up."

"Sir, how was your R&R?" Bowe asked. Tennessee grunted and hoisted his cup.

"I oughta kick your face in, Bowe. I got forty-nine days and a wake-up left. Be careful how you play the game." Hardin had jerked their chains so abruptly, the men stood silent.

Weapons sounded from the foxholes.

Hardin stood and started to inventory his rucksack. Before twilight every swinging-dick on Firebase Corregidor would be dancing within a range of fears consistent with his assessment of the combat situation.

"Wallers wants to talk with you, Captain," Stubbs said, his face buried in a new cigarette.

Hardin searched his memory, then closed his eyes and said, "What about?"

"Playin' saxophone music." Hardin smiled. His saxophone player was stepping out on the town.

Wallers packed a restless smile, anticipating his escape. Hardin smiled a smile he could not control. Instantly Wallers grew from a sketch to a friend. The gentle black man with the shy demeanor stood-to, ready to slide on downstream. He was a tall man who never seemed to look down at his friends. Even as he stood next to Hardin he made his Captain seem the taller.

The war was plain enough for Wallers. Bucks died in Black English.

"Where do ya think you're goin', Wallers?" Sax started to offer his best, so Hardin held up a hand. "You were in on tyin' me up, messin' with my program. Guess that means I owe ya." Sax started to rethink his situation. Hardin grinned and offered him some coffee.

"That was just for fun, Captain," he said.

"Has it been six months, Sax? How do ya figure those thirty-five-minute hours you been loggin' adds up to a full day?"

"I've been steady at it, Captain," Sax said, shrugging with his palms.

Hardin held out a fist, buoyed by the man's simplicity. "I'm glad ya made it kid. When you get to that band in Saigon, or wherever, you play a song for me." Sax agreed, hoping he knew the music. "'The Shadow of Your Smile'—for the men we used to know. For Bucks."

"I can't mend a Piper's wing. Not here in Vietnam, maybe never again." Sax gave Hardin an uncustomary pat on the shoulder, then said, "Thanks for taking care of the man for us, Captain. Chuck too."

Hardin held out a fist, and Sax smiled.

"You did your part, Sax. Take care of yourself. The rear area's got beaucoup drugs."

"I can dig it." Sax hit Hardin's fist again, stepped into a slide to the right and bounced into a long stride. Specialist Fourth Class Byron "Sax" Wallers would play his music with more flat and diminished chords, trying to outpace the echoes.

As if Hardin could forget, their faces were ranked in rigid file, black, brown and white. Rap, PeeWee, and Blood: from the rear, they looked like animals too long in the trace: sloppy rucksack, canted helmet, ripped pants, scarred muddy boots, and one draggin' ass.

Parched and forsaken, their hands ripe with time; they slept curled in their equipment. Their eyes were but toneless lenses. A small white tag hung on each of their regrets showing the price they had paid for surviving—five cents.

Enough money—perhaps.

And there was his father's grave. The flowered eagle stood tall, guarding the flank. A shadow ran long into a formless background. Crisp white roses filled a crystal blue vase. An arch of tiny blue crystals framed his headstone.

* * *

Airborne Enroute to the Tam Quan Valley. 1450 Hours.

Fog billowed away from the chopper as the company lifted out of Firebase Corregidor. Buffeted by winds and cold air, Hardin barely noticed the An Lao River 800 feet below his boots. Winds continued to gust as the aircraft set onto a ridge above the valley.

The monsoon was gathering.

The night laager was separated from the surrounding jungle. With one foxhole dug into a well-used trail and the night cool enough for a sweater, Stubbs stated the obvious. "How come no one's makin' any noise?"

"I don't know."

"Not one man cooked tonight."

Sometime after midnight a Claymore exploded. Daylight exposed the mutilated body of a trail watcher and the remnants of his carbine and bamboo chair: Dubitski's payback. Blood and Pops buried the carcass in the foxhole cut into the trail, booby-trapped the body with two frags, and left the man's feet sticking out of the ground in the middle of the trail.

"They'll dig this dude up fer sure." Amps was talking to himself, looking down the trail into a tunnel of vegetation at Chuck's bare feet. Hardin shook his head.

"A foot stool," Amps declared. "Look here Tennessee, you can sit down." Amps gathered the dead man's feet under his ass and sat down, delighted with his clever way.

"You better quit fuckin' around, Amps, his buddy's not far away."

Thirty minutes later the booby trap exploded and a collective "Chuck is stupid" rippled through the jungle.

* * *

After two days of cooling air, the company was extracted for a tour of berm security on bunkers#1 through #18 at Landing Zone English.

Hardin spent the first day fending off Uncle's suggestions concerning the remedial concessions he could offer to mollify the reporter's prejudicial allegation.

With Uncle looking on, Captain Edward Hardin stood to a brace before the brigade IG, listening to Stubbs recount the Viet Cong ambush and finding a picture that was taken by the reporter. The Inspector General accepted written affidavits from Hardin and Stubbs, along with a second copy of the picture.

"I don't know, Captain. That IG looks like trouble to me."

"I got forty-four and a wake-up, Stubbs. He can't do much."

* * *

Berm security was a concert of long days, quiet nights, and boring commo checks. Throughout, Hardin played subaltern to a staff major from brigade headquarters who claimed to be the Berm Commander.

Relentless, in an Elkhorn Creek sort of way, Amps fed the Berm Miester obscure logic that was curious and contradictory. Gradually, the very idea of Amps' existence became annoying.

* * *

At 2212 hours on the third night, with Tennessee and Amps enjoying Leech Dick's version of the footstool-in-the-trail story, PeeWee reported incoming fire from bunkers three through twelve. Green tracers jumped from a friendly village and raced over the rice paddy.

Hardin requested permission to return fire.

Studying the Berm Meister's face as it contracted into a spongy cud, Hardin shook at the laughter and keyed the hook. "Lima, Mike, November: get down, do not return fire, friendly villages, over." The far edge of the rice paddy south of the firebase was alight with sporadic muzzle flashes.

Hardin plunged a boyish cheek into the major's face. "Hiding is a bad business."

"Negative." The major was shaken, requesting guidance from his counterpart at brigade headquarters. He would not accept the responsibility of firing into a pacified village.

"Tennessee can tell you about gettin' shot by friendlies, Major. His old lady tried to blow off his nuts." Tennessee pushed at the memory and left the bunker.

The major shifted his chair closer to the radio table. His eyebrows curled over a deeply lined face. Uncertainty governed his voice as the sharp cracks increased without challenge.

"You need troops that don't want to shoot back, Major. We've got to return fire."

"Negative."

The major sat away from Hardin's insistence, sorting the possible outcomes. Hardin decided to threaten him with paybacks and mustered an expression of false resentment.

"Rifle companies aren't into hearts and minds. They're into dead bodies."

For Berm Meister the mere thought of firing into a village, just when he had attained the upper ranks of wisdom, left his mind adrift. The risks could not be reconciled.

"That's a friendly village, Captain." The incoming fire intensified.

"Have you ever been in that village, Major?"

"This is the first fire from that village since the brigade moved in." The comment was so illogical Hardin had to pause.

"Are old women firin' those AKs?" The major turned and sat down.

Hardin jumped up with a clatter to measure the major's reaction, then spoke with a more abrasive tone. "Where do ya think the first mortar round is gonna land? Maybe the general's trailer will take a couple hits."

With his hope hiding under a field table and his career at that proverbial fork in his planning guide, the enemy situation was overwhelming the major's rear-echelon ass, and he was alone, trapped with felonious ruffians who craved the hostility.

Amps, pretending to be on the land-line telephone, said with alarm, "No, sir, the major just wanted to know if your trailer was on fire."

The major turned his back on Hardin and spoke into the rapidly accelerating drum of AK fire. "I have direct orders from the General not to fire into that village." At bottom, the core of the major's longevity was wrapped in well-crafted avoidance.

Hardin had to deal the Berm Meister out of the game. He found Tennessee standing outside trying to smoke his first cigarette.

"Tell the S-4 to get a basic load of ammo on the road and give us a heads-up."

"All right!" Tennessee's eyes conveyed instant adhesion. Finally, the company would wake the Berm Meister with their protocols, and then relegate him to a paper heap.

"Have the berm stand by for a 'Bring the Max'." These code words allowed the platoons to expend their ammunition, knowing a resupply was on the way, which meant the major's career was over.

"Things are gonna get shit-hot." Amps could not conceal his contempt.

"Sorry 'bout that," Tennessee said, practicing his speech for the inquisition, struck silly by the thought of having the major by the bag.

"Relax, it'll be awhile. Contact that duster and get him ready to fire." The duster was an ancient piece of work: a tracked armored vehicle with twin 40mm cannons that fired alternately, and sounded like the steady pounding of a bass drum.

This particular duster was commanded by a first lieutenant commissioned into the air defense artillery branch of the Army who, with one youthful lapse, summoned the flimsy remnants of his heritage, disappeared in Kuala Lumpur, then reemerged as an authority on Asian contradictions.

At first his extended R&R went unnoticed. The IG inspection forced an examination of his records, producing sudden envy, and enough parasite-drag to ditch his career. Except for Mondays, which was the day he was escorted to town, his whereabouts was a comic interlude at the brigade's evening briefing.

His biggest offense was the revulsion his OCS lineage splattered against the general's mounting sense of territorial purpose. Brigade staff-patches had fashioned a positive pacification scenario through months of partially illuminated logic, ringing each village on their briefing map with a hidden complex of formless non-matter. Staff-patches were like ghosts picking at the layers of time to expose an awakening, a scenario too precious for the file-cabinet minds of the OCS unwashed, those infantry-blue, partially commissioned "Whip-and-Chills."

Hardin continued to badger the Berm Meister with requests to return fire. AKs continued to pick at the perimeter. With each report the major grew more solicitous, as if lost urgency equated to a greater sense of purpose.

Expecting the rush of a B-40 rocket or the distant tattoo of mortar tubes, Hardin kept announcing his concerns over the airways. Tennessee paced the command bunker wondering why his captain let his friends take so much abuse.

Finally Hardin developed a wedge. "Be nice to use a little mobile artillery." Hardin was referring to the duster, and the major relaxed just enough.

When the major relaxed and said, "Yes, if we had any," Hardin grabbed the hand set.

"Lima, Mike, November. Bring the Max." Bunkers #1 through #14 erupted with fire. The duster started firing two seconds later.

Initially the Berm Meister thought the enemy had mounted a full-scale assault. He alerted and sprang out of his chair. "Listen to that duster," he screamed. "The duster, the duster! Shut him off! Shut him off!" The lieutenant running the duster had turned off his radio.

Hardin left for the berm with Tennessee driving the jeep.

"Charlie Six, this is Puff. We're on station west of you, ten minutes out. We have six pistols and twenty-eight thousand rounds a pistol. Where can we help?" Holy shit, Hardin laughed. Puff was a C-130 filled with mini-guns. Puff could put the big dog's hose on Charlie, one round per square inch.

"Thanks for checkin' in Puff. Small-arms fire is comin' from the village to the south of the firebase, five or six locations. We're good for now. Hang around a bit, maybe Chuck's got a surprise for us."

"We can stay on station for five-zero minutes. We'll stay on your push."

After eight minutes, the time required for Berm Meister to find the duster, the duster stopped firing. Charlie Company stopped firing in stages as they ran out of ammunition.

"What do you think, Stubbs?"

"That major wasn't havin' much fun."

The next morning Hardin's ass was boot-locked before the Grand Wizard and flogged for promiscuous uncontrolled fire into a pacified village. The major's career was over. Having spent the night at Firebase Corregidor, the Old Man was off the hook. With his ring on high he sat in the corner of the general's office, content to witness the inquisition.

At bottom were the AK holes in the general's air-conditioned trailer. That, and only an insubordinate young disposable with ten-plus months in the woods could have pulled it off. The general packed a wry grin, using words Hardin had never heard before. With forty-one days and a wake-up left in country he had found an ally—his commanding general.

"What happened?" Stubbs, assuming his captain had been flogged, left his question confused by an erratic sucking on his most significant scrap of tobacco.

"Same-same the horse shit." From his expression, Stubbs was experiencing a moment of muffled suspension.

"You're kiddin." Stubbs shot his cigarette butt through the first door of the TOC and laughed. "There's too much goin' on back here."

"You sound surprised, Top." Amps and Tennessee were listening. "I think that major bought the farm. He's definitely history."

Hardin needed to tighten security to get Fish out of the bush. He didn't want to worry more about this man, but he had to—he promised Bucks. The rest—Rap, The Frenchman, Amps, Blood, Leech Dick, PeeWee, LeCotte, Boyle, Boo, Doc, Lightning, Tag, Reynolds, Packrat, Sergeant Snorkel, Linus, Grumpy, Wolfman, Knapp, and Pops—would take their turn as equals, as grunts.

Fatigue pushed at his heart and his boots were heavy with the mud he thought he had kicked free. Packrat was Hardin's problem because he got caught smoking dope by the marijuana police and sentenced to hump the outback. Packrat was a good point man.

Rehashing the general's words, Hardin found Maggie fostering the notion that he had been relieved of his command. Maggie had constructed scenes of Hardin's desperation, leaving the two-year captain at the mercy of his directives.

"You havin' a good day, Maggie?" Hardin asked.

"I am." Armed with an arsenal of adjectives, he was primed to the point of actively seeking Hardin's demise. Ridicule was Maggie's repayment for Hardin's infuriating protocol.

"What's next for Charlie Company?"

"The company is going to be inserted east of the Tigers in the morning, then into an AO north of English. Hard telling what your sorry ass will be doing."

The Old Man noted Maggie's gleeful tone when he entered the briefing room. He stopped, straightened his uniform, and sat down.

"Let's not fire up any of these villages. The General has direct orders from Abrams not to shoot into these areas. He knows they're not pacified."

Watching the gas bleed out of Maggie's nuts, Hardin asked, "What's the PZ time?"

"0700 hundred on the airstrip." Hardin looked at the Old Man and grinned. Maggie was finger-weaving the end of his pointer.

Hardin said, "There's only booby traps and stragglers in the Tiger Mountains, Colonel, no matter what the intell suggests. Might be a tunnel in one of those ravines."

* * *

Charlie Company hiked in the sun in the U-shaped valley, took a bath in their favorite bomb crater, and turned south, skirting the coast through a familiar palm grove.

The coffeecake was gone.

Heading toward the old woman and her dead sons, Tag slowed the pace.

Sunrise broke across the South China Sea, firing orange shafts of light through the open gardens of the village. The gray mists turned white and scurried into nothing as offshore winds pushed at the flanks of the Tiger Mountains.

Quietly the villagers set about their day, registering the GI's presence with an occasional glance. Stubbs studied one sector of the village and then another, gauging the movement of the people, watching for hand signals or other forms of coordination.

"Stubbs, look at this." Waiting for Stubbs to sit down, Hardin continued. "Look at the map. So far we've had enemy contact in five AOs: the Crow's Foot, the upper reaches of the Fishhook, the Tam Quan, the rice paddies north of the Tigers, and right here, this village on the southeast edge of the Tigers. We're gonna get hit today—I can feel it."

"If that old woman knows we're comin', it's gonna get nasty."

"She knows we're comin'."

Scurrying mists gave way to odd motions, intermittent air currents, and changing air pressures. The grass was too soft and too uniform. Suddenly and deliberately, Hardin stopped, his search jumping from point to point as he dropped into a full squat. The lush grass was tinged with the echoes of running feet.

I can feel men running, Hardin thought, keying the handset.

"Lima, this is where that hasty ambush blew up. Ya got to billy-goat this ridge, over."

Time clicked away. Death traced the worn folds of his map sheet. The morning was too tranquil, like being blessed with exhaustion. The villagers watched in spurts. Twice Tag started, then stopped. Hardin's friends were on point.

Why couldn't he stop them from entering the sequence, the flow of events?

There she stood. The small spare old woman was staring at him with cold assurance, singing his death with a lyrical whine. He had mocked her dead sons and thrown her to the interrogators. She sank into a deep squat, centered in her doorway, talking into the deeper shadows.

How did she get him back so soon?

Hardin's hand shook as he keyed the net, "Tag, put the barber up front. We got trouble."

"We can stop, clover Lima out around us," Tag said.

"Lima, you read that?" Hardin asked.

"We'll swing wide right and work a clover counterclockwise." GIs stopped in an elongated bubble, signaling the old woman.

"Stubbs, what's goin' on?" Hardin searched the old woman's face.

"I don't know. I haven't felt like this since the night Anderson got hit."

"They've been tipped off." The explosion sounded like a mortar round, a sickening hollow wump. The old woman exposed her blackened teeth, her account not settled.

"Amps, we got a friendly down. Need a dust-off."

Tennessee looked at Hardin with a burning fatalism. "It's Pops," he said, waiting for a response, allowing the pain to find its way.

"Yeah, I know." Hardin wanted to strike out. He leaned against a palm tree to gain his balance, the fever forcing sweat from his body. The old woman stood into the recess of her hootch and disappeared.

"Lima, how's Pops?"

"He's hit, but he's gonna make it." Amps threw the handset into the dirt. "He's gonna make it." The words were meaningless.

Hardin shed his rucksack, handed Amps his map, and started running. He would kill the old woman later: put his weapon under her jaw and blow her head off.

Halfway to his friend, breaking trail as if the war would wait, a dust-off dropped out of the sky and extracted what was left of Pops. The fabric of a platoon had been shredded by deceit. Hardin's heartbeat reached for the throb of the chopper blades as he crashed ahead. Suddenly, he stood in the spill of the kill zone, examining the faces of the ambush.

Blood's eyes conveyed his intentions. Fish was bartering with PeeWee's hysteria. Hardin screamed to control his rage. Pops' blood hung in large drops at the end of a pungent leaf—the remnants of his grace. Fish soaked the blood from the leaf with his drive-on rag.

"Just bad luck." Boyle spoke without a stutter.

"Give me that steel pot," Hardin said. Pops' stew-pot lay open to the sky. LeCotte shoved a cherry aside and grabbed the helmet.

"Somebody's gonna die for this," Reynolds said.

"Damn straight," LeCotte said.

Pops ran cross-compartment, never tracing a ridge. The Viet Cong had been running in front of Pops and set their booby trap on the fly. Hardin scanned the chest-high scrub covering the crest of the ridge. He sat alone absorbing the sorrow—sipping coffee, reading Dig-it's letter, picking at the details of the reporter's picture, holding Sweet Cheek's shroud line, Joe's drive-on rag, and Pops' helmet. He stomped around to tire himself out.

The company detailed the village with their vengeance. Hardin's orders were clear: only burn the old woman's hootch and do not kill the civilians or the livestock.

With Fish at his side, he handed the picture to the old woman. She accepted the picture without expression, her eyes a deep black. Nothing could hide her hatred. Hardin nodded ever so slightly, took the picture and said, "Get fat if ya can, Mama San."

With a sigh, he turned and arched his brow. That he could have been standing on Highlands Road in his pinstripes and cleats seemed impossible. Yet in this village in Vietnam, so filled with despair, he cursed himself for letting his home get so far away.

The flight to LZ English passed unnoticed. The precepts of his conscience had gained weight as he sat on his bunk alone—to cry if he remembered how, out of fear, out of shame, for his friend Pops. When they met again, he would cook. Sitting in the spill of Linda's smile, her beauty set time aside. His centerfold was smiling, too, at a soldier a world away—his world. Time and distance, mixed with the misery of circumstance, left the partings of Hardin's life cobbled such that his heart embraced sorrow and shunned the prospect of joy.

His eyes had filled with tears when Pops read Dig-it's letter, stirring an evening stew. His voice had cracked when he set the letter at its folds and ran a finger over the bloodstained salutation. "God knows why you feel alone, El Tee. I'd expect you to take the letter to my mom."

Pops didn't leave a letter.

Stubbs stared out over the rice shoots, reflecting, weighing the day, and turning Pops' death into denial and shame. His answers were few. The one he couldn't dismiss was coated with the best of regrets. He could taste a notion. It was bitter. A new man would fill the rank, and the rice paddy would be calm, filled to its dikes, waiting, waving to the wind.

Pops wasn't a man to find beauty where he stood. He had lived where new men had died, on this ridge and that. He was schooled in war, a crafty fighter, and a quiet thief—a prophet.

Vacant in heart, the other men stared at the medevac's trail, wondering how it could be that Pops had died. Silence sat atop a cocked-lip grin—Pops' grin. A new man stepped from a colored poster, deaf, dumb, and practically blind. He couldn't hear the war or taste the smells.

The sweaty leather of Stubbs' face wrinkled with contempt.

CHAPTER THIRTY-TWO

Stubbs

Rice Paddies North of Landing Zone English.

Morning fell out as Hardin expected it would, that he had an opportunity of comparing his memory of Pops with that of Bucks and Hippie and the rest. Pops held his ground, trading slang for slang, relieved of his duty when the company landed in the rice paddies north of LZ English.

Laagered in an eighty-foot wide drainage ditch, two days went by with 109 GIs rotating outposts and calling in negative attitudes.

Hardin admired the rural dignity Pops had carried, the simplicity of his appearance and his council now the standard. Tag had assumed Pops' mantle using Reynolds as his enforcer. That lasted until Fish decided Tag was too agreeable, and that a patriarch had to evolve. Besides, as Fish explained, the man might be black. Rap maybe.

New faces appeared at one foxhole and then the next—never seedy, roughly handsome in a foolish way. Their vetting was severe now. Rap and Fish held court—one with the look of a stuffed doll, one the look of a vulture. The new brown-skin GIs were given a choice. Most chose Fish because PeeWee was his secretary.

That and they were intrigued by PeeWee's version of Mexican Golf.

First Platoon got a Sergeant First Class, an E-7—a short, slender, second-tour, airborne master-blaster with a French handle and a sarcastic mouth. Pleased as though his assignment was well planned, Le Beau immediately exposed LeCotte for the Canadian he really was.

* * *

"Are you huntin' trouble, stud?" Hardin said, his expression firing darts at the stranger's face. The new man stepped away from Hardin's rucksack.

"Sarge told me to get Pops' helmet so we could cook some stew."

"Touch my shit again and I'll rip your throat out." The cherry let his innocent grin fade and stepped into an expression an apprentice might find in a tool shed. Blood, who fancied his role as headmaster, was peeling a wedge, crop in hand, intent on breaking the new man's face.

"This dickhead work for you, Blood?"

"Cherries don't work for nobody. This dumb ass is still tryin' to figure out how to shit in one spot. Did you talk to the man, or just start messin' with his shit?" Hollering, as if his rule had expanded, Blood screamed, "Well, Dip Shit, you're gettin' off to a real bad start." Blood looked away and then at Hardin. "You want me to deal with him, Captain?"

Hardin handed Blood the helmet.

"You're lucky, Cherry Boy. That man is crazy." The headmaster and his charge, side by side—old and new, one drawn to the weight, one unable to wait. "Ask around about the last fuckin' new guy he didn't like."

Tennessee laughed. "That cherry's gonna have a long tour."

Playing at being emphatically confused, Amps screamed at the trunk of a palm tree, scuffing its base to gain its attention. "Fuckin' new guys are stupid!" Holding a frag, he stood with his hands extended, inviting the tree to respond. When the tree stood silent, he feigned impatience, and said, "I'm not shittin' ya. That motherfucker is stupid."

When the palm tree continued to ignore him, Amps pulled Leech Dick next to the tree and said, "Tell him, Leech Dick. Tell this thatch-hatchin' mother fucker cherry-boy is stupid."

* * *

Guarding his instinct, as if that might help, Stubbs assembled the platoon leaders. Acting like the curator of an upcoming exhibit, he pictured the old woman and her dead sons appraising his work. He waited for Bowe to unwind before he gave Hardin a nod.

Speaking with an urgency he did not feel, Hardin said, "Well girls, it's time to gin up a gunfight. I want six 300-meter light clovers to run out of this perimeter five minutes prior to first light. Set the clovers tonight. Go straight out as best as the paddies will allow. Rotate clockwise."

"How many per clover?"

"Does your mama know you're here, Bowe? I don't care—small change. Don't fire up your flanks unless you know where your neighbor is." The lieutenants exchanged looks. "These clovers gotta be run fast. Chuck won't be ready."

Under a blunt sky, the cloverleaf patrols left the bubble within seconds of each other, moving swiftly through the adjoining hootches and along the paddy dikes. Within minutes, four of the six patrols had contact, killing three VC—one riding a bicycle, one climbing out of bed, one running into jungle. And a blood trail.

A deceleration colored each returning clover. The farmers were clearly Viet Cong.

"Lima, keepin' up can wear an old man out." Stubbs knew Hardin wasn't Lima.

"You got a ticket to ride, Stubbs—anytime."

Stubbs flipped his cigarette butt at the blue-line. "I've had enough."

"You can buy the beer, Stubbs."

Captain Edward Hardin and Sergeant First Class Oscar Stubbs, the best of friends, would tie their ribbons to a grog cart and gas on for days. They had danced down war's trace, the heat and the roar and the stench. The blood, well that was just for show.

Stubbs was a good man, the best. Through road apples and dead GIs, he managed his war with dignity and courage. He stood by his young lieutenant and his even younger captain, determined to be a soldier. He won every game of pinochle they played. He suffered the jokes about working for a kid, tempering intruders with a note of caution.

Detached and somewhat annoyed by it all, he brokered the unit's trust, dismissing those who might betray his men. Blessed with a heightened sense of reality, his men were never tethered to the-needs-of-the-service. A professional noncommissioned officer, he was the NCO the Army hoped would lead the way. To a man, the company would miss his steady council and his absorbing presence. They had not given a second thought to his orders.

Oscar B. Stubbs would have led brigades in wars past, a profoundly loyal gentleman.

As Hardin stared into the rolling boil in his canteen cup, he heard Pops say, "Hang on to Stubbs, El Tee." Pops and Hardin would talk again.

Somewhere between Pops' council and Dig-it's laugh, Hardin found himself standing in his father's den at Number #10, Highlands Road.

The Major laughed a short laugh as if to point out his amazement, then he thrust a picture into the glow of the desk lamp, and said, "Murphy liked to mimic Poston's walk, and his laugh. John Poston and I were part of the original eight liaison officers. Six liaison officers landed on the beaches at Normandy on D-Day, myself, Johnny, and four others."

"Here's a picture of Johnny taken in Belgium, in 1944, just before the Battle of the Bulge. Right next to the jeep. We had to wear ties."

"Johnny died in an ambush four days after the war ended. I can hear his laughter still. Johnny liked to have a pint or two, and sing songs as loud as he could."

Hardin could recite his father's stories. The Major's den, and Grandpa Karl's farm were his windows of home, windows set in fluid frames. Could they be re-glazed? Would Aunt Dorothy's roses resist his boots as they had his cleats?

Leery optics and a bowel filled with fiber kept Hardin in a fowl mood. "Amps, saddle up and move us 600 meters southwest."

"Who's first?" If gunplay were on the menu, the point squad would know within the first fifty meters when most of the GIs were still in the gully.

"Mike, in five minutes." Amps issued the orders. His speech gained momentum as Tag and the point squad broke into open ground. "Tag, Six wants high steppin'. Spread out, slack with a gun, over." Hardin didn't say it, but Amps had it right.

Within a hundred meters Tag killed an old man he swore was packing a weapon when he ran from a hootch. Maybe he was thinking of Pops when he fired. Or maybe he was thinking of the Viet Cong who were sleeping within a hare's breath of his foxhole. Unwilling to speculate on Tag's thoughts, Hardin decided Tag probably knew exactly what his target was about.

With the company resting in the shade of a palm grove, Stubbs gathered the platoon leaders and directed them to a hootch. An old woman sat in silence behind them holding a bamboo basket, her expression waiting for a turn of the sun. She seemed to enjoy her discomfort.

A second old woman in mauve silken rags hoisted a bamboo pole onto her shoulder, catching her stride. Spotting Hardin, she hesitated. Grime set the creases of her expression into a web of toil. In the quiet of the day this slatternly soul made the village seem more empty than it would have had she not been there. She shuffled down a trail and vanished.

"That old bag recognized me." Hardin spoke with a whisper, handing Stubbs the reporter's picture, suggesting that he show it to the three lieutenants. As if hooked in tandem, the three men scratched for a durable memory, wanting to retain their rage for Pops while calculating Stubbs' meaning and the meaning of the picture.

Wondering if he was once as new as they seemed, Hardin laid an open palm toward the empty village and said, "That picture is a wanted poster. There are copies spread across this delta." He lowered his head into his hands and tried to rub reason into his day. A rush of anger tightened his chest, his mouth instantly dry. Tired of juggling truth and half-truth, and angry beyond his ability to stand still, he said, "We just killed a man that was carryin' a hoe."

"Chuck is here, I can feel him," Bowe said.

"Damn straight," Dillon said. "We got paybacks for, Pops."

"Pops' honor is clean. Nobody is going to fuck with his honor," Hardin screamed, standing as if someone had tried to steal his weapon, searching for the GIs guarding the perimeter. Satisfied with his obligations, he said, "I got paybacks for Pops. You fuckers didn't know him."

Hours later, hiding at the junction of two dust-gray rice paddy dikes, his mattress a hard-beaten hollow of clay, Hardin stared at the sky, brooding. Thrusts of clay stretched away from his boots in a rayed pattern. *This may as well be my grave,* he thought.

Vietnam's old faces—there was an endless supply. Reflecting on his probable death at the hands of a thrombotic old wretch, Hardin decided McNamara was cunning beyond his credits; an acidic influence.

Being a religious sort, Robert-Bob believed everything he could imagine.

Laughing for no reason, Hardin discovered a branding symbol stamped on his P-38 can opener. His extra dick was stamped with a US\Shelby Corp. trademark. Holding the can opener off angle to the sun, he found an arc pierced by an arrow—a rocking arrow.

"Got to pay attention, Eddie," he said. Speaking into a gathering wind, he examined his weapon for secret words or numbers. Arguing the dimensions of his superstition, remnants of Dak To stood-to. The wounded never seemed to heal. Gravity drew at their frames.

* * *

Morning brought three cloverleaf patrols and Leech Dick inspecting the speed bump on his hog. In time, a tracer would have grazed his pecker and shattered his radio. The veterans at the American Legion Hall would laugh on cue, demanding a picture to verify the account.

"Captain, Uncle's on the hook."

"Charlie Six, this is Five Yankee." Uncle was stretching a serious tone, a cautious base with precise enunciation, casting pictures in a magic lantern.

"Hello, Uncle. Why don't you steal a slick and bring out some of the good times?"

"Here's a good time, Stud. One of your medics got word to the Old Man that you've got seventy-eight cases of advanced jungle rot."

Well, big fuckin' deal, Hardin thought. *How about the ass rot, the foot fungus, the boils, the dysentery, and the memory rot? Hell, I have to wipe the back of my hand before I can wipe my ass.*

So fuckin' what?

"My medic did that?" Either Doc Taylor or Doc Cosmo was a whore. "Any of the rest of these assholes talkin' to you?" Hardin was going to butt-stomp the quisling bastard into a fucking whisper for creating this backwash.

"Extraction in thirty minutes, you're in near the beach north of the Tigers. Saltwater and sun should dry things out." A stitch of caution came clumping in Uncle's voice.

"That vill's been hot before," Hardin said.

"Starblazer's got the gunship lead. Intell says it's cold."

Rear-echelon foreplay between the Tiger Mountains and the mouth of the An Lao River. Staff weans were stalking the company at a leisurely pace. The landing zone was one village north of the old woman's hootch.

"Does anybody at higher-higher know about this insertion?" A silence extended itself into some off-mike grumbling as Uncle waited for his RTOs to handle an artillery request.

"No, this is my operation. Be on a pickup zone in thirty minutes."

Hardin gave Stubbs a nod. "Find Doc Taylor."

Packing a face you could never quite remember, his face bound by wire-rimmed sunglasses, and his cock at grips with a foe, Doc Taylor ambled through his day. He did not care a wit about the war, or what Hardin wanted.

"What's happenin', Chuckles?" With a slight pause Hardin smiled. Only a slow dog would hang a handle like Chuckles on his company commander.

Hardin nodded through the steam off his coffee, centered his stare on his latest love child, and said with a grin, "You hippie fuck. Tell me a story about jungle rot."

"Seventy-nine cases: boils so deep we're usin' Tampax to plug the holes."

"You told Uncle we had seventy-eight cases."

"Yeah, well, you're supposed to know better. Some of the dudes have it pretty bad, need to dry out. I slid a note to the resupply pilot."

"You bought the boys a beach party, Doc: South China Sea, white sand, surf."

"Far out." Hardin was thankful that Taylor had cheek and angry that Taylor had not given him a heads-up.

* * *

The northern slopes of the Tiger Mountains lay muted in dust. The rice paddies were dry. Lost in the boredom of yet another chopper ride, the pagoda's white spire caught his eye.

Listening for the bell, he noted the location of the night ambush, and the kill zone that took Andy's leg.

With outposts in place, joyful dolts, deeming the day to be the best day ever, dug foxholes in the scrub grass near the fringe of the beach. Sandbags blossomed, as if the whole affair was so obvious. Staring with unfocused eyes, Hardin could barely see the surf.

Curious to know how a three-month man named Norman Ballick had been chosen to replace Tennessee, Amps warned that Norman required remedial wiring to treat his conspicuous wandering. Amps asked Fish to shoot the man so that Packrat could take the radio.

That's when Fish laughed and told Amps that Packrat didn't know a handset from a hand-job, and that Amps should go fuck himself.

Stubbs liked Norman Ballick because he was nearly underfoot and never spoke. He was a studious sort, the type of GI who found significance in any decision, then agonized over the difference. Incremental analysis was his cup-of-joe—taking words as he might from a broad basket, then gauging them with a caliper so fine his conclusions brought zits to his forehead.

Armed with the most valiant disregard for logic, he would be crazy within a week, uncertainty badgering even his well-founded conclusions.

At length, the thing being done, Hardin decided to mess with the professor. "Tell the platoons to get fifty percent of the studs into the pool, Bull-lock."

Reacting with indignation, Ballick began working a finger into his ear and looking at a map of the new area of operations. His body leaned backward until he adjusted his feet and assumed a brace. He was so stiff an AK round would blow him right out of his boots.

"Fifty percent?" He asked, promoting an impossible tone with a wrinkled brow.

"The last RTO who stood around me pickin' his ass got shot." He sank into a full squat, questioning Hardin's order. "Here's the way combat works, Bull-lock. You do what I tell ya, or I kick your ass. Now, fifty percent in the pool."

"Yes, sir." Hardin tapped on the RTO's map, causing Ballick to wait for a question. Relieved, as if a problem had been solved, he stared at the bottom of his foxhole.

"Everything you see on that map belongs to Chuck. His favorite targets are GIs carryin' radios, that's you, and GIs readin' maps, that's also you." Ballick laid his map in the sand, looking for a reason to pick it up.

"You can reduce the probability of being a primary target by fifty percent by getting rid of the map." He nodded and bounced a bit on his haunches. "I'm not gonna listen to your shit anyway, Bull-lick. You'll still be a cherry when I leave this dump." Hardin reached over and grabbed the hook.

"Lima, Mike, November, this is Six. I want half the studs in the pool."

"Roger, out. Roger, out. Roger, out."

"Easy money, Balls-itch. Push the button and they jump through their ass." With Stubbs organizing his kitchen, Hardin said, "Top, go check the OPs. Make sure we got six rucks on the one facin' that vill."

"On the way." Stubbs flipped his smoke into Hardin's foxhole and moved out.

"There ya go, Balls-itch? He's an E-7. He's been in the army longer then you've been alive. When I tell Top to do something, he doesn't ask me why. It's easy."

"Yes, sir."

"Keep the studs spread out, Balls-itch. Don't let 'em stand above the crest of this beach, where the grass rolls into those paddies. Keep talkin' to 'em, the outposts, and the squads. You got to ride 'em, or they'll relax."

"Yes, Sir. Sir, I don't like being called Balls-itch."

Hardin laughed, and said, "Balls-itch, learn this first. No one gives a shit what you like. You're gonna answer to whatever I call ya. Am I clear?"

"Yes sir." Balls-itch was a professor, a studious grunt. Tucked in the corner of his foxhole, he laid his map in the sand, ran a hand over it to flatten the folds, and began to study. With a flash of absolute rage and a silent scream, Hardin drove his K-Bar through the map.

"If you call me 'sir' out here again, Fuck Stick, I'm gonna end your ride. I told ya to put that fuckin' map away. You're not gonna get me killed because you're fuckin' stupid." Drawing his knife through his RTO's map, Hardin was pleased with its edge. Admiring his knife, he said, "I might give up a grin now and then, Jackass, but I'm not a nice guy."

GIs laughed and screamed as they paddled their rubber whores over the crest of the breakers. Open water drag-racing pit four and five GIs against the incoming tide.

The village elders stared in disbelief.

The old woman of Tiger Mountain would conclude her enemy would not be foolish enough to swim and lay around for two consecutive days. These GIs would surely leave in the morning. She would have the local Viet Cong platoon lay in ambush tomorrow, one kilometer west of the beach.

The hope that a day's rest might mend the rot that bored at their hearts, although romantic, became plausible when the company stayed on the beach for a second day. Moving a squad with a machine gun team into the village to monitor the activity, Stubbs initiated a search for a copy of the reporter's picture. As time wore on, and the day wore out, squads and fire teams reformed.

"We're movin' in the mornin', Doc. I think we're makin' the locals crazy."

"Two days won't get it done."

"How come we're not gettin' any clap out of this town?"

"Hard tellin'. Troops are moochin' Darvon, that kind of shit."

Twilight began with a sunset so pure the perimeter fell silent. Squatting near the crest of the beach, Hardin found himself staring at a striated band of orange-gold sky. The mountains seemed carved from coal. Gray rice paddies, lime-green palm trees, and the black-faced ridge that was the Fishhook were topped with a brilliant gold icing.

The sky ran east from the ridge dragging itself from deep blue to purple, to gray-black where it met the South China Sea. A Caribou popped over the black-faced ridge, its silhouette muted in the gold light. Far off to the east, under the churning clouds of the brooding monsoon, a flock of aluminum geese crabbed against a stiff head wind.

Discouraged, Hardin registered his find, wishing he could join the pilots for Happy Hour.

Nature's grace, distilled from the compost of man's hatred, seemed to caution these travelers. Numb and without emotion, the war had not turned out as Hardin had imagined. Beauty, now an abstract, was artificial, diminished because it was less apparent. Never quite free of this notion, he searched the rooftops of the village. For what, he did not know.

Twilight's trance ended with the sound of boots. Grumpy, Packrat, and Linus were scrambling away from their foxhole, hollering. A cobra had chased a frog out of the rice paddy and was eating the frog in the bottom of their digs. Three of America's finest, paratroopers to their core, armed with M-16s, were in retreat, run off by a six-foot snake.

Blood fragged the snake and blustered his disgust.

Nightfall began with a series of lizard calls, millions of stars, and one short burst of AK fire. Grumpy fired one round from his M-16 to demonstrate his furry before Fish pounced on his back, leaving indelible prints in his face.

* * *

As the morning made no sense, the sunrise forced light through the gathering clouds. Shadows of tired men stood over the crest of the beach. The sea was still, calmed by a slack tide. The wind from the sea blew in gusts. The sea, the beach, and the village seemed set apart—as if governed by separate rhythms, they were dancing together.

Unwilling to leave, Hardin was growling and cussing as he finished his coffee, studying the pattern of foxholes on the beach—Charlie Company's seal. Numbed by a mounting isolation, he glanced at his watch for no reason he could muster, then shouldered his rucksack. Maybe if he died, his friends would be less of a target.

With the cobra's head pinned to the front of his helmet by his camouflage band, Tag led the charge through the village, turned west into the rice paddy, and then into the vegetation along the northern foot of the Tiger Mountains.

The morning slipped away with the cobra's fangs still dripping. Sitting on his rucksack Stubbs handed Hardin a copy of the reporter's picture he had discovered under a roof strut. He looked over the wide expanse of rice paddy, then lit a smoke, gauging the effects of his offering.

"That reporter thinks he can hide," Stubbs said.

"I'm gettin' the feelin' that reporter didn't copy this picture, Stubbs."

"That don't matter. Blamin' him makes me feel better."

* * *

At 1523 hours, after seven hours of busting dry brush, the point squad mounted a bald, thirty-foot plateau, overlooking rice paddies on three sides.

"Tag, stop the parade. Lima's got a busted ruck."

"This place don't feel good, Captain." Amps had started chewing tobacco.

The company dug in contrary to habit. First Platoon took the northern sector at the finger end of the plateau facing the An Lao River.

Sitting against the trunk of a palm tree on the western rim of the plateau, talking with the Missouri contingent of Second Platoon, scanning the rice paddy, Hardin spotted the field where Andy lost his leg. As he said good-bye again, the image of the dog handler's outstretched arm appeared on the face of the palm grove, the man's hand cinched around the leash.

It was Stubbs' stories that kept this image fresh.

Jerking the leash from the handler's fist, as if separating him from his dead scout dog might somehow wake him, Hardin found himself dragging Dig-it's body, all the while listening to Shadow sing "The Shadow of Your Smile." When the muffled concussion of a buried 105mm artillery shell pushed across the plateau, he ran toward the billowing dust. Jungle boots never weighed so much.

Packrat lay shredded in the bottom of the shell crater, charred with black powder. Reynolds stood without moving, stunned, his frame covered with scraps of his friend. As if awakened he began screaming into the depression, "Oh, God! Oh, God!" gasping and throwing his rage.

Doc Taylor threw a piece of bone fragment into the air. Packrat didn't notice. He was a lacerated tangle of meat, blood, torn limbs, and blackened flesh. Two medics worked to stop his death—morphine, tourniquets and a poncho.

Stubbs pushed GIs away from the crater—booby traps came in pairs. "Get back to your positions, goddammit!" He yelled again, this time pushing LeCotte and Boyle.

Reynolds placed a cigarette between Packrat's charred lips and said good-bye. The cigarette waited for him to look away, then fell into the confusion. As if miming the explosion, Reynolds threw his hands into the air. Talking, he lingered near the crater.

"He's fucked, ain't he, Doc?"

"Shut up, Reynolds," Stubbs said, continuing to clear GIs from around the crater.

When the medics pulled Packrat out of the hole, his lifeless body gliding on a poncho, Grumpy screamed and threw his arms into the air. Grumpy had been standing between Packrat and Reynolds negotiating radio watch schedules. When the booby trap exploded Packrat set sail, flying, waving his limbs and throwing his boots, his helmet arcing from his head.

Struck by the odor of blood, Hardin confronted Stubbs, his voice quietly strained. "Stubbs, if ya know I'm makin' a mistake, ya gotta do somethin' about it."

Stubbs lit a cigarette and waited for the smoke to clear his mouth before he spoke. "God damn you, Captain. Shit is gonna get dealt our way and you ain't gonna stop that. We're all gonna die. Just that some of us jokers will still be walkin' when it's over."

"Give me a cigarette, Stubbs." Stubbs gave Hardin the finger and walked away.

The skids of the dust-off kissed the ground. Packrat was gone.

When an ordinance demolition team found two more 105mm booby traps buried near the shell crater with the firing devices triggered, silence flowed across the plateau.

Hardin jerked the hook off of Amps' shoulder strap. "Lima, Charlie Six."

"Lima, go." Dillon's voice seemed glued to the radio.

"Did you get a ruck off that medevac?"

"The bad ruck was Packrat's. They're gonna bury him in it."

Quick-fire had seized the men of First Platoon. They lost Pops and Packrat to the soulless indifference of an old woman's promise. They would allow that Hardin had payback for Pops. They would not allow any interference in their retribution for Packrat.

This kind of sequential purchase caused vibrations that spooked GIs for years.

When a GI's time was up, sorry 'bout that. Packrat's rucksack caused the company to stop. Packrat had traded his turn on OP when the company was on the beach so he could go swimming a second day. Packrat had picked the small depression to establish his OP. Packrat, not Reynolds or Grumpy, had stepped on the one booby trap that was properly wired.

Packrat had run out of time.

Hardin recited the Lord's Prayer to cover his Christian obligations, decided he was still tempted by pussy's simple delights, and wished for Chuck to excuse him while he went home.

Hours later, glancing absently around the perimeter, holding Joe's drive-on rag, he found himself waiting for another man to explode.

Relieved, as if any amount of money would do, he had earned the loneliness sunset brought, the vacant time that keyed so many memorial permutations—that combinatorial juggling of still-framed death, with screams more powerful from their rotting, the symphony bounding into a goose-stepped coda of funereal precision, chinking his armor.

Tears welled in his eyes. When he played war as a child, his imaginary buddy's name was Joe. They welcomed their glorious wounds. Hardin would lie on his back, practicing his agonies, moaning into the neighbor's woods. Joe would hear him and drag him back to friendly lines in the nick of time.

Death was such a close call.

Those were Dig-It's eyes: bright pools shining in the hollow of Pops' helmet, framed in a colloquy of Black English, continually adjusting their sense of doubt.

Top's mailbag slid over the edge of the cargo deck. The chopper was on fire. The old woman had the mailbag. She was reading the mail.

CHAPTER THIRTY-THREE

Starblazer

Charlie Company Night Laager. North of the Tiger Mountains.

Words of humor survived the day—hard, cruel, furious words.

"Packrat's dead," Stubbs said to no one, surveying the pattern of hootches that rimmed the rice paddy north of the Tiger Mountains. Tiring of the talk of revenge, no one knew these ragged men better than their Field First Sergeant. Pops and Packrat were the best point men to ever hump a ruck—since Bucks and Hippie, that is. And before that there were Nasty and Drips.

Viet Cong guerrillas controlling the flanks of the Tiger Mountains had taken out Pops and Packrat with artillery-shell pressure booby traps. Within a moment, they lost their legs. Packrat was lucky—he was dead. Word from the hospital in Qui Nhon listed Pops as wounded in action.

Permitting his expression an odd sense of recognition, Stubbs took a conclusive drag, exhaling away from his line of sight. The Headquarters Company first sergeant had the grit he needed to hone his war on marijuana. A GI caught smoking dope was dead.

* * *

Hardin put Fish and his attitude on drag, and the company dropped off the plateau into the hootches surrounding the large rice paddy on the north-central side of the mountains.

Tag slowed the pace to allow the heat and the tedium to mellow emotions, and to search the village for a reason to challenge its existence. The villagers were accommodating, drawing water from wells, watching as the quest drew one GI and then another through their home.

Tag stopped in the center of the village to show the children his cobra.

Stubbs alerted momentarily when a young boy ran from a hootch, frightened by LeCotte. The hootch was empty when he entered. The thatch walls were firm, supporting woven reed beds along two walls. The rice bin in the floor next to the door was full. Dillon grabbed Stubbs' arm to keep him from leaving the hootch. The rice bins in the other hootches were nearly empty.

"Stubbs, get Reynolds," Dillon said, stepping into the shadows.

"What's up, El Tee?" Reynolds asked.

"Stand off-angle and empty a magazine into that rice bin."

Instantly, Reynolds turned cold, looking for a bulge in the top layer of rice. Estimating where a man's head might be, he took an electric step, muzzle down, he emptied his weapon.

The rice bin erupted. AK rounds spit rice into a funnel and burst through the roof of the hootch. As if he might yell, a Viet Cong soldier forced his head and shoulders out of the rice. Reynolds' boot found what was left of his life.

The dead soldier slumped, his blood staining the rice.

Fish grabbed the AK as Stubbs bounded back into the hootch.

"Leave him in the rice. Find that kid who's runnin' around this hootch."

"He took off," Blood said, evaluating the blood-soaked rice.

Watching Reynolds search the rice bins a second time, Hardin decided to move west 400 hundred meters and dig in. Dillon wanted to backtrack a squad and ambush the village. His request denied, he put PeeWee and Fish on the OP covering the backtrack, then gave Fish a nod.

* * *

PeeWee sank into the grass, working the kinks out of the weeds in front of his face. A cold surge of fear pushed across the trail. It had taken an hour for the OP to get back to the perimeter of the village.

The trip flare hung from a vine like a dead snake. Counting the scuff-marks on the trail, PeeWee waited, listening before he exposed himself again.

Fish waited until the serenity of the jungle became intolerable. He jumped out of the brush, spitting at PeeWee's stupidity, then assaulted the trip flare with certain justice. He wrapped the wire into a jumble, then gingerly released the end. The wire held taunt.

Satisfied the trip flare would give them time to clear the village; they began to search for the boy. Why, they didn't know.

Of late the searching wasn't enough.

"Don't slit her throat, PeeWee." Fish warned the rest of the team out of the hootch.

"How big?" PeeWee said.

"She ain't the one." Fish moved closer to his friend.

"How big, Fisherman?"

"She didn't kill Packrat."

The glint from a knife flashed and Fish threw himself into PeeWee, knocking his friend off the old woman, sending his body reeling. The woman ran out of the hootch and along a vacant path, stoically frail, a frightened soul hiding in the crease of a painful smile.

With no mind for the boy, Fish drew the team back to the OP location. PeeWee had snapped. Fish led him back to the company laager, leaving LeCotte to run the outpost.

Celebrating PeeWee's lunacy, Fish laughed like he was trying to swallow a mouthful of Coke, forcing the fumes out of his nose. He laughed again and told PeeWee he was loco. "Maybe so," PeeWee said. Then PeeWee told Fish that the rotten holes in his gringo teeth were from eating too many boom-boom girls. Fish reckoned that this might be true.

No matter where, they sat together. Alone this time, they sat near their foxhole, secure and safe, yet fearful that someone might catch them happy.

PeeWee sliced a salami stick in silence, sitting in his kitchen between his helmet and his rucksack. His mind was clear. He slit the old woman's throat. He smiled when his knife pierced her wrinkled skin. Somehow she didn't notice.

No matter. The old woman wouldn't kill any more of his friends.

It didn't take long to become friends or enemies in such a place, the distinction measured in broken words. Fish and PeeWee were kindred friends—they worshipped being dead. Yet as crazy as Fish had become, he could still measure the worth of an old woman or a child.

"Tennessee, you've been diggin' deep. What's your problem?" Hardin asked.

"Bullshit's gettin' spooky."

"You best stay in that hole. We're gonna get hit tonight." Hardin set his rucksack at the back rim of the foxhole and knelt down to examine Joe's rag.

"What do ya think, Sarge, Chuck out drivin' around?" Tennessee asked.

"Feels like it. Get 'em in a hole." As if twilight weren't enough, GIs wandered from foxhole to foxhole, judging the day before being isolated by the night. Hand signals stopped the chatter and started a reaction that brought weapons to the ready.

With the sun dropping behind the Fishhook, a VC squad opened fire on the perimeter from an island of hootches across 150 meters of watered rice paddy. Within a second, machine gunners returned fire.

The paddy-sea boiled as red tracer rounds threw water into the air.

"Scramble a gunship team," Hardin yelled.

Fish screamed in anguish. A little girl's feet kicked into the air, her tiny body suspended for a moment in the fading light. He keyed the net, and screamed again, "Dinks are takin' off."

Heat from the AK rounds ripping the vegetation near his head followed Hardin as he bolted out of his foxhole, stepping on Amps' hand and yelling at Tennessee. Yelling "Cease fire," he zigzagged through Lima's sector and landed on the machine gunner still firing.

"Lightning, shut it off!" Hardin raced back to the radio.

"Mike, this is Six, take a squad light out to those hootches. Ya gotta hurry."

Eight pennies, a pocket full of loose change, ran down the long dike, silhouetted like deer on a bald ridge. Fingers lay ready to re-start suppression fires, leaning on triggers, eyes searching. Targets across black open water were farther than expected.

The radio barked. “Tennessee, we got kids and women down.”

“Dust-off’s on the way, Mike One,” Amps replied.

“We’ve got a Hollywood and a couple bleeders. One kid’s fucked.”

Amps drew his head away from the handset as if he might find cleaner air.

Hardin stalked the radios, waiting to explode, with Ballick analyzing his conduct. “Fuck you, Balls-itch, you god-bobbing puke.”

Hardin threw his steel pot into the foxhole grazing Amps. “God damn, greasy cocksuckers. Motherfuckin’ no-good, rat bastards. The next dink I find I’m gonna blow his pig-fuckin’ brains out.” Hardin was screaming into the fading light: at himself.

“Starblazer, Charlie Five.” Stubbs stared at Hardin as if seeing himself.

“Starblazer is here.” Hardin barged into his foxhole to retrieve his helmet.

“Cover my loose change back home would ya?” The dust-off was out of sight and eight frightened men were on a full-speed rawhide, running from the night.

“We see your pennies, Charlie Five. We got ’em covered. We’ll give ya a fire power demo on that low ridge to the west. We’ll drop down on your push, over.”

A moment later, and he was leading the band.

“Gentlemen, this is Starblazer. The first weapon is the 2.75 inch, 40mm rocket. Keep your eyes on the woods.” One pass and then another, taking the GIs’ minds off of slaughtering children. Starblazer expended his rockets and swung north over the perimeter and then the open paddy.

“The next weapon system is the Vulcan machine gun, the mini-gun.” The two gunships banked west along a blackened ridgeline.

When the shadows groaned and the Vulcans pissed red tracers into the unblemished vegetation, quiet cheers jumped from the foxholes, their mind’s eye following the rounds into a blunted gathering of simulated vengeance.

“Amps, this is Mike One, we’re in.”

“Thanks for callin.” Hardin could feel Ballick trying to prime him with impatience.

“I heard, Balls-itch. Get a commo check.”

Starblazer was winding full power, heading north toward the An Lao River, and back on the battalion net. The shadow of the two slicks raced across the surface of the water and jumped into a palm grove. The gunship crew would be drinking beer within the hour.

“Charlie Six, Starblazer, here. Hope the show gave the folks somethin’ to cuddle with.” His voice was shocked with a familiar rhythm, a familiar understanding.

"Roger that. Catchy tune." The pilot laughed a bit-part promise and let his charm melt into a hesitation, relieved that his support was helpful.

"Shake it off, Charlie Six. VC been killin' kids for thirty years. Bad things are gonna happen when there's a gunfight." Hardin stood dumb, listening to his father's voice bark from the handset, telling him to shake-it-off, piece-a-cake, take care of yourself. Hardin hung onto the sound, his focus suspended above the paddy sheen.

"Chalks away, Starblazer."

"Keep lookin' back to the left, boys. Chuck's comin' at ya."

"See ya in Piccadilly, Starblazer." Hardin waited to hear his father's voice again, keen to trap the words, his shoulders braced against the back of his foxhole.

"Take care of yourself, Pal."

His father was gone, and Starblazer had called him "Pal." Plowing between emotion and reason, he stood suddenly shaken, restless with exuberant fear. He could not keep a train of thought. Crazy with frustration, the blurring vagueness of his prolonged exposure to combat, to the ruthless slaughter of children, had finally drawn him to the edge.

His father's dreams raced to their end, then simmered in confusion, heavy like the mud he kicked from his boots. Even though his father died of a tortured heart, his words rang clear. The Major had fashioned a world Hardin could not find.

It was his punishment, and his father's offense.

Changes in Hardin were obvious at the end of this day. His fire for war was a feckless flame, gleaned from books with Eastern words. He had come as far as East would go to kill the strangers the Major said would fight. The journey had been a lonesome one. If he were not blessed with death, he would rue those Eastern words for their certitude.

A heavy veil had been forming for days. And then it rained—a pelting drum that brought the sky so low he could wash his face with the clouds. Rot was jumping from the jungle floor.

No man moved throughout the night. Spent as spent could be, Hardin was fighting to keep his grief concealed. He did not want to sleep, fearful that his dream might come true. He was thankful he could not see their tiny faces, or see them bleeding in the mud. He could hear their small screams, or was he screaming?

Little children were so dear, even a soldier's frown could harm them.

In a dream so clear, his father sat in his den telling a story. Pipe smoke curled away from the lines around his eyes.

"Richard Hardin, my granddad, your great granddad, was killed in the Boer War, in an ambush fighting in the Transvaal, in South Africa, in 1902. He died a long way from his home near Lands End and Cornwall, England. The old boy was one of the King's Welshman: a soldier, a Brownjob in the 24th Foot."

Mixed as they were in a cloud of pipe smoke, pictures of World War II filled the night.

* * *

Morning brought anger for Packrat, anger for the children, and a truckload of guilt. With no apparent purpose, the company moved to the west and stopped. The radio barked.

"Charlie, Mike Six, we left a Claymore at the laager."

Hardin grabbed the handset. "Roger, break, break. Lima, send some pennies back to police it up. Ya gotta fly."

"Roger, that." Fish and PeeWee were on drag, close to the night laager. Within a minute, a fire team full of M-16s belched the morning to a brace.

"Charlie, we got a wounded dink and a blood trail rollin' up the Claymore, over."

"What'd he say?" Ballick froze and handed Hardin the hook.

"Say again, Lima." A burst of M-16 fire left the jungle silent.

"We got a dead dink, a blood trail, and the Claymore. Ya want us to pursue, over?"

"Negative, close it up."

When the old woman's army used children as shields, righteous men registered their right to retribution—paybacks. And because retribution was a personal charge, any Viet Cong caught half-steppin' near the Tiger Mountains would die of high-velocity shock.

At bottom, a vicious tone settled over the day. GIs braced with aggression looked for someone to kill. By late afternoon the company settled into a patch of low scrub, ignoring the rain. The sunlight that had set the mountains in vivid profile had vanished behind the chill of graying skies. On schedule, after brief trysts into the Philippines, the monsoon took hold of the An Lao River basin.

Grumpy had fallen into a morose silence; his eyes hollowed, he sparred with a childhood he could not remember. He was communing with an archangel who found his guilt laughable.

* * *

Morning stand-to brought clearing skies, chilling air, and jungle vegetation moving in awkward triumph as the sun baked the moisture from its veins. Hardin stood among the old influences, perched on an open patch of wet clay, watching steam rise from Amps' back. The air near the jungle floor smelled like spoiled eggs. Leeches were boiling from the earth, sending GIs into a flurry of cock-saving rituals.

When a search-and-destroy mission is reduced to the fits and starts of a jungle that is too quiet, tempers accelerated and men like Tag and Reynolds unleashed their K-bars. When Leech Dick exposed his cock, as Fish explained it for the ninth time, Reynolds tackled the radio operator and Tag cut the buttons off his pants, warning that the next casualty would be his cock.

Leech Dick, suffering the incompatibility of Tag's stupidity and anything Fish might muster, read his dog tags. Drinking his morning coffee, he spoke the words to ensure that he remembered his name. His dog tags said he was a Baptist.

Stubbs cautioned Tag, sidestepping the GIs scattered in the brush, signaling that the unit was being followed. No one cared.

GIs lay in the shady spots, soaked with a burning sweat, drinking the dank-smelling water as fast as four children could raise the bucket. Staring into the well, Stubbs imagined a cold mountain stream. With no sense of relief, he realized the water had more body than pea soup.

Snow-melt didn't have particulate that stained the tin-ware.

Hardin drank from a wooden ladle, his eyes level with the young girl's face, searching for signs of recognition, her eyes too black to read. He smiled his best smile, the one he was saving for his little girl, and gave her a chocolate wafer. She turned into a scamper, then turned into a smile. Tooth for tooth she was a beautiful little girl.

* * *

Dirty, tired, and scared, fighting a mild dysentery and jungle rot, he laughed with the men who counted on a teenage captain to get them through Vietnam's war. He listened to their banter. PeeWee, The Frenchman, and LeCotte sat in a cluster, schooling a new man, sharing their smokes and their wisdom.

"Yeah, that's the captain. No, we're not shittin' ya. Young lookin' maybe. Don't be fuckin' off. That dude's got eleven months in the woods. Ask around, he's good luck. We got fewer casualties then anyone. Dig it, Chuck has tried. Don't be walkin' on a trail. Start bitchin' and see what happens. The dude'll kick in your face. Dig it! Ask around—he hates cherries."

And that's how the story was told. One GI to another, they had to believe in someone, in something. With Joe—and Hardin, and Stubbs—a GI got both: a man and his luck. Hardin let the water boil for an extra minute adding coffee to hide the bugs.

With three hours in the can, the company cut along the base of the plateau where Packrat got wasted and prepared for a resupply with an OP near the crest.

"Charlie Six, this is Six, we're sending out a resupply. Extraction at first light."

"What's the drill?" Hardin asked, promoting a fatalistic tone.

"NVA were spotted west of the Fishhook." West of the Fishhook—holy shit.

Casting an eye over the perimeter, allowing each man to say his name, Hardin spoke to Tennessee. "It's time for you to leave." Pulling out a map of the upper An Lao Valley he found his friend's expression unnerving. Premonition was the kiss of death.

A weighted silence was quickly replaced with the foolery of unemployed convalescents. Hardin turned his head aside, for, with a rush, he pushed at his memory of home. He stood in the jungle in his pinstripes and cleats. Amps was pitching that day.

"And take Amps with ya."

Yelling a duet of hallooning nonsense, ecstatic, as if without reason, Amps and Tennessee danced with joy, demonstrating their best moves. Tennessee was more composed. Amps gave his power pack a toss, pausing to see if his cock had a spark. Neither man could hide his relief.

The slick brought food, mail, ammunition, and shoulder-fired rockets.

Nodding allegiance to the confederates, Hardin said, "Look for us." Tennessee stuck out a fist. Amps stood off a ways, lecturing a palm tree on the finer points of servitude.

"Thanks, Captain." Tennessee loved guzzling with the upper chambers.

"Meet us when we rotate in." Hardin's rucksack seemed heavier as his expression conveyed the affection of a final journey.

Tennessee tried a hopeful shrug, then made a pale effort at nonchalance. "Just another walk in the woods. Like those night assaults." Every grunt knew the valleys west of the Fishhook were stone-cold death. "Captain, we never did figure how things crossed our mind, dodgin' all those thoughts of pussy." Amps exuded a gracious concurrence, coaxing his friend.

"Mercy! I was on top when she shot me." Hardin smiled as if he knew better, then studied Tennessee's face. "Your baby girl's waitin' on ya, Captain."

Hardin pointed at the chopper, and said, "You best get steppin."

Fish was next.

* * *

What alone should have given notice, six insertion choppers circled high above the Fishhook, buffeted by gusting winds, waiting on station while three F-100's dumped high-explosive ordinance into the seam of a rugged ravine.

Measuring the riverbed and the patch of reed grass where Walker was killed, Hardin replayed the firefight. He was dragging the dead radio operator, running down the river, when the door gunner slapped his shoulder.

"Hey!" The copilot jerked on his rucksack. "It's a one-slick LZ."

"We're first," Hardin yelled.

The copilot turned back to the radio. By the time the slick started down, Hardin was standing out on the skid, singing, and looking for enemy movement in the narrow ravine. The ridge on the north flank of the shell crater was laced with jagged rock. Jumping into the debris at the bottom of the crater, he hesitated while the other five men cleared the skids.

The high-explosive ordinance had befuddled the largest colony of fire ants in Southeast Asia. Enraged ants attacked the GIs, doing chin-ups to the chorus from Lil' Abner, their bite transmitting immediate shock. Sucking air through clinched teeth, GIs crab-walked out of the crater, dragging their rucksacks. Within forty meters Hardin was naked to his boots. The stinging intensified as he shook out his shirt and brushed the ants from his thighs.

Stubbs fell in the crater trying to clear the skid, started cussing when he lost his smoke, then started running. To hell with security.

"Damn, those little bastards hurt," Stubbs said, lighting a smoke.

"I saw you grab your nuts, take off your gear, and turn around—all at the same time."

"Fuck you." Stubbs was short for the bush, and a little testy.

"Captain, a FAC pilot wants to know somethin' about the bomb crater," Ballick said, annoyed that he didn't have the answer.

"What did you call me?" Hardin let the question linger, then he grabbed Balls-itch's map and slit it in two with his K-bar. Satisfied, he keyed the hook.

"This is Charlie Six, say again, over."

"This is FAC One-Niner. Higher-higher wants a crater analysis." Stubbs was counting the welts on his chest when Hardin started laughing.

"You're considerable, Balls-itch. What's your analysis of the crater?" Ballick looked confused and on the spot. "Look on your map, maybe that'll help. That map is gonna get somebody killed."

"I don't know how to analyze a crater." With a cultivated expression of shame, Ballick held the two halves of his map as if he might read them.

"FAC One-Niner, this is Charlie Six, what's your real name, and just what in hell do ya want to know?"

"The girls call me Thumper. How big a hole, collateral damage, that sort of stuff."

"Collateral has four syllables, and the girl's hole is crawling with fire ants."

"That's not good. Give me a couple of numbers, Charlie Six."

"Eight and twenty, Thumper."

"Blackbirds are good. Good luck, Charlie Six." Thumper was signing off, flying across a restless sky, romancing those needles of doubt, and racing toward a ready-board and more proportionate logic: a hot meal, a warm cot, and intuitive results, sally-fucking those randy little trotters at Cam Rahn Bay while minding the watch fires for more justified Christians.

"Tickle her fancy, Thumper, and have one for us."

"Fancy has a snap-cracker like a hooded cobra. About the size of a good cigar." Forward Air Control pilot—FAC One-Niner—Thumper—laughed into his handset while he used a grease pencil to scribble eight and twenty on his windscreen.

"Like a soggy cigar, eh Thumper?" Hardin smiled, brushing a fire ant from his arm.

"It's just needle, ball, and airspeed for me. Tally Ho, boys."

Ballick took the hook and spit chewing tobacco into the brush. He was inventing bush-bogies, which kept a grid coordinate on his lips.

The perimeter fell into fear. Nothing was humorous about this tunnel-colored valley. A trail ran the crest of the ridge above the landing zone. Sandal scuffs of indeterminate age headed east, toward the Fishhook. The trail bed was damp and hard-beaten, with weeds and stiff ground cover lining its shoulders. The canopy was layered, blocking all but those abrasive bits of light.

The vibrations of motionless symmetry would pass undetected.

Rucksacks lowered themselves as GIs sank away, drawn as they were by the silence. This jungle was breathing. Hardin wiped the pus from his hand, adjusted his knees into a squat, winced at the cramping in his gut, and searched the jungle floor across a small saddle.

He shivered suddenly, involuntarily.

Even the NVA would avoid such a place.

Billowed movement in the canopy converted linear shafts of light into a ripple, as the eye chased one flutter, and then another. Patches of light wobbled in circuits around the recesses, each recess requiring an evaluation. Hardin's gaze kept returning to the damp edges of the trail. A bamboo stake in the nuts would not be good.

Flashes of Dak To and Kontum framed his vision.

Men moved without breathing, communicating with the tail of their eyes. After five hours and forty-three minutes of ridge-running the flanks of the trail, Tag led the unit down to a vigorous blue-line to look for trail intersections.

Hardin sat plop-legged on his rucksack with his back fastened to the base of a tree, looking over a steep, rocky riverbank. The first rain of the season left the air with a taste that rivaled overcooked parsnips. Like animals wallowing in their own dung, not one man could keep from moving. The heavy stench produced a warmth that livened the senses.

First wet and then cold, the sun baked the canopy. The jungle floor was much darker after a rain—much darker, and much harder to define.

Stubbs flipped his smoke into the river, smiling as it ran free. Hardin and Stubbs exchanged glances, instantly realizing the cigarette butt could bring trouble.

"You know what they call us, Stubbs? What the staff-patches call us if we live through a firefight and can still walk and talk?" Hardin's shoulders shivered, lifting him away from the tree. He searched across the blue-line for movement and signaled Tag to do the same.

Satisfied, he whispered. "You know what those bastards call us, Stubbs?"

"Must be good."

"'Effectives.' They call us 'effectives.' So to leave this dump early we've gotta become ineffective, which should be easy if the wizards put us much farther out in the woods."

"A good dog would have trouble in these parts."

"The way to be combat-effective is to kill these commie rice-balls, and if we do that we're gonna get whacked, and then be classified as ineffective, which means we can't possibly be effective." Ballick was struggling with the logic, so Hardin continued.

"What should really frost ya, Stubbs, is the army thinks Chuck's runnin' outta time."

"Not many dinks are wearin' watches," Stubbs said, and lit another smoke.

"I read an after-action report from Dak To that was posted in the TOC. Forty-three studs from Alpha Company were executed by the NVA—shot in the face at close range. Up 'til then, they were effective, effectively fucked."

"There weren't any names on that report, Stubbs, not one name. No names, just numbers: seventy-six KIA, forty-three executed, four effectives extracted."

"Yeah, well, I'm short, so we're gonna tighten things up," Stubbs said, looking into an empty cigarette pack. Deciding it was still empty he showed it to Fish and held his hand out until Fish filled his palm with a new pack of Luckys.

* * *

After three days, the freshly peeled grapefruit skins Tag found were not as interesting as the twelve-slick extraction. *Ah yes,* Hardin thought, *LZ English, that mass of high-profile coagulate, that pudding sludge of Kiwi black and bad data.*

Hardin found Uncle walking to the mess tent.

"I got twenty-six days and a wake-up, Uncle, so get fat if ya can."

"You're short. Guess we better put you on the berm for one last go-round." The old friends laughed, knowing if the general got another slice of Hardin's ass, there wouldn't be anything left to ship home. "You're on the berm starting tonight."

"Is the Old Man gonna leave town or hang around for the show?" Uncle shook his head, smiling as he looked over the airstrip, watching a Caribou land.

"I think there's a bounty on your head. Worth about ten grand they say," Uncle said.

"Good rumor." Uncle nodded, his brow cautioning Hardin.

"The bounty was intell we got from a VC snatched north of the Tigers." The old woman of Tiger Mountain had an ample supply of recruits. "MPs found a copy of this picture in Bong Son last week," Uncle said, showing Hardin a copy of the reporter's picture.

Hardin took a copy of the picture out of his pocket and handed it to Uncle. "That reporter took that picture the morning I ran him out of the field—same man I punched out by the aid station."

"The prejudicial allegation was dropped."

Uncle stood to a brace, weighing the possibility that the reporter posted the bounty. Changing subjects, Uncle said, "We don't have rotation orders for you. Most orders are ninety days out. Guess the army thinks you're havin' a good time."

"I know when my tour's over, Uncle." Hardin clenched his right hand into a fist to ease the pain. Pus joined with the fire-ant welts.

"What's the deserter's name, Uncle?"

Uncle wasn't a lying man. He was a truthful man, a marvel of sorts. He weighed the garish quotes each day, the impersonal lies, the glories that clothed men and villages in achievements absurd to all except the authors, glories that were the fancy of wars past.

A soldier without an Army, Uncle set his jaw to the horizon, angry yet satisfied that Hardin was the man he was. The burden of hiding the missing man was gaining weight. With three months left on his extended tour of duty, Uncle had decided to keep the deserter and Hardin's imaginary friend alive—the deserter because he had to and Ragman for the hell of it.

"The deserter had a name yesterday," Uncle said. "Maybe it will come to me."

Revenge and saving face were the Celestial way. Hardin had assaulted the reporter, desecrated the memory of the old woman's sons, ended the career of a staff-patch, and humiliated the White Mice. The reporter or an old woman, a staff-patch or the White Mice: the bounty was, well, a fancy bit of intell—a rear-echelon story perhaps

And, Maggie—well, he was another story.

CHAPTER THIRTY-FOUR

Memories

Landing Zone English. 1120 Hours.

The shower was cold, the fatigues were refreshing, and the chow was a problem. Hardin found himself separated from the troops; their refitting activities shrouded in quiet conversations, deliberately secret. Worse, with GIs insulating themselves against his leaving, he had lost most of his sources of feedback: Pops, Stubbs, Amps and Tennessee.

He still had Rap and Fish.

The company mounted the perimeter berm at 1600 hours in a light rain amidst gusts of grab-ass and folly. Hardin sat alone in the command bunker looking at a *Playboy.* With a hesitant step, a GI stood-to, the pain in his face reflecting what might happen next.

"Sir." With his voice cracking and his lips split and bleeding, his words hung in the dim light. Someone had beaten his head into a swollen knob.

"What do you want, stud?"

"My squad leader pounded me. I need a transfer." Apologetic, he fought his tears, knowing that talking to the company commander might complicate his life.

"You talk to Sergeant Stubbs?" His expression fell into a hopeless spiral. Hardin's eyes began to vibrate as he stood, inviting the man to be a soldier.

"No, sir." Sensing his commander's changing mood, the GI stepped away.

"Stand up, goddammit. Sympathy in this man's army is in the dictionary between shit and syphilis. Shit and syphilis. And that's all the sympathy you're gonna get. That's the way it works, stud. Talk to Stubbs."

* * *

Except for those moments he found himself reflecting on the confines of a woman's thighs, Captain Edward Hardin's humor was dedicated to helping his men survive Vietnam's war. To his delight, the new battalion commander had maintained the traditions of the Gross Table, and with the support of the junior officers, mealtime slander was well received.

The underlings did enjoy the Table's founder coming by to fire-up their zeal.

Tonight would be rewarding. The brigade commanding general was coming for dinner and drinks. The old goat would surely remember Hardin's smiling face and the shape of his quivering ass.

The Gross Table was posted with a "reserved" sign and situated one layer from the head table to ensure that slanging proclamations would be baffled before reaching home. Except for well-timed emissions, the table's crust was limited to mimicking the general's table manners, and comments about the pussy leather belt generals liked to wear.

Members of the Gross Table were young officers. Their staff sergeants were associate members. Once a week they invited the surgeon to join them and once a month they invited the chaplain, logic being that alcohol was medicinal, and the blood of Christ couldn't hurt.

Valorous to a man, the last Monday of the month they read their citations aloud. Mother was their inspiration, his Silver Star being the rear-echelon equivalent of the Victoria Cross. Cocktail olives were clusters. Tracer rounds were for valor. Lieutenant Orshanski was awarded one hundred belted tracer rounds for scheduling a general's visit without telling the Old Man.

Throwing salt over their shoulders, they pledged their confusion, using their water glasses as finger bowls, sprinkling holy water on their placard, vowing to keep their letters under the rose until Hardin said otherwise or hell wouldn't have it.

Orshanski sat with tracer rounds hanging around his neck.

After dinner the general told a story, each episode followed by his singing a string of "Oh, very wells." With nine episodes, the more "Oh, very wells" the general sang, the more energized Orshanski became.

"Listen up," Orshanski declared. "When he finishes, we start a chorus of 'Oh, fuck ya then, Oh, fuck ya thens,' and run out about a dozen. Then we chug our beer and can-slam the table."

Six officers and two sergeants sat primed for a career change.

The last "Oh, very well" had barely hit the sandbags when the Gross Table jumped the general's tale. The Old Man looked like he was going to power-shit cement. When the insurgents slammed their cans in unison, the mess hall united in coherent shock, waiting first for the Old Man, and then for the general.

Uncle grabbed his balls and shouted, "A toast." Uncle stood-to and the head table followed. "A toast to the infantry grunt." The chaplain wasn't holding a drink.

"The grunt." As one they chimed and drank a toast. Hardin's can was empty.

Generals in Vietnam were like emperors in World War II, so removed from reality they could logically declare the grunt the root cause of their problems. General 'Very Well' would find empty magazines confusing and blood trails intriguing. The image of his enemy dragging like a dog off into the jungle, surely defeated, would spark his courage.

* * *

Amps and Tennessee stopped by the berm command bunker to continue saying good-bye. They laughed at the puckered man assigned as Berm Meister.

"Brigade wants to talk to you, Captain." The major shrugged, feigning ignorance, then turned away, fussing with an unruly thought.

"Really? Is it the general?" Hardin asked.

"I don't think so." The stranger had been warned of the farcings of Charlie Company.

Hardin shot two puffs of air into the handset and announced himself. "Charlie Six."

"Brigade S-5 has identified a national who crawls inside the wire in front of bunker #14. When his sister bangs on a pot, he goes home. Don't fire him up."

Bunker #14 was centered on the perimeter of the brigade helipad. Revetments for eight UH-1 Hueys stretched from bunker #11 to bunker #16. Tennessee started laughing.

"If he crawls inside the wire while this outfit's on the berm, he is crazy. Someone's gonna light up his sorry ass," Hardin said.

"Negative, don't shoot him."

"Roger, out." Hardin threw the handset on the floor.

Amps and Leech Dick could not control their laughter. "Now we got dinks bangin' on pots. It's a setup, Major. One of these nights you're gonna lose those slicks," Amps declared.

"Negative. That village is pacified." This negative was more personal.

"You ever been in that village, Major?" Hardin asked. "No, of course not. Why don't you let Chuck sit on that bunker? Let's take out that stretch of wire. Be more neighborly."

"Don't fire at him, Captain." Spitting his words, the major was losing his composure.

"No problem, Major. No matter what happens tonight, Charlie Company isn't going to shoot at anybody. Chuck can have this dump." Excited, Amps and Leech Dick began trading jokes about Crazy Eddie and his musical pots.

Finally in charge, the major's shoulders expanded as his forearms formed a corral for his radio and his ass worked its way across his chair. Situated for war, he said, "Brigade said not to fire, so we don't fire." He knew Charlie Company had organized the last uprising against a friendly village, and he knew he was in deep shit.

Tennessee tried to lighten the atmosphere. "The moon's pretty bright. Crazy Eddie's gonna be playin' happy pots. He'll be hard at it. The smoke never lies."

"By God, that's it," Amps exclaimed. "His sister lets him crawl inside the wire and jack off. Then they celebrate by bangin' on a pot and smokin' dope."

"Major, why don't you have the S-5 send a 'Hearts and Minds' guy out to bunker #14? Have him spend the night, maybe strike up a conversation with Crazy Eddie," Tennessee said, setting the perfect trap. The major had to respond. If he didn't ask for help from brigade and the dude was shot inside the wire, Charlie Company was covered.

Hardin laughed. "You gotta keep breathin', Major."

The radio handset whispered, "Charlie Six, November Two, we got movement."

"What bunker are you on, November Two?" Leech Dick asked, stifling a laugh.

"Fourteen." The major sat erect.

"You're not gonna believe this, November Two," Leech Dick said. "There's this crazy dude named Eddie who lives with his sister in that friendly village. Crazy Eddie likes to step inside the wire and watch the moon while he's smokin' a little rope. After a couple fat-ones his sister bangs on a pot, and Eddie goes home and smokes his sister."

"Roger, that. I don't know what the hell you're smokin', but if that asshole puts his hands on that next roll of wire, he's fuckin' history."

The major was in the cleavage phase of kissing his radio, begging the brigade S-5 for help. His dreams of a command assignment in Garmish, Germany, were fading fast.

Leech Dick dropped the handset on the floor and kicked it around the chair leg. Then he grabbed it and keyed the net. "Well, November Two, what can I say? Nobody wants to play guns so you be cool. Hopefully, Eddie won't frag your sorry ass. What's he's doin'?"

"Dude's in a deep-dink squat, knee caps to armpits, smokin' a joint, lookin' at the moon."

"Charlie Six, Nifty November here. I'm at bunker #14, we got it handled." Bowe's words were precise enough to close the major's eyes and he sat back in relief.

"Which one is it, Nifty, here or there?" Leech Dick asked.

"What are you talkin' about, Kilo?"

"First you told me you were here, and then you told me you were at bunker #14. The berm commander told me it was neither here nor there. Which is it, Nifty?"

"Roger, out." And that's the way it worked. Jungle Central had saved another friendly.

"Balls-itch, watch the radios. I'm gonna drink beer," Hardin said.

Vietnam's war was buckled to sandbag hovels, with tertiary spasms of ambition prompting an educated paralysis within the upper ranks of America's greatest generation: great men throttled by cleanliness, orderliness, godliness and territorial simplicities. They were a starched and spit-shined claque, packaging crusades with outcomes that were contradictory, and incomplete.

The "Overall Boys and the Sunbonnet Girls" were having their way with "Mother Westwind's" brood. Johnny Woodchuck, Ready Fox, Peter Rabbit—these were their warriors.

Secretaries and generals used their secrets and their clothing as tools to control the protocol of weary grunts. Battle Bullshit's postulate was absolute. Only a grunt could be guilty of shooting the wrong person, or visiting a whorehouse—essentially the same offense.

Whether he was a grunt or a proper officer, Hardin did not know. If he could avoid the District Police, the White Mice, and the villages around the Tiger Mountains, he might leave Vietnam alive—and in one piece.

* * *

First light was the darkest Hardin had seen.

Offshore winds blew a cold mist across the ground and filled the sky with black gusting clouds. Hardin laughed as he left the mess tent. Twenty-five days and a wake-up remained on his tour of combat duty, and Fish was the only veteran of the Battle for Dak To still in the jungle. With any luck, monsoon rains would shut down the war.

He spent the day writing letters in the corner of his bunker, and talking to his men. No longer were the veterans eager to absorb or foil the ramblings of an officer so willing to leave. Their secrets had become secret. The black troops, with their heads cocked down, were cultivating a bitter silence. Rap was available for consultation, but the din of Black English was formidable now and had a purpose. The new men, the freshly cracked shells, were a stain-resistant blend of resentment and mistrust.

If Hardin's replacement tried to win the war with the lives of these black, brown, and white men, he would be isolated and dealt with immediately.

Vietnam's war in the fall of 1968 was changing. News from the World was confusing at best, and yet more men were being drafted than ever before. With nothing to win, the new men didn't have a sense of humor and didn't have a prayer.

A sullen rot of combat humor had carried armies into battle for centuries. The grunts of Vietnam, the grunts of Charlie Company, needed the best stuff, especially when the rains came to shrivel their day.

And, rain it did.

Here was the monsoon, the muddy monsoon, dressed like a water buffalo full of rage, scattering rats and snakes into a frenzy, stirring the countryside into a waxy, putrid soup. A grim hard monsoon. Acid winds sent clouds crashing into the ridgelines in the west. The sky was in motion and the river delta was filling like a swamp's backwater.

GIs were giddy with relief, yelling over the roar on the roof. Naked, with jungle boots for thongs, they showered in the Company street. The monsoon surpassed pussy as the topic at cards. It was a natural, "Whose gonna fight in this shit?"

It rained harder each minute. Wearing a helmet was not possible. The roar bent the mind into a hush. The ground was a rolling boil.

Four days of rain pushed the An Lao River to its reaches, flooding the villages, turning the rice paddies into an endless sea of mud, rats, fire ants, snakes, and leeches. The river was an unctuous flow, carrying tons of clay-brown particulate to the sea.

Ground-level visibility was zero.

Hootches perched on clay platforms and bamboo poles were connected by occasional dikes and small wooden boats. Perched inches above standard flooding, the doorways were filled with dormant faces, watching, and fending off the displaced critters.

Water poured in sheets off the orderly room tent. The air was so moist the strike of the typewriter key punched holes in the paper. Hardin sat dumb. Hoping the monsoon would last until he left the country, he laughed as water ran down the crack of his ass, pooled under his nuts, and drained off of his chair.

* * *

Water pooled at Stubbs' feet, running from the ventilation holes on the inside of his jungle boots. Soaked, he took off his shirt and headed for the latrine. Rivulets carved the ground. Water sprayed through the screens of the latrine. The shit-paper roll was a soggy sponge.

Stubbs had taken the company radios to the battalion commo shack to be fitted with new contacts, sealing the handsets in waterproof bags. He was worried. Exhausted, he fell into a trance. His search traced the perimeter of LZ English and the first layer of palm trees beyond the bunkers. Diluted by falling water, the horizon lay hidden from view.

Kneaded in the red clays of Dak To, Stubbs now faced death in a graying delta. Clumps of raucous clouds whirled at paddy level, badgering palm leaves, as the wind burst dense formations into scattering displays. The horizon was a quilt of desperation, light and dark grays, engaging, threatening.

Mud flowed in squirts from the latrine screens, marched down the shiplap walls in front of Stubbs, then raced to the floor. He relaxed, and found he was so tired he could barely inhale. His hands had taken to shivering. He could do anything with his hands, anything except hold a cigarette. He sat alone, perched, waiting for the boiling of his bowels, watching the rain. The roar of the tin roof deafened his senses.

The six howitzers of the 155mm artillery battery dug in next to the mess tent cut loose. The latrine's foundation settled, then fell through a shift, and the guns let go again.

Who in hell is in contact, Stubbs thought? Unable to see, unable to hear, unable to get a dust-off, wounds clogged with mud and leeches. Who wants to die in this crap? Let the dinks have this dump, Stubbs said to himself. What in hell are we doin' here?

* * *

"Captain, a runner from brigade left this," Stubbs said.

Hardin reached for the large manila envelope, and said, "Maybe it's my orders." It was an enlarged copy of the reporter's photograph showing Hardin sitting on the airstrip.

"Don't that beat all," Stubbs whispered.

"You think the bounty's for real, Stubbs?"

"Uncle said the allegations were dropped. Maybe the sorry bitch found a better way to pay you back." Unable to mask his concern, Stubbs took a drag on his cigarette, then took the picture and dropped it on his desk. "I don't guess it makes much difference. The bastards haven't killed ya yet."

"I think it's the White Mice."

"Don't sweat it, Captain. From now on, they're all trouble."

* * *

As if the roar of the rain was not enough, bullshit consumed those who ventured out. Finding Tennessee reduced to a wrinkled nub, showering in front of the TOC with Johnson's Baby Shampoo, Hardin pointed at the obvious and hollered, "That's why she shot ya. You're nothin' but a foreskin." Tennessee gave Hardin the bone and reached for the shampoo.

"Where's the Old Man?" Tennessee pointed at the TOC and turned away.

Bronx and the artillery RTOs sat in their dry fatigues; their ponchos hung on hooks near the entryway. They didn't expect to get wet beyond convenience, and they certainly were relaxed. The passageway to the briefing room was stacked with cases of grenades.

Hardin stood-to, stripped to the waist and dripping wet. Maggie's expectations had fashioned a jail cell for Hardin. He despised the young captain, and now the insubordinate clown stood-to, out of uniform, with his tits exposed.

"Don't they have shirts down your way?" Maggie asked.

"My way isn't down anywhere, Major. You get excited lookin' at nice firm nipples, Major? Here, have a poke."

"You're pushing your luck, Captain." The cloth sandbags in the briefing room were leaking again. Hardin listened to the sound of an empty magazine bouncing off a tree trunk.

"No, Major, you're pushin' my luck. The problem you have, Major, is I already have a weapon, and the Old Man is going send me out in the mud anyway."

Maggie Warbucks returned to writing his briefing, so Hardin took a red pushpin from the situation map and left the briefing room to bum a Coke.

No sooner had he opened the soda when Maggie said, "Look here, Hardin, I don't want a beef with you. I do think you should have more regard for authority."

Hardin handed his accuser the red pushpin with a wry grin and a slight nod.

"I have respect for Charlie. He's dedicated and he's good. I have no respect for soldiers unwilling to walk outside the wire, Major."

"We're both in this thing, Hardin. I get frustrated, too."

"Yeah, maybe so. But us grunts," Hardin caught his temper, then continued. "Us grunts, we get the memories. And that's the wrinkle, Maggie."

Maggie wouldn't imagine that Hardin spent time holding his good luck charms, saying the Lord's Prayer, singing about San Francisco, counting slices of salami, wondering when Chuck would catch him too relaxed to care, or catch him mesmerized by the shadow of Dig-it's smile.

"Do you have a fond memory, Maggie?"

"I don't know," he said with a questioning crease. "I suppose."

"A memory that's precious." Hardin opened his palms, coaxing the major's spirit. "A moment you hold close to your vest."

"Yes, I guess. The night my wife and I celebrated our first anniversary."

"When that night comes to mind can you enjoy the sounds, the smells, the warmth of her touch? Can you replay your moment to its end?" Hardin's eyes began to dance and his heart raced. He wanted to grab the man and scream sense into his unwrinkled brain.

"Yes, it's a moment I hang on to."

"Grunts can't do that, Maggie. My friends and I can't do that. At times we can't even find the memory. When we try, someone screams medic and someone else dies."

"What do you want from me, Hardin?"

"Stop pushin' our luck. It's easy enough to die in this dump without someone featuring our courage as a briefing highlight."

Maggie turned in relief when the Old Man and Uncle entered the radio room arguing, throwing water as they took off their ponchos. Uncle acknowledged

Hardin's bare tits with a wry nod. The Old Man started with a yell, still fighting the monsoon's roar.

"Firebase Corregidor is out of food. Brigade tried a parachute drop, but the load was scattered by high winds up and down that ridge overlooking the Fish-hook. The general's orders are clear—get a rifle company out there with extra rations."

While the Old Man searched for a reaction, Hardin's thoughts were lost in the calmness of shock. The very idea of dancing in the rain made no sense. Corregidor in the fall—foxholes filled with water, monsoon winds, and one-hundred-plus GIs out of food.

Hardin shook the words loose. "That's a long walk. We'll have to go light. If we get hit, we're screwed." The Old Man wasn't listening. Charlie Company was going for a swim whether the mission was feasible or not.

"Each man packs twenty lerp rations, ten for the firebase."

"Do the slick drivers know they're gonna fly in this weather?"

Knowing the answer made no difference, the Old Man embraced the despair, then let his conclusions embrace the general's mantle.

"Lift off is 0800 hours. Any questions?" Maggie took a red pushpin from the cloth sandbag and stuck it in the situation map near Firebase Corregidor.

"One thing's certain, Colonel. If the chopper insertion isn't west of the An Lao River, we'll never make Corregidor."

Uncle acknowledged Hardin's words, and the meeting ended. The mission was paybacks for the mad-minute on the berm. The commanding general was squaring the sheet.

* * *

Stubbs had ordered the platoon leaders to gather in the orderly room. They barged through the door with a measure of relief, pausing to look back into the rain.

"This is bullshit." Dillon yelled, pointing at the waterfalls on the sides of the tent. "I bet that deserter's thinkin' about a dry cot."

"Wait til ya hear what Big Dog's gonna do to us in the mornin'," Stubbs said.

"You're kiddin'?"

"We'll wait for Bowe. Don't want to tranquilize ya twice."

Bowe stood bent by the storm. Somehow he was shorter for the boonies than Hardin. He was being transferred to supply. Leech Dick opened the screen door to Bowe shaking his head, trying to unravel his long, bony body from his poncho.

When he stopped moving, he settled into a chair, crossed his legs, then his arms, and gave those gathered his most disgusting appraisal.

"Corregidor is socked in and out of food," Hardin said, measuring reactions. There were none. "We're goin' out from the airstrip in the mornin'. Each man carries twenty lerps, ten for the firebase. Make sure you're up on heat tabs and C-four."

"Who's gonna fly in this shit? Who's fuckin' idea is this?" Dillon asked, laughing.

"The general's. Make sure the studs have a working air mattress, poncho, trip flares, and smokes. Top, get extra handsets, and batteries. Think of anything else?" Hardin asked.

Stubbs flipped his smoke out the door. The cigarette was out before it hit the ground.

"Look at those major-league tits." Dillon moved his unit around with his inner thighs, smiling and waving his tongue at the *Playboy* centerfold. Then he gave his program a hand check and showed off his treasure.

"No way, she ain't touchin' my dick," Leech Dick said, laughing.

"She-it, I'd low-crawl out to Corregidor just to get a sniff," Dillon said, kissing the picture. "Oh yeah, mud, rain, Chuck, nothing could keep me from servin' her some chow." Bowe smiled and uncrossed his legs. Who could be serious with an absurd mission like this?

Twenty-one days and a wake-up: Hardin was short for the war.

"First light on the airstrip."

Stubbs lit a smoke and pointed at Hardin. "Sir, you're gettin' too short for this. The Frenchman is out of the bush. Anyone else you want me to work on?"

"Remember that cherry-boy in An Khe? Second Platoon? Blew up that dink right after he got off the chopper: cried for days?"

"Yeah, short 'n stocky, eyebrows. Fish called him Short Round."

"His teeth rotted off. Nothin' left but brown stubs."

"You're kiddin." Stubbs gave his cigarette an inquisitive puckering, wondering how a man's teeth could rot off.

"Get him to that dentist by the airstrip. Get him out of the jungle." Stubbs started to leave. "Top, see if battalion aid's got any glasses for me."

"Why don't you tell the Old Man to find a replacement?"

"The White Mice play for both teams. I'm safer outside the wire." Stubbs started to leave. "Top, check on the DEROS of the studs who worked for us in First Platoon. I want to get as many out of the bush as I can."

"I checked. Rap's close, then LeCotte and PeeWee. Rap could go in a week."

* * *

Real chicken eggs would help buoy the enthusiasm that drove Hardin to survive. The table location had changed, but the Gross Table's placard stood tall.

"You ready?" The Old Man sat down with his coffee.

"Sir, this table demands a certain type of behavior." Hardin chopped his eggs into a scramble. The Old Man laughed and stirred his coffee, his eyes coursing the mess hall.

"I won't stay long." They agreed.

"Yes, sir, we're ready. Not very effective, but we're ready. Maggie sent us on those night combat assaults without food. Now Bravo's short. I think you have to watch his act," Hardin said, toasting the point with a fork full of eggs.

"I'm a little pissed. The weather guy told us monsoon rains were coming in."

"Maggie's a good man. He just doesn't get it." The Old Man nodded and stirred his coffee. "Why did you do that?" Hardin said, pointing at the coffee cup.

"What?" A cook was refilling the juice pitcher and replenishing the fresh-fruit tray.

"Stir your black coffee?"

"How do you know it's black?"

"I watched you pour it. There's nothin' in it but that spoon."

"Couldn't tell you. I do it all the time." The Old Man smiled and stirred his coffee again, banging the spoon on the sides of the cup for effect. Stubbs entered the back door of the mess tent, stepping past the chow line, shedding his poncho on the way.

"Top, how come Fish isn't out of the bush?" Hardin asked.

"He extended for six months to get a second R&R. Said he's havin' a good time." Stubbs poured himself a cup of coffee and said, "You're on the airstrip in forty minutes, Captain." Top sat down and gave his Colonel a nod. "Sir."

"Morning, First Sergeant," the Old Man said, banging his spoon on the side of his coffee cup. "First Sergeant, does Charlie Company have any problem with blacks?"

Hardin looked at Stubbs with tiring eyes as his resentment surged. Amid the gruesome details of Dak To marched Boyle stuttering, Dig-it's letter, Bucks' bloody chest, Lightning's smile, and Boo outrunning the horns of "All Hell."

Rap would kill Whitey. That's the way Battle Bullshit worked.

Hardin was determined to stand silent, but his mouth started moving on its own. "Yes sir, I got a problem with blacks. They're hard to see at night and I can't understand a word they say."

Stubbs sat into a brace as the second box of road apples hit the table.

"No sir," Stubbs said. "It's not like it is back here."

"Come out with us, Colonel," Hardin said. "Within ten meters you'll know Chuck doesn't care whose packin' a ruck. Too bad you didn't meet Bucks, one of the best buck sergeants ever. African Golf was his delight. I'll let you work with Rap. He's the blackest goddamn buck sergeant in the army. Rap has packed a rucksack from Dak To to Bong Son."

Rap would stir the colonel's coffee, talk about his mama too.

"When the monsoon stops, I'll do that." The Old Man stirred his coffee again.

"That coffee's black and you keep messin' with it. Maybe you're the one packin' around a problem, somethin' you gotta get off your mind." Hardin stood away from the table, waiting.

"You do have a way of making a point, Captain."

Standing near the door of the mess tent, judging his commander to be polished crud, Hardin noted a slight tremor in Stubbs' hand and asked, "What in hell was that about?"

Stubbs' head popped through the hole in his poncho, stripping the cigarette from his mouth. "Shit." Stubbs shook the cigarette to the floor. "The brothers get together back here and scare hell out of these rear-area jokers."

"I bet they do. See ya in a few days, Stubbs." Hardin turned, then stopped, taking Dig-it's letter out of his helmet liner. "Put this with my stationary on the field table next to my bunk."

"No sweat, Lima," Stubbs said, his eyes framing a curious expression.

"I'm not Lima, Stubbs. I'm Charlie Six. If I don't make it back, Stubbs, you deliver that letter to the man's mother. I promised the man, Stubbs."

"I can do that."

"One more thing, Stubbs. Reynolds has been packin' around a secret since, Ban Me Thuot. A secret he swore with Drips. Find out what it is."

"I can do that. I'll take care of your wife for ya too, Lima. If ya don't make it back."

"See ya around, Stubbs." Hardin smiled a smile of fatigue as he was consumed by a wall of rain. Grandpa Karl would shoot Stubbs if he came calling.

Removed by a lifetime of ritual, Hardin stood-to, surrounded by the men of Charlie Company, beaten by a rain no man could fathom. With his father's worry beads in one hand and Dig-it's rosary around his neck, he wished for luck, whispered the Lord's Prayer, counted the beads, and started singing, "The shadow of your smile, when you are gone."

Joe's drive-on rag was finally getting washed.

* * *

Number #10, Highlands Road. Bremerton, Washington. September 1960.

The Major enjoyed the letters from his son. Court was stationed at Fort Bragg, North Carolina, assigned as the Officer in Charge of the third week of parachute training—jump week. Dad's memories of the 6th British Airborne's heroics in Normandy made Court's position as Officer in Charge of jump week training all the more significant.

One of Court's West Point classmates had volunteered to be an advisor to the Army of South Vietnam. The Major advised Court with a phone call: "Wait and see how the situation plays out, Pal." Eddie found out later that Lieutenant Train died in Vietnam, in an ambush in June of 1962, one week before Eddie finished his first year of college.

The Major's counsel took on a hard edge. When he found out that Court had taken part in a classified mission as a member of a fourteen man HALO team, jumping into Laos from ten thousand feet, operating for three weeks gathering intelligence, then being extracted by helicopter from a remote pickup zone, he started calling his friends.

Jumping from an airplane contracted by Flying Tiger Airlines and carrying civilian passports, the recon team was fully exposed.

Each member of the team had written five letters to their families. The letters had been flown to England and posted in the overseas mail as a cover for the operation.

The Major was proud of his son.

CHAPTER THIRTY-FIVE

The Muddy Monsoon

Airstrip. Landing Zone English. 0635 Hours.

Water flowed down the crack of Hardin's ass, forming a vortex under his nuts that made his butt cheeks slap like plastic paddles when he walked. "This has got to be a joke," he said, wiping his face as if that might help him find his boots. Standing in ankle-deep water under a blackening sky, the airstrip was a long, wind-driven mess.

A constant chill had replaced the grime that came from going unwashed for weeks.

With twenty-one days and a wake-up left on his combat tour, a new fear had blossomed. Not a matter of fear as much as a matter of betrayal. The old woman and the Viet Cong were one. Hardin could kill either and be the braver for it. He could kill the deserter and be commended for it. The reporter and the staff-patch were untouchable, too obvious. The White Mice were off-limits, and yet they were uniquely capable of working on both sides of the wire.

Had paranoia set sail? Or was Hardin magnifying the danger from fight to fight to garner kudos by rescuing himself from Saint Peter just in the nick of time? Deciding the District Police had purloined the reporter's picture to deflect suspicion, LZ English had become more dangerous than the jungle.

Deciding the White Mice were chump compared to fighting in the mountains against the North Vietnamese, he chided himself for being self-absorbed. There was a bounty on his life, and he put it in place. In his pursuit of his father's fortunes he had fashioned the fate he wished for, a valiant death.

The men in his charge had weighed their options and withdrew in disbelief. His leaving and his death were no longer mutually exclusive events. It was not happiness or sorrow his men longed for. It was satisfaction. Excepting a few—Fish and PeeWee, LeCotte and Boyle, Rap and Blood, Tag and Leech Dick, Lightning—the men had become unwitting conspirators.

Laughing, Hardin found LeCotte worshipping his soiled mind, pissing on Boyle's leg, waving his cock around with perverted joy.

The choppers flew in from the north, into the teeth of an unforgiving wind. The eight slicks hovered above the airstrip as one. Unable to establish a cushion of air beneath the airframes, the slicks rocked from side to side, the pilots fighting to set the skids on the deck.

GIs stood off, waiting for the slicks to find a home before they raced under the blades. Water flew off the ends of the main rotor blades, forming a surreal cone.

"Get fat if you can," Hardin said, securing his place behind the copilot in the right door of the second slick. He looked for a friendly face. Fish and PeeWee had his back.

The slick surged forward, then stalled, tossed by changing currents, floundering at the mercy of a storm that was racing through the trough that was the An Lao River. Gusts tossed the slick like an unruly kite, driving rain into PeeWee's face one second and lurching away the next.

The airframe pitched left and fell in an instant, leaving PeeWee's helmet suspended for a moment near the end of the main rotor blade before it fell into the clouds. The last thing visible was the pack of Lucky Strikes trapped under his camouflage band. PeeWee sat clutching the door gunner's chair; his black eyes locked in fear.

The pilots flew at treetop level to find the river's course, then gained altitude, mindful of the river's trace. With the ceiling less than one hundred feet, the clouds and the river were one. The band of vegetation that lined the river seemed like a veneer. The ridges that formed the An Lao Valley stood 400 feet, hidden from view.

Worried men gripped the inside shell of the aircraft, catching their weight as the chopper bounced from gust to gust. A sudden change in direction forced the pilots to lean into their instruments as the chopper accelerated to full power. Flying blind, the pilots scrubbed the mission, picked separate vectors, and flew back to LZ English.

Deuce-and-a-half trucks idled in line to transport the company along the north bank of the An Lao River. The drivers leaned into their windshields. The wiper blades were useless.

Water lapped at the sandbags of bunker #1. The perimeter concertina wire curled through the surf. The chop on the surface of the paddy changed direction suddenly, turned calm, and then churned into a running surf. Villages lost definition: a hootch here and a hootch there. Old women and children bunched into doorways as the trucks rolled by.

The dirt road ended at the remnants of a small concrete bridge that had fallen into a raging tributary. With the aid of a small boat, the company crossed the tributary hand-over-hand on a rope ferry. Standing on the roadway, Hardin managed a feeble shiver. A greasy sheen covered his body.

The valley had become a sewage pond, filled with a cold, waxy sludge, spiced with crustaceans, boasting a retched smell. Critters were on the move—rats and cobras were swimming. Watching through sheets of gusting rain, the villagers across the river were struck by the stupidity. Viet Cong foot traffic from the mountains had come to a standstill.

Calf-deep water stretched west 800 meters to a tree line and the company's designated river crossing point. Rather than risk the open water, Hardin turned uphill into the canopy of a finger valley to laager for the night.

He planned to cross the ridge and enter the valley on its flank at first light.

With gravity in full fig, the layered parasols redirected the monsoon rain. Large leaves caught the rain and released it in a cascading parody of cleansing. Hundreds of waterfalls pounded the jungle floor, forcing unbelieving men to search from sound to sound. The roar magnified the absence of sanity, forcing GIs into a mortal slouch as they slogged uphill.

Stupid and miserable, a foul, gray mud claimed one boot and then another. Having gained eight pounds and three inches, a man could die in the monsoon, a treat for the rats.

Dysfunctional lighters, helmets lined with matchbooks, useless glasses, waterlogged rucksacks, shoulders rubbed raw, ammunition soaked in oily magazines, prune-textured hands, white-rotted sores, soured streams, and bones chilled to a shiver.

With two-man poncho tents for foxholes, GIs lay on the ground daring their enemy to make it worse. Trenches were dug to redirect the water. Mud bags were stacked three high.

Off the ground and out of the rain, Hardin leaned on an elbow and sipped coffee, looking up hill into a black-green wall of vegetation, pocked with even darker shadows. The jungle floor was in constant motion. The drum in the canopy had gained a morbid cadence.

His enemy would be killing his men and re-stacking their sandbags before he could see their faces. If he screamed, no one would hear him.

Hardin whispered, "What a shithole."

Thankful for the day, and too cold to sleep, he waited.

Packed and weathered like bleached raisins, with mud the dress of the day, GIs turned downhill, following gravity's call. Leech Dick fought with his handset. Sealed in a plastic bag at twilight, he found it soaked and unusable. The drainage ditch next to the perimeter had grown into an obstacle. The company would have to enter the valley at its mouth.

With time forcing the pace, Tag led the charge back to the river. The cobra head buckled to the front of his helmet had assumed an expression much like his own—one of wrinkled bullshit.

GIs stood silent. The open water on the valley floor now stretched for a kilometer. The water was waist deep. The designated crossing point on the An Lao River was shrouded in clouds. If the crossing was successful, the firebase was a two-day hump.

Dillon plowed into the water. Tag followed him, spreading the formation. Once they found the edge of the submerged tributary, they secured a rope to the only tree in the valley, the only aiming point, and began crossing the rope—one by one, five minutes per man.

Halfway through First Platoon's crossing, a tree limb boasting a mammoth pod of fire ants rammed Boyle's air mattress. The ants exploded over his body like fire racing across a pool of gasoline. Holding the rope, Boyle rolled into the water, losing his rucksack, the squad radio, his helmet, and his M-16. Covered with fire ants, the air mattress sailed toward the sea.

LeCotte thought it was funny.

With Tag on the far side of the valley, First Platoon wading like ducks on a pond, and half the company still on the rope, GIs were spread across 800 meters of open water. The probability of becoming a target was increasing rapidly.

When enemy fire sounded from the far tree line the GIs were ready. AK rounds lanced the water near the rope. The artillery recon sergeant called for supporting fire and Bowe's machine gunners began suppressive fire two fingers right of Tag's smoke.

Yellow smoke fought for altitude as the wind and rain battered the valley. The company would never reach the An Lao River without taking significant casualties. Hardin stood calm, unruffled by the steep shafts tracing the water around him. He was not afraid.

"Lima Six, withdraw the point and get your ass back here."

"Roger, out."

Amid the chaos a new man ducked under water, rattled off the requisite Hail Marys, leaped out of the water with his M-16 at the ready and pulled the trigger. The weapon blew up. The bottom of the magazine blew off, spewing the following spring and the ammunition into the water, twisting the bolt housing into pot-metal pasta.

Drill instructors and armorers alike proscribed this submerged-ambush move. Underwater gunplay was hazardous to your face. This man's face held an empty expression.

"Get the fuck away from me, you dumb bastard." Leech Dick wasn't impressed.

First Platoon was returning fire and falling back in stages. The point squad had made the tree line, and now were running with Dillon. Splashing, falling, returning fire, reloading, falling: there was no place to hide.

Tag's voice screamed from Leech Dick's handset. "We're out of the tree line. Give us some fuckin' help, Leech Dick."

"Shift fires left, Red-Leg," Dillon yelled. "Spread the guns. Keep poundin' the woods." Hardin waited for Dillon to finish his transmission, then keyed the net.

"Break, break. Bowe—have your guns put rounds in the tree line on both flanks of Tag's withdrawal."

"Lima's got a man down," Leech Dick screamed, pointing into the open water.

"Fuck me, scramble Starblazer." Hardin spotted the wounded man, chiding himself for being clinical. Blood had the wounded man in tow, along with Reynolds. Hand over hand, Hardin re-crossed the rope and waded to higher ground. GIs plowed through the water, running under an umbrella of fire.

Red tracer rounds from four machine guns spread over the retreating men like long fingers, pounding the enemy positions in the tree line. High-explosive artillery rounds fired with a one-second delay marched down the tree line, then reversed their course and marched again. How Starblazer found the fight was anybody's guess, but he flew in, singing his song, slamming the jungle with rockets and so many tracer rounds it look like the trees were growing smaller.

Cheers found their way across the water as one by one the point squad lowered themselves into the debris and re-crossed the rope, each man taking a turn on anchor. Leech inspections were continuous. Spoors from the jungle flush coated their faces. The air was heavy with the stench of uprooted rot. The fight was over.

The company lost four M-16s and a radio at the rope crossing.

Sergeant Snorkel, the company's Shake-and-Bake buck sergeant, was hit in the right shoulder. Back in the nest, he sat on a clay knob, wincing as medics mothered his wound. He smiled a sloppy expression of joy, knowing he had escaped death and was going home. With a dap for Tag and a grin for the LeCotte, he gave a nod when Fish handed him his weapon. He knew his war was over.

Involuntarily looking back over the expanse of water, Sergeant Snorkel sat erect. Arching his back, he gave up a wry grin, watching the monsoon wash his wound.

With an expression of smug satisfaction, Hardin returned the grin, and asked, "Are you gonna make it, Buck Sergeant?"

"Yes, sir. The shoulder hurts, but that dust-off's gonna make things sweet."

"I guess the catfish must be jumpin'," Hardin said.

"They damn sure are, Captain."

"Well, goddammit. If you're not fuckin' dyin', where's my rucksack? And don't tell me it's in that fuckin' river." Captain Joe's drive-on rag, Sweet Cheeks' shroud line, Squeak's bag of dew, the bird spider fang, Nuts' overseas cap, all had gone missing.

Defensive, as if reaching for the words, the big man's hands shot out, and he said, "No way, Captain. I ditched your ruck in the mud when we pulled out."

At that point Hardin realized his worry beads were gone. The eighteen ebony spheres had been disintegrating for the past week.

"You left my rucksack in the mud. Chuck is fuckin' with my stuff. You just gave my shit to Chuck, is that what you're sayin,' Buck Sergeant?"

Doc Taylor was bandaging Snorkel's wound, laughing at Hardin's assault.

"I pumped a magazine into it before I cut out." Hardin winced at the thought of his old friend taking eighteen rounds, then leaned on the big man's good shoulder.

"That sounds like somethin' LeCotte would do, or Boyle."

"They coulda. I know I shot it up a bunch."

"Well, Shake 'n Bake, you got a ticket to ride. You're goin' back to the world. Your feet won't touch brass but you're a damn good man. One of the best."

Hardin hit the big man's extended fist. When he looked out across the squall-driven paddy, the muds of Dak To flashed with scenes of helpless wounded, begging for water. The image of Nuts, then Hippie, and then Bucks appeared against the cloudy backdrop. A jarring mind-switch forced him to search the far tree line.

Charlie cut Joe's drive-on rag off his rucksack and Sweet Cheeks' shroud line, then laughed when he found Squeak's bag of dew. A second man was wearing Nuts' overseas cap.

Bad luck was in full fig.

The company fell back to the washed-out bridge, its port of embarkation, to laager for the night. Leech Dick requested nine pair of boots, five quarter-pound sticks of C-4, four M-16s, a radio, and a poncho for Hardin's hootch.

The mood was one of relief. With the mission scrubbed, a friend was going home.

* * *

By the time the resupply slick found the laager, Hardin was the only man not under a poncho. He greeted the chopper in a driving rain, reached for a hog-tied clatter of boots, missed the netted bag as he fell forward, his outstretched hand landing on the skid, grounding the chopper, electrifying his shriveled weans.

With his balls spinning in tight circles, he tried to step back. The skid slammed into the ground, driving his foot into the mud. The crew chief threw the boots and other supplies next to his shoulder and gave him a thumbs-up. When the slick lifted off he was lying in the mud. Too cold to sleep, he spent the night nursing hot coffee, singing to himself, and watching the river.

The faces marched along the riverbank, so many unconnected deaths. Pop's smile was painted on Dig-it's face, and Packrat was speaking with it: "Where are we goin,' El Tee?"

A haunting glow framed the river's course. Palm trees and hootches flashed in and out of focus. With no mind for laughter, he was relieved to find Dig-it's rosary sheltered from harm by his drive-on rag. He let the rosary cling to his P-38 and dog tags—a place of honor. Dig-it's laughter rang with a distant cheer.

Dying without regret was the most treasured end for an infantry platoon leader. For his tour of duty, Edward Hardin stood-to as Lima Six, Delta Six, Delta one, and Charlie Six. No matter the call sign, he had done his best. And even though a decision he made put Bucks in harm's way, he knew he had not made a mistake. *Still,* he thought, *When Big Bucks was alive, I was a younger man.*

The balance of the survivors of the Battle for Dak To, the Hill People, were safe in the world, with one exception. And who could account for a man like, Fish. Though men were dead, they encouraged Hardin from their graves, their bodies tangled in an endless jungle, their unblemished faces now whole in his mind.

The one man not smiling was Sam. Porfirio Rapada's Philippine heritage seemed to demand a more somber tone.

Morning brought modest weather and resupply choppers for Firebase Corregidor. With the company mucking back to LZ English, the war had come to a stop: too much mud, too much water, and microdinks claiming the dry spots.

Landing Zone English was pleated with erosion ditches, each with its own rust colored delta, the visual manifestation of eroding memories, washed into a compost of shattered bodies, connected one to another by a weary footprint.

Was this decay measurable? As the raven flies, Hardin had crossed one thousand miles of the sorcerer's ground, clutching at symbols of enduring guilt, courting an unearned mortality. But a yard was never three feet in a jungle clogged with insatiable energy: the true measure of his step given to an integral of emotion that could only be modified by instinct.

Yet, his steps kept coming, and his boots still had soles.

"Stubbs, check their feet. Make sure the weapons get cleaned. And check the radios, handsets, trip flares."

"I hear ya lost your rucksack, Captain."

"I'm becoming part of this sewer."

"An old master sergeant's been assigned to the company. Says he's goin' to the field when ya go back out." Stubbs shook his head, and flipped his cigarette into the air.

"Any word on my replacement?"

"Nothin'. They're gonna extend ya until they can figure out how to get ya killed."

"How's Tennessee doin'?"

"Don't see him much. He's been goin' to town, smilin'." Stubbs opened the screen door, lighting another smoke.

Before the screen door settled in its frame, the new master sergeant entered the orderly room from the rear of the tent. He stood five-eight, was thin, in his mid-fifties, with gray hair, a crew cut, and glasses. Visibly shocked by Hardin's youth, he gathered himself.

"Sir, I'm Master Sergeant Greenwell. I'm your new Field First Sergeant." Hardin dropped the old man's modest handshake. Hardin was at the end of his tether.

"How do ya know that?"

Holy horseshit; the young whippersnapper had a bite. Greenwell's best bet was bib overalls, faded bib overalls.

"I just figured since Stubbs was doin' that job, you'd want a replacement."

"Stubbs and I go way back—Dak To."

Offended by Hardin's sarcasm, the old man started to protest. Hardin cut him off.

"Get the studs refit. I'll give ya a shot. Fair warning—I got nineteen and a wake-up."

"Yes, sir, I know." *You don't know shit,* Hardin thought. The old sergeant moved out smartly, eager to militarize the boonie rats.

Hardin arrived early for the evening briefing and found Maggie broiling a war story over a strange captain, flying low cover in his C&C slick during a night combat assault. He waited until Maggie was using both hands to choreograph the most dangerous maneuver of his slick before he popped into Maggie's combat-secrets room.

"Hello, Maggie." Hardin looked at the stranger. "You tellin' war stories again, Maggie? Did he tell ya the story about the submarine?"

"This is the commander of Charlie Company," Maggie said. "Hardin, the good captain here is from the 525th Military Intelligence. He wants the intell on this area."

"Really? Don't you guys know what's goin' on?"

"My boss runs a trap line from here to Saigon. He told me to check you guys out."

The Old Man and Uncle entered the briefing room acting as if they should have been listening. Searching for a bright spark, Hardin could only laugh. His laughter brought a challenge from Maggie. With a side-nod, Uncle told Hardin to clear the area.

* * *

Hours later Hardin found the intell captain wired to a shot of whiskey, fondling the placard announcing the Gross Table.

"What's your intell on a man from this outfit who went missing near An Khe last May?"

"What? You're jokin', right?"

"Yeah, it's probably a joke. That, or a fuckin' secret."

Stubbs sat down. "Captain, can I talk to ya?" Stubbs looked at the stranger.

"Wha'd'a ya got, Stubbs?"

"Bowe is bein' transferred out of the field. We'll get replacements tomorrow."

Hardin pushed himself away from Stubbs' announcement, anxious to know what the transfers meant, what the paper soldiers were playing at. Beckett and Bowe were so new, the farther one stood from their leaving, the smaller they became.

Hardin gathered a sigh and asked, "Did we get more boots?"

"Yes, sir, we're tight. You're on the airstrip at first light to breakdown a firebase and hump the woods." Stubbs grabbed a beer at the bar. "Put this on the captain's tab."

After Stubbs stumbled back into the rain, Captain Thomas asked, "A man is missing?"

"I don't know if it's true."

"Jesus Christ. Someone's gotta know."

"I got enough trouble. You didn't hear it from me," Hardin said.

"Fair enough. Where's your next assignment?"

"Posting—the British call it a posting. I don't have orders."

"Jesus Christ. I'd be pissed."

"You and Jesus must be pretty tight," Hardin said, prompting a facetious nod. "Besides, only dead men have orders."

* * *

The rain had stopped. The wind slapped at the slicks as they settled onto the grassy plateau, the morning sky crowded with rushing gray clumps. Delta Company had cleared the firebase at first light, heading west into the An Lao Valley.

Disturbed by the serenity, Leech Dick and Balls-itch began arguing about their pestering habits, and Greenwell, with PeeWee's help, started lecturing Fish on how to pack for a hike.

"You better tie him up before Fish shoots him," Tag said, talking over his cup of coffee through a comfortable cloud of steam.

"He is steppin' kinda wide." Hardin lit the C-4 under his canteen cup and stared at the flame. "Leech Dick, tell Greenwell I want to talk to him." Hardin watched his RTO deliver the message and then waited fifteen minutes before the old soldier stood-to.

"Sir, do you want to talk to me?" A gust of wind waved through the savanna.

"Sit down, First Sergeant."

"I need to supervise packin' that wire. If they do it right, we can use it again."

"Fuck that wire. Sit down," Hardin said, his voice now unfriendly. "Ya know, Greenwell," he said, cleaning his glasses. "This is my twenty-second pair of glasses."

Hardin's expression chiseled itself chip by chip as he stared across the plateau. The grass was bent low under the offshore winds. He had lost his loneliness in his hatred for this new man.

Putting on the glasses, he stared at the old sergeant for a moment, then adjusted his watchband. "This is my eighth watch. My granddad's watch was smashed at seven-nineteen in the morning when a friend of mine named Dig-it was killed. Dig-it wasn't his Christian name. Dig-it was his real name."

Hardin searched the old soldier's eyes for a sense of recognition.

Finding none, he asked, "Do you know what I'm saying, First Sergeant?"

"Sir, these men will respond to whatever I call them."

"Is First Sergeant the name you prefer, Greenwell?"

"I don't know what you mean, Captain."

Hardin lifted his coffee cup up to his mouth with a nod, siphoned a sip through the steam, and fixed the old soldier with his eyes. Then he settled through a slow shrug, scrubbed at his face, and said, "Greenwell, I have the best platoon sergeants in the brigade. You stay out of their way. You don't tell any soldier what to do, and before you tell a platoon sergeant what to do, you clear it with me."

"Sir, with all due respect. I'm the First Sergeant. This is my company."

"No old man, this is Charlie Company." Hardin waved a hand around the perimeter and then leveled his focus on the old soldier. "Your illusions might work in Saigon, or behind the wire. But in the jungle these men waltz through a lonesome dance. Survival depends on individuals being willing to run through a tunnel of fire just to find a radio. There is no respect for rank out here, only respect for courage and luck."

The old soldier stood into a self-gratifying silence. "Goddamn you, old man," Hardin said with a gust. "You don't seem to have a clue."

"What do you want me to do, Captain?" Greenwell's voice had a hardened tone.

"I want you to get on that resupply chopper and leave."

* * *

Rap moved with an undirected stride, his M-16 slung over his right shoulder, barrel down. He knew he was short, but he would never ask.

"Rap, got a minute?" Mister David "Rap" Brown, of the Chicago Browns, an officer in the P-Blackstone Rangers, stood-to in silence, waiting for Hardin's comment. "There's a slick comin' with hot chow. I want you to get on it, and don't come back."

Hardin stood up and held out his fist. Rap responded immediately. His eyes set themselves on fire and he turned away.

"One thing." Rap turned, this time his chin was raised, knowing there was a string. "Thanks for hangin' with me." Unable to back off, Rap nodded his gesture of peace.

"Forget about Whitey, Rap," Hardin said, staring at a far tree line.

"The brothers in the world are lookin' for that Kansas motherfucker."

"Is that deserter for real, Rap?"

"If he was a brother, I'd know for sure." Rap shrugged ever so slightly, breathing as if he were making up his mind. Satisfied, he said, "Word is the dude was shot in Ban Me Thuot." Rap raised his jaw, reevaluating his message.

"Whose word?"

"Big Bucks—Mex, too." For a moment, a brief moment, Rap's trust was accessible.

Hardin looked out over the grass-covered plateau and let his search sink into the Tam Quan Valley. He was looking for something, for what he did not know. Deceit crept into his thoughts, then laughed as if Fish might one day be sane.

Protecting his men from themselves might not be possible. Alone, he looked at Rap, and said, "You got a few minutes. Best get your shit straight."

"Reynolds is a bad dude, El Tee. Motherfucker'll kill anybody."

"Rap, I know it's hard to believe, but I'm a captain, now."

The proud black man gave up a grin and turned into the wind. His stride was never longer. Boyle and Lightning laughed with excitement. Boo laughed as if he had lost his dog. After the rains, and losing Sergeant Snorkel, Rap was their victory. Fish and Tag stood as one, paying their respects. Rap handed Tag the last letter Rap had received from Tag's parents, shook Tag's hand, and turned toward the chopper.

Blood listened to the news with a sense of gain. The occasion contained an opportunity for him to expand his domain. The GIs who scared him now were Fish and Reynolds.

They were loners.

Rap sat well away from the resupply slick until the mermite cans of hot chow were unloaded. Then he bounded onto the cargo deck. He had finished his tour of duty. He had fought Vietnam's war, knowing the black men in the unit were his to command. He had kept the company from racial strife. Hardin didn't know who would take up the slack. He did know he would never see Rap again.

The P-Blackstone Rangers from South 63rd Street in Chicago were getting a good man.

Bucks, Mex, Rap, and Blood—they were the guts of Hardin's platoon. The buck sergeants, the fire-team leaders—two blacks, a brown, and a white.

* * *

The company humped through a blustery mist, headed north for 600 meters, and dug in. Clouds barged across the plateau. Stiff and wet, the grass near Hardin's foxhole danced and sang throughout the night. Unable to sleep, he listened for his fate.

At first light the company moved northeast toward the Tam Quan Valley.

"We got a slick inbound. Ten minutes out. New officers for Second and Third Platoons." Balls-itch was excited. Lieutenants of unknown origin, fresh eggs. High-paid grunts.

"Here we go again," Hardin whispered to himself. "Spread the platoons, Leech Dick. Two hundred meters at ten, two and six on the clock." With wide-open grass, he wanted as much warning as the terrain would allow.

The slick pilot scoffed into the radio. "We got lemon smoke."

"Lemon wins you a drip-free ride on two cracks a day." Leech Dick was a sick man.

The lieutenants eased onto the skids as if they were holding hands, then hopped into the grass, knowing they were going to land on a booby trap. When the Huey hovered away, their expression fell numb. Six GIs had come to meet them and not one of them looked old enough to be out of high school.

Hardin sat on his helmet smiling at their discomfort, letting the new men analyzed their situation. "Are ya fuckin' lost?" he asked, offering them a seat. They looked to be in good shape, each with a worried sparkle in his eye. The black officer would get Third Platoon. He looked like an athlete. The white officer, the wiry one with the Ranger tab, would get Second Platoon.

Hardin held up a finger, and said, "Two things to remember. The first is stay off the low high grounds that overlook the rice paddies. They're booby-trapped. Chuck knows we like to defend high ground. Second, don't walk on the trails or paddy dikes. Do either one and I'll kill ya myself."

"These are my people. Don't make any mistakes. If ya get in trouble let your platoon sergeant help. Your squad leaders know more about Chuck than you do—make sure they know ya believe in them. Any questions?"

"What about maps?" *Holy shit. These clowns are stupid,* Hardin thought.

"You don't have maps?" They shook their heads in synchrony. "You let the sorry bastards send you to the bush without a map?" They looked at each other.

"That's your first fuckin' mistake. I just got done tellin' ya not to make any mistakes. They send privates to the bush without maps. You dickheads are supposed to know better." Hardin's subalterns were sobering into expressions of attentive idiocy.

"Yes, sir." They were a duet, DUO—Dickheads of Unknown Origin.

"Yes sir. Yes sir. Fuck-a-bunch of 'yes sirs.'" They knew Fort Benning was bullshit now. "Empty your rucksacks. I want to see what you're packin."

The lieutenants dumped their rucksacks as if good reason might lead to good form. Stupid, as if low tide required a tight measure, lieutenants one and two displayed their gear: four pair of socks, three white T-shirts, four underwear briefs, and a bar of soap. No smoke grenades, no flares, no compass, no frags, no knife, no C-4, and twelve magazines of ammunition each.

"Who helped you pack for this hike?" Hardin's eyes gave out traces of minced sanity.

"We've been talking it over between us."

Hardin shook his gaze into the clouded horizon, pointed at one and then the other, and said, "Before this day is over you find a compass, two frags, two smoke grenades, a trip flare, ten more magazines, and a map. My name is Charlie Six."

"Yes, sir." Another chorus.

"Don't ever call me 'sir' out here again."

Hardin's new friends had no idea what to say, so he continued. "We're in summer uniform. That means no underwear, unless you want your nuts festered with jungle rot. And get rid of that rank on your helmet. Chuck's already lookin' for ya."

The new officers looked older than Hardin, and much happier.

"Yes, sir."

"Holy fuck, you're stupid. Third Platoon's over that way 200 meters and Second's over there same distance. Call me when you're ready."

Stuffing their rucksacks as if a drill sergeant was screaming at their backs, they raced to avoid further criticism. They stood in unison but they couldn't see any good-guys.

"Sir, how do we get into the platoon perimeters?"

"What are ya gonna do, sneak up on 'em? Are you gonna stand around and hold hands? Get steppin' goddammit." Hardin keyed the handset.

"Lima, Charlie Six, pick it up and chogey on over."

"Roger, out." The lieutenants hadn't moved.

"Pollock—you're call-sign is Mike Six, Second Platoon. And you, you black asshole that keeps callin' me 'sir.' Gray—you're call-sign is November Six, Third

Platoon. Listen up. Never leave one of my men behind, even if he's dead. Ya hear what I'm sayin'? Never."

"You leave one of my men behind and I'll kill ya where ya stand."

Hardin stood up and looked at Pollock and then at Gray. "Your troops come first. Dig your own foxholes, cook your own chow, and hump extra gun ammo. Rank doesn't mean jack outside the wire."

Hardin shook their hands, and grinned. "I'm glad ya came to fight. Listen to your troops—they're still alive."

The walk alone to their platoons would scare the hell out of them. They would search the blades of grass, straining to get a first glimpse of their GIs. The walk would teach them caution, and most of all, make them appreciate the security of their platoon.

Ground visibility was unlimited when Tag and the point squad led out to the east. Tag crossed a ridge overlooking the Tam Quan and dropped into a draw dotted with large boulders, forcing the company to split their files. Pollock skirted the north side of the crease, and Gray skirted the south, each platoon led by half of the point squad. Alpha Company's drag-man had been killed in the early morning. Hardin didn't expect to find much.

"Mike Six, November Six, don't fire across this draw," Leech Dick said.

"Mike Six, Wilco over. November Six, Wilco over."

Leech Dick laughed quietly and started a private conversation with the RTOs. By nightfall the word "Wilco" would be history.

Tag and Tee-N stopped the point teams near the bottom of the crease when they spotted the roof of a hootch. The platoons sat straddled on well-used trails on their respective side of the draw, eighty meters apart. Hardin moved to the center of Pollock's platoon, and Dillon moved up behind Gray.

Hardin had just sat down when Leech Dick rolled onto his belly, pointing down the trail, sighting his M-16. He whispered, "Sin loi, motherfucker."

A natty looking man with a straw hat and pajamas was ditty-bopping up the trail right into Second Platoon's perimeter, sandal-slapping the trail with his AK at sling arms, barrel down. The man yawned, then walked between two GIs, unable to control his steps.

His eyes grew wide, frozen in shock.

A strange grin crossed his face. The instant Pollock stood up to place him under arrest, using the army's "Halt, who goes there?" jingle, Chuck threw the barrel of his AK into an upward arc. His chest erupted. The force of the rounds fired from seven M-16s brought his sandals off the ground, throwing his body downhill like so much pig slop. Within seconds he was stripped of his weapon and money, and kicked into a pile.

Pollock hadn't moved. Without his grace, his platoon had killed Chuck, an enemy he thought too wily to find. No prisoner, no interrogation—just bang, you're dead.

"Leech Dick, we're gonna hold up here. Have Gray and Dillon run a clover counterclockwise." Leech Dick was a lot like Squeak. He loved his sly smirk.

"Nothin' to this combat shit, is there, Pollock," Hardin said, taking up a full squat next to the lieutenant, looking down the trail, over the body. "Were ya standin' up to shake the fucker's hand, or what? That fuckin' AK-47 will flat tear your ass apart."

Pollock whispered carefully, "Damn."

"It's 'Battle Bullshit,' that's fer sure." Hardin motioned down the trail.

"That VC was half-steppin," Pollock said.

"You won't catch many of 'em day-dreamin'. Dink was headin' somewhere up in these hills, a base camp we didn't find. He came from the Tam Quan without a rucksack. He'd 'a been at that base camp before dark."

"Yes, sir."

"Also means this trail is probably clean of booby traps. The first hootches you find on this trail are VC. There are punji pits near those hootches. He's probably fuckin' some betel-nut honey just down the road."

"Yes, sir."

"He's got well-worn treads on his sandals, a fairly new AK, and good money. The paymaster's somewhere here about. Look here."

Hardin led Pollock down the trail to a point where Chuck was still in full stride. "See the way these scuff marks pattern the direction he was movin'? Every trail will tell ya somethin'. You best learn how to cut a trail, how to backtrack."

"What about the money?"

"The studs will spend the money. They'll pack the AK. Eventually it'll get turned in. Some rear-area jockey will take it home for a trophy. Rear area's big on war stories."

"Happens fast."

"Move uphill off the trail and forward fifty meters. Always move your men after a contact, always. We'll sit tight while Dillon and Gray run clovers. Call me Six."

Thirty minutes later Gray's cherry got popped—all M-16 fire.

"Charlie, November Kilo. We got three VC dead, jumped a trail watcher and some rice bearers. We're runnin' after the rest, over"

"Negative, circle up. Do not pursue. Break, break. Lima, freeze November in place and break off northeast. See if those dinks are runnin' toward the Tam Quan. Take Tag with you."

"We're steppin."

"Pollock, billy-goat east another hundred meters."

Hardin monitored the hand signals as the platoon moved rapidly along the side of the draw, mindful that this trail had two directions. They settled in above the first set of hootches and set an OP fifty meters on a backtrack uphill.

"Charlie, Lima, we got punji pits. The barber's says we got beaucoup VC."

"Circle up. Bust the pits and torch the hootches."

The hootch fire fixed Dillon's location near the north side of the draw. The surprise was over. The VC would fold away and wait. The three platoons rallied at Gray's location on the south side of the draw and pushed into the rice paddies along the base of the mountains, moving south by southeast.

"Pick a spot to laager, Pollock," Hardin said. "The rest will move south 500 meters. You'll have to be quiet because any dinks following the company will stumble into to your foxholes."

Second Platoon took the lead for 400 meters heading south and stopped to laager.

Tag led the company away from Pollock's laager hoping the Viet Cong would assume all of the GIs had left the area. With Second Platoon digging in on a low high ground right in front of his eyes, Hardin dropped his rucksack and started running.

"You fuckin' dumb ass. Ya kill one dink and ya think ya own the fuckin' place." Pollock's face shook with confusion.

"I told ya to never take my people on these low high grounds. Never, goddammit. You understand? Never!" Pollock stepped back. "You get one of my people killed because you're fuckin' stupid, and I'll rip your heart out." Hardin stepped into his face.

"Booby traps, booby traps, booby traps, Dumb Ass, they're full of booby traps."

"Yes, sir."

"Fuck-a-bunch of 'yes, sirs.' Get off this fuckin' hill." Hardin stomped away and moved the rest of the unit 700 meters south and east. He was enjoying his evening meal when Dillon and Gray came to visit.

"Gray, did you and the Pollock come in country together?"

Leech Dick interrupted, "Bravo's new oscar is on that slick in the south."

When the lone Huey started to hover down on a small knoll at the base of a ridge, Hardin tapped Dillon's arm and said, "Watch this." The skids bounced on the knoll, stabilized, then landed on a booby trap. The chopper slid sideways, rolled below the crest of the hill, and slammed into a rice paddy.

"Sector, this is Casper Two. We're hit." Leech Dick turned up the volume on the radio. "We had six SOBs, delivered three, got three wounded, gonna bring 'em in if we can."

"Sector Nine, roger. We're scrambling Starblazer."

The slick rocked back and forth to free its skids from the mud, hovered up out of the water, turned into its fall, nosed down, fighting for altitude, barely clearing the palm trees.

With a deep sigh, Gray said, "It's been a long day." Looking over the rim of his canteen cup, he said, "The pilot called 'em SOBs."

"Souls-on-Board. That's us. That pilot would die tryin' to help, any day we asked him to. Those rotors will sound as sweet as your mama's sigh before it's over."

"Yeah. Those rotors already sound pretty good."

"Tell me somethin', Lieutenant. How did a man as black as you get a name like Gray? Can you iron that out for me?" Hardin grinned. Gray shook his head.

"I don't know, Captain. You're the first white boy to asked me that."

Hardin chuckled. Thank God the man had sand. "White boy, is it? Just try to keep track of where you're headed. I'll help ya if I can, but there may not be enough time. Tighten up the studs, Gray. Let's have good OPs."

Hardin gave Leech Dick an approving look, and said, "You sure ya didn't put that leech on your cock. Decorate the wild root for the hogs you like bangin'?"

"Tennessee said I'd be hearin' about that. I'll be glad when you're gone, Captain."

"No you won't. Are you gonna tell your wife how ya got that speed bump? Could be a great story, a sympathy deal. A bullet grazin' Old George while you were jackin' off."

"I'll think of somethin."

"We all got a story."

CHAPTER THIRTY-SIX

Friendly Fire

Battalion Mess. Landing Zone English.

Safe and somewhat ashamed, Uncle struggled with the decaying confines of Landing Zone English. He was a chopper pilot and an infantry officer, a lethal combination for a man fighting Vietnam's war. Promoted from his trade, he was relegated to a paper war—prejudicial allegations, IG inspections, reports of survey, and deserters who could not be explained. For sixteen months he watched officers come and go, most wounded or killed.

Whiskey helped him smile.

Covering Hardin's journey had become a hobby for Uncle, a worrisome hobby. Revered and hated, after forty-two combat assaults without ventilation, the young captain was an anomaly. Uncle laughed at a memory. His crew chief had nearly killed Hardin when he dropped a case of M-16 ammunition through the canopy. In the roar of that battle Hardin had taken the time to roll onto his back and give Uncle the bone.

After eleven months of combat Uncle could still see Hardin's middle finger perched next to a ruthless grin. Laughing now through a rush of instinct, Uncle pledged his future to intercepting papers that might put Hardin into tight quarters, content that the Army's demands weren't worth fulfilling.

Brigade and battalion staff-patches relied on Uncle for weekly updates on the probability that Hardin would end up in the stockade. Betting pools were adjusted daily. With eighteen days left in country, odds were turning: Hardin's luck might hold.

"How are the new platoon leaders?" Uncle asked, deciding the balance of Hardin's sanity was worth a good tickle.

"They're stupid. They think Maggie's a wizard."

"Word is the bounty's real," Uncle said, weighing Hardin's reaction.

"I don't care. Brigade get my orders?"

"Not a word. We've sent out several queries." Hardin gave his old friend a rousing "That's pure shit" look and left the mess tent.

Showered, he retreated to his bunker, put Dig-it's letter in his father's footlocker, and put pen to paper to write home. With Linda nursing their baby girl, one more lie would put him out of the jungle and make preparations for the holidays more enjoyable.

Fevered dreams ransacked the night, his grave inset on the left-hand verge of each scene—the crystal blue vase, the white roses. His father's grave loomed in a shadow, alive with mold. Sleep came in spurts. He was too exhausted to care. Relieved by first light, Captain Edward Hardin stood-to. He had once again watched his friends die, one at a time.

No longer calm, he spent the day expecting death. Once-routine events now were threatening. The White Mice were quartered fewer than one hundred meters from his bunker. Saturated, wondering about the day, he needed to pass the baton.

A chopper overhead pounded heavy air, the pulse hammered at his chest. Odd bits of laughter were remote. Lightning's smile was curled at its edge. Hardin was detaching, pushing away. GIs pranced like holographs, floating in animated planes, pestering their Lord for a slice of his luck.

Somehow their God knew of Vietnam.

"Captain." Stubbs kicked the edge of Hardin's chair. "Captain." Hardin stood up. "Sir, the Old Man wants you at the TOC."

"You still hangin' around, Stubbs?"

"Next week. Rap left for Cam Rahn Bay yesterday."

"What's happenin', Stubbs?"

"The company's goin' back out to the Tigers."

"You gotta be jokin'."

"Someone's fuckin' ya, Captain. The brigade IG and a civilian interviewed Tennessee and Amps, along with Rap, about those VC who died in that hasty ambush at the south end of the Tigers. Questions about executing prisoners."

"The old woman's sons. It's the White Mice, Stubbs. The District Police."

"Someone big enough to get a general to dance," Stubbs said.

"Shit, the Gross Table can do that. This war ain't over, Stubbs."

"I'm goin' home next week." Stubbs held out an open palm and lit a smoke.

Refreshed for a moment by a fine spray of rain, Hardin ran the calculations on his friend and decided the old sergeant was still trustworthy. Hesitating, then deciding, he said, "The word is that the deserter was killed in Ban Me Thuot, by a GI." Stubbs stepped to his right as if to catch his balance. Hardin cocked his head sensing that his friend was relieved by the news.

"That shit would be hard to keep quiet," Stubbs said, mustering a narrow eye.

"Not for Drips and Mex. Not for the Hill People. Not for Fish."

Nodding his concurrence, Stubbs asked, "Who killed him?" Stubbs lit a smoke, conspiring with himself before he allowed his eye to find his captain.

"Hard tellin.' Maybe one of the Hill People. Maybe Tag. Could have been anybody in the platoon or the point squad." Hardin waited for Stubbs' expression to stop calculating, then said, "Rap told me. Told me to watch out for Reynolds."

Stubbs held his cigarette as if it were made of glass, then set his ear to the perimeter. "Reynolds joined the outfit after Ban Me Thuot. No matter. We're gonna shut this down, Captain. I don't want to know what happened. And you and I didn't have this conversation."

* * *

The Tactical Operations Center drummed with excitement. The radio operators jabbered, coordinating dust-offs as staffers ran about, grease pencils at the ready. Four South Vietnamese Army officers scribbled on note pads, gathering each other with complimentary gestures. Maggie stood-to smiling, anticipating an invigorating round of face time.

Hardin stopped at the radio table.

"What's goin on, Bronx?" Bronx tossed Hardin a Coke.

"Bravo Six is dead. Stumbled into the resupply slick's main rotor blade."

A sudden knot seized Hardin's gut, the superstitious confines of his inner world riven by this final betrayal. His rucksack, Captain Joe's drive-on rag, Sweet Cheeks' shroud line, Squeak's bag of dew, Nuts' overseas cap, his grandfather's watch, a last pair of glasses, his father's worry beads—all consumed by the jungle. And now, a Huey's main rotor, its percussive warmth so dear, brought death.

Captain Anthony Foster hurried toward the sound of the rotor. The wind freshened his face. He was smiling, thankful for the pilot's effort, bathing in the rotor wash. He did not suspect his trusted friend. He stumbled to his death, relaxed and relieved.

Empty, Hardin measured the confines of the Tactical Operations Center. He assumed his enemy was in the bunker. Leaning against the back wall of the briefing room, tucked in the corner against the sandbags, he searched for a strained expression. The Old Man, Uncle, Maggie, and a wad of South Vietnamese officers all found his stare before they sat down.

One ARVN officer hesitated before he smiled.

Fiercely suspicious to the point of parsing postures, Hardin's war, like his father's words, had been reduced to a single phrase: "Take care of yourself, Pal." VC—Victoria Cross or Viet Cong. In the end the difference would be captured in a split second.

The lectern, the briefing map, the push pins, and the TOC—all were but props.

Renting allies for search and destroy missions in Viet Cong controlled villages when the rice paddies were full of water, rats, cobras, leeches, and floating gaggles of pissed-off fire ants, was not smart. Trusting the South Vietnamese was not smart either, yet they stood in the battalion briefing room as honored guests. M-16s were issued to the South Vietnamese Army in the Bong Son area of operations two weeks ago. Alpha Company lost three men to M-16 fire that day.

"Gentlemen." The Old Man stood-to, sliding his hands to the top of the lectern, his head cocked toward the only black push-pin on the briefing map. Maggie rose with a pointer aimed at the push-pin, his chin braced in solemn intensity. "We lost Bravo Six today," the Old Man said. "An accident. We have got to be more careful."

Realizing the Old Man intended to move on, Uncle stood and left the briefing. Bravo Six—Captain Anthony Foster—was a footnote. He was an Ineffective. That's all he could be. His was an ignominious death, embarrassing in some circles.

Would they argue the worth of his death, or were there too many dead grunts?

The briefing continued. It had dramatic speech. Some of it was true. Some of it was classified. The smoke grew dense as if to hide the harshly exclaimed charges.

Avoiding the conclusions, and thought when he could, Hardin surveyed the briefing room. The energetic warriors could not avoid themselves, let alone temporize their pride. And yet their personalities failed to hold the day. The story of Anthony Foster's death filled itself with hesitancy and spilled into denial, given to bad luck for a time and then to recrimination.

Before Hardin could object, the Old Man's voice rang with an accelerating tone. "Gentlemen, for the first time in Two Corps, or the central region of South Vietnam, an American infantry company will be placed under the operational control of a South Vietnamese infantry battalion." The Old Man looked at the South Vietnamese officers as if to judge his presentation.

International pride, the cousin that was the war, had set sail.

"Holy shit," Hardin said to himself, his calculations racing through the palm groves around the base of the Tiger Mountains.

"Lots of people will be watching this operation. Let's do it right."

"How long is the operation?" Stubbs asked, gauging his captain's chances.

"Fourteen days. Charlie Company will search between the north end of the Tiger Mountains and the An Lao River from LZ English to the South China Sea." Hardin wanted to slit Maggie's throat.

"Charlie Company and an ARVN battalion?" Stubbs asked.

Conjuring visions of well-planned friendly fire, Hardin moved toward the briefing map.

"They're deploying two rifle companies and a detachment of White Mice."

Hardin wrote down the radio frequencies and confronted the South Vietnamese officers with Bronx at his side. Extending a copy of the reporter's photograph, he searched their eyes for signs of recognition. The bastards had seen the photograph before.

Hardin confronted the American advisor.

"Whose idea was this operation?" The advisor was a US Army First Lieutenant.

"Came from your brigade. What's the big deal?"

Incensed by the advisor's derisive nature, Hardin flew into a rage. "You keep those people away from me, or I'll deal ya myself."

The advisor stepped away, surprised and shaken by Hardin's vicious tone.

Somehow Hardin's four-inch K-Bar had found the palm of his right hand. If Uncle's intell concerning the ten thousand dollar bounty was accurate, this search and destroy operation was a trap.

"I don't like you, asshole," Hardin said, forcing the man to catch his step. "And, I don't like your friends. Stay outta rifle range. I got a kid from Alabama who'll take your head off."

Hardin left the advisor standing in a perfect circle of white rocks near the battalion flagpole. He was looking for the one man he trusted who was still in the bush. Fish lay in a corner, suffering a hangover, nursing a can of beer, slobbering on about the whores by the airstrip, and assaulting LeCotte with unconnected insults.

"What's happenin', Captain?"

"Step outside, Fish—we gotta talk." Fish sobered instantly.

Hardin explained the operation, the rumored bounty on his life, the reporter's prejudicial allegation, that the reporter's picture had been found at four separate enemy contacts, the IG inquiry about executing the two VC who died at their own hand in the hasty ambush, and that no one knew about the man missing from Delta Company outside of the brigade.

Fish stood with his childish grin wired to a pair of eyeballs crazed with hate. Hardin continued. "The next fourteen days are gonna be dicey. The landing zone is that plateau where Packrat got wasted. You're gonna work the point with Tag, or we're gonna get whacked. Tell Tee-N and Blood, and anyone else you trust."

"Blood and Tag gotta know. Tee-N's on R&R. We can have Reynolds keep an eye on the White Mice. That way some villager won't end up with their throat slit."

"Someone's gonna die, Fish."

"The Mice are the dudes runnin' the whores by the airstrip."

* * *

Hardin ate a large meal and drank beer until he could not stand. Morning found him clutching a great reek of garlic, gargling bile, sitting in the right door of the second slick gassing the door gunner, facing an invisible dragon, watching the Tiger Mountains consume the horizon.

Nearly running off of Packrat's plateau, Fish guided the company west, away from the South China Sea, through the village with the white stucco pagoda and Andy's bell. Fish altered the pace and direction so often, Balls-Itch wore his hand set out calling in loc-stats.

For eight days Fish moved the company in and out of the villages, securing water, then searching the dense copse-filled draws at the base of the Tiger Mountains.

Hardin laughed at the madness, playing hide and seek by triangulating between Andy's bell, Packrat's plateau, and the island hootches where the kids were wasted in the cross fire. At the center of the triangle was the kill zone where Andy lost his leg and four GIs died.

On the ninth day the three platoons split up and ran to the points of the triangle. First Platoon continued their run, occupying the village 400 meters south of the island hootches. LeCotte and Boyle started arguing over a box of Chuckles candy. Boyle kicked his rucksack in frustration, setting off his M-79 grenade launcher and blowing apart the floor of a nearby hootch.

Boyle stared in disbelief. The hootch floor had a false chamber. Six inches below what appeared to be hard-beaten clay, rice was hidden in heavy plastic wrap, waiting to be bagged and transported into the mountains to feed NVA troops. The company demolished the village, one hootch at a time, bagging nine tons of rice.

"It's tough to get ambushed if you're not movin'," Hardin mused. Hardin drank his coffee in the bottom of a foxhole large enough for a squad, exposing himself to take a piss and welcome cloverleaf patrols back into the nest.

Six days and a wake-up.

Late in the night Leech Dick tripped over his rucksack and fell into their foxhole, crushing Hardin's glasses, leaving the pieces in a neat pile at the leading edge of the foxhole. Logic being that the captain could use the largest shard to get a fix on a target. Blind, as if his point of view might improve, Hardin held his tongue in check.

Leech Dick owed him a dose of greater courage and that couldn't be a bad thing.

First light of the eleventh day began with Hardin fumbling through his most simple rituals. The C-Ration toilet paper had a contentious edge, refusing to arrange itself in sufficient quantity to address his needs. And his head decided to rattle like a walnut inside a drum when he tipped it to the left. He tried to play a tune with it but the walnut had no sense.

"The ARVN battalion commander is 300 meters east of us. He's comin' for a look-see at the rice collection," Leech Dick said, laughing when Hardin looked through the twisted rims of his glasses and gave him the finger.

Vietnamese colonels spent most of their day standing next to their future, looking in a mirror, admiring the well-dressed, well-decorated ARVN officers they had become. Inspecting the rice-bagging operation, as if this particular rice was suspicious, the old boy spoke to himself, pestering his aide with obscure inflections and witless grins. The advisor formed the balance of the clerisy, mounting each move with a dip of his shoulders as an attendant might serve a queen.

An entourage of lesser Vietnamese soldiers, emitting an odor of stale fish, milled around the village in a wad, passing out temporary smiles and envious vowels, summarizing each encounter by gathering in a tighter circle and speaking in tongues.

Hardin watched the ARVN commander from the recess of a hootch, laughing as Fish greeted the colonel, introducing himself as the platoon leader. Hardin's laughter stopped when the advisor appeared escorting the reporter—the general's baby boy. Fish continued his charade, signaling Blood and Tag as he drew the colonel aside, forcing the advisor and the reporter to huddle with Tag.

With the reporter snapping pictures, Fish caught sight of the advisor's hand gestures. Fixing the colonel with an excuse-me gesture, he braced the two men, pushing them into the shadow of a palm tree.

"You two are the company's targets for this operation. Don't let us catch ya alone."

Blood stepped to the reporter's side, locking the man's left elbow in his right hand, guiding the man into a hootch. "You're gonna stay with the company for the rest of this operation. Your friends will think you're in good hands."

Fish and the advisor returned to the Vietnamese colonel, with Fish suggesting tactics as if they had decided on a plan that might work. As the advisor translated, Fish smiled and gave up a slight bow.

As expected, the colonel did not like the plan. Instead, Charlie Company would search north toward the An Lao River on a route that included the island hootches, Andy's night ambush site, and Joe's bell. Fish agreed to the plan as the best tactical decision possible, commending the colonel as a tactical genius.

Watching the Vietnamese clear the village, Hardin stepped to Fish's side. The reporter snapped a picture, smiling through a burst of energy. As if orchestrated by forces unseen, PeeWee and Reynolds appeared at the reporter's side. PeeWee whispered in his ear, then laughed at the man's discomfort.

Dillon grabbed PeeWee's arm. "Easy PeeWee. I'll handle this." Noticeably vulnerable, the reporter tried to brace himself. Dillon held up a copy of the reporter's picture, and said, "Why is this picture in the hands of every dink in this province?" The reporter's face fell through a series of false expressions: truth or half-truth, his own doing.

"Don't have a clue."

The butt of Dillon's weapon slammed into the lens of the reporter's camera, driving the camera into his chest. The reporter stepped, then fell over a large basket.

"Try lyin' to me again. You're gonna help us here, or you're gonna die here."

"I gave the negatives from that day's shoot to your brigade, to some goddamn psy-ops major. The man requested the film."

Hardin listened, correlating anomalous data, looking for a lapse of confidence, his eyes dancing. The stale smell of contempt mingled with the rot of the jungle floor. Taking a step forward, he cocked his head in a questioning shrug. Then spoke, suppressing a scream.

"What did this major look like?"

With a quietly strained voice, the reporter described the average white male. Mixing his grin with rage, Hardin forced the reporter's eyes into a slightly sharper focus, then slammed his helmet on the reporter's shoulder. The man winced and sat against the well.

"Nothin' to this combat shit, is there?" Hardin said.

Blood nodded his approval. Fish removed the film from the reporter's rucksack.

With eyes hot enough to melt steel, Hardin sank into a deep squat, far angrier for the man's arrogance. "You're gonna stay with the company for the rest of this operation. If one of us gets whacked, you're gonna get shot. What people like you don't understand is that us grunts are already dead. So killin' you won't mean nothin."

Hardin laughed an inexplicable laugh, releasing the tension in his throat. Then just as abruptly he screamed at the reporter. "Odds are, you're a fuckin' dead man."

Fish and Blood pulled the man to his feet and escorted him to the confines of First Platoon's sector. PeeWee and Reynolds had started a game of mumblety-peg. There was nowhere to run.

"What a dumb ass," Leech Dick said, shaking his head.

"Believe this, Leech Dick. We've bagged four AKs and nine tons of rice, and these dinks haven't found shit. Chuck's gotta turn over his own, or he's gotta bang us."

"We're not gonna shoot him, are we Captain?" Leech Dick asked, as if to judge himself.

"No. I just want to shit-scare him for a while."

"I'll tell Reynolds and Fish," Leech Dick said, relieved. "And PeeWee."

With Fish and Tag at the charge, the company nearly ran past the white pagoda. By the time the bell rang a third time the company had reached the south bank of the An Lao River, 200 meters away. Hidden from the river behind a verge of six-foot grass, GIs dug in, content to spend the last night of the operation in a well-constructed laager.

Hardin's replacement, a stocky man with a ruddy complexion, roan-colored hair, and an oversized nose, had flown out on the resupply chopper to work with the company for the last day of the operation. When he announced that he was on his second tour, Fish told him he was stupid. As if to promote his declaration, Fish challenged the captain to a game of mumblety-peg, Fish would throw first, the winner being the man without a knife stuck in his foot.

Advising Fish of his officer rank and the charge he intended to file, Fish laughed and declared that the captain's name would be Martha in honor of the tree Hardin was fond of.

"You normally dig in this early, Hardin?" Martha asked.

"Look, Martha. I don't want to talk to you. You're givin' me a bad feelin'. How long were you in the bush on your first tour?" Hardin noted the man's arrogance.

"Four months, in the mountains."

"I got jungle rot that's four months old. You're either a lifer or you're stupid. Whatever your story is, most of these studs have been in the bush longer than you have, and they're smarter than you, Ace. No way in hell would they come back."

"My unit was in the mountains. We had our share," he said.

"That means you're an art major. You know—the art of warfare. So, Captain Major, this is how it goes. This isn't the mountains. And at this point, when we dig and when we move is none of your business."

"You're right."

"This is my twelfth month in Charlie's jungle. I know I'm right. And, goddammit, if you plan on usin' a foxhole tonight, ya better fuckin' dig one. Nobody gets a free ride."

Hardin turned to Leech Dick. "Have LeCotte make some stew."

"Right on."

"I'd invite you to dinner, Martha, but I think you're a fuckin' jerk."

"You treat all your replacements this way?"

"You're the first replacement I've ever had," Hardin said, looking for humor in the man's eyes. When he found loose stuffing, he said, "Here's how this outfit works. Stay off the trails, ridges, and low hills around the rice paddies. Don't chase Chuck. Everyone fights and everyone digs. Forget the regs on the firebase—and never lie to another grunt."

“That’s it? Those are the rules?”

“If you break the rules these men will know.”

Hardin spent the next hour trying to say something to his friends—Boyle, Lightning, Boo, Wolfman, Reynolds, LeCotte, PeeWee, Fish, Blood, Grumpy, Linus, Mr. Monty, Pebbles, Stormy Norm, Balls-itch, Leech Dick and the three Docs.

“How do ya like it?” Doc Taylor handed Hardin a three-by-five colored glossy picture of a dink a gunship blew apart near the beach, when the company went for a swim. Doc had the negative made into a Christmas Card.

“I knew there was religious significance to this war,” Hardin said. Below the picture was a scene of Bethlehem and the inscription: *Peace on Earth, Christians: 1 Buddhists: 0.*

“Who made the card, Doc?”

“A buddy of mine in the World.”

“Thanks, Doc.” Dillon sank into a deep squat, pouring coffee into Hardin’s cup.

“We got problems. The Vietnamese want us to move at twilight and set up a blocking force. They say they’re gonna push some bad guys toward us.”

“And give the Gringos the glory? Bullshit.” Hardin pulled out his map. “Where does the Emperor want us to set up?” Dillon pointed to a spot on the map fewer than fifty meters from the location where the night ambush had blown off Andy’s leg.

“Tell me a story.”

“I say we dig deeper,” Dillon said.

“Good call. That location is where Captain Joe got hit the last time the company stomped around in the dark.” Hardin’s expression locked with laughter: three-on-a-match and all that. The reporter’s eyes were red with shock and his nose looked like an outcrop. Reynolds was trying to work the kinks out of his right hand. And Martha was digging a hole.

“Leech Dick, get the Advisor on the hook.”

“I got him on hold. Told him we were busy.”

Hardin grabbed the hook. “This is Charlie Six, say again, over.”

“Roger, set up a blocking position by 2100 hours.”

“This is Charlie Six, roger out.”

“I thought we weren’t movin.” Balls-itch arched his back, shaking his head, checking his map, and stirring his beef and rice. Martha stood erect, shovel silent, staring at Hardin.

“We’re not,” Hardin said, throwing the words at his replacement. “Give me some Tabasco, Balls-itch.” He hesitated, then tossed the bottle to Hardin.

“You just told that advisor we were movin.” Balls-itch held up his map as evidence. “You gave him a roger out.”

"You piss me off, ya know that, Balls-Itch? I told the man I understood his message and the conversation was over." Hardin solicited a grin from Leech Dick.

"He thinks we're movin."

"I got one and a wake-up, and that's what I want him to think." Martha shook his head slowly. He would have obeyed the order. He was bad luck wrapped in a seamless bag.

The night danced from one sound to the next. Hardin watched a slice of the river, careful to monitor the far bank. Patches of cloud raced from the sea, countering the river's flow.

The North Star glowed, as if on guard.

The tiny blue crystals on Willie Spencer's watch sparkled in the starshine.

At 0400 hours, Leech Dick woke the fire teams. Charlie Company would greet this first light with all hands awake, rucksacks secured. GIs cussed in silence as they packed in the dark. The company moved out rapidly at first light with Tag and Fish at the charge. Dillon occupied the designated blocking position minutes before the ARVN Advisor called.

"Charlie Six, where's your blocking force?" The lead element of South Vietnamese infantry was bogged down in a rice paddy, 200 meters east of the ambush site.

"A main element has been in place all night."

"Roger, Charlie Six."

Charlie Company sat at the base of the Tiger Mountains, knowing they had been set up. The South Vietnamese had moved throughout the night and were so far away they could not have known Dillon wasn't in place unless they had a separate unit waiting for him. But, they couldn't cop to having a unit waiting in ambush without proving they were—Viet Cong.

The advisor called again. "Charlie Six, we have a LRRP team in the Tigers reporting a hundred NVA in the open, full equipment. We're requesting firecracker rounds from the ARVN artillery. The battery is gun-target to your location, heads up."

A short round would hit the company. The bounty was for real.

Hardin motioned to the artillery FO. "What's a firecracker?"

"Firecracker rounds explode in the air, releasing bomblets that saturate a target." The first six firecracker rounds exploded over head and dozens of bomblets fell through the air. The last scheduled day for the operation and Charlie Company was a target of opportunity.

Leech Dick handed Hardin the hook. "It's Maggie."

"Well Maggie, what is it now?" Hardin asked.

"Higher-higher wants a Bomb-Damage-Assessment on that firecracker."

"Do you know what he's talkin' about, Red-Leg?" Hardin asked the artillery FO.

"I can do a BDA."

The company climbed the gully west of the ridge, popping up on the ridge at intervals until they found a spot where men had spent the night. The next knoll south was shredded. Small bomblets hung like ornaments in the waist-high vegetation.

"What's the deal, Red-Leg?"

"Firecracker has a twenty-nine percent dud ratio."

"Do the BDA from here, long-range Etch A Sketch. We're leavin' in five." Hardin could feel his enemy's surveillance. Snipers were his next problem. He was down to the final hours and seconds of his tour and he was spooked beyond reason.

Red-Leg drew the BDA overlay, and the company moved off the ridge into the paddy.

"You have to sign the overlay." The FO gave Hardin a pen. He signed the overlay with the alias, Peter Pan. "BDAs don't mean much."

"Kinda like this fuckin' war."

Hardin checked his watch: 0732 hours. Setting an ear to the shattered crstal, listening for his time, he had lived thirteen minutes longer than Dig-it lived on his last day. But he stood five-and-a-half kilometers east of LZ English, with the An Lao River to cross, and a detachment of White Mice on the loose.

"Three Yankee, answer the phone." Leech Dick's voice was frustrated. "Send us some slicks. Give us a ride home."

"Wait one, Charlie Kilo." Hardin handed his Claymore bag of magazines to LeCotte. He had one magazine in his weapon and seven magazines in the bandoleer across his chest.

"Charlie Six, this is Sector Nine, Six says walk." Hardin threw the handset in the dirt.

"Don't talk to that bastard." Leech Dick stuck the hook in the side pocket of his rucksack and turned off his radio.

A platoon of Vietnamese infantry was operating between the company and LZ English. Their location was unknown. Maggie would figure Hardin had it coming. So would Martha.

"Leech Dick, what happened to Miller?" Hardin asked, checking his weapon.

"He died in a car wreck in Australia, on R&R."

"No shit. Keep these beads, Leech Dick, for luck." Hardin slipped Dig-it's rosary into the side pocket on Leech Dick's rucksack. "I just realized Miller was gone."

Hardin shivered through a series of short breaths, crazy with fear, his friends now suspects. The hootches and palm trees seemed too small, out of proportion. Open paddies, and open stretches of grass lay in wait, hiding hundreds of spider holes. Tree lines challenged his step. As the day stretched on, Fish forced the reporter to walk at Hardin's side, explaining to the man that he was a human shield.

By the time the company crossed the An Lao River, Hardin was exhausted. His bandoleer of ammunition was gone. He had one magazine left. He knew if he looked, the magazine would be empty. Dillon and Fish were running the company.

At 1545 hours Hardin trudged up the slope between the hootches bordering the airstrip. The muddy alley that led to the airstrip seemed narrow. Whores chanted their antes, reaching for the GIs, their chants surreal, in and out of harmony, their echoes reaching across the PSP as his boots bounced free.

He dropped his weapon and rucksack, along with his helmet, on the orderly room porch. Hardin was enraged, then relieved, and then enraged again. Bronx pointed toward the briefing room when Hardin entered the TOC. Uncle and Maggie were not prepared for his hostility.

"Thanks for the ride, Maggot."

"That was the Old Man."

"Bullshit, you're the fuckin' dreamer." Uncle motioned Hardin into the briefing room where he had beer on ice.

"I'll buy ya a beer. Sit down and stop callin' my S-3 a maggot."

"Don't do anymore deals with the Vietnamese. They're VC."

"You're spooked. Maybe the rumors are takin' on their own life."

"Maybe. I figure the White Mice posted the bounty. Word is they're runnin' the whores by the airstrip." Maggie entered the room and stood behind the lectern. He smelled of soap.

"That makes more sense than anything I've heard so far," Uncle said, opening a beer.

"When's the change of command ceremony?"

Uncle spoke with a positive nod. "Noon sounds good."

"No, sir," Maggie declared. "The new Charlie Company commander wanted to be moved out to the field. They should be lifting off the airstrip any time."

A tail of foam hung in the light above the lectern as Hardin's beer can hit the cloth sandbag and Maggie's pushpins.

"You just don't get it, do ya, Maggot," Hardin screamed. "You fuckin' puke! I didn't get to say good-bye."

* * *

Hardin ran as fast as his boots would allow. Catching but traces of his friends, he stood-to, crying as he gave LeCotte and Lightning a thumbs-up. LeCotte returned his gesture with a salute, nudging Boyle to do the same.

Thank God three men knew he cared.

After a year of combat, fighting to keep his men alive, Captain Edward Hardin stood alone. The slicks were taking his keepsakes and dumping them into the fire. The trail of choppers led south and then west from the airstrip as far as the eye could see.

The chopping sound faded: his hopes, too. He stood on the airstrip looking over the paddies after his friends, hollow, and empty. As his memory lashed out at this last bit of grief, Stubbs mounted the PSB with a conniving bounce.

"Stubbs, you're still here."

"The game's over, Captain, and we don't know the score," Stubbs said, pushing smoke with his words. The choppers arced to the left toward the Tiger Mountains, then dropped below the palm trees. Stubbs rolled an AK bolt over in his hand, as if his message might be too late. Would he side with his men and their beleaguered captain, or would he talk to the IG?

"Who are we now, Stubbs?" Hardin asked, expecting the best from his old friend.

Instantly, as if grazing fire had cleared his conscience, Stubbs sided with his El Tee against the army he loved—his El Tee, his Captain. His men and their secret would be held from harm.

"We're Effectives, Captain." Stubbs said, lighting a smoke. Not knowing how best to tell his story, Stubbs decided to mend some other business first.

"I told Fish and Blood you didn't know they were goin' back out." Waiting for Hardin to stop looking at the horizon, he continued. "I gave Fish your dog tags like you asked, for luck. He got choked up when he read your father's tag."

Instantly, Hardin couldn't breathe. He didn't remember giving the tags to Stubbs or asking him to pass them on to Fish. Try as he might, he had difficulty drawing air into his lungs. The emotion of the day swept through his chest. His friends were just over there.

Finding Stubbs holding his arm, he shrugged and stepped away. Not angry, more surprised, he asked, "Who are we now, Stubbs?"

"I don't know, Captain. Soldiers, I guess." Stubbs dropped his head as if he were ashamed, as if his life's work had been gutted, as if further effort at excellence was futile. With smoke in his voice, he said, "Reynolds told me to give you this." Stubbs handed Hardin a well-oiled bolt from an AK-47.

"Reynolds is a tough one, a real piece of work. This bolt a souvenir, or what?"

"I guess it could be," Stubbs said, working the ash of his cigarette into a perfect cone.

"You got somethin' on your mind, Stubbs?"

"Drips gave that bolt to Reynolds when he left country. Made Reynolds promise to give it to you when you were goin' home. Drips killed the deserter in Ban Me Thuot, in the back of a whore house in a drunken rage. Bucks took the bolt from the man's AK."

"Fuck me. Let's hope—let's hope the man he killed was the deserter," Hardin said, rolling the bolt over in his hand. "So that's how the story goes—one more memory." Hardin let himself remember Drips, his loyalty, and the Hill People in turn—Squeak, Sweet Cheeks, Shadow, Mex, Bucks, Ski, and Fish.

Thankful, as if his friends knew he had done his best, he looked again toward the Tiger Mountains and said, "The man is missing in action."

Relieved, Stubbs said, "Maybe that's best."

"Best." Hardin looked west toward the Crow's Foot and then toward the Fish Hook. Shaking his head, he said, "Best isn't part of this war, Top Sergeant."

Outside the world, on a vacant airstrip, near the village of Bong Son, in South Vietnam, Sergeant First Class Oscar B. Stubbs tended an ox cart filled with rice. The harvest was long since over. He would tend the wain ropes from day to day as if his cargo were destined for home. He would stand-to at each crossroad waiting for orders, then muster his will and drive-on again.

From ridgeline to valley and ridgeline hence, he would tend the memory of his men, first one and then another. Nuts, Hippie, McGregor, Bucks, and Packrat, they were his men, too.

Their honor was clean, each man in turn.

* * *

Walking toward the mess tent to settle a score, Hardin's heart ached as the emotions he had reserved for his friends bled into a dark pool. He traced the silhouette of the Tiger Mountains to find Pops and Packrat. He found Stubbs standing stock still, barely a shadow.

* * *

Master Sergeant Greenwell was posting permanent orders on the company bulletin board. "Well, Captain, this is my company now. The new commander is a hard charger."

"That man is stupid. But that's not your biggest problem, Greenwell. Your new captain likes ham and lima beans." Hardin stuck his grin in the old sergeant's face to force the man to tighten the straps on his bib overalls. When he didn't respond, Hardin said, "Where's the company goin'?"

"Back into the villages north of the Tiger Mountains."

"You're not the only lifer who draws his courage from dead grunts."

* * *

The Old Man, Uncle, and Maggie were gathered in the mess tent, conjuring over a beer. They greeted him with handshakes all around. With a whiskey in tow he forced a chair into the circle and sat as close to Maggie as space would allow.

"I am sorry I missed your face with that can of beer, Maggie, because someone needs to make an impression on you."

"Your tour is over, Captain Hardin. Time to pack your bags and head back to the States. Back to your family," Maggie said, coaxing support from the Old Man.

"I'm gonna speak slowly, Major, because I know you're lost. My tour was not a timed event. My tour was a duty to my men." Uncle leaned back and the Old Man leaned in.

"Many men are fighting this war, Captain Hardin," Maggie said.

"You're not, Maggie. And you just sent my men into a Viet Cong village with a new captain and you told the dumb bastard that the village was pacified."

"He's on his second tour."

Hardin reached out and crushed Maggie's can sending beer skating across the table. Resentment filled his eyes, challenging the Old Man's gesture of conciliation. Then he continued. "Your new boy spent four months in the mountains, two years ago. Time and this war have changed. The VC have been in Binh Dinh Province for five decades. Ho Chi Minh grew up in this province. Those villages are not pacified."

"Captain Hardin, those men are not your problem."

"Well, Major, now I know you're stupid. Those men will always be my problem. We lost a dog that's still my problem."

With a box of Rambler's Road Apples in free-fall, Uncle said, "Come on Hardin, let's give Charlie Company a call and see how they're doing." Hardin declined Uncle's offer with a grin and a handshake. Old friends they were, sure enough.

At 0314 hours Uncle woke Hardin from a confusing sleep. "Wake up Hardin. Charlie Company got hit. One GI is dead, First Platoon."

"Find yourself a new ops officer." Hardin railed at the laces of his boots. "I'm gonna kill the one ya got. I'm gonna rip his throat out and stuff it up his sorry ass."

The ride to the aid station seemed a moment as the jeep picked its way past the brigade TOC. The harsh cones of light refracting off the empty metal tables set the background in the aid station aglow. With but one man to fondle, their hands quickly parsed the reasons.

The screen door of the aid station seemed to open itself.

"Don't touch him, Major," Hardin said, jarring Maggie when he stepped forward.

"Go back to the TOC, Major. You're not needed here," the Old Man said.

Lightning, Lima's ebony warrior, Lima's six-foot-four-inch, slender, black machine gunner, with the modest unassuming smile, and the loyal stride, was dead. Lightning lay quiet now, painted with an expression Hardin had not seen before: an expression of peaceful contempt. He must have met Hippie and Dig-it by now, and those other good men. Bucks.

Hardin cried as he placed Lightning's right hand by his side. His fingers hung in an odd array, his arm tense. The fungus in the jungle rot on his hand was moving. Hardin thought about Bucks' baseball dreams and his games of dice, then gave Lightning a pat on the shoulder.

Looking at the members of the triage team to fix their responsibility, he whispered. "Take care of yourself, Lightning. Say 'Hi' to Hippie, and Bucks, and the rest for me."

Hardin found Lightning's dog tags and took one for his own. The only word on the tag was Lightning. With tears he could not hide, Hardin looked into the mist of the triage tent, knowing he would miss Lightning dearly.

The Old Man and Uncle were waiting in the jeep when Hardin left the aid station. He stopped outside the door to let his eyes find their way.

Locating the two men, he registered his disgust. Handing Lightning's dog tag to Uncle, he said, "Give this to Fish for me, would you, Uncle? If you don't know who Fish is, it's high time you met a good soldier."

Watching Uncle's sorrow swell to meet his own, Hardin turned and stepped into the night, singing: "The shadow of your smile, when you are gone."

* * *

Number #10, Highlands Road. Bremerton, Washington. September 1961.

The Major read Court's letter, puffing on his pipe, tamping the coals with his right index finger. Smoke rolled through the hood on his reading lamp like an old stone chimney. The story of being ambushed by Viet Cong guerrillas and the death of Court's friend in South Vietnam had the Major searching the more solemn entries in his D-Day journal.

"Was Lieutenant Train a friend of Court's?"

"I think so, Pal. There's always a first man and there's always a last man. The ones in between don't seem as bad." The Major puffed on his pipe.

"I hope Court doesn't go to Vietnam."

"I'm with you there, Pal. Johnny Poston may have been the last casualty in the war against the Jerries. Johnny was killed four days after the war ended, ambushed by a Werewolf Team of German youth. We buried Johnny in Belgium."

"I remember the picture of the funeral, Pops."

The Major knocked his pipe against a glass ashtray, then thoughtfully refilled the bowl. "It took years for me to get past losing my friend. It still hurts at times."

* * *

Landing Zone English.

Hardin slept a weary sleep and woke up in defeat. The fatigues he had worn for Captain Joe's departure seemed fresh and crisp as he put them on. The walk to the mess tent for the evening meal seemed a mile, all uphill.

The loyal followers of the Gross Table were waiting for him. Grins changed to smiles and laughter as he was proclaimed Royal Dickhead of the Gross Table, as a formal change of command was held. The best meal he ever had and he couldn't even remember what it was.

Hours later, full of beer and clutching a scroll presented to him commemorating some of his lighter moments, Hardin broke up the celebration with handclasps and promises all around to write. Black humor would survive. Lieutenant Orshanski was clearly a dickhead.

The dead never slept any better than Hardin did that night.

* * *

Veterans Hospital. American Lake, Washington. 1995.

The nurse tells me he cried last night, almost all night. He is sleeping peacefully when I go in, and doesn't move as I take the machine from his hand and put in a new tape.

Transcribing this tape is a trial for me. I see the trap coming, as does he. Our own people, or our allies, are coaxing him to his death, a "friendly" death for him and his men. Who will be left to tell the story? What generation do they come from that they would foster deceit before acknowledging that the war they fashioned was misdirected: discomposed?

Who, here, has committed the atrocity? Against whom? Are we not all of us the victims; are we not all of us to blame?

Will this grunt's postulate be confused with time, or will Battle Bullshit become the hallmark for his war? Who will judge these grunts and weigh their contribution?

You and I? Or will we stand in solitude, fondling our rituals, and hide behind our chiseled pride?

Who is to blame? My God—they were only boys.

That night, as I see him, I burst into tears, and we hold each other for a long time. Monty was a piker compared to grunts like these.

* * *

Vietnam. October 1968.

In the morning, Hardin was alone. The ride on the Caribou to Cam Rahn Bay, which should have been so deliriously joyful, was lonely instead.

Hardin managed to have a space made for him on the Pan Am manifest by getting a rear-echelon soldier bumped. He wanted to go home.

They left the airspace of the Republic of South Vietnam as they had come. The stewardess was a round-eye, and Hardin was a grunt. Would he learn to be anything else?

* * *

Postscript.

Martha, Hardin's replacement, was killed twelve days after assuming command. Carrying an AK-47 and wearing a black T-shirt, Martha walked into a recon platoon ambush.

Balls-itch was only wounded. Hardin was relieved. Fish and PeeWee, Boyle and LeCotte, Blood and Reynolds, Boo and Tag, and Grumpy, Linus, Wolfman, Doc and the rest were standing tall.

Hardin laughed to ease his soul, then whispered, "Get fat if you can, boys."

In July of 1969, while working as an operations officer for the ROTC Summer Camp at Fort Lewis, Washington, Hardin used the resignation of his Regular Army Commission, as his formal declaration of disdain. No longer would he fight Vietnam's war.

By August, 1969, he was twenty-three days late reporting back to the ROTC Detachment at the University of California, at Davis. Actually, he was AWOL, but no one wanted to report the misconduct of J. T. Ragman.

In September of 1969, while teaching small-unit tactics for the ROTC detachment, Hardin was ordered to be Survival Assistance Officer for the Davis, California, area.

The first family's son was dead and the Army knew it, but the body was so mutilated Hardin was ordered to visit the family in his dress-green uniform and inform the parents that their son was missing in action. One week later he was ordered to revisit the family and inform them that their son was dead. The casket was stamped non-viewable.

The second family's son was dead and viewable, so the family didn't have to spend a week wondering where he had gone.

The very sight of Hardin's uniform destroyed these families in one imperious moment.

One year later, in September of 1970, Captain Edward Hardin was honorably discharged from the United States Army at the Processing Station at Oakland Army Terminal, given the lowest Officer Efficiency Report ever recorded: 65/120, a fifty-four percent rating.

Someone was finally listening.

* * *

Rutherfordton, North Carolina. September 1972.

Buoyed by his honorable discharge, Hardin mustered the courage to visit Dig-it's mom.

The small, well-kept home stood steeped in resolve as he unlatched the gate and started up the path to the concrete steps. The sitting porch was full of flowers, like the breakfast nook at his grandmother's house. Dig-it's letter pushed at his heart as he rang the bell. He prayed, as if on the cusp of a dream: fearful of what he had to do. With the third ring of the bell, footsteps sounded on a wood floor, and a slow, gentle hand worked the knob.

Edward Hardin could only stare at the beauty of Mrs. Johnson.

Dig-it's joy flashed in her eyes as she smiled and extended a welcoming hand. Eddie thought she might laugh at him and spin into a dance. As he told the story, Dig-it's mother smiled with her eyes. Gracious and forgiving, she reached for Eddie's hand.

His chest ached and he began to cry.

Her grace and beauty were like rose buds.

When Eddie handed her Dig-it's letter, the home filled with a quieting grief. Her gentle soul absorbed the hellish detail. Her eyes were like pools. She rubbed first one and then the other in a way that made him hold his breath.

Her touch, her delicate gestures were so natural, reflecting the dignity of Dig-it's being. Her hands caressed the blood-stained print, over and over again. Hardin followed the words as her finger moved across the page, her eyes welling with love and pain.

Hours later filled with cake and coffee, he embraced the pulse of an inner strength he had not had in years. Dig-it's mom gave him a hug. No longer would she wonder how her son had died, or if someone cared. Eddie looked back over the porch, wondering if he could come back. He waved instead; knowing this visit was a memory he could hold on to.

* * *

Superior Court House. Martinez, California. 1987.

Years later, pestered by guilt for having lived, Hardin sat down to write and finally say good-bye. In reality, it was Packrat's murder trial that forced his words.

In the spring of 1987, Packrat came back to life with no legs, a partial right hand, a body full of holes, and a mind full of war and drugs. With foxholes in his front yard and guns in his house, Packrat killed a rookie policeman trying to do his duty.

With one trial to escape the gas chamber and one trial to find a home, Packrat was given life in Soledad prison without the possibility of parole. With Grumpy, Linus, Doc, Reynolds, Knapp, Wolfman, and Hardin in tow, under the eye of a prison guard, Packrat said he saw a Viet Cong soldier where a policeman fell.

Who do you see when you are afraid?

* * *

Veterans Hospital. American Lake, Washington. 1995.

Years earlier, Hardin had bought a '77 Chevy Camero with 25,586 original miles on it. The car had been garaged for twelve years under a dust cover, washed once a week, waxed once a month, and driven twice a year. Linda filled the tank and Hardin handed the keys to his son. Karl's first car—a real treasure. As the young man pulled out of the parking lot, he looked back once and gave his dad a thumbs-up.

Hardin flashed on LeCotte's final salute and watched to the end of the street, where his son turned the corner and drove into his day.

So that's it. I treasured that car. I never realized that my dad did too. I never knew a lot of things about him—that he cared so deeply about so much. He lies here now, totally exhausted, just a matter of days now. His good friend Drips passed away last Sunday. He smiled when we told him. Their names won't be on the wall.

Godspeed.

Glossary

Digger	An Australian infantryman
Dogface	An American infantryman, WW II
Brownjob	A British Royal Air Force term for the British infantryman
Grunt	An American infantryman, Vietnam
GI	General Issue: an American Soldier
El Tee	Infantry Lieutenant
Top	Company First Sergeant
First Shirt	Company First Sergeant
CQ	Charge-of Quarters (a runner that works for the first sergeant)
TOC	Tactical Operations Center
Prick-25	PRC-25, the standard infantry platoon radio
RTO	Radio operator
Kilo	Radio operator
Push	Radio frequency
Freek	Radio frequency
Hook	Radio handset
Sit-rep	Situation report
Op-con	Operational control. Subject to the operational orders of another unit
Op-ord	Operations order. Same as the five-paragraph field order.
Drive-on Rag	A bandage worn around the neck like a tie
FUO	Fever of Unknown Origin
Dustoff	A Huey medevac helicopter
Slick	A Huey transport helicopter
Jungle penetrator	Cable lowered into the jungle with a litter basket to extract wounded
PSB	Metal decking used for airstrips and helipads
APC	Armored Personnel Carrier

AO	Area of Operation
Comics	Maps
Loc-stat	Location status
Klick	Kilometer
Point of Origin	Map grid intersection used to locate a unit's position
Papa Oscar	Radio term for Point of Origin.
Blue-line	Creek, Stream, or River
LZ	Landing Zone
PZ	Pickup Zone
Laager	A night defensive position
OP	Outpost
Oscar Papa	Radio term for Outpost
Bush	Ambush
Clover	Light recon patrol with a trace the shape of a cloverleaf
LRRP	Long Range Recon Patrol
Sky Soldiers	173rd Airborne Brigade, the 503rd Airborne Infantry
SF	Special Forces
Master Blaster	Master Parachutist
HALO	High Altitude-Low Opening
SOG	Special Operations Group
Mermite can	An insulated food container
Lerp	Dehydrated long range patrol ration
C-Rations	Canned rations
FAC	Forward Air Controller
Red-leg	Friendly artillery
FO	Forward Observer
Def-con	Defensive concentration for artillery fires
BDA	Bomb Damage Assessment
Battery-one	One shell fired from each of the six guns in an artillery battery
Battery-two	Two shells fired from each gun
Claymore	An antipersonnel mine
Clacker	Claymore firing device

Frag	A fragmentation grenade
Smoke Grenade	Yellow, Green, and Purple (Lemon, Lime, and Grape)
ARVN	Vietnamese Army
VC	Viet Cong
NVA	North Vietnamese Army
Chieu Hois	Enemy soldiers that changed sides
Sin loi	Sorry
Punji	A sharpened bamboo stake
DEROS	Date Expected to Rotate Overseas (to leave country)
FNG	Fucking New Guy, Cherry
REMF	Rear echelon mother fucker
DX	Direct Exchange
MARS	Mobile Army Radio Station
MIA	Missing in Action
KIA	Killed in Action
WIA	Wounded in Action
PFC	E-3 Private First Class
Spec Four	E-4 Specialist Fourth Class
Sgt.	E-5 Buck Sergeant
SSG	E-6 Staff Sergeant
SFC	E-7 Sergeant First Class
Master Sergeant	E-8 First Sergeant
Sergeant Major	E-9
OCAR	Officer Career Army

www.garypriskauthor.com